# THE OFFICIAL®
## OVERSTREET
# COMIC
# BOOK
## PRICE GUIDE
## COMPANION

# THE OFFICIAL

# OVERSTREET

# COMIC

# BOOK

## PRICE GUIDE
## COMPANION

By
## ROBERT M. OVERSTREET

**FOURTH EDITION**

HOUSE OF COLLECTIBLES • NEW YORK

This is a registered trademark of Random House, Inc.

© 1990 by Robert Overstreet

Cover art Captain America and Red Skull: ™ and © 1990 by Marvel Entertainment Group, Inc. All rights reserved.

All rights reserved under International and Pan-American Copyright Conventions.

Published by: House of Collectibles
201 East 50th Street
New York, New York 10022

Distributed by Ballantine Books, a division of Random House, Inc., New York, and simultaneously in Canada by Random House of Canada Limited, Toronto.

Manufactured in the United States of America

Library of Congress Catalog Card Number: 88-647216

ISBN: 0-876-37827-0

Fourth edition: November 1990

10 9 8 7 6 5 4 3 2 1

# TABLE OF
# CONTENTS

*An Overview to Comic Book Collecting*                          1
  Introduction                                        3
  Grading Comic Books                                 5
  Storage of Comic Books                              8
  How to Start Collecting                            10
  Collecting Back Issues                             11
  Proper Handling of Comic Books                     12
  Terminology                                        13
  How to Sell Your Comics                            15
  Where to Buy and Sell                              17
  Directory of Comic and Nostalgia Shops             18
  Comic Book Conventions                             55
    Comic Book Convention Calendar for 1991 56
  A Chronology of the Development of the
     American Comic Book, by M. Thomas Inge   59
  How to Use This Book                                68

*Comic Book Listings*                                          69

*Big Little Books*                                            469
  Introduction                                      471
  How to Use the Listings                           473
  Grading                                           474
  A Word on Pricing                                 476
  Big Little Book Listings                          478

# ACKNOWLEDGMENTS

Larry Bigman (Frazetta-Williamson data); Glenn Bray (Kurtzman data); Dan Malan and Charles Heffelfinger (Classic Comics data); Gary Carter (DC data); J. B. Clifford Jr. (E. C. data); Gary Coddington (Superman data); Wilt Conine (Fawcett data); Dr. S. M. Davidson (Cupples & Leon data); Al Dellinges (Kubert data); Kevin Hancer (Tarzan data); Charles Heffelfinger and Jim Ivey (March of Comics listing); R. C. Holland and Ron Pussell (Seduction and Parade of Pleasure data); Grant Irwin (Quality data); Richard Kravitz (Kelly data); Phil Levine (giveaway data); Fred Nardelli (Frazetta data); Michelle Nolan (love comics data); Mike Nolan (MLJ, Timely, Nedor data); George Olshevsky (Timely data); Richard Olson (LOA data); Scott Pell ('50s data); Greg Robertson (National data); Frank Scigliano (Little Lulu data); Gene Seger (Buck Rogers data); Rick Sloane (Archie data); David R. Smith, Archivist, Walt Disney Productions (Disney data); Don and Maggie Thompson (Four Color listing); Mike Tiefenbacher, Jerry Sinkovec, and Richard Yudkin (Atlas and National data); Raymond True (Classic Comics data); Jim Vadeboncoeur Jr. (Williamson and Atlas data); Kim Weston (Disney and Barks data); Cat Yronwode (Spirit data); Andrew Zerbe and Gary Behymer (M. E. data).

My appreciation must also be extended to Ron Pussell, Bruce Hamilton, Steve Geppi, Jon Warren, James Payette, Joe Vereneault, Jay Maybruck, Terry Stroud, Hugh O'Kennon, John Snyder, Walter Wang, Gary Carter and Gary Colabuono for pricing research; to Tom Inge for his "Chronology of the American Comic Book"; to Kevin Maguire for his outstanding cover art; and to Bill Spicer for his kind permission to reprint portions of his and Jerry Bails' America's Four Color Pastime.

# An Overview to Comic Book Collecting

# INTRODUCTION

Comic book values listed in this reference work were recorded from convention sales, dealers' lists, adzines, and by special contact with dealers and collectors from coast to coast. Prices paid for rare comics vary considerably from one locale to another. We have attempted to list a realistic average between the lowest and highest range observed. The reader should keep in mind that the prices listed only reflect the market just prior to publication. Any new trends that have developed since the preparation of this book would not be shown.

The values listed are reports, not estimates. Each new edition of the guide is actually an average report of sales that occurred during the year; not an estimate of what we feel the books will be bringing next year. Even though many prices listed will remain current throughout the year, the wise user of this book would keep abreast of current market trends to get the fullest potential out of his invested dollar.

All titles are listed as if they were one word, ignoring spaces, hyphens and apostrophes. Page counts listed will always include covers.

IMPORTANT. Prices listed in this book are in U. S. currency and are for your reference only. This book is not a dealer's price list, although some dealers may base their prices on the values listed. The true value of any comic book is what you are willing to pay. Prices listed herein are an indication of what collectors (not dealers) would probably pay. For one reason or another, these collectors might want certain books badly, or else need specific issues to complete their runs and so are willing to pay more. Dealers are not in a position to pay the full prices listed, but work on a percentage depending largely on the amount of investment required and the quality of material offered. Usually they will pay from 20 to 70 percent of the list price depending on how long it will take them to sell the collection after making the investment; the higher the demand and better the condition, the more the percentage. Most dealers are faced with expenses such as advertising, travel, telephone and mailing, plus convention costs. These costs all go in before the books are sold. The high demand books usually sell right away but there are many other titles that are difficult to sell due to low demand. Sometimes a dealer will have cost tied up in this type of material for several years before finally moving it. Remember, his position is that of handling, demand and overhead. Most dealers are victims of these economics.

Everyone connected with the publication of this book advocates the collecting of comic books for fun and pleasure, as well as for nostalgia, art, and cultural values. Second to this is investment, which, if wisely placed in the best quality books (condition and contents considered), will yield dividends over the long term.

# GRADING COMIC BOOKS

Before a comic book's true value can be assessed, its condition or state of preservation must be determined. In most comic books, the better the condition, the more desirable the book. The scarcer first and/or origin issues in MINT condition will bring several times the price of the same book in POOR condition. The grading of a comic book is done by simply looking at the book and describing its condition, which may range from absolutely perfect newsstand condition (MINT) to extremely worn, dirty, and torn (POOR). Numerous variables influence the evaluation of a comic's condition and **all** must be considered in the final evaluation. More important characteristics include tears, missing pieces, wrinkles, stains, yellowing, brittleness, tape repairs, water marks, spine roll, writing, and cover luster. The significance of each of these is described more fully in the grading scale definitions. Whenever in doubt, consult with a reputable dealer or experienced collector in your area. The following grading guide is given to aid the panelologist.

**MINT (M):** Absolutely perfect in every way, regardless of age. The cover has full luster, is crisp, cut square and shows no imperfections of any sort. The cover and all pages are extra white and fresh; the spine is tight, flat, and clean; not even the slightest blemish can be detected around staples, along spine and edges or at corners. Arrival dates pencilled on the cover are usually acceptable. As comics must be truly perfect to be in this grade, they are obviously extremely scarce and seldom are offered for sale. Books prior to 1963 in this grade can bring 20 to 500 percent more.

**NEAR MINT (NM):** Like new or newsstand condition, as above, but with very slight loss of luster, or a slight off-centered cover, or a minor printing error. Could have slight color fading, or a minor blemish that keeps it out of the Mint category, and white to extra white cover and pages. Any defects noticeable would be very minor. This grade is also very rare in books prior to 1963.

**VERY FINE (VF):** Slight wear beginning to show; possibly a small wrinkle or a minor stress line at staples or where cover has been opened a few times; still clean and flat with most of cover gloss retained. Very slight yellowing acceptable.

**FINE (F):** Tight cover with some wear, but still relatively flat, clean and shiny with no subscription crease, writing on cover, yellowed margins or tape repairs. Stress lines around staples and along spine beginning to show; minor color flaking possible at spine, staples, edges or corners. Slight yellowing acceptable.

**VERY GOOD (vg):** Obviously a read copy with original printing lustre and gloss almost gone; some discoloration, but not soiled; some signs of wear and minor markings, but none that deface the cover; usually needs slight repair around staples and along spine, which could be rolled; cover could have a minor tear or crease where a corner was folded under or a loose centerfold; no chunks missing. Slight yellowing acceptable.

**GOOD (g):** An average used copy complete with both covers and no panels missing; slightly soiled or marked with possible creases, minor tears or splits, rolled spine and small color flaking, but perfectly sound and legible. A well-read copy, but perfectly acceptable with no chunks missing. **Minor** tape repairs usually occur and slight browning (no brittleness) acceptable, although tape repairs should be considered a defect and priced accordingly.

**FAIR (f):** Very heavily read and soiled, but complete with possibly a small chunk out of cover; tears needing repairs and multiple folds and wrinkles likely; damaged by the elements, but completely sound and legible, bringing 50-70% of good price.

**POOR (p):** Damaged; heavily weathered; soiled; or otherwise unsuited for collection purposes.

**COVERLESS (c):** Coverless comics turn up frequently, are usually hard to sell and in many cases are almost worthless. It takes ingenuity and luck to get a good price; e.g., color xerox covers will increase the salability. A cover of an expensive book is scarcer and worth more. However, certain "high demand" issues could bring up to 30 percent of the good price.

IMPORTANT: Comics in all grades with fresh extra white pages usually bring more. Books with defects such as pages or panels missing, coupons cut, torn or taped covers and pages, brown or brittle pages, restapled, taped spines, pages or covers, water-marked, printing defects, rusted staples, stained, holed, or other imperfections that distract from the original beauty, are worth less than if free of these defects.

Many of the early strip reprint comics were printed in hardback with dust jackets. Books with dust jackets are worth more. The value can increase from 20 to 50 percent depending on the rarity of the book. Usually, the earlier the book, the greater the percentage. Unless noted, prices listed are without dust jackets. The condition of the dust jacket should be graded independently of the book itself.

# STORAGE OF
# COMIC BOOKS

Acids left in comic book paper during manufacture are the primary cause of aging and yellowing. Improper storage can accelerate the aging process.

The importance of storage is proven when looking at the condition of books from large collections that have surfaced over the past few years. In some cases, an entire collection has brown or yellowed pages approaching brittleness. Collections of this type were probably stored in too much heat or moisture, or exposed to atmospheric pollution (sulfur dioxide) or light. On the other hand, other collections of considerable age (30 to 50 years) have emerged with snow white pages and little sign of aging. Thus, we learn that proper storage is imperative to insure the long life of our comic book collections.

Store books in a dark, cool place with an ideal relative humidity of 50 percent and a temperature of 40 to 50 degrees or less. Air conditioning is recommended. Do not use regular cardboard boxes, since most contain harmful acids. Use acid-free boxes instead. Seal books in Mylar (Mylar is a registered trademark of the DuPont Company) or other suitable wrappings or bags and store them in the proper containers or cabinets, to protect them from heat, excessive dampness, ultraviolet light (use tungsten filament lights), polluted air, and dust.

Many collectors seal their books in plastic bags and store them in a cool dark room in cabinets or on shelving. Plastic bags should be changed every two to three years, since most contain harmful acids. Cedar chest storage is recommended, but the ideal method of storage is to stack your comics (preferably in Mylar bags) vertically in acid-free boxes. The boxes can be arranged on shelving for easy access. Storage boxes, plastic bags, backing boards, Mylar bags, archival supplies, etc., are available from dealers.

# HOW TO START
# COLLECTING

Most collectors of comic books begin by buying new issues in mint condition directly off the newsstand or from their local comic store. (Subscription copies are available from several mail-order services.) Each week new comics appear on the stands that are destined to become true collector's items. The trick is to locate a store that carries a complete line of comics. In several localities this may be difficult. Most panelologists frequent several magazine stands in order not to miss something they want. Even then, it pays to keep in close contact with collectors in other areas. Sooner or later, nearly every collector has to rely upon a friend in Fandom to obtain for him an item that is unavailable locally.

Before you buy any comic to add to your collection, you should carefully inspect its condition. Unlike stamps and coins, defective comics are generally not highly prized. The cover should be properly cut and printed. Remember that every blemish or sign of wear depreciates the beauty and value of your comics.

The serious panelologist usually purchases extra copies of popular titles. He may trade these multiples for items unavailable locally (for example, foreign comics), or he may store the multiples for resale at some future date. Such speculation is, of course, a gamble, but unless collecting trends change radically in the future, the value of certain comics in mint condition should appreciate greatly, as new generations of readers become interested in collecting.

# COLLECTING
# BACK ISSUES

In addition to current issues, most panelologists want to locate back issues. Some energetic collectors have had great success in running down large hoards of rare comics in their home towns. Occasionally, rare items can be located through agencies that collect old papers and magazines, such as the Salvation Army. The lucky collector can often buy these items for much less than their current market value. Placing advertisements in trade journals, newspapers, etc., can also produce good results. However, don't be discouraged if you are neither energetic nor lucky. Most panelologists build their collections slowly but systematically by placing mail orders with dealers and other collectors.

Comics of early vintage are extremely expensive if they are purchased through a regular dealer or collector, and unless you have unlimited funds to invest in your hobby, you will find it necessary to restrict your collecting in certain ways. However you define your collection, you should be careful to set your goals well within your means.

# PROPER HANDLING
# OF COMIC BOOKS

Before picking up an old, rare comic book, caution should be exercised to handle it properly. Old comic books are very fragile and can be easily damaged. Because of this, many dealers hesitate to let customers personally handle their rare comics. They would prefer to remove the comic from its bag and show it to the customer themselves. In this way, if the book is damaged, it would be the dealer's responsibility—not the customer's. Remember, the slightest crease or chip could render an otherwise Mint book to Near Mint or even Very Fine. The following steps are provided to aid the novice in the proper handling of comic books: 1. Remove the comic from its protective sleeve or bag very carefully. 2. Gently lay the comic (unopened) in the palm of your hand so that it will stay relatively flat and secure. 3. You can now leaf through the book by carefully rolling or flipping the pages with the thumb and forefinger of your other hand. Caution: Be sure the book always remains relatively flat or slightly rolled. Avoid creating stress points on the covers with your fingers and be particularly cautious in bending covers back too far on Mint books. 4. After examining the book, carefully insert it back into the bag or protective sleeve. Watch corners and edges for folds or tears as you replace the book.

# TERMINOLOGY

Many of the following terms and abbreviations are used in the comic book market and are explained here:

**a**—Story art; **a(i)**—Story art inks; **a(p)**—Story art pencils; **a(r)**—Story art reprint.
**B&W**—Black and white art.
**Bondage cover**—Usually denotes a female in bondage.
**c**—Cover art; **c(i)**—Cover inks; **c(p)** —Cover pencils; **c(r)**—Cover reprint.
**Cameo**—When a character appears briefly in one or two panels.
**Colorist**—Artist who applies color to the pen and ink art.
**Con**—A convention or public gathering of fans.
**Cosmic Aeroplane**—Refers to a large collection discovered by Cosmic Aeroplane Books.
**Debut**—The first time that a character appears anywhere.
**Drug propaganda story**—Where comic makes an editorial stand about drug abuse.
**Drug use story**—Shows the actual use of drugs: shooting, taking a trip, harmful effects, etc.
**Fanzine**—An amateur fan publication.
**File Copy**—A high grade comic originating from the publisher's file.
**First app.**—Same as debut.
**Flashback**—When a previous story is being recalled.
**G. A.**—Golden Age (1930s—1950s).
**Headlight**—Protruding breasts.
**i**—Art inks.
**Infinity cover**—Shows a scene that repeats itself to infinity.

**Inker**—Artist who does the inking.

**Intro**—Same as debut.

**JLA**—Justice League of America.

**JSA**—Justice Society of America.

**Lamont Larson**—Refers to a large high grade collection of comics. Many of the books have Lamont or Larson written on the cover.

**Logo**—The title of a strip or comic book as it appears on the cover or title page.

**Mile High**—Refers to a large NM-Mint collection of comics originating from Denver, Colorado (Edgar Church collection).

**nd**—No date.

**nn**—No number.

**N. Y. Legis. Comm.**—New York Legislative Committee to Study the Publication of Comics (1951).

**Origin**—When the story of the character's creation is given.

**p**—Art pencils.

**Penciler**—Artist who does the pencils.

**POP—Parade of Pleasure**, book about the censorship of comics.

**Poughkeepsie**—Refers to a large collection of Dell Comics' "file copies" believed to have originated from Poughkeepsie, NY.

**R or r**—Reprint.

**Rare**—10 to 20 copies estimated to exist.

**Reprint comics**—Comic books that contain newspaper strip reprints.

**S. A.**—Silver Age (1956—Present).

**Scarce**—20 to 100 copies estimated to exist.

**Silver proof**—A black & white actual size print on thick glossy paper given to the colorist to indicate colors to the engraver.

**S&K**—Simon and Kirby (artists).

**SOTI—Seduction of the Innocent**, book about the censorship of comics.

**Splash panel**—A large panel that usually appears at the front of a comic story.

**Very rare**—1 to 10 copies estimated to exist.

**X-over**—When one character crosses over into another's strip.

**Zine**—See Fanzine.

# HOW TO SELL
# YOUR COMICS

If you have a collection of comics for sale, large or small, the following steps should be taken. (1) Make a detailed list of the books for sale, being careful to grade them accurately, showing any noticeable defects; i.e., torn or missing pages, centerfolds, etc. (2) Decide whether to sell or trade wholesale to a dealer all in one lump or to go through the long laborious process of advertising and selling piece by piece to collectors. Both have their advantages and disadvantages.

In selling to dealers, you will get the best price by letting everything go at once—the good with the bad—all for one price. Simply select names either from ads in this book or from some of the adzines mentioned below. Send them your list and ask for bids. The bids received will vary depending on the demand, rarity and condition of the books you have. The more in demand, and better the condition, the higher the bids will be.

On the other hand, you could become a "dealer" and sell the books yourself. Order a copy of one or more of the adzines. Take note how most dealers lay out their ads. Type up your ad copy, carefully pricing each book (using the *Guide* as a reference). Send finished ad copy with payment to adzine editor to be run. You will find that certain books will sell at once while others will not sell at all. The ad will probably have to be retyped, remaining books repriced, and run again. Price books according to how fast you want them to move. If you try to get top dollar, expect a much longer period of time. Otherwise, the better deal you give the collector, the faster they will move. Remember, in being your own dealer, you will have overhead expenses in postage, mailing supplies and advertising cost. Some books might even be returned for refund due to misgrading, etc.

In selling all at once to a dealer, you get instant cash, immediate profit, and eliminate the long process of running several ads to dispose of the books; but if you have patience, and a small amount of business sense, you could realize more profit selling them directly to collectors yourself.

# WHERE TO BUY
# AND SELL

Most of the larger cities have comic specialty shops that buy and sell old comic books. *The Comics Buyers Guide*, a weekly tabloid, published by Krause Publications, 700 E. State St., Iola, WI 54997, is the best source for buying and selling. This publication is full of ads buying and selling comic books. Comic book conventions are now held the year round in most of the larger cities. These conventions are an excellent source for buying and selling comic books. If you are an inexperienced collector, be sure to compare prices before you buy. Never send large sums of cash through the mail. Send money orders or checks for your personal protection. Beware of bargains, as the items advertised sometimes do not exist, but are only a fraud to get your money.

Learn how to grade properly. You will find that dealers vary considerably in how they grade their comics. For your own protection, your first order to a dealer should consist of an inexpensive book as a test of his grading. This initial order will give you a clue as to how the dealer grades as well as the care he takes in packaging his orders and the promptness in which he gets the order to you.

# DIRECTORY OF
# COMIC AND
# NOSTALGIA SHOPS

This is a current up-to-date list, but is not all-inclusive. We cannot assume any responsibility in your dealings with these shops. This list is provided for your information only. When planning your trips, it would be advisable to make appointments in advance.

**ALABAMA:**

**Camelot Books**
2201 Quintard Ave.
Anniston, AL 36201
PH:205-236-3474

**Discount Comic Book Shop**
1301 Noble St.
Anniston, AL 36201
PH:205-238-8373

**Gold Dragon Comics**
3970 Government Blvd.
Mobile, AL 36693
PH:205-661-4060

**Sincere Comics**
3738 Airport Blvd.
Mobile, AL 36608
PH:205-342-2603

## ARIZONA:

**Atomic Comics**
1318 West Southern #9
Mesa, AZ 85202
PH:602-649-0807

**Books, Comics & Records**
535 E. Southern Ave.
Mesa, AZ 85202
PH:602-962-5751

**AAA Best Comics, Etc.**
8336 N. Seventh St., B-C
Phoenix, AZ 85020
PH:602-997-4012

**All About Books & Comics**
529 E. Camelback
Phoenix, AZ 85012
PH:602-277-0757

**All About Books & Comics West**
4208 W. Dunlap
Phoenix, AZ 85051
PH:602-435-0410

**CRC Collectibles**
3033 North 24th St.
Phoenix, AZ 85016-7800
PH:602-957-8833

**Lost Dutchman Comics**
5805 N. 7th St.
Phoenix, AZ 85014
PH:602-263-5249

**All About Books & Comics III**
4000 N. Scottsdale Rd. #102
Scottsdale, AZ 85251
PH:602-994-1812

**The ONE Book Shop**
120-A East University Drive
Tempe, AZ 85281
PH:602-967-3551

**The Comic Corner**
P.O. Box 58779
Tucson, AZ 85732-8779
PH:602-790-2625

**Fantasy Comics**
6001 E. 22nd St.
Tucson, AZ 85711
PH:602-748-7483

**Fantasy Comics**
2745 N. Campbell
Tucson, AZ 85719
PH:602-325-9790

## ARKANSAS:

**Rock Bottom Used Book Shop**
418 W. Dickson St.
Fayetteville, AR 72701
PH:501-521-2917

**Paperbacks Plus**
2207 Rogers Ave.
Fort Smith, AR 72901
PH:501-785-5642

**The Comic Book Store**
1400 S. University, Suite #1
Little Rock, AR 72204
PH:501-661-1516

**Pie-Eyes**
5223 W. 65th St.
Little Rock, AR 72209
PH:501-568-1414

**Collector's Edition Comics**
5310 MacArthur Drive
North Little Rock, AR 72118
PH:501-753-2586

**TNT Collectors Hut**
503 W. Hale Ave.
Osceola, AR 72370
PH:501-563-5760


## CALIFORNIA:

**Comic Heaven**
24 W. Main St.
Alhambra, CA 91801
PH:818-289-3945

**Comic Relief**
2138 University Ave.
Berkeley, CA 94704
PH:415-843-5002

**Fantasy Kingdom**
1802 W. Olive Ave.
Burbank, CA 91506
PH:818-954-8432

**Graphitti Comics & Games**
4325 Overland Ave.
Culver City, CA 90230
PH:213-559-2058

**Thrill Books, Comics & Games**
629 First St.
Encinitas, CA 92024
PH:619-753-4299

**Comic Gallery**
675-B N. Broadway
Escondido, CA 92025
PH:619-745-5660

**The Comic Castle**
330 - 5th St.
Eureka, CA 95501
PH:707-444-2665

**Adventureland Comics**
106 N. Harbor Blvd.

Fullerton, CA 92632
PH:714-738-3698

**Comic Castle**
107 W. Amerige
Fullerton, CA 92632
PH:714-879-6160

**Comics Unlimited**
12913 Harbor Blvd.
Garden Grove, CA 92640
PH:714-638-2040

**Geoffrey's Comics**
15530 Crenshaw Blvd.
Gardena, CA 90249
PH:213-538-3198

**Shooting Star Comics & Games**
700 E. Colorado Blvd.
Glendale, CA 91205
PH:818-502-1535

**Comics Unlimited**
21505 Norwalk Blvd.
Hawaiian Gardens, CA 90716
PH:213-865-4474

**The American Comic Book Co.**
3972 Atlantic Ave.
Long Beach, CA 90807
PH:213-426-0393

**Pacific Fantasy Comics**
5622 East Second St.
Long Beach, CA 90803
PH:213-434-5136

**Another World**
1615 Colorado Blvd.
Los Angeles, CA 90041
PH:213-257-7757

**Cheap Comics - 2**
7779 Melrose Ave.
Los Angeles, CA 90046
PH:213-655-9323

**Golden Apple Comics**
7711 Melrose Ave.
Los Angeles, CA 90046
PH:213-658-6047

**Golden Apple Comics**
8934 West Pico Blvd.
Los Angeles, CA 90035
PH:213-274-2008

**Graphitti-Westwood—UCLA**
960 Gayley Ave.
Los Angeles, CA 90024
PH:213-824-3656

**Wonderworld Cards, Comics
and Art**
1579 El Camino
Millbrae, CA 94030
PH:415-871-2674

**Bonanza Books & Comics**
Roseburg Square Center
813 W. Roseburg Ave.
Modesto, CA 95350-5058
PH:209-529-0415

**Archive Comics**
5148 Colfax Ave.
North Hollywood, CA 91601
PH:818-763-8044

**The Comic Book Store**
11517 Burbank Blvd.
North Hollywood, CA 90000
PH:818-509-2901

**Ninth Nebula:
The Comic Book Store**
11517 Burbank Blvd.

North Hollywood, CA 91601
PH:818-509-2901

**Golden Apple Comics**
8958-8962 Reseda Blvd.
Northridge, CA 91324
PH:818-993-7804

**Freedonia Funnyworks**
350 S. Tustin Ave.
Orange, CA 92666
PH:714-639-5830

**Desert Comics**
406 N. Palm Canyon Drive
Palm Springs, CA 92262
PH:619-325-5805

**Lee's Comics**
3429 Alma St.
(In Alma Plaza)
Palo Alto, CA 94306
PH:415-493-3957

**Funtime Comics & Fantasy**
147 Pomona Mall East
Pomona, CA 91766
PH:714-629-8860

**Galaxy Comics & Cards**
1503 Aviation Blvd.
Redondo Beach, CA 90278
PH:213-374-7440

**Markstu Discount Comics**
3642 - 7th St.
Riverside, CA 92501
PH:714-684-8544

**Players Baseball Cards &
Comics**
9462 Magnolia Ave.
Riverside, CA 92503
PH:714-688-5040

**Comic Gallery**
4224 Balboa Ave.
San Diego, CA 92117
PH:619-483-4853

**Comics and Da-Kind**
1643 Noriega St.
San Francisco, CA 94122
PH:415-753-9678

**Com-X & Card-X**
**The Comic and Card Exchange**
1610 Irving St.
San Francisco, CA 94122

**Gary's Corner Bookstore**
1051 So. San Gabriel Blvd.
San Gabriel, CA 91776
PH:818-285-7575

**Comics Pendragon**
1189 Branham Lane
San Jose, CA 95118
PH:408-265-3323

**The Comic Shop**
2164 E. 14th St.
San Leandro, CA 94577
PH:415-483-0205

**Lee's Comics**
2222 S. El Camino Real
San Mateo, CA 94403
PH:415-571-1489

**San Mateo Wonderworld Cards**
**Comics & Art**
106 S. B St.
San Mateo, CA 94401
PH:415-344-1536

**Comic Castle**
724 N St.
Sanger, CA 93657
PH:209-875-5160

**Brian's Books**
3225 Cabrillo Ave.
Santa Clara, CA 95127
PH:408-985-7481

**R & K Comics**
3153 El Camino Real
Santa Clara, CA 95051
PH:408-554-6512

**Atlantis Fantasyworld**
610-F Cedar St.
Santa Cruz, CA 95060
PH:408-426-0158

**Markgraf's Comic Books**
440 S. Broadway
Santa Maria, CA 93454
PH:805-925-7470

**Hi De Ho Comics & Fantasy**
525 Santa Monica Blvd.
Santa Monica, CA 90401
PH:213-394-2820

**Superhero Universe VIII**
Sycamore Plaza
2955-A5 Cochran St.
Simi Valley, CA 93065
PH:805-583-3027

**Cheap Comics - 1**
12123 Garfield Ave.
South Gate, CA 90280
PH:213-408-0900

**Graphitti - The Valley!**
12080 Ventura Pl., No. 3
Studio City, CA 91604
PH:818-980-4976

**Superhero Universe IV**
18722 Ventura Blvd.
Tarzana, CA 93156
PH:818-774-0969

**J & K Comics and Toys**
3535 Torrance Blvd., No. 9
Torrance, CA 90503-4815
PH:213-540-9685

**Silver City Comics**
4671 Torrance Blvd. at Anza
Torrance, CA 90503
PH:213-542-8034

**Roleplayers**
5933 Adobe Rd.
29 Palms, CA 92277
PH:619-367-6282

**Hi De Ho Comics & Fantasy**
64 Windward Ave.
Venice, CA 90291
PH:213-399-6206

**The Second Time Around**
391 E. Main St.
Ventura, CA 93001
PH:805-643-3154

**Comic Castle**
14464 - 7th St.
Victorville, CA 92392
PH:619-245-8006

**Graphitti - South Bay!**
Airport/Marina Hotel (Rear)
8639 Lincoln Blvd., No. 102
Westchester, L. A., CA 90045
PH:213-641-8661

**Comics Unlimited**
16344 Beach Blvd.
Westminster, CA 92683
PH:714-841-6646

**Comics Unlimited**
14153 Whittier Blvd.
Whittier, CA 90605
PH:213-945-1733

**COLORADO:**

**Colorado Comic Book Co.**
220 N. Tejon St.
Colorado Springs, CO 80903
PH:719-635-2516

**Colorado Comic Book Co./
Heroes & Dragons**
The Citadel #2158
Colorado Springs, CO 80909
PH:719-550-9570

**CONNECTICUT:**

**Outer Limit Comic Shop**
Rt. 37 - 52½ Pembroke Rd.
Danbury, CT 06811
PH:203-746-1068

**The Bookie**
206 Burnside Ave.
East Hartford, CT 06108
PH:203-289-1208

**A Timeless Journey**
402 Elm St.
Stamford, CT 06902
PH:203-353-1720

**DELAWARE:**

**Captain Blue Hen Comics, Cards
& Games**
Baycourt Plaza, Rt. 113
Dover, DE 19901
PH:302-734-3222

**Comicmania**
1616 W. Newport Pike
Stanton, DE 19804
PH:302-995-1971

## FLORIDA:

**The Funny Farm**
422 26th St. W.
Bradenton, FL 34205
PH:813-747-7714

**Time Machine II**
Southwood Mall
5748 - 14 St. W.
Bradenton, FL 34207
PH:813-758-3684

**Comics Etc.**
1271 Semoran Blvd., Suite 125
Lake Howell Square
Casselberry, FL 32707
PH:407-679-5665

**Comics and Cards**
7778 Wiles Rd.
Coral Springs, FL 33071
PH:305-752-0580

**Acevedo's Collectables**
4761 S. University Drive
Davie, FL 33328
PH:305-434-0540

**Cliff's Books**
209 N. Woodland Blvd. (17-92)
De Land, FL 32720
PH:904-734-6963

**Intergalactic Comics & Collectibles**
109 E. Semoran Blvd.
Fern Park, FL 32720
PH:407-260-0017

**Novel Ideas**
804 West University Ave.
Gainesville, FL 32601
PH:904-374-8593

**Novel Ideas**
3206 S.W. 35th Blvd.
Butler Plaza
Gainesville, FL 32608
PH:904-377-2694

**Charlie's Comics**
1255 West 46th St.
Hialeah, FL 33012
PH:305-557-5994

**Coliseum of Comics**
1180 E. Vine St.
Kissimmee, FL 32741
PH:407-870-5322

**Past—Present—Future Comics**
6186 S. Congress Ave., Suite A4
Lantana, FL 33462
PH:407-433-3068

**Geppi's Comic World**
2200 East Bay Drive #203
Largo, FL 34641
PH:813-585-0226

**Phil's Comic Shoppe**
614 S. State Rd. 7
Margate, FL 33063
PH:305-977-6947

**Frank's Comic Book & Baseball Card Store**
2678 S.W. 87 Ave.
Miami, FL 33165
PH:305-226-5072

**Comic Warehouse, Inc.**
1029 Airport Rd. N., #B-6
Naples, FL 33942
PH:813-643-1020

**Tropic Comics South, Inc.**
742 N.E. 167th St.
N. Miami Beach, FL 33161
PH:305-940-8700

**Adventure Into Comics**
841 Bennett Rd.
Orlando, FL 32803
PH:407-896-4047

**Cartoon Museum**
4300 S. Semoran, Suite 109
Orlando, FL 32822-2453
PH:407-273-0141

**Coliseum of Comics**
4103 S. Orange Blossom Trail
Orlando, FL 32809
PH:407-422-5757

**Coliseum of Comics**
5306 Silver Star Rd.
Orlando, FL 32808
PH:407-298-9411

**Enterprise 1701**
2814 Corrine Drive
Orlando, FL 32803
PH:407-896-1701

**Past-Present-Future Comics North**
4270 Northlake Blvd.
Palm Beach Gardens, FL 33410

**Sincere Comics, Inc.**
Town & Country Plaza
3300 N. Pace Blvd.
Pensacola, FL 32505
PH:904-432-1352

**Tropic Comics, Inc.**
313 S. State Rd. 7
Plantation, FL 33317
PH:305-587-8878

**Comics U.S.A.**
3231 N. Federal Highway
Pompano Beach, FL 33064
PH:305-942-1455

**Comic & Gaming Exchange**
8432 W. Oakland Park Blvd.
Sunrise, FL 33351
PH:305-742-0777

**David T. Alexander's Comic Books and Baseball Cards**
(By Appointment Only)
P.O. Box 273086
Tampa, FL 33618
PH:813-968-1805

**New England Comics**
Northdale Court
15836 N. Dale Mabry Highway
Tampa, FL 33618
PH:813-264-1848

**Tropic Comics North, Inc.**
1018 - 21st St. (U.S. 1)
Vero Beach, FL 32960
PH:407-562-8501

## GEORGIA:

**Fischer's Book Store**
6569 Riverdale Rd.
Riverdale, GA 30274
PH:404-997-7323

**Starbase 1**
1517½ N. Ashley St.
Valdosta, GA 31602
PH:1-800-526-5490

## HAWAII:

**Jelly's Comics & Books**
98-199 Kam. Hwy.
Aiea, HI 96701
PH:808-486-5600

**Jelly's Comics & Books**
404 Piikoi St.
Honolulu, HI 96814
PH:808-538-7771

**Compleat Comics Company**
1728 Kaahumanu Ave.
Wailuku, Maui, HI 96793
PH:808-242-5875

## IDAHO:

**King's Komix Kastle**
1706 N. 18th St. (appointments)
Boise, ID 83702
PH:208-343-7142

**King's Komix Kastle II**
2560 Leadville (drop in)
Mail: 1706 N. 18th
Boise, ID 83702
PH:208-343-7055

**New Mythology Comics &
Science Fiction**
1725 Broadway
Boise, ID 83706
PH:208-344-6744

## ILLINOIS:

**Friendly Frank's Distribution**
(Wholesale Only)
727 Factory Rd.
Addison, IL 60101

**Friendly Frank's Comics**
11941 S. Cicero
Alsip, IL 60658
PH:312-371-6760

**All-American Comic Shops 3**
9118 Ogden Ave.
Brookfield, IL 60513
PH:708-387-9588

**Moondog's Comicland**
1231 W. Dundee Rd.
Plaza Verde
Buffalo Grove, IL 60090
PH:708-259-6060

**Amazing Fantasy**
1856 Sibley Blvd.
Calumet City, IL
PH:708-891-2260

**All-American Comic Shops 6**
6457 W. Archer Ave.
Chicago, IL 60638
PH:312-586-5090

**Comics for Heroes** (Main Store)
1702 W. Foster
Chicago, IL 60640
PH:312-769-4745

**Comics for Heroes**
3937 W. Lawrence
Chicago, IL 60625
PH:312-478-8585

**For the Love of Toons**
3954 N. Avondale
Chicago, IL 60613
PH:312-549-6430

**Larry's Comic Book Store**
1219 W. Devon Ave.
Chicago, IL 60660
PH:312-274-1832

**Larry Laws** (by appointment
only)
(Call First) (Mail Order)
831 Cornelia
Chicago, IL 60657
PH:312-477-9247

**Joe Sarno's Comic Kingdom**
5941 W. Irving Park Rd.
Chicago, IL 60634
PH:312-545-2231

**Yesterday**
1143 W. Addison St.
Chicago, IL 60613
PH:312-248-8087

**All-American Comic Shops 5**
1701 N. Larkin Ave.
Hillcrest Shopping Center
Crest Hill, IL 60435
PH:815-744-2094

**Moondog's Comicland**
114 S. Waukegan Rd.
Deerbrook Mall
Deerfield, IL 60015
PH:708-272-6080

**The Paper Escape**
205 W. First St.

Dixon, IL 61021
PH:815-284-7567

**GEM Comics**
156 N. York Rd.
Elmhurst, IL 60126
PH:708-833-8787

**All-American Comic Shops, Ltd.**
3514 W. 95th St.
Evergreen Park, IL 60642
PH:708-425-7555

**More Fun Comics**
650 Roosevelt Rd., Suite #112
Glen Ellyn, IL 60137
PH:708-469-6141

**Fiction House**
Dixie Hwy.
Homewood, IL
PH:708-206-1330

**Moondog's Comicland**
139 W. Prospect Ave.
Mt. Prospect, IL 60056
PH:708-398-6060

**Moondog's Comicland**
Randhurst Shopping Center
Mt. Prospect, IL 60056
PH:708-577-8668

**All-American Comic Shops 2**
14620 S. LaGrange Rd.
Orland Park, IL 60462
PH:708-460-5556

**All-American Comic Shops 4**
22305 S. Central Park
Central Court Plaza
Park Forest, IL 60466
PH:708-748-2509

**Tomorrow Is Yesterday**
5600 N. Second St.
Rockford, IL 61111
PH:815-633-0330

**Moondog's Comicland**
1455 W. Schaumburg Rd.
Schaumburg Plaza
Schaumburg, IL 60194
PH:708-529-6060

**Family Book**
3123 So. Dirksen Pkwy.
Springfield, IL 62703
PH:217-529-1709

**Unicorn Comics & Cards**
216 S. Villa Ave.
Villa Park, IL 60181
PH:708-279-5777

**Heroland Comics**
6963 W. 111th St.
Worth, IL 60482
PH:708-448-2937

# INDIANA:

**Pen Comics & Entertainment Store**
7 North 5th Ave.
Beech Grove, IN 46107
PH:317-782-3450

**25th Century Five & Dime**
106 E. Kirkwood, P.O. Box 7
Bloomington, IN 47402
PH:812-332-0011

**The Bookstack**
112 W. Lexington Ave.
Elkhart, IN 46516
PH:219-293-3815

**Spider's Web**
51815 State Rd. 19 N.
Elkhart, IN 46514
PH:219-264-9178

**Collector's Carnival**
2030 E. Morgan
Evansville, IN 47711
PH:812-925-3290

**Books, Comics and Things**
2212 Maplecrest Rd.
Fort Wayne, IN 46815
PH:219-749-4045

**Books, Comics and Things**
5950 West Jefferson Blvd.
Time Corners
Fort Wayne, IN 46804
PH:219-436-0159

**Broadway Comic Book and Baseball Card Shop**
2423 Broadway
Fort Wayne, IN 46807
PH:219-744-1456

**Friendly Frank's Distr., Inc.**
(Wholesale only)
3990 Broadway
Gary, IN 46408
PH:219-884-5052

**Friendly Frank's Comics**
220 Main St.
Hobart, IN 46342
PH:219-942-6020

**Comic Carnival & Nostalgia Emporium**
6265 N. Carrollton Ave.
Indianapolis, IN 46220
PH:317-253-8882

**Comic Carnival & Nostalgia Emporium**
5002 S. Madison Ave.
Indianapolis, IN 46227
PH:317-787-3773

**Comic Carnival & Nostalgia Emporium**
982 N. Mitthoeffer Rd.
Indianapolis, IN 46229
PH:317-898-5010

**Comic Carnival & Nostalgia Emporium**
3837 N. High School Rd.
Indianapolis, IN 46254
PH:317-293-4386

**Tenth Planet**
204 Route 30
Schereville, IN
PH:219-322-2902

## IOWA:

**Oak Leaf Comics**
5219 University Ave.
Cedar Falls, IA 50613
PH:319-277-1835

**Comic World & Baseball Cards**
1626 Central Ave.
Dubuque, IA 52001
PH:319-557-1897

**Oak Leaf Comics**
23 - 5th S.W.
Mason City, IA 50401
PH:515-424-0333

**The Comiclogue**
520 Elm St., P.O. Box 65304
West Des Moines, IA 50265
PH:515-279-9006

## KANSAS:

**Kwality Books, Comics & Games**
1111 Massachusetts St.
Lawrence, KS 66044
PH:913-843-7239

**1,000,000 Comix Inc.**
5332 West 95th St.
Prairie Village, KS 66207
PH:913-383-1777

**Prairie Dog Comics East**
Oxford Square Mall
6100 E. 21st St., Suite 190
Wichita, KS 67208
PH:316-688-5576

**Prairie Dog Comics West**
Central Heights Mall
7387 West Central
Wichita, KS 67212
PH:316-722-6316

## KENTUCKY:

**Pac-Rat's, Inc.**
Greenwood Station
1051 Bryant Way, Suites C & D
Bowling Green, KY 42103
PH:502-782-8092

**Comic Book World**
7130 Turfway Rd.
Florence, KY 41042
PH:606-371-9562

**The Great Escape**
2433 Bardstown Rd.
Louisville, KY 40205
PH:502-456-2216


## LOUISIANA:

**Comic Book Emporium**
5201 Nicholson Drive, Suite H
Baton Rouge, LA 70816
PH:504-767-1227

**B.T. & W.D. Giles**
P.O. Box 271
Keithville, LA 71047
PH:318-925-6654

**Bookworm of N.O.E.**
7011 Read Rd.
New Orleans, LA 70127
PH:504-242-7608

**Excalibur Comics, Cards &
Games**
9066 Mansfield Rd.
Shreveport, LA 71118
PH:318-686-7076

**Comix Plus**
637 Carollo Drive
Slidell, LA 70458
PH:504-649-4376


## MAINE:

**Lippincott Books**
624 Hammond St.
Bangor, ME 04401
PH:207-942-4398

**Moonshadow Comics**
10 Exchange St.

Portland, ME 04101
PH:207-772-3870

**Moonshadow Comics**
The Maine Mall
Maine Mall Rd.
South Portland, ME 04106
PH:207-772-4605

**Book Barn**
U.S. Route 1
Wells, ME 04090
PH:207-646-4926


## MARYLAND:

**Universal Comics**
5300 East Drive
Arbutus, MD 21227
PH:301-242-4578

**Comic Book Kingdom, Inc.**
4307 Harford Rd.
Baltimore, MD 21214
PH:301-426-4529

**Geppi's Comic World**
7019 Security Blvd.
Hechinger's Square
at Security Mall
Baltimore, MD 21207
PH:301-298-1758

**Geppi's Comic World**
Harbor Place
Upper Level, Light St. Pavilion
301 Light St.
Baltimore, MD 21202
PH:301-547-0910

**Mindbridge, Ltd. I**
1786 Merritt Blvd.
Merritt Park Shopping Center
Baltimore, MD 21222
PH:301-284-7880

**Mike's Clubhouse**
108 S. Main St.
Bel Air, MD 21014
PH:301-838-6255

**Big Planet Comics**
4865 Cordell Ave. (2nd Floor)
Bethesda, MD 20814
PH:301-654-6856

**The Magic Page**
7416 Laurel-Bowie Rd. (Rt. 197)
Bowie, MD 20715
PH:301-262-4735

**Alternate Worlds**
9924 York Rd.
Cockeysville, MD 21030
PH:301-666-3290

**The Closet of Comics**
7319 Baltimore Ave. (U.S. 1)
College Park, MD 20740
PH:301-699-0498

**Comic Classics**
365 Main St.
Laurel, MD 20707
PH:301-792-4744, 490-9811

**Mindbridge, Ltd. II**
9847 Belair Rd. (Route 1)
Perry Hall, MD 21128
PH:301-256-7880

**The Closet of Comics**
Calvert Village Shopping Center
Prince Frederick, MD 20678
PH:301-535-4731

**Geppi's Comic World**
8317 Fenton St.
Silver Spring, MD 20910
PH:301-588-2546

**Barbarian**
11254 Triangle Lane
Wheaton, MD 20902
PH:301-946-4184


## MASSACHUSETTS:

**New England Comics**
168 Harvard Ave.
Allston (Boston), MA 02134
PH:617-783-1848

**Comically Speaking**
1322 Mass. Ave.
Arlington, MA 02174
PH:617-643-XMEN

**Bargain Books and Collectibles**
247 So. Main St.
Attleboro, MA 02703
PH:508-226-1668

**Ayer Comics & Baseball Cards**
28 Main St
Ayer, MA 01432
PH:508-772-4994

**Superhero Universe III**
41 West St.
Boston, MA 02111

**New England Comics**
748 Crescent St.
East Crossing Plaza
Brockton, MA 02402
PH:508-559-5068

**New England Comics**
316 Harvard St.
Brookline, MA 02146
PH:617-566-0115

**Superhero Universe I**
1105 Massachusetts Ave.
Cambridge, MA 02138
PH:617-354-5344

**Michael Richards**
P.O. Box 455
Dorchester, MA 02122
PH:617-436-7995

**World of Fantasy**
529 Broadway
Everett, MA 02149
PH:617-381-0411

**That's Entertainment**
387 Main St.
Fitchburg, MA 01420
PH:508-342-8607

**Bop City Comics**
80 Worcester Rd. (Route 9)
Marshalls Mall
Framingham, MA 01701
PH:508-872-2317

**New England Comics**
12A Pleasant St.
Malden, MA 02148
PH:617-322-2404

**New England Comics**
714 Washington St.
Norwood, MA 02062
PH:617-769-4552

**Imagine That Bookstore**
58 Dalton Ave.
Pittsfield, MA 01201
PH:413-445-5934

**New England Comics**
13B Court St.
Plymouth, MA 02360
PH:508-746-8797

**New England Comics**
1350 Hancock St.
Quincy, MA 02169
PH:617-770-1848

**Pages of Reading**
25 Harnden St.
Reading, MA 01867
PH:617-944-9613

**Park Nostalgia**
1242 Wilbur Ave.
Somerset, MA 02725
PH:508-673-0303

**Blaine's Comics**
1 Winter St.
(352 Bldg. Main St.)
Stoneham, MA 02180
PH:617-438-5813

**The Outer Limits**
457 Moody St.
Waltham, MA 02154
PH:617-891-0444

**Golden Age Buyers**
457 Moody St. Dept. 09
Waltham, MA 02154
PH:617-891-0444

**Mayo Beach Bookstore**
Kendrick Ave., Mayo Beach
Wellfleet, MA 02667
PH:508-349-3154

**Fabulous Fiction Book Store**
984 Main St.
Worcester, MA 01603
PH:508-754-8826

**That's Entertainment**
151 Chandler St.
Worcester, MA 01609
PH:508-755-4207

## MICHIGAN:

**Dave's II Comics & Collectibles**
623 E. William
Ann Arbor, MI 48017
PH:313-665-6969

**Tom & Terry Comics**
508 Lafayette Ave.
Bay City, MI 48708
PH:517-895-5525

**Harley Yee** (By appointment)
P.O. Box 19578
Detroit, MI 48219-0578
PH:313-533-2731

**Curious Book Shop**
307 E. Grand River Ave.
East Lansing, MI 48823
PH:517-332-0112

**Comix Corner - East**
32004 Utica Rd.
Fraser, MI 48026
PH:313-296-2758

**Argos Book Shop**
1405 Robinson Rd. S.E.
Grand Rapids, MI 49506
PH:616-454-0111

**Tardy's Collector's Corner, Inc.**
2009 Eastern Ave. S.E.
Grand Rapids, MI 49507
PH:616-247-7828, 247-0245

**Comix Corner - West**
861 E. Auburn Rd.
Rochester Hills, MI 48063
PH:313-852-3356

**Dave's Comics & Collectibles**
407 S. Washington
Royal Oak, MI 48067
PH:313-548-1230

**Book Stop**
1160 Chicago Drive S.W.
Wyoming, MI 49509-1004
PH:616-245-0090

## MINNESOTA:

**Collector's Connection**
21 East Superior St.
Duluth, MN 55802
PH:218-722-9551

**College of Comic Book Knowledge**
3151 Hennepin Ave. S.
Minneapolis, MN 55408
PH:612-822-2309

**Midway Book & Comic**
1579 University Ave.
St. Paul, MN 55104
PH:612-644-7605

## MISSISSIPPI:

**Gulf Coast Comics**
Petit Bois Specialty Center
240 Eisenhower Drive, C-1
Biloxi, MS 39531
PH:601-388-2991

**Sharon Zocchi's Retail Games and Comics**
2803 Pass Rd. (near the airbase)
Biloxi, MS 39531
PH:601-374-6632

**Star Store**
4212 N. State St.
Jackson, MS 39206
PH:601-362-8001

**Spanish Trail Books**
1006 Thorn Ave.
Ocean Springs, MS 39564
PH:601-875-1444

## MISSOURI:

**Parallel Worlds**
12th & Virginia, P.O. Box 2802
(Joplin Flea Market)
Joplin, MO 64803
PH:417-781-5130

**B &R Comix Center**
4747 Morganford
St. Louis, MO 63116
PH:314-353-4013

**Mo's Comics and Stories**
4530 Gravois
St. Louis, MO 63116
PH:314-353-9500

**The Book Rack**
300 W. Olive
Springfield, MO 65806
PH:417-865-4945

## MONTANA:

**Marvel-Us Comics**
600 15th St. South
Great Falls, MT 59405
PH:406-771-1535

**The Book Exchange**
2335 Brooks
Trempers Shopping Center
Missoula, MT 59801
PH:406-728-6342

## NEBRASKA:

**Dragon's Lair**
8316 Blondo St.
Omaha, NE 68137
PH:402-399-9141

**Dragon's Lair Too**
13826 T Plaza
Omaha, NE 68137
PH:402-895-5653

**Star Realm**
7305 South 85th St.
Omaha, NE 68128
PH:402-331-4844

## NEVADA:

**Page After Page**
1412 E. Charleston Blvd.
Las Vegas, NV 89104
PH:702-384-1690

**Fandom's Comicworld of Reno**
2001 East Second St.
Reno, NV 89502
PH:702-786-6663

**Stella Enterprises**
126 "B" St.
P.O. Box 251
Sparks, NV 89432
PH:702-359-7812

## NEW HAMPSHIRE:

**James F. Payette**
P.O. Box 750
Bethlehem, NH 03574
PH:603-869-2097

**Comic Store**
643 Elm St.
Manchester, NH 03101
PH:603-668-6705

**Comic Store**
300 Main St.
Simoneau Plaza
Nashua, NH 03060
PH:603-881-4855

## NEW JERSEY:

**The Comic Zone**
71 Rtc. 73 & Day Ave.
Berlin, NJ 08009
PH:609-768-8186

**Collector's Cove**
27 Watsessing Ave.
Bloomfield, NJ 07003
PH:201-748-9263

**Rainbow Collectibles**
Laurel Hill Plaza
Clementon, NJ 08021
PH:609-627-1711

**Steve's Comic Relief**
1555 St. George Ave. off Rt. 35
Colonia, NJ 07067
PH:201-382-3736

**Steve's Comic Relief**
24 Mill Run Plaza
Off Route 130
Delran, NJ 08075
PH:609-461-1770

**Thunder Rd. Comics & Cards**
Parkway Plaza
831 Parkway Ave.
Ewing Township, NJ 08618
PH:609-771-1055

**Shore Video Comics & Baseball Cards**
615 Lacey Rd.
Forked River, NJ 08731
PH:609-693-3831

**1,000,000 Comix Inc.**
629 Palisade Ave.
Fort Lee, NJ
(call info re phone #)

**Star Spangled Comics**
U.S. Rt. 22 - King George Plaza
Green Brook, NJ 08812
PH: Call information

**Thunder Rd. Comics & Cards**
3694 Nottingham Way
Hamilton Square, NJ 08690
PH:609-587-5353

**Steve's Comic Relief**
106 Clifton Ave. off Route 9
Lakewood, NJ 08701
PH:201-363-3899

**Steve's Comic Relief**
156-A Mercer Mall off Route 1
Lawrenceville, NJ 08648
PH:609-452-7548

**The Hobby Shop**
Route 34
Strathmore Shopping Center
Matawan, NJ 07747
PH:201-583-0505

**Comic Museum**
58 High St.
Mount Holly, NJ 08060
PH:609-261-0996

**Comicrypt**
521 White Horse Pike
Oaklyn, NJ 08107
PH:609-858-3877

**Passaic Book Center**
594 Main Ave.
Passaic, NJ 07055
PH:201-778-6646

**Fantasy Zone Comics**
80 Broad St.
Red Bank, NJ 07701
PH:201-842-4940

**Sparkle City** (appointment only)
P.O. Box 67
Sewell, NJ 08080
PH:609-881-1174

**Philip M. Levine and Sons, Rare
& Esoteric Books**
P.O. Box 246 (appointment only)
Three Bridges, NJ 08887
PH:201-788-0532

**Mr. Collector**
327 Union Blvd.
Totowa, NJ 07512
PH:201-595-0900

**TemDee**
15 Whitman Square
Black Horse Pike
Turnersville, NJ 08012
PH:609-228-8645

**Comics Plus**
Ocean Plaza
Hwy. 35 & Sunset Ave.
Wanamassa, NJ 07712
PH:201-922-3308

**1,000,000 Comix Inc.**
875 Mantua Pike
Southwood Shopping Centre
Woodbury Heights, NJ 08096
PH:609-384-8844

**NEW MEXICO:**

**Over the Rainbow Comics and
Cards**
1560-F Juan Tabo, N.E.
Albuquerque, NM 87112
PH:505-292-1374

**Captain Comic's Specialty Shop**
109 W. 4th St.
Clovis, NM 88101
PH:505-769-1543

**NEW YORK:**

**Earthworld Comic Inc.**
327 Central Ave.
Albany, NY 12206
PH:518-465-5495

**FantaCo Enterprises Inc.**
21 Central Ave. - Level Two
Albany, NY 12210
PH:518-463-3667

**FantaCo Archival Research Center**
21 Central Ave. - Sublevel One
Albany, NY 12210
PH:518-463-1400

**FantaCo Comic Shop**
21 Central Ave. - Level One
Albany, NY 12210
PH:518-463-1400

**FantaCon Organization Offices**
21 Central Ave. - Level One
Albany, NY 12210
PH:518-463-1400

**FantaCo Publications**
21 Central Ave. - Level Two
Albany, NY 12210
PH:518-463-3667

**FantaCo 1990: Year of the Zombie Headquarters**
21 Central Ave. - Level Two
Albany, NY 12210
PH:518-463-3667

**Collector's Comics**
167 Deer Park Ave.
Babylon, NY 11702
PH:516-321-4347

**Long Island Comics**
1670-D Sunrise Hwy.
Bay Shore, NY 11706
PH:516-665-4342

**Fordham Comics**
390 East Fordham Rd.
Bronx, NY 10458
PH:212-933-9245

**Wow Comics**
652 E. 233rd St.
Bronx, NY 10466
PH:212-231-0913

**Wow Comics**
642 Pelham Parkway S.
Bronx, NY 10462
PH:212-829-0461

**Brain Damage Comics**
1289 Prospect Ave.
Brooklyn, NY 11218
PH:718-438-1335

**Metro Comics**
138 Montague St.
Brooklyn, NY 11201
PH:718-935-0911

**Metropolis Comics**
(by appointment)
P. O. Box 165
Brooklyn, NY 11214
PH:718-837-2538

**Pinocchio Discounts**
1814 McDonald Ave. near Ave. P
Brooklyn, NY 11223
PH:718-645-2573

**World of Fantasy**
737 Long Island Ave. at Deer Park Ave.
Deer Park, NY 11729
PH:516-586-7314

**The Book Stop**
384 East Meadow Ave.
East Meadow, NY 11554
PH:516-794-9129

**Comics for Collectors**
211 West Water St.
Elmira, NY 14901
PH:607-732-2299

**Fantazia**
2 So. Central Ave.
Hartsdale, NY 10530
PH:914-946-3306

**Comics for Collectors**
148 The Commons
Ithaca, NY 14850
PH:607-272-3007

**Bush Hobbies**
Park Plaza Shopping Center
299-12 Hawkins Ave.
Lake Ronkonkoma, NY 11779
PH:516-981-0253

**Bailey's Comics**
106 N. Wellwood Ave.
Lindenhurst, NY 11757
PH:516-957-7276

**Long Beach Books, Inc.**
17 E. Park Ave.
Long Beach, NY 11561
PH:516-432-2265

**Comics & Hobbies**
156 Mamaroneck Ave.
Mamaroneck, NY 10543
PH:914-698-9473

**Action Comics**
318 E. 84th St.
(Between 1st & 2nd Ave.)
New York, NY 10028
PH:212-249-7344

**Big Apple Comics**
2489 Broadway (92 - 93 St.)
New York, NY 10025
PH:212-724-0085

**Forbidden Planet**
821 Broadway at 12th St.
New York, NY 10003
PH:212-475-6161

**Forbidden Planet**
227 E. 59th St. & 3rd Ave.
New York, NY 10022
PH:212-751-4386

**Funny Business**
656 Amsterdam Ave.
(corner 92nd St.)
New York, NY 10025
PH:212-799-9477

**Golden Age Express**
2489 Broadway (92-93)
New York, NY 10025
PH:212-769-9570

**Jim Hanley's Universe**
At A&S Plaza, 5th & 6th Floors
901 Ave. of the Americas (at 33rd
St.)
New York, NY 10001
PH:212-268-7088

**Jerry Ohlinger's Movie Material
Store, Inc.**
242 West 14th St.
New York, NY 10011
PH:212-989-0869

**Pinnacle Bag Co.**
P.O. Box 6639 Grand Central Sta.
New York, NY 10163
PH:718-539-8603

**St. Mark's Comics**
11 St. Mark's Pl.
New York, NY 10003
PH:212-598-9439 or 212-353-3300

**West Side Comics &Video**
107 West 86 St.
New York, NY 10024
PH:212-724-0432

**Corner-Stone Bookshop**
110 Margaret St.
Plattsburgh, NY 12901
PH:518-561-0520

**Fantastic Planet**
24 Oak St.
Plattsburgh, NY 12901
PH:518-563-2946

**Flash Point — "The Science
Fiction & Fantasy Shop"**
Harbor Square Mall
134 Main St.
Port Jefferson, NY 11777
PH:516-331-9401

**Amazing Comics**
12 Gillette Ave.
Sayville, NY 11782
PH:516-567-8069

**Comix 4-U, Inc.**
1675 Broadway
Schenectady, NY 12306
PH:518-372-6612, 452-0801

**Electric City Comics**
1704 Van Vranken Ave.
Schenectady, NY 12308
PH:518-377-1500

**Clearly Chaotic Comix Co.**
(By appointment only)
168 Portage Ave.
Staten Island, NY 10314
PH:718-667-9056

**Jim Hanley's Universe**
at the Staten Island Mall
2655 Richmond Ave.
Staten Island, NY 10314
PH:718-983-5752

**Comic Book Heaven**
48-14 Skillman Ave.

Sunnyside, Queens, NY 11104
PH:718-899-4175

**Dream Days Comic Book Shop**
312 South Clinton St.
Syracuse, NY 13202
PH:315-475-3995

**Michael Sagert**
P.O. Box 456 - Downtown
Syracuse, NY 13201
PH:315-475-3995

**Twilight Book & Game
Emporium, Inc.**
1401 North Salina St.
Syracuse, NY 13208
PH:315-471-3139

**Aquilonia Comics**
459 Fulton St.
Troy, NY 12180
PH:518-271-1069

**Collector's Comics**
3247 Sunrise Hwy.
Wantagh, NY 11793
PH:516-783-8700


# NORTH CAROLINA:

**Super Giant Books**
344 Merrimon Ave.
Asheville, NC 28801
PH:704-254-2103

**Heroes Aren't Hard to Find**
Corner Central Ave. & The Plaza
P.O. Box 9181
Charlotte, NC 28299
PH:704-375-7462

**Heroes Aren't Hard to Find**
Carmel Commons Shopping Ctr.
6648 Carmel Rd.
Charlotte, NC 28226
PH:704-542-8842

**Heroes Aren't Hard to Find**
Mail Order Subscription &
Wholesale
P.O. Box 9181
Charlotte, NC 28299
PH:704-376-5766

**New Dimension Comics**
2609 Central Ave.
Charlotte, NC 28205
PH:704-377-4376

**New Dimension Comics Whse.**
Mailorder-Conventions-Wholesale
2611 Central Ave.
Charlotte, NC 28205
PH:704-372-4376

**Heroes Are Here**
208 S. Berkeley Blvd.
Goldsboro, NC 27530
PH:919-751-3131

**Acme Comics**
348 S. Elm St.
Greensboro, NC 27401
PH:919-272-5994

**Parts Unknown—The Comic
Book Store**
The Cotton Mill Square
801 Merritt Drive/Spring Garden
St.
Greensboro, NC 27407
PH:919-294-0091

**Heroes Are Here, Too**
116 E. Fifth St.

Greenville, NC 27858
PH:919-757-0948

**The Nostalgia News Stand**
919 Dickinson Ave.
Greenville, NC 27834
PH:919-758-6909

**Tales Resold**
3936 Atlantic Ave.
Raleigh, NC 27604
PH:919-878-8551

**The Booktrader**
121 Country Club Rd.
Rocky Mount, NC 27801
PH:919-443-3993

**Bargain Bookstore II**
Delwood Rd.
Waynesville, NC 28786
PH:704-452-2539

**Heroes Aren't Hard to Find**
Silas Creek Crossing Shop. Ctr.
3234 Silas Creek Parkway
Winston-Salem, NC 27103
PH:919-765-4370

## NORTH DAKOTA:

**Collector's Corner**
306 N. 4th St.
Grand Forks, ND 58203
PH:701-772-2518

## OHIO:

**C. C. Books**
4651 Whipple Ave. N.W.
Canton, OH 44718
PH:216-492-9606

**Comics, Cards & Collectables**
533 Market Ave. North
Canton, OH 44702
PH:216-456-8907

**Comic Book World**
5526 Colerain Ave.
Cincinnati, OH 45239
PH:513-541-8002

**Collectors Warehouse Inc.,**
5437 Pearl Rd.
Cleveland, OH 44129
PH:216-842-2896

**Bookie Parlor**
2920 Wayne Ave.
Dayton, OH 45420
PH:513-256-6806

**Troll and Unicorn Comics and Games**
5460 Brandt Pike
Huber Heights, OH 45424
PH:513-233-6535

**Bigg Fredd's Coins & Collectables**
162 West Main St.
(1 Block E. of U.S. 33 on U.S. 22)
Lancaster, OH 43130
PH:614 653-5555

**Comic Book City**
2601 Hubbard Rd.
Madison, OH 44057
PH:216-428-4786

**L. A. Comics & Collectibles**
6672 Pearl Rd.
Parma Heights, OH 44130
PH:216-884-0666

**Toy Scouts, Inc. (Mail Order)**
P.O. Box 268

Seville, OH 44273
PH:216-769-2523

**Monarch Cards & Comics**
2620 Airport Hwy.
Toledo, OH 43609
PH:419-382-1451

**Funnie Farm Bookstore**
328 N. Dixie Drive
Airline Shopping Center
Vandalia, OH 45377
PH:513-898-2794

**Dark Star Books**
231 Xenia Ave.
Yellow Springs, OH 45387
PH:513-767-9400


# OKLAHOMA:

**Comic Archives**
1914 E. Second St.
Edmond, OK 73034
PH:405-348-6800

**Comic Archives**
Heismen Sq., 1221 E. Alameda
(in Bargain Time Store)
Norman, OK 73071
PH:405-360-6866

**Planet Comics & SF**
918 W. Main
Norman, OK 73069
PH:405-329-9695

**New World**
6219 N. Meridian Ave.
Oklahoma City, OK 73112
PH:405-721-7634

**New World**
4420 S.E. 44th St.
Oklahoma City, OK 73135
PH:405-677-2559

**Planet Comics & SF**
2112 S.W. 74th
Oklahoma City, OK 73159
PH:405-682-9144

**Comic Empire of Tulsa**
3122 S. Mingo Rd.
Tulsa, OK 74146
PH:918-664-5808

**Comics, Cards & Collectibles**
4618 East 31st St.
Tulsa, OK 74135
PH:918-749-8500

**Starbase 21**
2130 S. Sheridan Rd.
Tulsa, OK 74129
PH:918-838-3388

**Want List Comics**
Box 701932 (appointment only)
Tulsa, OK 74170-1932
PH:918-299-0440

## OREGON:

**ComicCave**
100 Will Dodge Way
Ashland, OR 97520
PH:503-488-3901

**Pegasus Books**
4390 S.W. Lloyd
Beaverton, OR 97005
PH:503-643-4222

**Emerald City Comics**
770 E. 13th

Eugene, OR 97401
PH:503-345-2568

**Nostalgia Collectibles**
527 Williamette St.
Eugene, OR 97401
PH:503-484-9202

**House of Fantasy**
2005 E. Burnside
P.O. Box 472
Gresham, OR 97030
PH:503-661-1815

**Nelscott Books**
3412 S.E. Hwy. 101
Lincoln City, OR 97367
PH:503-994-3513

**More Fun**
413 E. Main
Medford, OR 97501
PH:503-776-1200

**The Comic Shop**
(Mail Order Service)
P.O. Box 22081
Milwaukie, OR 97222

**It Came From Outer Space**
10812 S.E. Oak St.
Milwaukie, OR 97222
PH:503-786-0865

**Pegasus Books & Video**
10902 S.E. Main St.
Milwaukie, OR 97222
PH:503-652-2752

**Armchair "Family" Bookstore**
3205 S.E. Milwaukie Ave.
Portland, OR 97202
PH:503-238-6680

**Future Dreams - Burnside**
1800 East Burnside
Portland, OR 97214
PH:503-231-8311

**Future Dreams - Gateway**
10508 N.E. Halsey
Portland, OR 97220
PH:503-255-5245

**Future Dreams Comic Art
Reading Library**
10506 N.E. Halsey
Portland, OR 97220
PH:503-256-1885

**Pegasus Books & Video**
1401 S.E. Division
Portland, OR 97214
PH:503-233-0768

**Pegasus Books**
5015 N.E. Sandy Blvd.
Portland, OR 97213
PH:503-284-4693

**Rackafratz Comics & Cards**
3760 Market
Salem, OR 97301
PH:503-371-1320

## PENNSYLVANIA:

**Cap's Comic Cavalcade**
1980 Catasauqua Rd.
Allentown, PA 18103
PH:215-264-5540

**Dreamscape Comics**
404 West Broad St.
Bethlehem, PA 18018
PH:215-867-1178

**Dreamscape Comics**
9 East Third St.
Bethlehem, PA 18015
PH:215-865-4636

**Showcase Comics**
839 W. Lancaster Ave.
Bryn Mawr, PA 19010
PH:215-527-6236

**Comic Universe**
Bazaar of All Nations, Store 228
Clifton Heights, PA 19018
PH:215-259-9943

**Mr. Monster's Comic Crypt &
House of Horrors**
1805 Washington Blvd.
Easton, PA 18042
PH:215-250-0659

**Comic Universe**
446 MacDade Blvd.
Folsom, PA 19033
PH:215-461-7960

**Comic Universe**
395 Lancaster Ave.
Frazer, PA 19355
PH:215-889-3320

**Golden Unicorn Comics**
860 Alter St.
Hazleton, PA 18201
PH:717-455-4645

**Ott's Trading Post**
201 Allegheny St.
Hollidaysburg, PA 16648
PH:814-696-3494

**Charlie's Collectors Corner**
100-D West Second St.
Hummelstown, PA 17036
PH:717-566-7216

**Captain Blue Hen Comics, Cards & Games**
1800 Lincoln Hwy. East
Lancaster, PA 17602
PH:717-397-8011

**The Comic Store**
Station Square
28 McGovern Ave.
Lancaster, PA 17602
PH:717-397-8737

**Steve's Comic Relief**
4153 Woerner Ave.
Near 5 Points
Levittown, PA 19057
PH:215-945-7954

**Chris Bass t/a Japanimation Super Store**
3407 Kensington Ave.
Philadelphia, PA 19134
PH:215-634-5167

**Fat Jack's Comicrypt I**
2006 Sansom St.
Philadelphia, PA 19103
PH:215-963-0788

**Fat Jack's Comicrypt II**
7598 Haverford Ave.
Philadelphia, PA 19151
PH:215-473-6333

**Fat Jack's Comicrypt III**
5736 North 5th St.
Philadelphia, PA19120
PH:215-924-8210

**Sparkle City Comics**
Philadelphia, PA
(Philly area by appointment)
PH:609-881-1174

**Adventures in Comics**
1368 Illinois Ave.
Pittsburgh, PA 15216
PH:412-531-5644

**BEM: The Store**
622 South Ave.
Pittsburgh, PA 15221
PH:412-243-2736

**Eide's Comics and Records**
940 Penn Ave.
Pittsburgh, PA 15222
PH:412-261-3666

**Eide's Comics and Records**
2713 Murray Ave.
Pittsburgh, PA 15217
PH:412-422-4666

**Book Swap**
110 South Fraser St.
State College, PA 16801
PH:814-234-6005

**The Comic Store - West**
Northwest Plaza
915 Loucks Rd.
York, PA 17404


# RHODE ISLAND:

**TheAnnex**
314 Broadway
Newport, RI 02840
PH:401-847-4607

**Starship Excalibur**
60 Washington St.
Providence, RI 02903
PH:401-273-8390

**Starship Excalibur**
834 Hope St.
Providence, RI 02906
PH:401-861-1177

**Superhero Universe II**
187 Angell St.
Providence, RI 02906
PH:401-331-5637

**Starship Excalibur**
830-832 Post Rd., Warwick Plaza
Warwick, RI 02888
PH:401-941-8890

## SOUTH CAROLINA:

**Super Giant Comics & Records**
Market Place/Cinema Center
3466 Clemson Blvd.
Anderson, SC 29621
PH:803-225-9024

**Silver City**
904 Knox Abbott Drive
Cayce, SC 29033
PH:803-791-4021

**Book Exchange**
1219 Savannah Hwy.
Charleston, SC 29407
PH:803-556-5051

**Final Frontier Comics & Games**
1670 Olde Towne Rd.
Charleston, SC 29407
PH:803-766-9504

**New Dimension Comics**
1930 Main St.
Columbia, SC
PH:803-779-4376

**Heroes Aren't Hard to Find**
1415-A Laurens Rd.
Greenville, SC 29607
PH:803-235-3488

**New Dimension Comics**
1608 Laurens Rd.
Greenville, SC
PH:803-271-1104

**Haven for Heroes**
1131 Dick Pond Rd.
Myrtle Beach, SC 29575
PH:803-238-9975

**Super Giant Comics**
Suite 24 - 660 Spartan Blvd.
Spartanburg, SC 29301
PH:803-576-4990

## TENNESSEE:

**Comics and Curios #1**
3472 Brainerd Rd.
Chattanooga, TN 37411
PH:615-698-1710

**Comics and Curios #2**
629 Signal Mountain Rd.
Chattanooga, TN

**Collector's Choice**
3405 Keith St., Shoney's Plaza
Cleveland, TN 37311
PH:615-472-6649

**Big D's Baseball Cards & Comics**
323 N. Washington Ave.
Cookeville, TN 38501
PH:615-528-6070

**Marnello's Comics & Cards**
451 E. Elk Ave.
Elizabethton, TN 37643
PH:615-542-6564

**Gotham City Comics**
7869 Farmington Blvd.
Germantown, TN 38138
PH:901-757-9665

**Comics and Curios #3**
5131-B Hixson Pike
Hixson, TN

**Mountain Empire Collectibles III**
1210 N. Roan St.
Johnson City, TN 37602
PH:615-929-8245

**Mountain Empire Collectibles II**
1451 E. Center St.
Kingsport, TN 37664
PH:615-245-0364

**Collector's Choice**
2104 Cumberland Ave.
Knoxville, TN 37916
PH:615-546-2665

**The Great Escape**
Gallatin Rd. at Old Hickory Blvd.
Madison, TN 37115
PH:615-865-8052

**Comics and Collectibles**
4750 Poplar Ave.
Memphis, TN 38117
PH:901-683-7171

**Memphis Comics & Records**
665 So. Highland
Memphis, TN 38111
PH:901-452-1304

**Collector's World**
1511 East Main St.
Murfreesboro, TN 37130
PH:615-895-1120

**Collector's World**
5751 Nolensville Rd.
Nashville, TN 37211
PH:615-333-9458

**The Great Escape**
1925 Broadway
Nashville, TN 37203
PH:615-327-0646

**Walt's Paperback Books**
2604 Franklin Rd.
Nashville, TN 37204
PH:615-298-2506

## TEXAS:

**Lone Star Comics Books & Games**
511 East Abram St.
Arlington, TX 76010
PH:817-Metro 265-0491

**Lone Star Comics Books & Games**
5721 W. I-20 at Green Oaks Blvd.
Arlington, TX 76016
PH:817-478-5405

**Dollar Video**
813 Conrad Hilton Ave.
Cisco, TX 76437
PH:817-442-1998

**Lone Star Comics Books & Games**
11661 Preston Forest Village
Dallas, TX 75230
PH:214-373-0934

**Remember When**
2431 Valwood Pkwy.
Dallas, TX 75234
PH:214-243-3439

**Lone Star Comics Books & Games**
3014 West 7th St.
Fort Worth, TX 76107
PH:817-654-0333

**B & D Trophy Shop**
4404 N. Shepherd
Houston, TX 77018
PH:713-694-8436

**Nan's Games and Comics, Too!**
2011 Southwest Freeway (U.S. 59)
Houston, TX 77098-4805
PH:713-520-8700

**Third Planet Books**
2439 Bissonnet
Houston, TX 77005
PH:713-528-1067

**Third Planet Books**
3806 S. Shaver
Houston, TX 77587
PH:713-941-1490

**Lone Star Comics Books & Games**
2550 N. Beltline Rd.
Irving, TX 75062
PH:214-659-0317

**Alan's**
2525-B Judson Rd.

Longview, TX75601
PH:214-753-0493

**Lone Star Comics Books & Games**
3600 Gus Thomasson, Suite 107
Mesquite, TX 75150
PH:214-681-2040

**Comics & Records Unlimited**
226 Bitters Rd., Suite 102
San Antonio, TX 78216
PH:512-545-9063

**Comics & Records Unlimited**
6856 Ingram Rd.
San Antonio, TX 78238
PH:512-522-9063

**The Book Cellar**
2 S. Main St.
Temple, TX 76501
PH:817-773-7545

**Excalibur Comics, Cards & Games**
2811 State Line Ave.
Texarkana, TX 75503
PH:214-792-5767

**Bankston's Comics**
1321 S. Valley Mills Drive
Waco, TX 76711
PH:817-755-0070

**UTAH:**

**The Bookshelf**
2456 Washington Blvd.
Ogden, UT 84401
PH:801-621-4752

**Comics Utah**
1956 S. 1100 East
Salt Lake City, UT 84105
PH:801-487-5390

**Comics Utah**
2985 W. 3500 South
Salt Lake City, UT 84119
PH:801-966-8581

## VERMONT:

**Comics Outpost**
27 Granite St.
Barre, VT 05641
PH:802-476-4553

**Comics City, Inc.**
6 No. Winooski Ave.
Burlington, VT 05401
PH:802-865-3828

**Earth Prime Comics**
154 Church St.
Burlington, VT 05401
PH:802-863-3666

## VIRGINIA:

**Capital Comics Center
Storyland, U.S.A.**
2008 Mt. Vernon Ave.
Alexandria, VA 22301 (D.C. area)
PH:703-548-3466

**Geppi's Crystal City Comics**
1675 Crystal Square Arcade
Arlington, VA 22202
PH:703-521-4618

**Mountain Empire Collectibles I**
509 State St.
Bristol, VA 24201
PH:703-466-6337

**Burke Centre Books**
5741 Burke Centre Pkwy.
Burke, VA 22015
PH:703-250-5114

**Fantasia Comics and Records**
1419½ University Ave.
Charlottesville, VA 22903
PH:804-971-1029

**Fantasia Comics and Records II**
1861 Seminole Trail
Charlottesville, VA 22901
PH:804-974-7512

**Trilogy Shop #3**
3580-F Forest Haven Ln.
Chesapeake, VA 23321
PH:804-483-4173

**Zeno's Books**
1112 Sparrow Rd.
Chesapeake, VA 23225
PH:804-420-2344

**Hole in the Wall Books**
905 West Broad St.
Falls Church, VA 22046
PH:703-536-2511

**Marie's Books and Things**
1701 Princess Anne St.
Fredericksburg, VA 22401
PH:703-373-5196

**Bender's Books & Cards**
22 South Mallory St.
Hampton, VA 23663
PH:804-723-3741

**Franklin Farm Books**
13320-I Franklin Farm Rd.
Herndon, VA 22071
PH:703-437-9530

**Trilogy Shop #2**
700 E. Little Creek Rd.
Norfolk, VA 23518
PH:804-587-2540

**Ward's Comics**
3405 Clifford St.
Portsmouth, VA 23707
PH:804-397-7106

**Dave's Comics**
7019-E Three Chopt Rd.
Richmond, VA 23226
PH:804-282-1211

**Nostalgia Plus**
5610 Patterson Ave.
Richmond, VA 23221
PH:804-282-5532

**B & D Comic Shop**
3514 Williamson Rd. N.W.
Roanoke, VA 24012
PH:703-563-4161

**Trilogy Shop #1**
5773 Princess Anne Rd.
Virginia Beach, VA 23462
PH:804-490-2205

**Trilogy Shop #4**
867 S. Lynnhaven Rd.
Virginia Beach, VA 23452
PH:804-468-0412

**Zeno's Books**
338 Constitution Drive
Virginia Beach, VA 23462
PH:804-490-1517

**WASHINGTON:**

**Psycho 5 Comics & Cards**
221 Bellevue Way N.E.
Bellevue, WA 98004
PH:206-462-2869

**Paperback Exchange**
2100 N. National Ave.
Chehalis, WA 98532
PH:206-748-4792

**Geepy's Comics**
618 Bridge
Clarkston, WA 99403
No Phone

**Everett Comics & Cards**
2934½ Colby Ave.
Everett, WA 98201
PH:206-252-8181

**Tales of Kirkland**
128-A Park Lane
Kirkland, WA 98033
PH:206-822-7333

**Olympic Card & Comic Shop**
321 S. Sound Center
Lacey, WA 98503
PH:206-459-7721

**Coin House**
777 Stevens Drive
Richland, WA 99352

**The Comic Character Shop**
Old Firehouse Antique Mall
110 Alaskan Way South
Seattle, WA 98104
PH:206-283-0532

**Corner Comics**
6521 N.E. 181st
Seattle, WA 98155
PH:206-486-XMEN

**Corner Comics II**
5226 University Way N.E.
Seattle, WA 98105
PH:206-525-9394

**Gemini Book Exchange and Comic Center**
9614 - 16th Ave. S.W.
Seattle, WA 98106
PH:206-762-5543

**Golden Age Collectables, Ltd.**
1501 Pike Place Market
401 Lower Level
Seattle, WA 98101
PH:206-622-9799

**Psycho 5 Comics & Cards**
12513 Lake City Way N.E.
Seattle, WA 98125
PH:206-367-1620

**Rocket Comics & Collectibles**
119 N. 85th
Seattle, WA 98103
PH:206-784-7300

**Zanadu Comics**
1923 3rd Ave.
Seattle, WA 98101
PH:206-443-1316

**Zanadu Comics**
4518 University Way N.E.
2nd Floor Arcade Bldg.
Seattle, WA 98105
PH:206-632-0989

**The Book Exchange**
K-Mart Center, N. 6504 Division
Spokane, WA 99208
PH:509-489-2053

**The Book Exchange**
University City East
E. 10812 Sprague
Spokane, WA 99206
PH:509-928-4073

**Lady Jayne's Comics & Books**
6611 S. 12th
Tacoma, WA 98465
PH:206-564-6168

**Pegasus Books**
813 Grand Blvd.
Vancouver, WA 98661
PH:206-693-1240

**Galaxy Comics**
1720 - 5th St., Suite D
Wenatchee, WA 98801
PH:509-663-4330

## WEST VIRGINIA:

**Downtown Baseball Cards**
415 Neville St.
(Mail: 117 Monroe Ave.)
Beckley, WV 25801
PH:304-252-2134

**Cheryl's Comics & Toys**
5216½ MacCorkle Ave. S.E.
Charleston, WV 25304
PH:304-925-7269

**Comic World**
613 West Lee St.
Charleston, WV 25302
PH:304-343-3874

**Comic World**
1204 - 4th Ave.
Huntington, WV 25701
PH:304-522-3923

**Books and Things**
2506 Pike St.
Parkersburg, WV 26101
PH:304-422-0666

**Triple Play Cards, Comics & Collectibles**
335 - 4th Ave.
South Charleston, WV 25303
PH:304-744-2602

## WISCONSIN:

**Cover To Cover**
511 South Barstow St.
Eau Claire, WI 54701
PH:715-832-4252

**River City Cards & Comics**
115 South 6th St.
La Crosse, WI 54601
PH:608-782-5540

**Capital City Comics**
1910 Monroe St.
Madison, WI 53711
PH:608-251-8445

**20th Century Books**
108 King St.
Madison, WI 53703
PH:608-251-6226

**Incredible Comics**
4429 W. Lisbon Ave.
Milwaukee, WI 53208
PH:414-445-7006, 786-0112

**Polaris Comics**
4935 W. Center St.
Milwaukee, WI 53210
PH:414-442-0494

## AUSTRALIA

**Nostalgia Old Comic Shop**
48 Balmoral Rd.
Mortdale, NSW 2223, Australia
PH: (02) 57-5332

## CANADA:

## ALBERTA:

**Another Dimension**
324 - 10 St. N.W.
Calgary, Alberta, Can. T2N 1V8
PH:403-283-7078

**Another Dimension**
#1 - 3616 - 52 Ave. N.W.
Calgary, Alberta, Can. T2L 1V9
PH:403-282-7120

**Another Dimension**
2108B - 33 Ave. S.W.
Calgary, Alberta, Can. T2T 1Z6
PH:403-246-6768

**Another Dimension**
7610 Elbow Drive S.W.
Calgary, Alberta, Can. T2V 1K2
PH:403-255-2588

**Comic Legends** -Head Office
#205, 908 17th Ave. S.W.
Calgary, Alberta, Can. T2T 0A3
PH:403-245-5884

**Comic Legends**
#8, 10015 Oakfield Drive S.W.
Calgary, Alberta, Can.
PH:403-251-5964


## BRITISH COLUMBIA:

**L.A. Comics & Books**
371 Victoria St.
Kamloops, B.C., Can. V2C 2A3
PH:604-828-1995

**Page After Page**
1763 Harvey Ave.
Kelowna, B.C., Can. V1Y 6G4
PH:604-860-6554

**Ted's Paperback & Comics**
269 Leon Ave.
Kelowna, B.C., Can. V1Y 6J1
PH:604-763-1258

**Island Fantasy**
#29 Market Square
560 Johnson St.
Victoria, B.C., Can. V8W 3C6
PH:604-381-1134


## MANITOBA:

**International Comic Book Co.**
**Calvin Slobodian**
859 - 4th Ave.
Rivers, Man., Can. R0K 1X0
PH:204-328-7846

**Collector's Slave**
156 Imperial Ave.
Winnipeg, Man., Can. R2M 0K8
PH:204-237-4428

**Comic Factory II**
380 Donald St.
Winnipeg, Man., Can. R3B 2J2
PH:204-957-1978

**Doug Sulipa's Comic World**
374 Donald St.
Winnipeg, Man., Can. R3B 2J2
PH:204-943-3642


## NEW BRUNSWICK:

**1,000,000 Comix, Inc.**
345 Mountain Rd.
Moncton, N.B., Can. E1C 2M4
PH:506-855-0056


## NOVA SCOTIA:

**Members Only Comic Service**
(Mail Order Service Only)
6257 Yale St.
Halifax, N.S., Can. B3L 1C9
PH:902-423-MOCS/FAX 423-6627

**1,000,000 Comix, Inc.**
6251 Quinpool Rd.
Halifax, N.S., Can. B3L 1A4
PH:902-425-5594


## ONTARIO:

**1,000,000 Comix, Inc.**
2400 Guelph Line
Burlington, Ont., Can. L7P 4M7
PH:416-332-5600

**Starlite Comics and Books**
132 Westminster Drive South
Cambridge (Preston),
Ont., Can. N3H 1S8
PH:519-653-6571

**Comic King**
26 King St.
Dryden, Ont., Can.
PH:807-223-3254

**D. Farrell** (by appointment only)
2 Dalston Rd.
Etobicoke, Toronto, Ont., Can.
M8W 4R3
PH:416-251-1659

**Lookin' For Heroes**
93 Ontario St. S.
Kitchener, Ont., Can. N2G 1W5
PH:519-570-0873

**Books 'N' Stuff**
104 William St. N.
Lindsay, Ont., Can. K9V 4A5
PH:705-328-3491

**Bid Time Return**
183 Dundas St.
London, Ont., Can. N6A 1G4
PH:519-679-0295

**Endless Adventure**
400 Richmond St.
London, Ont., Can. N6A 3C7
PH:519-660-8521

**Endless Adventure**
White Oaks Mall
1105 Wellington Rd.
London, Ont., Can. N6E 1V4
PH:519-649-4572

**1,000,000 Comix, Inc.**
2150 Burnhamthorpe Rd.
South Common Mall
Mississauga, Ont., Can. L5L 3A2
PH:416-828-8208

**Comic King**
705 Victoria Ave. East
Victoriaville Mall
Thunder Bay, Ont., Can.
PH:807-623-6499

**Queen's Comics**
1009 Kingston Rd.
Toronto, Ont., Can. M4E 1T3
PH:416-698-8757

**Ken Mitchell Comics**
(by appointment only)
710 Conacher Drive
Willowdale, Ont., Can. M2M 3N6
PH:416-222-5808

## QUEBEC:

**Capitaine Quebec - Dollard**
4305 Blvd. St. Jean
D.D.O., Que., Can. H9H 2A4
PH:514-620-1866

**Capitaine Quebec - Snowdon**
5108 Decarie
Montreal, Que., Can. H3X 2H9
PH:514-487-0970

**Capitaine Quebec - Centre-Ville**
1837 St. Catherine O.
Montreal, Que., Can. H3H 1M2
PH:514-939-9970

**Cosmix**
11819 Laurentien Blvd.
Montreal, Que., Can. H4J 2M1
PH:514-337-6183

**Komico Inc.**
4210 Decarie
Montreal, Que., Can. H4A 3K3
PH:514-489-4009

**Multinational Comics/Cards**
8918A Lajeunesse
Montreal, Que., Can. H2M 1R9
PH:514-385-6273

**1,000,000 Comix, Inc.**
Corporate Headquarters
6290 Somerled
Montreal, Que., Can. H3X 2B6
PH:514-486-1175

**1,000,000 Comix, Inc.**
372 Sherbrooke St. West
Montreal, Que., Can.
PH:514-844-9313

**1,000,000 Comix, Inc.**
1260 Dollard St., LaSalle
Montreal, Que., Can. H8N 2P2
PH:514-366-1233

**1,000,000 Comix, Inc.**
1539 Van Horne
Montreal, Que., Can.
PH:514-277-5788

**1,000,000 Comix, Inc.**
3846 Jean-Talon
Montreal, Que., Can.
PH:514-725-1355

**Comix Plus (1,000,000 affil.)**
1475 McDonald
St. Laurent, Que., Can.
PH:514-334-0732

**Capitaine Quebec - Verdun**
4422 Wellington
Verdun, Que., Can. H4G 1W5
PH:514-768-1351

**Premiere Issue**
27 "A" D'Autevil
(Vieux Quebec), Quebec City,
Que., Can. G1R 4B9
PH:418-692-3985


## ENGLAND

**Stateside Comics**
(By Appointment)
P.O. Box 1108
London N11 1RW, England
PH:London 449 5535 & London
368 1837

# COMIC BOOK
# CONVENTIONS

As is the case with most other aspects of comic collecting, comic book conventions, or cons as they are referred to, were originally conceived as the comic-book counterpart to science-fiction fandom conventions. There were many attempts to form successful national cons prior to the time of the first one that materialized, but they were all stillborn. It is interesting that after only three relatively organized years of existence, the first comic con was held. Of course, its magnitude was nowhere near as large as most established cons held today.

What is a comic con? As might be expected, there are comic books to be found at these gatherings. Dealers, collectors, fans, whatever they call themselves, can be found trading, selling, and buying the adventures of their favorite characters for hours on end. Additionally, if at all possible, cons have guests of honor, usually professionals in the field of comic art, either writers, artists, or editors. The committees put together panels for the con attendees where the assembled pros talk about certain areas of comics, most of the time fielding questions from the assembled audience. At cons one can usually find displays of various and sundry things, usually original art. There might be radio listening rooms; there is most certainly a daily showing of different movies, usually science-fiction or horror type. Of course, there is always the chance to get together with friends at cons and just talk about comics; one also has a good opportunity to make new friends who have similar interests and with whom one can correspond after the con.

It is difficult to describe accurately what goes on at a con. The best way to find out is to go to one or more if you can.

The addresses below are those currently available for conventions to be held in the upcoming year. Unfortunately, addresses for certain major conventions are unavailable as this list is being compiled. Once again, the best way to keep abreast of conventions is through the various adzines. Please remember when writing for convention information to include a self-addressed, stamped envelope for reply. Most conventions are non-profit, so they appreciate the help. Here is the list:

# COMIC BOOK CONVENTION
# CALENDAR FOR 1991

**ATLANTA FANTASY FAIR XVII**, Aug. 1991, Omni Hotel, Atlanta, GA. Info: Atlanta Fantasy Fair, 691 Spring Forest Dr., Lawrenceville, GA 30243. PH: (404) 961-2347.

**ATLANTA SPRING COMICS FAIR V** (Mar. 1991), Info: The Atlanta Spring Comics Fair, c/o The Atlanta Fantasy Fair, 691 Spring Forest Dr., Lawrenceville, GA 30243. PH: (404) 961-2347.

**BIG-D Super Comic & Collectibles Show** (Formerly CHILDHOOD TREASURES) July 1991-Dallas Sheraton Park Central Hotel, Hwy. 635 & Coit Rd. Write Don Maris, Box 111266, Arlington, TX 76007. PH: (817) 261-8745.

**CAROLINA CON X**, Sept. 1991, Ramada Hotel, 1001 S. Church St., Greenville, SC. Sponsored by The Carolina Pictorial Fiction Assn. Send SASE to Steve Harris, 100 E. Augusta Place, Greenville, SC 29605.

**CHICAGO - Baseball Card & Comic Book Show**. Held monthly at University of Illinois at Chicago. For more info call Rich at (708) 837-0375.

**CHICAGO COMICON**—Larry Charet, 1219-A West Devon Ave., Chicago, IL 60660. PH: (312) 274-1832.

**CREATION CON**, 249-04 Hillside Ave., Bellerose, NY 11426. PH: (718) 343-0202. Holds major conventions in the following cities: Atlanta, Boston, Cincinnati, Cleveland, Detroit, London, Los Angeles, Philadelphia, Rochester, San Francisco, and Washington, DC. Write or call for details.

**DALLAS FANTASY FAIR**, A Bulldog Prod. Convention. For info: Lary Lankford, P.O. Box 820488, Dallas, TX 75382. PH: (214) 349-3367.

**DETROIT AREA COMIC BOOK/BASEBALL CARD SHOWS**. Held every 2-3 weeks in Royal Oak and Livonia, MI. Write: Michael Goldman, Suite 231, 19785 W. 12 Mile Rd., Southfield, MI 48076. PH: (313) 350-2633.

**EL PASO FANTASY FESTIVAL**—c/o Rita's Fantasy Shop, No. 34 Sunrise Center, El Paso, TX 79904. PH: (915) 757-1143. Late July-Early August.

**FANTACON 1991**, Sept., 1991, Empire State Plaza Convention Center, between State and Madison, Albany, NY. For info: Tom Skulan, FantaCo Organization Offices, 21 Central Ave., Albany, NY 12210-1391. Please send SASE with inquiry or call (518) 463-1400.

**ISLAND NOSTALGIA COMIC BOOK/BASEBALL CARD SHOWS**, Hauppauge, NY-Holiday Inn off L.I.E. exit 55, 10-4 P.M., 1740 Express Drive South, Hauppauge, NY, For more info call Dennis (516) 724-7422 or Day of Shows only (516) 234-3030, ext. 450.

**KANSAS CITY COMIC CONVENTION** (Formerly MO-KAN COMICS FESTIVAL)—c/o Kansas City Comic Book Club, 734 North 78th St., Kansas City, KS 66112.

**LONG ISLAND COMIC BOOK & COLLECTOR'S MARKET CONVENTION** (held monthly). Rockville Centre Holiday Inn, 173 Sunrise Hwy., NY. For info: Cosmic Comics & Books of Rockville Centre, 139 N. Park Ave., Rockville Centre, NY 11570. PH: (516) 763-1133.

**LOS ANGELES COMIC BOOK & SCIENCE FICTION CONVENTION**, held monthly. For information contact: Bruce Schwartz, 1802 West Olive Ave., Burbank, CA 91506. PH: (818) 954-8432.

**MOBI-CON 91**, June 1991, The Days Inn (I-65 and Airport), Mobile, AL 36608. For more info: Christie Nelson, P.O. Box 161257, Mobile, AL 36616. PH: (205) 342-9073 or 661-4060.

**THE ORIGINAL LONG ISLAND MONTHLY COMIC BOOK & BASEBALL CARD SHOW**, held 1st Sunday each month at the Coliseum Motor Inn, 1650 Hempstead Turnpike, East Meadow, Long Island, NY. Contact: Perry Albert, P.O. Box 66, Fredonia, NY 14063. PH: (716) 672-2913.

**ORLANDO CON**, Sept. 1991, International Inn, Orlando, FL. Info: Jim Ivey, 4300 S. Semoran, Suite 109, Orlando, FL 32822-2453. PH: (407) 273-0141.

**SAN DIEGO COMIC-CON**, Box 17066, San Diego, CA 92117. July 4th week, 1991, San Diego Convention Center.

**THE SCENIC CITY COMICS & COLLECTIBLES FAIR**, April, Chattanooga at Eastgate Mall, Mark Derrick, 3244 Castle Ave., Chattanooga, TN 37412. PH: (615) 624-3704.

Schenectady, New York, **THE CAPITAL DISTRICT ANNUAL SHOW**, S.A.S.E. with inquiry or call Jared Nathanson at (518) 372-6612 or write: Comix 4-U, Inc., 1121 State St., 2nd Floor, Schenectady, NY 12304.

**SEATTLE CENTER CON**, Apr, July, Oct, 1991, Box 2043, Kirkland, WA, 98033. PH: (206) 822-5709 or 827-5129.

**SEATTLE QUEST NORTHWEST**, Seattle, WA. Write: Ron Church or Steve Sibra, P.O. Box 82676, Kenmore, WA 98028.

**THE SUNDAY FUNNIES**, Will Murray, 334 E. Squantum St., Quincy, MA 02171. PH: (617) 328-5224.

# A CHRONOLOGY OF THE DEVELOPMENT OF THE AMERICAN COMIC BOOK

By M. Thomas Inge

**Precursors:** The facsimile newspaper strip reprint collections constitute the earliest "comic books." The first of these was a collection of Richard Outcault's **Yellow Kid** from the Hearst **New York American** in March 1897. Commercial and promotional reprint collections, usually in cardboard covers, appeared through the 1920s and featured such newspaper strips as **Mutt and Jeff, Foxy Grandpa, Buster Brown,** and **Barney Google**. During 1922 a reprint magazine, **Comic Monthly**, appeared with each issue devoted to a separate strip, and from 1929 to 1930 George Delacorte published 36 issues of **The Funnies** in tabloid format with original comic pages in color, becoming the first four-color comic newsstand publication.

**1933:** The Ledger syndicate published a small broadside of their Sunday comics on 7″ × 9″ plates. Employees of Eastern Color Printing

Company in New York, sales manager Harry I. Wildenberg and salesman Max C. Gaines, saw it and figured that two such plates would fit a tabloid page, which would produce a book about 7½″ × 10″ when folded. Thus, 10,000 copies of **Funnies on Parade**, containing 32 pages of Sunday newspaper reprints, were published for Proctor and Gamble to be given away as premiums. Some of the strips included were: **Joe Palooka, Mutt and Jeff, Hairbreadth Harry, and Reg'lar Fellas**. M. C. Gaines was very impressed with this book and convinced Eastern Color that he could sell a lot of them to such big advertisers as Milk-O-Malt, Wheatena, Kinney Shoe Stores, and others to be used as premiums and radio giveaways. So, Eastern Color printed **Famous Funnies: A Carnival of Comics**, and then **Century of Comics**, both as before, containing Sunday newspaper reprints. Mr. Gaines sold these books in quantities of 100,000 to 250,000.

**1934:** The giveaway comics were so successful that Mr. Gaines believed that youngsters would buy comic books for ten cents like the "Big Little Books" coming out at that time. So, early in 1934, Eastern Color ran off 35,000 copies of **Famous Funnies, Series 1**, 64 pages of reprints for Dell Publishing Company to be sold for ten cents in chain stores. Selling out promptly on the stands, Eastern Color, in May 1934, issued **Famous Funnies** No. 1 (dated July 1934) which became, with issue No. 2 in July, the first monthly comic magazine. The title continued for over 20 years through 218 issues, reaching a circulation peak of nearly one million copies. At the same time, Mr. Gaines went to the sponsors of Percy Crosby's **Skippy**, who was on the radio, and convinced them to put out a Skippy book, advertise it on the air, and give away a free copy to anyone who bought a tube of Phillip's toothpaste. Thus, 500,000 copies of **Skippy's Own Book of Comics** were run off and distributed through drugstores everywhere. This was the first four-color comic book of reprints devoted to a single character.

**1935:** Major Malcolm Wheeler-Nicholson's National Periodical Publications issued in February a tabloid-sized comic publication called **New Fun**, which became **More Fun** after the sixth issue and converted to the normal comic-book size after issue eight. **New Comics** was the first comic book of a standard size to publish original material and continued publication until 1949. **Mickey Mouse Magazine** began in the summer, to become **Walt Disney's Comics and Stories** in 1940, and combined original material with reprinted newspaper strips in most issues.

**1936:** In the wake of the success of **Famous Funnies**, other publishers, in conjunction with the major newspaper strip syndicates, inaugurated more reprint comic books: **Popular Comics** (News-Tribune, February), **Tip Top Comics** (United Features, April), **King Comics** (King

Features, April), and **The Funnies** (new series, NEA, October). Four issues of **Wow Comics**, from David McKay and Henle Publications, appeared, edited by S. M. Iger and including early art by Will Eisner, Bob
Kane, and Alex Raymond. The first non-reprint comic book devoted to a
single theme was **Detective Picture Stories** issued in December by The
Comics Magazine Company.

**1937:** The second single-theme title, **Western Picture Stories**, came
in February from The Comics Magazine Company, and the third was **Detective Comics**, an offshoot of **More Fun**, which began in March to be
published to the present. The book's initials, "D.C.," have long served to
refer to National Periodical Publications, which was purchased from Major Nicholson by Harry Donenfeld late this year.

**1938:** "DC" copped a lion's share of the comic book market with the
publication of **Action Comics** No. 1 in June which contained the first appearance of Superman by writer Jerry Siegel and artist Joe Shuster, a dis-
covery of Max C. Gaines. The "man of steel" inaugurated the "Golden
Era" in comic book history. Fiction House, a pulp publisher, entered the
comic book field in September with **Jumbo Comics**, featuring Sheena,
Queen of the Jungle, and appearing in over-sized format for the first
eight issues.

**1939:** The continued success of "DC" was assured in May with the
publication of **Detective Comics** No. 27, containing the first episode of
Batman by artist Bob Kane and writer Bill Finger. **Superman Comics** appeared in the summer. Also, during the summer, a black and white premium comic titled **Motion Picture Funnies Weekly** was published to be
given away at motion picture theaters. The plan was to issue it weekly
and to have continued stories so that the kids would come back week after week not to miss an episode. Four issues were planned but only one
came out. This book contains the first appearance and origin of the Sub-
Mariner by Bill Everett (8 pages), which was later reprinted in **Marvel
Comics**. In November, the first issue of **Marvel Comics** came out, featuring the Human Torch by Carl Burgos and the Sub-Mariner reprint with
color added.

**1940:** The April issue of **Detective Comics** No. 38 introduced Robin
the Boy Wonder as a sidekick to Batman, thus establishing the "Dynamic
Duo" and a major precedent for later costume heroes who would also
have boy companions. **Batman Comics** began in the spring. Over 60 different comic book titles were being issued, including **Whiz Comics** begun in February by Fawcett Publications. A creation of writer Bill Parker
and artist C. C. Beck, **Whiz's** Captain Marvel was the only superhero ever
to surpass Superman in comic book sales. Drawing on their own popular

pulp magazine heroes, Street and Smith Publications introduced **Shadow Comics** in March and **Doc Savage Comics** in May. A second trend was established with the summer appearance of the first issue of **All-Star Comics**, which brought several superheroes together in one story and in its third issue that winter would announce the establishment of the Justice Society of America.

**1941:** Wonder Woman was introduced in the spring issue of **All-Star Comics** No. 8, the creation of psychologist William Moulton Marston and artist Harry Peter. **Captain Marvel Adventures** began this year. By the end of 1941, over 160 titles were being published, including **Captain America** by Jack Kirby and Joe Simon, **Police Comics** with Jack Cole's Plastic Man and later Will Eisner's Spirit, **Military Comics** with Blackhawk by Eisner and Charles Cuidera, **Daredevil Comics** with the original character by Charles Biro, **Air Fighters** with Airboy also by Biro, and **Looney Tunes & Merrie Melodies** with Porky Pig, Bugs Bunny, and Elmer Fudd, reportedly created by Bob Clampett for the Leon Schlesinger Productions animated films and drawn for the comics by Chase Craig. Also, Albert Kanter's Gilberton Company initiated the **Classics Illustrated** series with **The Three Musketeers.**

**1942:** **Crime Does Not Pay** by editor Charles Biro and publisher Lev Gleason, devoted to factual accounts of criminals' lives, began a different trend in realistic crime stories. **Wonder Woman** appeared in the summer. John Goldwater's character Archie, drawn by Bob Montana, first published in **Pep Comics**, was given his own magazine **Archie Comics**, which has remained popular for over 40 years. The first issue of **Animal Comics** contained Walt Kelly's "Albert Takes the Cake," featuring the new character of Pogo. In mid-1942, the undated Dell Four Color title, No. 9, **Donald Duck Finds Pirate Gold**, appeared with art by Carl Barks and Jack Hannah. Barks, also featured in **Walt Disney's Comics and Stories**, remained the most popular delineator of Donald Duck and later introduced his greatest creation, Uncle Scrooge, in **Christmas on Bear Mountain** (Dell Four Color No. 178). The fantasy work of George Carlson appeared in the first issue of **Jingle Jangle Comics**, one of the most imaginative titles for children ever to be published.

**1945:** The first issue of **Real Screen Comics** introduced the Fox and the Crow by James F. Davis, and John Stanley began drawing the **Little Lulu** comic book based on a popular feature in the **Saturday Evening Post** by Marjorie Henderson Buell from 1935 to 1944. Bill Woggon's Katy Keene appears in issue No. 5 of **Wilbur Comics** to be followed by appearances in **Laugh, Pep, Suzie** and her own comic book in 1950. The popularity of Dick Briefer's satiric version of the Frankenstein monster, originally drawn for **Prize Comics** in 1941, led to the publication of **Frankenstein** by Prize publications.

**1950:** The son of Max C. Gaines, William M. Gaines, who earlier had inherited his father's firm, Educational Comics (later Entertaining Comics), began publication of a series of well-written and masterfully drawn titles which would establish a "New Trend" in comics magazines: **Crypt of Terror** (later **Tales from the Crypt, April), The Vault of Horror** (April), **The Haunt of Fear** (May), **Weird Science** (May), **Weird Fantasy** (May), **Crime SuspenStories** (October), and **Two-Fisted Tales** (November), the latter stunningly edited by Harvey Kurtzman.

**1952:** In October "E.C." published the first number of **Mad** under Kurtzman's creative editorship, thus establishing a style of humor which would inspire other publications and powerfully influence the underground comic book movement of the 1960s.

**1953:** All Fawcett titles featuring Captain Marvel were ceased after many years of litigation in the courts during which National Periodical Publications claimed that the super-hero was an infringement on the copyrighted Superman.

**1954:** The appearance of Fredric Wertham's book, **Seduction of the Innocent,** in the spring was the culmination of a continuing war against comic books fought by those who believed they corrupted youth and de-based culture. The U.S. Senate Subcommittee on Juvenile Delinquency investigated comic books and in response the major publishers banded together in October to create the Comics Code Authority and adopted, in their own words, "the most stringent code in existence for any communications media." Before the Code took effect, more than 1,000,000,000 issues of comic books were being sold annually.

**1955:** In an effort to avoid the Code, "E.C." launched a "New Direction" series of titles, such as **Impact, Valor, Aces High, Extra, M.D.,** and **Psychoanalysis,** none of which lasted beyond the year. **Mad** was changed into a larger magazine format with issue No. 24 in July to escape the Comics Code entirely, and "E.C." closed down its line of comic books altogether.

**1956:** Beginning with the Flash in **Showcase** No. 4, Julius Schwartz began a popular revival of "DC" superheroes which would lead to the "Silver Age" in comic book history.

**1957:** Atlas reduced the number of titles published by two-thirds, with **Journey into Mystery** and **Strange Tales** surviving, while other publishers did the same or went out of business. Atlas would survive as a part of the Marvel Comics Group.

**1960:** After several efforts at new satire magazines (**Trump** and

**Humbug**), Harvey Kurtzman, no longer with Gaines, issued in August the first number of another abortive effort, **Help!**, where the early work of underground cartoonists Jay Lynch, Skip Williamson, Gilbert Shelton, and Robert Crumb appeared.

**1961:** Stan Lee edited in November the first **Fantastic Four**, featuring Mr. Fantastic, the Human Torch, the Thing, and the Invisible Girl, and inaugurated an enormously popular line of titles from Marvel Comics featuring a more contemporary style of superhero.

**1962:** Lee introduced **The Amazing Spider-Man** in August, with art by Steve Ditko, **The Hulk** in May, and **Thor** in August, the last two produced by Dick Ayers and Jack Kirby.

**1963:** Marvel's **The X-Men**, with art by Jack Kirby, began a successful run in November, but the title would experience a revival and have an even more popular reception in the 1980s.

**1965:** James Warren issued **Creepy**, a larger black and white comic book, outside Comics Code's control, which emulated the "E.C." horror comic line. Warren's **Eerie** began in September and **Vampirella** in September 1969.

**1967:** Robert Crumb's **Zap** No. 1 appeared, the first popular underground comic book to achieve wide popularity, although the undergrounds had began in 1962 with **Adventures of Jesus** by Foolbert Sturgeon (Frank Stack) and 1964 with **God Nose** by Jack Jackson.

**1970:** Editor Roy Thomas at Marvel begins **Conan the Barbarian** based on fiction by Robert E. Howard with art by Barry Smith, and Neal Adams began to draw for "DC" a series of **Green Lantern/Green Arrow** stories which would deal with relevant social issues such as racism, urban poverty, and drugs.

**1972: The Swamp Thing** by Berni Wrightson begins in November from "DC."

**1973:** In February, "DC" revived the original Captain Marvel with new art by C. C. Beck and reprints in the first issue of **Shazam** and in October **The Shadow** with scripts by Denny O'Neil and art by Mike Kaluta.

**1974:** "DC" began publication in the spring of a series of over-sized facsimile reprints of the most valued comic books of the past under the general title of "Famous First Editions," beginning with a reprint of **Action** No. 1 and including afterwards **Detective Comics** No. 27, **Sensation Comics** No. 1, **Whiz Comics** No. 2, **Batman** No. 1, **Wonder Woman** No. 1, **All-Star Comics** No. 3, **Flash Comics** No. 1, and **Superman** No. 1. Mike Friedrich, an independent publisher, released **Star Reach** with work by Jim Starlin, Neal Adams, and Dick Giordano, with ownership of the characters and stories invested in the creators themselves.

**1975:** In the first collaborative effort between the two major comic book publishers of the previous decade, Marvel and "DC" produced together an over-sized comic-book version of **MGM's Marvelous Wizard of Oz** in the fall, and then the following year in an unprecedented crossover produced **Superman vs. the Amazing Spider-Man**, written by Gerry Conway, drawn by Ross Andru, and inked by Dick Giordano.

**1976:** Frank Brunner's Howard the Duck, who had appeared earlier in Marvel's **Fear** and **Man-Thing**, was given his own book in January, which, because of distribution problems, became an over-night collector's item. After decades of litigation, Jerry Siegel and Joe Shuster were given financial recompense and recognition by National Periodical Publications for their creation of Superman, after several friends of the team made a public issue of the case.

**1977:** Stan Lee's **Spider-Man** was given a second birth, fifteen years after his first, through a highly successful newspaper comic strip, which began syndication on January 3 with art by John Romita. This invasion of the comic strip by comic book characters continued with the appearance on June 6 of Marvel's **Howard the Duck**, with story by Steve Gerber and visuals by Gene Colan. In an unusually successful collaborative effort, Marvel began publication of the comic book adaption of the George Lucas film **Star Wars**, with script by Roy Thomas and art by Howard Chaykin, at least three months before the film was released nationally on May 25. The demand was so great that all six issues of **Star Wars** were reprinted at least seven times, and the installments were reprinted in two volumes of an over-sized Marvel Special Edition and a single paperback volume for the book trade. Dave Sim, with an issue dated December, began self-publication of his **Cerebus the Aardvark**, the success of which would help establish the independent market for non-traditional black-and-white comics.

**1978:** In an effort to halt declining sales, Warner Communications drastically cut back on the number of "DC" titles and overhauled its distribution process in June. The interest of the visual media in comic book characters reached a new high with the Hulk, Spider-Man, and Doctor Strange, the subjects of television shows; with various projects begun to produce film versions of Flash Gordon, Dick Tracy, Popeye, Conan, The Phantom, and Buck Rogers; and with the movement reaching an outlandish peak of publicity with the release of **Superman** in December. Two significant applications of the comic book format to traditional fiction appeared this year: **A Contract with God and Other Tenement Stories** by Will Eisner and **The Silver Surfer** by Stan Lee and Jack Kirby. Eclipse Enterprises published Paul Gulacy's **Sabre**, the first graphic album produced for the direct sales market, and initiated a policy of paying royalties and granting copyrights to comic book creators. Another self-publishing project, Wendy Pini's **Elfquest**, was so popular that it achieved bookstore distribution. The magazine **Heavy Metal** brought to American attention the avant-garde comic book work of European artists.

**1980:** Publication of the November premier issue of **The New Teen Titans**, with art by George Perez and story by Marv Wolfman, brought back to widespread popularity a title originally published by "DC" in 1966.

**1981:** The distributor Pacific Comics began publishing titles for direct sales through comic shops with the inaugural issue of Jack Kirby's **Captain Victory and the Galactic Rangers** and offered royalties to artists and writers on the basis of sales. "DC" would do the same for regular newsstand comics in November (with payments retroactive to July 1981), and Marvel followed suit by the end of the year. The first issue of **Raw**, irregularly published by Art Spiegelman and Francoise Mouly, carried comic book art into new extremes of experimentation and innovation with work by European and American artists. With issue No. 158, Frank Miller began to write and draw Marvel's **Daredevil** and brought a vigorous style of violent action to comic book pages.

**1982:** The first slick format comic book in regular size appeared, **Marvel Fanfare** No. 1, with a March date. Fantagraphics Books began publication in July of **Love and Rockets** by Mario, Gilbert, and Jaime Hernandez and brought a new ethnic sensibility and sophistication in style and content to comic book narratives for adults.

**1983:** This year saw more comic book publishers, aside from Marvel and DC, issuing more titles than have existed in the past 40 years; most small independent publishers relying on direct sales, such as Americomics, Capital, Eagle, Eclipse, First, Pacific, and Red Circle; and with Archie, Charlton, and Whitman publishing on a limited scale. Frank Miller's mini-series **Ronin** demonstrated a striking use of sword-play and martial arts typical of Japanese comic book art, and Howard Chaykin's stylish but controversial **American Flagg** appeared with an October date on its first issue.

**1984:** A publishing, media, and merchandising phenomenon began with the appearance of the first issue of **Teenage Mutant Ninja Turtles** from Mirage Studios by Kevin Eastman and Peter Laird.

**1985:** Ohio State University's Library of Communication and Graphic Arts hosted the first major exhibition devoted to the comic book May 19 through August 2. In what was billed as an irreversible decision, the silver age superheroine Supergirl was killed in the seventh (October) issue of **Crisis on Infinite Earths**, a limited series intended to reorganize and simplify the DC universe on the occasion of the publisher's 50th anniversary.

**1986:** In recognition of its twenty-fifth anniversary, Marvel began publication of several new ongoing titles comprising Marvel's "New Universe," a self-contained fictional world. DC attracted extensive publicity and media coverage with its revisions of the character of **Superman** by John Byrne and of **Batman** in the **Dark Knight** series by Frank Miller. **Watchmen**, a limited-series graphic novel by Alan Moore and artist Dave Gibbons, began publication with a September issue from DC and Marvel's **The 'Nam**, written by Vietnam veteran Doug Murray and pencilled by Michael Golden, began with its December issue. DC issued guidelines in December for labelling their titles as either for mature readers or for readers of all ages; in response, many artists and writers publicly objected or threatened to resign.

**1987:** Art Spiegelman's **Maus: A Survivor's Tale** was nominated for the National Book Critics Circle Award in biography, the first comic book to be so honored. A celebration of Superman's fiftieth birthday began with the opening of an exhibition on his history at the Smithsonian's Museum of American History in Washington, D.C., in June, and a symposium on "The Superhero in America" in October.

**1988:** Superman's birthday celebration continued with a public party in New York and a CBS television special in February, a cover story in **Time** magazine in March (the first comic book character to appear on the cover), and an international exposition in Cleveland in June. With issue number 601 for May 24, **Action Comics** became the first modern weekly comic book, which ceased publication after 42 issues with the December 13 number. In August, DC initiated a new policy of allowing creators of new characters to retain ownership of them rather than rely solely on work-for-hire.

**1989:** The fiftieth anniversary of Batman was marked by the release of the film **Batman**, starring Michael Keaton as Bruce Wayne and Jack Nicholson as the Joker; it grossed more money in the weekend it opened than any other motion picture in film history to that time.

**Note:** A special word of thanks is due Gerard Jones for his suggestions and contributions to the above chronology.

# HOW TO USE
# THIS BOOK

The author of this book has included a selection of key titles covering a variety of subjects that are mostly collected. The comic book titles are listed alphabetically for easy reference. All key issues and important contents are pointed out and priced in three grades—good, fine and near mint.

Most comic books listed are priced in groups: 11-20, 21-30, 31-50, etc. The prices listed in the right-hand column are for each single comic book in that grouping.

The prices shown represent the current range, but since prices do change constantly, the values in this book should be used as a guide only.

A general selection of titles is represented here, so for more detailed information please consult *The Official Overstreet Comic Book Price Guide*, master guide.

# Comic Book
# Listings

# A

**ABBOTT AND COSTELLO** (. . . Comics)
Feb, 1948 - No. 40, Sept?, 1956 (Mort Drucker art in most issues)
St. John Publishing Co.

|  | Good | Fine | N-Mint |
|---|---|---|---|
| 1 | 22.00 | 65.00 | 154.00 |
| 2 | 11.50 | 34.00 | 80.00 |
| 3-9 (#8, 8/49; #9, 2/50) | 6.50 | 19.50 | 45.00 |
| 10-Son of Sinbad story by Kubert (new) | 13.00 | 40.00 | 90.00 |
| 11,13-20 (#11, 10/50; #13, 8/51; #15, 12/52) | 4.00 | 12.00 | 28.00 |
| 12-Movie issue | 5.50 | 16.50 | 38.00 |
| 21-30: 28 r-#8. 30-Painted-c | 3.00 | 9.00 | 21.00 |
| 31-40: #33, 38-r | 2.30 | 7.00 | 16.00 |
| 3-D #1 (11/53)-Infinity-c | 19.00 | 57.00 | 132.00 |

**ACE COMICS**
April, 1937 - No. 151, Oct-Nov, 1949
David McKay Publications

| | Good | Fine | N-Mint |
|---|---|---|---|
| 1-Jungle Jim by Alex Raymond, Blondie, Ripley's Believe It Or Not, Krazy Kat begin | 158.00 | 395.00 | 950.00 |
| 2 | 50.00 | 150.00 | 350.00 |
| 3-5 | 36.00 | 107.00 | 250.00 |
| 6-10 | 26.00 | 77.00 | 180.00 |
| 11-The Phantom begins (In brown costume, 2/38) | 32.00 | 95.00 | 225.00 |
| 12-20 | 19.00 | 57.00 | 135.00 |
| 21-25,27-30 | 16.00 | 48.00 | 110.00 |
| 26-Origin Prince Valiant (begins series?) | 44.00 | 132.00 | 310.00 |
| 31-40: 37 Krazy Kat ends | 11.50 | 34.00 | 80.00 |
| 41-60 | 10.00 | 30.00 | 70.00 |
| 61-64, 66-76-(7/43; last 68 pgs.) | 8.50 | 25.50 | 60.00 |
| 65-(8/42; Flag-c) | 9.00 | 27.00 | 63.00 |
| 77-84 (3/44; all 60 pgs.) | 7.00 | 21.00 | 50.00 |
| 85-99 (52 pgs.) | 6.00 | 18.00 | 42.00 |
| 100 (7/45; last 52 pgs.) | 7.00 | 21.00 | 50.00 |
| 101-134: 128-11/47; Brick Bradford begins. 134-Last Prince Valiant (All 36 pgs.) | 5.00 | 15.00 | 35.00 |
| 135-151: 135-6/48; Lone Ranger begins | 4.00 | 12.00 | 28.00 |

*Action Comics #29, © DC Comics*

**ACTION COMICS** ( . . . Weekly No. 601 -642)
6/38 - No. 583, 9/86; No. 584, 1/87 - Present
National Periodical Publ./Detective Comics/DC Comics

|  | Good | Fine | VF-NM |
|---|---|---|---|
| 1-Origin & 1st app. Superman | 6000.00 | 15,000.00 | 32,500.00 |
| *(Only one known copy exists in mint condition which has not sold)* | | | |

|  | Good | Fine | N-Mint |
|---|---|---|---|
| 1(1976,1983)-Giveaway; paper cover, 16 pgs. in color; reprints complete | | | |
|     Superman story from #1 ('38) | .70 | 2.00 | 4.00 |
| 1(1987 Nestle Quik giveaway; 1988, 50 cent-c) | | .25 | .50 |
| 2 | 800.00 | 2000.00 | 4800.00 |
| 3 (Scarce) | 635.00 | 1590.00 | 3800.00 |
| 4 | 435.00 | 1090.00 | 2600.00 |
| 5 (Rare) | 535.00 | 1340.00 | 3200.00 |
| 6-1st Jimmy Olsen (called office boy) | 435.00 | 1090.00 | 2600.00 |
| 7,10-Superman covers | 535.00 | 1340.00 | 3200.00 |
| 8,9 | 367.00 | 920.00 | 2200.00 |

|  | Good | Fine | N-Mint |
|---|---|---|---|
| 11,12,14:14-Clip Carson begins, ends #41 | 192.00 | 480.00 | 1150.00 |
| 13-Superman cover; last Scoop Scanlon | 267.00 | 670.00 | 1600.00 |
| 15-Superman cover | 267.00 | 670.00 | 1600.00 |
| 16 | 148.00 | 370.00 | 890.00 |
| 17-Superman cover; last Marco Polo | 200.00 | 500.00 | 1200.00 |
| 18-Origin 3 Aces; 1st X-Ray Vision? | 140.00 | 350.00 | 840.00 |
| 19-Superman covers begin | 183.00 | 450.00 | 1100.00 |
| 20-'S' left off Superman's chest | 168.00 | 420.00 | 1000.00 |
| 21,22,24,25 | 105.00 | 260.00 | 630.00 |
| 23-1st app. Luthor & Black Pirate; Black Pirate by Moldoff; 1st mention of | | | |
| The Daily Planet? (4/40) | 153.00 | 380.00 | 920.00 |
| 26-30 | 82.00 | 205.00 | 490.00 |
| 31,32 | 63.00 | 158.00 | 375.00 |
| 33-Origin Mr. America | 75.00 | 190.00 | 450.00 |
| 34-40:37-Origin Congo Bill. 40-Intro/1st app. Star Spangled Kid & Stripesy | | | |
|  | 62.00 | 155.00 | 375.00 |
| 41 | 58.00 | 145.00 | 350.00 |
| 42-Origin Vigilante; Bob Daley becomes Fat Man; origin Mr. America's | | | |
| magic flying carpet | 83.00 | 210.00 | 500.00 |
| 43-50: 44-Fat Man's i.d. revealed to Mr. America. 45-Intro. Stuff | | | |
|  | 58.00 | 145.00 | 350.00 |
| 51-1st app. The Prankster | 50.00 | 125.00 | 300.00 |
| 52-Fat Man & Mr. America become the Ameri-commandos; origin Vigi- | | | |
| lante retold | 58.00 | 145.00 | 350.00 |
| 53-60:56-Last Fat Man. 59-Kubert Vigilante begins?, ends #70. 60-First | | | |
| app. Lois Lane as Superwoman | 43.00 | 110.00 | 255.00 |
| 61-63,65-70:63-Last 3 Aces | 39.00 | 100.00 | 235.00 |
| 64-Intro Toyman | 43.00 | 110.00 | 255.00 |
| 71-79: 74-Last Mr. America | 33.00 | 83.00 | 200.00 |
| 80-2nd app. & 1st Mr. Mxyztplk-c (1/45) | 58.00 | 145.00 | 350.00 |
| 81-90:83-Intro Hocus & Pocus | 33.00 | 83.00 | 200.00 |
| 91-99: 93-X-Mas-c. 99-1st small logo(7/46) | 30.00 | 75.00 | 180.00 |
| 100 | 67.00 | 170.00 | 400.00 |
| 101-Nuclear explosion-c | 37.00 | 92.00 | 225.00 |
| 102-120: 105,117-X-Mas-c | 30.00 | 75.00 | 180.00 |
| 121-126,128-140: 135,136,138-Zatara by Kubert | | | |
|  | 28.00 | 70.00 | 170.00 |
| 127-Vigilante by Kubert; Tommy Tomorrow begins | | | |
|  | 43.00 | 110.00 | 225.00 |

|                                                                    | Good | Fine | N-Mint |
|--------------------------------------------------------------------|------|------|--------|
| 141-157,159-161: 156-Lois Lane as Super Woman. 160-Last 52 pgs.    |      |      |        |
|                                                                    | 28.00 | 70.00 | 170.00 |
| 158-Origin Superman                                                | 32.00 | 80.00 | 195.00 |
| 162-180: 168,176-Used in **POP,** pg. 90                           | 16.00 | 48.00 | 110.00 |

181-201:191-Intro. Janu in Congo Bill. 198-Last Vigilante. 201-Last precode

| issue                                                              | 16.00 | 48.00 | 110.00 |
| 202-220                                                            | 13.00 | 40.00 | 90.00 |
| 221-240:224-1st Golden Gorilla story                               | 10.00 | 30.00 | 70.00 |

241,243-251:248-Congo Bill becomes Congorilla. 251-Last Tommy Tomor-

| row                                                                | 8.00 | 24.00 | 55.00 |

242-Origin & 1st app. Brainiac (7/58); 1st mention of Shrunken City of

| Kandor                                                             | 40.00 | 120.00 | 275.00 |

252-Origin & 1st app. Supergirl (5/59); Re-intro Metallo (see Superboy

| #49 for 1st app.)                                                  | 57.00 | 170.00 | 400.00 |
| 253-2nd app. Supergirl                                             | 10.00 | 30.00 | 70.00 |
| 254-1st meeting of Bizarro & Superman                              | 11.00 | 33.00 | 75.00 |

255-1st Bizarro Lois & both Bizarros leave Earth to make Bizarro World

|                                                                    | 8.50 | 25.50 | 60.00 |

256-261: 259-Red Kryptonite used. 261-1st X-Kryptonite which gave
Streaky his powers; last Congorilla in Action; origin & 1st app.

| Streaky The Super Cat                                              | 4.30 | 13.00 | 30.00 |
| 262-266,268-270: 263-Origin Bizarro World                         | 3.60 | 11.00 | 25.00 |

267(8/60)-3rd Legion app; 1st app. Chameleon Boy, Colossal Boy, & Invis-

| ible Kid                                                           | 29.00 | 86.00 | 200.00 |
| 271-275,277-282: Last 10 cent issue                               | 3.15 | 9.50 | 22.00 |

276(5/61)-6th Legion app; 1st app. Brainiac 5, Phantom Girl, Triplicate
Girl, Bouncing Boy, Sun Boy, & Shrinking Violet; Supergirl joins Le-

| gion                                                               | 10.00 | 30.00 | 70.00 |
| 283(12/61)-Legion of Super-Villains app.                           | 4.30 | 13.00 | 30.00 |
| 284(1/62)-Mon-el app.                                              | 4.30 | 13.00 | 30.00 |

285(2/62)-12th Legion app; Brainiac 5 cameo; Supergirl's existence re-

| vealed to world                                                    | 4.30 | 13.00 | 30.00 |

286-290: 286(3/62)-Legion of Super Villains app. 287(4/62)-14th Legion
app.(cameo). 288-Mon-el app.; r-origin Supergirl. 289(6/62)-16th Legion app.(Adult); Lightning Man & Saturn Woman's marriage 1st revealed. 290(7/62)-17th Legion app; Phantom Girl app.

|                                                                    | 2.30 | 7.00 | 16.00 |

291,292,294-299: 292-2nd app. Superhorse (see Adv. 293). 297-Monel app;

| 298-Legion app.                                                    | 1.50 | 4.50 | 10.00 |
| 293-Origin Comet(Superhorse)                                       | 3.15 | 9.50 | 22.00 |

|  | Good | Fine | N-Mint |
|---|---|---|---|
| 300 | 1.70 | 5.00 | 12.00 |

301-303,305-308,310-320: 306-Brainiac 5, Mon-el app. 307-Saturn Girl app. 314-r-origin Supergirl; J.L.A. x-over. 317-Death of Nor-Kan of Kandor.

| 319-Shrinking Violet app. | 1.00 | 3.00 | 6.00 |
|---|---|---|---|
| 304-Origin & 1st app. Black Flame | 1.00 | 3.00 | 6.00 |
| 309-Legion app. | 1.00 | 3.00 | 7.00 |

321-333,335-340: 336-Origin Akvar(Flamebird). 340-Origin, 1st app. Para-

| site | .70 | 2.10 | 4.20 |
|---|---|---|---|

334-Giant G-20; origin Supergirl, Streaky, Superhorse & Legion (all-r)

|  | 1.15 | 3.50 | 8.00 |
|---|---|---|---|
| 341-346,348-359 | .60 | 1.75 | 3.50 |

347,360-Gnt. Supergirl G-33, G-45; 347-Origin Comet-r. 360-Legion-r;

| r-origin Supergirl | .90 | 2.75 | 5.50 |
|---|---|---|---|

361-372,374-380: 365-Legion app. 370-New facts about Superman's origin. 376-Last Supergirl in Action. 377-Legion begins

|  | .35 | 1.00 | 2.00 |
|---|---|---|---|
| 373-Giant Supergirl G-57; Legion-r | .70 | 2.00 | 4.00 |

381-402: 392-Last Legion in Action. Saturn Girl gets new costume. 393-402-All Superman issues

|  | .25 | .75 | 1.50 |
|---|---|---|---|

403-413: All 52 pg. issues; 411-Origin Eclipso-(r). 413-Metamorpho be-gins, ends #418

|  | .25 | .75 | 1.50 |
|---|---|---|---|

414-424: 419-Intro. Human Target. 421-Intro Capt. Strong; Green Arrow begins. 422,423-Origin Human Target

|  | .25 | .75 | 1.50 |
|---|---|---|---|
| 425-Neal Adams-a; Atom begins | .35 | 1.00 | 2.00 |
| 426-436,438,439,442,444-450 | .25 | .75 | 1.50 |
| 437,443-100 pg. giants | .35 | 1.00 | 2.00 |
| 440-1st Grell-a on Green Arrow | .70 | 2.00 | 4.00 |
| 441-Grell-a on Green Arrow continues | .40 | 1.25 | 2.50 |

451-499: 454-Last Atom. 458-Last Green Arrow. 487-488, 44 pgs. 487-1st app. Microwave Man; origin Atom retold

|  | .25 | .75 | 1.50 |
|---|---|---|---|

500-Infinity-c; Superman life story; $1.00 size; 68 pgs.; shows Legion stat-ues in museum

|  |  | .60 | 1.20 |
|---|---|---|---|

501-551,554-582: 511-514-New Airwave. 513-The Atom begins. 517-Aquaman begins; ends #541. 521-Intro. & 1st app. The Vixen. 532-New Teen Titans cameo. 535,536-Omega Men app.; 536-New Teen Titans cameo. 544-(Mando paper, 68 pgs.)-Origins New Luthor & Brainiac; Omega Men cameo. 546-J.L.A. & New Teen Titans guest. 551-Starfire becomes Red-Star

|  |  | .50 | 1.00 |
|---|---|---|---|
| 552-Animal Man-c & app. (2/84) | 1.15 | 3.50 | 7.00 |
| 553-Animal Man-c & app. (3/84) | .75 | 2.25 | 4.50 |

|                                                                 | Good | Fine | N-Mint |
|-----------------------------------------------------------------|------|------|--------|
| 583-Alan Moore scripts                                          | 1.30 | 4.00 | 8.00   |
| 584-Byrne-a begins; New Teen Titans app.                        | .25  | .75  | 1.50   |
| 585-597, 599: 586-Legends x-over. 596-Millenium                 |      | .50  | 1.00   |
| 598-1st app. Checkmate                                          | .50  | 1.50 | 3.00   |
| 600-($2.50, 84 pgs., 5/88)                                      | .70  | 2.00 | 4.00   |

601-642-Weekly issues ($1.50, 52 pgs.); 601-Re-intro The Secret Six.

| 611-614: Catwoman. 613-618: Nightwing                           | .25  | .75  | 1.50   |

643-Superman & monthly issues begin again; Perez-c/a/scripts begin;

| Cover swipe Superman #1                                         | .25  | .75  | 1.50   |
| 644-649                                                         |      | .40  | .80    |
| 650-$1.50, 52 pgs.                                              | .25  | .75  | 1.50   |
| 651-660                                                         |      | .50  | 1.00   |
| Annual 1 (10/87)-Art Adams-c/a(p)                              | 1.00 | 3.00 | 6.00   |
| Annual 2 (7/89, $1.75, 68 pgs.)-Perez-c/a(i)                   | .35  | 1.00 | 2.00   |

## ADVANCED DUNGEONS & DRAGONS
Dec, 1988- Present ($1.25, color) (Newsstand #1 is Holiday, 1988-89)
DC Comics

| 1-Based on TSR role playing game                               | 1.85 | 5.50 | 11.00  |
| 2                                                              | 1.35 | 4.00 | 8.00   |
| 3                                                              | .85  | 2.50 | 5.00   |
| 4-10: Later issues $1.50 cover                                 | .50  | 1.50 | 3.00   |
| 11-15                                                          | .35  | 1.00 | 2.00   |
| 16-24                                                          | .25  | .75  | 1.50   |

## ADVENTURE COMICS (Formerly New Adventure)
No. 32, 11/38 - No. 490, 2/82; No. 491, 9/82 - No. 503, 9/83
National Periodical Publications/DC Comics

32-Anchors Aweigh (ends #52), Barry O'Neil (ends #60, not in #33), Captain Desmo (ends #47), Dale Daring (ends #47), Federal Men (ends #70), The Golden Dragon (ends #36), Rusty & His Pals (ends #52) by Bob Kane, Todd Hunter (ends #38) and Tom Brent (ends #39) begin

|                                                                | 93.00 | 235.00 | 560.00 |
| 33-38: 37-c-used on Double Action 2                            | 58.00 | 145.00 | 350.00 |

39(1/39)-Jack Wood begins, ends #42: 1st mention of Marijuana in comics

|                                                                | 64.00 | 160.00 | 385.00 |

40-Intro. & 1st app. The Sandman. Socko Strong begins, ends #54

|                                                                | 600.00 | 1500.00 | 3600.00 |

*Adventure Comics #73, © DC Comics*

|  | Good | Fine | N-Mint |
|---|---|---|---|
| 41 | 150.00 | 375.00 | 900.00 |
| 42-47: 47-Steve Conrad Adventurer begins, ends #76 | | | |
|  | 100.00 | 250.00 | 600.00 |
| 48-Intro. & 1st app. The Hourman by Bernard Baily | | | |
|  | 567.00 | 1420.00 | 3400.00 |
| 49,50: 50-Cotton Carver by Jack Lehti begins, ends #59? | | | |
|  | 100.00 | 250.00 | 600.00 |
| 51-60: 53-Intro Jimmy "Minuteman" Martin & the Minutemen of America in Hourman; ends #78. 58-Paul Kirk Manhunter begins, ends #72 | | | |
|  | 93.00 | 235.00 | 560.00 |
| 61-Intro/1st app. Starman by Jack Burnley | 367.00 | 920.00 | 2200.00 |
| 62-65,67,68: 67-Origin The Mist | 75.00 | 190.00 | 450.00 |
| 66-Origin Shining Knight | 102.00 | 255.00 | 615.00 |
| 69-Intro. Sandy the Golden Boy (Sandman's sidekick) by Bob Kane; Sandman dons new costume | 95.00 | 240.00 | 570.00 |
| 70-Last Federal Men | 79.00 | 200.00 | 475.00 |
| 71-Jimmy Martin becomes costume aide to the Hourman; intro Hourman's Miracle Ray machine | 75.00 | 190.00 | 450.00 |

| | Good | Fine | N-Mint |
|---|---|---|---|
| 72-1st Simon & Kirby Sandman | 300.00 | 750.00 | 1800.00 |
| 73-Origin Manhunter by Simon & Kirby; begin new series | | | |
| | 350.00 | 875.00 | 2100.00 |
| 74-76: 74-Thorndyke replaces Jimmy, Hourman's assistant | | | |
| | 100.00 | 250.00 | 600.00 |
| 77-Origin Genius Jones; Mist story | 100.00 | 250.00 | 600.00 |
| 78-80-Last Simon & Kirby Manhunter & Burnley Starman | | | |
| | 100.00 | 250.00 | 600.00 |
| 81-90: 83-Last Hourman. 84-Mike Gibbs begins, ends #102 | | | |
| | 63.00 | 160.00 | 375.00 |
| 91-Last Simon & Kirby Sandman | 56.00 | 140.00 | 335.00 |
| 92-99,101,102 Last Starman, Sandman, & Genius Jones. Most-S&K-c. 92- | | | |
| Last Manhunter | 42.00 | 105.00 | 250.00 |
| 100 | 67.00 | 170.00 | 400.00 |
| 103-Aquaman, Green Arrow, Johnny Quick, Superboy begin; 1st small | | | |
| logo (4/46) | 167.00 | 420.00 | 1000.00 |
| 104 | 52.00 | 130.00 | 315.00 |
| 105-110 | 43.00 | 110.00 | 260.00 |
| 111-120:113-X-Mas-c | 37.00 | 92.00 | 225.00 |
| 121-126,128-130:128-1st meeting Superboy-Lois Lane | | | |
| | 30.00 | 75.00 | 180.00 |
| 127-Brief origin Shining Knight retold | 33.00 | 85.00 | 200.00 |
| 131-140: 132-Shining Knight 1st return to King Arthur time; origin aide Sir | | | |
| Butch | 27.00 | 68.00 | 160.00 |
| 141,143-149 | 27.00 | 68.00 | 160.00 |
| 142-Origin Shining Knight & Johnny Quick retold | | | |
| | 30.00 | 75.00 | 180.00 |
| 150,151,153,155,157,159,161,163-All have 6-pg. Shining Knight stories by | | | |
| Frank Frazetta. 159-Origin Johnny Quick | | | |
| | 43.00 | 110.00 | 260.00 |
| 152,154,156,158,160,162,164-169: 166-Last Shining Knight. 168-Last 52 | | | |
| pgs. | 20.00 | 60.00 | 140.00 |
| 170-180 | 18.50 | 56.00 | 130.00 |
| 181-199: 189-B&W and color illo in **POP** | 17.00 | 51.00 | 120.00 |
| 200 | 22.00 | 64.00 | 150.00 |
| 201-209: 207-Last Johnny Quick (not in 205). 209-Last Pre-code issue; ori- | | | |
| gin Speedy | 16.50 | 50.00 | 115.00 |
| 210-1st app. Krypto (Superdog) | 121.00 | 363.00 | 845.00 |
| 211-220 | 13.00 | 40.00 | 90.00 |
| 221-246: 237-1st Intergalactic Vigilante Squadron(Legion Tryout) | | | |
| | 11.50 | 34.00 | 80.00 |

|                                                                                              | Good  | Fine   | N-Mint  |
|----------------------------------------------------------------------------------------------|-------|--------|---------|
| 247(4/58)-1st Legion of Super Heroes app.; 1st app. Cosmic Boy, Lightning Boy (later Lightning Lad in #267), & Saturn Girl (origin) | 215.00 | 645.00 | 1600.00 |
| 248-252,254,255: 248-255-All have Kirby Green Arrow. 255-Intro. Red Kryptonite in Superboy (used in #252 but with no effect) | 7.00  | 21.00  | 50.00   |
| 253-Superboy & Robin 1st meet                                                                | 950   | 28.50  | 66.00   |
| 256-Origin Green Arrow by Kirby                                                              | 26.50 | 80.00  | 185.00  |
| 257-259                                                                                      | 7.00  | 21.00  | 50.00   |
| 260-Origin Aquaman retold (1st S.A. app.)                                                    | 21.50 | 64.50  | 150.00  |
| 261-266,268,270: 262-Origin Speedy in Green Arrow. 270-Congorilla begins ends #281,283       | 5.50  | 16.50  | 38.00   |
| 267(12/59)-2nd Legion of Super Heroes; Lightning Boy now called Lightning Lad; new costumes for Legion | 54.00 | 161.00 | 375.00  |
| 269-Intro. Aqualad; last Green Arrow (not in #206)                                           | 9.30  | 28.00  | 65.00   |
| 271-Origin Luthor                                                                            | 11.50 | 34.50  | 80.00   |
| 272-274,277-280: 279-Intro White Kryptonite in Superboy. 280-1st meeting Superboy-Lori Lemaris | 4.00  | 12.00  | 28.00   |
| 275-Origin Superman-Batman team retold (see World's Finest #94)                             | 6.50  | 19.50  | 45.00   |
| 276-(9/60) Re-intro Metallo (3rd app?); story similar to Superboy #49                       | 4.00  | 12.00  | 28.00   |
| 281,284,287-289: 281-Last Congorilla. 284-Last Aquaman in Adv. 287,288-Intro. Dev-Em, the Knave from Krypton. 287-1st Bizarro Perry White & J. Olsen. 289-Legion cameo (statues) | 3.50  | 10.50  | 24.00   |
| 282(3/61)-5th Legion app; intro/origin Star Boy                                             | 9.30  | 28.00  | 65.00   |
| 283-Intro. The Phantom Zone                                                                  | 5.50  | 16.50  | 38.00   |
| 285-1st Bizarro World story (ends #299) in Adv. (See Action #255)                           | 6.50  | 19.50  | 45.00   |
| 286-1st Bizarro Mxyzptlk                                                                     | 5.15  | 16.50  | 36.00   |
| 290(11/61)-8th Legion app; origin Sunboy in Legion (last 10 cent issue)                     | 8.50  | 25.50  | 60.00   |
| 291,292,295-298: 292-1st Bizarro Lana Lang & Lucy Lane. 295-1st Bizarro Titano               | 3.00  | 9.00   | 21.00   |
| 293(2/62)-13th Legion app; Mon-el & Legion Super Pets (intro & origin) app. (1st Superhorse). 1st Bizarro Luthor & Kandor | 6.00  | 18.00  | 42.00   |

| | Good | Fine | N-Mint |
|---|---|---|---|
| 294-1st Bizarro M. Monroe, Pres. Kennedy | 4.50 | 14.00 | 32.00 |
| 299-1st Gold Kryptonite(8/62) | 3.15 | 9.50 | 22.00 |
| 300-Legion series begins; Mon-el leaves Phantom Zone (temporarily), joins Legion | 26.50 | 80.00 | 185.00 |
| 301-Origin Bouncing Boy | 8.85 | 26.50 | 62.00 |
| 302-305: 303-1st app. Matter Eater Lad. 304-Death of Lightning Lad in Legion | 4.70 | 14.00 | 33.00 |
| 306-310: 306-Intro. Legion of Substitute Heroes. 307-Intro. Element Lad in Legion. 308-1st app. Lightning Lass in Legion | 3.70 | 11.00 | 26.00 |
| 311-320: 312-Lightning Lad back in Legion. 315-Last new Superboy story; Colossal Boy app. 316-Origins & powers of Legion given. 317-Intro. Dream Girl in Legion; Lightning Lass becomes Light Lass; Hall of Fame series begins. 320-Dev-Em 2nd app. | 2.85 | 8.50 | 20.00 |
| 321-Intro Time Trapper | 2.15 | 6.50 | 15.00 |
| 322-330: 327-Intro Timber Wolf in Legion. 329-Intro Legion of Super Bizarros | 1.85 | 5.50 | 13.00 |
| 331-340: 337-Chlorophyll Kid & Night Girl app. 340-Intro Computo in Legion | 1.70 | 5.00 | 12.00 |
| 341-Triplicate Girl becomes Duo Damsel | 1.15 | 3.50 | 8.00 |
| 342-345,347,350,351: 345-Last Hall of Fame; returns in 356,371. 351-1st app. White Witch | 1.00 | 3.00 | 7.00 |
| 346,348,349: 346-1st app. Karate Kid, Princess Projectra, Ferro Lad, & Nemesis Kid. 348-Origin Sunboy; intro Dr. Regulus in Legion. 349-Intro Universo & Rond Vidar | 1.15 | 3.50 | 8.00 |
| 352,354-360: 355-Insect Queen joins Legion (4/67) | 1.00 | 3.00 | 6.00 |
| 353-Death of Ferro Lad in Legion | 1.50 | 4.50 | 10.00 |
| 361-364,366,368-370: 369-Intro Mordru in Legion | .75 | 2.25 | 4.50 |
| 365,367,371,372: 365-Intro Shadow Lass; lists origins & powers of L.S.H. 367-New Legion headquarters. 371-Intro. Chemical King. 372-Timber Wolf & Chemical King join | .90 | 2.75 | 5.50 |
| 373,374,376-380: Last Legion in Adv. | .75 | 2.25 | 4.50 |
| 375-Intro Quantum Queen & The Wanderers | .90 | 2.75 | 5.50 |
| 381-389,391-400: 381-Supergirl begins. 399-Unpubbed G.A. Black Canary story. 400-New costume for Supergirl | | .60 | 1.20 |
| 390-Giant Supergirl G-69 | .70 | 2.00 | 4.00 |
| 401,402,404-410: 409-420-52 pg. issues | | .60 | 1.20 |

|  | Good | Fine | N-Mint |
|---|---|---|---|
| 403-68 pg. Giant G-81 | .70 | 2.00 | 4.00 |
| 411,413,414: 413-Hawkman by Kubert; G.A. Robotman-r/Det. 178; | | | |
| Zatanna begins, ends #421 | | .40 | .80 |
| 412-Animal Man origin reprint/Str. Advs. #180 | | | |
|  | 1.00 | 3.00 | 6.00 |
| 415,420,421-Animal Man reprints | .35 | 1.00 | 2.00 |
| 416-Giant DC-10. GA-r | | .60 | 1.20 |
| 417-Morrow Vigilante; Frazetta Shining Knight r-/Adv. #161; origin The | | | |
| Enchantress | | .60 | 1.20 |
| 418,419,422-424: Last Supergirl in Adv. | | .40 | .80 |
| 425-New look, content change to adventure; Toth-a, origin Capt. Fear | | | |
|  | .25 | .75 | 1.50 |
| 426-458: 427-Last Vigilante. 435-Mike Grell's 1st comic work ('74). | | | |
| 440-New Spectre origin | | .40 | .80 |
| 459-466($1.00 size, 68 pgs.) | | .45 | .90 |
| 467-490: 467-Starman by Ditko, Plastic Man begin, end 478. 469, | | | |
| 470-Origin Starman | | .40 | .80 |
| 491-499: 491-100 pg. Digest size begins | | .60 | 1.20 |
| 500-All Legion-r (Digest size, 148 pgs.) | .25 | .80 | 1.60 |
| 501-503-G.A.-r | | .60 | 1.20 |

## ADVENTURES INTO THE UNKNOWN
Fall, 1948 - No. 174, Aug, 1967 (No. 1-33·52 pgs.)
American Comics Group

*(1st continuous series horror comic; see Eerie #1)*

| 1-Guardineer-a; adapt. of 'Castle of Otranto' by Horace Walpole | | | |
|---|---|---|---|
|  | 48.00 | 145.00 | 335.00 |
| 2 | 21.50 | 64.00 | 150.00 |
| 3-Feldstein-a, 9 pgs. | 23.00 | 68.00 | 160.00 |
| 4,5 | 13.00 | 40.00 | 90.00 |
| 6-10 | 10.00 | 30.00 | 70.00 |
| 11-16,18-20:13-Starr-a | 7.00 | 21.00 | 50.00 |
| 17-Story similar to movie 'The Thing' | 10.00 | 30.00 | 70.00 |
| 21-26,28-30 | 6.50 | 19.50 | 45.00 |
| 27-Williamson/Krenkel-a, 8 pgs. | 14.00 | 42.00 | 100.00 |
| 31-50: 38-Atom bomb panels | 4.30 | 13.00 | 30.00 |
| 51(1/54) - 59 (3-D effect issues) | 10.00 | 30.00 | 70.00 |
| 60-Woodesque-a by Landau | 3.15 | 9.50 | 22.00 |
| 61-Last pre-code issue (1-2/55) | 2.85 | 8.50 | 20.00 |

|  | Good | Fine | N-Mint |
|---|---|---|---|
| 62-70 | 2.15 | 6.50 | 15.00 |
| 71-90 | 1.50 | 4.50 | 10.00 |
| 91,95,96(#95 on inside),107,116-All contain Williamson-a | | | |
|  | 2.85 | 8.50 | 20.00 |
| 92-94,97-99,101-106,108-115,117-127: 109-113,118-Whitney painted-c | | | |
|  | 1.35 | 4.00 | 8.00 |
| 100 | 2.00 | 6.00 | 12.00 |
| 128-Williamson/Krenkel/Torres-a(r) | 2.00 | 6.00 | 12.00 |
| 129-150 | 1.00 | 3.00 | 6.00 |
| 151-153: 153-Magic Agent app. | .70 | 2.00 | 4.00 |
| 154-Nemesis series begins (origin), ends #170 | | | |
|  | 1.00 | 3.00 | 6.00 |
| 155-167,169-174: 157-Magic Agent app. | .70 | 2.00 | 4.00 |
| 168-Ditko-a(p) | 1.00 | 3.00 | 6.00 |

**ADVENTURES OF DEAN MARTIN AND JERRY LEWIS, THE** (The
   Adventures of Jerry Lewis No. 41 on)
July-Aug, 1952 - No. 40, Oct, 1957
National Periodical Publications

| 1 | 36.00 | 107.00 | 250.00 |
|---|---|---|---|
| 2 | 17.00 | 51.00 | 120.00 |
| 3-10 | 9.30 | 28.00 | 65.00 |
| 11-19: Last precode (2/55) | 5.00 | 15.00 | 35.00 |
| 20-30 | 3.65 | 11.00 | 25.00 |
| 31-40 | 2.85 | 8.50 | 20.00 |

**ADVENTURES OF JERRY LEWIS, THE** (Advs. of Dean Martin & Jerry
   Lewis No. 1-40)
No. 41, Nov, 1957 - No. 124, May-June, 1971
National Periodical Publications

| 41-60 | 2.30 | 7.00 | 16.00 |
|---|---|---|---|
| 61-80: 68,74-Photo-c | 1.70 | 5.00 | 12.00 |
| 81-91,93-96,98-100: 89-Bob Hope app. | 1.00 | 3.00 | 7.00 |
| 92-Superman cameo | 1.15 | 3.50 | 8.00 |
| 97-Batman/Robin x-over; Joker-c/story | 2.00 | 6.00 | 14.00 |
| 101-104-Neal Adams c/a; 102-Beatles app. | 2.65 | 8.00 | 18.00 |
| 105-Superman x-over | 1.00 | 3.00 | 7.00 |
| 106-111,113-116 | .70 | 2.00 | 4.00 |

| | Good | Fine | N-Mint |
|---|---|---|---|
| 112-Flash x-over | .85 | 2.50 | 5.00 |
| 117-Wonder Woman x-over | .85 | 2.50 | 5.00 |
| 118-124 | .50 | 1.50 | 3.00 |

**ADVENTURES OF SUPERMAN** (Formerly Superman)
No. 424, Jan, 1987 - Present
DC Comics

| | | | |
|---|---|---|---|
| 424 | .45 | 1.35 | 2.70 |
| 425-449: 426-Legends x-over. 432-1st app. Jose Delgado who becomes Gangbuster in #434. 436-Byrne scripts begin. 436,437-Millennium x-over. 438-New Brainiac app. | | .50 | 1.00 |
| 450-472: 457-Perez plots | | .40 | .80 |
| Annual 1: 1(9/87)-Starlin-c. | .25 | .70 | 1.40 |
| Annual 2 (1990, $2.00, 68 pgs.) | .35 | 1.00 | 2.00 |

**ADVENTURES OF THE FLY** (The Fly, No. 2; Fly Man No. 32-39)
Aug, 1959 -No. 30, Oct, 1964; No. 31, May, 1965
Archie Publications/Radio Comics

| | | | |
|---|---|---|---|
| 1-Shield app.; origin The Fly; S&K-c/a | 33.70 | 101.00 | 235.00 |
| 2-Williamson, S&K, Powell-a | 18.50 | 55.50 | 130.00 |
| 3-Origin retold; Davis, Powell-a | 12.00 | 36.00 | 84.00 |
| 4-Neal Adams-a(p)(1 panel); S&K-c; Powell-a; Shield x-over | 8.50 | 25.50 | 60.00 |
| 5-10: 7-Black Hood app. 8,9-Shield x-over. 9-1st app. Cat Girl.10-Black Hood app. | 5.00 | 15.00 | 35.00 |
| 11-13,15-20: 16-Last 10 cent issue. 20-Origin Fly Girl retold | 2.85 | 8.50 | 20.00 |
| 14-Intro. & origin Fly Girl | 4.30 | 13.00 | 30.00 |
| 21-31: 23-Jaguar cameo. 29-Black Hood cameo. 30-Comet x-over in Fly Girl. 31-Black Hood, Shield, Comet app. | 2.15 | 6.50 | 15.00 |

**ADVENTURES OF THE JAGUAR, THE**
Sept, 1961 - No. 15, Nov, 1963
Archie Publications (Radio Comics)

| | | | |
|---|---|---|---|
| 1-Origin Jaguar (1st app?) | 11.00 | 33.00 | 75.00 |
| 2,3: 3-Last 10 cent issue | 5.00 | 15.00 | 35.00 |
| 4,5-Catgirl app. | 3.60 | 11.00 | 25.00 |

|  | Good | Fine | N-Mint |
|---|---|---|---|
| 6-10: 6-Catgirl app. | 2.65 | 8.00 | 18.00 |
| 11-15: 13,14-Catgirl, Black Hood app. in both | 2.00 | 6.00 | 14.00 |

**AIRBOY COMICS** (Air Fighters Comics No. 1-22)
V2#11, Dec, 1945 - V10#4, May, 1953 (No V3#3)
Hillman Periodicals

| | Good | Fine | N-Mint |
|---|---|---|---|
| V2#11 | 26.00 | 77.00 | 180.00 |
| 12-Valkyrie app. | 17.00 | 51.00 | 120.00 |
| V3#1,2(no #3) | 13.00 | 42.00 | 100.00 |
| 4-The Heap app. in Skywolf | 11.50 | 34.00 | 80.00 |
| 5-8: 6-Valkyrie app; | 10.00 | 30.00 | 70.00 |
| 9-Origin The Heap | 11.50 | 34.00 | 80.00 |
| 10,11 | 10.00 | 30.00 | 70.00 |
| 12-Skywolf & Airboy x-over; Valkyrie app. | 13.00 | 40.00 | 90.00 |
| V4#1-Iron Lady app. | 11.50 | 34.00 | 80.00 |
| 2,3,12: 2-Rackman begins | 7.00 | 21.00 | 50.00 |
| 4-Simon & Kirby-c | 8.50 | 25.50 | 60.00 |
| 5-11-All S&K-a | 10.00 | 30.00 | 70.00 |
| V5#1-9: 4-Infantino Heap. 5-Skull-c | 5.00 | 15.00 | 35.00 |
| 10,11: 10-Origin The Heap | 5.00 | 15.00 | 35.00 |
| 12-Krigstein-a(p) | 6.50 | 19.50 | 45.00 |
| V6#1-3,5-12: 6,8-Origin The Heap | 5.00 | 15.00 | 35.00 |
| 4-Origin retold | 5.70 | 17.00 | 40.00 |
| V7#1-12: 7,8,10-Origin The Heap | 5.00 | 15.00 | 35.00 |
| V8#1-3,6-12 | 4.00 | 12.00 | 28.00 |
| 4-Krigstein-a | 6.50 | 19.50 | 45.00 |
| 5(#100) | 5.00 | 15.00 | 35.00 |
| V9#1-6,8-12: 2-Valkyrie app. | 4.00 | 12.00 | 28.00 |
| 7-One pg. Frazetta ad | 4.50 | 14.00 | 32.00 |
| V10#1-4 | 4.00 | 12.00 | 28.00 |

**AIR FIGHTERS COMICS** (Airboy Comics #23 (V2#11) on)
Nov, 1941; No. 2, Nov, 1942 - V2#10, Fall, 1945
Hillman Periodicals

| | Good | Fine | N-Mint |
|---|---|---|---|
| V1#1-(Produced by Funnies, Inc.); Black Commander only app. | | | |
| | 90.00 | 270.00 | 630.00 |

| | Good | Fine | N-Mint |
|---|---|---|---|
| 2(11/42)-(Produced by Quality artists & Biro for Hillman); Origin Airboy & Iron Ace; Black Angel, Flying Dutchman & Skywolf begin; Fuje-a; Biro c/a | 140.00 | 420.00 | 980.00 |
| 3-Origin The Heap & Skywolf | 71.00 | 213.00 | 500.00 |
| 4 | 50.00 | 150.00 | 350.00 |
| 5,6 | 37.00 | 110.00 | 260.00 |
| 7-12 | 28.00 | 86.00 | 200.00 |
| V2#1,3-9: 5-Flag-c; Fuje-a. 7-Valkyrie app. | 26.50 | 80.00 | 185.00 |
| 2-Skywolf by Giunta; Flying Dutchman by Fuje; 1st meeting Valkyrie & Airboy (She worked for the Nazis in beginning) | 32.00 | 95.00 | 225.00 |
| 10-Origin The Heap & Skywolf | 32.00 | 95.00 | 225.00 |

**ALF** (TV)
Mar, 1988 - Present ($1.00, color)
Marvel Comics

| | | | |
|---|---|---|---|
| 1-Post-a; photo-c | 1.00 | 3.00 | 6.00 |
| 2-Post-a | .70 | 2.00 | 4.00 |
| 3-5 | .35 | 1.00 | 2.00 |
| 6-36: 6-Photo-c. 26-Infinity-c | | .60 | 1.20 |
| Annual 1 ($1.75, 68 pgs.)-Evolutionary War | .60 | 1.75 | 3.50 |
| Annual 2 (1989, $2.00, 68 pgs.) | .35 | 1.00 | 2.00 |
| Annual 3 (1990, $2.00, 68 pgs.) | .35 | 1.00 | 2.00 |
| Holiday Special 1 ($1.75, 1988, 68 pgs.) | .30 | .90 | 1.75 |
| Holiday Special 2 ($2.00, Winter/90, 68 pgs.) | .35 | 1.00 | 2.00 |
| Spring Special 1 (Spr/89, $1.75, 68 pgs.) | .30 | .90 | 1.75 |

**ALL-AMERICAN COMICS** (. . . Western #103-126)
April, 1939 - No. 102, Oct, 1948
National Periodical Publications/All-American

| | | | |
|---|---|---|---|
| 1-Hop Harrigan, Scribbly, Toonerville Folks, Ben Webster, Spot Savage, Mutt & Jeff, Red White & Blue, Adv. in the Unknown, Tippie, Reg'lar Fellers, Skippy, Bobby Thatcher, Mystery Men of Mars, Daiseybelle, & Wiley of West Point begin | 217.00 | 545.00 | 1300.00 |
| 2-Ripley's Believe It or Not begins, ends #24 | 83.00 | 210.00 | 500.00 |
| 3-5: 5-The American Way begins, ends #10 | 58.00 | 145.00 | 350.00 |

| | Good | Fine | N-Mint |
|---|---|---|---|
| 6,7: 6-Last Spot Savage; Popsicle Pete begins, ends #26, 28. 7 Last Bobby | | | |
| Thatcher | 47.00 | 120.00 | 280.00 |
| 8-The Ultra Man begins | 75.00 | 190.00 | 450.00 |
| 9,10: 10-X-Mas-c | 53.00 | 135.00 | 315.00 |
| 11-15: 12-Last Toonerville Folks. 15-Last Tippie & Reg'lar Fellars | | | |
| | 43.00 | 110.00 | 260.00 |
| 16-(Rare)-Origin & 1st app. Green Lantern and begin series, created by | | | |
| Martin Nodell | 1670.00 | 4180.00 | 10,000.00 |
| *(Prices vary widely on this book)* | | | |
| 17-(Scarce)-2nd Green Lantern | 467.00 | 1170.00 | 2800.00 |
| 18-N.Y. World's Fair-c/story | 233.00 | 585.00 | 1400.00 |
| 19-Origin/1st app. The Atom; Last Ultra Man | | | |
| | 367.00 | 920.00 | 2200.00 |
| 20-Atom dons costume; Hunkle becomes Red Tornado; Rescue on Mars | | | |
| begins, ends #25; 1 pg. origin Green Lantern | | | |
| | 158.00 | 395.00 | 950.00 |
| 21-23: 21-Last Wiley of West Point & Skippy. 23-Last Daiseybelle; 3 Idiots | | | |
| begin, end #82 | 112.00 | 280.00 | 670.00 |
| 24-Sisty & Dinky become the Cyclone Kids; Ben Webster ends. Origin Dr. | | | |
| Mid-Nite & Sargon, The Sorcerer in text with app. | | | |
| | 120.00 | 300.00 | 720.00 |
| 25-Origin & 1st story app. Dr. Mid-Nite by Stan Asch; Hop Harrigan be- | | | |
| comes Guardian Angel; last Adventure in the Unknown | | | |
| | 233.00 | 585.00 | 1400.00 |
| 26-Origin/1st story app. Sargon, the Sorcerer | | | |
| | 133.00 | 335.00 | 800.00 |
| 27: #27-32 are misnumbered in indicia with correct No. appearing on | | | |
| cover. Intro. Doiby Dickles, Green Lantern's sidekick | | | |
| | 142.00 | 355.00 | 850.00 |
| 28-Hop Harrigan gives up costumed i.d. | 75.00 | 190.00 | 450.00 |
| 29,30 | 75.00 | 190.00 | 450.00 |
| 31-40: 35-Doiby learns Green Lantern's i.d. | 56.00 | 140.00 | 335.00 |
| 41-50: 50-Sargon ends | 49.00 | 125.00 | 295.00 |
| 51-60: 59-Scribbly & the Red Tornado ends | 42.00 | 105.00 | 250.00 |
| 61-Origin Solomon Grundy | 150.00 | 375.00 | 900.00 |
| 62-70: 70-Kubert Sargon; intro Sargon's helper, Maximillian O'Leary | | | |
| | 39.00 | 100.00 | 235.00 |
| 71-Last Red White & Blue | 31.00 | 78.00 | 185.00 |

|                                                                              | Good   | Fine   | N-Mint  |
|------------------------------------------------------------------------------|--------|--------|---------|
| 72-88,90-99: 72-Black Pirate begins (not in #74-82); last Atom. 73- Winky, Blinky & Noddy begins, ends #82. 90-Origin Icicle. 99-Last Hop Harrigan | 31.00 | 78.00 | 185.00 |
| 89-Origin Harlequin                                                          | 38.00  | 95.00  | 225.00  |
| 100-1st app. Johnny Thunder by Alex Toth                                     | 58.00  | 145.00 | 350.00  |
| 101-Last Mutt & Jeff                                                         | 44.00  | 110.00 | 265.00  |
| 102-Last Green Lantern, Black Pirate & Dr. Mid-Nite                          | 50.00  | 125.00 | 300.00  |

**ALL-AMERICAN WESTERN** (Formerly All-American Comics)
No. 103, Nov, 1948 - No. 126, June-July, 1952 (103-121: 52 pgs.)
National Periodical Publications

|                                                                              | Good   | Fine   | N-Mint  |
|------------------------------------------------------------------------------|--------|--------|---------|
| 103-Johnny Thunder & his horse Black Lightning continues by Toth, ends #126; Foley of The Fighting 5th, Minstrel Maverick, & Overland Coach begin; Capt. Tootsie by Beck | 21.50 | 64.00 | 150.00 |
| 104-Kubert-a                                                                 | 14.00  | 43.00  | 100.00  |
| 105,107-Kubert-a                                                             | 12.00  | 36.00  | 85.00   |
| 106,108-110,112: 112-Kurtzman "Pot-Shot Pete," 1 pg.                         | 9.30   | 28.00  | 65.00   |
| 111,114-116-Kubert-a                                                         | 10.00  | 30.00  | 70.00   |
| 113-Intro. Swift Deer, J. Thunder's new sidekick; classic Toth-c; Kubert-a  | 11.50  | 34.00  | 80.00   |
| 117-120,122-125                                                              | 8.00   | 24.00  | 56.00   |
| 121-Kubert-a                                                                 | 8.00   | 24.00  | 56.00   |
| 126-Last issue                                                               | 8.00   | 24.00  | 56.00   |

**ALL-FLASH** (. . . Quarterly No.1-5)
Summer, 1941 - No. 32, Dec-Jan, 1947-48
National Periodical Publications/All-American

|                                                                              | Good   | Fine   | N-Mint  |
|------------------------------------------------------------------------------|--------|--------|---------|
| 1-Origin The Flash retold by E. Hibberd                                      | 333.00 | 835.00 | 2000.00 |
| 2-Origin recap                                                               | 117.00 | 295.00 | 700.00  |
| 3,4                                                                          | 76.00  | 190.00 | 455.00  |
| 5-Winky, Blinky & Noddy begins, ends #32                                     | 58.00  | 145.00 | 350.00  |
| 6-10                                                                         | 50.00  | 125.00 | 300.00  |

*All-Flash #8, © DC Comics*

|  | Good | Fine | N-Mint |
|---|---|---|---|
| 11-13: 12-Origin The Thinker. 13-The King app. | | | |
|  | 42.00 | 105.00 | 250.00 |
| 14-Green Lantern cameo | 47.00 | 120.00 | 280.00 |
| 15-20: 18-Mutt & Jeff begins, ends #22 | 38.00 | 95.00 | 225.00 |
| 21-31 | 32.00 | 80.00 | 190.00 |
| 32-Origin The Fiddler; 1st Star Sapphire | 39.00 | 100.00 | 235.00 |

**ALL-SELECT COMICS** (Blonde Phantom No. 12 on)
Fall, 1943 - No. 11, Fall, 1946
Timely Comics (Daring Comics)

| 1-Capt. America, Human Torch, Sub-Mariner begin; Black Widow app. | | | |
|---|---|---|---|
|  | 208.00 | 520.00 | 1250.00 |
| 2-Red Skull app. | 88.00 | 220.00 | 525.00 |
| 3-The Whizzer begins | 58.00 | 145.00 | 350.00 |
| 4,5-Last Sub-Mariner | 49.00 | 125.00 | 295.00 |
| 6-9: 6-The Destroyer app. 8-No Whizzer | 40.00 | 100.00 | 240.00 |

|  | Good | Fine | N-Mint |
|---|---|---|---|
| 10-The Destroyer & Sub-Mariner app.; last Capt. America & Human Torch issue | 40.00 | 100.00 | 240.00 |
| 11-1st app. Blonde Phantom; Miss America app.; all Blonde Phantom-c by Shores | 66.00 | 165.00 | 395.00 |

**ALL STAR COMICS** (All Star Western No. 58 on)
Summer, 1940 - No. 57, Feb-Mar, 1951; No. 58, Jan-Feb, 1976-No. 74, Sept-Oct, 1978
National Periodical Publ./All-American/DC Comics

| | Good | Fine | N-Mint |
|---|---|---|---|
| 1-The Flash (No. 1 by Harry Lampert), Hawkman(by Shelly), Hourman, The Sandman, The Spectre, Biff Bronson, Red White & Blue begin; Ultra Man's only app. | 667.00 | 1670.00 | 4000.00 |
| 2-Green Lantern, Johnny Thunder begin | 317.00 | 795.00 | 1900.00 |
| 3-Origin Justice Society of America; Dr. Fate & The Atom begin, Red Tornado cameo; last Red White & Blue | 1250.00 | 3125.00 | 7500.00 |
| 4 | 317.00 | 795.00 | 1900.00 |
| 5-Intro. & 1st app. Shiera Sanders as Hawkgirl | 267.00 | 670.00 | 1600.00 |
| 6-Johnny Thunder joins JSA | 233.00 | 585.00 | 1400.00 |
| 7-Batman, Superman, Flash cameo; last Hourman; Doiby Dickles app. | 233.00 | 585.00 | 1400.00 |
| 8-Origin & 1st app. Wonder Woman (added as 8pgs. making book 76 pgs.; origin cont'd in Sensation #1); Dr. Fate dons new helmet; Dr. Mid-Nite, Hop Harrigan text stories & Starman begin; Shiera app.; Hop Harrigan JSA guest | 450.00 | 1125.00 | 2700.00 |
| 9-Shiera app. | 183.00 | 460.00 | 1100.00 |
| 10-Flash, Green Lantern cameo, Sandman new costume | 183.00 | 460.00 | 1100.00 |
| 11-Wonder Woman begins; Spectre cameo; Shiera app. | 175.00 | 440.00 | 1050.00 |
| 12-Wonder Woman becomes JSA Secretary | 175.00 | 440.00 | 1050.00 |
| 13-15: Sandman w/Sandy in No. 14 & 15; 15-Origin Brain Wave; Shiera app. | 158.00 | 400.00 | 950.00 |
| 16-19: 19-Sandman w/Sandy | 117.00 | 295.00 | 700.00 |
| 20-Dr. Fate & Sandman cameo | 117.00 | 295.00 | 700.00 |
| 21-Spectre & Atom cameo; Dr. Fate by Kubert; Dr. Fate, Sandman end | 100.00 | 250.00 | 600.00 |

| | Good | Fine | N-Mint |
|---|---|---|---|
| 22,23: 22-Last Hop Harrigan; Flag-c. 23-Origin Psycho Pirate; last Spectre | | | |
| & Starman | 100.00 | 250.00 | 600.00 |
| 24-Flash & Green Lantern cameo; Mr. Terrific only app.; Wildcat, JSA | | | |
| guest; Kubert Hawkman begins | 100.00 | 250.00 | 600.00 |
| 25-27:25-The Flash & Green Lantern start again. 27-Wildcat, JSA guest | | | |
| | 93.00 | 235.00 | 560.00 |
| 28-32 | 80.00 | 200.00 | 480.00 |
| 33-Solomon Grundy, Hawkman, Doiby Dickles app. | | | |
| | 150.00 | 375.00 | 900.00 |
| 34,35-Johnny Thunder cameo in both | 73.00 | 220.00 | 440.00 |
| 36-Batman & Superman JSA guests | 158.00 | 475.00 | 950.00 |
| 37-Johnny Thunder cameo; origin Injustice Society; last Kubert | | | |
| Hawkman | 83.00 | 210.00 | 500.00 |
| 38-Black Canary begins; JSA Death issue | 92.00 | 230.00 | 550.00 |
| 39,40: 39-Last Johnny Thunder | 59.00 | 150.00 | 355.00 |
| 41-Black Canary joins JSA; Injustice Society app. | | | |
| | 57.00 | 145.00 | 345.00 |
| 42-Atom & the Hawkman don new costumes | 57.00 | 145.00 | 345.00 |
| 43-49 | 57.00 | 145.00 | 345.00 |
| 50-Frazetta art, 3 pgs. | 63.00 | 160.00 | 380.00 |
| 51-56: 55-Sci/fi story | 57.00 | 145.00 | 345.00 |
| 57-Kubert-a, 6 pgs. (Scarce) | 67.00 | 170.00 | 405.00 |
| V12#58-74(1976-78)-Flash, Hawkman, Dr. Mid-Nite, Wildcat, Dr. Fate, | | | |
| Green Lantern, Star Spangled Kid, & Robin app.; intro Power Girl. | | | |
| 58-JSA app. 69-1st app. Huntress | | .25 | .50 |

## ALL TOP COMICS
1945; No. 2, Sum, 1946 - No. 18, Mar, 1949
Fox Features Synd.

| | Good | Fine | N-Mint |
|---|---|---|---|
| 1-Cosmo Cat & Flash Rabbit begin | 10.00 | 30.00 | 70.00 |
| 2 | 5.00 | 15.00 | 35.00 |
| 3-7 | 3.50 | 10.50 | 25.00 |
| 8-Blue Beetle, Phantom Lady, & Rulah, Jungle Goddess begin | | | |
| (11/47); Kamen-c | 57.00 | 170.00 | 400.00 |
| 9-Kamen-c | 34.00 | 103.00 | 240.00 |
| 10-Kamen bondage-c | 36.00 | 107.00 | 250.00 |
| 11-13,15-17: 15-No Blue Beetle | 26.00 | 77.00 | 180.00 |

|  | Good | Fine | N-Mint |
|---|---|---|---|

14-No Blue Beetle; used in **SOTI**, illo-"Corpses of colored people strung
up by their wrists"                              32.00      95.00     225.00
18-Dagar, Jo-Jo app; no Phantom Lady or Blue Beetle
                                                 21.50      64.00     150.00

**ALL WESTERN WINNERS** (Formerly All Winners; becomes Western
   Winners with No. 5; see Two-Gun Kid No. 5)
No. 2, Winter, 1948-49 - No. 4, April, 1949
Marvel Comics (CDS)

2-Black Rider (Origin & 1st app.) & his horse Satan, Kid Colt & his horse
   Steel, & Two-Gun Kid & his horse Cyclone begin
                                                 18.50      56.00     130.00
3-Anti-Wertham editorial                         13.00      40.00      90.00
4-Black Rider i.d. revealed                      13.00      40.00      90.00

**ALL WINNERS COMICS** (All Teen #20)
Summer, 1941 - No. 19, Fall, 1946; No. 21, Winter, 1946-47
(no No. 20) (No. 21 continued from Young Allies No. 20)
USA No. 1-7/WFP No. 10-19/YAI No. 21

1-The Angel & Black Marvel only app.; Capt. America by Simon & Kirby
   Human Torch & Sub-Mariner begin (#1 was advertised as All Aces)
                                                315.00     790.00    1890.00
2-The Destroyer & The Whizzer begin; Simon & Kirby Captain America
                                                150.00     375.00     900.00
3,4                                             117.00     295.00     700.00
5,6: 6-The Black Avenger only app.; no Whizzer story
                                                 78.00     195.00     470.00
7-10                                             65.00     165.00     390.00
11-18: 12-Last Destroyer; no Whizzer story; no Human Torch #14-16
                                                 41.00     105.00     245.00
19-(Scarce)-1st app. & origin All Winners Squad
                                                 98.00     245.00     590.00
21-(Scarce)-All Winners Squad; bondage-c  91.00   230.00     545.00
      *(2nd Series - August, 1948, Marvel Comics (CDS))*
         *(Becomes All Western Winners with No. 2)*
1-The Blonde Phantom, Capt. America, Human Torch, & Sub-Mariner
   app.                                          68.00     205.00     480.00

**ALPHA FLIGHT** (See X-Men #120,121)
Aug, 1983 - Present (#52-on are direct sale only)
Marvel Comics Group

|  | Good | Fine | N-Mint |
|---|---|---|---|
| 1-Byrne-a begins (52 pgs.)-Wolverine & Nightcrawler cameo | | | |
|  | .85 | 2.50 | 5.00 |
| 2-Vindicator becomes Guardian; origin Marrina & Alpha Flight | | | |
|  | .40 | 1.25 | 2.50 |
| 3-5: 3-Concludes origin Alpha Flight | .35 | 1.10 | 2.20 |
| 6-11: 6-Origin Shaman. 7-Origin Snowbird. 10,11-Origin Sasquatch | | | |
|  | .35 | 1.00 | 2.00 |
| 12-Double size; death of Guardian | .40 | 1.25 | 2.50 |
| 13-Wolverine app. | 1.35 | 4.00 | 8.00 |
| 14-16: 16-Wolverine app. | .25 | .75 | 1.50 |
| 17-X-Men x-over; Wolverine cameo | .85 | 2.50 | 5.00 |
| 18-28: 20-New headquarters. 25-Return of Guardian. 28-Last Byrne issue | | | |
|  | .25 | .75 | 1.50 |
| 29-32,35-39 |  | .65 | 1.30 |
| 33,34: 33-X-Men (Wolverine) app. 34-Origin Wolverine | | | |
|  | .70 | 2.00 | 4.00 |
| 40-49,51,54-64 |  | .65 | 1.30 |
| 50-Double size | .20 | .70 | 1.40 |
| 52,53-Wolverine app. | .70 | 2.00 | 4.00 |
| 65-74,76-90: 65-Begin $1.50-c. 71-Intro The Sorcerer (villain). 74- Wolverine, Spider-Man & The Avengers app. | .25 | .75 | 1.50 |
| 75-Double size ($1.95, 52 pgs.) | .35 | 1.00 | 1.95 |

**AMAZING FANTASY**
No. 15, Aug, 1962 (Sept, 1962 shown in indicia)
Marvel Comics Group (AMI)

| | Good | Fine | N-Mint |
|---|---|---|---|
| 15-Origin & 1st app. of Spider-Man by Ditko; Kirby/Ditko-c | | | |
|  | 320.00 | 1280.00 | 3200.00 |

**AMAZING-MAN COMICS**
No. 5, Sept, 1939 - No. 27, Feb, 1942
Centaur Publications

5(No.1)(Rare)-Origin/1st app. A-Man the Amazing Man by Bill Everett;
    The Cat-Man by Tarpe Mills (also No. 8), Mighty Man by Filchock,

|  | Good | Fine | N-Mint |
|---|---|---|---|
| Minimidget & sidekick Ritty, & The Iron Skull by Burgos begins | | | |
|  | 750.00 | 1875.00 | 4500.00 |
| 6-Origin The Amazing Man retold; The Shark begins; Ivy Menace by Tarpe Mills app. | 217.00 | 545.00 | 1300.00 |
| 7-Magician From Mars begins; ends #11 | 133.00 | 400.00 | 800.00 |
| 8-Cat-Man dresses as woman | 84.00 | 253.00 | 590.00 |
| 9-Magician From Mars battles the 'Elemental Monster,' swiped into The Spectre in More Fun 54 & 55 | 82.00 | 245.00 | 575.00 |
| 10,11: 11-Zardi, the Eternal Man begins; ends #16; Amazing Man dons costume; last Everett issue | 70.00 | 210.00 | 490.00 |
| 12,13 | 68.00 | 204.00 | 475.00 |
| 14-Reef Kinkaid, Rocke Wayburn (ends #20), & Dr. Hypno (ends #21) begin; no Zardi or Chuck Hardy | 54.00 | 160.00 | 375.00 |
| 15,17-20: 15-Zardi returns; no Rocke Wayburn. 17-Dr. Hypno returns; no Zardi | 39.00 | 118.00 | 275.00 |
| 16-Mighty Man's powers of super strength & ability to shrink & grow explained; Rocke Wayburn returns; no Dr. Hypno; Al Avison (a character) begins, ends #18 (a tribute to the famed artist) | | | |
|  | 42.00 | 126.00 | 295.00 |
| 21-Origin Dash Dartwell (drug-use story); origin & only app. T.N.T. | | | |
|  | 39.00 | 118.00 | 275.00 |
| 22-Dash Dartwell, the Human Meteor & The Voice app; last Iron Skull & The Shark; Silver Streak app. | 39.00 | 118.00 | 275.00 |
| 23-Two Amazing Man stories; intro/origin Tommy the Amazing Kid; The Marksman only app. | 42.00 | 126.00 | 295.00 |
| 24,27: 24-King of Darkness, Nightshade, & Blue Lady begin; end #26; 1st App. Super-Ann | 39.00 | 118.00 | 275.00 |
| 25,26 (Scarce)-Meteor Martin by Wolverton in both; 26-Electric Ray app. | | | |
|  | 72.00 | 215.00 | 505.00 |

**AMAZING SPIDER-MAN, THE** (See Amazing Fantasy, Marvel Team-Up, Spectacular . . . , Spider-Man Vs. Wolverine, Web of Spider-Man)
March, 1963 - Present
Marvel Comics Group

| | Good | Fine | N-Mint |
|---|---|---|---|
| 1-Retells origin by Steve Ditko; F.F. x-over; intro. John Jameson & The Chameleon; Kirby-c | 320.00 | 1280.00 | 3200.00 |
| 1-Reprint from the Golden Record Comic set | 6.50 | 19.50 | 45.00 |
| with record. . . . | 14.00 | 42.00 | 100.00 |

*The Amazing Spider-Man #161,*
*© Marvel Comics*

| | Good | Fine | N-Mint |
|---|---|---|---|
| 2-Intro the Vulture & the Terrible Tinkerer | | | |
| | 145.00 | 435.00 | 1000.00 |
| 3-Human Torch cameo; intro. & 1st app. Doc Octopus; Dr. Doom & Ant-Man app. | 100.00 | 300.00 | 700.00 |
| 4-Origin & 1st app. The Sandman; Intro. Betty Brant & Liz Allen | | | |
| | 65.00 | 195.00 | 450.00 |
| 5-Dr. Doom app. | 57.00 | 171.00 | 400.00 |
| 6-1st app. Lizard | 65.00 | 195.00 | 450.00 |
| 7,8,10: 8-Fantastic 4 app. 10-1st app. Big Man & Enforcers | | | |
| | 43.00 | 130.00 | 300.00 |
| 9-1st app. Electro (origin) | 46.00 | 138.00 | 325.00 |
| 11,12: 11-1st app. Bennett Brant | 26.00 | 78.00 | 180.00 |
| 13-1st app. Mysterio | 32.00 | 96.00 | 225.00 |
| 14-Intro The Green Goblin; Hulk x-over | 65.00 | 195.00 | 450.00 |
| 15-Intro Kraven the Hunter | 28.00 | 85.00 | 200.00 |
| 16,18,19: 18-Fant.-4 app; 19-Intro. Ned Leeds | | | |
| | 18.00 | 54.00 | 125.00 |

AMAZING SPIDER-MAN, THE    95

|  | Good | Fine | N-Mint |
|---|---|---|---|
| 17-2nd app. Green Goblin | 28.00 | 85.00 | 200.00 |
| 20-Intro & origin The Scorpion | 20.00 | 60.00 | 140.00 |
| 21,22: 22-1st app. Princess Python | 14.00 | 42.00 | 100.00 |
| 23-3rd app. The Green Goblin | 17.85 | 53.50 | 125.00 |
| 24,25: 25-1st app. Spencer Smythe | 12.85 | 38.50 | 90.00 |
| 26-4th app. The Green Goblin; 1st app. Crime Master; dies in #27 |  |  |  |
|  | 15.70 | 47.00 | 110.00 |
| 27-5th app. The Green Goblin | 15.70 | 47.00 | 110.00 |
| 28-Origin/1st app. Molten Man | 14.00 | 42.00 | 100.00 |
| 29,30 | 12.00 | 36.00 | 85.00 |
| 31-38: 31-Intro. Harry Osborn, Gwen Stacy & Prof. Warren. 36-1st app. Looter. 37-Intro. Norman Osborn. 38-Last Ditko issue. |  |  |  |
|  | 8.50 | 25.50 | 60.00 |
| 39-Green Goblin-c & app. | 9.30 | 28.00 | 65.00 |
| 40-Origin Green Goblin | 10.70 | 32.00 | 75.00 |
| 41,43-49: 41-1st app. Rhino. 46-Intro. Shocker |  |  |  |
|  | 5.00 | 15.00 | 35.00 |
| 42-1st app. Mary Jane Watson | 6.50 | 19.50 | 45.00 |
| 50-Intro. Kingpin | 16.00 | 48.00 | 112.00 |
| 51-2nd app. Kingpin | 4.70 | 14.00 | 33.00 |
| 52-60: 52-Intro. Joe Robertson. 56-Intro. Capt. George Stacy. 57,58-Ka-Zar app. 59-Intro. Brainwasher (alias Kingpin) |  |  |  |
|  | 3.00 | 9.00 | 21.00 |
| 61-80: 67-Intro. Randy Robertson. 73-Intro. Silvermane. 78-Intro. Prowler |  |  |  |
|  | 2.00 | 6.00 | 14.00 |
| 81-89,91-93,95,99: 83-Intro. Schemer & Vanessa (Kingpin's wife). 93-Intro. Arthur Stacy | 1.85 | 5.50 | 13.00 |
| 90-Death of Capt. Stacey | 2.40 | 7.20 | 17.00 |
| 94-Origin retold | 3.00 | 9.00 | 21.00 |
| 96-98-Drug books not approved by CCA | 4.00 | 12.00 | 28.00 |
| 100-Anniversary issue | 9.30 | 28.00 | 65.00 |
| 101-Intro. Morbius | 2.50 | 7.50 | 18.00 |
| 102-Origin Morbius (52 pgs.) | 2.50 | 7.50 | 18.00 |
| 103-112,115-118: 108-Intro. Sha-Shan. 110-Intro. Gibbon. 111-Kraven the Hunter app. | 1.60 | 4.80 | 11.00 |
| 113,114,119,120: 113-Intro. Hammerhead | 1.70 | 5.00 | 12.00 |
| 121-Death of Gwen Stacy (r-/in Marvel Tales #98) |  |  |  |
|  | 6.50 | 19.50 | 45.00 |
| 122-Death of Green Goblin (r-/in Marvel Tales #99) |  |  |  |
|  | 10.70 | 32.00 | 75.00 |
| 123-128: 124-Intro. Man Wolf, origin in #125 | 1.70 | 5.00 | 10.00 |

|  | Good | Fine | N-Mint |
|---|---|---|---|
| 129-1st app. The Punisher (2/74) | 36.00 | 108.00 | 250.00 |
| 130-133,137-140: 139-Intro. Grizzly | 1.15 | 3.50 | 7.00 |
| 134-Punisher cameo; intro Tarantula | 2.40 | 7.20 | 17.00 |
| 135-Punisher app. | 6.50 | 19.50 | 45.00 |
| 136-Reappearance of Green Goblin | 2.15 | 6.50 | 15.00 |
| 141-160: 143-Intro. Cyclone | 1.15 | 3.50 | 7.00 |
| 161-Nightcrawler app. from X-Men; Punisher cameo | | | |
|  | 1.60 | 4.80 | 11.00 |
| 162-Punisher, Nightcrawler app. | 2.85 | 8.50 | 20.00 |
| 163-173,176-188: 167-1st app. Will O' The Wisp. 171-Nova app. 177-180-Green Goblin app. 181-Origin retold; gives life history of Spider-Man | .70 | 2.10 | 4.20 |
| 174,175-Punisher app. | 2.00 | 6.00 | 14.00 |
| 189,190-Byrne-a(p) | .85 | 2.50 | 5.00 |
| 191-193,195-199,203-219: 196-Faked death of Aunt May. 203-2nd Dazzler app. 210-Intro. & 1st app. Madame Web. 212-Intro. Hydro Man | .70 | 2.10 | 4.20 |
| 194-1st Black Cat | .95 | 2.80 | 5.60 |
| 200-Giant origin issue | 1.70 | 5.00 | 12.00 |
| 201,202-Punisher app. | 2.15 | 6.50 | 15.00 |
| 220-237: 226,227-Black Cat returns. 236-Tarantula dies. 235-Origin Will-'O-The-Wisp | .70 | 2.00 | 4.00 |
| 238-1st app. Hobgoblin | 3.15 | 9.50 | 22.00 |
| 239-2nd app. Hobgoblin | 1.70 | 5.00 | 10.00 |
| 240-250: 241-Origin The Vulture | .50 | 1.50 | 3.00 |
| 251-Last old costume | 1.00 | 3.00 | 6.00 |
| 252-Spider-Man dons new costume (5/84); ties with Spectacular Spider-Man #90 for 1st new costume | 1.35 | 4.00 | 8.00 |
| 253-1st app. The Rose | .85 | 2.50 | 5.00 |
|  | .60 | 1.75 | 3.50 |
| 255-260: 259-Spidey back to old costume | .50 | 1.50 | 3.00 |
| 261-274,276-283: 261-Hobgoblin app. | .35 | 1.00 | 2.00 |
| 275-Origin-r by Ditko ($1.25, double-size) | .85 | 2.50 | 5.00 |
| 284-Punisher cameo; Gang War story begins | .70 | 2.00 | 4.00 |
| 285-Punisher app. | 2.00 | 6.00 | 12.00 |
| 286-288,290-292: 288-Last Gang War | .60 | 1.75 | 3.50 |
| 289-Double-size, origin Hobgoblin | 1.70 | 5.00 | 10.00 |
| 293,294-Part 2 & 5 of Kraven story from Web of Spider-Man | 1.00 | 3.00 | 6.00 |
| 295-297 | .70 | 2.00 | 4.00 |

|  | Good | Fine | N-Mint |
|---|---|---|---|
| 298-Todd McFarlane-c/a begins, ends #325 | 5.00 | 15.00 | 30.00 |
| 299-McFarlane-a | 2.50 | 7.50 | 15.00 |
| 300 ($1.50, 52 pgs.; 25th Anniversary)-Last black costume | | | |
|  | 5.00 | 15.00 | 30.00 |
| 301-305: 301 ($1.00 issues begin). 304-1st bi-weekly issue | | | |
|  | 2.50 | 7.50 | 15.00 |
| 306-315: 306-Cover swipe from Action #1. 312-Hobgoblin app. | | | |
|  | 1.70 | 5.00 | 10.00 |
| 316-323,325: 319-Bi-weekly begins again | 1.00 | 3.00 | 6.00 |
| 324-McFarlane-c only | 1.00 | 3.00 | 6.00 |
| 326,327,329: 327-Cosmic. | .35 | 1.00 | 2.00 |
| 328-Last McFarlane issue; Hulk x-over | | | |
|  | 1.00 | 3.00 | 6.00 |
| 330,331-Punisher app. | .50 | 1.50 | 3.00 |
| 332-342 |  | .50 | 1.00 |
| Annual 1 (1964)-Origin Spider-Man; Intro. Sinister Six; Kraven the Hunter | | | |
| app. | 21.00 | 63.00 | 150.00 |
| Annual 2 | 8.50 | 25.50 | 60.00 |
| Special 3,4 | 3.60 | 11.00 | 25.00 |
| Special 5-8 (12/71) | 1.70 | 5.00 | 12.00 |
| King Size 9 ('73)-Green Goblin app. | 1.35 | 4.00 | 8.00 |
| Giant-Size 1(7/74)-Kirby/Ditko-r plus new-a | | | |
|  | 1.35 | 4.00 | 8.00 |
| Giant-Size 2(10/74), 3(1/75), 5(7/75), 6(9/75) | | | |
|  | .70 | 2.00 | 4.00 |
| Giant-Size 4(4/75)-Third Punisher app. | 5.70 | 17.00 | 40.00 |
| Annual 10(6/76)-Old Human Fly app. | .85 | 2.50 | 5.00 |
| Annual 11(9/77), 12(8/78) | .85 | 2.50 | 5.00 |
| Annual 13(11/79)-Byrne-a | 1.00 | 3.00 | 6.00 |
| Annual 14(12/80)-Miller-c/a(p), 40 pgs. | 1.15 | 3.50 | 7.00 |
| Annual 15(1981)-Miller-c/a(p); Punisher app. | | | |
|  | 2.50 | 7.50 | 15.00 |
| Annual 16-20: 16(12/82)-Origin/1st app. new Capt. Marvel (female hero- | | | |
| ine). 17(12/83). 18 ('84). 19(11/85). 20(11/86)-Origin Iron Man of 2020 | | | |
|  | .70 | 2.00 | 4.00 |
| Annual 21('87)-Special wedding issue (direct sale, no bar codes) | | | |
|  | 1.00 | 3.00 | 6.00 |
| Annual 21-Wedding issue (newsstand) | .85 | 2.50 | 5.00 |
| Annual 22('88, $1.75, 68 pgs.)-Intro/1st app. Speedball; Evolutionary War | | | |
| x-over | 1.00 | 3.00 | 6.00 |

|                                                                          | Good  | Fine   | N-Mint |
|--------------------------------------------------------------------------|-------|--------|--------|
| Annual 23 ('89, $2.00, 68 pgs.)-Atlantis Attacks; origin Spider-Man retold; She-Hulk app.; Byrne-c | .70 | 2.00 | 4.00 |
| Annual 24 ('90, $2.00, 68 pgs.)                                          | .35   | 1.00   | 2.00   |

## AMERICA'S BEST COMICS
Feb, 1942 - No. 31, July, 1949
Nedor/Better/Standard Publications

|                                                                          | Good  | Fine   | N-Mint |
|--------------------------------------------------------------------------|-------|--------|--------|
| 1-The Woman in Red, Black Terror, Captain Future, Doc Strange, The Liberator, & Don Davis, Secret Ace begin | 57.00 | 170.00 | 400.00 |
| 2-Origin The American Eagle; The Woman in Red ends                       | 31.00 | 95.00  | 220.00 |
| 3-Pyroman begins                                                         | 22.00 | 65.00  | 155.00 |
| 4                                                                        | 20.00 | 60.00  | 140.00 |
| 5-Last Captain Future-not in #4; Lone Eagle app.                         | 17.00 | 51.00  | 120.00 |
| 6,7: 6-American Crusader app. 7-Hitler, Mussolini & Hirohito-c           | 16.00 | 48.00  | 110.00 |
| 8-Last Liberator                                                         | 12.00 | 36.00  | 85.00  |
| 9-The Fighting Yank begins; The Ghost app.                               | 12.00 | 36.00  | 85.00  |
| 10-14: 10-Flag-c. 14-American Eagle ends                                 | 11.00 | 32.00  | 75.00  |
| 15-20                                                                    | 10.00 | 30.00  | 70.00  |
| 21-Infinity-c                                                            | 8.50  | 25.50  | 60.00  |
| 22-Capt. Future app.                                                     | 8.50  | 25.50  | 60.00  |
| 23-Miss Masque begins; last Doc Strange                                  | 11.50 | 34.00  | 80.00  |
| 24-Miss Masque bondage-c                                                 | 10.00 | 30.00  | 70.00  |
| 25-Last Fighting Yank; Sea Eagle app.                                    | 8.50  | 25.50  | 60.00  |
| 26-The Phantom Detective & The Silver Knight app.; Frazetta text illo & some panels in Miss Masque | 11.50 | 34.00 | 80.00 |
| 27-31: 27,28-Commando Cubs. 27-Doc Strange. 28-Tuska Black Terror. 29-Last Pyroman | 8.50 | 25.50 | 60.00 |

## ANIMAL COMICS
Dec-Jan, 1941-42 - No. 30, Dec-Jan, 1947-48
Dell Publishing Co.

|                                                                          | Good  | Fine   | N-Mint |
|--------------------------------------------------------------------------|-------|--------|--------|
| 1-1st Pogo app. by Walt Kelly (Dan Noonan art in most issues)            | 86.00 | 257.00 | 600.00 |
| 2-Uncle Wiggily begins                                                   | 36.00 | 107.00 | 250.00 |

| | Good | Fine | N-Mint |
|---|---|---|---|
| 3,5 | 25.00 | 75.00 | 175.00 |
| 4,6,7-No Pogo | 14.00 | 42.00 | 100.00 |
| 8-10 | 17.00 | 51.00 | 120.00 |
| 11-15 | 11.00 | 32.00 | 75.00 |
| 16-20 | 7.00 | 21.00 | 50.00 |
| 21-30: 25-30-"Jigger" by John Stanley | 5.00 | 15.00 | 35.00 |

**ANIMAL MAN** (Also see Strange Adventures #180)
Sept, 1988 - Present ($1.25, color)
DC Comics

| | | | |
|---|---|---|---|
| 1-All have Brian Bolland-c | 2.50 | 7.50 | 15.00 |
| 2 | 1.50 | 4.50 | 9.00 |
| 3,4 | .85 | 2.50 | 5.00 |
| 5-10: 6-Invasion tie-in | .60 | 1.75 | 3.50 |
| 11-15 | .40 | 1.25 | 2.50 |
| 16-20 | .35 | 1.00 | 2.00 |
| 21-30 | .25 | .75 | 1.50 |

**ANNIE OAKLEY** (Also see Two-Gun Kid & Wild Western)
Spring, 1948 - No. 4, 11/48; No. 5, 6/55 - No. 11, 6/56
Marvel/Atlas Comics (MPI No. 1-4/CDS No. 5 on)

| | | | |
|---|---|---|---|
| 1 (1st Series, '48)-Hedy Devine app. | 16.00 | 47.00 | 110.00 |
| 2 (7/48, 52 pgs.)-Kurtzman-a, "Hey Look," 1pg; Intro. Lana; Hedy Devine app; Captain Tootsie by Beck | 11.00 | 32.00 | 75.00 |
| 3,4 | 8.50 | 25.50 | 60.00 |
| 5 (2nd Series)(1955)-Reinman-a | 5.70 | 17.00 | 40.00 |
| 6-8: 6,8-Woodbridge-a | 4.30 | 13.00 | 30.00 |
| 9-Williamson-a, 4 pgs. | 4.30 | 13.00 | 30.00 |
| 10,11: 11-Severin-c | 3.60 | 11.00 | 25.00 |

**ANNIE OAKLEY AND TAGG** (TV)
1953- No. 18, Jan-Mar, 1959; July, 1965 (all photo-c)
Dell Publishing Co./Gold Key

| | | | |
|---|---|---|---|
| 4-Color 438 (#1) | 7.00 | 21.00 | 50.00 |
| 4-Color 481,575 | 5.00 | 15.00 | 35.00 |
| 4(7-9/55)-10 | 4.00 | 12.00 | 28.00 |

|  | Good | Fine | N-Mint |
|---|---|---|---|
| 11-18(1-3/59) | 3.60 | 11.00 | 25.00 |
| 1(7/65-Gold Key)-Photo-c | 3.00 | 9.00 | 21.00 |

**ANTHRO** (See Showcase #74)
July-Aug, 1968 - No. 6, July-Aug, 1969
National Periodical Publications

| 1-Howie Post-a in all | 1.50 | 4.50 | 10.00 |
| 2-6: 6-Wood-c/a (inks) | 1.00 | 3.00 | 6.00 |

**AQUAMAN** (See Adventure, Brave & the Bold, Detective, Justice
    League of America, More Fun #73, Showcase #30, & World's Finest)
Jan-Feb, 1962 - No. 56, Mar-Apr, 1971; No. 57, Aug-Sept, 1977 - No. 63,
    Aug-Sept, 1978
National Periodical Publications/DC Comics

| 1-Intro. Quisp | 21.00 | 63.00 | 145.00 |
| 2 | 9.50 | 28.50 | 66.00 |
| 3-5 | 6.50 | 19.50 | 45.00 |
| 6-10 | 4.30 | 13.00 | 30.00 |
| 11-20: 11-Intro. Mera. 18-Aquaman weds Mera; JLA cameo | | | |
|  | 2.85 | 8.50 | 20.00 |
| 21-32,34-40: 23-Birth of Aquababy. 26-Huntress app.(3-4/66). 29-Intro Ocean Master, Aquaman's stepbrother | 1.60 | 4.80 | 11.00 |
| 33-Intro. Aqua-Girl | 1.85 | 5.50 | 13.00 |
| 41-47,49 | .85 | 2.50 | 5.00 |
| 48-Origin reprinted | .90 | 2.70 | 5.50 |
| 50-52-Deadman by Neal Adams | 1.60 | 4.80 | 11.00 |
| 53-56('71): 56-Intro Crusader | .60 | 1.75 | 3.50 |
| 57('77)-63: 58-Origin retold | .35 | 1.00 | 2.00 |

**AQUAMAN**
Feb, 1986 - No. 4, May, 1986 (mini-series)
DC Comics

| 1-New costume | .85 | 2.50 | 5.00 |
| 2-4 | .50 | 1.50 | 3.00 |
| Special 1 ('88, $1.50, 52 pgs.) | .35 | 1.00 | 2.00 |

**AQUAMAN**
June, 1989 - No. 5, Oct, 1989 ($1.00, mini-series)
DC Comics

|  | Good | Fine | N-Mint |
|---|---|---|---|
| 1-5: Giffen plots/breakdowns; Swan-p |  | .60 | 1.20 |
| Special 1(Legend of . . . , $2.00, 1989, 52 pgs.)-Giffen plots/breakdowns-<br>Swan-p | .35 | 1.00 | 2.00 |

**ARCHIE COMICS** (Archie No. 158 on) (See Jackpot, Little . . . , & Pep)
    (First Teen-age comic) (Radio show 1st aired 6/2/45, by NBC)
Winter, 1942-43 - No. 19, 3-4/46; No. 20, 5-6/46 - Present
MLJ Magazines No. 1-19/Archie Publ. No. 20 on

| | Good | Fine | N-Mint |
|---|---|---|---|
| 1 (Scarce)-Jughead, Veronica app. | 330.00 | 830.00 | 2000.00 |
| 2 | 107.00 | 320.00 | 750.00 |
| 3 (60 pgs.) | 75.00 | 225.00 | 525.00 |
| 4,5 | 54.00 | 162.00 | 375.00 |
| 6-10 | 37.00 | 110.00 | 260.00 |
| 11-20: 15,17,18-Dotty & Ditto by Woggon. 16-Woggon-a | 23.00 | 70.00 | 160.00 |
| 21-30: 23-Betty & Veronica by Woggon (1st app?). 25-Woggon-a | 16.00 | 48.00 | 110.00 |
| 31-40 | 10.00 | 30.00 | 70.00 |
| 41-50 | 7.00 | 21.00 | 50.00 |
| 51-70 (1954): 51,65-70-Katy Keene app. | 4.00 | 12.00 | 28.00 |
| 71-99: 72-74-Katy Keene app. | 2.35 | 7.00 | 16.00 |
| 100 | 3.00 | 9.00 | 18.00 |
| 101-130 (1962) | 1.15 | 3.50 | 8.00 |
| 131-160 | .70 | 2.00 | 4.00 |
| 161-200 | .35 | 1.00 | 2.00 |
| 201-240 |  | .50 | 1.00 |
| 241-282 |  | .30 | .60 |
| 283-Cover/story plugs "International Children's Appeal" which was a<br>fraudulent charity, according to TV's 20/20 news program broadcast<br>July 20, 1979 |  | .60 | 1.25 |
| 284-376: 300-Anniversary issue |  | .25 | .50 |
| Annual 1('50)-116 pgs. (Scarce) | 75.00 | 225.00 | 525.00 |
| Annual 2('51) | 40.00 | 120.00 | 280.00 |
| Annual 3('52) | 22.00 | 65.00 | 154.00 |
| Annual 4,5(1953-54) | 16.00 | 48.00 | 110.00 |

| | Good | Fine | N-Mint |
|---|---|---|---|
| Annual 6-10(1955-59) | 9.00 | 27.00 | 62.00 |
| Annual 11-15(1960-65) | 4.00 | 12.00 | 28.00 |
| Annual 16-20(1966-70) | 1.15 | 3.50 | 7.00 |
| Annual 21-26(1971-75) | .45 | 1.25 | 2.50 |
| Annual Digest 27('75)-55('83-'89)(. . . Magazine #35 on) | | | |
| | .50 | 1.00 | |

## ARCHIE'S GIRLS, BETTY AND VERONICA (Becomes Betty & Veronica)
1950 - No. 347, 1987
Archie Publications (Close-Up)

| | Good | Fine | N-Mint |
|---|---|---|---|
| 1 | 65.00 | 195.00 | 455.00 |
| 2 | 32.00 | 95.00 | 225.00 |
| 3-5 | 18.00 | 54.00 | 125.00 |
| 6-10: 10-2pg. Katy Keene app. | 14.00 | 42.00 | 100.00 |
| 11-20: 11,13,14,17-19-Katy Keene app. 20-Debbie's Diary, 2 pgs. | | | |
| | 9.00 | 27.00 | 62.00 |
| 21-30: 27-Katy Keene app. | 7.00 | 21.00 | 50.00 |
| 31-50 | 5.00 | 15.00 | 35.00 |
| 51-74 | 3.00 | 9.00 | 21.00 |
| 75-Betty & Veronica sell souls to Devil | 6.00 | 18.00 | 42.00 |
| 76-99 | 1.70 | 5.00 | 12.00 |
| 100 | 2.30 | 7.00 | 16.00 |
| 101-140: 118-Origin Superteen. 119-Last Superteen story | | | |
| | .85 | 2.50 | 5.00 |
| 141-180 | .35 | 1.00 | 2.00 |
| 181-220 | | .50 | 1.00 |
| 221-347: 300-Anniversary issue | | .30 | .60 |
| Annual 1 (1953) | 40.00 | 120.00 | 280.00 |
| Annual 2(1954) | 17.00 | 51.00 | 120.00 |
| Annual 3-5 ('55-'57) | 13.00 | 40.00 | 90.00 |
| Annual 6-8 ('58-'60) | 9.00 | 27.00 | 62.00 |

## ARCHIE'S PAL, JUGHEAD
1949 - No. 126, Nov, 1965
Archie Publications

| | Good | Fine | N-Mint |
|---|---|---|---|
| 1 | 60.00 | 180.00 | 420.00 |
| 2 | 30.00 | 90.00 | 210.00 |
| 3-5 | 20.00 | 60.00 | 140.00 |

|  | Good | Fine | N-Mint |
|---|---|---|---|
| 6-10: 7-Suzie app. | 12.00 | 36.00 | 84.00 |
| 11-20 | 9.00 | 27.00 | 62.00 |
| 21-30: 23-25,28-30-Katy Keene app. 28-Debbie's Diary app. | | | |
|  | 5.70 | 17.00 | 40.00 |
| 31-50 | 3.50 | 10.50 | 24.00 |
| 51-70 | 2.65 | 8.00 | 18.00 |
| 71-100 | 1.50 | 4.50 | 9.00 |
| 101-126 | 1.00 | 3.00 | 6.00 |
| Annual 1 (1953) | 28.00 | 85.00 | 200.00 |
| Annual 2 (1954) | 17.00 | 51.00 | 120.00 |
| Annual 3-5 (1955-57) | 12.00 | 36.00 | 84.00 |
| Annual 6-8 (1958-60) | 8.00 | 24.00 | 56.00 |

**ASTONISHING** (Marvel Boy No. 1,2)
No. 3, April, 1951 - No. 63, Aug, 1957
Marvel/Atlas Comics(20CC)

|  | Good | Fine | N-Mint |
|---|---|---|---|
| 3-Marvel Boy continues | 28.00 | 85.00 | 200.00 |
| 4-6-Last Marvel Boy; 4-Stan Lee app. | 22.00 | 65.00 | 154.00 |
| 7-10 | 6.00 | 18.00 | 42.00 |
| 11,12,15,17,20 | 5.00 | 15.00 | 35.00 |
| 13,14,16,19-Krigstein-a | 5.70 | 17.00 | 40.00 |
| 18-Jack The Ripper story | 5.70 | 17.00 | 40.00 |
| 21,22,24 | 4.00 | 12.00 | 28.00 |
| 23-E.C. swipe-'The Hole In The Wall' from Vault Of Horror #16 | | | |
|  | 5.00 | 15.00 | 35.00 |
| 25-Crandall-a | 5.00 | 15.00 | 35.00 |
| 26-29: 29-Decapitation-c | 3.50 | 10.50 | 24.00 |
| 30-Tentacled eyeball story | 5.70 | 17.00 | 40.00 |
| 31-37-Last pre-code issue | 3.00 | 9.00 | 21.00 |
| 38-43,46,48-52,56,58,59,61 | 2.00 | 6.00 | 14.00 |
| 44-Crandall swipe/Weird Fantasy #22 | 3.50 | 10.50 | 24.00 |
| 45,47-Krigstein-a | 3.50 | 10.50 | 24.00 |
| 53,54: 53-Crandall, Ditko-a. 54-Torres-a | 3.00 | 9.00 | 21.00 |
| 55-Crandall, Torres-a | 3.50 | 10.50 | 24.00 |
| 57-Williamson/Krenkel-a, 4 pgs. | 4.50 | 13.50 | 32.00 |
| 60-Williamson/Mayo-a, 4 pgs. | 4.50 | 13.50 | 32.00 |
| 62-Torres, Powell -a | 2.30 | 7.00 | 16.00 |
| 63-Last issue; Woodbridge-a | 2.30 | 7.00 | 16.00 |

**ASTONISHING TALES**
Aug, 1970 - No. 36, July, 1976 (#1-7: 15 cents; #8: 25 cents)
Marvel Comics Group

|  | Good | Fine | N-Mint |
|---|---|---|---|
| 1-Ka-Zar by Kirby(p) & Dr. Doom by Wood begin; Kraven the Hunter-c/ story | 1.10 | 3.25 | 6.50 |
| 2-Kraven the Hunter-c/story; Kirby, Wood-a | .50 | 1.50 | 3.00 |
| 3-6: Smith-p; Wood-a-#3,4. 5-Red Skull app. | 1.00 | 3.00 | 6.00 |
| 7,8: 8-(52 pgs.)-Last Dr. Doom | .50 | 1.50 | 3.00 |
| 9-Lorna-r | .25 | .75 | 1.50 |
| 10-Smith-a(p) | .40 | 1.25 | 2.50 |
| 11-Origin Ka-Zar & Zabu | .25 | .75 | 1.50 |
| 12-Man-Thing by Neal Adams (apps. #13 also) | .40 | 1.25 | 2.50 |
| 13-24: 20-Last Ka-Zar. 21-It! the Living Colossus begins, ends #24. | | .50 | 1.00 |
| 25-Deathlok the Demolisher begins (1st app.); Perez 1st work, 2pgs. (8/74) | .60 | 1.75 | 3.50 |
| 26-36:29-Origin Guardians of the Galaxy | | .60 | 1.20 |

**ASTRO BOY** (TV)
August, 1965 (12 cents)
Gold Key

| | Good | Fine | N-Mint |
|---|---|---|---|
| 1(10151-508) | 14.00 | 42.00 | 100.00 |

**ATOM, THE** (. . . & the Hawkman #80 on; see All-American, Brave & the Bold, Detective, Flash Comics #80, Showcase & World's Finest)
June-July, 1962- No. 38, Aug-Sept, 1968
National Periodical Publications

| | Good | Fine | N-Mint |
|---|---|---|---|
| 1-Intro Plant-Master | 43.00 | 130.00 | 300.00 |
| 2 | 13.00 | 40.00 | 90.00 |
| 3-1st Time Pool story; 1st app. Chronos (origin) | 10.30 | 31.00 | 72.00 |
| 4,5: 4-Snapper Carr x-over | 7.70 | 23.00 | 54.00 |
| 6-10: 7-Hawkman x-over. 8-Justice League, Dr. Light app. | 6.00 | 18.00 | 42.00 |
| 11-15 | 4.30 | 13.00 | 30.00 |

*The Atom #8, © DC Comics*

|  | Good | Fine | N-Mint |
|---|---|---|---|
| 16-20: 19-Zatanna x-over | 2.85 | 8.50 | 20.00 |
| 21-28,30 | 1.70 | 5.00 | 12.00 |
| 29-Golden Age Atom x-over (1st S.A. app.) | 4.30 | 13.00 | 30.00 |
| 31-38: 31-Hawkman x-over. 36-G.A. Atom x-over. 37-Intro. Major Mynah | | | |
|     Hawkman cameo | 1.40 | 4.25 | 8.50 |

**ATOM & HAWKMAN, THE** (Formerly The Atom)
No. 39, Oct-Nov, 1968 - No. 45, Oct-Nov, 1969
National Periodical Publications

| 39-45: 43-1st app. Gentlemen Ghost, origin-44 | | | |
|---|---|---|---|
| | 1.20 | 3.50 | 7.00 |

**AUTHENTIC POLICE CASES**
Feb, 1948 - No. 38, Mar, 1955
St. John Publishing Co.

| | Good | Fine | N-Mint |
|---|---|---|---|
| 1-Hale the Magician by Tuska begins | 12.00 | 36.00 | 84.00 |
| 2-Lady Satan, Johnny Rebel app. | 8.00 | 24.00 | 56.00 |
| 3-Veiled Avenger app.; blood drainage story plus 2 Lucky Coyne stories; used in **SOTI**, illo. from Red Seal #16 | 17.00 | 51.00 | 120.00 |
| 4,5: 4-Masked Black Jack app. 5-Late 1930s Jack Cole-a(r); transvesticism story | 7.00 | 21.00 | 50.00 |
| 6-Matt Baker-c; used in **SOTI**, illo-"An invitation to learning," r-in Fugitives From Justice #3; Jack Cole-a | 17.00 | 51.00 | 120.00 |
| 7,8,10-14: 7-Jack Cole-a; Matt Baker art begins #8; Vic Flint in #10-14 | 7.00 | 21.00 | 50.00 |
| 9-No Vic Flint | 5.70 | 17.00 | 40.00 |
| 15-Drug-c/story; Vic Flint app.; Baker-c | 7.00 | 21.00 | 50.00 |
| 16,18,20,21,23 | 3.70 | 11.00 | 26.00 |
| 17,19,22-Baker-c | 3.85 | 11.50 | 27.00 |
| 24-28 (All 100 pages): 26-Transvestism | 11.00 | 32.00 | 75.00 |
| 29,30 | 2.45 | 7.25 | 17.00 |
| 31,32,37-Baker-c | 2.85 | 8.50 | 20.00 |
| 33-Transvestism; Baker-c | 3.70 | 11.00 | 26.00 |
| 34-Drug-c by Baker | 3.70 | 11.00 | 26.00 |
| 35-Baker-c/a(2) | 3.50 | 10.50 | 24.00 |
| 36-Vic Flint strip-r; Baker-c | 2.65 | 8.00 | 18.00 |
| 38-Baker-c/a | 3.50 | 10.50 | 24.00 |

**AVENGERS, THE** (See Solo Avengers, Tales Of Suspense, West Coast
    Avengers & X-Men Vs. . . . )
Sept, 1963 - Present
Marvel Comics Group

| | Good | Fine | N-Mint |
|---|---|---|---|
| 1-Origin The Avengers (Thor, Iron Man, Hulk, Ant-Man, Wasp) | 117.00 | 351.00 | 820.00 |
| 2 | 40.00 | 120.00 | 275.00 |
| 3 | 25.00 | 75.00 | 175.00 |
| 4-Revival of Captain America who joins the Avengers; 1st Silver Age app. of Captain America (3/64) | 55.00 | 165.00 | 385.00 |
| 4-Reprint from the Golden Record Comic set | 5.00 | 15.00 | 35.00 |
|     with record. . . . | 11.00 | 32.00 | 75.00 |
| 5-Hulk leaves | 16.50 | 50.00 | 115.00 |
| 6-10: 6-Intro The Masters of Evil. 8-Intro Kang. 9-Intro Wonder Man who dies in same story | 13.00 | 40.00 | 90.00 |

| | Good | Fine | N-Mint |
|---|---|---|---|
| 11-Spider-Man-c + x-over | 9.30 | 28.00 | 65.00 |
| 12-16: 15-Death of Zemo. 16-New Avengers line-up (Hawkeye, Quicksilver; Scarlet Witch join; Thor, Iron Man, Giant-Man & Wasp leave) | | | |
| | 8.30 | 25.00 | 58.00 |
| 17-19: 19-Intro Swordsman; origin Hawkeye | 6.00 | 18.00 | 42.00 |
| 20-22: Wood inks | 4.30 | 13.00 | 30.00 |
| 23-30: 28-Giant-Man becomes Goliath | 2.85 | 8.50 | 20.00 |
| 31-40 | 1.70 | 5.00 | 12.00 |
| 41-52,54-56: 48-Intro/Origin new Black Knight. 52-Black Panther joins Intro The Grim Reaper. 54-Intro new Masters of Evil | | | |
| | 1.30 | 4.00 | 9.00 |
| 53-X-Men app. | 1.60 | 4.80 | 11.00 |
| 57-Intro. The Vision | 3.70 | 11.00 | 26.00 |
| 58-Origin The Vision | 2.65 | 8.00 | 18.00 |
| 59-67: 59-Intro. Yellowjacket. 60-Wasp & Yellowjacket wed. 63-Goliath becomes Yellowjacket; Hawkeye becomes the new Goliath. 65-Last 12 cent issue. 66,67: B. Smith-a | 1.50 | 4.50 | 10.00 |
| 68-70 | 1.15 | 3.50 | 7.00 |
| 71-1st Invaders; Black Knight joins | 1.10 | 3.25 | 6.50 |
| 72-82,84-91: 80-Intro. Red Wolf. 87-Origin The Black Panther. 88-Written by Harlan Ellison | .90 | 2.75 | 5.50 |
| 83,92: 83-Intro. The Liberators (Wasp, Valkyrie, Scarlet Witch, Medusa & Black Widow). 92-Neal Adams-c | 1.10 | 3.25 | 6.50 |
| 93-(52 pgs.)-Neal Adams-c/a | 4.50 | 14.00 | 32.00 |
| 94-96-Neal Adams-c/a | 2.75 | 8.25 | 19.00 |
| 97-G.A. Capt. America, Sub-Mariner, Human Torch, Patriot, Vision, Blazing Skull, Fin, Angel, & new Capt. Marvel x over | | | |
| | 1.35 | 4.00 | 8.00 |
| 98-Goliath becomes Hawkeye; Smith c/a(i) | 1.85 | 5.50 | 13.00 |
| 99-Smith/Sutton-a | 1.85 | 5.50 | 13.00 |
| 100-Smith-c/a; featuring everyone who was an Avenger | | | |
| | 3.70 | 11.00 | 26.00 |
| 101-106,108,109: 101-Harlan Ellison scripts | .75 | 2.25 | 4.50 |
| 107-Starlin-a(p) | .85 | 2.50 | 5.00 |
| 110,111-X-Men app. | 1.20 | 3.50 | 7.00 |
| 112-1st app. Mantis | 1.00 | 3.00 | 6.00 |
| 113-120: 116-118-Defenders/Silver Surfer app. | .70 | 2.00 | 4.00 |

|  | Good | Fine | N-Mint |
|---|---|---|---|
| 121-130: 123-Origin Mantis | .60 | 1.75 | 3.50 |
| 131-133,136-140: 136-Ploog-r/Amaz. Advs.#12 | .50 | 1.50 | 3.00 |
| 134,135-True origin The Vision | .50 | 1.50 | 3.00 |
| 141-149: 144-Origin & 1st app. Hellcat | .40 | 1.25 | 2.50 |
| 150-Kirby-a(r); new line-up: Capt. America, Scarlet Witch, Iron Man, Wasp, Yellowjacket, Vision & The Beast | .40 | 1.25 | 2.50 |
| 151-163: 151-Wonderman returns with new costume | .35 | 1.15 | 2.30 |
| 164-166-Byrne-a | .75 | 2.25 | 4.50 |
| 167-180 | .35 | 1.00 | 2.00 |
| 181-191-Byrne-a. 181-New line-up: Capt. America, Scarlet Witch, Iron Man, Wasp, Vision, Beast & The Falcon. 183-Ms. Marvel joins. 185-Origin Quicksilver & Scarlet Witch | .45 | 1.30 | 2.60 |
| 192-202: Perez-a. 195-1st Taskmaster. 200-Double size; Ms. Marvel leaves | .35 | 1.00 | 2.00 |
| 203-262,264-271,273: 211-New line-up: Capt. America, Iron Man, Tigra, Thor, Wasp & Yellowjacket. 213-Yellowjacket leaves. 215, 216-Silver Surfer app. 216-Tigra leaves. 217-Yellowjacket & Wasp return. 221-Hawkeye & She-Hulk join. 227-Capt. Marvel (female) joins; origins of Ant-Man, Wasp, Giant-Man, Goliath, Yellowjacket, & Avengers. 230-Yellowjacket quits. 231-Ironman leaves. (Eros) joins. 234-Origin Quicksilver, Scarlet Witch. 238-Origin Blackout. 240-Spider-Woman revived. 250-($1.00, 52 pgs.) 232-Starfox | .60 |  | 1.20 |
| 263-1st app. X-Factor (1/86)(story continues in Fantastic Four #286) | .70 | 2.00 | 4.00 |
| 272-Alpha Flight guest star | .35 | 1.00 | 2.00 |
| 274-299: 291-$1.00 issues begin |  | .60 | 1.20 |
| 300 ($1.75, 68 pgs.)-Thor joins | .30 | .90 | 1.80 |
| 301-304,306-328: 302-Re-intro Quasar |  | .50 | 1.00 |
| 305-Byrne scripts begin | .35 | 1.00 | 2.00 |

**AVENGERS SPOTLIGHT** (Formerly Solo Avengers)
No. 21, Aug, 1989 - Present (.75-$1.00, color)
Marvel Comics

| 21 (75 cents)-Byrne-c/a | .50 | 1.00 |
|---|---|---|
| 22-40 ($1.00): 26-Acts of Vengeance story | .50 | 1.00 |

**AVENGERS WEST COAST** (Formerly West Coast Avengers)
No. 48, Sept, 1989 - Present ($1.00, color)
Marvel Comics

|  | Good | Fine | N-Mint |
|---|---|---|---|
| 48-50: Byrne-c/a & scripts continue. 50-Re-intro original Human Torch | | | |
|  | | .55 | 1.10 |
| 51-66: 54-Cover swipe Fantastic Four #1 | | .50 | 1.00 |

# B

**BABY HUEY, THE BABY GIANT**
9/56 - No. 97, 10/71; No. 98, 10/72; No. 99, 10/80
Harvey Publications

|  | Good | Fine | N-Mint |
|---|---|---|---|
| 1-Infinity-c | 20.00 | 60.00 | 140.00 |
| 2 | 10.00 | 30.00 | 70.00 |
| 3-Baby Huey takes anti-pep pills | 6.00 | 18.00 | 42.00 |
| 4,5 | 4.35 | 13.00 | 30.00 |
| 6-10 | 2.15 | 6.50 | 15.00 |
| 11-20 | 1.35 | 4.00 | 9.00 |
| 21-40 | 1.00 | 3.00 | 7.00 |
| 41-60 | .70 | 2.00 | 4.00 |
| 61-79(12/67) | .35 | 1.00 | 2.00 |
| 80(12/68) - 95-All 68 pg. Giants | .50 | 1.50 | 3.00 |
| 96,97-Both 52 pg. Giants | .50 | 1.50 | 3.00 |
| 98,99-regular size |  | .50 | 1.00 |

**BATGIRL SPECIAL** (See Teen Titans #50)
1988 (One shot, color, $1.50, 52 pgs)
DC Comics

| 1-Batman: The Killing Joke tie-in | 1.25 | 3.75 | 7.50 |
|---|---|---|---|

**BATMAN** (See The Brave & the Bold, Cosmic Odyssey, Detective,
80-Page Giants, The Joker, Justice League of America #250, Justice
League Int., Legends of the Dark Knight, Shadow of the . . . , Star
Spangled, 3-D Batman, Untold Legend of . . . , & World's Finest)
Spring, 1940 - Present
National Periodical Publ./Detective Comics/DC Comics

1-Origin The Batman retold by Bob Kane; see Detective #33 for 1st origin; 1st app. Joker & The Cat (Catwoman)

|  | Good | Fine | N-Mint |
|---|---|---|---|
|  | 2420.00 | 6050.00 | 14500.00 |
| *(Prices vary widely on this book)* | | | |
| 2 | 667.00 | 1670.00 | 4000.00 |
| 3-1st Catwoman in costume; 1st Puppetmaster app. | | | |
|  | 450.00 | 1125.00 | 2700.00 |
| 4 | 367.00 | 920.00 | 2200.00 |

*Batman #426, © DC Comics*

|  | Good | Fine | N-Mint |
|---|---|---|---|
| 5-1st app. of the Batmobile with its bat-head front | | | |
|  | 280.00 | 700.00 | 1680.00 |
| 6-10: 8-Infinity-c | 205.00 | 515.00 | 1230.00 |
| 11-Classic Joker-c (2nd Joker-c, 6-7/42) | 225.00 | 565.00 | 1350.00 |
| 12-15: 13-Jerry Siegel, creator of Superman appears in a Batman story | | | |
|  | 167.00 | 420.00 | 1000.00 |
| 16-IntroAlfred (4-5/43) | 233.00 | 585.00 | 1400.00 |
| 17-20: 18-Hitler, Hirohito, Mussolini-c | 105.00 | 265.00 | 630.00 |
| 21,22,24,26,28-30: 22-1st Alfred solo | 97.00 | 245.00 | 580.00 |
| 23-Joker-c/story | 130.00 | 325.00 | 780.00 |
| 25-Joker-c; only Joker/Penguin team-up | 121.00 | 305.00 | 730.00 |
| 27-Christmas-c | 100.00 | 250.00 | 600.00 |
| 31,32,34-36,38,39: 32-Origin Robin retold | 62.00 | 155.00 | 370.00 |
| 33-Christmas-c | 74.00 | 185.00 | 445.00 |
| 37,40-Joker-c/stories | 83.00 | 210.00 | 500.00 |
| 41-43,45,46: 45-Christmas-c | 52.00 | 130.00 | 315.00 |
| 44-Joker-c/story | 83.00 | 210.00 | 500.00 |

| | Good | Fine | N-Mint |
|---|---|---|---|
| 47-1st detailed origin The Batman | 167.00 | 420.00 | 1000.00 |
| 48-1000 Secrets of Batcave; r-in #203 | 56.00 | 140.00 | 335.00 |
| 49-Joker-c/story; 1st Vicki Vale & Mad Hatter | | | |
| | 83.00 | 210.00 | 500.00 |
| 50-Two-Face impostor app. | 52.00 | 130.00 | 315.00 |
| 51,53,54,56-60: 57-Centerfold is a 1950 calendar | | | |
| | 47.00 | 120.00 | 285.00 |
| 52,55-Joker-c/stories | 64.00 | 160.00 | 385.00 |
| 61-Origin Batman Plane II | 47.00 | 120.00 | 285.00 |
| 62-Origin Catwoman | 58.00 | 145.00 | 350.00 |
| 63-65,67-72: 65-Catwoman-c. 68-Two-Face app. 72-Last 52 pgs. | | | |
| | 37.00 | 95.00 | 225.00 |
| 66,73-Joker-c/stories | 50.00 | 125.00 | 300.00 |
| 74-77,79,80: 74-Used in **POP**, pg. 90 | 37.00 | 95.00 | 225.00 |
| 78-(8-9/53)-Ron Kar, The Man Hunter from Mars story-the 1st lawman of Mars to come to Earth (green skinned) | 47.00 | 120.00 | 280.00 |
| 81-89: 84-Two-Face app. 86-Intro Batmarine (Batman's submarine). 89-Last Pre-Code issue | 37.00 | 95.00 | 225.00 |
| 90,91,93-99 | 25.00 | 65.00 | 150.00 |
| 92-1st app. Bat-Hound | 28.00 | 70.00 | 170.00 |
| 100 | 112.00 | 280.00 | 680.00 |
| 101-104,106-109 | 20.00 | 60.00 | 140.00 |
| 105-1st Batwoman in Batman | 26.00 | 78.00 | 185.00 |
| 110-Joker story | 25.00 | 75.00 | 175.00 |
| 111-120: 113-1st app. Fatman | 14.00 | 42.00 | 100.00 |
| 121,122,124-126,128-130: 129-Origin Robin retold; Bondage-c | | | |
| | 11.50 | 34.00 | 80.00 |
| 123,127-Joker stories. 127-Superman cameo | 14.00 | 42.00 | 100.00 |
| 131-135,137-139,141-143: Last 10 cent issue. 131-Intro 2nd Batman & Robin series. 133-1st Bat-Mite in Batman. 134-Origin The Dummy. 139-Intro old Bat-Girl | 8.50 | 25.50 | 60.00 |
| 136-Joker-c/story | 13.00 | 40.00 | 90.00 |
| 140,144-Joker stories | 9.30 | 28.00 | 65.00 |
| 145,148-Joker-c/stories | 10.00 | 30.00 | 70.00 |
| 146,147,149,150 | 6.50 | 19.50 | 45.00 |
| 151,153,154,156-158,160-162,164-170: 164-New Batmobile; New look & Mystery Analysts series begins | 4.50 | 14.00 | 32.00 |
| 152-Joker story | 5.15 | 15.50 | 36.00 |
| 155-1st Silver Age Penguin | 8.50 | 25.50 | 60.00 |
| 159,163-Joker-c/stories | 6.50 | 19.50 | 45.00 |

|                                                                                      | Good  | Fine   | N-Mint |
|--------------------------------------------------------------------------------------|-------|--------|--------|
| 171-Riddler app.(5/65), 1st since 12/48                                              | 36.00 | 108.00 | 250.00 |
| 172-175,177,178,180,181,183,184: 181-Batman & Robin poster insert; intro. Poison Ivy | 2.35  | 8.50   | 20.00  |
| 176-80-Pg. Giant G-17; Joker-c/story                                                 | 4.00  | 12.00  | 28.00  |
| 179-2nd Riddler app.                                                                 | 7.15  | 21.50  | 50.00  |
| 182-80 Pg. Giant G-24; Joker-c/story                                                 | 3.60  | 11.00  | 25.00  |
| 185-80 Pg. Giant G-27                                                                | 3.15  | 9.50   | 22.00  |
| 186,188-192,194-197,199: 197-New Bat-Girl app.                                       | 1.70  | 5.00   | 12.00  |
| 187-80 Pg. Giant G-30; Joker-c/story                                                 | 3.50  | 10.50  | 24.00  |
| 193-80-Pg. Giant G-37; Batcave blueprints                                            | 2.00  | 6.00   | 14.00  |
| 198-80-Pg. Giant G-43; Joker story; Origin-r                                         | 2.35  | 7.00   | 16.00  |
| 200-Joker story; retells origin of Batman & Robin                                    | 14.00 | 42.00  | 100.00 |
| 201-Joker story                                                                      | 2.00  | 6.00   | 14.00  |
| 202,204-207,209,210                                                                  | 1.35  | 4.00   | 8.00   |
| 203-80 Pg. Giant G-49; r/#48, 61, & Det. 185                                         | 1.50  | 4.50   | 9.00   |
| 208,218: 208-80 Pg. Giant G-55; New origin Batman by Gil Kane. 218-80 Pg. Giant G-67 | 1.50  | 4.50   | 9.00   |
| 211,212,214-217: 216-Alfred given a new last name-"Pennyworth." (see Det. 96)        | 1.35  | 4.00   | 8.00   |
| 213-80-Pg. Giant G-61; origin Alfred, Joker(r/Det. 168), Clayface; new origin Robin  | 3.60  | 11.00  | 25.00  |
| 219-Neal Adams-a                                                                     | 2.35  | 7.00   | 16.00  |
| 220,221,224-227,229-231                                                              | 1.15  | 3.50   | 7.00   |
| 222-Beatles take-off                                                                 | 1.70  | 5.00   | 12.00  |
| 223,228,233-80-Pg. Giants G-73,G-79,G-85                                             | 1.50  | 4.50   | 9.00   |
| 232,237: 232-N. Adams-a, Intro/1st app. Ras Al Ghul. 237-G.A. Batman-r; Wrightson/Ellison plots; N. Adams-a | 2.30  | 7.00   | 16.00  |
| 234-N. Adams-a; 1st Silver Age app. Two-Face; 52 pg. issues begin, end #242          | 3.60  | 11.00  | 25.00  |
| 235,236,239-242: 239-Xmas-c. 241-r-Batman #5                                         | 1.00  | 3.00   | 6.00   |
| 238-DC-8 100 pg. Super Spec.; unpubbed G.A. Atom, Sargon, Plastic Man stories; Doom Patrol origin-r; Batman, Legion, Aquaman-r; N. Adams-c | 1.15  | 3.50   | 7.00   |
| 243-245-Neal Adams-a                                                                 | 1.70  | 5.00   | 12.00  |
| 246-250,252,253: 253-Shadow app.                                                     | 1.00  | 3.00   | 6.00   |
| 251-N. Adams-c/a; Joker-c/story                                                      | 3.50  | 10.50  | 24.00  |
| 254,256-259,261-All 100 pg. editions; part-r                                         | 1.15  | 3.50   | 7.00   |

|  | Good | Fine | N-Mint |
|---|---|---|---|
| 255-N. Adams-c/a; tells of Bruce Wayne's father who wore bat costume & fought crime (100 pgs.) | 1.50 | 4.50 | 10.00 |
| 260-Joker-c/story (100pgs.) | 2.15 | 6.50 | 15.00 |
| 262-285,287-290,292,293,295-299: 262-68pgs. 266-Catwoman back to old costume | .60 | 1.80 | 3.60 |
| 286,291,294-Joker-c/stories | 1.00 | 3.00 | 6.00 |
| 300-Double-size | .85 | 2.50 | 5.00 |
| 301-320,322-352,354-356,358,360-365,367,369,370: 304-(44 pgs.). 311-Batgirl reteams w/Batman. 316-Robin returns. 323,324-Catman & Catwoman app. 332-Catwoman's 1st solo. 345-New Dr. Death app. 361-1st app. Harvey Bullock | .60 | 1.80 | 3.60 |
| 321,353,359-Joker-c/stories | 1.00 | 3.00 | 6.00 |
| 357-1st app. Jason Todd (3/83); see Det. 524 | 1.15 | 3.50 | 8.00 |
| 366-Jason Todd 1st in Robin costume; Joker-c/story | 4.20 | 12.50 | 25.00 |
| 368-1st new Robin in costume (Jason Todd) | 3.35 | 10.00 | 20.00 |
| 371-399,401-403: 386,387-Intro Black Mask (villain). 401-2nd app. Magpie | .50 | 1.50 | 3.00 |
| 400 ($1.50, 64 pgs.)-Dark Knight special; intro by Steven King; Art Adams/ Austin-a | 3.00 | 9.00 | 18.00 |
| 404-Miller scripts begin (end 407); Year 1 | 1.70 | 5.00 | 10.00 |
| 405-407: 407-Year 1 ends (See Det. for Year 2) | 1.00 | 3.00 | 6.00 |
| 408-410: New Origin Jason Todd (Robin) | 1.00 | 3.00 | 6.00 |
| 411-416,421-425: 415,416-Millennium tie-ins. 416-Nightwing-c/story. 423-McFarlane-c | .50 | 1.50 | 3.00 |
| 417-420: "Ten Nights of the Beast" storyline | 2.50 | 7.50 | 15.00 |
| 426-($1.50, 52 pgs.)-"A Death In The Family" storyline begins, ends #429 | 5.00 | 15.00 | 30.00 |
| 427,428: 428-Death of Robin (Jason Todd) | 3.35 | 10.00 | 20.00 |
| 429-Joker-c/story; Superman app. | 1.35 | 4.00 | 8.00 |
| 430-432 | .30 | .90 | 1.80 |
| 433-435-"Many Deaths of the Batman" story by John Byrne-c/scripts | .50 | 1.50 | 3.00 |
| 436-Year 3 begins (ends #439); origin original Robin retold by Nightwing (Dick Grayson) | .85 | 2.50 | 5.00 |
| 436-2nd print |  | .50 | 1.00 |
| 437-439: 437-Origin Robin continued | .50 | 1.50 | 3.00 |
| 440,441: "A Lonely Place of Dying" Parts 1 & 3; 440-1st app. Timothy Drake? | .25 | .70 | 1.40 |
| 442-1st app. New Robin(Timothy Drake) | .50 | 1.50 | 3.00 |

| | Good | Fine | N-Mint |
|---|---|---|---|
| 443-458 | | .50 | 1.00 |
| Annual 1(8-10/61)-Swan-c | 27.50 | 82.50 | 190.00 |
| Annual 2 | 11.00 | 32.00 | 75.00 |
| Annual 3(Summer, '62)-Joker-c/story | 12.00 | 36.00 | 85.00 |
| Annual 4,5 | 5.70 | 17.00 | 40.00 |
| Annual 6,7(7/64) | 4.30 | 13.00 | 30.00 |
| Annual 8(10/82) | .85 | 2.50 | 5.00 |
| Annual 9(7/85), 10(8/86), 12('88, $1.50) | .55 | 1.65 | 3.30 |
| Annual 11('87, $1.25)-Alan Moore scripts | .85 | 2.50 | 5.00 |
| Annual 13('89, $1.75, 68 pgs.)-Gives history of Bruce Wayne, Dick Grayson, Jason Todd, Alfred, Comm. Gordon, Barbara Gordon (Batgirl) & Vicki Vale; Morrow-i | .35 | 1.10 | 2.20 |
| Annual 14('90, $2.00, 68 pgs.)-Origin Two-Face | | | |
| | .35 | 1.00 | 2.00 |

**BATMAN: ARKHAM ASYLUM** (See Saga of Swamp Thing #52, 53)
1989 ($24.95, hardcover, mature readers, 132 pgs.)
DC Comics

| | | | |
|---|---|---|---|
| nn-Joker-c/story | 5.00 | 15.00 | 30.00 |
| nn-Soft cover ($14.95) | 2.50 | 7.50 | 15.00 |

**BATMAN FAMILY, THE**
Sept-Oct, 1975 - No. 20, Oct-Nov, 1978 (No. 1-4, 17 on: 68 pages)
(Combined with Detective Comics with No. 481)
National Periodical Publications/DC Comics

| | | | |
|---|---|---|---|
| 1-Origin Batgirl-Robin team-up (The Dynamite Duo); reprints plus one new story begins; N. Adams-a(r) | .85 | 2.50 | 5.00 |
| 2-5: 3-Batgirl & Robin learn each's i.d. | .50 | 1.50 | 3.00 |
| 6,9-Joker's daughter on cover | .85 | 2.50 | 5.00 |
| 7,8,10,14-16: 10-1st revival Batwoman | .50 | 1.50 | 3.00 |
| 11-13: Rogers-p. 11-New stories begin; Man-Bat begins | .85 | 2.50 | 5.00 |
| 17-($1.00 size)-Batman, Huntress begin | .50 | 1.50 | 3.00 |
| 18-20: Huntress by Staton in all. 20-Origin Ragman retold | .30 | .90 | 1.75 |

**BATMAN: SON OF THE DEMON**
Sept, 1987 (80 pgs., hardcover, $14.95)
DC Comics

| | Good | Fine | N-Mint |
|---|---|---|---|
| 1-Hardcover | 10.00 | 30.00 | 60.00 |
| Limited signed & numbered hard-c (1,700) | 15.00 | 45.00 | 90.00 |
| Softcover w/new-c ($8.95) | 2.50 | 7.50 | 15.00 |
| Softcover, 2ndprint (1989, $9.95)-4th print | 1.70 | 5.00 | 10.00 |

**BATMAN: THE CULT**
1988 - No. 4, Nov, 1988 ($3.50, color, deluxe mini-series)
DC Comics

| | | | |
|---|---|---|---|
| 1-Wrightson-a/painted-c in all | 3.00 | 9.00 | 18.00 |
| 2 | 2.30 | 7.00 | 14.00 |
| 3,4 | 2.00 | 6.00 | 12.00 |

**BATMAN: THE DARK KNIGHT RETURNS**
March, 1986 - No. 4, 1986
DC Comics

| | | | |
|---|---|---|---|
| 1-Miller story & a(p); set in the future | 7.50 | 22.50 | 45.00 |
| 1-2nd printing | 1.70 | 5.00 | 10.00 |
| 1-3rd printing | .70 | 2.00 | 4.00 |
| 2-Carrie Kelly becomes Robin (female) | 4.00 | 12.00 | 24.00 |
| 2-2nd printing | 1.00 | 3.00 | 6.00 |
| 2-3rd printing | .60 | 1.80 | 3.60 |
| 3-Death of Joker | 1.70 | 5.00 | 10.00 |
| 3-2nd printing | .70 | 2.00 | 4.00 |
| 4-Death of Alfred | 1.00 | 3.00 | 6.00 |

**BATMAN: THE KILLING JOKE** (Also see Batgirl Special)
1988 ($3.50, 52 pgs. color, deluxe, adults)
DC Comics

| | | | |
|---|---|---|---|
| 1-Bolland-c/a; Alan Moore scripts | 4.35 | 13.00 | 26.00 |
| 1-2nd thru 8th printings | .85 | 2.50 | 5.00 |

**BATMAN: THE OFFICIAL COMIC ADAPTATION OF THE WARNER
    BROS. MOTION PICTURE**
1989 ($2.50, $4.95, 68 pgs.) (Movie adaptation)
DC Comics

| | | | |
|---|---|---|---|
| 1-Regular format ($2.50)-Ordway-c/a | .70 | 2.00 | 4.00 |

| | Good | Fine | N-Mint |
|---|---|---|---|
| 1-Prestige format ($4.95)-Diff.-c, same in sides | | | |
| | 1.00 | 3.00 | 6.00 |

## BEVERLY HILLBILLIES (TV)
4-6/63 - No. 18, 8/67; No. 19; No. 20, 10/70; No. 21, Oct, 1971
Dell Publishing Co.

| | Good | Fine | N-Mint |
|---|---|---|---|
| 1-Photo c-1-3,5,8-14,17-21 | 5.70 | 17.00 | 40.00 |
| 2 | 2.80 | 8.50 | 20.00 |
| 3-10 | 2.15 | 6.50 | 15.00 |
| 11-21: 19-Reprints #1 | 1.70 | 5.00 | 12.00 |

## BEWARE THE CREEPER (See Brave & the Bold & Showcase)
May-June, 1968 - No. 6, March-April, 1969
National Periodical Publications

| | Good | Fine | N-Mint |
|---|---|---|---|
| 1-Ditko c/a-1-5 | 2.65 | 8.00 | 18.00 |
| 2-6 | 1.50 | 4.50 | 10.00 |

## BILL BOYD WESTERN (See Hopalong Cassidy & Western Hero)
Feb, 1950 - No. 23, June, 1952 (1-3,7,11,14-on: 36 pgs.) (Movie star)
Fawcett Publications

| | Good | Fine | N-Mint |
|---|---|---|---|
| 1-Bill Boyd & his horse Midnite begin; photo front/back-c | | | |
| | 21.00 | 64.00 | 150.00 |
| 2-Painted-c | 13.00 | 40.00 | 90.00 |
| 3-Photo-c begin, end #23; last photo back-c | 12.00 | 36.00 | 84.00 |
| 4-6(52 pgs.) | 9.50 | 28.50 | 65.00 |
| 7,11(36 pgs.) | 7.50 | 22.50 | 53.00 |
| 8-10,12,13(52 pgs.) | 8.00 | 24.00 | 56.00 |
| 14-22 | 6.50 | 19.50 | 45.00 |
| 23-Last issue | 7.00 | 21.00 | 50.00 |

## BILLY THE KID ADVENTURE MAGAZINE
Oct, 1950 - No. 30, 1955
Toby Press

| | Good | Fine | N-Mint |
|---|---|---|---|
| 1-Williamson/Frazetta, 4 pgs; photo-c | 14.00 | 42.00 | 100.00 |
| 2-Photo-c | 3.60 | 11.00 | 26.00 |

|  | Good | Fine | N-Mint |
|---|---|---|---|
| 3-Williamson/Frazetta "The Claws of Death," 4 pgs. plus Williamson-a | | | |
|  | 17.00 | 51.00 | 120.00 |
| 4,5,7,8,10: 7-Photo-c | 2.15 | 6.50 | 15.00 |
| 6-Frazetta story assist on "Nightmare"; photo-c | | | |
|  | 7.00 | 21.00 | 50.00 |
| 9-Kurtzman Pot-Shot Pete; photo-c | 5.50 | 16.50 | 38.00 |
| 11,12,15-20 | 2.00 | 6.00 | 14.00 |
| 13-Kurtzman r-/John Wayne 12 (Genius) | 2.30 | 7.00 | 16.00 |
| 14-Williamson/Frazetta; r-of #1, 2 pgs. | 5.00 | 15.00 | 35.00 |
| 21,23-30 | 1.50 | 4.50 | 10.00 |
| 22-Williamson/Frazetta r(1 pg.)-/#1; photo-c | 1.85 | 8.00 | 18.00 |

**BLACK CAT COMICS** ( . . . Western No. 16-19; . . . Mystery No. 30 on)
June-July, 1946 - No. 29, June, 1951
Harvey Publications (Home Comics)

| | Good | Fine | N-Mint |
|---|---|---|---|
| 1-Kubert-a | 25.00 | 75.00 | 175.00 |
| 2-Kubert-a | 14.00 | 42.00 | 100.00 |
| 3,4: 4-The Red Demons begin (The Demon #4 & 5) | | | |
|  | 10.00 | 32.00 | 70.00 |
| 5,6-The Scarlet Arrow app. in ea. by Powell; S&K-a in both. 6-Origin Red Demon | 13.00 | 40.00 | 90.00 |
| 7-Vagabond Prince by S&K plus 1 more story | | | |
|  | 13.00 | 40.00 | 90.00 |
| 8-S&K-a; Kerry Drake begins, ends #13 | 11.00 | 34.00 | 80.00 |
| 9-Origin Stuntman (r-/Stuntman #1) | 14.00 | 43.00 | 100.00 |
| 10-20: 14,15,17-Mary Worth app. plus Invisible Scarlet O'Neil-#15,20, 24 | | | |
|  | 9.00 | 27.00 | 62.00 |
| 21-26 | 7.00 | 21.00 | 50.00 |
| 27-Used in **SOTI**, pg. 193; X-Mas-c | 9.00 | 27.00 | 62.00 |
| 28-Intro. Kit, Black Cat's new sidekick | 9.00 | 27.00 | 62.00 |
| 29-Black Cat bondage-c; Black Cat stories | 8.00 | 24.00 | 56.00 |

**BLACK CAT MYSTERY** (Formerly Black Cat; . . . Western Mystery #54;
. . . Western #55, 56; . . . Mystery #57; . . . Mystic #58-62; Black Cat #63-65)
No. 30, Aug, 1951 - No. 65, April, 1963
Harvey Publications

| | Good | Fine | N-Mint |
|---|---|---|---|
| 30-Black Cat on cover only | 7.00 | 21.00 | 50.00 |

| | Good | Fine | N-Mint |
|---|---|---|---|
| 31,32,34,37,38,40 | 4.50 | 14.00 | 32.00 |
| 33-Used in **POP**, pg. 89; electrocution-c | 5.70 | 17.00 | 40.00 |
| 35-Atomic disaster cover/story | 6.00 | 18.00 | 42.00 |
| 36,39-Used in **SOTI**: #36-Pgs. 270,271; #39-Pgs. 386-388 | | | |
| | 8.50 | 25.50 | 60.00 |
| 41-43 | 4.50 | 14.00 | 32.00 |
| 44-Eyes, ears, tongue cut out; Nostrand-a | 5.00 | 15.00 | 35.00 |
| 45-Classic "Colorama" by Powell; Nostrand-a | 8.50 | 25.50 | 60.00 |
| 46-49,51-Nostrand-a in all | 5.50 | 16.50 | 38.00 |
| 50-Check-a; Warren Kremer?-c showing a man's face burning away | | | |
| | 8.50 | 25.50 | 60.00 |
| 52,53 (r-#34 & 35) | 3.70 | 11.00 | 26.00 |
| 54-Two Black Cat stories | 5.50 | 16.50 | 38.00 |
| 55,56-Black Cat app. | 3.50 | 10.50 | 24.00 |
| 57(7/56)-Simon?-c | 2.85 | 8.50 | 20.00 |
| 58-60-Kirby-a(4) | 5.00 | 15.00 | 35.00 |
| 61-Nostrand-a; "Colorama" r-/45 | 4.00 | 12.00 | 28.00 |
| 62(3/58)-E.C. story swipe | 2.85 | 8.50 | 20.00 |
| 63-Giant(10/62); Reprints; Black Cat app.; origin Black Kitten | | | |
| | 4.50 | 14.00 | 32.00 |
| 64-Giant(1/63); Reprints; Black Cat app. | 4.50 | 14.00 | 32.00 |
| 65-Giant(4/63); Reprints; Black Cat app. | 4.50 | 14.00 | 32.00 |

**BLACKHAWK** (Formerly Uncle Sam No. 1-8; Also see Military Comics & Modern Comics)
No. 9, Winter, 1944 - No. 243, 10-11/68; No. 244, 1-2/76 - No. 250, 1-2/77; No. 251, 10/82 - No. 273, 11/84
Comic Magazines (Quality) No. 9-107(12/56); National Periodical Publ. No. 108(1/57)-250; DC Comics No. 251 on

| | | | |
|---|---|---|---|
| 9 (1944) | 103.00 | 310.00 | 725.00 |
| 10 (1946) | 46.00 | 140.00 | 325.00 |
| 11-15: 14-Ward-a; 13,14-Fear app. | 33.00 | 100.00 | 235.00 |
| 16-20: 20-Ward Blackhawk | 28.00 | 86.00 | 200.00 |
| 21-30 | 21.00 | 62.00 | 145.00 |
| 31-40: 31-Chop Chop by Jack Cole | 16.00 | 48.00 | 110.00 |
| 41-49,51-60 | 11.00 | 32.00 | 75.00 |
| 50-1st Killer Shark; origin in text | 13.50 | 40.00 | 95.00 |
| 61-Used in **POP**, pg. 91 | 11.00 | 32.00 | 75.00 |

*Blackhawk #26, © DC Comics*

|  | Good | Fine | N-Mint |
|---|---|---|---|
| 62-Used in **POP**, pg. 92 & color illo | 11.00 | 32.00 | 75.00 |
| 63-65,67-70,72-80: 70-Return of Killer Shark. 75-Intro. Blackie the Hawk | | | |
|  | 9.50 | 28.50 | 65.00 |
| 66-B&W and color illos in **POP** | 10.00 | 30.00 | 70.00 |
| 71-Origin retold; flying saucer-c; A-Bomb panels | | | |
|  | 10.00 | 30.00 | 70.00 |
| 81-86: Last precode (3/55) | 8.00 | 24.00 | 56.00 |
| 87-92,94-99,101-107 | 5.50 | 16.50 | 38.00 |
| 93-Origin in text | 7.00 | 21.00 | 50.00 |
| 100 | 7.00 | 21.00 | 50.00 |
| 108-Re-intro. Blackie, the Hawk, their mascot; not in #115 | | | |
|  | 21.50 | 64.50 | 150.00 |
| 109-117 | 5.00 | 15.00 | 35.00 |
| 118-Frazetta r-/Jimmy Wakely 4, 3 pgs. | 6.50 | 19.50 | 45.00 |
| 119-130 | 2.30 | 7.00 | 16.00 |
| 131-142,144-163,165,166: 133-Intro. Lady Blackhawk. 166-Last 10 cent issue | | | |
| sue | 1.60 | 4.80 | 11.00 |

| | Good | Fine | N-Mint |
|---|---|---|---|
| 143-Kurtzman r-/Jimmy Wakely 4 | 1.70 | 5.00 | 12.00 |
| 164-Origin retold | 1.70 | 5.00 | 12.00 |
| 167-180 | .85 | 2.50 | 5.00 |
| 181-190,198: 198-Origin retold | .70 | 2.00 | 4.00 |
| 191-197,199-202,204-210: Combat Diary series begins. 197-New look for | | | |
|    Blackhawks | .50 | 1.50 | 3.00 |
| 203-Origin Chop Chop (12/64) | .60 | 1.75 | 3.50 |
| 211-243(1968):228-Batman, Green Lantern, Superman, The Flash cameos. | | | |
|    230-Blackhawks become superheroes. 242-Return to old costumes | | | |
| | .50 | 1.50 | 3.00 |
| 244 ('76) -250; 250-Chuck dies | .25 | .75 | 1.50 |
| 251-264: 251-Origin retold; Black Knights return. 252-Intro Domino. | | | |
|    253-Part origin Hendrickson. 258-Blackhawk's Island destroyed. | | | |
|    259-Part origin Chop-Chop | .50 | | 1.00 |
| 265-273 (75 cent cover price) | .50 | | 1.00 |

## BLACKHAWK
Mar, 1988 - No. 3, May, 1988 ($2.95, mini-series)
DC Comics

| | Good | Fine | N-Mint |
|---|---|---|---|
| 1-3: Chaykin painted-c/a | .40 | 1.25 | 2.50 |

## BLACKHAWK
March, 1989 - No. 16, Aug, 1990 ($1.50, color, mature readers)
DC Comics

| | Good | Fine | N-Mint |
|---|---|---|---|
| 1-6,8-16 | .25 | .75 | 1.50 |
| 7-($2.50, 52 pgs.)-story-r/Military #1 | .40 | 1.25 | 2.50 |
| Annual 1 (1989, $2.95, 68 pgs.)-Recaps origin of Blackhawk, Lady | | | |
|    Blackhawk, and others | .50 | 1.50 | 3.00 |

## BLACK RIDER (Formerly Western Winners)
No. 8, 3/50 - No. 18, 1/52; No. 19, 11/53 - No. 27, 3/55
Marvel/Atlas Comics (CDS No. 8-17/CPS No. 19 on)

| | Good | Fine | N-Mint |
|---|---|---|---|
| 8 (#1)-Black Rider & his horse Satan begin; 36 pgs; photo-c | | | |
| | 17.00 | 51.00 | 120.00 |
| 9-52 pgs. begin, end #14 | 8.50 | 25.50 | 60.00 |
| 10-Origin Black Rider | 11.00 | 32.00 | 75.00 |
| 11-14(Last 52 pgs.) | 6.00 | 18.00 | 42.00 |
| 15-19: 19-Two-Gun Kid app. | 5.50 | 16.50 | 38.00 |

|                                                                              | Good  | Fine   | N-Mint |
|------------------------------------------------------------------------------|-------|--------|--------|
| 20-Classic-c; Two-Gun Kid app.                                               | 6.00  | 18.00  | 42.00  |
| 21-26: 21-23-Two-Gun Kid app. 24,25-Arrowhead app. 26-Kid Colt app.          |       |        |        |
|                                                                              | 4.30  | 13.00  | 30.00  |
| 27-Last issue; last precode. Kid Colt app. The Spider (a villain) burns to   |       |        |        |
|     death                                                 | 4.50  | 14.00  | 32.00  |

**BLACK TERROR** (See America's Best & Exciting Comics)
Wint, 1942-43 - No. 27, June, 1949
Better Publications/Standard

|                                                     | Good  | Fine   | N-Mint |
|-----------------------------------------------------|-------|--------|--------|
| 1-Black Terror, Crime Crusader begin                | 60.00 | 180.00 | 425.00 |
| 2                                                   | 30.00 | 90.00  | 210.00 |
| 3                                                   | 22.00 | 65.00  | 154.00 |
| 4,5                                                 | 17.00 | 51.00  | 120.00 |
| 6-10: 7-The Ghost app.                              | 13.00 | 40.00  | 90.00  |
| 11-20: 20-The Scarab app.                           | 11.00 | 34.00  | 80.00  |
| 21-Miss Masque app.                                 | 12.00 | 36.00  | 84.00  |
| 22-Part Frazetta-a on one Black Terror story        | 13.00 | 40.00  | 90.00  |
| 23,25-27                                            | 11.00 | 32.00  | 75.00  |
| 24-1/4 pg. Frazetta-a                               | 11.00 | 34.00  | 80.00  |

**BLONDE PHANTOM** (Formerly All-Select #1-11)
No. 12, Winter, 1946-47 - No. 22, March, 1949
Marvel Comics (MPC)

|                                                         | Good  | Fine   | N-Mint |
|---------------------------------------------------------|-------|--------|--------|
| 12-Miss America begins, ends #14                        | 46.00 | 140.00 | 325.00 |
| 13-Sub-Mariner begins                                   | 31.00 | 94.00  | 220.00 |
| 14,15; 14-Male Bondage-c; Namora app. 15-Kurtzman's "Hey Look" |       |        |        |
|                                                         | 27.00 | 81.00  | 190.00 |
| 16-Captain America with Bucky app.; Kurtzman's "Hey Look" |       |        |        |
|                                                         | 30.00 | 90.00  | 210.00 |
| 17-22: 22-Anti Wertham editorial                        | 26.00 | 77.00  | 180.00 |

**BLONDIE COMICS** ( . . . Monthly #16-141; see Ace & Magic Comics)
Spring, 1947 - No. 163, Nov, 1965; No. 164, Aug, 1966 - No. 175, Dec, 1967;
   No. 177, Feb, 1969 - No. 222, Nov, 1976
David McKay #1-15/Harvey #16-163/King #164-175/Charlton #177 on

|   |       |       |       |
|---|-------|-------|-------|
| 1 | 10.00 | 30.00 | 70.00 |
| 2 | 5.00  | 15.00 | 35.00 |

|                                              | Good | Fine  | N-Mint |
|----------------------------------------------|------|-------|--------|
| 3-5                                          | 3.70 | 11.00 | 26.00  |
| 6-10                                         | 2.85 | 8.50  | 20.00  |
| 11-15                                        | 2.00 | 6.00  | 14.00  |
| 16-(3/50; 1st Harvey)                        | 2.30 | 7.00  | 16.00  |
| 17-20                                        | 1.70 | 5.00  | 12.00  |
| 21-30                                        | 1.30 | 4.00  | 9.00   |
| 31-50                                        | 1.00 | 3.00  | 7.00   |
| 51-80                                        | .85  | 2.60  | 6.00   |
| 81-100                                       | .75  | 2.50  | 5.00   |
| 101-124,126-130                              | .70  | 2.00  | 4.00   |
| 125 (80 pgs.)                                | 1.00 | 3.00  | 7.00   |
| 131-136,138,139                              | .50  | 1.50  | 3.00   |
| 137,140-(80 pages)                           | .85  | 2.60  | 6.00   |
| 141-166(#148,155,157-159,161-163 are 68 pgs.)| .85  | 2.60  | 6.00   |
| 167-One pg. Williamson ad                    | .35  | 1.00  | 2.00   |
| 168-175,177-222 (no #176)                    |      | .50   | 1.00   |

**BLUE BEETLE, THE** (Also see All Top & Mystery Men)
Winter, 1939-40 - No. 60, Aug, 1950
Fox Publ. No. 1-11, 31-60; Holyoke No. 12-30

| | Good | Fine | N-Mint |
|---|---|---|---|
| 1-Reprints from Mystery Men 1-5; Blue Beetle origin; Yarko the Great-r/ from Wonder/Wonderworld 2-5 all by Eisner; Master Magician app.; (Blue Beetle in 4 different costumes) | 142.00 | 355.00 | 850.00 |
| 2-K-51-r by Powell/Wonderworld 8,9 | 55.00 | 165.00 | 385.00 |
| 3-Simon-c | 38.00 | 115.00 | 265.00 |
| 4-Marijuana drug mention story | 28.00 | 84.00 | 195.00 |
| 5-Zanzibar The Magician by Tuska | 24.00 | 72.00 | 168.00 |
| 6-Dynamite Thor begins; origin Blue Beetle | 22.00 | 65.00 | 154.00 |
| 7,8-Dynamo app. in both. 8-Last Thor | 20.00 | 60.00 | 140.00 |
| 9,10-The Blackbird & The Gorilla app. in both. 10-Bondage/hypo-c | | | |
| | 18.00 | 54.00 | 125.00 |
| 11(2/42)-The Gladiator app. | 18.00 | 54.00 | 125.00 |
| 12(6/42)-The Black Fury app. | 18.00 | 54.00 | 125.00 |
| 13-V-Man begins, ends #18; Kubert-a | 21.00 | 62.00 | 148.00 |
| 14,15-Kubert-a in both. 14-Intro. side-kick (c/text only), Sparky (called Spunky #17-19) | 20.00 | 60.00 | 140.00 |
| 16-18 | 15.00 | 45.00 | 105.00 |
| 19-Kubert-a | 18.00 | 54.00 | 125.00 |

|  | Good | Fine | N-Mint |
|---|---|---|---|
| 20-Origin/1st app. Tiger Squadron; Arabian Nights begin | | | |
|  | 18.00 | 54.00 | 125.00 |
| 21-26: 24-Intro. & only app. The Halo. 26-General Patton story & photo | | | |
|  | 12.00 | 36.00 | 84.00 |
| 27-Tamaa, Jungle Prince app. | 10.00 | 30.00 | 70.00 |
| 28-30(2/44) | 8.00 | 24.00 | 56.00 |
| 31(6/44), 33-40: "The Threat from Saturn" serial in #34-38 | | | |
|  | 6.50 | 19.50 | 45.00 |
| 32-Hitler-c | 8.00 | 24.00 | 56.00 |
| 41-45 | 5.25 | 15.50 | 36.00 |
| 46-The Puppeteer app. | 5.70 | 17.00 | 40.00 |
| 47-Kamen & Baker-a begin | 34.00 | 100.00 | 235.00 |
| 48-50 | 27.00 | 81.00 | 190.00 |
| 51,53 | 25.00 | 75.00 | 175.00 |
| 52-Kamen bondage-c | 34.00 | 100.00 | 235.00 |
| 54-Used in **SOTI**. Illo-"Children call these 'headlights' comics" | | | |
|  | 54.00 | 163.00 | 380.00 |
| 55,57(7/48)-Last Kamen issue | 25.00 | 75.00 | 175.00 |
| 56-Used in **SOTI**, pg. 145 | 23.00 | 70.00 | 160.00 |
| 58(4/50)-60-No Kamen-a | 4.30 | 13.00 | 30.00 |

**BLUE BEETLE**
V2 No. 1, 6/64 - V2 No. 5, 3-4/65; V3 No. 50, 7/65 - V3 No. 54, 2-3/66; No. 1,
6/67 - No. 5, 11/68
Charlton Comics

| V2#1-Origin Dan Garrett-Blue Beetle | 3.60 | 11.00 | 25.00 |
|---|---|---|---|
| 2-5, V3#50-54 | 2.50 | 7.50 | 17.00 |
| 1(1967)-Question series begins by Ditko | 5.70 | 17.00 | 40.00 |
| 2-Origin Ted Kord-Blue Beetle; Dan Garrett x-over | | | |
|  | 2.15 | 6.50 | 15.00 |
| 3-5 (All Ditko-c/a in #1-5) | 1.70 | 5.00 | 12.00 |

**BLUE BOLT**
June, 1940 - No. 101 (V10 No.2), Sept-Oct, 1949
Funnies, Inc. No. 1/Novelty Press/Premium Group of Comics

V1#1-Origin Blue Bolt by Joe Simon, Sub-Zero, White Rider & Super
Horse, Dick Cole, Wonder Boy & Sgt. Spook
|  | 110.00 | 330.00 | 770.00 |

|  | Good | Fine | N-Mint |
|---|---|---|---|
| 2-Simon-a | 65.00 | 195.00 | 455.00 |
| 3-1pg. Space Hawk by Wolverton; S&K-a | 50.00 | 150.00 | 350.00 |
| 4,5-S&K-a in each; 5-Everett-a begins on Sub-Zero | | | |
|  | 42.00 | 125.00 | 295.00 |
| 6,8-10-S&K-a | 38.00 | 115.00 | 265.00 |
| 7-S&K c/a | 40.00 | 120.00 | 280.00 |
| 11,12 | 18.00 | 54.00 | 125.00 |

V2#1-Origin Dick Cole & The Twister; Twister x-over in Dick Cole, Sub-Zero, & Blue Bolt. Origin Simba Karno who battles Dick Cole through V2#5 & becomes main supporting character V2#6 on; battle-c

|  | Good | Fine | N-Mint |
|---|---|---|---|
|  | 12.00 | 36.00 | 84.00 |
| 2-Origin The Twister retold in text | 9.00 | 27.00 | 62.00 |
| 3-5: 5-Intro. Freezum | 7.00 | 21.00 | 50.00 |
| 6-Origin Sgt. Spook retold | 6.00 | 18.00 | 42.00 |
| 7-12: 7-Lois Blake becomes Blue Bolt's costume aide; last Twister | | | |
|  | 5.00 | 15.00 | 35.00 |
| V3#1-3 | 4.00 | 12.00 | 28.00 |
| 4-12: 4-Blue Bolt abandons costume | 3.50 | 10.50 | 24.00 |
| V4#1-Hitler, Tojo, Mussolini-c | 4.00 | 12.00 | 28.00 |
| V4#2-12: 3-Shows V4#3 on-c, V4#4 inside (9-10/43). 8-Last Sub-Zero | | | |
|  | 2.65 | 8.00 | 18.00 |
| V5#1-8, V6#1-3,5-10, V7#1-12 | 1.70 | 5.00 | 12.00 |
| V6#4-Racist cover | 2.30 | 7.00 | 16.00 |
| V8#1-6,8-12, V9#1-5,7,8 | 1.50 | 4.50 | 10.00 |
| V8#7,V9#6,9-L. B. Cole-c | 2.00 | 6.00 | 14.00 |
| V10#1(#100) | 1.70 | 5.00 | 12.00 |
| V10#2(#101)-Last Dick Cole, Blue Bolt | 1.70 | 5.00 | 12.00 |

**BLUE RIBBON COMICS** (. . . Mystery Comics No. 9-18)
Nov, 1939 - No. 22, March, 1942 (1st MLJ series)
MLJ Magazines

| | Good | Fine | N-Mint |
|---|---|---|---|
| 1-Dan Hastings, Richy the Amazing Boy, Rang-A-Tang the Wonder Dog begin; Little Nemo app. (not by W. McCay); Jack Cole-a(3) | | | |
|  | 118.00 | 354.00 | 825.00 |
| 2-Bob Phantom, Silver Fox (both in #3), Rang-A-Tang Club & Cpl. Collins begin; Jack Cole-a | 50.00 | 150.00 | 350.00 |
| 3-J. Cole-a | 32.00 | 95.00 | 225.00 |
| 4-Doc Strong, The Green Falcon, & Hercules begin; origin & 1st app. The Fox & Ty-Gor, Son of the Tiger | 38.00 | 115.00 | 265.00 |

|  | Good | Fine | N-Mint |
|---|---|---|---|
| 5-8: 8-Last Hercules; 6,7-Biro, Meskin-a. 7-Fox app. on-c | | | |
|  | 22.00 | 65.00 | 154.00 |
| 9-(Scarce)-Origin & 1st app. Mr. Justice | 100.00 | 300.00 | 700.00 |
| 10-12: 12-Last Doc Strong | 43.00 | 130.00 | 300.00 |
| 13-Inferno, the Flame Breather begins, ends #19. Devil-c | | | |
|  | 43.00 | 130.00 | 300.00 |
| 14,15,17,18: 15-Last Green Falcon | 38.00 | 115.00 | 265.00 |
| 16-Origin & 1st app. Captain Flag | 70.00 | 210.00 | 490.00 |
| 19-22: 20-Last Ty-Gor. 22-Origin Mr. Justice retold | | | |
|  | 32.00 | 95.00 | 225.00 |

**BOB COLT** (Movie star)
Nov, 1950 - No. 10, May, 1952
Fawcett Publications

| | Good | Fine | N-Mint |
|---|---|---|---|
| 1-Bob Colt, his horse Buckskin & sidekick Pablo begin; photo front/ back-c begin | 20.00 | 60.00 | 140.00 |
| 2 | 13.00 | 40.00 | 90.00 |
| 3-5 | 11.50 | 34.00 | 80.00 |
| 6-Flying Saucer story | 10.00 | 30.00 | 70.00 |
| 7-10: 9-Last photo back-c | 8.50 | 25.50 | 60.00 |

**BOB STEELE WESTERN** (Movie star)
Dec, 1950 - No. 10, June, 1952
Fawcett Publications

| | Good | Fine | N-Mint |
|---|---|---|---|
| 1-Bob Steele & his horse Bullet begin; photo front/back-c begin | 20.00 | 60.00 | 140.00 |
| 2 | 13.00 | 40.00 | 90.00 |
| 3-5: 4-Last photo back-c | 11.50 | 34.00 | 80.00 |
| 6-10: 10-Last photo-c | 8.50 | 25.50 | 60.00 |

**BONANZA** (TV)
June-Aug, 1960 - No. 37, Aug, 1970 (All Photo-c)
Dell/Gold Key

| | Good | Fine | N-Mint |
|---|---|---|---|
| 4-Color 1110 | 7.00 | 21.00 | 50.00 |
| 4-Color 1221,1283, & #01070-207, 01070-210 | 5.70 | 17.00 | 40.00 |
| 1(12/62-Gold Key) | 5.70 | 17.00 | 40.00 |
| 2 | 3.50 | 10.50 | 24.00 |

| | Good | Fine | N-Mint |
|---|---|---|---|
| 3-10 | 2.65 | 8.00 | 18.00 |
| 11-20 | 2.00 | 6.00 | 14.00 |
| 21-37: 29-Reprints | 1.30 | 4.00 | 9.00 |

## BORIS KARLOFF TALES OF MYSTERY (. . . Thriller No. 1,2)
No. 3, April, 1963 - No. 97, Feb, 1980 (TV)
Gold Key

| | Good | Fine | N-Mint |
|---|---|---|---|
| 3-8,10-(Two #5's, 10/63,11/63) | 1.15 | 3.50 | 8.00 |
| 9-Wood-a | 1.50 | 4.50 | 10.00 |
| 11-Williamson-a, Orlando-a, 8 pgs. | 1.50 | 4.50 | 10.00 |
| 12-Torres, McWilliams-a; Orlando-a(2) | 1.00 | 3.00 | 7.00 |
| 13,14,16-20 | .70 | 2.00 | 5.00 |
| 15-Crandall,Evans-a | .85 | 2.60 | 6.00 |
| 21-Jones-a | .85 | 2.60 | 6.00 |
| 22-30: 23-Reprint; photo-c | .50 | 1.50 | 3.00 |
| 31-50 | .35 | 1.00 | 2.00 |
| 51-74: 74-Origin & 1st app. Taurus | | .60 | 1.20 |
| 75-79,87-97: 78,81-86,88,90,92,95,97-Reprints | | .40 | .80 |
| 80-86-(52 pages) | | .40 | .80 |

## BORIS KARLOFF THRILLER (TV) (Becomes Boris Karloff Tales . . . )
Oct, 1962 - No. 2, Jan, 1963 (80 pages)
Gold Key

| | Good | Fine | N-Mint |
|---|---|---|---|
| 1-Photo-c | 3.00 | 9.00 | 21.00 |
| 2 | 2.85 | 8.50 | 20.00 |

## BOY COMICS (Captain Battle No. 1 & 2; Boy Illustories No.43-108)
No. 3, April, 1942 - No. 119, March, 1956
Lev Gleason Publications (Comic House)

| | Good | Fine | N-Mint |
|---|---|---|---|
| 3(No.1)-Origin Crimebuster, Bombshell & Young Robin Hood; Yankee Longago, Case 1001-1008, Swoop Storm, & Boy Movies begin; intro. Iron Jaw | 100.00 | 300.00 | 700.00 |
| 4-Hitler, Tojo, Mussolini-c | 43.00 | 130.00 | 300.00 |
| 5 | 36.00 | 107.00 | 250.00 |
| 6-Origin Iron Jaw; origin & death of Iron Jaw's son; Little Dynamite begins, ends #39 | 68.00 | 205.00 | 475.00 |
| 7,9: 7-Flag & Hitler, Tojo, Mussolini-c | 30.00 | 90.00 | 210.00 |

|  | Good | Fine | N-Mint |
|---|---|---|---|
| 8-Death of Iron Jaw | 34.00 | 100.00 | 235.00 |
| 10-Return of Iron Jaw; classic Biro-c | 43.00 | 130.00 | 300.00 |
| 11-14 | 20.00 | 60.00 | 140.00 |
| 15-Death of Iron Jaw | 24.00 | 73.00 | 170.00 |
| 16,18-20 | 13.00 | 40.00 | 90.00 |
| 17-Flag-c | 14.00 | 42.00 | 100.00 |
| 21-26 | 8.50 | 25.50 | 60.00 |
| 27-29-(68 pages). 28-Yankee Longago ends | 9.30 | 28.00 | 65.00 |
| 30-Origin Crimebuster retold | 11.50 | 34.00 | 80.00 |
| 31-40: 32(68pgs.)-Swoop Storm, Young Robin Hood ends. 34-Suicide | | | |
| cover/story | 4.30 | 13.00 | 30.00 |
| 41-50 | 2.85 | 8.50 | 20.00 |
| 51-59: 57-Dilly Duncan begins, ends #71 | 2.15 | 6.50 | 15.00 |
| 60-Iron Jaw returns | 2.65 | 8.00 | 18.00 |
| 61-Origin Crimebuster & Iron Jaw retold | 3.50 | 10.50 | 24.00 |
| 62-Death of Iron Jaw explained | 3.70 | 11.00 | 26.00 |
| 63-72 | 2.00 | 6.00 | 14.00 |
| 73-Frazetta 1-pg. ad | 2.15 | 6.50 | 15.00 |
| 74-88: 80-1st app. Rocky X of the Rocketeers; becomes "Rocky X" #101; | | | |
| Iron Jaw, Sniffer & the Deadly Dozen begin, end #118 | | | |
|  | 1.70 | 5.00 | 12.00 |
| 89-92-The Claw serial app. in all | 2.00 | 6.00 | 14.00 |
| 93-Claw cameo; Check-a(Rocky X) | 2.85 | 8.50 | 20.00 |
| 94-97,99 | 1.70 | 5.00 | 12.00 |
| 98-Rocky X by Sid Check | 3.15 | 9.50 | 22.00 |
| 100 | 2.65 | 8.00 | 18.00 |
| 101-107,109,111,119: 111-Crimebuster becomes Chuck Chandler. | | | |
| 119-Last Crimebuster | 1.70 | 5.00 | 12.00 |
| 108,110,112-118-Kubert-a | 2.65 | 8.00 | 18.00 |

**BOY COMMANDOS** (See Detective #64 & World's Finest Comics #8)
Winter, 1942-43 - No. 36, Nov-Dec, 1949
National Periodical Publications

| 1-Origin Liberty Belle; The Sandman & The Newsboy Legion x-over in | | | |
|---|---|---|---|
| Boy Commandos; S&K-a, 48 pgs. | 158.00 | 395.00 | 950.00 |
| 2-Last Liberty Belle; S&K-a, 46 pgs. | 64.00 | 193.00 | 450.00 |
| 3-S&K-a, 45 pgs. | 46.00 | 137.00 | 320.00 |
| 4,5 | 27.00 | 80.00 | 185.00 |
| 6-8,10: 6-S&K-a | 17.00 | 51.00 | 120.00 |

| | Good | Fine | N-Mint |
|---|---|---|---|
| 9-No S&K-a | 11.50 | 34.00 | 80.00 |
| 11-Infinity-c | 12.00 | 36.00 | 84.00 |
| 12-16,18-20 | 9.50 | 28.50 | 65.00 |
| 17-Sci/fi c/story | 10.00 | 30.00 | 70.00 |
| 21,22,24,25: 22-Judy Canova x-over | 6.00 | 18.00 | 42.00 |
| 23-S&K c/a (all) | 8.00 | 24.00 | 56.00 |
| 26-Flying Saucer story (3-4/48)-4th of this theme | | | |
| | 6.50 | 19.50 | 45.00 |
| 27,28,30 | 6.00 | 18.00 | 42.00 |
| 29-S&K story (1) | 7.00 | 21.00 | 50.00 |
| 31-35: 32-Dale Evans app. on-c & story. 34-Intro. Wolf, their mascot | | | |
| | 4.30 | 13.00 | 30.00 |
| 36-Intro The Atomobile c/sci-fi story | 5.70 | 17.00 | 40.00 |

*The Brave and the Bold #38, © DC Comics*

**BRAVE AND THE BOLD, THE**
Aug-Sept, 1955 - No. 200, July, 1983
National Periodical Publications/DC Comics

| | Good | Fine | N-Mint |
|---|---|---|---|
| 1-Viking Prince by Kubert, Silent Knight, Golden Gladiator begin | | | |
| | 82.00 | 245.00 | 575.00 |
| 2 | 37.00 | 110.00 | 250.00 |
| 3,4 | 20.00 | 60.00 | 140.00 |
| 5-Robin Hood begins | 14.00 | 42.00 | 100.00 |
| 6-10: 6-Robin Hood by Kubert; Golden Gladiator last app.; Silent Knight; no Viking Prince | | | |
| | 15.00 | 45.00 | 105.00 |
| 11-22: 22-Last Silent Knight | 11.50 | 34.00 | 80.00 |
| 23-Viking Prince origin by Kubert | 14.00 | 42.00 | 100.00 |
| 24-Last Viking Prince by Kubert | 14.00 | 42.00 | 100.00 |
| 25-27-Suicide Squad | 6.50 | 19.50 | 45.00 |
| 28-(2-3/60)-Justice League intro./1st app.; origin Snapper Carr | | | |
| | 175.00 | 525.00 | 1225.00 |
| 29,30-Justice League | 68.00 | 204.00 | 475.00 |
| 31-33-Cave Carson | 5.70 | 17.00 | 40.00 |
| 34-1st app./origin Silver-age Hawkman & Byth by Kubert | | | |
| | 22.00 | 66.00 | 155.00 |
| 35,36-Hawkman by Kubert; origin Shadow Thief #36 | | | |
| | 8.00 | 24.00 | 55.00 |
| 37-39-Suicide Squad. 38-Last 10 cent issue | 4.50 | 14.00 | 32.00 |
| 40,41-Cave Carson Inside Earth; #40 has Kubert art | | | |
| | 4.50 | 14.00 | 32.00 |
| 42,44-Hawkman by Kubert | 6.50 | 19.50 | 45.00 |
| 43-1st origin S.A. Hawkman by Kubert | 9.30 | 28.00 | 65.00 |
| 45-49-Strange Sports Stories by Infantino | 1.35 | 4.00 | 8.00 |
| 50-The Green Arrow & Manhunter From Mars; team-ups begin | | | |
| | 6.50 | 19.50 | 45.00 |
| 51-Aquaman & Hawkman | 1.50 | 4.50 | 10.00 |
| 52-Sgt. Rock by Kubert, Haunted Tank, Johnny Cloud, & Mlle. Marie | | | |
| | 1.50 | 4.50 | 10.00 |
| 53-Atom & The Flash by Toth | 1.70 | 5.00 | 12.00 |
| 54-Kid Flash, Robin & Aqualad; 1st app./origin Teen Titans (6-7/64) | | | |
| | 13.00 | 39.00 | 90.00 |
| 55-Metal Men & The Atom | .75 | 2.25 | 4.50 |
| 56-The Flash & Manhunter From Mars | .75 | 2.25 | 4.50 |
| 57-Intro & Origin Metamorpho | 5.00 | 15.00 | 35.00 |
| 58-Metamorpho by Fradon | 1.50 | 4.50 | 10.00 |
| 59-Batman & Green Lantern | 3.60 | 11.00 | 25.00 |
| 60-Teen Titans (2nd app.)-1st app. new Wonder Girl (DonnaTroy), who joins Titans (6-7/65) | | | |
| | 5.00 | 15.00 | 35.00 |

|  | Good | Fine | N-Mint |
|---|---|---|---|
| 61,62-Origin Starman & Black Canary by Anderson. 62-Huntress app. | | | |
|  | 1.35 | 4.00 | 8.00 |
| 63-Supergirl & Wonder Woman | .75 | 2.25 | 4.50 |
| 64-Batman Versus Eclipso (1966) | 1.50 | 4.50 | 10.00 |
| 65-Flash & Doom Patrol | .85 | 2.50 | 5.00 |
| 66-Metamorpho & Metal Men | .85 | 2.50 | 5.00 |
| 67-Batman & The Flash by Infantino; Batman team-ups begin, end #200 | | | |
|  | 1.15 | 3.50 | 7.00 |
| 68-Batman/Joker/Riddler/Penguin-c/story | 1.70 | 5.00 | 12.00 |
| 69-78: Batman team-ups | 1.15 | 3.50 | 7.00 |
| 79-Batman-Deadman by Neal Adams | 2.15 | 6.50 | 15.00 |
| 80-Batman-Creeper; N. Adams-a | 1.85 | 5.50 | 13.00 |
| 81-Batman-Flash; N. Adams-a | 1.85 | 5.50 | 13.00 |
| 82-Batman-Aquaman; N. Adams-a; origin Ocean Master retold | | | |
|  | 1.85 | 5.50 | 13.00 |
| 83-Batman-Teen Titans; N. Adams-a | 3.15 | 9.50 | 22.00 |
| 84-Batman(GA)-Sgt. Rock; N. Adams-a | 1.85 | 5.50 | 13.00 |
| 85-Batman-Green Arrow; 1st new costume for Green Arrow by Neal | | | |
| Adams | 1.85 | 5.50 | 13.00 |
| 86-Batman-Deadman; N. Adams-a | 1.85 | 5.50 | 13.00 |
| 87-92: Batman team-ups | .70 | 2.00 | 4.00 |
| 93-Batman-House of Mystery; N. Adams-a | 1.85 | 5.50 | 13.00 |
| 94-Batman-Teen Titans | .85 | 2.50 | 5.00 |
| 95-99: 97-Origin Deadman-r | .70 | 2.00 | 4.00 |
| 100-Batman-Gr. Lantern-Gr. Arrow-Black Canary-Robin; Deadman by | | | |
| N. Adams (52 pgs., 25 cents) | 1.70 | 5.00 | 12.00 |
| 101-Batman-Metamorpho; Kubert Viking Prince | | | |
|  | .50 | 1.50 | 3.00 |
| 102-Batman-Teen Titans; N. Adams-a(p) | .85 | 2.50 | 5.00 |
| 103-110: Batman team-ups | .50 | 1.50 | 3.00 |
| 111-Batman/Joker-c/story | 1.35 | 4.00 | 8.00 |
| 112-117: all 100 pgs.; Batman team-ups | .70 | 2.00 | 4.00 |
| 118-Batman/Wildcat/Joker-c/story | 1.15 | 3.50 | 7.00 |
| 119-128,131-140: Batman team-ups | .40 | 1.25 | 2.50 |
| 129,130-Batman/Joker-c/stories | 1.35 | 4.00 | 8.00 |
| 141-Batman vs. Joker c/story | 1.15 | 3.50 | 7.00 |
| 142-190,192-199: 148-Xmas-c. 149-Batman-Teen Titans. 150-Anniversary issue; Superman. 179-LSH. 182-Batman/Robin. 181-Hawk & Dove. 183-Riddler. 187-Metal Men. 196-Origin Ragman retold. 197-Earth II Batman & Catwoman marry | .35 | 1.00 | 2.00 |

|  | Good | Fine | N-Mint |
|---|---|---|---|
| 191-Batman/Joker-c/story | .85 | 2.50 | 5.00 |

200-Double-sized (64 pgs.); printed on Mando paper; Earth One & Earth
    Two Batman team-up; Intro/1st app. Batman & The Outsiders

|  | 1.00 | 3.00 | 6.00 |
|---|---|---|---|

## BRENDA STARR
No. 13, 9/47; No. 14, 3/48; V2 No.3, 6/48 - V2 No. 12, 12/49
Four Star Comics Corp./Superior Comics Ltd.

| | Good | Fine | N-Mint |
|---|---|---|---|
| V1#13-By Dale Messick | 32.00 | 95.00 | 225.00 |
| 14-Kamen bondage-c | 32.00 | 95.00 | 225.00 |
| V2#3-Baker-a? | 26.00 | 77.00 | 180.00 |
| 4-Used in **SOTI**, pg. 21; Kamen bondage-c | | | |
| | 28.00 | 85.00 | 200.00 |
| 5-10 | 21.50 | 64.00 | 150.00 |
| 11,12 (Scarce) | 27.00 | 80.00 | 185.00 |

## BROTHER POWER, THE GEEK (See Saga of Swamp Thing Annual)
Sept-Oct, 1968 - No. 2, Nov-Dec, 1968
National Periodical Publications

| | | | |
|---|---|---|---|
| 1-Origin; Simon-c(i?) | 2.00 | 6.00 | 14.00 |
| 2 | 1.50 | 4.50 | 9.00 |

## BUCK JONES (Also see Crackajack Funnies & Master Comics #7)
No. 299, Oct, 1950 - No. 850, Oct, 1957 (All Painted-c)
Dell Publishing Co.

4-Color 299(#1)-Buck Jones & his horse Silver-B begin; painted back-c be-
    gins, ends #5

| | 8.50 | 25.50 | 60.00 |
|---|---|---|---|
| 2(4-6/51) | 4.50 | 14.00 | 32.00 |
| 3-8(10-12/52) | 3.50 | 10.50 | 24.00 |
| 4-Color 460,500,546,589 | 3.50 | 10.50 | 24.00 |
| 4-Color 652,733,850 | 2.30 | 7.00 | 16.00 |

## BUCK ROGERS (Also see Famous Funnies)
Winter, 1940-41 - No. 6, Sept, 1943
Famous Funnies

|                                                                 | Good   | Fine   | N-Mint |
|-----------------------------------------------------------------|--------|--------|--------|
| 1-Sunday strip reprints by Rick Yager; begins with strip #190; Calkins-c | | | |
|                                                                 | 121.00 | 365.00 | 850.00 |
| 2 (7/41)-Calkins-c                                              | 72.00  | 215.00 | 500.00 |
| 3 (12/41), 4 (7/42)                                            | 57.00  | 170.00 | 400.00 |
| 5-Story continues with Famous Funnies No. 80; 1/2 Buck Rogers, 1/2 Sky | | | |
| Roads                                                          | 51.00  | 152.00 | 360.00 |
| 6-Reprints of 1939 dailies; contains B.R. story "Crater of Doom" (2 pgs.) | | | |
| by Calkins not reprinted from Famous Funnies                   | | | |
|                                                                 | 51.00  | 152.00 | 360.00 |

**BUCK ROGERS**
No. 100, Jan, 1951 - No. 9, May-June, 1951
Toby Press

|                                                  | Good  | Fine  | N-Mint |
|--------------------------------------------------|-------|-------|--------|
| 100(7)                                           | 14.00 | 42.00 | 100.00 |
| 101(8), 9-All Anderson-a('47-'49-r/dailies)      | 11.50 | 34.00 | 80.00  |

**BUCK ROGERS** (. . . in the 25th Century No. 5 on) (TV)
10/64; No. 2, 7/79 - No. 16, 5/82 (no No. 10)
Gold Key/Whitman No. 7 on

|                                                  | Good  | Fine  | N-Mint |
|--------------------------------------------------|-------|-------|--------|
| 1(10128-410)-Painted-c; 12 cents                 | 2.65  | 8.00  | 18.00  |
| 2(8/79)-Movie adaptation                         | .35   | 1.00  | 2.00   |
| 3-9,11-16: 3,4-Movie adaptation; 5-new stories   |       | .50   | 1.00   |

**BUGS BUNNY**
1942 - No. 245, 1983
Dell Publishing Co./Gold Key No. 86-218/Whitman No. 219 on

Large Feature Comic 8(1942)-(Rarely found in fine-mint condition)

|                                                         | Good  | Fine   | N-Mint |
|---------------------------------------------------------|-------|--------|--------|
|                                                         | 56.00 | 167.00 | 390.00 |
| 4-Color 33 ('43)                                        | 32.00 | 95.00  | 220.00 |
| 4-Color 51                                              | 18.50 | 56.00  | 130.00 |
| 4-Color 88                                              | 11.50 | 34.00  | 80.00  |
| 4-Color 123('46),142,164                                | 6.50  | 19.50  | 45.00  |
| 4-Color 187,200,217,233                                 | 5.50  | 16.50  | 38.00  |
| 4-Color 250-Used in **SOTI**, pg. 309                   | 5.50  | 16.50  | 38.00  |
| 4-Color 266,274,281,289,298('50)                        | 4.30  | 13.00  | 30.00  |
| 4-Color 307,317(#1),327(#2),338,347,355,366,376,393     |       |        |        |
|                                                         | 3.50  | 10.50  | 24.00  |

|  | Good | Fine | N-Mint |
|---|---|---|---|
| 4-Color 407,420,432 | 2.30 | 7.00 | 16.00 |
| 28(12-1/52-53)-30 | 1.50 | 4.50 | 10.00 |
| 31-50 | .85 | 2.60 | 6.00 |
| 51-85(7-9/62) | .75 | 2.25 | 5.00 |
| 86(10/62)-88-Bugs Bunny's Showtime-(80 pgs.) (25 cents) | | | |
| | 2.00 | 6.00 | 16.00 |
| 89-100 | .70 | 2.00 | 4.00 |
| 101-120 | .40 | 1.25 | 2.50 |
| 121-140 | .35 | 1.00 | 2.00 |
| 141-170 | | .60 | 1.20 |
| 171-228,230-245 | | .30 | .60 |
| 229-Swipe of Barks story/WDC&S 223 | | .35 | .70 |

**BULLETMAN** (See Master Comics & Nickel Comics)
Sum, 1941 - #12, 2/12/43; #14, Spr, 1946 - #16, Fall, 1946 (nn 13)
Fawcett Publications

| | | | |
|---|---|---|---|
| 1 | 142.00 | 425.00 | 850.00 |
| 2 | 70.00 | 210.00 | 490.00 |
| 3 | 50.00 | 150.00 | 350.00 |
| 4,5 | 41.00 | 124.00 | 290.00 |
| 6-10: 7-Ghost Stories as told by the night watchman of the cemetery be- | | | |
| gins; Eisnerish-a | 36.00 | 107.00 | 250.00 |
| 11,12,14-16 (nn 13) | 30.00 | 90.00 | 210.00 |

**BULLWINKLE** (TV) ( . . . and Rocky No. 20 on) (Jay Ward)
3-5/62 - #11, 4/74; #12, 6/76 - #19, 3/78; #20, 4/79 - #25, 2/80
Dell/Gold Key

| | | | |
|---|---|---|---|
| 4-Color 1270 (3-5/62) | 7.00 | 21.00 | 50.00 |
| 01-090-209 (Dell, 7-9/62) | 7.00 | 21.00 | 50.00 |
| 1(11/62, Gold Key) | 5.00 | 15.00 | 35.00 |
| 2(2/63) | 4.00 | 12.00 | 28.00 |
| 3(4/72)-11(4/74-Gold Key) | 1.15 | 3.50 | 8.00 |
| 12(6/76)-reprints | .70 | 2.00 | 4.00 |
| 13(9/76), 14-new stories | .85 | 2.60 | 6.00 |
| 15-25 | .70 | 2.00 | 4.00 |
| Mother Moose Nursery Pomes 01-530-207 (5-7/62-Dell) | | | |
| | 5.00 | 15.00 | 35.00 |

**BULLWINKLE** (. . . & Rocky No. 2 on) (TV)
July, 1970 - No. 7, July, 1971
Charlton Comics

|       | Good | Fine | N-Mint |
|-------|------|------|--------|
| 1     | 1.50 | 4.50 | 10.00  |
| 2-7   | .85  | 2.60 | 6.00   |

# C

**CAPTAIN ACTION**
Oct-Nov, 1968 - No. 5, June-July, 1969
National Periodical Publications

|  | Good | Fine | N-Mint |
|---|---|---|---|
| 1-Origin; Wood-a; based on Ideal toy | 2.00 | 6.00 | 14.00 |
| 2-5: 2,3,5-Kane/Wood-a | 1.35 | 4.00 | 8.00 |
| . . . & Action Boy('67)-Ideal Toy Co. giveaway | | | |
|  | 2.00 | 6.00 | 14.00 |

*Captain America Annual #8, © Marvel Comics*

**CAPTAIN AMERICA** (Formerly Tales of Suspense #1-99; Captain
America and the Falcon #134-223) (See Avengers #4)
No. 100, April, 1968 - Present
Marvel Comics Group

|  | Good | Fine | N-Mint |
|---|---|---|---|
| 100-Flashback on Cap's revival with Avengers & Sub-Mariner | | | |
|  | 23.00 | 70.00 | 160.00 |
| 101 | 5.00 | 15.00 | 35.00 |
| 102-108 | 3.15 | 9.50 | 22.00 |
| 109-Origin Capt. America | 4.00 | 12.00 | 28.00 |
| 110,111,113-Steranko-c/a. 110-Rick becomes Cap's partner. 110-Hulk x-over. 111-Death of Steve Rogers. 113-Cap's funeral | | | |
|  | 5.00 | 15.00 | 35.00 |
| 112-Origin retold | 1.60 | 4.80 | 11.00 |
| 114-120: 117-1st app. The Falcon | 1.30 | 4.00 | 9.00 |
| 121-140: 121-Retells origin. 133-The Falcon becomes Cap's partner; origin Modok. 137,138-Spider-Man x-over. 140-Origin Grey Gargoyle retold | | | |
|  | 1.15 | 3.50 | 7.00 |
| 141-171,176-179: 143-(52 pgs.). 155-Origin; redrawn with Falcon added. 164-1st app. Nightshade. 176-End of Capt. America | | | |
|  | .70 | 2.00 | 4.00 |
| 172-175-X-Men x-over | 1.35 | 4.00 | 8.00 |
| 180-200: 180-Intro & origin of Nomad. 181-Intro & origin of new Capt. America. 183-Death of New Cap; Nomad becomes Cap. 186-True origin The Falcon | | | |
|  | .60 | 1.75 | 3.50 |
| 201-240,242-246: 244,245-Miller-c | .40 | 1.25 | 2.50 |
| 241-Punisher app.; Miller-c | 7.00 | 21.00 | 48.00 |
| 247-255-Byrne a. 255-Origin; Miller-c | .60 | 1.75 | 3.50 |
| 256-331: 269-1st Team America | .35 | 1.00 | 2.00 |
| 332-Old Cap resigns | 1.70 | 5.00 | 10.00 |
| 333-Intro new Captain | 1.10 | 3.30 | 6.60 |
| 334 | .90 | 2.75 | 5.50 |
| 335-340: 339-Fall of the Mutants tie-in | .85 | 2.50 | 5.00 |
| 341-343,345-349 | .30 | .85 | 1.70 |
| 344-Double size, $1.50 | .35 | 1.10 | 2.20 |
| 350 (68 pgs., $1.75)-Return of Steve Rogers (original Cap) to original costume | | | |
|  | .70 | 2.00 | 4.00 |
| 351-354: 351-Nick Fury app. | .30 | .85 | 1.70 |
| 355-380 | | .50 | 1.00 |
| Giant Size 1(12/75, 68pg.)-r stories/T.O.S #59-63 | | | |
|  | .75 | 2.20 | 4.40 |
| Special 1(1/71), 2(1/72)-Colan-r/Not Brand Echh | | | |
|  | 1.30 | 3.85 | 7.70 |
| Annual 3-7: 3(4/76), 4(1977, 52 pgs.)-Kirby-c/a, 5(1981, 52 pgs.), 6 (11/82, 52 pgs.), 7('83, 52 pgs.) | | | |
|  | .30 | .95 | 1.90 |

|                                        | Good   | Fine    | N-Mint  |
|----------------------------------------|--------|---------|---------|
| Annual 8(9/86)-Wolverine featured      | 2.50   | 7.50    | 15.00   |
| Annual 9 ('90, $2.00, 68 pgs.)         | .35    | 1.00    | 2.00    |

**CAPTAIN AMERICA COMICS** (See All Winners & Marvel Mystery)
Mar, 1941 - No. 75, Jan, 1950; No. 76, 5/54 - No. 78, 9/54 (No. 74 & 75
    titled Capt. America's Weird Tales)
Timely/Marvel Comics (TCI 1-20/CmPS 21-68/MjMC 69-75/Atlas Comics
    PrPI 76-78)

|                                                                              | Good    | Fine    | N-Mint  |
|------------------------------------------------------------------------------|---------|---------|---------|
| 1-Origin & 1st app. Captain America & Bucky by S&K; Hurricane, Tuk           |         |         |         |
| the Caveboy begin by S&K; Red Skull app. Hitler-c                            |         |         |         |
|                                                                              | 1500.00 | 3750.00 | 9000.00 |
| *(Prices vary widely on this book)*                                          |         |         |         |
| 2-S&K Hurricane; Tuk by Avison (Kirby splash)                                |         |         |         |
|                                                                              | 483.00  | 1210.00 | 2900.00 |
| 3-Red Skull app; Stan Lee's 1st text                                         | 350.00  | 875.00  | 2100.00 |
| 4                                                                            | 233.00  | 585.00  | 1400.00 |
| 5                                                                            | 217.00  | 545.00  | 1300.00 |
| 6-Origin Father Time; Tuk the Caveboy ends                                   |         |         |         |
|                                                                              | 183.00  | 460.00  | 1100.00 |
| 7-Red Skull app                                                              | 183.00  | 460.00  | 1100.00 |
| 8-10-Last S&K issue (S&K centerfold #6-10)                                   |         |         |         |
|                                                                              | 150.00  | 375.00  | 900.00  |
| 11-Last Hurricane, Headline Hunter; Al Avison Captain America begins,        |         |         |         |
| ends #20                                                                     | 117.00  | 295.00  | 700.00  |
| 12-The Imp begins, ends #16; Last Father Time                                |         |         |         |
|                                                                              | 117.00  | 295.00  | 700.00  |
| 13-Origin The Secret Stamp; classic-c                                        | 125.00  | 315.00  | 750.00  |
| 14,15                                                                        | 117.00  | 295.00  | 700.00  |
| 16-Red Skull unmasks Cap                                                     | 125.00  | 315.00  | 750.00  |
| 17-The Fighting Fool only app.                                               | 100.00  | 250.00  | 600.00  |
| 18,19-Human Torch begins #19                                                 | 89.00   | 225.00  | 535.00  |
| 20-Sub-Mariner app.; no H. Torch                                             | 89.00   | 225.00  | 535.00  |
| 21-25: 25-Cap drinks liquid opium                                            | 79.00   | 200.00  | 475.00  |
| 26-30: 27-Last Secret Stamp; last 68 pg. issue? 28-60 pg. issues begin?      |         |         |         |
|                                                                              | 71.00   | 180.00  | 425.00  |
| 31-36,38-40                                                                  | 64.00   | 160.00  | 385.00  |
| 37-Red Skull app.                                                            | 67.00   | 170.00  | 400.00  |
| 41-45,47: 41-Last Jap War-c. 47-Last German War-c                            |         |         |         |
|                                                                              | 56.00   | 140.00  | 335.00  |

|  | **Good** | **Fine** | **N-Mint** |
|---|---|---|---|
| 46-German Holocaust-c | 56.00 | 140.00 | 335.00 |
| 48-58,60 | 52.00 | 130.00 | 310.00 |
| 59-Origin retold | 75.00 | 190.00 | 450.00 |
| 61-Red Skull c/story | 67.00 | 170.00 | 400.00 |
| 62,64,65: 65-"Hey Look" by Kurtzman | 52.00 | 130.00 | 310.00 |
| 63-Intro/origin Asbestos Lady | 56.00 | 140.00 | 335.00 |
| 66-Bucky is shot; Golden Girl teams up with Captain America & learns his i.d.; origin Golden Girl | 63.00 | 160.00 | 380.00 |
| 67-Captain America/Golden Girl team-up; Mxyztplk swipe; last Toro in Human Torch | 52.00 | 130.00 | 310.00 |
| 68,70-Sub-Mariner/Namora, and Captain America/Golden Girl team- up in each. 70-Science fiction c/story | 52.00 | 130.00 | 310.00 |
| 69-73: 69-Human Torch/Sun Girl team-up. 71-Anti Wertham editorial; The Witness, Bucky app. | 52.00 | 130.00 | 310.00 |
| 74-(Scarce)(1949)-Titled "C.A.'s Weird Tales"; Red Skull app. | 81.00 | 205.00 | 485.00 |
| 75(2/50)-Titled "C.A.'s Weird Tales"; no C.A. app.; horror cover/stories | 55.00 | 140.00 | 330.00 |
| 76-78(1954); Human Torch/Toro story | 35.00 | 90.00 | 210.00 |

**CAPTAIN MARVEL** (See Marvel Super-Heroes #12)
May, 1968 - No. 19, Dec, 1969; No. 20, June, 1970 - No. 21, Aug, 1970; No. 22, Sept, 1972 - No. 62, May, 1979
Marvel Comics Group

| | | | |
|---|---|---|---|
| 1 | 7.00 | 21.00 | 50.00 |
| 2 | 1.70 | 5.00 | 12.00 |
| 3-5 | 1.50 | 4.50 | 10.00 |
| 6-11: 11-Smith/Trimpe-c; Death of Una | .85 | 2.50 | 5.00 |
| 12-24: 17-New costume | .60 | 1.80 | 3.60 |
| 25-Starlin-c/a | 1.35 | 4.00 | 8.00 |
| 26-Starlin-c/a | 1.00 | 3.00 | 6.00 |
| 27-34-Starlin-c/a. 29-C.M. gains more powers. 34-C.M. contracts cancer, which eventually kills him | .75 | 2.25 | 4.50 |
| 35-62: 36-Origin recap; Starlin-a (3 pgs.). 39-Origin Watcher. 41,43-Wrightson part inks; #43-c(i) | | .50 | 1.00 |
| Giant-Size 1 (12/75)-r/Capt. Marvel #17 & 20 | .50 | 1.50 | 3.00 |

**CAPTAIN MARVEL**
Nov, 1989 ($1.50, color, one-shot, 52 pgs.)
Marvel Comics

|  | Good | Fine | N-Mint |
|---|---|---|---|
| 1-Super-hero from Avengers; new powers | .25 | .75 | 1.50 |

**CAPTAIN MARVEL ADVENTURES** (See Special Edition Comics)
1941 - No. 150, Nov, 1953
Fawcett Publications

| | Good | Fine | N-Mint |
|---|---|---|---|
| nn(#1)-Captain Marvel & Sivana by Jack Kirby. The cover was printed on unstable paper stock and is rarely found in Fine or Mint condition; blank inside-c | 1167.00 | 2925.00 | 7000.00 |
| *(Prices vary widely on this book)* | | | |
| 2-(Advertised as #3, which was counting Special Edition Comics as the real #1); Tuska-a | 157.00 | 470.00 | 1100.00 |
| 3-Metallic silver-c | 81.00 | 245.00 | 570.00 |
| 4-Three Lt. Marvels app. | 59.00 | 178.00 | 415.00 |
| 5 | 51.00 | 152.00 | 355.00 |
| 6-10 | 39.00 | 118.00 | 275.00 |
| 11-15: 13-Two-pg. Capt. Marvel pin-up. 15-Comic cards on back-c begin, end #26 | 30.00 | 90.00 | 210.00 |
| 16,17: 17-Painted-c | 27.00 | 81.00 | 190.00 |
| 18-Origin & 1st app. Mary Marvel & Marvel Family; painted-c (12/11/42) | 41.00 | 122.00 | 285.00 |
| 19-Mary Marvel x-over; Christmas-c | 25.00 | 75.00 | 175.00 |
| 20,21-With miniature comic attached to-c | 65.00 | 195.00 | 455.00 |
| 20,21-Without miniature | 21.50 | 64.00 | 150.00 |
| 22-Mr. Mind serial begins | 39.00 | 118.00 | 275.00 |
| 23-25 | 21.00 | 62.00 | 145.00 |
| 26-30: 26-Flag-c | 17.00 | 51.00 | 120.00 |
| 31-35: 35-Origin Radar | 16.00 | 48.00 | 110.00 |
| 36-40: 37-Mary Marvel x-over | 13.00 | 40.00 | 95.00 |
| 41-46: 42-Christmas-c. 43-Capt. Marvel 1st meets Uncle Marvel; Mary Batson cameo. 46-Mr. Mind serial ends | 12.00 | 36.00 | 84.00 |
| 47-50 | 11.00 | 32.00 | 75.00 |
| 51-53,55-60: 52-Origin & 1st app. Sivana Jr.; Capt. Marvel Jr. x-over | 8.00 | 24.00 | 56.00 |
| 54-Special oversize 68-pg. issue | 10.00 | 30.00 | 70.00 |
| 61-The Cult of the Curse serial begins | 11.00 | 32.00 | 75.00 |

|                                                                 | Good | Fine | N-Mint |
|-----------------------------------------------------------------|------|------|--------|
| 62-66-Serial ends; Mary Marvel x-over in #65. 66-Atomic War-c   |      |      |        |
|                                                                 | 7.00 | 21.00 | 50.00 |
| 67-77,79: 69-Billy Batson's Christmas; Uncle Marvel, Mary Marvel, Capt. Marvel Jr. x-over. 71-Three Lt. Marvels app. 79-Origin Mr. Tawny |      |      |        |
|                                                                 | 6.50 | 19.50 | 45.00 |
| 78-Origin Mr. Atom                                              | 7.00 | 21.00 | 50.00 |
| 80-Origin Capt. Marvel retold                                   | 11.50 | 34.00 | 80.00 |
| 81-84,86-90: 81,90-Mr. Atom app. 82-Infinity-c. 86-Mr. Tawny app. |      |      |        |
|                                                                 | 7.00 | 21.00 | 50.00 |
| 85-Freedom Train issue                                          | 8.50 | 25.50 | 60.00 |
| 91-99: 96-Mr. Tawny app.                                        | 5.70 | 17.00 | 40.00 |
| 100-Origin retold                                               | 12.00 | 36.00 | 84.00 |
| 101-120: 116-Flying Saucer issue (1/51)                         | 5.70 | 17.00 | 40.00 |
| 121-Origin retold                                               | 7.00 | 21.00 | 50.00 |
| 122-141,143-149: 138-Flying Saucer issue (11/52). 141-Pre-code horror story "The Hideous Head-Hunter" | 5.70 | 17.00 | 40.00 |
| 142-Used in **POP**, pgs. 92,96                                 | 5.70 | 17.00 | 40.00 |
| 150-(Low distribution)                                          | 11.00 | 32.00 | 75.00 |

**CAPTAIN MARVEL, JR.** (See Marvel Family, Master & Whiz Comics)
Nov, 1942 - No. 119, June, 1953 (nn 34)
Fawcett Publications

| 1-Origin Capt. Marvel Jr. retold (Whiz No. 25); Capt. Nazi app. |        |        |        |
|-----------------------------------------------------------------|--------|--------|--------|
|                                                                 | 110.00 | 332.00 | 775.00 |
| 2-Vs. Capt. Nazi; origin Capt. Nippon                           | 55.00  | 165.00 | 385.00 |
| 3,4                                                             | 41.00  | 122.00 | 285.00 |
| 5-Vs. Capt. Nazi                                                | 31.00  | 94.00  | 220.00 |
| 6-10: 8-Vs. Capt. Nazi. 9-Flag-c. 10-Hitler-c                   | 24.00  | 73.00  | 170.00 |
| 11,12,15-Capt. Nazi app.                                        | 19.00  | 58.00  | 135.00 |
| 13,14,16-20: 16-Capt. Marvel & Sivana x-over. 19-Capt. Nazi & Capt. Nippon app. | 13.50 | 41.00 | 95.00 |
| 21-30: 25-Flag-c                                                | 9.30   | 28.00  | 65.00  |
| 31-33,36-40: 37-Infinity-c                                      | 6.00   | 18.00  | 42.00  |
| 35-#34 on inside; cover shows origin of Sivana Jr. which is not on inside. Evidently the cover to #35 was printed out of sequence and bound with contents to #34 | 6.00 | 18.00 | 42.00 |
| 41-50                                                           | 4.30   | 13.00  | 30.00  |
| 51-70: 53-Atomic Bomb story                                     | 3.70   | 11.00  | 26.00  |
| 71-99,101-104: 104-Used in **POP**, pg. 89                      | 3.15   | 9.50   | 22.00  |

|  | Good | Fine | N-Mint |
|---|---|---|---|
| 100 | 3.70 | 11.00 | 26.00 |
| 105-114,116-119: 119-Electric chair-c | 3.15 | 9.50 | 22.00 |
| 115-Injury to eye-c; Eyeball story w/ injury-to-eye panels | | | |
|  | 4.50 | 14.00 | 32.00 |

**CAPTAIN MIDNIGHT** (Radio, films, TV) (See The Funnies & Popular)
Sept, 1942 - No. 67, Fall, 1948
Fawcett Publications

| 1-Origin Captain Midnight; Captain Marvel cameo on cover | | | |
|---|---|---|---|
|  | 108.00 | 325.00 | 650.00 |
| 2 | 46.00 | 140.00 | 325.00 |
| 3-5 | 32.00 | 95.00 | 225.00 |
| 6-10: 9-Raboy-c. 10-Raboy Flag-c | 22.00 | 65.00 | 155.00 |
| 11-20: 11,17-Raboy-c | 14.00 | 43.00 | 100.00 |
| 21-30 | 11.50 | 34.00 | 80.00 |
| 31-40 | 8.50 | 25.50 | 60.00 |
| 41-59,61-67: 54-Sci/fi theme begins? | 6.50 | 19.50 | 45.00 |
| 60-Flying Saucer issue (2/48)-3rd of this theme; see Shadow Comics | | | |
| V7#10 & Boy Commandos #26 | 10.00 | 30.00 | 70.00 |

**CASPER, THE FRIENDLY GHOST** (Becomes Harvey Comics Hits No. 61
   (No. 6), and then continued with Harvey issue No. 7)
9/49 - No. 3, 8/50; 9/50 - No. 5, 5/51
St. John Publishing Co.

| 1(1949)-Origin & 1st app. Baby Huey | 50.00 | 150.00 | 350.00 |
|---|---|---|---|
| 2,3 | 27.00 | 81.00 | 190.00 |
| 1(9/50) | 35.00 | 105.00 | 245.00 |
| 2-5 | 22.00 | 65.00 | 155.00 |

**CASPER, THE FRIENDLY GHOST** (Paramount Picture Star . . . )
No. 7, Dec, 1952 - No. 70, July, 1958
Harvey Publications (Family Comics)

   **Note:** No. 6 is Harvey Comics Hits No. 61 (10/52)

| 7-Baby Huey begins, ends #9 | 17.00 | 51.00 | 120.00 |
|---|---|---|---|
| 8-10: 10-Spooky begins(1st app.), ends #70? | 8.50 | 25.50 | 60.00 |
| 11-19: 19-1st app. Nightmare (4/54) | 5.70 | 17.00 | 40.00 |

| | Good | Fine | N-Mint |
|---|---|---|---|
| 20-Wendy the Witch begins (1st app., 5/54) | 6.50 | 19.50 | 45.00 |
| 21-30: 24-Infinity-c | 4.50 | 14.00 | 32.00 |
| 31-40 | 3.75 | 11.25 | 26.00 |
| 41-50 | 3.00 | 9.00 | 21.00 |
| 51-70 | 2.30 | 7.00 | 16.00 |

**CAT, THE**
Nov, 1972 - No. 4, June, 1973
Marvel Comics Group

| | | | |
|---|---|---|---|
| 1-Origin The Cat; Mooney-a(i); Wood-c(i)/a(i) | .75 | 2.25 | 4.50 |
| 2-Mooney-a(i), 3-Everett inks | .50 | 1.50 | 3.00 |
| 4-Starlin/Weiss-a(p) | .50 | 1.50 | 3.00 |

**CATMAN COMICS** (Crash No. 1-5)
5/41 - No. 17, 1/43; No. 18, 7/43 - No. 22, 12/43; No. 23, 3/44 - No. 26,
    11/44; No. 27, 4/45 - No. 30, 12/45; No. 31, 6/46 - No. 32, 8/46
Holyoke Publishing Co./Continental Magazines V2#12, 7/44 on

| | Good | Fine | N-Mint |
|---|---|---|---|
| 1(V1#6)-Origin The Deacon & Sidekick Mickey, Dr. Diamond & Rag-Man; The Black Widow app.; The Catman by Chas. Quinlan & Blaze Baylor begin | 64.00 | 192.00 | 450.00 |
| 2(V1#7) | 31.00 | 92.00 | 215.00 |
| 3(V1#8), 4(V1#9): 3-The Pied Piper begins | 24.00 | 73.00 | 170.00 |
| 5(V2#10)-Origin Kitten; The Hood begins (c-redated), 6,7(V2#11,12) | 19.00 | 58.00 | 135.00 |
| 8(V2#13,3/42)-Origin Little Leaders; Volton by Kubert begins (his 1st comic book work) | 27.00 | 80.00 | 185.00 |
| 9(V2#14) | 17.00 | 50.00 | 120.00 |
| 10(V2#15)-Origin Blackout; Phantom Falcon begins | 17.00 | 50.00 | 120.00 |
| 11(V3#1)-Kubert-a | 17.00 | 50.00 | 120.00 |
| 12(V3#2) - 15, 17, 18(V3#8, 7/43) | 13.00 | 40.00 | 90.00 |
| 16 (V3#5)-Hitler, Tojo, Mussolini, Stalin-c | 14.00 | 42.00 | 100.00 |
| 19 (V2#6)-Hitler, Tojo, Mussolini-c | 14.00 | 42.00 | 100.00 |
| 20(V2#7) - 23(V2#10, 3/44) | 13.00 | 40.00 | 90.00 |
| nn(V3#13, 5/44)-Rico-a; Schomburg bondage-c | 11.50 | 34.00 | 80.00 |
| nn(V2#12, 7/44) | 11.50 | 34.00 | 80.00 |

|  | Good | Fine | N-Mint |
|---|---|---|---|
| nn(V3#1, 9/44)-Origin The Golden Archer; Leatherface app. | | | |
|  | 10.00 | 30.00 | 70.00 |
| nn(V3#2, 11/44)-L. B. Cole-c | 16.00 | 48.00 | 110.00 |
| 27-Origin Kitten retold; L. B. Cole Flag-c | 17.00 | 51.00 | 120.00 |
| 28-Catman learns Kitten's I.D.; Dr. Macabre, Deacon app.; L. B. Cole-c/a | | | |
|  | 19.00 | 58.00 | 135.00 |
| 29-32-L. B. Cole-c; bondage-#30 | 16.00 | 48.00 | 110.00 |

**CATWOMAN** (Also see Action Comics Weekly #611-614 & Batman)
Feb, 1989 - No. 4, May, 1989 ($1.50, mini-series, mature readers)
DC Comics

| | | | |
|---|---|---|---|
| 1 | 2.00 | 6.00 | 12.00 |
| 2 | 1.70 | 4.00 | 8.00 |
| 3,4: 3-Batman cameo. 4-Batman app. | .60 | 1.75 | 3.50 |

**CENTURY OF COMICS**
1933 (100 pages) (Probably the 3rd comic book)
Eastern Color Printing Co.

Bought by Wheatena, Milk-O-Malt, John Wanamaker, Kinney Shoe Stores,
  & others to be used as premiums and radio giveaways. No publisher
  listed. nn-Mutt & Jeff, Joe Palooka, etc. reprints

|  | 433.00 | 1085.00 | 2600.00 |
|---|---|---|---|

**CEREBUS BI-WEEKLY**
Dec. 2, 1988 - No. 26, Nov. 11, 1989 ($1.25, B&W)
Aardvark-Vanaheim

| | | | |
|---|---|---|---|
| 1-Reprints Cerebus #1 | .25 | .75 | 1.50 |
| 2-26-Reprints Cerebus #2-26 |  | .60 | 1.25 |

**CEREBUS JAM**
Apr, 1985
Aardvark-Vanaheim

| | | | |
|---|---|---|---|
| 1-Eisner, Austin-a | .60 | 1.75 | 3.50 |

*Cerebus the Aardvark #31, © Aardvark-Vanaheim*

**CEREBUS THE AARDVARK**
Dec, 1977 - Present
Aardvark-Vanaheim

|  | Good | Fine | N-Mint |
|---|---|---|---|
| 1-2000 print run; most copies poorly printed | | | |
|  | 54.00 | 162.50 | 325.00 |

**Note:** There is a counterfeit version known to exist. It can be distinguished from the original in the following ways: inside cover is glossy instead of flat, black background on the front cover is blotted or spotty. These counterfeits sell for between $50.00 and $70.00.

|  | Good | Fine | N-Mint |
|---|---|---|---|
| 2 | 22.50 | 67.50 | 135.00 |
| 3-Origin Red Sophia | 18.30 | 55.00 | 110.00 |
| 4-Origin Elrod the Albino | 12.50 | 37.50 | 75.00 |
| 5,6 | 10.85 | 32.50 | 65.00 |
| 7-12: 11-Origin Capt. Coachroach | 7.50 | 22.50 | 45.00 |
| 13-15: 14-Origin Lord Julius | 4.15 | 12.50 | 25.00 |
| 16-20 | 2.50 | 7.50 | 15.00 |
| 21-Scarcer | 11.70 | 35.00 | 70.00 |

|                                               | **Good** | **Fine** | **N-Mint** |
|-----------------------------------------------|----------|----------|------------|
| 22-Low distribution, no cover price           | 3.35     | 10.00    | 20.00      |
| 23-28                                         | 1.85     | 5.50     | 11.00      |
| 29,30                                         | 2.15     | 6.50     | 13.00      |
| 31-Origin Moonroach                           | 2.50     | 7.50     | 15.00      |
| 32-40                                         | 1.00     | 3.00     | 6.00       |
| 41-50,52: 52-Cutey Bunny app.                 | .85      | 2.50     | 5.00       |
| 51-Not reprinted; Cutey Bunny app.            | 3.00     | 9.00     | 18.00      |
| 53-Intro. Wolveroach (cameo)                  | 1.15     | 3.50     | 7.00       |
| 54-Wolveroach 1st full story                  | 1.70     | 5.00     | 10.00      |
| 55,56-Wolveroach app.                         | 1.15     | 3.50     | 7.00       |
| 57-60                                         | .60      | 1.75     | 3.50       |
| 61,62: Flaming Carrot app.                    | .85      | 2.50     | 5.00       |
| 63-68                                         | .70      | 2.00     | 4.00       |
| 69-75                                         | .55      | 1.60     | 3.20       |
| 76-79                                         | .50      | 1.50     | 3.00       |
| 80-85                                         | .45      | 1.25     | 2.50       |
| 86-136: 104-Flaming Carrot app.               | .35      | 1.00     | 2.00       |

## CHALLENGERS OF THE UNKNOWN (See Showcase #6, 7, 11 & 12)
4-5/58 - No. 77, 12-1/70-71; No. 78, 2/73 - No. 80, 6-7/73; No. 81, 6-7/77 -
No. 87, 6-7/78
National Periodical Publications/DC Comics

|                                               | **Good** | **Fine** | **N-Mint** |
|-----------------------------------------------|----------|----------|------------|
| 1-Kirby/Stein-a(2)                            | 70.00    | 210.00   | 485.00     |
| 2-Kirby/Stein-a(2)                            | 36.00    | 72.00    | 250.00     |
| 3-Kirby/Stein-a(2)                            | 30.00    | 90.00    | 210.00     |
| 4-8-Kirby/Wood-a plus c-#8                    | 25.00    | 75.00    | 175.00     |
| 9,10                                          | 12.00    | 36.00    | 85.00      |
| 11-15: 14-Origin Multi-Man                    | 7.85     | 23.50    | 55.00      |
| 16-22: 18-Intro. Cosmo, the Challengers Space pet. 22-Last 10 cent issue | | | |
|                                               | 5.50     | 16.50    | 38.00      |
| 23-30                                         | 2.15     | 6.50     | 15.00      |
| 31-40: 31-Retells origin of the Challengers   | 1.50     | 4.50     | 10.00      |
| 41-60: 43-New look begins. 48-Doom Patrol app. 49-Intro. Challenger Corps. 51-Sea Devils app. 55-Death of Red Ryan. 60-Red Ryan returns | | | |
|                                               | .85      | 2.50     | 5.00       |
| 61-63,66-73: 69-Intro. Corinna                | .50      | 1.50     | 3.00       |
| 64,65-Kirby origin-r, parts 1 & 2             | .50      | 1.50     | 3.00       |
| 74-Deadman by Tuska/N. Adams                  | 1.30     | 4.00     | 8.00       |
| 75-87: 82-Swamp Thing begins                  | .25      | .75      | 1.50       |

**CHAMBER OF CHILLS** (. . . of Clues No. 27 on)
No. 21, June, 1951 - No. 26, Dec, 1954
Harvey Publications/Witches Tales

|  | Good | Fine | N-Mint |
|---|---|---|---|
| 21 (#1) | 10.00 | 30.00 | 70.00 |
| 22,24 | 6.00 | 18.00 | 42.00 |
| 23-Excessive violence; eyes torn out | 7.00 | 21.00 | 50.00 |
| 5(2/52)-Decapitation, acid in face scene | 7.00 | 21.00 | 50.00 |
| 6-Woman melted alive | 5.70 | 17.00 | 40.00 |
| 7-Used in **SOTI**, pg. 389; decapitation/severed head panels | | | |
|  | 5.00 | 15.00 | 35.00 |
| 8-10: 8-Decapitation panels | 4.30 | 13.00 | 30.00 |
| 11,12,14 | 3.50 | 10.50 | 24.00 |
| 13,15-24-Nostrand-a in all; c-#20. 13,21-Decapitation panels. 18-Atom bomb panels | 5.70 | 17.00 | 40.00 |
| 25,26 | 3.00 | 9.00 | 21.00 |

**CHAMBER OF CLUES** (Formerly Chamber of Chills)
No. 27, Feb, 1955 - No. 28, April, 1955
Harvey Publications

| | | | |
|---|---|---|---|
| 27-Kerry Drake r-/No. 19; Powell-a | 4.30 | 13.00 | 30.00 |
| 28-Kerry Drake | 2.30 | 7.00 | 16.00 |

**CHAMPIONS, THE**
October, 1975 - No. 17, Jan, 1978
Marvel Comics Group

| | | | |
|---|---|---|---|
| 1-The Angel, Black Widow, Ghost Rider, Hercules, Ice Man (The Champions) begin; Kane/Adkins-c; Venus x-over | .85 | 2.50 | 5.00 |
| 2-10,16: 2,3-Venus x-over | .25 | .75 | 1.50 |
| 11-15,17-Byrne-a | .50 | 1.50 | 3.00 |

**CHECKMATE** (See Action Comics #598)
April, 1988 - Present ($1.25)
DC Comics

| | | | |
|---|---|---|---|
| 1 | .60 | 1.75 | 3.50 |
| 2 | .40 | 1.25 | 2.50 |

|                                                        | Good  | Fine   | N-Mint |
|--------------------------------------------------------|-------|--------|--------|
| 3-5                                                    | .30   | .90    | 1.75   |
| 6-20: 13-on are $1.50, new format                      | .25   | .75    | 1.50   |
| 21-34                                                  |       | .60    | 1.25   |

## CISCO KID, THE (TV)
July, 1950 - No. 41, Oct-Dec, 1958
Dell Publishing Co.

| 4-Color 292(#1)-Cisco Kid, his horse Diablo, & sidekick Pancho & his |       |        |        |
|---------------------------------------------------------------------|-------|--------|--------|
| horse Loco begin; painted-c begin                                   | 9.30  | 28.00  | 65.00  |
| 2(1/51)-5                                                           | 4.50  | 14.00  | 32.00  |
| 6-10                                                                | 3.70  | 11.00  | 26.00  |
| 11-20                                                               | 3.00  | 9.00   | 21.00  |
| 21-36-Last painted-c                                                | 2.65  | 8.00   | 18.00  |
| 37-41: All photo-c                                                  | 5.00  | 15.00  | 35.00  |

## CLASSIC X-MEN (Becomes X-Men Classic #46 on)
Sept, 1986 - No. 45, Mar, 1990 (#27 on: $1.25)
Marvel Comics Group

| 1-Begins-r of New X-Men w/Art Adams-c                    | .90   | 2.75   | 5.50   |
|----------------------------------------------------------|-------|--------|--------|
| 2-4                                                      | .60   | 1.75   | 3.50   |
| 5-10                                                     | .50   | 1.50   | 3.00   |
| 11-15                                                    | .40   | 1.25   | 2.50   |
| 16,18-20                                                 | .35   | 1.00   | 2.00   |
| 17-Wolverine-c                                           | .75   | 2.25   | 4.50   |
| 21-25,27-30: 27-r/X-Men #121                             | .25   | .75    | 1.50   |
| 26-r/X-Men #120; Wolverine app.                          | .35   | 1.00   | 2.00   |
| 31-42,44,45: 35-r/X-Men #129 (1st Kitty Pryde)           |       | .65    | 1.30   |
| 43-Byrne-c/a(r); $1.75, double-size                      | .35   | 1.00   | 2.00   |

## CLUE COMICS
Jan, 1943 - No. 15 (V2 No.3), May, 1947
Hillman Periodicals

| 1-Origin The Boy King, Nightmare, Micro-Face, Twilight, & Zippo |       |        |        |
|-----------------------------------------------------------------|-------|--------|--------|
|                                                                 | 42.00 | 126.00 | 295.00 |
| 2                                                               | 22.00 | 65.00  | 155.00 |
| 3                                                               | 17.00 | 51.00  | 120.00 |
| 4                                                               | 14.00 | 42.00  | 100.00 |

| | Good | Fine | N-Mint |
|---|---|---|---|
| 5 | 12.00 | 36.00 | 84.00 |
| 6,8,9: 8-Palais-c/a(2) | 9.30 | 28.00 | 65.00 |
| 7-Classic torture-c | 13.00 | 40.00 | 90.00 |
| 10-Origin The Gun Master | 10.00 | 30.00 | 70.00 |
| 11 | 6.00 | 18.00 | 42.00 |
| 12-Origin Rackman; McWilliams-a, Guardineer-a(2) | | | |
| | 8.50 | 25.50 | 60.00 |
| V2#1-Nightro new origin; Iron Lady app.; Simon & Kirby-a | | | |
| | 13.00 | 40.00 | 90.00 |
| V2#2-S&K-a(2)-Bondage/torture-c; man attacks & kills people with electric iron. Infantino-a | | | |
| | 13.00 | 40.00 | 90.00 |
| V2#3-S&K-a(3) | 13.00 | 40.00 | 90.00 |

## COMIC CAVALCADE

Winter, 1942-43 - No. 63, June-July, 1954 (Contents change with No. 30, Dec-Jan, 1948-49 on)
All-American/National Periodical Publications

| | Good | Fine | N-Mint |
|---|---|---|---|
| 1-The Flash, Green Lantern, Wonder Woman, Wildcat, The Black Pirate by Moldoff (also #2), Ghost Patrol, and Red White & Blue begin; Scribbly app., Minute Movies | 217.00 | 545.00 | 1300.00 |
| 2-Mutt & Jeff begin; last Ghost Patrol & Black Pirate; Minute Movies | | | |
| | 108.00 | 270.00 | 650.00 |
| 3-Hop Harrigan & Sargon, the Sorcerer begin; The King app. | | | |
| | 80.00 | 200.00 | 480.00 |
| 4,5: 4-The Gay Ghost, The King, Scribbly, & Red Tornado app. 5-Christmas-c | 67.00 | 170.00 | 400.00 |
| 6-10: 7-Red Tornado & Black Pirate app.; last Scribbly. 9-X-mas-c | | | |
| | 50.00 | 125.00 | 300.00 |
| 11,12,14-20: 12-Last Red White & Blue. 15-Johnny Peril begins, ends #29. 19-Christmas-c | 42.00 | 105.00 | 255.00 |
| 13-Solomon Grundy app. | 72.00 | 180.00 | 435.00 |
| 21-23 | 42.00 | 105.00 | 255.00 |
| 24-Solomon Grundy x-over in Green Lantern | 50.00 | 125.00 | 300.00 |
| 25-29: 25-Black Canary app.; Xmas-c. 26-28-Johnny Peril app. 28-Last Mutt & Jeff. 29-Last Flash, Wonder Woman, Green Lantern & Johnny Peril; Wonder Woman invents "Thinking Machine"; 1st computer in comics? | 32.00 | 80.00 | 190.00 |
| 30-The Fox & the Crow, Dodo & the Frog & Nutsy Squirrel begin | | | |
| | 20.00 | 60.00 | 140.00 |

|  | Good | Fine | N-Mint |
|---|---|---|---|
| 31-35 | 9.00 | 27.00 | 62.00 |
| 36-49 | 7.00 | 21.00 | 48.00 |
| 50-62(Scarce) | 9.00 | 27.00 | 62.00 |
| 63(Rare) | 16.00 | 48.00 | 110.00 |

## COMICS, THE
March, 1937 - No. 11, 1938 (Newspaper strip reprints)
Dell Publishing Co.

| | | | |
|---|---|---|---|
| 1-1st Tom Mix in comics; Wash Tubbs, Tom Beatty, Myra North, Arizona Kid, Erik Noble & International Spy w/Doctor Doom begin | | | |
| | 64.00 | 193.00 | 450.00 |
| 2 | 34.00 | 103.00 | 240.00 |
| 3-11: 3-Alley Oop begins | 28.00 | 85.00 | 200.00 |

## COMICS AND STORIES (See Walt Disney's . . . )

## COMICS MAGAZINE, THE (. . . Funny Pages #3) (Funny Pages #6 on)
May, 1936 - No. 5, Sept, 1936 (Paper covers)
Comics Magazine Co.

| | | | |
|---|---|---|---|
| 1: Dr. Mystic, The Occult Detective by Siegel & Shuster (1st episode continues in More Fun #14); 1pg. Kelly-a; Sheldon Mayer-a | | | |
| | 200.00 | 500.00 | 1200.00 |
| 2: Federal Agent by Siegel & Shuster; 1pg. Kelly-a | | | |
| | 90.00 | 270.00 | 620.00 |
| 3-5 | 75.00 | 225.00 | 525.00 |

## CONAN, THE BARBARIAN
Oct, 1970 - Present
Marvel Comics Group

| | | | |
|---|---|---|---|
| 1-Origin/1st app. Conan by Barry Smith; Kull app. | | | |
| | 15.00 | 45.00 | 105.00 |
| 2 | 5.70 | 17.00 | 40.00 |

*Conan, the Barbarian #100, © Marvel Comics*

|  | Good | Fine | N-Mint |
|---|---|---|---|
| 3-(low distribution in some areas) | 9.15 | 27.50 | 64.00 |
| 4,5 | 4.30 | 13.00 | 30.00 |
| 6-10: 8-Hidden panel message, pg. 14. 10-52 pgs.; Black Knight-r; Kull story by Severin | 2.85 | 8.50 | 20.00 |
| 11-13: 11-52 pgs. 12-Wrightson c(i) | 2.15 | 6.50 | 15.00 |
| 14,15-Elric app. | 3.15 | 9.50 | 22.00 |
| 16,19,20: 16-Conan-r/Savage Tales #1 | 1.70 | 5.00 | 12.00 |
| 17,18-No Barry Smith-a | 1.15 | 3.50 | 7.00 |
| 21,22: 22-has r-from #1 | 1.50 | 4.50 | 10.00 |
| 23-1st app. Red Sonja | 1.85 | 5.50 | 13.00 |
| 24-1st full story Red Sonja; last Smith-a | 1.85 | 5.50 | 13.00 |
| 25-John Buscema-c/a begins | 1.15 | 3.50 | 7.00 |
| 26-30 | .70 | 2.00 | 4.00 |
| 31-36,38-40 | .40 | 1.25 | 2.50 |
| 37-Neal Adams-c/a | .85 | 2.50 | 5.00 |
| 41-43,46-49: 48-Origin retold | .30 | .85 | 1.70 |
| 44,45-N. Adams-i(Crusty Bunkers). 45-Adams-c | .35 | 1.00 | 2.00 |

|  | Good | Fine | N-Mint |
|---|---|---|---|
| 50-57,59,60: 59-Origin Belit | .30 | .85 | 1.70 |
| 58-2nd Belit app. (see Giant-Size #1) | .50 | 1.50 | 3.00 |
| 61-99: 68-Red Sonja story cont'd from Marvel Feature #7. 84-Intro. Zula. 85-Origin Zula. 87-R/Savage Sword of Conan #3 in color | | | |
|  | | .60 | 1.20 |
| 100-(52 pg. Giant)-Death of Belit | .40 | 1.25 | 2.50 |
| 101-114,116-193 | | .50 | 1.00 |
| 115-Double size | | .60 | 1.20 |
| 194-199,201-240: 196-200,204-Red Sonja app. | | .50 | 1.00 |
| 200-Double size ($1.50) | .25 | .75 | 1.50 |
| Giant Size 1(9/74)-Smith r-/#3; start adaptation of Howard's "Hour of the Dragon." 1st app. Belit; new-a also #1-4 | .70 | 2.00 | 4.00 |
| Giant Size 2(12/74)-Smith r-/#5; Sutton-a; Buscema-c (Giants 1-5 all have 68 pgs.) | .70 | 2.00 | 4.00 |
| Giant Size 3-5: 3(4/75-Smith r-/#6; Sutton-a), 4(6/75; Smith r-/#7), 5('75; Smith r-/#14,15; Kirby-c) | .35 | 1.00 | 2.00 |
| King Size 1(9/73, 35 cents, 52 pgs.)-Smith r-/#2,4; Smith-c | | | |
|  | 1.00 | 3.00 | 6.00 |
| Annual 2(6/76)-50 cents; new stories | .40 | 1.25 | 2.50 |
| Annual 3(2/78)-reprints | .35 | 1.00 | 2.00 |
| Annual 4(10/78), 5(12/79)-Buscema-a/part-c | .25 | .75 | 1.50 |
| Annual 6(10/81)-Kane-c/a | .25 | .75 | 1.50 |
| Annual 7-11: 7(11/82), 8(2/84), 9(12/84), 10(2/87), 11(2/88) | | | |
|  | | .60 | 1.25 |
| Special Edition 1(Red Nails) | .50 | 1.50 | 3.00 |

**COPS** (TV)
Aug, 1988 - No. 15, Aug, 1989 ($1.00, color)
DC Comics

| | Good | Fine | N-Mint |
|---|---|---|---|
| 1 ($1.50) Based on Hasbro Toys | .35 | 1.10 | 2.20 |
| 2-7 | | .60 | 1.25 |
| 8-15: 14-Orlando-c(p) | | .50 | 1.00 |

**COSMIC BOY** (See The Legion of Super-Heroes)
Dec, 1986 - No. 4, Mar, 1987 (mini-series)
DC Comics

| | Good | Fine | N-Mint |
|---|---|---|---|
| 1-Legends tie-in, all issues | .25 | .75 | 1.50 |
| 2-4 | | .50 | 1.00 |

## COSMIC ODYSSEY
1988 - No. 4, 1988 (Squarebound, $3.50, color)
DC Comics

|  | Good | Fine | N-Mint |
|---|---|---|---|
| 1-4: Superman, Batman, Green Lantern app. | .70 | 2.00 | 4.00 |

## CRACKAJACK FUNNIES
June, 1938 - No. 43, Jan, 1942
Dell Publishing Co.

| | Good | Fine | N-Mint |
|---|---|---|---|
| 1-Dan Dunn, Freckles, Myra North, Wash Tubbs, Apple Mary, The Nebbs, Don Winslow, Tom Mix, Buck Jones, Major Hoople, Clyde Beatty, Boots begin | 82.00 | 245.00 | 575.00 |
| 2 | 38.00 | 115.00 | 270.00 |
| 3 | 27.00 | 81.00 | 190.00 |
| 4,5 | 22.00 | 65.00 | 154.00 |
| 6-8,10 | 17.00 | 51.00 | 120.00 |
| 9-(3/39)-Red Ryder strip-r begin by Harman; 1st app. in comics & 1st cover app. | 24.00 | 73.00 | 170.00 |
| 11-14 | 15.00 | 45.00 | 105.00 |
| 15-Tarzan text feature begins by Burroughs (9/39); not in #26,35 | 16.00 | 48.00 | 115.00 |
| 16-24 | 12.00 | 36.00 | 84.00 |
| 25-The Owl begins; in new costume #26 by Frank Thomas | 27.00 | 81.00 | 190.00 |
| 26-30: 28-Owl-c. 29-Ellery Queen begins | 21.00 | 62.00 | 145.00 |
| 31-Owl covers begin | 19.00 | 57.00 | 132.00 |
| 32-Origin Owl Girl | 21.00 | 62.00 | 145.00 |
| 33-38: 36-Last Tarzan issue | 14.00 | 42.00 | 100.00 |
| 39-Andy Panda begins (intro/1st app.) | 16.00 | 48.00 | 110.00 |
| 40-43: 42-Last Owl cover | 13.00 | 40.00 | 90.00 |

## CRACK COMICS (. . . Western No. 63 on)
May, 1940 - No. 62, Sept, 1949
Quality Comics Group

| | Good | Fine | N-Mint |
|---|---|---|---|
| 1-Origin The Black Condor by Lou Fine, Madame Fatal, Red Torpedo, Rock Bradden & The Space Legion; The Clock, Alias the Spider, Wizard Wells, & Ned Brant begin; Powell-a; Note: Madame Fatal is a man dressed up as a woman | 171.00 | 515.00 | 1200.00 |

|  | Good | Fine | N-Mint |
|---|---|---|---|
| 2 | 86.00 | 257.00 | 600.00 |
| 3 | 63.00 | 188.00 | 440.00 |
| 4 | 54.00 | 163.00 | 380.00 |
| 5-10: 5-Molly The Model begins. 10-Tor, the Magic Master begins | | | |
|  | 42.00 | 126.00 | 295.00 |
| 11-20: 18-1st app. Spitfire? | 37.00 | 110.00 | 260.00 |
| 21-24-Last Fine Black Condor | 28.00 | 85.00 | 200.00 |
| 25,26 | 18.50 | 56.00 | 130.00 |
| 27-Intro & origin Captain Triumph by Alfred Andriola (Kerry Drake artist) | | | |
|  | 37.00 | 110.00 | 260.00 |
| 28-30 | 16.00 | 48.00 | 110.00 |
| 31-39: 31-Last Black Condor | 9.30 | 28.00 | 65.00 |
| 40-46 | 6.50 | 19.50 | 45.00 |
| 47-57,59,60-Capt. Triumph by Crandall | 7.50 | 22.50 | 52.00 |
| 58,61,62-Last Captain Triumph | 5.50 | 16.50 | 38.00 |

**CRACK WESTERN** (Formerly Crack Comics)
No. 63, Nov, 1949 - No. 84, May, 1953 (36 pgs., 63-68,74-on)
Quality Comics Group

| | Good | Fine | N-Mint |
|---|---|---|---|
| 63(#1)-Two-Gun Lil (origin & 1st app.)(ends #84), Arizona Ames, his horse Thunder (sidekick Spurs & his horse Calico), Frontier Marshal (ends #70), & Dead Canyon Days (ends #69) begin; Crandall-a | | | |
|  | 8.50 | 25.50 | 60.00 |
| 64,65-Crandall-a | 6.00 | 18.00 | 42.00 |
| 66,68-Photo-c. 66-Arizona Ames becomes A. Raines (ends #84) | | | |
|  | 6.00 | 18.00 | 42.00 |
| 67-Randolph Scott photo-c; Crandall-a | 7.00 | 21.00 | 50.00 |
| 69(52 pgs.)-Crandall-a | 6.00 | 18.00 | 42.00 |
| 70(52 pgs.)-The Whip (origin & 1st app.) & his horse Diablo begin (end #84); Crandall-a | | | |
|  | 6.00 | 18.00 | 42.00 |
| 71(52 pgs.)-Frontier Marshal becomes Bob Allen F. Marshal (ends #84); Crandall-c/a | | | |
|  | 7.00 | 21.00 | 50.00 |
| 72(52 pgs.)-Tim Holt photo-c | 6.00 | 18.00 | 42.00 |
| 73(52 pgs.)-Photo-c | 4.50 | 14.00 | 32.00 |
| 74,77,79,80,82 | 3.00 | 9.00 | 21.00 |
| 75,76,78,81,83-Crandall-c | 4.50 | 14.00 | 32.00 |
| 84-Crandall c/a | 6.50 | 19.50 | 45.00 |

**CRASH COMICS** (Catman Comics No. 6 on)
May, 1940 - No. 5, Nov, 1940
Tem Publishing Co.

| | Good | Fine | N-Mint |
|---|---|---|---|
| 1-The Blue Streak, Strongman (origin), The Perfect Human, Shangra begin; Kirby-a | 93.00 | 280.00 | 650.00 |
| 2-Simon & Kirby-a | 43.00 | 130.00 | 300.00 |
| 3-Simon & Kirby-a | 35.00 | 105.00 | 245.00 |
| 4-Origin & 1st app. The Catman; S&K-a | 57.00 | 170.00 | 400.00 |
| 5-S&K-a | 35.00 | 105.00 | 245.00 |

**CRIME DOES NOT PAY** (Formerly Silver Streak Comics No. 1-21)
No. 22, June, 1942 - No. 147, July, 1955 (1st crime comic)
Comic House/Lev Gleason/Golfing (Title inspired by film)

| | Good | Fine | N-Mint |
|---|---|---|---|
| 22(23 on cover, 22 on indicia)-Origin The War Eagle & only app.; Chip Gardner begins; No. 22 rebound in Complete Book of True Crime (Scarce) | 82.00 | 245.00 | 575.00 |
| 23 (Scarce) | 46.00 | 140.00 | 325.00 |
| 24-Intro. & 1st app. Mr. Crime (Scarce) | 38.00 | 115.00 | 270.00 |
| 25-30 | 21.00 | 62.00 | 145.00 |
| 31-40 | 12.00 | 36.00 | 84.00 |
| 41-Origin & 1st app. Officer Common Sense | 8.00 | 24.00 | 56.00 |
| 42-Electrocution-c | 9.30 | 28.00 | 65.00 |
| 43-46,48-50: 44,45,50 are 68 pg. issues | 6.50 | 19.50 | 45.00 |
| 47-Electric chair-c | 9.30 | 28.00 | 65.00 |
| 51-62,65-70 | 3.50 | 10.50 | 24.00 |
| 63,64-Possible use in **SOTI**, pg. 306. #63-Contains Biro-Gleason's self censorship code of 12 listed restrictions (5/48) | 3.50 | 10.50 | 24.00 |
| 71-99: 87-Chip Gardner begins, ends #99 | 2.30 | 7.00 | 16.00 |
| 100 | 2.65 | 8.00 | 18.00 |
| 101-104,107-110: 102-Chip Gardner app. | 1.70 | 5.00 | 12.00 |
| 105-Used in **POP**, pg. 84 | 1.70 | 5.00 | 12.00 |
| 106,114-Frazetta, 1 pg. | 2.00 | 6.00 | 14.00 |
| 111-Used in **POP**, pgs. 80,81 & injury-to-eye story illo | 1.70 | 5.00 | 12.00 |
| 112,113,115-130 | 1.30 | 4.00 | 9.00 |
| 131-140 | 1.15 | 3.50 | 8.00 |
| 141,142-Last pre-code issue; Kubert-a(1) | 2.30 | 7.00 | 16.00 |

|                                      | Good  | Fine   | N-Mint |
|--------------------------------------|-------|--------|--------|
| 143,147-Kubert-a, one each           | 2.30  | 7.00   | 16.00  |
| 144-146                              | 1.00  | 3.00   | 7.00   |
| 1(Golfing-1945)                      | 1.50  | 4.50   | 10.00  |

**CRIME MUST PAY THE PENALTY** (Formerly Four Favorites; Penalty No. 47,48)
No. 33, Feb, 1948; No. 2, June, 1948 - No. 48, Jan, 1956
Ace Magazines (Current Books)

| | Good | Fine | N-Mint |
|---|---|---|---|
| 33(#1, 2/48)-Becomes Four Teeners #34? | 9.30 | 28.00 | 65.00 |
| 2(6/48)-Extreme violence; Palais-a? | 5.70 | 17.00 | 40.00 |
| 3-'Frisco Mary' story used in Senate Investigation report, pg. 7 | | | |
| | 3.00 | 9.00 | 21.00 |
| 4,8-Transvestism story | 5.00 | 15.00 | 35.00 |
| 5-7,9,10 | 2.30 | 7.00 | 16.00 |
| 11-20 | 1.70 | 5.00 | 12.00 |
| 21-32,34-40,42-48 | 1.50 | 4.50 | 10.00 |
| 33(7/53)-"Dell Fabry-Junk King"-drug story; mentioned in **Love and Death** | 3.00 | 9.00 | 21.00 |
| 41-Drug story-"Dealers in White Death" | 3.00 | 9.00 | 21.00 |

**CRIMES BY WOMEN**
June, 1948 - No. 15, Aug, 1951; 1954
Fox Features Syndicate

| | Good | Fine | N-Mint |
|---|---|---|---|
| 1 | 43.00 | 130.00 | 300.00 |
| 2 | 22.00 | 65.00 | 154.00 |
| 3-Used in **SOTI**, pg. 234 | 22.00 | 65.00 | 154.00 |
| 4,5,7,9,11-15 | 20.00 | 60.00 | 140.00 |
| 6-Classic girl fight-c; acid-in-face panel | 23.00 | 70.00 | 160.00 |
| 8-Used in **POP** | 20.00 | 60.00 | 140.00 |
| 10-Used in **SOTI**, pg. 72 | 20.00 | 60.00 | 140.00 |
| 54(M.S. Publ.-'54)-Reprint | 9.00 | 27.00 | 62.00 |

**CRIME SMASHERS**
Oct, 1950 - No. 15, Mar, 1953
Ribage Publishing Corp. (Trojan Magazines)

| | Good | Fine | N-Mint |
|---|---|---|---|
| 1-Used in **SOTI**, pg. 19,20, & illo-"A girl raped and murdered"; Sally the Sleuth begins | 30.00 | 90.00 | 210.00 |

|                                                        | Good  | Fine   | N-Mint |
|--------------------------------------------------------|-------|--------|--------|
| 2-Kubert-c                                             | 14.00 | 42.00  | 100.00 |
| 3,4                                                    | 11.50 | 34.00  | 80.00  |
| 5-Wood-a                                               | 17.00 | 51.00  | 120.00 |
| 6,8-11                                                 | 9.00  | 27.00  | 62.00  |
| 7-Female heroin junkie story                           | 10.00 | 30.00  | 70.00  |
| 12-Injury to eye panel; 1 pg. Frazetta                 | 11.00 | 32.00  | 75.00  |
| 13-Used in POP, pgs. 79,80; 1 pg. Frazetta             | 9.00  | 27.00  | 62.00  |
| 14,15                                                  | 9.00  | 27.00  | 62.00  |

**CRIME SUSPENSTORIES** (Formerly Vault of Horror No. 12-14)
No. 15, Oct-Nov, 1950 - No. 27, Feb-Mar, 1955
E. C. Comics

15-Identical to #1 in content; #1 printed on outside front cover. #15 (formerly "The Vault of Horror") printed and blackened out on inside front cover with Vol. 1, No. 1 printed over it.

|                                                        | Good  | Fine   | N-Mint |
|--------------------------------------------------------|-------|--------|--------|
|                                                        | 70.00 | 210.00 | 495.00 |
| 1                                                      | 55.00 | 165.00 | 385.00 |
| 2                                                      | 34.00 | 100.00 | 235.00 |
| 3-5                                                    | 23.00 | 70.00  | 160.00 |
| 6-10                                                   | 17.00 | 51.00  | 120.00 |
| 11,12,14,15                                            | 12.00 | 36.00  | 84.00  |
| 13,16-Williamson-a                                     | 15.00 | 45.00  | 105.00 |
| 17-Williamson/Frazetta-a, 6 pgs.                       | 17.00 | 52.00  | 120.00 |
| 18,19: 19-Used in SOTI, pg. 235                        | 10.00 | 30.00  | 70.00  |

20-Cover used in SOTI, illo-"Cover of a children's comic book"

|                                                        | 13.00 | 40.00  | 90.00  |
|--------------------------------------------------------|-------|--------|--------|
| 21,25-27                                               | 7.00  | 21.00  | 50.00  |

22,23-Used in Senate investigation on juvenile delinquency. 22-Ax decapitation-c

|                                                        | 11.00 | 33.00  | 76.00  |
|--------------------------------------------------------|-------|--------|--------|

24-'Food For Thought' similar to 'Cave In' in Amazing Detective Cases #13 ('52)

|                                                        | 7.00  | 21.00  | 50.00  |
|--------------------------------------------------------|-------|--------|--------|

**CRISIS ON INFINITE EARTHS**
Apr, 1985 - No. 12, Mar, 1986 (12 issue maxi-series)
DC Comics

1-1st DC app. Blue Beetle & Detective Karp from Charlton; Perez-c on all

|                                                        | .70   | 2.00   | 4.00   |
|--------------------------------------------------------|-------|--------|--------|
| 2                                                      | .50   | 1.50   | 3.00   |

|  | Good | Fine | N-Mint |
|---|---|---|---|
| 3 | .40 | 1.25 | 2.50 |
| 4-6: 6-Intro Charlton's Capt. Atom, Nightshade, Question, Judomaster, Peacemaker & Thunderbolt | .35 | 1.00 | 2.00 |
| 7-Double size; death of Supergirl | .40 | 1.25 | 2.50 |
| 8-Death of Flash | .40 | 1.25 | 2.50 |
| 9-11: 9-Intro. Charlton's Ghost. 10-Intro. Charlton's Banshee, Dr. Spectro, Image, Punch & Jewellee | .35 | 1.00 | 2.00 |
| 12-Double size; deaths of Dove, Kole, Lori Lemaris, Sunburst, G.A. Robin & Huntress; Kid Flash becomes new Flash | .50 | 1.50 | 3.00 |

# D

**DAFFY** (. . . Duck No. 18 on) (See Looney Tunes)
#457, 3/53 - #30, 7-9/62; #31, 10-12/62 - #145, 1983 (No #132,133)
Dell Publishing Co./Gold Key No. 31-127/Whitman No. 128 on

|  | Good | Fine | N-Mint |
|---|---|---|---|
| 4-Color 457(#1)-Elmer Fudd x-overs begin | 2.15 | 6.50 | 15.00 |
| 4-Color 536,615('55) | 1.50 | 4.50 | 10.00 |
| 4(1-3/56)-11('57) | 1.15 | 3.50 | 8.00 |
| 12-19(1958-59) | .85 | 2.50 | 6.00 |
| 20-40(1960-64) | .70 | 2.00 | 4.00 |
| 41-60(1964-68) | .35 | 1.00 | 2.00 |
| 61-90(1969-73)-Road Runner in most |  | .60 | 1.20 |
| 91-131,134-145(1974-83) |  | .40 | .80 |

**DALE EVANS COMICS** (Also see Queen of the West . . . )
Sept-Oct, 1948 - No. 24, July-Aug, 1952 (No. 1-19: 52 pgs.)
National Periodical Publications

|  | Good | Fine | N-Mint |
|---|---|---|---|
| 1-Dale Evans & her horse Buttermilk begin; Sierra Smith begins by Alex Toth; photo-c | 23.00 | 70.00 | 160.00 |
| 2-Alex Toth-a; photo-c | 14.00 | 42.00 | 100.00 |
| 3-11-Alex Toth-a (photo c-4-14) | 12.00 | 36.00 | 85.00 |
| 12-24 | 6.50 | 19.50 | 45.00 |

**DAMAGE CONTROL**
5/89 - #4, 8/89; V2#1, 12/89 - #4, 2/90 ($1.00, color, both mini-series)
Marvel Comics

|  | Good | Fine | N-Mint |
|---|---|---|---|
| 1-4: 4-Wolverine app. |  | .60 | 1.20 |
| V2#1-4: 2,4-Punisher app. | .25 | .75 | 1.50 |

**DANIEL BOONE** (TV)
Jan, 1965 - No. 15, Apr, 1969
Gold Key

|  | Good | Fine | N-Mint |
|---|---|---|---|
| 1 | 1.50 | 4.50 | 10.00 |
| 2-5 | .85 | 2.50 | 5.00 |
| 6-15: 4,6-Fess Parker photo-c | .70 | 2.00 | 4.00 |

*Daredevil #257, © Marvel Comics*

**DAREDEVIL** (. . . & the Black Widow #92-107 on-c only)
April, 1964 - Present
Marvel Comics Group

|  | Good | Fine | N-Mint |
|---|---|---|---|
| 1-Origin Daredevil; r-/in Marvel Super Heroes #1, 1966. Death of Battling Murdock; intro Foggy Nelson & Karen Page | | | |
|  | 88.00 | 264.00 | 620.00 |
| 2-Fantastic Four cameo | 36.00 | 108.00 | 250.00 |
| 3-Origin, 1st app. The Owl | 21.00 | 63.00 | 150.00 |
| 4,5: 5-Wood-a begins; new costume | 12.00 | 36.00 | 85.00 |
| 6,8-10: 8-Origin & 1st app. Stilt-Man | 9.30 | 28.00 | 65.00 |
| 7-Dons new red costume | 10.30 | 31.00 | 72.00 |
| 11-15: 12-Romita's 1st work at Marvel. 13-Facts about Ka-Zar's origin; Kirby-a | 5.70 | 17.00 | 40.00 |
| 16,17-Spider-Man x-over | 5.15 | 15.50 | 36.00 |
| 18-20: 18-Origin & 1st app. Gladiator | 3.50 | 10.50 | 24.00 |
| 21-30: 24-Ka-Zar app. | 2.65 | 8.00 | 18.00 |

|  | Good | Fine | N-Mint |
|---|---|---|---|
| 31-40 | 2.15 | 6.50 | 15.00 |
| 41-49: 41-Death Mike Murdock. 43-vs. Capt. America | | | |
|  | 1.30 | 4.00 | 9.00 |
| 50-53: 50-52-Smith-a. 53-Origin retold | 1.60 | 4.80 | 11.00 |
| 54-56,58-60 | 1.00 | 3.00 | 6.00 |
| 57-Reveals i.d. to Karen Page | 1.15 | 3.50 | 7.00 |
| 61-99: 62-1st app. Nighthawk. 81-Oversize issue; Black Widow begins | | | |
|  | .85 | 2.50 | 5.00 |
| 100-Origin retold | 1.60 | 4.80 | 11.00 |
| 101-106,108-113,115-120 | .40 | 1.25 | 2.50 |
| 107,114: 107-Starlin-c. 114-1st app. Deathstalker | | | |
|  | .50 | 1.50 | 3.00 |
| 121-130,132-137: 124-1st app. Copperhead; Black Widow leaves. 126-1st | | | |
| New Torpedo | .35 | 1.00 | 2.00 |
| 131-Origin Bullseye | 1.70 | 5.00 | 10.00 |
| 138-Byrne-a | .50 | 1.50 | 3.00 |
| 139-157: 142-Nova cameo. 148-30 & 35 cent issues exist. 150-1st app. Pala- | | | |
| din. 151-Reveals i.d. to Heather Glenn. 155-Black Widow returns. | | | |
| 156-1960s Daredevil app. | .35 | 1.00 | 2.00 |
| 158-Frank Miller art begins (5/79); origin/death of Deathstalker (See | | | |
| Spect. Spider-Man for Miller's 1st D.D. | 6.00 | 18.00 | 36.00 |
| 159 | 2.50 | 7.50 | 15.00 |
| 160,161 | 1.50 | 4.50 | 9.00 |
| 162-Ditko-a, no Miller-a | .40 | 1.25 | 2.50 |
| 163,164: 163-Hulk cameo. 164-Origin | 1.35 | 4.00 | 8.00 |
| 165-167,170 | 1.00 | 3.00 | 6.00 |
| 168-Intro/origin Elektra | 2.65 | 8.00 | 16.00 |
| 169-Elektra app. | 1.35 | 4.00 | 8.00 |
| 171-175: 174,175-Elektra app. | .70 | 2.00 | 4.00 |
| 176-180-Elektra app. | .50 | 1.50 | 3.00 |
| 181-Double size; death of Elektra | .60 | 1.75 | 3.50 |
| 182-184-Punisher app. by Miller | 1.15 | 3.50 | 7.00 |
| 185-191: 187-New Black Widow. 189-Death of Stick. 190-Double size; | | | |
| Elektra returns, part origin. 191-Last Miller Daredevil | | | |
|  | .25 | .75 | 1.50 |
| 192-195,197-210: 208-Harlan Ellison scripts | | .60 | 1.20 |
| 196-Wolverine app. | 1.00 | 3.00 | 6.00 |
| 211-225 | | .50 | 1.00 |
| 226-Frank Miller plots begin | .25 | .75 | 1.50 |
| 227-Miller scripts begin | .70 | 2.00 | 4.00 |

|  | Good | Fine | N-Mint |
|---|---|---|---|
| 228-233-Last Miller scripts | .35 | 1.00 | 2.00 |
| 234-240,242-247,250,251,253-256,258,259 |  | .50 | 1.00 |
| 241-Todd McFarlane-a(p) | .35 | 1.00 | 2.00 |
| 248,249-Wolverine app. | .40 | 1.25 | 2.50 |
| 252-(Double size, 52 pgs.)-Fall of the Mutants | .40 | 1.25 | 2.50 |
| 257-Punisher app. | .50 | 1.50 | 3.00 |
| 260-Double size | .35 | 1.00 | 2.00 |
| 261-288: 272-Intro Shotgun (villain) |  | .50 | 1.00 |
| Giant Size 1 ('75) | .50 | 1.50 | 3.00 |
| Special 1(9/67, 25 cents, 68 pgs.)-new art | 1.50 | 4.50 | 10.00 |
| Special 2,3: 2(2/71, 25 cents, 52 pgs.)-Entire book has Powell/Wood-r; |  |  |  |
| Wood-c. 3(1/72)-reprints | .85 | 2.50 | 5.00 |
| Annual 4(10/76) | .50 | 1.50 | 3.00 |
| Annual 4(1989, $2.00, 68 pgs.)-Atlantis Attacks | .40 | 1.25 | 2.50 |
| Annual 5(1989, $2.00, 68 pgs.) | .35 | 1.00 | 2.00 |
| Annual 6(1990, $2.00, 68 pgs.)-Sutton-a | .35 | 1.00 | 2.00 |

**DAREDEVIL COMICS** (See Silver Streak Comics)
July, 1941 - No. 134, Sept, 1956 (Charles Biro stories)
Lev Gleason Publications (Funnies, Inc. No. 1)

(No. 1 titled "Daredevil Battles Hitler")
1-The Silver Streak, Lance Hale, Cloud Curtis, Dickey Dean, Pirate
    Prince team up with Daredevil and battle Hitler; Daredevil battles
    the Claw; Origin of Hitler feature story. Hitler photo app. on-c

|  | | | |
|---|---|---|---|
|  | 300.00 | 750.00 | 1800.00 |

2-London, Pat Patriot, Nightro, Real American No. 1, Dickie Dean, Pirate
    Prince, & Times Square begin; intro. & only app. The Pioneer, Cham-
    pion of America                          130.00     390.00     910.00
3-Origin of 13                               78.00      238.00     550.00
4                                            64.00      193.00     450.00
5-Intro. Sniffer & Jinx; Ghost vs. Claw begins by Bob Wood, ends #20

|  | 57.00 | 170.00 | 400.00 |
|---|---|---|---|

6-(#7 on indicia)                            50.00      150.00     350.00
7-10: 8-Nightro ends                         43.00      130.00     300.00
11-London, Pat Patriot end; bondage/torture-c

|  | 38.00 | 114.00 | 265.00 |
|---|---|---|---|

12-Origin of The Claw; Scoop Scuttle by Wolverton begins (2-4 pgs.),
    ends #22, not in #21                     57.00      170.00     400.00
13-Intro. of Little Wise Guys               57.00      170.00     400.00

| | Good | Fine | N-Mint |
|---|---|---|---|
| 14 | 28.00 | 85.00 | 200.00 |
| 15-Death of Meatball | 43.00 | 130.00 | 300.00 |
| 16,17 | 26.00 | 80.00 | 185.00 |
| 18-New origin of Daredevil-Not same as Silver Streak #6 | | | |
| | 57.00 | 170.00 | 400.00 |
| 19,20 | 24.00 | 70.00 | 165.00 |
| 21-Reprints cover of Silver Streak #6 (on inside) plus intro. of The Claw | | | |
|     from Silver Streak #1 | 34.00 | 103.00 | 240.00 |
| 22-30 | 14.00 | 42.00 | 100.00 |
| 31-Death of The Claw | 25.00 | 75.00 | 175.00 |
| 32-37: 34-Two Daredevil stories begin, end #68 | | | |
| | 9.30 | 28.00 | 65.00 |
| 38-Origin Daredevil retold from #18 | 19.00 | 58.00 | 135.00 |
| 39,40 | 9.30 | 28.00 | 65.00 |
| 41-50: 42-Intro. Kilroy in Daredevil | 5.70 | 17.00 | 40.00 |
| 51-69-Last Daredevil issue | 4.30 | 13.00 | 30.00 |
| 70-Little Wise Guys take over book; McWilliams-a; Hot Rock Flanagan be- | | | |
|     gins, ends #80 | 2.65 | 8.00 | 18.00 |
| 71-79,81: 79-Daredevil returns | 2.00 | 6.00 | 14.00 |
| 80-Daredevil x-over | 2.00 | 6.00 | 14.00 |
| 82,90-One page Frazetta ad in both | 2.30 | 7.00 | 16.00 |
| 83-89,91-99,101-134 | 1.70 | 5.00 | 12.00 |
| 100 | 3.00 | 9.00 | 21.00 |

**DARING COMICS** (Formerly Daring Mystery Comics)
No. 9, Fall, 1944 - No. 12, Fall, 1945
Timely Comics (HPC)

| | | | |
|---|---|---|---|
| 9-Human Torch & Sub-Mariner begin | 36.00 | 107.00 | 250.00 |
| 10-The Angel only app. | 32.00 | 95.00 | 220.00 |
| 11,12-The Destroyer app. | 32.00 | 95.00 | 220.00 |

**DARING MYSTERY COMICS** (Daring Comics No. 9 on)
Jan, 1940 - No. 8, Jan, 1942
Timely Comics (TPI 1-6/TCI 7,8)

1-Origin The Fiery Mask by Joe Simon; Monako, Prince of Magic, John
    Steele, Soldier of Fortune, Doc Doyle begin; Flash Foster & Barney
    Mullen, Sea Rover only app; bondage-c

| | 583.00 | 1460.00 | 3500.00 |
|---|---|---|---|

|  | Good | Fine | N-Mint |
|---|---|---|---|
| 2-(Rare)-Origin The Phantom Bullet & only app.; The Laughing Mask & Mr. E only app.; Trojak the Tiger Man begins, ends #6; Zephyr Jones & K-4 & His Sky Devils app., also #4 | 283.00 | 710.00 | 1700.00 |
| 3-The Phantom Reporter, Dale of FBI, Breeze Barton, Captain Strong & Marvex the Super-Robot only app.; The Purple Mask begins | 200.00 | 500.00 | 1200.00 |
| 4-Last Purple Mask; Whirlwind Carter begins; Dan Gorman, G-Man app. | 133.00 | 335.00 | 800.00 |
| 5-The Falcon begins; The Fiery Mask, Little Hercules app. by Sagendorf in the Segar style; bondage-c | 133.00 | 335.00 | 800.00 |
| 6-Origin & only app. Marvel Boy by S&K; Flying Flame, Dynaman, & Stuporman only app.; The Fiery Mask by S&K; S&K-c | 158.00 | 395.00 | 950.00 |
| 7-Origin The Blue Diamond, Captain Daring by S&K, The Fin by Everett, The Challenger, The Silver Scorpion & The Thunderer by Burgos; Mr. Millions app. | 158.00 | 395.00 | 950.00 |
| 8-Origin Citizen V; Last Fin, Silver Scorpion, Capt. Daring by Borth, Blue Diamond & The Thunderer; S&K-c; Rudy the Robot only app. | 125.00 | 315.00 | 750.00 |

**DARK SHADOWS** (TV)
March, 1969 - No. 35, Feb, 1976 (Photo-c: 2-7)
Gold Key

| | Good | Fine | N-Mint |
|---|---|---|---|
| 1(30039-903)-with pull-out poster (25 cents) | 9.70 | 29.00 | 68.00 |
| 2 | 4.70 | 14.00 | 33.00 |
| 3-with pull-out poster | 6.30 | 19.00 | 44.00 |
| 4-7: Last photo-c | 4.15 | 12.50 | 29.00 |
| 8-10 | 3.15 | 9.50 | 22.00 |
| 11-20 | 2.40 | 7.20 | 17.00 |
| 21-35: 30-last painted-c | 1.70 | 5.00 | 12.00 |
| Story Digest 1 (6/70) | 1.70 | 5.00 | 12.00 |

**DATE WITH DEBBI**
Jan-Feb, 1969 - No. 17, Sept-Oct, 1971; No. 18, Oct-Nov, 1972
National Periodical Publications

| | Good | Fine | N-Mint |
|---|---|---|---|
| 1 | 1.00 | 3.00 | 6.00 |
| 2-5 | .60 | 1.75 | 3.50 |
| 6-18 | .50 | 1.50 | 3.00 |

## DC COMICS PRESENTS
July-Aug, 1978 - No. 97, Sept, 1986 (Superman team-ups in all)
DC Comics

|  | Good | Fine | N-Mint |
|---|---|---|---|
| 1-12,14-25: 19-Batgirl | .25 | .75 | 1.50 |
| 13-Legion of Super Heroes (also in #43 & 80) | .40 | 1.25 | 2.50 |
| 26-(10/80)-Green Lantern; intro Cyborg, Starfire, Raven, New Teen Titans; Starlin-c/a; Sargon the Sorcerer back-up; 16 pgs. preview of the New Teen Titans | 1.15 | 3.50 | 7.00 |
| 27-40,42-71,73-76,79-84,86-97: 31,58-Robin. 35-Man-Bat. 52-Doom Patrol. 82-Adam Strange. 83-Batman & Outsiders. 86-88-Crisis x-over. 88-Creeper | .25 | .75 | 1.50 |
| 41-Superman/Joker-c/story | .50 | 1.50 | 3.00 |
| 72-Joker/Phantom Stranger-c/story | .50 | 1.50 | 3.00 |
| 77,78: 77,78-Animal Man app. (77-cover app.) | .70 | 2.00 | 4.00 |
| 85-Swamp Thing; Alan Moore scripts | .35 | 1.00 | 2.00 |
| Annual 1-4: 1(9/82)-G.A. Superman. 2(7/83)-Intro/origin Superwoman. 3(9/84)-Shazam. 4(10/85)-Superwoman | | .60 | 1.20 |

## DEFENDERS, THE (Also see Marvel Feature; The New . . . #140-on)
Aug, 1972 - No. 152, Feb, 1986
Marvel Comics Group

| | Good | Fine | N-Mint |
|---|---|---|---|
| 1-The Hulk, Doctor Strange, & Sub-Mariner begin | 2.40 | 7.20 | 17.00 |
| 2-5: 4-Valkyrie joins | .85 | 2.50 | 5.00 |
| 6-10: 9,10-Avengers app. 10-Thor-Hulk battle | .85 | 2.50 | 5.00 |
| 11-50: 15,16-Magneto & Brotherhood of Evil Mutants app. from X-Men. 31,32-Origin Nighthawk. 35-Intro. New Red Guardian. 44- Hellcat joins. 45-Dr. Strange leaves | .35 | 1.00 | 2.00 |
| 51-151: 55-Origin Red Guardian. 74-Nighthawk resigns. 77-Origin Omega. 78-Original Defenders return thru #101. 100-Double size. 104-The Beast joins. 106-Death of Nighthawk. 125-Double size; 1st app. Mad Dog; intro. new Defenders. 129-New Mutants cameo. 150-Double size; origin Cloud | | .50 | 1.00 |
| 152-Double size; ties in with X-Factor & Secret Wars II | .30 | .90 | 1.75 |

**DENNIS THE MENACE**
8/53 - #14, 1/56; #15, 3/56 - #31, 11/58; #32, 1/59 - #166, 11/79
Standard Comics/Pines No. 15-31/Hallden (Fawcett) No. 32 on

|  | Good | Fine | N-Mint |
|---|---|---|---|
| 1-1st app. Mr. & Mrs. Wilson, Ruff & Dennis' mom & dad; Wiseman- a, written by Fred Toole-most issues | 21.50 | 65.00 | 150.00 |
| 2 | 11.00 | 32.00 | 75.00 |
| 3-10 | 5.70 | 17.00 | 40.00 |
| 11-20 | 3.50 | 10.50 | 24.00 |
| 21-30: 22-1st app. Margaret w/blonde hair | 1.70 | 5.00 | 12.00 |
| 31-40: 31-1st app. Joey | 1.15 | 3.50 | 8.00 |
| 41-60 | .85 | 2.60 | 6.00 |
| 61-90 | .60 | 1.75 | 3.50 |
| 91-166 | .30 | 1.00 | 2.00 |

*Detective Comics #41, © DC Comics*

**DETECTIVE COMICS**
March, 1937 - Present
National Periodical Publications/DC Comics

|  | Good | Fine | N-Mint |
|---|---|---|---|
| 1-(Scarce)-Slam Bradley & Spy by Siegel & Shuster, Speed Saunders by Guardineer, Flat Foot Flannigan by Gustavson, Cosmo, the Phantom of Disguise, Buck Marshall, Bruce Nelson begin; Chin Lung-c from 'Claws of the Red Dragon' serial; Flessel-c (1st?) | 1900.00 | 4750.00 | 11,400.00 |
| (No copy is known to exist beyond NM condition) | | | |
| 2 (Rare) | 583.00 | 1460.00 | 3500.00 |
| 3 (Rare) | 483.00 | 1210.00 | 2900.00 |
| 4,5: 5-Larry Steele begins | 267.00 | 670.00 | 1600.00 |
| 6,7,9,10 | 180.00 | 450.00 | 1080.00 |
| 8-Mister Chang-c | 228.00 | 570.00 | 1370.00 |
| 11-17,19: 17-1st app. Fu Manchu in Det. | 153.00 | 385.00 | 920.00 |
| 18-Fu Manchu-c | 200.00 | 500.00 | 1200.00 |
| 20-The Crimson Avenger begins (intro. & 1st app.) | 217.00 | 545.00 | 1300.00 |
| 21,23-25 | 108.00 | 270.00 | 650.00 |
| 22-1st Crimson Avenger-c (12/38) | 150.00 | 375.00 | 900.00 |
| 26 | 125.00 | 315.00 | 750.00 |
| 27-The Batman & Commissioner Gordon begin (1st app.) by Bob Kane (5/39); Batman-c (1st) | 6000.00 | 15,000.00 | 32,500.00 |
| *(Only one copy known to exist beyond VF-NM condition which sold in 1988 for $35,000. Prices vary widely on this book.)* | | | |
| 27(1984)-Oreo Cookies giveaway (32 pgs., paper-c, r-/Det. 27, 38 & Batman No. 1 (1st Joker) | 1.15 | 3.50 | 7.00 |
| 28 | 767.00 | 2200.00 | 4600.00 |
| 29-Batman-c; Doctor Death app. | 833.00 | 2100.00 | 5000.00 |
| 30,32: 30-Dr. Death app. 32-Batman uses gun | 350.00 | 875.00 | 2100.00 |
| 31-Classic Batman-c; 1st Julie Madison, Bat Plane (Bat-Gyro) & Batarang | 833.00 | 2100.00 | 5000.00 |
| 33-Origin The Batman; Batman gunholster-c | 1083.00 | 2710.00 | 6500.00 |
| 34-Steve Malone begins; 2nd Crimson Avenger-c | 300.00 | 750.00 | 1800.00 |
| 35-37: 35-Batman-c begin. 35-Hypo-c. 36-Origin Hugo Strange. 37- Cliff Crosby begins | 333.00 | 835.00 | 2000.00 |

|  | Good | Fine | N-Mint |
|---|---|---|---|

38-Origin/1st app. Robin the Boy Wonder (4/40)

|  | 1000.00 | 2500.00 | 7000.00 |

39                                                                    283.00    710.00    1700.00

40-Origin & 1st app. Clay Face (Basil Karlo); 1st Clay Face cover app.
   (6/40)                                    333.00    835.00    2000.00

41-Robin's 1st solo                          183.00    450.00    1100.00

42-44: 44-Crimson Avenger-new costume        133.00    335.00     800.00

45-1st Joker story in Det. (3rd app.)        200.00    500.00    1200.00

46-50: 48-1st time car called Batmobile; Gotham City 1st mention. 49-Last
   Clay Face                                 122.00    305.00     735.00

51-57,59: 59-Last Steve Malone; 2nd Penguin; Wing becomes Crimson
   Avenger's aide                            100.00    250.00     600.00

58-1st Penguin app.; last Speed Saunders     183.00    450.00    1100.00

60-Intro. Air Wave                           108.00    270.00     650.00

61,63: 63-Last Cliff Crosby; 1st app. Mr. Baffle

|  | 92.00 | 230.00 | 550.00 |

62-Joker-c/story (1st Joker-c, 4/42)         120.00    300.00     720.00

64-Origin & 1st app. Boy Commandos by Simon & Kirby; Joker app.

|  | 250.00 | 625.00 | 1500.00 |

65-Boy Commandos-c                           125.00    315.00     750.00

66-Origin & 1st app. Two-Face               167.00    420.00    1000.00

67,70                                         78.00    195.00     470.00

68-Two-Face-c/story                           83.00    210.00     500.00

69-Joker-c/story                             103.00    260.00     620.00

71-Joker-c/story                              93.00    235.00     560.00

72-75: 73-Scarecrow-c/story. 74-1st Tweedledum & Tweedledee; S&K-a

|  | 70.00 | 175.00 | 420.00 |

76-Newsboy Legion & The Sandman x-over in Boy Commandos; S&K-a;
   Joker-c/story                             108.00    270.00     650.00

77-79: All S&K-a                              70.00    175.00     420.00

80-Two-Face app.; S&K-a                       73.00    185.00     440.00

81,82,84,86-90: 81-1st Cavalier app. 89-Last Crimson Avenger

|  | 63.00 | 160.00 | 380.00 |

83-1st "Skinny" Alfred; last S&K Boy Commandos? Most issues #84 on
   signed S&K are not by them                 71.00    180.00     425.00

85-Joker-c/story; Last Spy                     83.00    210.00     500.00

91,102-Joker-c/story                           78.00    195.00     470.00

92-99: 96-Alfred's last name 'Beagle' revealed, later changed to
   'Pennyworth'-Batman 214                    58.00    145.00     350.00

100 (6/45)                                     83.00     21.00     500.00

| | Good | Fine | N-Mint |
|---|---|---|---|
| 101,103-108,110-113,115-117,119,120: 114-1st small logo (8/46) | | | |
| | 53.00 | 135.00 | 320.00 |
| 109,114,118-Joker-c/stories | 72.00 | 180.00 | 430.00 |
| 121-123,125-127,129,130: 126-Electrocution-c | 51.00 | 128.00 | 305.00 |
| 124,128-Joker-c/stories | 67.00 | 170.00 | 400.00 |
| 131-136,139: 137-Last Air Wave | 43.00 | 110.00 | 260.00 |
| 137-Joker-c/story | 58.00 | 145.00 | 350.00 |
| 138-Origin Robotman (See Star Spangled No. 7, 1st app.); series ends No. | | | |
| 202 | 75.00 | 190.00 | 450.00 |
| 140-1st app. The Riddler (10/48) | 133.00 | 335.00 | 800.00 |
| 141,143-148,150: 150-Last Boy Commandos | 43.00 | 110.00 | 260.00 |
| 142-2nd Riddler app. | 67.00 | 170.00 | 400.00 |
| 149-Joker-c/story | 56.00 | 140.00 | 335.00 |
| 151-Origin & 1st app. Pow Wow Smith | 46.00 | 115.00 | 275.00 |
| 152,154,155,157-160: 152-Last Slam Bradley | 43.00 | 110.00 | 260.00 |
| 153-1st Roy Raymond app.; origin The Human Fly | | | |
| | 46.00 | 115.00 | 275.00 |
| 156(2/50)-The new classic Batmobile | 54.00 | 135.00 | 325.00 |
| 161-167,169-176: Last 52 pgs. | 46.00 | 115.00 | 275.00 |
| 168-Origin the Joker | 158.00 | 395.00 | 950.00 |
| 177-189,191-199,201-204,206-212,214-216: 185-Secret of Batman's utility | | | |
| belt. 187-Two-Face app. 202-Last Robotman & Pow Wow Smith. | | | |
| 216-Last precode (2/55) | 30.00 | 75.00 | 180.00 |
| 190-Origin Batman retold | 47.00 | 120.00 | 280.00 |
| 200 | 43.00 | 110.00 | 260.00 |
| 205-Origin Batcave | 45.00 | 115.00 | 270.00 |
| 213-Origin Mirror Man | 42.00 | 105.00 | 250.00 |
| 217-224 | 28.00 | 70.00 | 170.00 |
| 225-(11/55)-Intro. & 1st app. Martian Manhunter-John Jones, later | | | |
| changed to J'onn J'onzz; also see Batman #78 | | | |
| | 170.00 | 510.00 | 1200.00 |
| 226-Origin Martian Manhunter continued | 44.00 | 132.00 | 310.00 |
| 227-229 | 27.00 | 81.00 | 190.00 |
| 230-1st app. Mad Hatter | 32.00 | 96.00 | 225.00 |
| 231-Origin Martian Manhunter retold | 21.00 | 63.00 | 145.00 |
| 232,234,236-240 | 18.00 | 54.00 | 125.00 |
| 233-Origin & 1st app. Batwoman | 50.00 | 150.00 | 350.00 |
| 235-Origin Batman & his costume | 26.50 | 80.00 | 185.00 |
| 241-260: 246-Intro. Diane Meade, J. Jones' girl. 257-Intro. & 1st app. | | | |
| Whirly Bats | 13.50 | 40.00 | 95.00 |

|  | Good | Fine | N-Mint |
|---|---|---|---|
| 261-264,266,268-270: 261-1st app. Dr. Double X. 262-Origin Jackal | | | |
| | 10.00 | 30.00 | 70.00 |
| 265-Batman's origin retold | 14.85 | 44.50 | 104.00 |
| 267-Origin & 1st app. Bat-Mite | 11.00 | 32.00 | 75.00 |
| 271-280: 276-2nd Bat-Mite | 8.00 | 24.00 | 55.00 |
| 281-297: 287-Origin J'onn J'onzz retold. 292-Last Roy Raymond. 293-Aquaman begins, ends #300. 297-Last 10 cent issue (11/61) | | | |
| | 5.70 | 17.00 | 40.00 |
| 298-1st modern Clayface (Matt Hagen) | 9.30 | 28.00 | 65.00 |
| 299-326,329,330: 311-Intro. Zook in John Jones; 1st app. Catman. 322-Batgirl's 1st app. in Det. 326-Last J'onn J'onzz; intro. Idol Head of Diabolu | 3.15 | 9.50 | 22.00 |
| 327-Elongated Man begins, ends 383; 1st new Batman costume | | | |
| | 3.60 | 11.00 | 25.00 |
| 328-Death of Alfred | 5.70 | 17.00 | 40.00 |
| 331,333-340,342-358,360-364,366-368,370: 345-Intro The Block Buster. 351-Elongated Man new costume. 355-Zatanna x-over in Elongated Man. 356-Alfred brought back in Batman | 1.85 | 5.50 | 13.00 |
| 332,341,365-Joker-c/stories | 2.85 | 8.50 | 20.00 |
| 359-Intro/origin new Batgirl | 2.85 | 8.50 | 20.00 |
| 369-Neal Adams-a | 3.15 | 9.50 | 22.00 |
| 371-386,389,390 | 1.50 | 4.50 | 9.00 |
| 387-R/1st Batman story from #27; Joker-c | 2.85 | 8.50 | 20.00 |
| 388-Joker-c/story | 2.15 | 6.50 | 15.00 |
| 391-394,396,398,399,401,403,405,406,409: 392-1st app. Jason Bard. 401-2nd Batgirl/Robin team-up | 1.15 | 3.50 | 7.00 |
| 395,397,402,404,407,408,410-Neal Adams-a | 1.85 | 5.50 | 13.00 |
| 400-Origin & 1st app. Man-Bat; 1st Batgirl/Robin team-up; Neal Adams-a | | | |
| | 2.65 | 8.00 | 18.00 |
| 411-420: 414-52 pgs. begin, end #424. 418-Creeper x-over | | | |
| | 1.15 | 3.50 | 7.00 |
| 421-436: 424-Last Batgirl; 1st She-Bat. 426-426-Elongated Man app. 428,434-Hawkman begins, ends #467 | 1.00 | 3.00 | 6.00 |
| 437-New Manhunter begins by Simonson, ends #443 | | | |
| | 1.35 | 4.00 | 8.00 |
| 438-445 (All 100 pgs.): 439-Origin Manhunter. 440-G.A. Manhunter, Hawkman, Dollman, Gr. Lantern; Toth-a. 441-G.A. Plastic Man, Batman, Ibis-r. 442-G.A. Newsboy Legion, Bl. Canary, Elongated Man, Dr. Fate-r. 443-Origin The Creeper-r; death of Manhunter; G.A. Green | | | |

|                                                                      | Good | Fine | N-Mint |
|----------------------------------------------------------------------|------|------|--------|
| Lantern, Spectre-r. 444-G.A. Kid Eternity-r. 445-G.A. Dr. Midnite-r  |      |      |        |
|                                                                      | 1.15 | 3.50 | 7.00   |
| 446-465,469,470,480: 457-Origin retold & updated. 480-(44 pgs.)      |      |      |        |
|                                                                      | .85  | 2.50 | 5.00   |
| 466-468,471-474,478,479-Rogers-a; 478-1st app. 3rd Clayface (Preston |      |      |        |
| Payne). 479-(44 pgs.)                                                 | 1.50 | 4.50 | 9.00   |
| 475,476-Joker-c/stories; Rogers-a                                    | 2.70 | 8.00 | 16.00  |
| 477-Neal Adams-a(r); Rogers-a, 3pgs.                                 | 1.70 | 5.00 | 10.00  |

481-(Combined with Batman Family, 12/78-1/79)(Begin $1.00, 68 pg. issues, ends #495); 481-495-Batgirl, Robin solo stories.

|                                                                      | 1.35 | 4.00 | 8.00   |
|----------------------------------------------------------------------|------|------|--------|

482-Starlin/Russell, Golden-a; The Demon begins (origin-r), ends #485 (by Ditko #483-485)

|                                                                      | .85  | 2.50 | 5.00   |
|----------------------------------------------------------------------|------|------|--------|

483-40th Anniversary issue; origin retold; Newton Batman begins

|                                                                      | 1.00 | 3.00 | 6.00   |
|----------------------------------------------------------------------|------|------|--------|

484-499,501-503,505-523: 484-Origin Robin. 485-Death of Batwoman. 487-The Odd Man by Ditko. 489-Robin/Batgirl team-up. 490-Black Lightning begins. 491(492 on inside). 518-1st app. Deadshot? 519-Last Batgirl. 521-Green Arrow series begins. 523-Solomon Grundy app.

|                                                                      | .60  | 1.80 | 3.60   |
|----------------------------------------------------------------------|------|------|--------|
| 500-($1.50)-Batman/Deadman team-up                                   | 1.15 | 3.50 | 7.00   |
| 504-Joker-c/story                                                    | 1.00 | 3.00 | 6.00   |
| 524-2nd app. Jason Todd (cameo)(3/83)                                | .70  | 2.00 | 4.00   |
| 525-3rd app. Jason Todd (See Batman #357)                            | .50  | 1.50 | 3.00   |

526-Batman's 500th app. in Detective Comics (68 pgs., $1.50); contains 55 pg. Joker story

|                                                                      | 1.70 | 5.00 | 10.00  |
|----------------------------------------------------------------------|------|------|--------|

527-531,533,534,536-568,571: 536-2nd Deadshot? 542-Jason Todd quits as Robin (becomes Robin again #547). 549,550-Alan Moore scripts (Gr. Arrow). 554-1st new Black Canary. 566-Batman villains profiled. 567-Harlan Ellison scripts

|                                                                      | .40  | 1.25 | 2.50   |
|----------------------------------------------------------------------|------|------|--------|
| 532,569,570-Joker-c/stories                                          | .85  | 2.50 | 5.00   |

535-Intro new Robin (Jason Todd)-1st appeared in Batman

|                                                                      | .85  | 2.50 | 5.00   |
|----------------------------------------------------------------------|------|------|--------|
| 572 (60 pgs., $1.25)-50th Anniversary                                | .60  | 1.80 | 3.60   |
| 573                                                                  | .40  | 1.25 | 2.50   |
| 574-Origin Batman & Jason Todd retold                                | .70  | 2.00 | 4.00   |
| 575-Year 2 begins, ends #578                                         | 2.50 | 7.50 | 15.00  |
| 576-578: McFarlane-c/a                                               | 2.00 | 6.00 | 12.00  |

579-597,601-610: 579-New bat wing logo. 589-595-(52 pgs.)-Each contain free 16 pg. Batman stories. 604-607-Mudpack storyline; 604,

| | Good | Fine | N-Mint |
|---|---|---|---|
| 607-Contain Batman mini-posters | .25 | .75 | 1.50 |
| 598-Double-size, $2.95; "Blind Justice" storyline begins by Batman movie writer Sam Hamm, ends 600 | 1.85 | 5.50 | 11.00 |
| 599 | 1.35 | 2.00 | 4.00 |
| 600-($2.95, 84 pgs.)-50th Anniversary issue; 1 pg. N. Adams pin-up, among others | .85 | 2.50 | 5.00 |
| 608-624 | | .50 | 1.00 |
| Annual 1(1988, $1.50) | .85 | 2.50 | 5.00 |
| Annual 2(1989, $2.00, 68 pgs.) | .70 | 2.00 | 4.00 |

**DICK TRACY**
Jan, 1948 - No. 24, Dec, 1949
Dell Publishing Co.

| | | | |
|---|---|---|---|
| 1-('34-r) | 38.00 | 115.00 | 265.00 |
| 2,3 | 20.00 | 60.00 | 140.00 |
| 4-10 | 17.00 | 51.00 | 120.00 |
| 11-18: 13-Bondage-c | 13.00 | 40.00 | 90.00 |
| 19-1st app. Sparkle Plenty, B.O. Plenty & Gravel Gertie in a 3-pg. strip not by Gould | 14.00 | 42.00 | 100.00 |
| 20-1st app. Sam Catchem c/a not by Gould | 11.50 | 34.00 | 80.00 |
| 21-24-Only 2 pg. Gould-a in each | 11.50 | 34.00 | 80.00 |

**DICK TRACY** (Continued from Dell series)
No. 25, Mar, 1950 - No. 145, April, 1961
Harvey Publications

| | | | |
|---|---|---|---|
| 25 | 14.00 | 42.00 | 100.00 |
| 26-28,30: 28-Bondage-c | 11.50 | 34.00 | 80.00 |
| 29-1st app. Gravel Gertie in a Gould-r | 14.00 | 42.00 | 100.00 |
| 31,32,34,35,37-40 | 10.00 | 30.00 | 70.00 |
| 33-"Measles the Teen-Age Dope Pusher" | 11.50 | 34.00 | 80.00 |
| 36-1st app. B.O. Plenty in a Gould-r | 11.50 | 34.00 | 80.00 |
| 41-50 | 8.50 | 25.50 | 60.00 |
| 51-56,58-80: 51-2 pgs Powell-a | 8.00 | 24.00 | 56.00 |
| 57-1st app. Sam Catchem, Gould-r | 10.00 | 30.00 | 70.00 |
| 81-99,101-140 | 6.00 | 18.00 | 42.00 |
| 100 | 6.50 | 19.50 | 45.00 |
| 141-145 (25 cents) | 5.70 | 17.00 | 40.00 |

**DISNEY'S DUCKTALES** (TV)
Oct, 1988 - No. 13, May, 1990 (1,2,9-11: $1.50; 3-10: 95 cents, color)
Gladstone Publishing

|  | Good | Fine | N-Mint |
|---|---|---|---|
| 1-Barks-r | .45 | 1.40 | 2.80 |
| 2,3: 2-Barks-r | .30 | .90 | 1.80 |
| 4,5: 4,5-Barks-r | .30 | .85 | 1.70 |
| 6-8: 6-Barks-r. 7-Barks-r(1 pg.) |  | .55 | 1.10 |
| 9-11: ($1.50, 52 pgs.) 9-11-Barks-r | .25 | .75 | 1.50 |
| 12,13 ($1.95, 68 pgs.): Barks-r. 12-r/F.C. #495 | .35 | 1.00 | 2.00 |

**DOCTOR STRANGE** (Formerly Strange Tales #1-168)
No. 169, 6/68 - No. 183, 11/69; 6/74 - No. 81, 2/87
Marvel Comics Group

| | | | |
|---|---|---|---|
| 169(#1)-Origin; panel swipe/M.D. #1-c | 6.50 | 19.50 | 45.00 |
| 170-183: 177-New costume | 2.30 | 7.00 | 16.00 |
| 1(6/74)-Brunner-c/a | 2.15 | 6.50 | 15.00 |
| 2 | 1.40 | 4.25 | 8.00 |
| 3-5 | .85 | 2.50 | 5.00 |
| 6-26: 21-Origin-r/Strange Tales #169 | .30 | .90 | 1.80 |
| 27-81: 56-Origin retold. 78-New Costume | | .60 | 1.20 |
| Annual 1(1976)-New Russell-a | .35 | 1.00 | 2.00 |
| Giant Size 1(11/75)-r/Strange Tales #164-168 | .35 | 1.00 | 2.00 |

**DOCTOR STRANGE, SORCERER SUPREME**
Nov, 1988 - Present (Mando paper, $1.25-$1.50, direct sales only)
Marvel Comics

| | | | |
|---|---|---|---|
| 1 ($1.25) | .85 | 2.50 | 5.00 |
| 2-14,16-24 ($1.50): 3-New Defenders app. 5-Guice-a(p) begins. 11- Hobgoblin app. | .25 | .75 | 1.50 |
| 15-Unauthorized Amy Grant photo-c | 1.10 | 3.25 | 6.50 |

**DOLL MAN** (Also see Feature Comics #27)
Fall, 1941 - No. 7, Fall, '43; No. 8, Spring, '46 - No. 47, Oct, 1953
Quality Comics Group

| | | | |
|---|---|---|---|
| 1-Dollman & Justin Wright begin | 100.00 | 300.00 | 700.00 |
| 2-The Dragon begins; Crandall-a(5) | 52.00 | 155.00 | 365.00 |

|  | Good | Fine | N-Mint |
|---|---|---|---|
| 3 | 37.00 | 110.00 | 260.00 |
| 4 | 27.00 | 80.00 | 190.00 |
| 5-Crandall-a | 24.00 | 73.00 | 170.00 |
| 6,7(1943) | 19.00 | 58.00 | 135.00 |
| 8(1946)-1st app. Torchy by Bill Ward | 21.50 | 64.00 | 150.00 |
| 9 | 16.50 | 50.00 | 115.00 |
| 10-20 | 13.00 | 40.00 | 90.00 |
| 21-30 | 11.50 | 34.00 | 80.00 |
| 31-36,38,40: Jeb Rivers app. #32-34 | 9.30 | 28.00 | 65.00 |
| 37-Origin Dollgirl; Dollgirl bondage-c | 12.00 | 36.00 | 85.00 |
| 39-"Narcotics . . . the Death Drug"-c-/story | 10.00 | 30.00 | 70.00 |
| 41-47 | 6.50 | 19.50 | 45.00 |

*Donald Duck #250, © The Disney Company*

**DONALD DUCK** (Walt Disney's . . . #262 on)
1940 - #84, 9-11/62; #85, 12/62 - #245, 1984; #246, 10/86 - #279, 5/90
Dell Publishing Co./Gold Key No. 85-216/Whitman No. 217-245/Gladstone Publishing No. 246 on

|  | Good | Fine | N-Mint |
|---|---|---|---|
| 4-Color 4(1940)-Daily 1939 strip-r by Al Taliaferro | | | |
| | 328.00 | 985.00 | 2300.00 |
| Large Feature Comic 16(1/41?)-1940 Sunday strips-r in B&W | | | |
| | 157.00 | 470.00 | 1100.00 |
| Large Feature Comic 20('41)-Comic Paint Book, r-single panels from Large Feat. 16 at top of each page to color; daily strip-r across bottom of each page | 215.00 | 645.00 | 1500.00 |
| 4-Color 9('42)-"Finds Pirate Gold";-64 pgs. by Carl Barks & Jack Hannah (pgs. 1,2,5,12-40 are by Barks, his 1st comic book work; © 8/17/42) | | | |
| | 370.00 | 1115.00 | 2600.00 |
| 4-Color 29(9/43)-"Mummy's Ring" by Carl Barks; reprinted in Donald Duck Adventures #14 | 243.00 | 730.00 | 1700.00 |
| *(Prices vary widely on all above books)* | | | |
| 4-Color 62(1/45)-"Frozen Gold"; 52 pgs. by Carl Barks, reprinted in Donald Duck Adventures #4 | 120.00 | 360.00 | 840.00 |
| 4-Color 108(1946)-"Terror of the River"; 52 pgs. by Carl Barks | | | |
| | 90.00 | 270.00 | 630.00 |
| 4-Color 147(5/47)-in "Volcano Valley" by Carl Barks | | | |
| | 60.00 | 180.00 | 420.00 |
| 4-Color 159(8/47)-in "The Ghost of the Grotto"; 52 pgs. by Carl Barks (2); reprinted in D. Duck Advs. #9 | 54.00 | 160.00 | 375.00 |
| 4-Color 178(12/47)-1st Uncle Scrooge by Carl Barks | | | |
| | 64.00 | 192.00 | 450.00 |
| 4-Color 189(6/48)-by Carl Barks | 54.00 | 160.00 | 375.00 |
| 4-Color 199(10/48)-by Carl Barks | 54.00 | 160.00 | 375.00 |
| 4-Color 203(12/48)-by Carl Barks | 36.00 | 108.00 | 250.00 |
| 4-Color 223(4/49)-by Carl Barks | 50.00 | 150.00 | 350.00 |
| 4-Color 238(8/49), 256(12/49)-by Barks | 27.00 | 81.00 | 190.00 |
| 4-Color 263(2/50)-Two Barks stories | 27.00 | 81.00 | 190.00 |
| 4-Color 275(5/50), 282(7/50), 291(9/50), 300(11/50)-All by Carl Barks. 291 r/in Donald Duck Adventures #16 | 25.00 | 75.00 | 175.00 |
| 4-Color 308(1/51), 318(3/51)-by Barks | 21.00 | 63.00 | 147.00 |
| 4-Color 328(5/51)-by Carl Barks | 23.00 | 70.00 | 160.00 |
| 4-Color 339(7-8/51), 379-not by Barks | 4.35 | 13.00 | 30.00 |
| 4-Color 348(9-10/51), 356,394-Barks-c only | 6.00 | 18.00 | 42.00 |
| 4-Color 367(1-2/52)-by Barks | 20.00 | 60.00 | 140.00 |
| 4-Color 408(7-8/52), 422(9-10/52)-All by Carl Barks | | | |
| | 20.00 | 60.00 | 140.00 |
| 26(11-12/52)-In "Trick or Treat"; Barks-a | 22.00 | 65.00 | 154.00 |
| 27-30-Barks-c only | 4.30 | 13.00 | 30.00 |

|  | Good | Fine | N-Mint |
|---|---|---|---|
| 31-40 | 2.65 | 8.00 | 18.00 |
| 41-44,47-50 | 2.00 | 6.00 | 14.00 |
| 45-Barks-a, 6 pgs. | 7.00 | 21.00 | 50.00 |
| 46-"Secret of Hondorica" by Barks, 24 pgs. | 8.00 | 24.00 | 56.00 |
| 51-Barks, 1/2 pg. | 1.70 | 5.00 | 12.00 |
| 52-"Lost Peg-Leg Mine" by Barks, 10 pgs. | 6.50 | 19.50 | 45.00 |
| 53,55-59 | 1.60 | 4.80 | 11.00 |
| 54-"Forbidden Valley" by Barks, 26 pgs. | 7.50 | 22.00 | 52.00 |
| 60-"Donald Duck & the Titanic Ants" by Barks, 20 pgs. plus 6 more pgs. | | | |
|  | 6.50 | 19.50 | 45.00 |
| 61-67,69,70 | 1.30 | 4.00 | 9.00 |
| 68-Barks-a, 5 pgs. | 3.75 | 11.25 | 26.00 |
| 71-Barks-r, 1/2 pg. | 1.50 | 4.50 | 10.00 |
| 72-78,80,82-97,99,100: 96-Donald Duck Album | 1.15 | 3.50 | 8.00 |
| 79,81-Barks-a, 1pg. | 1.50 | 4.50 | 10.00 |
| 98-Reprints #46 (Barks) | 2.15 | 6.50 | 15.00 |
| 101-133: 112-1st Moby Duck | .85 | 2.50 | 6.00 |
| 134-Barks-r/#52 & WDC&S 194 | 1.00 | 3.00 | 7.00 |
| 135-Barks-r/WDC&S 198, 19 pgs. | .70 | 2.00 | 5.00 |
| 136-153,155,156,158 | .50 | 1.50 | 3.00 |
| 154-Barks-r(#46) | .70 | 2.00 | 5.00 |
| 157,159,160,164: 157-Barks-r(#45). 159-Reprints/WDC&S #192 (10 pgs.). | | | |
| 160-Barks-r(#26). 164-Barks-r(#79) | .40 | 1.25 | 2.50 |
| 161-163,165-170 | .25 | .75 | 1.50 |
| 171-173,175-187,189-191 | | .60 | 1.20 |
| 174,188: 174-R/4-Color #394. 188-Barks-r/#68 | .35 | 1.00 | 2.00 |
| 192-Barks-r(40 pgs.) from Donald Duck #60 & WDC&S #226,234 (52 pgs.). | | | |
|  | .40 | 1.25 | 2.50 |
| 193-200,202-207,209-211,213-218: 217 has 216 on-c | | | |
|  | | .50 | 1.00 |
| 201,208,212: 201-Barks-r/Christmas Parade #26, 16 pgs. 208-Barks-r/ #60 | | | |
| (6 pgs.). 212-Barks-r/WDC&S #130 | .35 | 1.00 | 2.00 |
| 219-Barks-r/WDC&S #106,107, 10 pgs. ea. | | .60 | 1.20 |
| 220-227,231-245 | | .35 | .70 |
| 228-230: 228-Barks-r/F.C. #275. 229-Barks-r/F.C. #282. 230-Barks-r/ #52 & | | | |
| WDC&S #194 | .25 | .75 | 1.50 |
| 246-(1st Gladstone issue)-Barks-r/FC #422 | 1.25 | 3.75 | 7.70 |
| 247-249: 248-Barks-r/DD #54. 249-Barks-r/DD #26 | | | |
|  | .45 | 1.40 | 2.80 |
| 250-Barks-r/4-Color #9, 64 pgs. | 1.10 | 3.30 | 6.60 |

|  | Good | Fine | N-Mint |
|---|---|---|---|
| 251-256: 251-Barks-r/'45 Firestone. 254-Barks-r/FC #328. 256-Barks-r/ FC | | | |
| #147 | .35 | 1.10 | 2.20 |
| 257-Barks-r/Vac. Parade #1 (52 pgs.) | .55 | 1.65 | 3.30 |
| 258-260 | .30 | .85 | 1.70 |
| 261-277: 261-Barks-r/FC #300. 275-Kelly-r/FC #92 | | .55 | 1.10 |
| 278 ($1.95, 68 pgs.)-Rosa-a; Barks-r/FC 263 | .35 | 1.00 | 2.00 |
| 279 ($1.95, 68 pgs.)-Rosa-c; Barks-r | .35 | 1.00 | 2.00 |

**DONALD DUCK ADVENTURES** (Walt Disney's . . . #4 on)
Nov, 1987 - No. 20, April, 1990
Gladstone Publishing

|  | Good | Fine | N-Mint |
|---|---|---|---|
| 1 | .55 | 1.65 | 3.30 |
| 2-r/F.C. #308 | .35 | 1.10 | 2.20 |
| 3,4,6,7,9-11,13,15-18: 3-r/F.C. #223. 4-r/F.C. #62. 9-r/F.C. #159. 16-r/F.C. | | | |
| #291; Rosa-c. 18-r/F.C. #318; Rosa-c | .30 | .85 | 1.70 |
| 5,8-Don Rosa-a | .35 | 1.10 | 2.20 |
| 12($1.50, 52 pgs)-Rosa-c/a w/Barks poster | .35 | 1.10 | 2.20 |
| 14-r/F.C. #29, "Mummy's Ring" | .40 | 1.25 | 2.50 |
| 19 ($1.95, 68 pgs.)-Barks-r/F.C. #199 | .35 | 1.00 | 2.00 |
| 20 ($1.95, 68 pgs.)-Barks-r/F.C. #189 plus-c(r) | .35 | 1.00 | 2.00 |

**DON WINSLOW OF THE NAVY** (See TV Teens; Movie, Radio, TV)
2/43 - #64, 12/48; #65, 1/51 - #69, 9/51; #70, 3/55 - #73, 9/55
Fawcett Publications/Charlton No. 70 on

|  | Good | Fine | N-Mint |
|---|---|---|---|
| 1-(68 pgs.)-Captain Marvel on cover | 42.00 | 125.00 | 290.00 |
| 2 | 21.00 | 62.00 | 145.00 |
| 3 | 14.00 | 42.00 | 100.00 |
| 4,5 | 11.50 | 34.00 | 80.00 |
| 6-Flag-c | 9.30 | 28.00 | 65.00 |
| 7-10: 8-Last 68 pg. issue? | 7.00 | 21.00 | 50.00 |
| 11-20 | 5.00 | 15.00 | 35.00 |
| 21-40 | 3.50 | 10.50 | 24.00 |
| 41-63 | 2.65 | 8.00 | 18.00 |
| 64(12/48)-Matt Baker-a | 2.85 | 8.50 | 20.00 |
| 65(1/51) - 69(9/51): All photo-c. 65-Flying Saucer attack | | | |
| | 3.70 | 11.00 | 26.00 |
| 70(3/55)-73: 70-73 r-/#26,58 & 59 | 2.30 | 7.00 | 16.00 |

**DOOM PATROL, THE** (My Greatest Adv. No. 1-85; see Showcase)
No. 86, 3/64 - No. 121, 9-10/68; 2/73 - No. 124, 6-7/73
National Periodical Publications

|  | Good | Fine | N-Mint |
|---|---|---|---|
| 86-1 pg. origin | 6.50 | 19.50 | 45.00 |
| 87-99: 88-Origin The Chief. 91-Intro. Mento. 99-Intro. Beast Boy who later became the Changeling in the New Teen Titans | | | |
|  | 4.30 | 13.00 | 30.00 |
| 100-Origin Beast Boy; Robot-Maniac series begins | | | |
|  | 5.25 | 16.00 | 37.00 |
| 101-110: 102-Challengers/Unknown app. 105-Robot-Maniac series ends. | | | |
| 106-Negative Man begins (origin) | 2.35 | 7.00 | 16.00 |
| 111-120 | 1.85 | 5.50 | 13.00 |
| 121-Death of Doom Patrol; Orlando-c | 6.50 | 19.50 | 45.00 |
| 122-124(reprints) | .35 | 1.00 | 2.00 |

**DOOM PATROL**
Oct, 1987 - Present
DC Comics

|  | Good | Fine | N-Mint |
|---|---|---|---|
| 1 | .40 | 1.25 | 2.50 |
| 2-9: 3-1st app. Lodestone. 4-1st app. Karma. 8-Art Adams-c(i) | | | |
|  |  | .50 | 1.00 |
| 10-18 ($1.00): 15,16-A. Adams-c(i). 18-Invasion |  | .50 | 1.00 |
| 19-New format, direct sale begins ($1.50) | .50 | 1.50 | 3.00 |
| 20-38 | .25 | .75 | 1.50 |
| . . . And Suicide Squad Special 1 ($1.50, 3/88) | | | |
|  | .35 | 1.00 | 2.00 |
| Annual 1 ('88, $1.50) | .25 | .75 | 1.50 |

**DRAGONLANCE**
Dec, 1988 - Present ($1.25-$1.50, color, Mando paper)
DC Comics

|  | Good | Fine | N-Mint |
|---|---|---|---|
| 1: Based on TSR game | 1.00 | 3.00 | 6.00 |
| 2 | .70 | 2.00 | 4.00 |
| 3-5 | .60 | 1.75 | 3.50 |
| 6-10: 6-Begin $1.50-c | .50 | 1.50 | 3.00 |
| 11-15 | .35 | 1.00 | 2.00 |
| 16-26 | .25 | .75 | 1.50 |

**DURANGO KID, THE**
Oct-Nov, 1949 - No. 41, Oct-Nov, 1955 (All 36 pgs.)
Magazine Enterprises

|  | Good | Fine | N-Mint |
|---|---|---|---|
| 1-Charles Starrett photo-c; Durango Kid & his horse Raider begin; Dan Brand & Tipi (origin) begin by Frazetta & continue through #16 | | | |
|  | 37.00 | 110.00 | 260.00 |
| 2(Starrett photo-c) | 25.00 | 75.00 | 175.00 |
| 3-5(All-Starrett photo-c) | 21.50 | 64.00 | 150.00 |
| 6-10 | 11.50 | 34.00 | 80.00 |
| 11-16-Last Frazetta issue | 8.50 | 25.50 | 60.00 |
| 17-Origin Durango Kid | 11.00 | 32.00 | 75.00 |
| 18-Fred Meagher-a on Dan Brand begins | 5.50 | 16.50 | 38.00 |
| 19-30: 19-Guardineer c/a (3) begin, end #41. 23-Intro. The Red Scorpion | | | |
|  | 5.50 | 16.50 | 38.00 |
| 31-Red Scorpion returns | 4.50 | 14.00 | 32.00 |
| 32-41-Bolle/Frazetta-a (Dan Brand) | 6.00 | 18.00 | 42.00 |

# E

**EERIE** (Strange Worlds No. 18 on)
No. 1, Jan, 1947; No. 1, May-June, 1951 - No. 17, Aug-Sept, 1954
Avon Periodicals

|  | Good | Fine | N-Mint |
|---|---|---|---|
| 1(1947)-1st horror comic; Kubert, Fugitani-a; bondage-c | | | |
|  | 38.00 | 115.00 | 265.00 |
| 1(1951)-Reprints story/'47 No. 1 | 21.50 | 64.00 | 150.00 |
| 2-Wood c/a; bondage-c | 24.00 | 70.00 | 165.00 |
| 3-Wood-c; Kubert, Wood/Orlando-a | 24.00 | 70.00 | 165.00 |
| 4,5-Wood-c | 21.50 | 64.00 | 150.00 |
| 6,13,14 | 8.00 | 24.00 | 56.00 |
| 7-Wood/Orlando-c; Kubert-a | 14.00 | 42.00 | 100.00 |
| 8-Kinstler-a; bondage-c; Phantom Witch Doctor story | | | |
|  | 8.50 | 25.50 | 60.00 |
| 9-Kubert-a; Check-c | 10.00 | 30.00 | 70.00 |
| 10,11-Kinstler-a | 8.00 | 24.00 | 56.00 |
| 12-25-pg. Dracula story from novel | 11.00 | 32.00 | 75.00 |
| 15-Reprints No. 1('51)minus-c (bondage) | 5.00 | 15.00 | 35.00 |
| 16-Wood-a r-/No. 2 | 6.50 | 19.50 | 45.00 |
| 17-Wood/Orlando & Kubert-a; reprints #3 minus inside & outside Wood-c | | | |
|  | 8.50 | 25.50 | 60.00 |

**80 PAGE GIANT** (. . . Magazine No. 1-15) (25 cents)
8/64 - No. 15, 10/65; No. 16, 11/65 - No. 89, 7/71 (All reprints)
National Periodical Publications (#1-56: 84 pgs.; #57-89: 68 pages)

|  | Good | Fine | N-Mint |
|---|---|---|---|
| 1-Superman Annual | 9.00 | 27.00 | 72.00 |
| 2-Jimmy Olsen | 3.75 | 11.25 | 30.00 |
| 3-Lois Lane | 2.15 | 6.50 | 17.00 |
| 4-Flash-G.A.-r; Infantino-a | 2.15 | 6.50 | 17.00 |
| 5-Batman; has Sunday newspaper strip; Catwoman-r; Batman's Life Story-r (25th anniversary special) | 3.15 | 9.50 | 25.00 |
| 6-Superman | 2.15 | 6.50 | 17.00 |
| 7-Sgt. Rock's Prize Battle Tales; Kubert c/a | 2.15 | 6.50 | 17.00 |
| 8-More Secret Origins-origins of JLA, Aquaman, Robin, Atom, & Superman; Infantino-a | 8.25 | 24.75 | 66.00 |
| 9-Flash(reprints Flash #123)-Infantino-a | 2.15 | 6.50 | 17.00 |

180

*80-Page Giant #5, © DC Comics*

| | Good | Fine | N-Mint |
|---|---|---|---|
| 10-Superboy | 2.15 | 6.50 | 17.00 |
| 11-Superman-All Luthor issue | 2.15 | 6.50 | 17.00 |
| 12-Batman; has Sunday newspaper strip | 2.65 | 8.00 | 21.00 |
| 13-Jimmy Olsen | 2.15 | 6.50 | 17.00 |
| 14-Lois Lane | 2.15 | 6.50 | 17.00 |
| 15-Superman and Batman; Joker-c/story | 3.15 | 9.50 | 25.00 |

**ELEKTRA: ASSASIN**
Aug, 1986 - No. 8, Mar, 1987 (limited series) (Adults)
Epic Comics (Marvel)

| | | | |
|---|---|---|---|
| 1-Miller scripts in all | .85 | 2.50 | 5.00 |
| 2 | .70 | 2.00 | 4.00 |
| 3-7 | .50 | 1.50 | 3.00 |
| 8 | .70 | 2.00 | 4.00 |

**ELEKTRA SAGA, THE**
Feb, 1984 - No. 4, June, 1984 ($2.00 cover; Baxter paper)
Marvel Comics Group

|  | Good | Fine | N-Mint |
|---|---|---|---|
| 1-4-r/Daredevil 168-190; Miller-c/a | 1.00 | 3.00 | 6.00 |

**EXCALIBUR** (Also see Marvel Comics Presents #31)
Oct, 1988 - Present ($1.50-$1.75, Baxter)
Marvel Comics

| | Good | Fine | N-Mint |
|---|---|---|---|
| 1($1.50)-X-Men spin-of | 1.70 | 5.00 | 10.00 |
| 2 | 1.00 | 3.00 | 6.00 |
| 3,4 | .70 | 2.00 | 4.00 |
| 5-10 | .50 | 1.50 | 3.00 |
| 11-15: 10,11-Rogers/Austin-a | .35 | 1.00 | 2.00 |
| 16-32 | .25 | .75 | 1.50 |
| . . . The Sword is Drawn nn ($3.25, 4/88) | 2.50 | 7.50 | 15.00 |
| . . . The Sword is Drawn nn ($3.50, 10/88)-2nd printing | | | |
| | 1.00 | 3.00 | 6.00 |
| . . . The Sword is Drawn nn ($4.50, 12/89)-3rd printing | | | |
| | .75 | 2.25 | 4.50 |
| . . . Mojo Mayhem nn ($4.50, 12/89)-Art Adams/Austin-c/a | | | |
| | .85 | 2.50 | 5.00 |

**EXCITING COMICS**
April, 1940 - No. 69, Sept, 1949
Nedor/Better Publications/Standard Comics

| | Good | Fine | N-Mint |
|---|---|---|---|
| 1-Origin The Mask, Jim Hatfield, Sgt. Bill King, Dan Williams begin | | | |
| | 64.00 | 193.00 | 450.00 |
| 2-The Sphinx begins; The Masked Rider app. | | | |
| | 28.50 | 85.00 | 200.00 |
| 3 | 24.00 | 73.00 | 170.00 |
| 4 | 19.00 | 57.00 | 135.00 |
| 5 | 15.00 | 45.00 | 105.00 |
| 6-8 | 12.00 | 36.00 | 84.00 |
| 9-Origin/1st app. of The Black Terror & sidekick Tim, begin series | | | |
| | 64.00 | 193.00 | 450.00 |
| 10-13 | 27.00 | 81.00 | 190.00 |

|                                                                              | Good  | Fine  | N-Mint |
|------------------------------------------------------------------------------|-------|-------|--------|
| 14-Last Sphinx, Dan Williams                                                 | 17.00 | 51.00 | 120.00 |
| 15-The Liberator begins (origin)                                             | 22.00 | 65.00 | 154.00 |
| 16-20: 20-The Mask ends                                                      | 12.00 | 36.00 | 84.00  |
| 21,23-30: 28-Crime Crusader begins, ends #58                                 |       |       |        |
|                                                                              | 11.50 | 34.00 | 80.00  |
| 22-Origin The Eaglet; The American Eagle begins                              |       |       |        |
|                                                                              | 12.00 | 36.00 | 84.00  |
| 31-38: 35-Liberator ends, not in 31-33                                       | 11.00 | 32.00 | 75.00  |
| 39-Origin Kara, Jungle Princess                                             | 16.00 | 48.00 | 110.00 |
| 40-50: 42-The Scarab begins. 49-Last Kara, Jungle Princess. 50- Last         |       |       |        |
|   American Eagle                                                             | 13.00 | 40.00 | 90.00  |
| 51-Miss Masque begins                                                        | 17.00 | 51.00 | 120.00 |
| 52-54: Miss Masque ends                                                      | 13.00 | 40.00 | 90.00  |
| 55-Judy of the Jungle begins (origin), ends #69; 1 pg. Ingels-a              |       |       |        |
|                                                                              | 17.00 | 51.00 | 120.00 |
| 56-58: All airbrush-c                                                        | 16.00 | 48.00 | 110.00 |
| 59-Frazetta art in Caniff style; signed Frank Frazeta (one t), 9 pgs.        |       |       |        |
|                                                                              | 21.50 | 64.00 | 150.00 |
| 60-66: 60-Rick Howard, the Mystery Rider begins. 66-Robinson/Meskin-a        |       |       |        |
|                                                                              | 12.00 | 36.00 | 84.00  |
| 67-69                                                                        | 8.00  | 24.00 | 56.00  |

# F

**FAMOUS FUNNIES**
1933 - No. 218, July, 1955
Eastern Color

|  | Good | Fine | N-Mint |
|---|---|---|---|
| **A Carnival of Comics** (probably the second comic book), 36 pgs., no date given, no publisher, no number; contains strip reprints of The Bungle Family, Dixie Dugan, Hairbreadth Harry, Joe Palooka, Keeping Up With the Jones, Mutt & Jeff, Reg'lar Fellers, S'Matter Pop, Strange As It Seems, and others. This book was sold by M. C. Gaines to Wheatena, Milk-O-Malt, John Wanamaker, Kinney Shoe Stores, & others to be given away as premiums and radio giveaways (1933). | 300.00 | 900.00 | 2100.00 |
| **Series 1**-(Very rare) (nd-early 1934) (68 pgs.) No publisher given (Eastern Color Printing Co.); sold in chain stores for 10 cents. 35,000 print run. Contains Sunday strip reprints of Mutt & Jeff, Reg'lar Fellers, Nipper, Hairbreadth Harry, Strange As It Seems, Joe Palooka, Dixie Dugan, The Nebbs, Keeping Up With the Jones, and others. Inside front and back covers and pages 1-16 of Famous Funnies Series 1, #s 49-64 reprinted from **Famous Funnies, A Carnival of Comics,** and most of pages 17-48 reprinted from **Funnies on Parade.** This was the first comic book sold. | 600.00 | 1800.00 | 4200.00 |
| **No. 1** (Rare) (7/34-on stands 5/34) - Eastern Color Printing Co. First monthly newsstand comic book. Contains Sunday strip reprints of Toonerville Folks, Mutt & Jeff, Hairbreadth Harry, S'Matter Pop, Nipper, Dixie Dugan, The Bungle Family, Connie, Ben Webster, Tailspin Tommy, The Nebbs, Joe Palooka, & others. | 450.00 | 1350.00 | 3150.00 |
| 2 (Rare) | 150.00 | 375.00 | 900.00 |
| 3-Buck Rogers Sunday strip reprints by Rick Yager begins, ends #218; not in No. 191-208; the number of the 1st strip reprinted is pg. 190, Series No. 1 | 200.00 | 500.00 | 1200.00 |
| 4 | 71.00 | 215.00 | 500.00 |
| 5 | 57.00 | 170.00 | 400.00 |
| 6-10 | 46.00 | 140.00 | 325.00 |
| 11,12,18-Four pgs. of Buck Rogers in each issue, completes stories in Buck Rogers #1 which lacks these pages; #18-Two pgs. of Buck Rogers reprinted in Daisy Comics #1 | 40.00 | 120.00 | 280.00 |

184

|  | Good | Fine | N-Mint |
|---|---|---|---|
| 13-17,19,20: 14-Has two Buck Rogers panels missing. 17-1st Christmas-c on a newsstand comic | 29.00 | 90.00 | 205.00 |
| 21,23-30: 27-War on Crime begins; part photo-c. 29-Xmas-c | 21.00 | 62.00 | 145.00 |
| 22-Four pgs. of Buck Rogers needed to complete stories in Buck Rogers #1 | 23.00 | 70.00 | 160.00 |
| 31,32,34,36,37,39,40 | 16.00 | 48.00 | 110.00 |
| 33-Careers of Baby Face Nelson & John Dillinger traced | 16.00 | 48.00 | 110.00 |
| 35-Two pgs. Buck Rogers omitted in Buck Rogers #2 | 17.00 | 51.00 | 120.00 |
| 38-Full color portrait of Buck Rogers | 16.00 | 48.00 | 110.00 |
| 41-60: 41,53-Xmas-c. 55-Last bottom panel, pg. 4 in Buck Rogers redrawn in Buck Rogers #3 | 11.00 | 32.00 | 75.00 |
| 61-64,66,67,69,70 | 9.30 | 28.00 | 65.00 |
| 65,68-Two pgs. Kirby-a-"Lightnin' & the Lone Rider" | 10.00 | 30.00 | 70.00 |
| 71,73,77-80: 80-Buck Rogers story continues from Buck Rogers #5 | 8.00 | 24.00 | 56.00 |
| 72-Speed Spaulding begins by Marvin Bradley (artist), ends #88. This series was written by Edwin Balmer & Philip Wylie and later appeared as film & book "When Worlds Collide" | 8.50 | 25.50 | 60.00 |
| 74-76-Two pgs. Kirby-a in all | 7.00 | 21.00 | 50.00 |
| 81-Origin Invisible Scarlet O'Neil; strip begins #82, ends #167 | 6.00 | 18.00 | 42.00 |
| 82-Buck Rogers-c | 7.00 | 21.00 | 50.00 |
| 83-87,90: 87 has last Buck Rogers full page-r. 90-Bondage-c | 6.00 | 18.00 | 42.00 |
| 88-Buck Rogers in "Moon's End" by Calkins, 2 pgs. (not reprints). Beginning with #88, all Buck Rogers pages have rearranged panels | 6.50 | 19.50 | 45.00 |
| 89-Origin Fearless Flint, the Flint Man | 6.50 | 19.50 | 45.00 |
| 91-93,95,96,98-99,101-110: 105-Series 2 begins (Strip Page #1) | 4.50 | 14.00 | 32.00 |
| 94-Buck Rogers in "Solar Holocaust" by Calkins, 3 pgs. (not reprints) | 5.50 | 16.50 | 38.00 |
| 97-War Bond promotion, Buck Rogers by Calkins, 2 pgs. (not reprints) | 5.50 | 16.50 | 38.00 |
| 100 | 5.50 | 16.50 | 38.00 |
| 111-130 | 3.70 | 11.00 | 26.00 |

| | Good | Fine | N-Mint |
|---|---|---|---|
| 131-150: 137-Strip page No. 110 1/2 omitted | 2.65 | 8.00 | 18.00 |
| 151-162,164-168 | 2.30 | 7.00 | 16.00 |
| 163-St. Valentine's Day-c | 2.85 | 8.50 | 20.00 |
| 169,170-Two text illos. by Williamson, his 1st comic book work | | | |
| | 5.50 | 16.50 | 38.00 |
| 171-180: 171-Strip pgs. 227,229,230, Series 2 omitted. 172-Strip Pg. 232 | | | |
| omitted | 2.30 | 7.00 | 16.00 |
| 181-190: Buck Rogers ends with start of strip pg. 302, Series 2 | | | |
| | 1.85 | 5.50 | 13.00 |
| 191-197,199,201,203,206-208: No Buck Rogers | | | |
| | 1.60 | 4.70 | 11.00 |
| 198,202,205-One pg. Frazetta ads; no Buck Rogers | | | |
| | 2.00 | 6.00 | 14.00 |
| 200-Frazetta 1 pg. ad | 2.15 | 6.50 | 15.00 |
| 204-Used in **POP**, pgs. 79,99 | 2.15 | 6.50 | 15.00 |
| 209-Buck Rogers begins with strip pg. 480, Series 2; Frazetta-c | | | |
| | 24.00 | 73.00 | 170.00 |
| 210-216: Frazetta-c. 211-Buck Rogers ads by Anderson begins, ends #217. | | | |
| #215-Contains B. Rogers strip pg. 515-518, series 2 followed by pgs. | | | |
| 179-181, Series 3 | 24.00 | 73.00 | 170.00 |
| 217,218-Buck Rogers ends with pg. 199, Series 2 | | | |
| | 3.15 | 6.50 | 15.00 |

**FANTASTIC COMICS**
Dec, 1939 - No. 23, Nov, 1941
Fox Features Syndicate

| | Good | Fine | N-Mint |
|---|---|---|---|
| 1-Intro/Origin Samson; Stardust, The Super Wizard, Space Smith, Sub Saunders (by Kiefer), Capt. Kidd begin | 120.00 | 360.00 | 835.00 |
| 2-Powell text illos | 59.00 | 178.00 | 415.00 |
| 3-5: 3-Powell text illos | 48.00 | 145.00 | 340.00 |
| 6-9: 6,7-Simon-c | 38.00 | 115.00 | 270.00 |
| 10-Intro/origin David, Samson's aide | 29.00 | 88.00 | 205.00 |
| 11-17: 16-Stardust ends | 23.00 | 70.00 | 160.00 |
| 18-Intro. Black Fury & sidekick Chuck; ends #23 | | | |
| | 26.00 | 77.00 | 180.00 |
| 19,20,22 | 23.00 | 70.00 | 160.00 |
| 21,23: 21-The Banshee begins(origin); ends #23; Hitler-c. 23-Origin The Gladiator | 26.00 | 77.00 | 180.00 |

*Fantastic Four #238, © Marvel Comics*

**FANTASTIC FOUR**
Nov, 1961 - Present
Marvel Comics Group

|  | Good | Fine | N-Mint |
|---|---|---|---|
| 1-Origin & 1st app. The Fantastic Four; origin The Mole Man | | | |
|  | 330.00 | 1320.00 | 3300.00 |
| 1-Golden Record Comic Set-r | 7.15 | 21.50 | 50.00 |
| with record. . . . | 14.30 | 43.00 | 100.00 |
| 2-Vs. The Skrulls (last 10 cent issue) | 123.00 | 370.00 | 860.00 |
| 3-Fantastic Four don costumes & establish Headquarters; brief 1 pg. origin; intro The Fantasticar | 94.00 | 282.00 | 655.00 |
| 4-1st Silver Age Sub-Mariner app. | 95.00 | 285.00 | 660.00 |
| 5-Origin & 1st app. Doctor Doom | 95.00 | 285.00 | 660.00 |
| 6-Sub-Mariner, Dr. Doom team up; 1st Marvel villain team-up | | | |
|  | 58.00 | 174.00 | 410.00 |
| 7-10: 7-1st app. Kurrgo. 8-1st app. Puppet-Master & Alicia Masters | | | |
|  | 44.00 | 132.00 | 310.00 |

|  | Good | Fine | N-Mint |
|---|---|---|---|
| 11-Origin The Impossible Man | 30.00 | 90.00 | 210.00 |
| 12-Fantastic Four Vs. The Hulk | 34.00 | 102.00 | 235.00 |
| 13-Intro. The Watcher; 1st app. The Red Ghost | | | |
| | 26.00 | 78.00 | 180.00 |
| 14-19: 17-Early Ant-Man app. (7/63). 18-Origin The Super Skrull. 19-Intro. Rama-Tut | | | |
| | 18.00 | 54.00 | 125.00 |
| 20-Origin The Molecule Man | 18.50 | 55.50 | 130.00 |
| 21-24,27: 21-Intro. The Hate Monger | 10.00 | 30.00 | 70.00 |
| 25,26-The Thing vs. The Hulk | 19.00 | 57.00 | 133.00 |
| 28-X-Men app. | 11.50 | 34.50 | 80.00 |
| 29,30: 30-Intro. Diablo | 7.00 | 21.00 | 48.00 |
| 31-40: 31-Avengers x-over. 33-1st app. Attuma. 35-Intro/1st app. Dragon Man. 36-Intro/1st app. Madam Medusa & the Frightful Four (Sandman, Wizard, Paste Pot Pete). 39-Wood inks on Daredevil | | | |
| | 5.15 | 15.50 | 36.00 |
| 41-47: 41-43-Frightful Four app. 44-Intro. Gorgan. 45-Intro. The Inhumans | | | |
| | 3.60 | 11.00 | 25.00 |
| 48-Origin/1st app. The Silver Surfer & Galactus (3/66) | | | |
| | 26.00 | 78.00 | 180.00 |
| 49-2nd app. Silver Surfer | 7.50 | 22.50 | 52.00 |
| 50-Silver Surfer battles Galactus | 12.15 | 36.50 | 85.00 |
| 51-54: 52-Intro. The Black Panther; origin-#53. 54-Inhumans cameo | | | |
| | 2.85 | 8.50 | 25.00 |
| 55-60: Silver Surfer x-over. 59,60-Inhumans cameo | | | |
| | 3.50 | 10.50 | 24.00 |
| 61-65,68-70: 61-Silver Surfer cameo | 2.65 | 8.00 | 18.00 |
| 66,67-1st app. & origin Him (Warlock) | 2.85 | 8.50 | 20.00 |
| 71,73,78-80 | 1.50 | 4.50 | 10.00 |
| 72,74-77: Silver Surfer app. in all | 2.00 | 6.00 | 14.00 |
| 81-88: 81-Crystal joins & dons costume. 82,83-Inhumans app. 84-87-Dr. Doom app. 88-Last 12 cent issue | 1.30 | 4.00 | 9.00 |
| 89-99,101,102 | 1.00 | 3.00 | 7.00 |
| 100 | 4.30 | 13.00 | 30.00 |
| 103-111: 108-Last Kirby issue | 1.00 | 3.00 | 6.00 |
| 112-Hulk Vs. Thing | 2.15 | 6.50 | 15.00 |
| 113-120 | .85 | 2.50 | 5.00 |
| 121-123-Silver Surfer x-over | 1.00 | 3.00 | 6.00 |
| 124-127,129-149,151-154,158-160: 126-Origin F.F. retold; cover swipe of F.F. #1. 129-Intro. Thundra. 130-Sue leaves F.F. 131-Quicksilver app. 132-Medusa joins. 133-Thundra Vs. Thing. 142-Kirbyish-a by Buckler | | | |

|  | Good | Fine | N-Mint |
|---|---|---|---|
| begins. 143-Dr. Doom app. 151-Origin Thundra. 159- Medusa leaves, | | | |
| Sue rejoins | .50 | 1.55 | 3.10 |
| 128-Four pg. insert of F.F. Friends & Fiends | .70 | 2.00 | 4.00 |
| 150-Crystal & Quicksilver's wedding | .70 | 2.00 | 4.00 |
| 155-157: Silver Surfer in all | .70 | 2.00 | 4.00 |
| 161-180: 164-The Crusader (old Marvel Boy) revived; origin #165. 176-Re- | | | |
| intro Impossible Man | .35 | 1.05 | 2.10 |
| 181-199: 190-191-F.F. breaks up | .25 | .80 | 1.60 |
| 200-Giant size-FF re-united | .70 | 2.00 | 4.00 |
| 201-208,219 | | .65 | 1.30 |
| 209-216,218,220,221-Byrne-a. 209-1st Herbie the Robot. 220-Brief origin | | | |
|  | .25 | .80 | 1.60 |
| 217-Dazzler app. by Byrne | .45 | 1.35 | 2.70 |
| 222-231 | | .65 | 1.30 |
| 232-Byrne-a begins | .50 | 1.55 | 3.10 |
| 233-235,237-249: All Byrne-a. 238-Origin Frankie Ray | | | |
|  | .40 | 1.25 | 2.50 |
| 236-20th Anniversary issue (11/81, 64 pgs., $1.00)-Brief origin F.F. | | | |
|  | .50 | 1.55 | 3.10 |
| 250,260: 250-Double size; Byrne-a; Skrulls impersonate New X-Men. | | | |
| 260-Alpha Flight app. | .50 | 1.55 | 3.10 |
| 251-259: Byrne-c/a. 252-Reads sideways; Annihilus app. | | | |
|  | .40 | 1.15 | 2.30 |
| 261-285: 261-Silver Surfer. 262-Origin Galactus. 264-Cover swipe of F.F. #1 | | | |
|  | .35 | 1.05 | 2.10 |
| 286-2nd app. X-Factor cont./Avengers #263 | .60 | 1.80 | 3.60 |
| 287-295: 292-Nick Fury app. | | .50 | 1.00 |
| 296-Barry Smith c/a; Thing rejoins | .35 | 1.05 | 2.10 |
| 297-305,307-318, 320-330: 312-X-Factor x-over. 327-Mr. Fantastic & Invisi- | | | |
| ble Girl return | | .50 | 1.00 |
| 306-New team begins | .25 | .75 | 1.50 |
| 319-Double size | .35 | 1.00 | 2.00 |
| 331-348: 334-Simonson-c/scripts begin. 337-Simonson-c/a/scripts begin | | | |
|  | .50 | 1.00 | |
| Giant-Size 2(8/74) - 4: Formerly Giant-Size Super-Stars | | | |
|  | .85 | 2.50 | 5.00 |
| Giant-Size 5(5/75), 6(8/75) | .50 | 1.50 | 3.00 |
| Annual 1('63)-Origin F.F.; Ditko-i | 26.00 | 78.00 | 180.00 |
| Annual 2('64)-Dr. Doom origin & x-over | 19.00 | 57.00 | 130.00 |
| Annual 3('65)-Reed & Sue wed | 8.30 | 25.00 | 58.00 |

| | Good | Fine | N-Mint |
|---|---|---|---|
| Special 4(11/66)-G.A. Torch x-over & origin retold | | | |
| | 3.60 | 11.00 | 25.00 |
| Special 5(11/67)-New art; Intro. Psycho-Man; Silver Surfer, Black Panther, Inhumans app. | 2.00 | 6.00 | 14.00 |
| Special 6(11/68)-Intro. Annihilus; no reprints; birth of Franklin Richards | | | |
| | 2.00 | 6.00 | 14.00 |
| Special 7(11/69) | 2.00 | 6.00 | 14.00 |
| Special 8(12/70), 9(12/71), 10('73) | .55 | 1.70 | 3.40 |
| Annual 11-20: 11(6/76), 12(2/78), 13(10/78), 14(1/80), 15(10/80), 16(10/81), 17(9/83), 18(11/84), 19(11/85), 20(9/87) | | | |
| | .40 | 1.15 | 2.30 |
| Annual 21(9/88)-Evolutionary War x-over | .55 | 1.70 | 3.40 |
| Annual 22(1989, $2.00, 64pg.)-Atlantis Attacks x-over; Sub-Mariner & The Avengers app. Buckler-a | .35 | 1.00 | 2.00 |
| Annual 23(1990, $2.00, 68 pgs.) | .35 | 1.00 | 2.00 |
| Special Edition 1 (5/84)-r/Annual #1; Byrne c/a | | | |
| | .35 | 1.05 | 2.10 |

**FANTASTIC FOUR ROAST**
May, 1982 (One Shot, Direct Sale)
Marvel Comics Group

| | Good | Fine | N-Mint |
|---|---|---|---|
| 1-Celebrates 20th anniversary of F. F. #1; Golden, Miller, Buscema, Rogers, Byrne, Anderson, Austin-c(i) | .60 | 1.80 | 3.60 |

**FANTASTIC FOUR VS. X-MEN**
Feb, 1987 - No. 4, Jun, 1987 (mini-series)
Marvel Comics

| | Good | Fine | N-Mint |
|---|---|---|---|
| 1 | .60 | 1.75 | 3.50 |
| 2-4: 4-Austin-a(i) | .40 | 1.25 | 2.50 |

**FANTASY MASTERPIECES** (Marvel Super Heroes No. 12 on)
Feb, 1966 - No. 11, Oct, 1967; Dec, 1979 - No. 14, Jan, 1981
Marvel Comics Group

| | Good | Fine | N-Mint |
|---|---|---|---|
| 1-Photo of Stan Lee (12 cent-c #1,2) | 2.65 | 8.00 | 18.00 |
| 2 | .85 | 2.50 | 5.00 |

|                                                                 | Good | Fine | N-Mint |
|-----------------------------------------------------------------|------|------|--------|
| 3-8: 3-G.A. Capt. America-r begin, end #6; 1st 25 cent Giant; Colan reprint. 7-Begin G.A. Sub-Mariner, Torch-r/M. Mystery. 8-Torch battles the Sub-Mariner r-/Marvel Mystery #9 | | | |
|                                                                 | 1.25 | 3.75 | 7.50   |
| 9-Origin Human Torch r-/Marvel Comics #1                        | 1.50 | 4.50 | 10.00  |
| 10,11: 10-R/origin & 1st app. All Winners Squad from All Winners #19. 11-R/origin of Toro (H.T. #1) & Black Knight | | | |
|                                                                 | 1.00 | 3.00 | 6.00   |
| V2#1(12/79)-52 pgs.; 75 cents; r-/origin Silver Surfer from S. Surfer #1 with editing; J. Buscema-a | .30 | .90 | 1.80 |
| 2-14-Silver Surfer-r                                            |      | .60  | 1.20   |

**FAWCETT'S FUNNY ANIMALS** (No. 1-26, 80-on titled "Funny Animals")
12/42 - #79, 4/53; #80, 6/53 - #83, 12?/53; #84, 4/54 - #91, 2/56
Fawcett Publications/Charlton Comics No. 84 on

| 1-Capt. Marvel on cover; intro. Hoppy The Captain Marvel Bunny, cloned from Capt. Marvel; Billy the Kid & Willie the Worm begin | | | |
|---------------------------------------------------------------|-------|-------|--------|
|                                                               | 26.00 | 77.00 | 180.00 |
| 2-Xmas-c                                                      | 12.00 | 36.00 | 84.00  |
| 3-5                                                           | 8.50  | 25.50 | 60.00  |
| 6,7,9,10                                                      | 5.70  | 17.00 | 40.00  |
| 8-Flag-c                                                      | 6.50  | 19.50 | 45.00  |
| 11-20                                                         | 3.70  | 11.00 | 26.00  |
| 21-40: 25-Xmas-c. 26-St. Valentines Day-c                    | 2.30  | 7.00  | 16.00  |
| 41-88,90,91                                                   | 1.60  | 4.70  | 11.00  |
| 89-Merry Mailman issue                                       | 2.00  | 6.00  | 14.00  |

**FEATURE COMICS** (Formerly Feature Funnies)
No. 21, June, 1939 - No. 144, May, 1950
Quality Comics Group

| 21-Strips continue from Feature Funnies                       | 23.00  | 70.00  | 160.00 |
|--------------------------------------------------------------|--------|--------|--------|
| 22-26: 23-Charlie Chan begins                                | 17.00  | 51.00  | 120.00 |
| 26-(nn, nd)-c-in one color, (10 cents, 36 pgs.; issue No. blanked out. 2 variations exist, each contain half of the regular #26) | | | |
|                                                              | 5.50   | 16.50  | 38.00  |
| 27-(Rare)-Origin/1st app. Dollman by Eisner                  |        |        |        |
|                                                              | 135.00 | 405.00 | 945.00 |
| 28-1st Fine Dollman                                          | 65.00  | 195.00 | 455.00 |

|  | Good | Fine | N-Mint |
|---|---|---|---|
| 29,30 | 40.00 | 120.00 | 280.00 |
| 31-Last Clock & Charlie Chan issue | 32.00 | 95.00 | 225.00 |
| 32-37: 32-Rusty Ryan & Samar begin. 34-Captain Fortune app. 37- Last | | | |
| Fine Dollman | 25.00 | 75.00 | 175.00 |
| 38-41: 38-Origin the Ace of Space. 39-Origin The Destroying Demon, ends | | | |
| #40. 40-Bruce Blackburn in costume | 18.00 | 54.00 | 125.00 |
| 42-USA, the Spirit of Old Glory begins | 12.00 | 36.00 | 84.00 |
| 43,45-50: 46-Intro. Boyville Brigadiers in Rusty Ryan. 48-USA ends | | | |
|  | 12.00 | 36.00 | 84.00 |
| 44-Dollman by Crandall begins, ends #63; Crandall-a(2) | | | |
|  | 17.00 | 51.00 | 120.00 |
| 51-60: 56-Marijuana story in "Swing Session." 57-Spider Widow begins. | | | |
| 60-Raven begins, ends #71 | 10.00 | 30.00 | 70.00 |
| 61-68 (5/43) | 9.50 | 28.50 | 65.00 |
| 69,70-Phantom Lady x-over in Spider Widow | | | |
|  | 10.00 | 30.00 | 70.00 |
| 71-80: 71-Phantom Lady x-over. 72-Spider Widow ends | | | |
|  | 6.50 | 19.50 | 45.00 |
| 81-99 | 5.50 | 16.50 | 38.00 |
| 100 | 6.50 | 19.50 | 45.00 |
| 101-144: 139-Last Dollman. 140-Intro. Stuntman Stetson | | | |
|  | 4.50 | 14.00 | 32.00 |

**FEATURE FUNNIES** (Feature Comics No. 21 on)
Oct, 1937 - No. 20, May, 1939
Harry 'A' Chesler

|  | Good | Fine | N-Mint |
|---|---|---|---|
| 1(V9/1-indicia)-Joe Palooka, Mickey Finn, The Bungles, Jane Arden, | | | |
| Dixie Dugan, Big Top, Ned Brant, Strange As It Seems, & Off the Rec- | | | |
| ord strip reprints begin | 138.00 | 412.00 | 825.00 |
| 2-The Hawk app. (11/37); Goldberg-c | 57.00 | 170.00 | 400.00 |
| 3-Hawks of Seas begins by Eisner, ends #12; The Clock begins; | | | |
| Christmas-c | 40.00 | 120.00 | 280.00 |
| 4,5 | 28.00 | 85.00 | 195.00 |
| 6-12: 11-Archie O'Toole by Bud Thomas begins, ends #22 | | | |
|  | 23.00 | 70.00 | 160.00 |
| 13-Espionage, Starring Black X begins by Eisner, ends #20 | | | |
|  | 25.00 | 75.00 | 175.00 |
| 14-20 | 20.00 | 60.00 | 140.00 |

**FELIX THE CAT** (See The Funnies, New Funnies & Popular Comics)
2-3/48 - No. 118, 11/61; 9-11/62 - No. 12, 7-9/65
Dell Publ. No. 1-19/Toby No. 20-61/Harvey No. 62-118/Dell

|  | Good | Fine | N-Mint |
|---|---|---|---|
| 1-(Dell) | 14.00 | 42.00 | 100.00 |
| 2 | 7.00 | 21.00 | 50.00 |
| 3-5 | 5.50 | 16.50 | 38.00 |
| 6-19(2-3/51-Dell) | 4.00 | 12.00 | 28.00 |
| 20-30(Toby): 28-(2/52) some copies have #29 on cover, #28 on inside | | | |
|  | 3.50 | 10.50 | 24.00 |
| 31,34,35-No Messmer-a | 1.70 | 5.00 | 12.00 |
| 32,33,36-61(6/55-Toby)-Last Messmer issue | 2.30 | 7.00 | 16.00 |
| 62(8/55)-100 (Harvey) | 1.00 | 3.00 | 7.00 |
| 101-118(11/61) | .85 | 2.50 | 6.00 |
| 12-269-211(#1, 9-11/62)(Dell) | 1.50 | 4.50 | 10.00 |
| 2-12(7-9/65)(Dell, TV) | .75 | 2.25 | 5.00 |
| 3-D Comic Book 1(1953-One Shot) | 20.00 | 60.00 | 140.00 |
| Summer Annual 2('52)-Early 1930s Sunday strip-r (Exist?) | | | |
|  | 17.00 | 51.00 | 120.00 |
| Summer Annual nn('53, 100 pgs., Toby)-1930s daily & Sunday-r | | | |
|  | 17.00 | 51.00 | 120.00 |
| Winter Annual 2('54, 100 pgs., Toby)-1930s daily & Sunday-r | | | |
|  | 11.50 | 34.00 | 80.00 |
| Summer Annual 3('55) (Exist?) | 10.00 | 30.00 | 70.00 |

**FIGHT COMICS**
Jan, 1940 - No. 86, Summer, 1953
Fiction House Magazines

| 1-Origin Spy Fighter, Starring Saber; Fine/Eisner-c; Eisner-a | | | |
|---|---|---|---|
|  | 90.00 | 270.00 | 625.00 |
| 2-Joe Louis life story | 39.00 | 118.00 | 275.00 |
| 3-Rip Regan, the Power Man begins | 36.00 | 107.00 | 250.00 |
| 4,5: 4-Fine-c | 27.00 | 81.00 | 190.00 |
| 6-10: 6,7-Powell-c | 22.00 | 65.00 | 154.00 |
| 11-14: Rip Regan ends | 20.00 | 60.00 | 140.00 |
| 15-1st Super American | 26.00 | 80.00 | 185.00 |
| 16-Captain Fight begins; Spy Fighter ends | 26.00 | 80.00 | 185.00 |
| 17,18: Super American ends | 23.00 | 70.00 | 160.00 |

| | Good | Fine | N-Mint |
|---|---|---|---|
| 19-Captain Fight ends; Senorita Rio begins (origin & 1st app.); Rip Carson, Chute Trooper begins | 23.00 | 70.00 | 160.00 |
| 20 | 17.00 | 51.00 | 120.00 |
| 21-30 | 11.50 | 34.00 | 80.00 |
| 31,33-35: 31-Decapitation-c | 10.00 | 30.00 | 70.00 |
| 32-Tiger Girl begins | 11.00 | 32.00 | 75.00 |
| 36-47,49,50: 44-Capt. Fight returns | 10.00 | 30.00 | 70.00 |
| 48-Used in **Love and Death** by Legman | 10.00 | 30.00 | 70.00 |
| 51-Origin Tiger Girl; Patsy Pin-Up app. | 16.00 | 48.00 | 110.00 |
| 52-60 | 8.00 | 24.00 | 56.00 |
| 61-Origin Tiger Girl retold | 10.00 | 30.00 | 70.00 |
| 62-65-Last Baker issue | 8.00 | 24.00 | 56.00 |
| 66-78: 78-Used in **POP**, pg. 99 | 7.00 | 20.00 | 48.00 |
| 79-The Space Rangers app. | 7.00 | 20.00 | 48.00 |
| 80-85 | 5.70 | 17.00 | 40.00 |
| 86-Two Tigerman stories by Evans; Moreira-a | 7.00 | 20.00 | 48.00 |

**FIGHTING AMERICAN**
Apr-May, 1954 - No. 7, Apr-May, 1955
Headline Publications/Prize

| | Good | Fine | N-Mint |
|---|---|---|---|
| 1-Origin Fighting American & Speedboy; S&K c/a(3) | 73.00 | 220.00 | 515.00 |
| 2-S&K-a(3) | 37.00 | 110.00 | 255.00 |
| 3,4-S&K-a(3) | 31.00 | 94.00 | 220.00 |
| 5-S&K-a(2); Kirby/?-a | 31.00 | 94.00 | 220.00 |
| 6-Four pg. reprint of origin, plus 2 pgs. by S&K | 28.00 | 85.00 | 200.00 |
| 7-Kirby-a | 26.00 | 79.00 | 185.00 |

**FIGHTING YANK** (See America's Best & Startling Comics)
Sept, 1942 - No. 29, Aug, 1949
Nedor/Better Publ./Standard

| | Good | Fine | N-Mint |
|---|---|---|---|
| 1-The Fighting Yank begins; Mystico, the Wonder Man app; bondage-c | 60.00 | 180.00 | 420.00 |
| 2 | 28.00 | 85.00 | 200.00 |
| 3 | 19.00 | 58.00 | 135.00 |
| 4 | 14.00 | 42.00 | 100.00 |

| | Good | Fine | N-Mint |
|---|---|---|---|
| 5-10: 7-The Grim Reaper app. | 12.00 | 36.00 | 84.00 |
| 11-20: 11-The Oracle app. 12-Hirohito bondage-c. 18-The American Eagle | | | |
| app. | 10.00 | 30.00 | 70.00 |
| 21,23,24: 21-Kara, Jungle Princess app. 24-Miss Masque app. | | | |
| | 11.50 | 34.00 | 80.00 |
| 22-Miss Masque-c/story | 14.00 | 42.00 | 100.00 |
| 25 Robinson/Meskin-a; strangulation, lingerie panel; The Cavalier app. | | | |
| | 14.00 | 42.00 | 100.00 |
| 26-29: All-Robinson/Meskin-a. 28-One pg. Williamson-a | | | |
| | 11.50 | 34.00 | 80.00 |

**FIRESTAR**
March, 1986 - No. 4, June, 1986 (From Spider-Man TV series)
Marvel Comics Group

| | | | |
|---|---|---|---|
| 1-X-Men & New Mutants app. | .35 | 1.00 | 2.00 |
| 2-Wolverine-c by Art Adams (p) | .60 | 1.75 | 3.50 |
| 3,4 | .25 | .75 | 1.50 |

**FLAME, THE** (See Wonderworld Comics)
Summer, 1940 - No. 8, Jan, 1942 (#1,2: 68 pgs; #3-8: 44 pgs.)
Fox Features Syndicate

| | | | |
|---|---|---|---|
| 1-Flame stories from Wonderworld #5-9; origin The Flame; Lou Fine-a, | | | |
| 36 pgs., r-/Wonderworld 3,10 | 142.00 | 425.00 | 850.00 |
| 2-Fine-a(2). Wing Turner by Tuska | 59.00 | 176.00 | 410.00 |
| 3-8: 3-Powell-a | 32.00 | 95.00 | 225.00 |

**FLASH, THE** (Formerly Flash Comics) (See Adventure, The Brave & the
Bold, Crisis on . . . , Green Lantern, Showcase & World's Finest)
No. 105, Feb-Mar, 1959 - No. 350, Oct, 1985
National Periodical Publications/DC Comics

| | | | |
|---|---|---|---|
| 105-Origin Flash (retold) & Mirror Master | 128.00 | 384.00 | 900.00 |
| 106-Origin Grodd & Pied Piper | 54.00 | 162.00 | 375.00 |
| 107 | 26.00 | 78.00 | 180.00 |
| 108,109 | 21.50 | 64.00 | 150.00 |
| 110-Intro/origin The Weather Wizard & Kid Flash who later becomes | | | |
| Flash in Crisis On Infinite Earths #12 | 30.00 | 90.00 | 210.00 |

*The Flash #289, © DC Comics*

|  | Good | Fine | N-Mint |
|---|---|---|---|
| 111 | 12.00 | 36.00 | 85.00 |
| 112-Intro & origin Elongated Man | 13.00 | 39.00 | 90.00 |
| 113-Origin Trickster | 11.50 | 34.50 | 80.00 |
| 114-Origin/1st app. Captain Cold | 11.00 | 33.00 | 77.00 |
| 115-120: 117-Origin Capt. Boomerang. 119-Elongated Man marries Sue Dearborn | 8.50 | 25.50 | 60.00 |
| 121,122: 122-Origin & 1st app. The Top | 6.50 | 19.50 | 45.00 |
| 123-Re-intro. Golden Age Flash; origins of both Flashes; 1st mention on Earth II where DC Golden Age heroes live | 41.50 | 124.50 | 290.00 |
| 124-Last 10 cent issue | 5.70 | 17.00 | 40.00 |
| 125-128,130: 128-Origin Abra Kadabra | 3.50 | 10.50 | 24.00 |
| 129-G.A. Flash x-over; J.S.A. cameo in flashback | 10.70 | 32.00 | 75.00 |
| 131-136,138-140: 136-1st Dexter Miles. 139-Origin Prof. Zoom. 140-Origin & 1st app. Heat Wave | 3.50 | 10.50 | 24.00 |
| 137-G.A. Flash x-over; J.S.A. cameo (1st real app. since 2-3/51); 1st Silver Age app. Vandall Savage | 8.50 | 25.50 | 60.00 |
| 141-150 | 1.50 | 4.50 | 10.00 |

|  | Good | Fine | N-Mint |
|---|---|---|---|
| 151-159: 151-G.A. Flash x-over | 1.35 | 4.00 | 8.00 |
| 160-80-Pg. Giant G-21-G.A.-r Flash & Johnny Quick | 1.60 | 4.80 | 11.00 |
| 161-168,170: 165-Silver Age Flash weds Iris West. 167-New facts about Flash's origin. 170-Dr. Mid-Nite, Dr. Fate, G.A. Flash x-over | 1.15 | 3.50 | 7.00 |
| 169-80-Pg. Giant G-34 | 1.50 | 4.50 | 10.00 |
| 171-177,179,180: 175-2nd Superman/Flash race | 1.00 | 3.00 | 6.00 |
| 178-80-Pg. Giant G-46 | 1.50 | 4.50 | 9.00 |
| 181-186,188-195,197-200: 186-Re-intro. Sargon | .70 | 2.00 | 4.00 |
| 187,196: 68-Pg. Giants G-58, G-70 | 1.10 | 3.25 | 6.50 |
| 201-204,206-210: 201-New G.A. Flash story. 208-52 pg. begin, end #213,215,216. 206-Elongated Man begins | .35 | 1.00 | 2.00 |
| 205-68-Pg. Giant G-82 | .90 | 2.75 | 5.50 |
| 211-213,216,220: 211-G.A. Flash origin-r/#104. 213-Reprints #137. 216-G.A. Flash x-over | .35 | 1.00 | 2.00 |
| 214-DC 100 Page Super Spectacluar DC-11; origin Metal Men-r/Showcase #37; never before pubbed G.A. Flash story | .70 | 2.00 | 4.00 |
| 215 (52 pgs.)-Flash-r/Showcase #4 | .35 | 1.00 | 2.00 |
| 217-219: Neal Adams-a in all. 217-Green Lantern/Green Arrow series begins. 219-Last Green Arrow | 1.00 | 3.00 | 6.00 |
| 221-225,227,228,230,231 | .25 | .75 | 1.50 |
| 226-Neal Adams-a | .60 | 1.75 | 3.50 |
| 229,232,233-(All 100 pgs.)-G.A. Flash-r & new-a | .40 | 1.25 | 2.50 |
| 234-274,277-288,290: 243-Death of The Top. 246-Last Green Lantern. 256-Death of The Top retold. 265-267-(44 pgs.). 267-Origin of Flash's uniform. 270-Intro The Clown. 286-Intro/origin Rainbow Raider | | .60 | 1.20 |
| 275,276-Iris West Allen dies | .35 | 1.00 | 2.00 |
| 289-Perez 1st DC art; new Firestorm series begins, ends #304 | | .35 | 1.00 | 2.00 |
| 291-299,301-305: 298-Intro/origin Shade | | .50 | 1.00 |
| 300-52pgs.; origin Flash retold | .35 | 1.00 | 2.00 |
| 306-Dr. Fate by Giffen begins, ends #313 | .35 | 1.00 | 2.00 |
| 307-313-Giffen-a. 309-Origin Flash retold | .25 | .75 | 1.50 |
| 314-349: 344-Origin Kid Flash | | .50 | 1.00 |
| 350-Double size ($1.25) | .55 | 1.60 | 3.20 |

|  | Good | Fine | N-Mint |
|---|---|---|---|
| Annual 1(10-12/63, 84 pgs.)-Origin Elongated Man & Kid Flash-r; origin Grodd, G.A. Flash-r | 21.50 | 64.50 | 150.00 |

**FLASH**
June, 1987 - Present (75 cents, $1.00 #17 on)
DC Comics

| | Good | Fine | N-Mint |
|---|---|---|---|
| 1-Guice c/a begins; New Teen Titans app. | 1.15 | 3.50 | 7.00 |
| 2 | .75 | 2.25 | 4.50 |
| 3-Intro. Kilgore | .40 | 1.25 | 2.50 |
| 4-6: 5-Intro. Speed McGee | .35 | 1.00 | 2.00 |
| 7-10: 7-1st app. Blue Trinity. 8,9-Millennium tie-ins. 9-1st app. The Chunk | .25 | .75 | 1.50 |
| 11-20: 12-Free extra 16 pg. Dr. Light story. 19-Free extra 16 pg. Flash story | | .55 | 1.10 |
| 21-46: 28-Capt. Cold app. 29-New Phantom Lady app. | | .50 | 1.00 |
| Annual 1 (9/87, $1.25), 2 (10/88, $1.50) | .35 | 1.00 | 2.00 |
| Annual 3 (7/89, $1.75, 68 pgs.)-Gives history of G.A., Silver Age, & new Flash in text | .30 | .90 | 1.75 |
| Special 1 ('90, $2.95, 84 pgs.) | .50 | 1.50 | 3.00 |

**FLASH COMICS** (The Flash No. 105 on) (Also see All-Flash)
Jan, 1940 - No. 104, Feb, 1949
National Periodical Publications/All-American

| | Good | Fine | N-Mint |
|---|---|---|---|
| 1-Origin The Flash by Harry Lampert, Hawkman by Gardner Fox, The Whip, & Johnny Thunder by Stan Asch; Cliff Cornwall by Moldoff, Minute Movies begin; Moldoff (Shelly) cover; 1st app. Shiera Sanders who later becomes Hawkgirl, #24; reprinted in Famous First Edition | 1170.00 | 2925.00 | 7000.00 |
| 2-Rod Rian begins, ends #11 | 300.00 | 750.00 | 1800.00 |
| 3-The King begins, ends #41 | 233.00 | 585.00 | 1400.00 |
| 4-Moldoff (Shelly) Hawkman begins | 200.00 | 500.00 | 1200.00 |
| 5 | 175.00 | 440.00 | 1050.00 |
| 6,7 | 142.00 | 355.00 | 850.00 |
| 8-10 | 108.00 | 270.00 | 650.00 |
| 11-20: 12-Les Watts begins; "Sparks" #16 on. 17-Last Cliff Cornwall | 83.00 | 210.00 | 500.00 |
| 21-23 | 70.00 | 175.00 | 420.00 |

|                                                                                       | Good   | Fine   | N-Mint  |
|---------------------------------------------------------------------------------------|--------|--------|---------|
| 24-Shiera becomes Hawkgirl                                                            | 82.00  | 205.00 | 490.00  |
| 25-30: 28-Last Les Sparks. 29-Ghost Patrol begins (origin, 1st app.), ends            |        |        |         |
| #104                                                                                  | 58.00  | 145.00 | 350.00  |
| 31-40: 35-Origin Shade                                                                | 50.00  | 125.00 | 300.00  |
| 41-50                                                                                 | 44.00  | 110.00 | 265.00  |
| 51-61: 59-Last Minute Movies. 61-Last Moldoff Hawkman                                 |        |        |         |
|                                                                                       | 37.00  | 95.00  | 225.00  |
| 62-Hawkman by Kubert begins                                                           | 50.00  | 125.00 | 300.00  |
| 63-70: 66-68-Hop Harrigan in all                                                      | 39.00  | 98.00  | 235.00  |
| 71-85: 80-Atom begins, ends #104                                                      | 39.00  | 98.00  | 235.00  |
| 86-Intro. The Black Canary in Johnny Thunder; rare in Mint due to black               |        |        |         |
| ink smearing on white cover                                                           | 100.00 | 250.00 | 600.00  |
| 87-90: 88-Origin Ghost. 89-Intro villain Thorn                                        |        |        |         |
|                                                                                       | 50.00  | 125.00 | 300.00  |
| 91,93-99: 98-Atom dons new costume                                                    | 63.00  | 160.00 | 380.00  |
| 92-1st solo Black Canary                                                              | 96.00  | 240.00 | 575.00  |
| 100 (10/48),103 (Scarce)-52 pgs. each                                                 | 103.00 | 260.00 | 620.00  |
| 101,102 (Scarce)                                                                      | 83.00  | 210.00 | 500.00  |
| 104-Origin The Flash retold (Scarce)                                                  | 200.00 | 500.00 | 1200.00 |

**FLASH GORDON**
No. 10, 1943 - No. 512, Nov, 1953
Dell Publishing Co.

| 4-Color 10(1943)-by Alex Raymond; reprints/"The Ice Kingdom"   |       |        |        |
|----------------------------------------------------------------|-------|--------|--------|
|                                                                | 55.00 | 165.00 | 385.00 |
| 4-Color 84(1945)-by Alex Raymond; reprints/"The Fiery Desert"  |       |        |        |
|                                                                | 33.00 | 100.00 | 230.00 |
| 4-Color 173,190: 190-Bondage-c                                 | 11.50 | 34.00  | 80.00  |
| 4-Color 204,247                                                | 9.00  | 27.00  | 62.00  |
| 4-Color 424                                                    | 6.50  | 19.50  | 45.00  |
| 2(5-7/53-Dell)-Evans-a                                         | 3.50  | 10.50  | 24.00  |
| 4-Color 512                                                    | 3.50  | 10.50  | 24.00  |

**FLASH GORDON**
9/66 - #11, 12/67; #12, 2/69 - #18, 1/70; #19, 10-11/78 - #37, 3/82 (Painted
  covers No. 19-30, 34)
King #1-11/Charlton #12-18/Gold Key #19-23/Whitman #24 on

|  | Good | Fine | N-Mint |
|---|---|---|---|
| 1-Williamson c/a(2); E.C. swipe/Incred. S.F. 32. Mandrake story | | | |
| | 1.70 | 5.00 | 12.00 |
| 2-Bolle, Gil Kane-c/a; Mandrake story | 1.30 | 4.00 | 9.00 |
| 3-Williamson-c | 1.50 | 4.50 | 10.00 |
| 4-Secret Agent X-9 begins, Williamson-c/a(3) | 1.50 | 4.50 | 10.00 |
| 5-Williamson c/a(2) | 1.50 | 4.50 | 10.00 |
| 6,8-Crandall-a. 8-Secret Agent X-9-r | 2.00 | 6.00 | 14.00 |
| 7-Raboy-a | 1.50 | 4.50 | 10.00 |
| 9,10-Raymond-r. 10-Buckler's 1st pro work (11/67) | | | |
| | 1.70 | 5.00 | 12.00 |
| 11-Crandall-a | 1.15 | 3.50 | 8.00 |
| 12-Crandall-c/a | 1.30 | 4.00 | 9.00 |
| 13-Jeff Jones-a | 1.30 | 4.00 | 9.00 |
| 14-17: 17-Brick Bradford story | .70 | 2.00 | 4.00 |
| 18-Kaluta-a (1st pro work?) | .85 | 2.50 | 5.00 |
| 19(9/78, G.K.), 20-30(10/80) | .35 | 1.00 | 2.00 |
| 30 (7/81; re-issue) | | .30 | .60 |
| 31-33: Movie adaptation; Williamson-a | | .50 | 1.00 |
| 34-37: Movie adaptation | | .40 | .80 |

**FLASH GORDON**
June, 1988 - No. 9, Holiday, 1988-'89 ($1.25, color, mini-series)
DC Comics

| | Good | Fine | N-Mint |
|---|---|---|---|
| 1-Painted-c | .35 | 1.00 | 2.00 |
| 2-9: 5-Painted-c | .25 | .75 | 1.50 |

**FLINTSTONES, THE** (TV)
No. 2, Nov-Dec, 1961 - No. 60, Sept, 1970 (Hanna-Barbera)
Dell Publ. Co./Gold Key No. 7 (10/62) on

| | Good | Fine | N-Mint |
|---|---|---|---|
| 2 | 3.70 | 11.00 | 26.00 |
| 3-6(7-8/62) | 2.65 | 8.00 | 18.00 |
| 7 (10/62; 1st GK) | 2.65 | 8.00 | 18.00 |
| 8-10: Mr. & Mrs. J. Evil Scientist begin? | 2.30 | 7.00 | 16.00 |
| 11-1st app. Pebbles (6/63) | 3.00 | 9.00 | 21.00 |
| 12-15,17-20 | 2.00 | 6.00 | 14.00 |
| 16-1st app. Bamm-Bamm (1/64) | 2.30 | 7.00 | 16.00 |
| 21-30: 24-1st app. The Grusomes | 1.70 | 5.00 | 12.00 |

|  | Good | Fine | N-Mint |
|---|---|---|---|
| 31-33,35-40: 31-Xmas-c. 33-Meet Frankenstein & Dracula. 39-Reprints | | | |
|  | 1.50 | 4.50 | 10.00 |
| 34-1st app. The Great Gazoo | 2.00 | 6.00 | 14.00 |
| 41-60: 45-Last 12 cent issue | 1.30 | 4.00 | 9.00 |
| At N. Y. World's Fair ('64)-J.W. Books (25 cents)-1st printing; no date on-c | | | |
|   (29 cent version exists, 2nd print?) | 2.30 | 7.00 | 16.00 |
| At N. Y. World's Fair (1965 on-c; re-issue). NOTE: Warehouse find in 1984 | | | |
|  | .50 | 1.50 | 3.00 |
| Bigger & Boulder 1(#30013-211) (Gold Key Giant, 11/62, 25 cents, 84 pgs.) | | | |
|  | 3.70 | 11.00 | 26.00 |
| Bigger & Boulder 2-(25 cents)(1966)-reprints B&B No. 1 | | | |
|  | 3.15 | 9.50 | 22.00 |
| . . . With Pebbles & Bamm Bamm(100 pgs., G.K.)-30028-511 (paper- c, | | | |
|   25 cents)(11/65) | 3.15 | 9.50 | 22.00 |

**FLINTSTONES, THE** (TV) (. . . & Pebbles)
Nov, 1970 - No. 50, Feb, 1977 (Hanna-Barbera)
Charlton Comics

|  | Good | Fine | N-Mint |
|---|---|---|---|
| 1 | 1.70 | 5.00 | 12.00 |
| 2 | 1.00 | 3.00 | 6.00 |
| 3-7,9,10 | .85 | 2.50 | 5.00 |
| 8-"Flintstones Summer Vacation," 52 pgs. (Summer, 1971) | | | |
|  | 1.00 | 3.00 | 6.00 |
| 11-20 | .70 | 2.00 | 4.00 |
| 21-50: 37-Byrne text illos (1st work). 42-Byrne-a, 2 pgs. | | | |
|  | .50 | 1.50 | 3.00 |

**FLY MAN** (Formerly Adventures of The Fly)
No. 32, July, 1965 - No. 39, Sept, 1966
Mighty Comics Group (Radio Comics) (Archie)

|  | Good | Fine | N-Mint |
|---|---|---|---|
| 32,33-Comet, Shield, Black Hood, The Fly & Flygirl x-over; re-intro. Wiz- | | | |
|   ard, Hangman #33 | 2.00 | 6.00 | 14.00 |
| 34-36: 34-Shield begins. 35-Origin Black Hood. 36-Hangman x-over in | | | |
|   Shield; re-intro. & origin of Web | 1.60 | 4.80 | 11.00 |
| 37-39: 37-Hangman, Wizard x-over in Flyman; last Shield issue. 38- Web | | | |
|   story. 39-Steel Sterling story | 1.60 | 4.80 | 11.00 |

**FORBIDDEN WORLDS**
7-8/51 - No. 34, 10-11/54; No. 35, 8/55 - No. 145, 8/67
American Comics Group

| | Good | Fine | N-Mint |
|---|---|---|---|
| 1-Williamson/Frazetta-a, 10 pgs. | 55.00 | 165.00 | 385.00 |
| 2 | 22.00 | 65.00 | 155.00 |
| 3-Williamson/Wood/Orlando-a, 7 pgs. | 26.00 | 77.00 | 180.00 |
| 4 | 12.00 | 36.00 | 85.00 |
| 5-Williamson/Krenkel-a, 8pgs. | 21.50 | 65.00 | 150.00 |
| 6-Harrison/Williamson-a, 8pgs. | 19.00 | 58.00 | 135.00 |
| 7,8,10 | 8.50 | 25.50 | 60.00 |
| 9-A-Bomb explosion story | 9.30 | 28.00 | 65.00 |
| 11-20 | 5.70 | 17.00 | 40.00 |
| 21-33: 24-E.C. swipe by Landau | 4.00 | 12.00 | 28.00 |
| 34(10-11/54)(Becomes Young Heroes #35 on)-Last pre-code issue; A-Bomb explosion story | 4.00 | 12.00 | 28.00 |
| 35(8/55)-62 | 2.15 | 6.50 | 15.00 |
| 63,69,76,78-Williamson-a in all; w/Krenkel #69 | 3.50 | 10.50 | 24.00 |
| 64,66-68,70-72,74,75,77,79-90 | 1.50 | 4.50 | 10.00 |
| 65-"There's a New Moon Tonight" listed in #114 as holding 1st record fan mail response | 1.70 | 5.00 | 12.00 |
| 73-Intro/1st app. Herbie by Whitney | 14.00 | 42.00 | 100.00 |
| 91-93,95,97-100 | 1.00 | 3.00 | 7.00 |
| 94-Herbie app. | 4.00 | 12.00 | 24.00 |
| 96-Williamson-a | 2.00 | 6.00 | 14.00 |
| 101-109,111-113,115,117-120 | .85 | 2.50 | 5.00 |
| 110,114,116-Herbie app. 114 contains list of editor's top 20 ACG stories. 116-Herbie goes to Hell | 2.00 | 6.00 | 14.00 |
| 121-124: 124-Magic Agent app. | .70 | 2.00 | 4.00 |
| 125-Magic Agent app.; intro. & origin Magicman series, ends #141 | 1.00 | 3.00 | 7.00 |
| 126-130 | .85 | 2.50 | 5.00 |
| 131-141: 133-Origin/1st app. Dragonia in Magicman (1-2/66); returns in #138. 136-Nemesis x-over in Magicman. 140-Mark Midnight app. by Ditko | .70 | 2.00 | 4.00 |
| 142-145 | .50 | 1.50 | 3.00 |

**FOREVER PEOPLE, THE**
Feb-Mar, 1971 - No. 11, Oct-Nov, 1972
National Periodical Publications

|  | Good | Fine | N-Mint |
|---|---|---|---|
| 1-Superman x-over; Kirby-c/a begins | 1.35 | 4.00 | 8.00 |
| 2-11: 4-9-G.A. reprints. 9,10-Deadman app. | .50 | 1.50 | 3.00 |

**FOUR MOST** (. . . Boys No. 32-41)
Winter, 1941-42 - V8#5(#36), 9-10/49; #37, 11-12/49 - #41, 6-7/50
Novelty Publications/Star Publications No. 37-on

| V1#1-The Target by Sid Greene, The Cadet & Dick Cole begin with origins | | | |
|---|---|---|---|
| retold; produced by Funnies Inc. | 45.00 | 135.00 | 315.00 |
| 2-Last Target | 21.50 | 64.00 | 150.00 |
| 3-Flag-c | 18.50 | 56.00 | 130.00 |
| 4-1 pg. Dr. Seuss (signed) | 14.00 | 42.00 | 100.00 |
| V2#1-4, V3#1-4 | 3.50 | 10.50 | 24.00 |
| V4#1-4 | 2.65 | 8.00 | 18.00 |
| V5#1-5: 1-The Target & Targeteers app. | 2.30 | 7.00 | 16.00 |
| V6#1-4,6: 1-White Rider & Super Horse begin | 2.30 | 7.00 | 16.00 |
| 5-L. B. Cole-c | 3.70 | 11.00 | 26.00 |
| V7#1,3,5, V8#1 | 2.30 | 7.00 | 16.00 |
| 2,4,6-L. B. Cole-c. 6-Last Dick Cole | 3.70 | 11.00 | 26.00 |
| V8#2,3,5-L. B. Cole-c/a | 5.00 | 15.00 | 35.00 |
| 4-L. B. Cole-a | 3.00 | 9.00 | 21.00 |
| 37-41: 38,39-L.B. Cole-c. 38-Johnny Weismuller life story | | | |
|  | 3.00 | 9.00 | 21.00 |

**FOX AND THE CROW** (See Comic Cavalcade, Real Screen Comics)
Dec-Jan, 1951-52 - No. 108, Feb-Mar, 1968
National Periodical Publications

| 1 | 50.00 | 150.00 | 350.00 |
|---|---|---|---|
| 2(Scarce) | 24.00 | 73.00 | 170.00 |
| 3-5 | 14.00 | 42.00 | 100.00 |
| 6-10 | 10.00 | 30.00 | 70.00 |
| 11-20 | 6.50 | 19.50 | 45.00 |
| 21-40: 22-Last precode (2/55) | 4.00 | 12.00 | 28.00 |
| 41-60 | 2.65 | 8.00 | 18.00 |
| 61-80 | 1.70 | 5.00 | 12.00 |

| | Good | Fine | N-Mint |
|---|---|---|---|
| 81-94 | 1.15 | 3.50 | 8.00 |
| 95-Stanley & His Monster begin (origin) | 1.70 | 5.00 | 12.00 |
| 96-99,101-108 | .85 | 2.50 | 6.00 |
| 100 | 1.15 | 3.50 | 8.00 |

**FRANKENSTEIN COMICS** (Also See Prize Comics)
Sum, 1945 - V5#5(#33), Oct-Nov, 1954
Prize Publications (Crestwood/Feature)

| | Good | Fine | N-Mint |
|---|---|---|---|
| 1-Frankenstein begins by Dick Briefer (origin); Frank Sinatra parody | | | |
| | 32.00 | 95.00 | 225.00 |
| 2 | 14.00 | 42.00 | 100.00 |
| 3-5 | 12.00 | 36.00 | 84.00 |
| 6-10: 7-S&K a(r)/Headline Comics. 8(7-8/47)-Superman satire | | | |
| | 11.00 | 32.00 | 75.00 |
| 11-17(1-2/49)-11-Boris Karloff parody-c/story. 17-Last humor issue | | | |
| | 8.00 | 24.00 | 56.00 |
| 18(3/52)-New origin, horror series begins | 11.00 | 32.00 | 75.00 |
| 19,20(V3#4, 8-9/52) | 6.50 | 19.50 | 45.00 |
| 21(V3#5), 22(V3#6) | 6.50 | 19.50 | 45.00 |
| 23(V4#1) - #28(V4#6) | 5.50 | 16.50 | 38.00 |
| 29(V5#1) - #33(V5#5) | 5.50 | 16.50 | 38.00 |

**FRIENDLY GHOST, CASPER, THE** (See Casper . . . )
Aug, 1958 - No. 224, Oct, 1982; No. 225, Oct, 1986 - Present
Harvey Publications

| | Good | Fine | N-Mint |
|---|---|---|---|
| 1-Infinity-c | 14.00 | 42.00 | 100.00 |
| 2 | 7.00 | 21.00 | 50.00 |
| 3-10: 6-Xmas-c | 4.00 | 12.00 | 28.00 |
| 11-20: 18-Xmas-c | 2.65 | 8.00 | 18.00 |
| 21-30 | 1.20 | 3.50 | 8.00 |
| 31-50 | .70 | 2.00 | 5.00 |
| 51-100: 54-Xmas-c | .55 | 1.60 | 3.20 |
| 101-159 | | .60 | 1.20 |
| 160-163: All 52 pg. Giants | .25 | .75 | 1.50 |
| 164-238: 173,179,185-Cub Scout Specials. 238-on $1.00 issues | | | |
| | | .35 | .70 |
| 239-252 ($1.00) | | .50 | 1.00 |

*Frontline Combat #5, © William M. Gaines*

**FRONTLINE COMBAT**
July-Aug, 1951 - No. 15, Jan, 1954
E. C. Comics

|  | Good | Fine | N-Mint |
|---|---|---|---|
| 1 | 36.00 | 110.00 | 255.00 |
| 2 | 24.00 | 73.00 | 170.00 |
| 3 | 18.00 | 54.00 | 125.00 |
| 4-Used in **SOTI**, pg. 257; contains "Airburst" by Kurtzman which is his personal all-time favorite story | 15.00 | 45.00 | 105.00 |
| 5 | 13.00 | 40.00 | 90.00 |
| 6-10 | 11.00 | 32.00 | 75.00 |
| 11-15 | 8.50 | 25.50 | 60.00 |

**FUNNIES, THE** (New Funnies No. 65 on)
Oct, 1936 - No. 64, May, 1942
Dell Publishing Co.

|                                                                    | Good  | Fine   | N-Mint |
|--------------------------------------------------------------------|-------|--------|--------|
| 1-Tailspin Tommy, Mutt & Jeff, Alley Oop (1st app?), Capt. Easy, Don Dixon begin | 92.00 | 230.00 | 550.00 |
| 2-Scribbly by Mayer begins                                         | 39.00 | 118.00 | 275.00 |
| 3                                                                  | 34.00 | 100.00 | 235.00 |
| 4,5: 4-Christmas-c                                                 | 28.00 | 84.00  | 195.00 |
| 6-10                                                               | 22.00 | 65.00  | 155.00 |
| 11-20: 16-Christmas-c                                              | 19.00 | 58.00  | 135.00 |
| 21-29                                                              | 16.50 | 50.00  | 115.00 |
| 30-John Carter of Mars (origin) begins by Edgar Rice Burroughs     | 50.00 | 150.00 | 350.00 |
| 31-44: 33-John Coleman Burroughs art begins on John Carter. 35-(9/39)-Mr. District Attorney begins-based on radio show | 28.00 | 84.00 | 195.00 |
| 45-Origin Phantasmo, the Master of the World & intro. his sidekick Whizzer McGee | 22.00 | 65.00 | 155.00 |
| 46-50: 46-The Black Knight begins, ends #62                        | 19.00 | 58.00  | 135.00 |
| 51-56-Last ERB John Carter of Mars                                 | 19.00 | 58.00  | 135.00 |
| 57-Intro. & origin Captain Midnight                                | 48.00 | 145.00 | 335.00 |
| 58-60                                                              | 20.00 | 60.00  | 140.00 |
| 61-Andy Panda begins by Walter Lantz                               | 21.50 | 65.00  | 150.00 |
| 62,63-Last Captain Midnight cover                                  | 19.00 | 57.00  | 135.00 |
| 64-Format change; Oswald the Rabbit, Felix the Cat, Li'l Eight Ball app.; origin & 1st app. Woody Woodpecker in Oswald; last Capt. Midnight | 39.00 | 118.00 | 275.00 |

**FUNNIES ON PARADE** (Premium)
1933 (Probably the 1st comic book) (36 pgs.; slick cover)
No date or publisher listed
Eastern Color Printing Co.

|                                                                    | Good   | Fine   | N-Mint  |
|--------------------------------------------------------------------|--------|--------|---------|
| nn-Contains Sunday page reprints of Mutt & Jeff, Joe Palooka, Hairbreadth Harry, Reg'lar Fellers, Skippy, & others (10,000 print run). This book was printed for Proctor & Gamble to be given away & came out before Famous Funnies or Century of Comics. | 300.00 | 900.00 | 2100.00 |

**FUNNY PAGES** (Formerly The Comics Magazine)
No. 6, Nov, 1936 - No. 42, Oct, 1940
Comics Magazine Co./Ultem Publ. (Chesler)/Centaur Publications

| | Good | Fine | N-Mint |
|---|---|---|---|
| V1#6 (nn, nd)-The Clock begins (2 pgs., 1st app.), ends #11 | | | |
| | 46.00 | 140.00 | 325.00 |
| 7-11 | 28.00 | 85.00 | 200.00 |
| V2#1 (9/37)(V2#2 on-c; V2#1 in indicia) | 23.00 | 70.00 | 160.00 |
| V2#2 (10/37)(V2#3 on-c; V2#2 in indicia) | 23.00 | 70.00 | 160.00 |
| 3(11/37)-5 | 23.00 | 70.00 | 160.00 |
| 6(1st Centaur, 3/38) | 36.00 | 110.00 | 250.00 |
| 7-9 | 26.00 | 77.00 | 180.00 |
| 10(Scarce)-1st app. of The Arrow by Gustavson (Blue costume) | | | |
| | 117.00 | 295.00 | 700.00 |
| 11,12 | 50.00 | 150.00 | 350.00 |
| V3#1-6 | 50.00 | 150.00 | 350.00 |
| 7-1st Arrow-c (9/39) | 61.00 | 182.00 | 425.00 |
| 8 | 50.00 | 150.00 | 350.00 |
| 9-Tarpe Mills jungle-c | 50.00 | 150.00 | 350.00 |
| 10-2nd Arrow-c | 55.00 | 165.00 | 385.00 |
| V4#1(1/40, Arrow-c)-(Rare)-The Owl & The Phantom Rider app.; origin Mantoka, Maker of Magic by Jack Cole. Mad Ming begins, ends #42. | | | |
| Tarpe Mills-a | 60.00 | 180.00 | 420.00 |
| 35-Arrow-c | 43.00 | 130.00 | 300.00 |
| 36-38-Mad Ming-c | 43.00 | 130.00 | 300.00 |
| 39-42-Arrow-c. 42-Last Arrow | 43.00 | 130.00 | 300.00 |

**FUNNY STUFF**
Summer, 1944 - No. 79, July-Aug, 1954
All-American/National Periodical Publications No. 7 on

| | Good | Fine | N-Mint |
|---|---|---|---|
| 1-The Three Mouseketeers & The "Terrific Whatzit" begin-Sheldon | | | |
| Mayer-a | 45.00 | 135.00 | 315.00 |
| 2-Sheldon Mayer-a | 21.50 | 65.00 | 150.00 |
| 3-5 | 13.00 | 40.00 | 90.00 |
| 6-10 (6/46) | 8.50 | 25.50 | 60.00 |
| 11-20: 18-The Dodo & the Frog begin? | 5.70 | 17.00 | 40.00 |
| 21,23-30: 24-Infinity-c | 4.30 | 13.00 | 30.00 |
| 22-Superman cameo | 14.00 | 42.00 | 100.00 |
| 31-79: 75-Bo Bunny by Mayer | 2.85 | 8.50 | 20.00 |

# G

**GABBY HAYES ADVENTURE COMICS**
Dec, 1953
Toby Press

|  | Good | Fine | N-Mint |
|---|---|---|---|
| 1-Photo-c | 6.00 | 18.00 | 42.00 |

**GABBY HAYES WESTERN** (Movie star) (See Monte Hale, Real Western
    Hero & Western Hero)
Nov, 1948 - No. 50, Jan, 1953; No. 51, Dec, 1954 - No. 59, Jan, 1957
Fawcett/Toby Press/Charlton Comics No. 51 on

| | Good | Fine | N-Mint |
|---|---|---|---|
| 1-Gabby & his horse Corker begin; Photo front/back-c begin | | | |
| | 23.00 | 70.00 | 165.00 |
| 2 | 11.50 | 34.00 | 80.00 |
| 3-5 | 8.50 | 25.50 | 60.00 |
| 6-10 | 7.00 | 21.00 | 50.00 |
| 11-20: 19-Last photo back-c? | 5.00 | 15.00 | 35.00 |
| 21-49 | 3.50 | 10.50 | 24.00 |
| 50-(1/53)-Last Fawcett issue; last photo-c? | 3.70 | 11.00 | 26.00 |
| 51-(12/54)-1st Charlton issue; photo-c | 3.70 | 11.00 | 26.00 |
| 52-59(Charlton '55-57): 53,55-Photo-c | 2.15 | 6.50 | 15.00 |

**GANG BUSTERS** (Radio/TV) (See Popular Comics #38)
Dec-Jan, 1947-48 - No. 67, Dec-Jan, 1958-59 (No. 1-23: 52 pgs.)
National Periodical Publications

| | Good | Fine | N-Mint |
|---|---|---|---|
| 1 | 31.00 | 92.00 | 215.00 |
| 2 | 13.00 | 40.00 | 90.00 |
| 3-8 | 8.00 | 24.00 | 56.00 |
| 9,10-Photo-c | 9.30 | 28.00 | 65.00 |
| 11-13-Photo-c | 7.00 | 21.00 | 50.00 |
| 14,17-Frazetta-a, 8 pgs. each. 14-Photo-c | 18.00 | 54.00 | 125.00 |
| 15,16,18-20 | 5.00 | 15.00 | 35.00 |
| 21-30: 26-Kirby-a | 3.70 | 11.00 | 26.00 |
| 31-44: 44-Last Pre-code (2-3/55) | 2.85 | 8.50 | 20.00 |
| 45-67 | 2.00 | 6.00 | 14.00 |

**GENE AUTRY COMICS** (Movie, radio star; singing cowboy) (Dell takes over with No. 11)
1941 (On sale 12/31/41) - No. 10, 1943 (68 pgs.)
Fawcett Publications

|  | Good | Fine | N-Mint |
|---|---|---|---|
| 1 (Rare)-Gene Autry & his horse Champion begin | | | |
|  | 142.00 | 355.00 | 850.00 |
| 2 | 48.00 | 145.00 | 335.00 |
| 3-5 | 36.00 | 110.00 | 255.00 |
| 6-10 | 31.00 | 92.00 | 215.00 |

**GENE AUTRY COMICS** (. . . & Champion No. 102 on)
No. 11, 1943 - No. 121, Jan-Mar, 1959 (TV - later issues)
Dell Publishing Co.

| | Good | Fine | N-Mint |
|---|---|---|---|
| 11,12(1943-2/44)-Continuation of Fawcett series (60 pgs. each); #11-photo back-c | 34.00 | 100.00 | 240.00 |
| 4-Color 47(1944, 60 pgs.) | 34.00 | 100.00 | 240.00 |
| 4-Color 57(11/44),66('45)(52 pgs. each) | 28.00 | 84.00 | 195.00 |
| 4-Color 75,83('45, 36 pgs. each) | 23.00 | 70.00 | 165.00 |
| 4-Color 93,100('45-46, 36 pgs. each) | 19.00 | 58.00 | 135.00 |
| 1(5-6/46, 52 pgs.) | 34.00 | 100.00 | 240.00 |
| 2(7-8/46)-Photo-c begin, end #111 | 17.00 | 51.00 | 120.00 |
| 3-5: 4-Intro Flapjack Hobbs | 13.00 | 40.00 | 90.00 |
| 6-10 | 9.30 | 28.00 | 65.00 |
| 11-20: 12-Line drawn-c. 20-Panhandle Pete begins | 6.50 | 19.50 | 45.00 |
| 21-29(36 pgs.) | 5.00 | 15.00 | 35.00 |
| 30-40(52 pgs.) | 5.00 | 15.00 | 35.00 |
| 41-56(52 pgs.) | 4.00 | 12.00 | 28.00 |
| 57-66(36 pgs.): 58-Xmas-c | 2.65 | 8.00 | 18.00 |
| 67-80(52 pgs.) | 3.00 | 9.00 | 21.00 |
| 81-90(52 pgs.): 82-Xmas-c. 87-Blank inside-c | 2.30 | 7.00 | 16.00 |
| 91-99(36 pgs. No. 91-on). 94-Xmas-c | 1.70 | 5.00 | 12.00 |
| 100 | 2.65 | 8.00 | 18.00 |
| 101-111-Last Gene Autry photo-c | 1.70 | 5.00 | 12.00 |
| 112-121-All Champion painted-c | 1.15 | 3.50 | 8.00 |

## GEORGIE COMICS (. . . & Judy Comics #20-35?)
Spring, 1945 - No. 39, Oct, 1952
Timely Comics/GPI No. 1-34

|  | Good | Fine | N-Mint |
|---|---|---|---|
| 1-Dave Berg-a | 8.00 | 24.00 | 56.00 |
| 2 | 4.00 | 12.00 | 28.00 |
| 3-5,7,8 | 2.65 | 8.00 | 18.00 |
| 6-Georgie visits Timely Comics | 3.15 | 9.50 | 22.00 |
| 9,10-Kurtzman's "Hey Look" (1 & ?); Margie app. | | | |
|  | 3.70 | 11.00 | 26.00 |
| 11,12: 11-Margie, Millie app. | 2.30 | 7.00 | 16.00 |
| 13-Kurtzman's "Hey Look," 3 pgs. | 3.50 | 10.50 | 24.00 |
| 14-Wolverton art, 1 pg. & Kurtzman's "Hey Look" | | | |
|  | 3.70 | 11.00 | 26.00 |
| 15,16,18-20 | 1.70 | 5.00 | 12.00 |
| 17,29-Kurtzman's "Hey Look," 1 pg. | 2.65 | 8.00 | 18.00 |
| 21-24,27,28,30-39: 21-Anti-Wertham editorial | 1.30 | 4.00 | 9.00 |
| 25-Painted cover by classic pin-up artist Peter Driben | | | |
|  | 3.15 | 9.50 | 22.00 |
| 26-Logo design swipe from Archie Comics | 1.30 | 4.00 | 9.00 |

## GET SMART (TV)
June, 1966 - No. 8, Sept, 1967 (All have Don Adams photo-c)
Dell Publishing Co.

|  | Good | Fine | N-Mint |
|---|---|---|---|
| 1 | 4.00 | 12.00 | 28.00 |
| 2-Ditko-a | 3.50 | 10.50 | 24.00 |
| 3-8: 3-Ditko-a(p) | 2.65 | 8.00 | 18.00 |

## GHOST RIDER (Also see Red Mask & Tim Holt)
1950 - No. 14, 1954
Magazine Enterprises

|  | Good | Fine | N-Mint |
|---|---|---|---|
| 1(A-1 #27)-Origin Ghost Rider | 34.00 | 103.00 | 240.00 |
| 2-5: 2(A-1 #29), 3(A-1 #31), 4(A-1 #34), 5(A-1 #37)-All Frazetta-c only | | | |
|  | 36.00 | 107.00 | 250.00 |
| 6,7: 6(A-1 #44), 7(A-1 #51) | 11.50 | 34.00 | 84.00 |
| 8,9: 8(A-1 #57)-Drug use story, 9(A-1 #69)-L.S.D. story | | | |
|  | 10.00 | 30.00 | 70.00 |

|  | Good | Fine | N-Mint |
|---|---|---|---|
| 10(A-1 #71)-vs. Frankenstein | 10.00 | 30.00 | 70.00 |
| 11-14: 11(A-1 #75), 12(A-1 #80, bondage-c), 13(A-1 #84), 14(A-1 #112) | | | |
|  | 8.00 | 24.00 | 55.00 |

## GHOST RIDER, THE
Feb, 1967 - No. 7, Nov, 1967 (Western hero) (All 12 cent-c)
Marvel Comics Group

| | Good | Fine | N-Mint |
|---|---|---|---|
| 1-Origin Ghost Rider; Kid Colt-r begin | 2.85 | 8.50 | 20.00 |
| 2-7: 6-Last Kid Colt-r; All Ayers-c/a(p) | 1.15 | 3.50 | 7.00 |

## GHOST RIDER (See The Champions & Marvel Spotlight)
Sept, 1973 - No. 81, June, 1983 (Super-hero)
Marvel Comics Group

| | Good | Fine | N-Mint |
|---|---|---|---|
| 1 | 2.85 | 8.50 | 20.00 |
| 2 | 1.70 | 5.00 | 10.00 |
| 3-5: 3-Ghost Rider gets new cycle; Son of Satan app. | | | |
| | 1.35 | 4.00 | 8.00 |
| 6-10: 10-Ploog-a; origin-r/Marvel Spotlight #5 | .85 | 2.50 | 5.00 |
| 11-19 | .70 | 2.00 | 4.00 |
| 20-Byrne-a | 1.10 | 3.25 | 6.50 |
| 21-30 | .50 | 1.50 | 3.00 |
| 31-50: 50-Double size | .35 | 1.00 | 2.00 |
| 51-81: 68-Origin | .25 | .75 | 1.50 |

## GHOST RIDER
May, 1990 - Present ($1.50, color)
Marvel Comics

| | Good | Fine | N-Mint |
|---|---|---|---|
| 1 ($1.95, 52 pgs.)-Origin | 1.50 | 4.50 | 9.00 |
| 2 | .85 | 2.50 | 5.00 |
| 3-4 | .30 | .90 | 1.80 |
| 5,6-Punisher app. | .25 | .75 | 1.50 |

## G. I. COMBAT
Oct, 1952 - No. 43, Dec, 1956
Quality Comics Group

|  | Good | Fine | N-Mint |
|---|---|---|---|
| 1-Crandall-c | 14.00 | 42.00 | 100.00 |
| 2 | 5.70 | 17.00 | 40.00 |
| 3-5,10-Crandall-c/a | 5.70 | 17.00 | 40.00 |
| 6-Crandall-a | 5.00 | 15.00 | 35.00 |
| 7-9 | 3.70 | 11.00 | 26.00 |
| 11-20 | 2.30 | 7.00 | 16.00 |
| 21-31,33,35-43 | 2.00 | 6.00 | 14.00 |
| 32-Nuclear attack-c | 4.00 | 12.00 | 28.00 |
| 34-Crandall-a | 3.60 | 11.00 | 25.00 |

## G. I. COMBAT
No. 44, Jan, 1957 - No. 288, Mar, 1987
National Periodical Publications/DC Comics

| | | | |
|---|---|---|---|
| 44 | 14.00 | 42.00 | 100.00 |
| 45 | 7.50 | 22.50 | 53.00 |
| 46-50 | 4.50 | 14.00 | 32.00 |
| 51-60 | 3.00 | 9.00 | 21.00 |
| 61-66,68-80 | 2.15 | 6.50 | 15.00 |
| 67-1st Tank Killer | 4.15 | 12.50 | 29.00 |
| 81,82,84-86 | 1.35 | 4.00 | 8.00 |
| 83-1st Big Al, Little Al, & Charlie Cigar | 2.15 | 6.50 | 15.00 |
| 87-1st Haunted Tank | 4.15 | 12.50 | 29.00 |
| 88-90: Last 10 cent issue | .85 | 2.50 | 5.00 |
| 91-113,115-120 | .55 | 1.60 | 3.20 |
| 114-Origin Haunted Tank | 1.40 | 4.20 | 8.40 |
| 121-137,139,140 | .35 | 1.05 | 2.10 |
| 138-Intro. The Losers (Capt. Storm, Gunner/Sarge, Johnny Cloud) in Haunted Tank (10-11/69) | .45 | 1.30 | 2.60 |
| 141-259: 151,153-Medal of Honor series by Maurer. 201-245,247-259 are $1.00 size. 232-Origin Kana the Ninja. 244-Death of Slim Stryker; 1st app. The Mercenaries. 246-(76 pgs., $1.50)-30th Anniversary issue. 257-Intro. Stuart's Raiders | .25 | .80 | 1.60 |
| 260-281 ($1.25, 52 pgs.). 264-Intro Sgt. Bullet and the Bravos of Vietnam; origin Kana | .30 | .85 | 1.70 |
| 282-288 (75 cents): 282-New advs. begin | .30 | .85 | 1.70 |

**GIGGLE COMICS** (Also see Ha Ha Comics)
Oct, 1943 - No. 99, Jan-Feb, 1955
Creston No.1-63/American Comics Group No. 64 on

|  | Good | Fine | N-Mint |
|---|---|---|---|
| 1 | 14.00 | 42.00 | 100.00 |
| 2 | 6.50 | 19.50 | 45.00 |
| 3-5: Ken Hultgren-a begins? | 4.50 | 14.00 | 32.00 |
| 6-10: 9-1st Superkatt | 3.70 | 11.00 | 26.00 |
| 11-20 | 2.30 | 7.00 | 16.00 |
| 21-40 | 1.85 | 5.50 | 13.00 |
| 41-54,56-59,61-99: 95-Spencer Spook app. | 1.50 | 4.50 | 10.00 |
| 55,60-Milt Gross-a | 1.85 | 5.50 | 13.00 |

**G. I. JOE AND THE TRANSFORMERS**
Jan, 1987 - No. 4, Apr, 1987 (mini-series)
Marvel Comics Group

|  | | | |
|---|---|---|---|
| 1 | .35 | 1.00 | 2.00 |
| 2-4 | .25 | .75 | 1.50 |

**G. I. JOE, A REAL AMERICAN HERO**
June, 1982 - Present
Marvel Comics Group

|  | | | |
|---|---|---|---|
| 1-Printed on Baxter paper | 3.00 | 9.00 | 18.00 |
| 2-Printed on reg. paper | 4.50 | 13.50 | 27.00 |
| 2-10: 2nd printings | .30 | .90 | 1.80 |
| 3-5 | 1.80 | 5.40 | 10.80 |
| 6,8 | 1.95 | 5.85 | 11.70 |
| 7,9,10 | 1.65 | 4.95 | 9.90 |
| 11-Intro Airborne | 1.20 | 3.60 | 7.20 |
| 12 | 1.80 | 5.40 | 10.80 |
| 13-15 | 1.50 | 4.50 | 9.00 |
| 14 (2nd printing) | .30 | .90 | 1.80 |
| 16 | 1.35 | 4.05 | 8.10 |
| 17-20 | .90 | 2.70 | 5.40 |
| 17-19 (2nd printings) | .25 | .70 | 1.40 |

| | Good | Fine | N-Mint |
|---|---|---|---|
| 21,22 | 1.15 | 3.40 | 6.80 |
| 23-25 | .60 | 1.80 | 3.60 |
| 21,23,25 (2nd printings) | .25 | .70 | 1.40 |
| 26,27-Origin Snake-Eyes | .90 | 2.70 | 5.40 |
| 26,27 (2nd printings) | | .45 | .90 |
| 28-30 | .60 | 1.80 | 3.60 |
| 29,30 (2nd printings) | | .45 | .90 |
| 31-35: 33-New headquarters | .50 | 1.55 | 3.10 |
| 36-40 | .40 | 1.25 | 2.50 |
| 34,35,36,37 (2nd printings) | | .45 | .90 |
| 41-49 | .30 | .95 | 1.90 |
| 50-Double size; intro Special Missions | .55 | 1.70 | 3.40 |
| 51-59: 59-$1.00 issues begin | .25 | .75 | 1.50 |
| 51 (2nd printing) | | .35 | .70 |
| 60-Todd McFarlane-a | .30 | .90 | 1.80 |
| 61-99,101-108: 94-96-Snake-Eyes app. | | .45 | .90 |
| 100 ($1.50, 52 pgs.) | .25 | .75 | 1.50 |
| Special Treasury Edition (1982)-r/#1 | 1.20 | 3.60 | 7.20 |
| ... Yearbook 1 ('84)-r/#1 | 1.05 | 3.15 | 6.30 |
| ... Yearbook 2 ('85) | .60 | 1.80 | 3.60 |
| ... Yearbook 3 ('86, 68 pgs.) | .45 | 1.35 | 2.70 |
| ... Yearbook 4 (2/88) | .25 | .80 | 1.60 |

## G. I. JOE ORDER OF BATTLE, THE
Dec, 1986 - No. 4, Mar, 1987 (mini-series)
Marvel Comics Group

| | Good | Fine | N-Mint |
|---|---|---|---|
| 1 | .55 | 1.60 | 3.20 |
| 2-4 | .30 | .90 | 1.80 |

## G. I. JOE SPECIAL MISSIONS (Indicia title: Special Missions)
Oct, 1986 - No. 28, Dec, 1989 ($1.00, color)
Marvel Comics Group

| | Good | Fine | N-Mint |
|---|---|---|---|
| 1 | .50 | 1.50 | 3.00 |
| 2 | .30 | .90 | 1.80 |

| | Good | Fine | N-Mint |
|---|---|---|---|
| 3-10 | .25 | .75 | 1.50 |
| 11-28 | | .50 | 1.00 |

## GODZILLA
August, 1977 - No. 24, July, 1979 (Based on movie series)
Marvel Comics Group

| | Good | Fine | N-Mint |
|---|---|---|---|
| 1-Mooney-i | .60 | 1.75 | 3.50 |
| 2-10: 2-Tuska-i. 3-Champions app. 4,5-Sutton-a | .35 | 1.10 | 2.20 |
| 11-24: 20-F.F. app. 21,22-Devil Dinosaur app. | .30 | .90 | 1.80 |

## GREEN ARROW (See Brave & the Bold, Green Lantern, Justice League
of America #4, Leading, More Fun, and World's Finest)
May, 1983 - No. 4, Aug, 1983 (Mini-series)
DC Comics

| | Good | Fine | N-Mint |
|---|---|---|---|
| 1-Origin; Speedy cameo | .50 | 1.50 | 3.00 |
| 2-4 | .35 | 1.00 | 2.00 |

## GREEN ARROW
Feb, 1988 - Present ($1.00, mature readers) (Painted-c #1-3)
DC Comics

| | Good | Fine | N-Mint |
|---|---|---|---|
| 1-Mike Grell scripts in all | 1.00 | 3.00 | 6.00 |
| 2 | .70 | 2.00 | 4.00 |
| 3 | .50 | 1.50 | 3.00 |
| 4,5 | .40 | 1.25 | 2.50 |
| 6-12 | .35 | 1.00 | 2.00 |
| 13-20 | .25 | .75 | 1.50 |
| 21-40: 27,28-Warlord app. | | .60 | 1.25 |
| Annual 1 ('88)-No Grell scripts | .35 | 1.00 | 2.00 |
| Annual 2 ('89, $2.50, 68 pgs.)-No Grell scripts; recaps origin Green Arrow, Speedy, Black Canary & others | .40 | 1.25 | 2.50 |
| Annual 3 (1990, $2.50, 68 pgs.) | .40 | 1.25 | 2.50 |

*Green Arrow: The Long Bow Hunters #2, © DC Comics*

## GREEN ARROW: THE LONG BOW HUNTERS
Aug, 1987 - No. 3, Oct, 1987 ($2.95, color, mature readers)
DC Comics

|  | Good | Fine | N-Mint |
|---|---|---|---|
| 1-Grell c/a | 2.50 | 7.50 | 15.00 |
| 1-2nd printing | .50 | 1.50 | 3.00 |
| 2 | 1.35 | 4.00 | 8.00 |
| 2-2nd printing | .50 | 1.50 | 3.00 |
| 3 | .85 | 2.50 | 5.00 |

## GREEN HORNET, THE
Nov, 1989 - Present ($1.75, color)
Now Comics

| | Good | Fine | N-Mint |
|---|---|---|---|
| 1 ($2.95, double-size)-Steranko painted-c; G.A. Green Hornet | | | |
| | 2.50 | 7.50 | 15.00 |
| 2-Green Hornet & Kato from '60s TV show | 1.70 | 5.00 | 10.00 |
| 3,4 | 1.00 | 3.00 | 6.00 |
| 5-Death of original ('30s) Green Hornet | .85 | 2.50 | 5.00 |
| 6-8 | .50 | 1.50 | 3.00 |
| 9-10 | .30 | .90 | 1.80 |

**GREEN HORNET COMICS** (. . . Racket Buster #44) (Radio, movies)
Dec, 1940 - No. 47, Sept, 1949 (See All New #13,14)
Helnit Publ. Co. (Holyoke) No. 1-6/Family Comics (Harvey) No. 7-on

| | Good | Fine | N-Mint |
|---|---|---|---|
| 1-Green Hornet begins (1st app.); painted-c | | | |
| | 117.00 | 350.00 | 820.00 |
| 2 | 54.00 | 160.00 | 375.00 |
| 3 | 43.00 | 130.00 | 300.00 |
| 4-6 (8/41) | 34.00 | 100.00 | 235.00 |
| 7 (6/42)-Origin The Zebra; Robin Hood & Spirit of 76 begin | | | |
| | 30.00 | 90.00 | 210.00 |
| 8-10 | 24.00 | 70.00 | 165.00 |
| 11,12-Mr. Q in both | 20.00 | 60.00 | 140.00 |
| 13-20 | 18.50 | 56.00 | 130.00 |
| 21-30: 24-Sci-Fi-c | 16.50 | 50.00 | 115.00 |
| 31-The Man in Black Called Fate begins | 17.00 | 51.00 | 120.00 |
| 32-36: 36-Spanking panel | 14.00 | 42.00 | 100.00 |
| 37-Shock Gibson app. by Powell; S&K Kid Adonis reprinted from | | | |
| Stuntman No. 3 | 16.00 | 48.00 | 110.00 |
| 38-Shock Gibson, Kid Adonis app. | 14.00 | 42.00 | 100.00 |
| 39-Stuntman story by S&K | 18.50 | 56.00 | 130.00 |
| 40,41 | 10.00 | 30.00 | 70.00 |
| 42-45,47-Kerry Drake in all. 45-Boy Explorers on cover only | | | |
| | 10.00 | 30.00 | 70.00 |
| 46-"Case of the Marijuana Racket" cover/story; Kerry Drake app. | | | |
| | 10.00 | 30.00 | 70.00 |

*Green Lantern #7 (Spring 1943), © DC Comics*

**GREEN LANTERN** (1st Series) (See All-American, All Flash Quarterly,
    All Star Comics & Comic Cavalcade)
Fall, 1941 - No. 38, May-June, 1949
National Periodical Publications/All-American

|  | Good | Fine | N-Mint |
|---|---|---|---|
| 1-Origin retold | 583.00 | 1460.00 | 3500.00 |
| 2-1st book-length story | 250.00 | 625.00 | 1500.00 |
| 3 | 192.00 | 480.00 | 1150.00 |
| 4 | 133.00 | 335.00 | 800.00 |
| 5 | 106.00 | 265.00 | 635.00 |
| 6-8: 8-Hop Harrigan begins | 92.00 | 230.00 | 550.00 |
| 9,10: 10-Origin Vandal Savage | 79.00 | 200.00 | 475.00 |
| 11-17,19,20: 12-Origin Gambler | 67.00 | 170.00 | 400.00 |
| 18-Christmas-c | 75.00 | 190.00 | 450.00 |
| 21-29: 27-Origin Sky Pirate | 56.00 | 140.00 | 335.00 |
| 30-Origin/1st app. Streak the Wonder Dog by Toth | | | |
|  | 56.00 | 140.00 | 335.00 |

|  | Good | Fine | N-Mint |
|---|---|---|---|
| 31-35 | 47.00 | 120.00 | 285.00 |
| 36-38: 37-Sargon the Sorcerer app. | 56.00 | 140.00 | 335.00 |

**GREEN LANTERN** (2nd series)  (See Adventure, Brave & the Bold,
    Flash, Justice League & Showcase; Green Lantern Corps #206 on)
7-8/60 - No. 89, 4-5/72; No. 90, 8-9/76 - No. 205, 10/86
National Periodical Publications/DC Comics

| | | | |
|---|---|---|---|
| 1-Origin retold; Gil Kane-a begins | 104.00 | 312.00 | 725.00 |
| 2-1st Pieface | 45.00 | 135.00 | 315.00 |
| 3 | 26.00 | 78.00 | 184.00 |
| 4,5: 5-Origin & 1st app. Hector Hammond; 1st 5700 A.D. story | | | |
| | 21.50 | 64.50 | 150.00 |
| 6-10: 6-Intro Tomar-re the alien G.L. 7-Origin Sinestro. 9-1st Jordan | | | |
|     Brothers; last 10 cent issue | 12.00 | 36.00 | 84.00 |
| 11-15: 13-Flash x-over. 14-Origin Sonar | 9.00 | 27.00 | 63.00 |
| 16-20: 16-Origin Star Sapphire. 20-Flash x-over | | | |
| | 7.50 | 22.50 | 53.00 |
| 21-30: 21-Origin Dr. Polaris. 23-1st Tattooed Man. 24-Origin Shark. 29-JLA | | | |
|     cameo; 1st Blackhand | 6.50 | 19.50 | 45.00 |
| 31-39 | 4.50 | 14.00 | 32.00 |
| 40-1st app. Crisis; 1st solo G.A. Green Lantern in Silver Age; origin The | | | |
|     Guardians | 30.00 | 90.00 | 200.00 |
| 41-44,46-50: 42-Zatanna x-over. 43-Flash x-over | | | |
| | 2.85 | 8.50 | 20.00 |
| 45-G.A. Green Lantern x-over | 3.70 | 11.00 | 26.00 |
| 51,53-58 | 1.60 | 4.80 | 11.00 |
| 52-G.A. Green Lantern x-over | 2.30 | 7.00 | 16.00 |
| 59-1st app. Guy Gardner | 12.50 | 37.50 | 88.00 |
| 60,62-75: 69-Wood inks | 1.35 | 4.00 | 8.00 |
| 61-G.A. Green Lantern x-over | 1.60 | 4.80 | 11.00 |
| 76-Begin Green Lantern/Green Arrow series by Neal Adams, ends #122 | | | |
| | 7.85 | 23.50 | 55.00 |
| 77 | 2.85 | 8.50 | 20.00 |
| 78-80 | 2.30 | 7.00 | 16.00 |
| 81-84: 82-One pg. Wrightson inks. 83-G.L. reveals i.d. to Carol Ferris. | | | |
|     84-N. Adams/Wrightson-a, 22 pgs. | 1.70 | 5.00 | 12.00 |
| 85,86(52 pgs.)-Drug propaganda books. 86-G.A. Green Lantern-r; Toth-a | | | |
| | 2.65 | 8.00 | 18.00 |
| 87(52 pgs.): 2nd app. Guy Gardner (cameo); 1st app. John Stewart (be- | | | |
|     comes Green Lantern in #182) | 1.50 | 4.50 | 9.00 |

|  | Good | Fine | N-Mint |
|---|---|---|---|
| 88(52 pgs.,'72)-Unpubbed G.A. Gr. Lantern story; Gr. Lant.-r/Showcase #23. N. Adams-a(1 pg.) | .50 | 1.50 | 3.00 |
| 89(52 pgs.)-G.A. Green Lantern-r | 1.15 | 3.50 | 7.00 |
| 90('76)-99 | .35 | 1.00 | 2.00 |
| 100-(Giant)-1st app. new Air Wave | .50 | 1.50 | 3.00 |
| 101-119: 107-1st Tales of the G.L. Corps story. 108-110 (44 pgs)-G.A. Gr. Lant. 111-Origin retold; G.A. Gr. Lantern app. 112-G.A. Gr. Lantern origin retold | .35 | 1.00 | 2.00 |
| 120-135,138-140,144-149: 132-Adam Strange begins new series, ends #147. 148-Tales of the G.L. Corps begins | .60 | 1.20 | |
| 136,137-1st app. Citadel; Space Ranger app. | .35 | 1.00 | 2.00 |
| 141-1st app. Omega Men | .50 | 1.50 | 3.00 |
| 142,143-The Omega Men app.; Perez-c | .35 | 1.00 | 2.00 |
| 150-Anniversary issue, 52 pgs.; no G.L. Corps | .35 | 1.00 | 2.00 |
| 151-170: 159-Origin Evil Star. 160,161-Omega Men app. 181-Hal Jordan resigns as G.L. 182-John Stewart becomes new G.L.; origin recap of Hal Jordan as G.L. | .50 | 1.00 | |
| 171-194,196-199,201-205: (75 cent cover). 185-Origin new G.L. (John Stewart). 188-I.D. revealed; Alan Moore back-up scripts. 191-1st app. Star Sapphire. 194-Crisis x-over; Guardians choose Guy Gardner to become new G.L. 199-Hal Jordan returns as a member of G.L. Corps (3 G.L.s now). 201-Green Lantern Corps begins (is cover title & says premiere issue) | .50 | 1.00 | |
| 195-Guy Gardner becomes Green Lantern; Crisis x-over | .70 | 2.00 | 4.00 |
| 200-Double-size | .35 | 1.00 | 2.00 |

**GREEN LANTERN CORPS, THE** (Formerly Green Lantern)
No. 206, Nov, 1986 - No. 224, May, 1988
DC Comics

|  | Good | Fine | N-Mint |
|---|---|---|---|
| 206-223: 220,221-Millennium tie-ins | | .50 | 1.00 |
| 224-Double size last issue | .25 | .75 | 1.50 |

**GREEN LANTERN: EMERALD DAWN**
Dec, 1989 - No. 6, May, 1990 ($1.00, color, mini-series)
DC Comics

|  | Good | Fine | N-Mint |
|---|---|---|---|
| 1-Origin retold | 1.50 | 4.50 | 9.00 |
| 2 | .75 | 2.25 | 4.50 |

| | Good | Fine | N-Mint |
|---|---|---|---|
| 3,4 | .40 | 1.25 | 2.50 |
| 5,6 | .25 | .75 | 1.50 |

**GREEN MASK, THE** (See Mystery Men)
Summer, 1940 - No. 9, 2/42; No. 10, 8/44 - No. 11, 11/44; V2#1, Spring,
    1945 - No. 6, 10-11/46
Fox Features Syndicate

| | Good | Fine | N-Mint |
|---|---|---|---|
| V1#1-Origin The Green Mask & Domino; reprints/Mystery Men No. | | | |
| 1-3,5-7; Lou Fine-c | 93.00 | 278.00 | 650.00 |
| 2-Zanzibar The Magician by Tuska | 44.00 | 133.00 | 310.00 |
| 3-Powell-a; Marijuana story | 27.00 | 81.00 | 190.00 |
| 4-Navy Jones begins, ends No. 6 | 22.00 | 65.00 | 154.00 |
| 5 | 19.00 | 58.00 | 135.00 |
| 6-The Nightbird begins, ends No. 9; bondage/torture-c | | | |
| | 16.50 | 50.00 | 115.00 |
| 7-9 | 13.00 | 40.00 | 90.00 |
| 10,11: 10-Origin One Round Hogan & Rocket Kelly | | | |
| | 11.50 | 34.00 | 80.00 |
| V2#1 | 8.50 | 25.50 | 60.00 |
| 2-6 | 6.50 | 19.50 | 45.00 |

**GROO THE WANDERER** (Sergio Aragones' . . . )
March, 1985 - Present
Epic Comics (Marvel)

| | Good | Fine | N-Mint |
|---|---|---|---|
| 1-Aragones-c/a begins | 2.35 | 7.00 | 14.00 |
| 2 | 1.70 | 5.00 | 10.00 |
| 3-5 | 1.10 | 3.30 | 6.60 |
| 6-10 | .85 | 2.50 | 5.00 |
| 11-20 | .55 | 1.65 | 3.30 |
| 21-26 | .35 | 1.10 | 2.20 |
| 27-35 ($1.00-c) | .35 | 1.10 | 2.20 |
| 36-48 ($1.50-c) | .30 | .85 | 1.70 |
| 49,51-72 ($1.00-c) | | .50 | 1.00 |
| 50-$1.50, double-size | .25 | .75 | 1.50 |

**GUARDIANS OF THE GALAXY**
June, 1990-Present ($1.00, color)
Marvel Comics

|  | Good | Fine | N-Mint |
|---|---|---|---|
| 1 | .25 | .75 | 1.50 |
| 2-6 |  | .50 | 1.00 |

**GUNSMOKE** (TV)
No. 679, 2/56 - No. 27, 6-7/61; 2/69 - No. 6, 2/70
Dell Publishing Co./Gold Key (All have James Arness photo-c)

| | Good | Fine | N-Mint |
|---|---|---|---|
| 4-Color 679(No. 1) | 6.00 | 18.00 | 42.00 |
| 4-Color 720,769,797,844 | 4.00 | 12.00 | 28.00 |
| 6(11-1/57-58), 7 | 4.00 | 12.00 | 28.00 |
| 8,9,11,12-Williamson-a in all, 4 pgs. each | 5.00 | 15.00 | 35.00 |
| 10-Williamson/Crandall-a, 4 pgs. | 5.00 | 15.00 | 35.00 |
| 13-27 | 3.70 | 11.00 | 26.00 |
| Gunsmoke Film Story (11/62-G.K. Giant) No. 30008-211 | | | |
| | 4.00 | 12.00 | 28.00 |
| 1 (Gold Key) | 2.15 | 6.50 | 15.00 |
| 2-6('69-70) | 1.15 | 3.50 | 8.00 |

# H

**HA HA COMICS** (Also see Giggle)
Oct, 1943 - No. 99, Jan, 1955
Scope Mag.(Creston Publ.) No. 1-80/American Comics Group

| | Good | Fine | N-Mint |
|---|---|---|---|
| 1 | 14.00 | 42.00 | 100.00 |
| 2 | 6.50 | 19.50 | 45.00 |
| 3-5: Ken Hultgren-a begins? | 4.50 | 14.00 | 32.00 |
| 6-10 | 3.70 | 11.00 | 26.00 |
| 11-20: 14-Infinity-c | 2.30 | 7.00 | 16.00 |
| 21-40 | 1.85 | 5.50 | 13.00 |
| 41-94,96-99: 49-Xmas-c | 1.50 | 4.50 | 10.00 |
| 95-3-D effect-c | 5.70 | 17.00 | 40.00 |

**HAPPY COMICS**
Aug, 1943 - No. 40, Dec, 1950
Nedor Publ./Standard Comics (Animated Cartoons)

| | | | |
|---|---|---|---|
| 1 | 11.50 | 34.00 | 80.00 |
| 2 | 5.50 | 16.50 | 38.00 |
| 3-10 | 3.70 | 11.00 | 26.00 |
| 11-19 | 2.15 | 6.50 | 15.00 |
| 20-31,34-37-Frazetta text illos in all; 2 in #34 & 35, 3 in #27,28,30 | | | |
| | 3.50 | 10.50 | 24.00 |
| 32-Frazetta-a, 7 pgs. plus two text illos; Roussos-a | | | |
| | 10.00 | 30.00 | 70.00 |
| 33-Frazetta-a(2), 6 pgs. each (Scarce) | 17.00 | 51.00 | 120.00 |
| 38-40 | 1.60 | 4.80 | 11.00 |

**HAUNT OF FEAR**
No. 15, May-June, 1950 - No. 28, Nov-Dec, 1954
E. C. Comics

| | | | |
|---|---|---|---|
| 15(#1, 1950) | 110.00 | 332.00 | 775.00 |
| 16 | 56.00 | 170.00 | 395.00 |
| 17-Origin of Crypt of Terror, Vault of Horror, & Haunt of Fear; used in **SOTI**, pg. 43; last pg. Ingels-a used by N.Y. Legis. Comm. | | | |
| | 56.00 | 170.00 | 395.00 |

*Haunt of Fear #17, © William M. Gaines*

|  | Good | Fine | N-Mint |
|---|---|---|---|
| 4 | 43.00 | 130.00 | 300.00 |
| 5-Injury-to-eye panel, pg. 4 | 32.00 | 95.00 | 225.00 |
| 6-10: 8-Shrunken head cover | 22.00 | 65.00 | 155.00 |
| 11-13,15-18 | 16.00 | 48.00 | 110.00 |
| 14-Origin Old Witch by Ingels | 22.00 | 65.00 | 155.00 |
| 19-Used in **SOTI**, ill.-"A comic book baseball game" & Senate investigation on juvenile delinquency | 21.00 | 62.00 | 150.00 |
| 20-Feldstein-r/Vault of Horror #12 | 14.00 | 42.00 | 100.00 |
| 21,22,25,27: 27-Cannibalism story | 9.30 | 28.00 | 65.00 |
| 23-Used in **SOTI**, pg. 241 | 11.00 | 32.00 | 75.00 |
| 24-Used in Senate Investigative Report, pg. 8 | 10.00 | 30.00 | 70.00 |
| 26-Contains anti-censorship editorial, 'Are you a Red Dupe?' | 10.00 | 30.00 | 70.00 |
| 28-Low distribution | 11.50 | 34.00 | 80.00 |

**HAVOK AND WOLVERINE**
Mar, 1989 - No. 4, Oct, 1989 ($3.50, mini-series, squarebound)
Epic Comics (Marvel)

|  | Good | Fine | N-Mint |
|---|---|---|---|
| 1-Mature readers, violent | .85 | 2.50 | 5.00 |
| 2-4 | .60 | 1.75 | 3.50 |

**HAWK AND DOVE**
Oct, 1988 - No. 5, Feb, 1989 ($1.00, color, mini-series)
DC Comics

| 1 | .75 | 2.25 | 4.50 |
|---|---|---|---|
| 2 | .50 | 1.50 | 3.00 |
| 3-5 | .35 | 1.00 | 2.00 |

**HAWK AND DOVE**
June, 1989 - Present ($1.00, color)
DC Comics

| 1 | .25 | .75 | 1.50 |
|---|---|---|---|
| 2-18 |  | .50 | 1.00 |

**HAWK AND THE DOVE, THE** (See Showcase #75 & Teen Titans)
Aug-Sept, 1968 - No. 6, June-July, 1969
National Periodical Publications

| 1-Ditko c/a-1,2 | 2.65 | 8.00 | 18.00 |
|---|---|---|---|
| 2-6: 5-Teen Titans cameo | 1.85 | 5.50 | 13.00 |

**HAWKMAN** (See Atom & Hawkman, The Brave & the Bold, Detective,
   Flash Comics & Justice League of America #31)
Apr-May, 1964 - No. 27, Aug-Sept, 1968
National Periodical Publications

| 1 | 23.00 | 70.00 | 160.00 |
|---|---|---|---|
| 2 | 8.50 | 25.50 | 60.00 |
| 3-5: 4-Zatanna x-over (origin & 1st app.) | 5.70 | 17.00 | 40.00 |
| 6-10: 9-Atom cameo; Hawkman & Atom learn each other's I.D.; 2nd app. | | | |
|     Shadow Thief | 3.60 | 11.00 | 25.00 |
| 11-15 | 2.15 | 6.50 | 15.00 |

| | Good | Fine | N-Mint |
|---|---|---|---|
| 16-27: Adam Strange x-over #18, cameo #19. 25-G.A. Hawkman-r | | | |
| | 1.50 | 4.50 | 10.00 |

**HAWKMAN** (Also see Mystery in Space, Showcase & World's Finest)
Aug, 1986 - No. 17, Dec, 1987
DC Comics

| | | | |
|---|---|---|---|
| 1 | .30 | .90 | 1.75 |
| 2-17: 10-Byrne-c | | .50 | 1.00 |
| Special #1 ('86, $1.25) | .25 | .75 | 1.50 |

**HAYWIRE**
Oct, 1988 - No. 13, Sept, 1989 ($1.25, color, mature readers)
DC Comics

| | | | |
|---|---|---|---|
| 1 | .30 | .90 | 1.80 |
| 2-13 | .25 | .75 | 1.50 |

**HEADLINE COMICS** (. . . Crime No. 32-39)
Feb, 1943 - No. 22, Nov-Dec, 1946; No. 23, 1947 - No. 77, Oct, 1956
Prize Publications

| | | | |
|---|---|---|---|
| 1-Yank & Doodle x-over in Junior Rangers | 18.00 | 54.00 | 125.00 |
| 2 | 7.00 | 21.00 | 50.00 |
| 3-Used in POP, pg. 84 | 6.50 | 19.50 | 45.00 |
| 4-7,9,10: 4,9,10-Hitler stories in each | 5.00 | 15.00 | 35.00 |
| 8-Classic Hitler-c | 8.00 | 24.00 | 56.00 |
| 11,12 | 3.50 | 10.50 | 24.00 |
| 13-15-Blue Streak in all | 3.70 | 11.00 | 26.00 |
| 16-Origin Atomic Man | 8.00 | 24.00 | 56.00 |
| 17,18,20,21: 21-Atomic Man ends | 4.30 | 13.00 | 30.00 |
| 19-S&K-a | 11.00 | 32.00 | 75.00 |
| 22-Kiefer-c | 2.30 | 7.00 | 16.00 |
| 23,24: (All S&K-a). 24-Dope-crazy killer story | | | |
| | 11.00 | 32.00 | 75.00 |
| 25-35-S&K c/a. 25-Powell-a | 7.00 | 21.00 | 50.00 |
| 36-S&K-a | 5.00 | 15.00 | 35.00 |
| 37-One pg. S&K, Severin-a | 2.85 | 8.50 | 20.00 |
| 38,40-Meskin-a | 2.00 | 6.00 | 14.00 |
| 39,41-43,45-48,50-55: 51-Kirby-c. 45-Kirby-a | 1.15 | 3.50 | 8.00 |

| | Good | Fine | N-Mint |
|---|---|---|---|
| 44-S&K-c; Severin/Elder, Meskin-a | 3.50 | 10.50 | 24.00 |
| 49-Meskin-a | 1.50 | 4.50 | 10.00 |
| 56-S&K-a | 2.85 | 8.50 | 20.00 |
| 57-77: 72-Meskin c/a(i) | 1.15 | 3.50 | 8.00 |

**HELLBLAZER** (John Constantine) (See Saga of Swamp Thing #37)
Jan, 1988 - Present ($1.25-$1.50, Adults)
DC Comics

| | | | |
|---|---|---|---|
| 1 | .85 | 2.50 | 5.00 |
| 2-5 | .60 | 1.75 | 3.50 |
| 6-10 | .40 | 1.15 | 2.25 |
| 11-20 | .30 | .90 | 1.80 |
| 21-36 | .25 | .75 | 1.50 |
| Annual 1 ('89, $2.95, 68 pgs.) | .70 | 2.00 | 4.00 |

**HEROIC COMICS** (Reg'lar Fellers . . . #1-15; New Heroic #41 on)
Aug, 1940 - No. 97, June, 1955
Eastern Color Printing Co./Famous Funnies (Funnies, Inc. No. 1)

| | Good | Fine | N-Mint |
|---|---|---|---|
| 1-Hydroman (origin) by Bill Everett, The Purple Zombie (origin) & Mann of India by Tarpe Mills begins | 50.00 | 150.00 | 350.00 |
| 2 | 25.00 | 75.00 | 175.00 |
| 3,4 | 21.50 | 64.00 | 150.00 |
| 5,6 | 16.00 | 48.00 | 110.00 |
| 7-Origin Man O'Metal, 1 pg. | 18.50 | 56.00 | 130.00 |
| 8-10: 10-Lingerie panels | 11.00 | 32.00 | 75.00 |
| 11,13: 13-Crandall/Fine-a | 9.30 | 28.00 | 65.00 |
| 12-Music Master (origin) begins by Everett, ends No. 31; last Purple Zombie & Mann of India | 11.00 | 32.00 | 75.00 |
| 14-Hydroman x-over in Rainbow Boy; also in No. 15; origin Rainbow Boy | 11.00 | 32.00 | 75.00 |
| 15-Intro. Downbeat | 11.00 | 32.00 | 75.00 |
| 16-20: 17-Rainbow Boy x-over in Hydroman. 19-Rainbow Boy x-over in Hydroman & vice versa | 7.00 | 21.00 | 50.00 |
| 21-30:25-Rainbow Boy x-over in Hydroman. 28-Last Man O'Metal. 29-Last Hydroman | 4.30 | 13.00 | 30.00 |
| 31,34,38 | 1.60 | 4.70 | 11.00 |
| 32,36,37-Toth-a, 3-4 pgs. | 2.85 | 8.50 | 20.00 |
| 33,35-Toth-a, 8 & 9 pgs. | 3.15 | 9.50 | 22.00 |

|  | Good | Fine | N-Mint |
|---|---|---|---|
| 39-42-Toth, Ingels-a | 3.15 | 9.50 | 22.00 |
| 43,46,47,49-Toth-a, 2-4 pgs. 47-Ingels-a | 2.15 | 6.50 | 15.00 |
| 44,45,50-Toth-a, 6-9 pgs. | 2.65 | 8.00 | 18.00 |
| 48,53,54 | 1.15 | 3.50 | 8.00 |
| 51-Williamson-a | 3.50 | 10.50 | 24.00 |
| 52-Williamson-a (3 pg. story) | 1.70 | 5.00 | 12.00 |
| 55-Toth-c/a | 2.15 | 6.50 | 15.00 |
| 56-60-Toth-c. 60-Everett-a | 1.85 | 5.50 | 13.00 |
| 61-Everett-a | 1.30 | 4.00 | 9.00 |
| 62,64-Everett-c/a | 1.50 | 4.50 | 10.00 |
| 63-Everett-c | 1.00 | 3.00 | 7.00 |
| 65-Williamson/Frazetta-a; Evans-a, 2 pgs. | 5.00 | 15.00 | 35.00 |
| 66,75,94-Frazetta-a, 2 pgs. each | 2.00 | 6.00 | 14.00 |
| 67,73-Frazetta-a, 4 pgs. each | 2.85 | 8.50 | 20.00 |
| 68,74,76-80,84,85,88-93,95-97 | .85 | 2.60 | 6.00 |
| 69,72-Frazetta-a (6 & 8 pgs. each) | 5.00 | 15.00 | 35.00 |
| 70,71,86,87-Frazetta, 3-4 pgs. each; 1 pg. ad by Frazetta in #70 | | | |
|  | 2.65 | 8.00 | 18.00 |
| 81,82-One pg. Frazetta art | 1.30 | 4.00 | 9.00 |
| 83-Frazetta-a, 1/2 pg. | 1.30 | 4.00 | 9.00 |

**HIT COMICS**
July, 1940 - No. 65, July, 1950
Quality Comics Group

| | Good | Fine | N-Mint |
|---|---|---|---|
| 1-Origin Neon, the Unknown & Hercules; intro. The Red Bee; Bob & Swab, Blaze Barton, the Strange Twins, X-5 Super Agent, Casey Jones & Jack & Jill (ends #7) begin | 175.00 | 525.00 | 1225.00 |
| 2-The Old Witch begins, ends #14 | 83.00 | 250.00 | 580.00 |
| 3-Casey Jones ends; transvestism story-'Jack & Jill' | 68.00 | 205.00 | 475.00 |
| 4-Super Agent (ends #17), & Betty Bates (ends #65) begin; X-5 ends | 57.00 | 170.00 | 400.00 |
| 5-Classic cover | 83.00 | 250.00 | 580.00 |
| 6-10: 10-Old Witch by Crandall, 4 pgs.-1st work in comics | 48.00 | 144.00 | 335.00 |
| 11-17: 13-Blaze Barton ends. 17-Last Neon; Crandall Hercules in all | 45.00 | 135.00 | 315.00 |
| 18-Origin Stormy Foster, the Great Defender; The Ghost of Flanders begins; Crandall-c | 48.00 | 144.00 | 335.00 |

|  | Good | Fine | N-Mint |
|---|---|---|---|
| 19,20 | 45.00 | 135.00 | 315.00 |
| 21-24: 21-Last Hercules. 24-Last Red Bee & Strange Twins | | | |
|  | 38.00 | 115.00 | 265.00 |
| 25-Origin Kid Eternity and begins by Moldoff | | | |
|  | 50.00 | 150.00 | 350.00 |
| 26-Blackhawk x-over in Kid Eternity | 39.00 | 118.00 | 275.00 |
| 27-29 | 22.00 | 65.00 | 155.00 |
| 30,31-"Bill the Magnificent" by Kurtzman, 11 pgs. in each | | | |
|  | 18.50 | 56.00 | 130.00 |
| 32-40: 32-Plastic Man x-over. 34-Last Stormy Foster | | | |
|  | 9.30 | 28.00 | 65.00 |
| 41-50 | 6.50 | 19.50 | 45.00 |
| 51-60-Last Kid Eternity | 5.70 | 17.00 | 40.00 |
| 61,63-Crandall c/a; Jeb Rivers begins #61 | 6.50 | 19.50 | 45.00 |
| 62 | 5.00 | 15.00 | 35.00 |
| 64,65-Crandall-a | 5.70 | 17.00 | 40.00 |

**HOPALONG CASSIDY** (Also see Bill Boyd Western, Master Comics, Real Western Hero & Western Hero; Bill Boyd starred as H. Cassidy in the movies; H. Cassidy in movies, radio & TV)
Feb, 1943; No. 2, Summer, 1946 - No. 85, Jan, 1954
Fawcett Publications

| 1 (1943, 68 pgs.)-H. Cassidy & his horse Topper begin (on sale 1/8/43)-Captain Marvel on-c | 125.00 | 315.00 | 750.00 |
|---|---|---|---|
| 2-(Sum, '46) | 37.00 | 110.00 | 260.00 |
| 3,4: 3-(Fall, '46, 52 pgs. begin) | 19.00 | 57.00 | 135.00 |
| 5-"Mad Barber" story mentioned in **SOTI**, pgs. 308,309 | | | |
|  | 18.00 | 54.00 | 125.00 |
| 6-10 | 14.00 | 42.00 | 100.00 |
| 11-19: 11,13-19-Photo-c | 11.00 | 32.00 | 76.00 |
| 20-29 (52 pgs.)-Painted/photo-c | 8.50 | 25.50 | 60.00 |
| 30,31,33,34,37-39,41 (52 pgs.)-Painted-c | 5.50 | 16.50 | 38.00 |
| 32,40 (36 pgs.)-Painted-c | 4.50 | 14.00 | 32.00 |
| 35,42,43,45 (52 pgs.)-Photo-c | 5.50 | 16.50 | 38.00 |
| 36,44,48 (36 pgs.)-Photo-c | 4.50 | 14.00 | 32.00 |
| 46,47,49-51,53,54,56 (52 pgs.)-Photo-c | 5.00 | 15.00 | 35.00 |
| 52,55,57-70 (36 pgs.)-Photo-c | 3.70 | 11.00 | 26.00 |
| 71-84-Photo-c | 2.85 | 8.50 | 20.00 |
| 85-Last Fawcett issue; photo-c | 3.50 | 10.50 | 24.00 |

## HOPALONG CASSIDY (TV)
No. 86, Feb, 1954 - No. 135, May-June, 1959 (All-36 pgs.)
National Periodical Publications

|  | Good | Fine | N-Mint |
|---|---|---|---|
| 86-Photo covers continue | 12.00 | 36.00 | 84.00 |
| 87 | 6.50 | 19.50 | 45.00 |
| 88-90 | 4.50 | 14.00 | 32.00 |
| 91-99 (98 has #93 on-c & is last precode issue, 2/55) | | | |
|  | 3.70 | 11.00 | 26.00 |
| 100 | 5.00 | 15.00 | 35.00 |
| 101-108-Last photo-c | 3.15 | 9.50 | 22.00 |
| 109-135: 124-Painted-c | 3.15 | 9.50 | 22.00 |

## HOT STUFF, THE LITTLE DEVIL
10/57 - No. 141, 7/77; No. 142, 2/78 - No. 164, 8/82; No. 165, 10/86 - No.
171, 11/87; No. 172, 11/88 - Present
Harvey Publications (Illustrated Humor)

| 1 | 13.00 | 40.00 | 90.00 |
|---|---|---|---|
| 2-1st app. Stumbo the Giant | 8.00 | 24.00 | 56.00 |
| 3-5 | 6.00 | 18.00 | 42.00 |
| 6-10 | 3.00 | 9.00 | 21.00 |
| 11-20 | 1.50 | 4.50 | 10.00 |
| 21-40 | .70 | 2.00 | 5.00 |
| 41-60 | .55 | 1.60 | 3.20 |
| 61-105 | .25 | .80 | 1.60 |
| 106-112: All 52 pg. Giants | .35 | 1.00 | 2.00 |
| 113-174 (10/89)-Later issues $1.00-c | | .40 | .80 |

## HOWDY DOODY (TV)
1/50 - No. 38, 7-9/56; No. 761, 1/57; No. 811, 7/57
Dell Publishing Co.

| 1-Photo-c; 1st TV comic? | 18.00 | 54.00 | 125.00 |
|---|---|---|---|
| 2-Photo-c | 8.50 | 25.50 | 60.00 |
| 3-5: All photo-c | 5.70 | 17.00 | 40.00 |
| 6-Used in SOTI, pg. 309; painted-c begin | 5.00 | 15.00 | 35.00 |
| 7-10 | 4.50 | 14.00 | 32.00 |
| 11-20 | 3.50 | 10.50 | 24.00 |

|  | Good | Fine | N-Mint |
|---|---|---|---|
| 21-38 | 2.30 | 7.00 | 16.00 |
| 4-Color 761,811 | 4.50 | 14.00 | 32.00 |

**HUEY, DEWEY AND LOUIE JUNIOR WOODCHUCKS** (Disney)
Aug, 1966 - No. 81, 1984 (See Walt Disney's C&S #125)
Gold Key No. 1-61/Whitman No. 62 on

|  | Good | Fine | N-Mint |
|---|---|---|---|
| 1 | 2.65 | 8.00 | 18.00 |
| 2,3(12/68) | 1.70 | 5.00 | 12.00 |
| 4,5(4/70)-Barks-r | 1.70 | 5.00 | 12.00 |
| 6-17-Written by Barks | 1.15 | 3.50 | 8.00 |
| 18,27-30 | .70 | 2.00 | 4.00 |
| 19-23,25-Written by Barks. 22,23,25-Barks-r | .85 | 2.50 | 5.00 |
| 24,26-Barks-r | .85 | 2.50 | 5.00 |
| 31-57,60-81: 41,70,80-Reprints | .25 | .75 | 1.50 |
| 58,59-Barks-r | .35 | 1.00 | 2.00 |

**HUMAN TORCH, THE** (Red Raven #1) (See Marvel Comics)
No. 2, Fall, 1940 - No. 15, Spring, 1944 (becomes Funny Tunes); No. 16,
Fall, 1944 - No. 35, Mar, 1949 (becomes Love Tales); No. 36, April,
1954 - No. 38, Aug, 1954
Timely/Marvel Comics (TP 2,3/TCI 4-9/SePI 10/SnPC 11-25/CnPC
26-35/Atlas Comics (CPC 36-38))

2(#1)-Intro & Origin Toro; The Falcon, The Fiery Mask, Mantor the Magician, & Microman only app.; Human Torch by Burgos, Sub-Mariner
by Everett begin (origin of each in text)

|  | Good | Fine | N-Mint |
|---|---|---|---|
|  | 583.00 | 1460.00 | 3500.00 |

*(Prices vary widely on this book)*

3(#2)-40 pg. H.T. story; H.T. & S.M. battle over who is best artist in text-
Everett or Burgos    233.00    585.00    1400.00
4(#3)-Origin The Patriot in text; last Everett Sub-Mariner; Sid Greene-a
175.00    440.00    1050.00
5(#4)-The Patriot app; Angel x-over in Sub-Mariner (Summer, 1941)
125.00    315.00    750.00
5-Human Torch battles Sub-Mariner (Fall,'41)
200.00    500.00    1200.00
6,7,9    82.00    205.00    490.00
8-Human Torch battles Sub-Mariner; Wolverton-a, 1 pg.
133.00    335.00    800.00

| | Good | Fine | N-Mint |
|---|---|---|---|
| 10-Human Torch battles Sub-Mariner; Wolverton-a, 1 pg. | | | |
| | 100.00 | 250.00 | 600.00 |
| 11-15 | 63.00 | 160.00 | 380.00 |
| 16-20: 20-Last War issue | 50.00 | 125.00 | 300.00 |
| 21-30 | 42.00 | 105.00 | 250.00 |
| 31-Namora x-over in Sub-Mariner (also #30); last Toro | | | |
| | 33.00 | 83.00 | 200.00 |
| 32-Sungirl, Namora app.; Sungirl-c | 33.00 | 83.00 | 200.00 |
| 33-Capt. America x-over | 35.00 | 90.00 | 210.00 |
| 34-Sungirl solo | 33.00 | 83.00 | 200.00 |
| 35-Captain America & Sungirl app. (1949) | 35.00 | 90.00 | 210.00 |
| 36-38(1954)-Sub-Mariner in all | 25.00 | 63.00 | 150.00 |

# I

**IBIS, THE INVINCIBLE** (See Whiz Comics)
1943 (Feb) - No. 2, 1943; No. 3, Wint, 1945 - No. 6, Spring, 1948
Fawcett Publications

|  | Good | Fine | N-Mint |
|---|---|---|---|
| 1-Origin Ibis; Raboy-c; on sale 1/2/43 | 75.00 | 225.00 | 525.00 |
| 2-Bondage-c | 37.00 | 110.00 | 260.00 |
| 3-Wolverton-a #3-6 (4 pgs. each) | 30.00 | 90.00 | 210.00 |
| 4-6: 5-Bondage-c. 6-Beck-c | 23.50 | 71.00 | 165.00 |

**I LOVE LUCY COMICS** (TV) (Also see The Lucy Show)
No. 535, Feb, 1954 - No. 35, Apr-June, 1962 (All photo-c)
Dell Publishing Co.

| | Good | Fine | N-Mint |
|---|---|---|---|
| 4-Color 535(#1) | 14.00 | 42.00 | 100.00 |
| 4-Color 559(#2, 5/54) | 11.00 | 32.00 | 75.00 |
| 3 (8-10/54) - 5 | 7.00 | 21.00 | 50.00 |
| 6-10 | 6.00 | 18.00 | 42.00 |
| 11-20 | 5.50 | 16.50 | 38.00 |
| 21-35 | 4.50 | 14.00 | 32.00 |

**INCREDIBLE HULK, THE** (See The Avengers & The Defenders #1)
May, 1962 - No. 6, Mar, 1963; No. 102, Apr, 1968 - Present
Marvel Comics Group

| | Good | Fine | N-Mint |
|---|---|---|---|
| 1-Origin & 1st app. (skin is grey colored) | 150.00 | 450.00 | 1050.00 |
| 2-1st Green skinned Hulk | 60.00 | 180.00 | 420.00 |
| 3-Origin retold | 45.00 | 135.00 | 315.00 |
| 4-6: 4-Brief origin retold. 6-Intro. Teen Brigade | | | |
| | 37.00 | 111.00 | 260.00 |
| 102-(Formerly Tales to Astonish)-Origin retold | | | |
| | 14.30 | 43.00 | 100.00 |
| 103,104 | 5.00 | 15.00 | 35.00 |
| 105-108: 105-1st Missing Link | 3.15 | 9.50 | 22.00 |
| 109,110 | 2.15 | 6.50 | 15.00 |
| 111-117: 117-Last 12 cent issue | 1.50 | 4.50 | 10.00 |
| 118-125 | 1.00 | 3.00 | 6.00 |

*The Incredible Hulk #4,* © *Marvel Comics*

| | Good | Fine | N-Mint |
|---|---|---|---|
| 126-140: 126-1st Barbara Norriss (Valkyrie). 131-1st Jim Wilson, Hulk's new sidekick. 136-1st Xeron, The Star-Slayer. 140-Written by Harlan Ellison; 1st Jarella, Hulk's love | .50 | 1.50 | 3.00 |
| 141-1st app. Doc Samson | .70 | 2.00 | 4.00 |
| 142-161,163-175,179: 145-(52 pgs.). 149-1st The Inheritor. 155-1st app. Shaper. 161-The Mimic dies. 163-1st app. The Gremlin. 164-1st app. Capt. Omen & Colonel John D. Armbruster. 166-1st Zzzax. 168-1st The Harpy. 169-1st Bi-Beast. 172-X-Men cameo; origin Juggernaut retold | .35 | 1.00 | 2.00 |
| 162-1st app. The Wendigo; Beast app. | .70 | 2.00 | 4.00 |
| 176-178-Warlock app. | .70 | 2.00 | 4.00 |
| 180-1st app. Wolverine (cameo) | 8.50 | 25.50 | 60.00 |
| 181-Wolverine app. | 35.00 | 105.00 | 245.00 |
| 182-Wolverine cameo; 1st Crackajack Jackson | 6.50 | 19.50 | 45.00 |
| 183-199: 185-Death of Col. Armbruster | .45 | 1.40 | 2.80 |

| | Good | Fine | N-Mint |
|---|---|---|---|
| 200-Silver Surfer app. | 1.70 | 5.00 | 10.00 |
| 201-240: 212-1st The Constrictor | .35 | 1.00 | 2.00 |
| 241-249,251-271: 271-Rocket Raccoon app. | | .60 | 1.20 |
| 250-Giant size; Silver Surfer app. | .35 | 1.00 | 2.00 |
| 272-Alpha Flight app. | .50 | 1.50 | 3.00 |
| 273-299,301-313: 278,279-Most Marvel characters app. (Wolverine in both). 279-X-Men & Alpha Flight cameos. 282-She-Hulk app. 293-F.F. app. 312-Origin Hulk | | .60 | 1.20 |
| 300-Double size | .35 | 1.00 | 2.00 |
| 314-Byrne-c/a begins, ends #319 | .85 | 2.50 | 5.00 |
| 315-319 | .35 | 1.00 | 2.00 |
| 320-323,325-329: 326-Grey vs. Green Hulk | | .60 | 1.20 |
| 324-1st app. Grey Hulk since earlier series | .75 | 2.25 | 4.50 |
| 330-1st McFarlane issue | 2.15 | 6.50 | 13.00 |
| 331-Grey Hulk series begins | 1.50 | 4.50 | 9.00 |
| 332-334,336-339: 336,337-X-Factor app. | 1.00 | 3.00 | 6.00 |
| 335-No McFarlane-a | .40 | 1.15 | 2.25 |
| 340-Wolverine-c/story by McFarlane | 2.50 | 7.50 | 15.00 |
| 341-345: 345-($1.50, 52 pgs.) | .70 | 2.00 | 4.00 |
| 346-Last McFarlane issue | .60 | 1.75 | 3.50 |
| 347-349,351-358,360-375 | | .50 | 1.00 |
| 350-Double size | .35 | 1.00 | 2.00 |
| 359-Wolverine app. (illusion only) | .25 | .75 | 1.50 |
| Giant-Size 1(1975) | .50 | 1.50 | 3.00 |
| Special 1(10/68, 68 pg.)-New-a; Steranko-c | 3.60 | 11.00 | 25.00 |
| Special 2(10/69, 25 cents, 68 pg.)-Origin retold | 1.70 | 5.00 | 12.00 |
| Special 3(1/71, 25 cents, 68 pg.) | .85 | 2.50 | 5.00 |
| Annual 4 (1/72) | .50 | 1.50 | 3.00 |
| Annual 5(10/76) | .35 | 1.00 | 2.00 |
| Annual 6 (11/77) | .25 | .75 | 1.50 |
| Annual 7(8/78)-Byrne/Layton-c/a; Iceman & Angel app. | .50 | 1.50 | 3.00 |
| Annual 8-16: 8(11/79). 9(9/80). 10('81). 11(10/82)-Miller, Buckler-a(p). 12(8/83). 13('84). 14('85). 15('86). 16('90) | .25 | .75 | 1.50 |
| . . . Versus Quasimodo (3/83, one-shot)-Based on Saturday morning cartoon | | .50 | 1.00 |

## INCREDIBLE HULK AND WOLVERINE, THE
Oct, 1986 (One shot, $2.50, color)
Marvel Comics Group

|  | Good | Fine | N-Mint |
|---|---|---|---|
| 1-r-/1st app. Wolverine & Incred. Hulk from Incred. Hulk #180,181; Wolverine back-up by Austin(i); Byrne-c | 1.35 | 4.00 | 8.00 |

## INDIAN CHIEF (White Eagle . . . )
No. 3, July-Sept, 1951 - No. 33, Jan-Mar, 1959 (All painted-c)
Dell Publishing Co.

|  | Good | Fine | N-Mint |
|---|---|---|---|
| 3 | 1.70 | 5.00 | 12.00 |
| 4-11: 6-White Eagle app. | 1.15 | 3.50 | 8.00 |
| 12-1st White Eagle(10-12/53)-Not same as earlier character |  |  |  |
|  | 1.70 | 5.00 | 12.00 |
| 13-29 | 1.00 | 3.00 | 7.00 |
| 30-33-Buscema-a | 1.15 | 3.50 | 8.00 |

## INFERIOR FIVE, THE (Inferior 5 #11, 12) (See Showcase #62, 63, 65)
3-4/67 - No. 10, 9-10/68; No. 11, 8-9/72 - No. 12, 10-11/72
National Periodical Publications (#1-10: 12 cents)

|  | Good | Fine | N-Mint |
|---|---|---|---|
| 1-Sekowsky-a(p) | 1.70 | 5.00 | 12.00 |
| 2-Plastic Man app.; Sekowsky-a(p) | 1.00 | 3.00 | 6.00 |
| 3-10: 10-Superman x-over | .85 | 2.50 | 5.00 |
| 11,12-Orlando-c/a; both r-/Showcase #62,63 | .85 | 2.50 | 5.00 |

## INFINITY, INC.
Mar, 1984 - No. 53, Aug, 1988 ($1.25; Baxter paper; 36 pgs.)
DC Comics

|  | Good | Fine | N-Mint |
|---|---|---|---|
| 1-Brainwave, Jr., Fury, The Huntress, Jade, Northwind, Nuklon, Obsidian, Power Girl, Silver Scarab & Star Spangled Kid begin |  |  |  |
|  | .60 | 1.75 | 3.50 |
| 2-5: 2-Dr. Midnite, G.A. Flash, W. Woman, Dr. Fate, Hourman, Gr. Lantern, Wildcat app. 5-Nudity panels | .35 | 1.10 | 2.20 |
| 6-10 | .30 | .95 | 1.90 |
| 11-13,38-49,51-53: 46,47-Millennium tie-ins | .25 | .80 | 1.60 |
| 14-Todd McFarlane-a (5/85) | .85 | 2.50 | 5.00 |
| 15-37-McFarlane-a (20,23,24: 5 pgs. only; 33: 2 pgs.); 18-24-Crisis x-over. |  |  |  |

|  | Good | Fine | N-Mint |
|---|---|---|---|
| 21-Intro new Hourman & Dr. Midnight. 26-New Wildcat app. 31-Star-Spangled Kid becomes Skyman. 32-Green Fury becomes Green Flame. 33-Origin Obsidian | .50 | 1.50 | 3.00 |
| 50 ($2.50, 52 pgs.) | .40 | 1.25 | 2.50 |
| Annual 1,2: 1(12/85)-Crisis x-over. 2('88, $2.00) | .35 | 1.00 | 2.00 |
| Special 1 ('87, $1.50) | .25 | .75 | 1.50 |

**IRON FIST** (Also see Marvel Premiere & Power Man)
Nov, 1975 - No. 15, Sept, 1977
Marvel Comics Group

|  | Good | Fine | N-Mint |
|---|---|---|---|
| 1-McWilliams-a(i); Iron Man app. | 1.85 | 5.50 | 11.00 |
| 2 | 1.00 | 3.00 | 6.00 |
| 3-5 | .75 | 2.25 | 4.50 |
| 6-10: 8-Origin retold | .60 | 1.80 | 3.60 |
| 11-13: 12-Capt. America app. | .45 | 1.40 | 2.80 |
| 14-1st app. Saber Tooth | 3.70 | 11.00 | 22.00 |
| 15-New X-Men app., Byrne-a | 3.00 | 9.00 | 18.00 |
| 15 (35 cent edition) | 4.15 | 12.50 | 25.00 |

**IRON MAN** (Also see The Avengers #1 & Tales of Suspense #39)
May, 1968 - Present
Marvel Comics Group

|  | Good | Fine | N-Mint |
|---|---|---|---|
| 1-Origin | 37.00 | 111.00 | 260.00 |
| 2 | 11.50 | 34.50 | 80.00 |
| 3 | 8.50 | 25.50 | 60.00 |
| 4,5 | 6.30 | 19.00 | 44.00 |
| 6-10 | 4.00 | 12.00 | 28.00 |
| 11-15: 15-Last 12 cent issue | 3.15 | 9.50 | 22.00 |
| 16-20 | 1.85 | 5.50 | 13.00 |
| 21-40: 22-Death of Janice Cord. 27-Intro Fire Brand. 33-Intro Spymaster | 1.70 | 5.00 | 10.00 |
| 41-46,48-50: 43-Intro The Guardsman. 46-The Guardsman dies. 50-Princess Python app. | 1.35 | 4.00 | 8.00 |
| 47-Origin retold; Smith-a(p) | 2.00 | 6.00 | 12.00 |
| 51-54 | 1.00 | 3.00 | 6.00 |
| 55,56-Starlin-a; 55-Starlin-c | 1.50 | 4.50 | 9.00 |
| 57-67,69,70: 59-Firebrand returns. 65-Origin Dr. Spectrum | .90 | 2.75 | 5.50 |

*Iron Man #169, © Marvel Comics*

|  | Good | Fine | N-Mint |
|---|---|---|---|
| 68-Starlin-c; origin retold | 1.00 | 3.00 | 6.00 |
| 71-99: 76 r-/#9. 86-1st app. Blizzard. 87-Origin Blizzard | | | |
|  | .75 | 2.20 | 4.40 |
| 100-Starlin-c | 1.50 | 4.50 | 9.00 |
| 101-117: 101-Intro DreadKnight. 109-1st app. new Crimson Dynamo. | | | |
| 110-Origin Jack of Hearts retold | .55 | 1.65 | 3.30 |
| 118-Byrne-a(p) | .90 | 2.75 | 5.50 |
| 119,120,123-128-Tony Stark recovers from alcohol problem. 120,121- Sub- | | | |
| Mariner x-over. 125-Ant-Man app. | .70 | 2.00 | 4.00 |
| 121,122,129-149: 122-Origin. 131,132-Hulk x-over | | | |
|  | .35 | 1.10 | 2.20 |
| 150-Double size | .50 | 1.50 | 3.00 |
| 151-168: 152-New armor. 161-Moon Knight app. 167-Tony Stark alcohol | | | |
| problem starts again | .30 | .85 | 1.70 |
| 169-New Iron Man (Jim Rhodes replaces Tony Stark) | | | |
|  | 1.35 | 4.00 | 8.00 |
| 170 | .75 | 2.20 | 4.40 |
| 171 | .35 | 1.10 | 2.20 |

|  | Good | Fine | N-Mint |
|---|---|---|---|
| 172-199: 172-Captain America x-over. 186-Intro Vibro. 190-Scarlet Witch app. 191-198-Tony Stark returns as original Iron Man. 192- Both Iron Men battle | .30 | .85 | 1.70 |
| 200-Double size ($1.25)-Tony Stark returns as new Iron Man (red & white armor) thru #230 | .70 | 2.00 | 4.00 |
| 201-224: 213-Intro new Dominic Fortune | .25 | .75 | 1.50 |
| 225-Double size ($1.25) | .90 | 2.75 | 5.50 |
| 226-243: 228-Vs. Capt. America. 231-Intro new Iron Man. 233-Ant-Man app. 243-T. Stark loses use of legs | .25 | .75 | 1.50 |
| 244-($1.50, 52 pgs.)-New Armor makes him walk | .75 | 2.20 | 4.40 |
| 245-249: 247-Hulk x-over | .25 | .75 | 1.50 |
| 250 ($1.50, 52 pgs.) | .30 | .85 | 1.70 |
| 251-264 |  | .50 | 1.00 |
| Giant Size 1('75)-Ditko-a(r) | .70 | 2.00 | 4.00 |
| Special 1(8/70)-Sub-Mariner x-over; Everett-c | 1.50 | 4.50 | 10.00 |
| Special 2(11/71) | .85 | 2.50 | 5.00 |
| Annual 3(6/76)-Man-Thing app. | .50 | 1.50 | 3.00 |
| Annual 5-9: 5(12/82). 6(11/83)-New Iron Man(J. Rhodes) app. 7(10/84). 8(10/86)-X-Factor app. 9(12/87) | .35 | 1.00 | 2.00 |
| Annual 10(8/89, $2.00, 68 pgs.)-Atlantis Attacks x-over; P. Smith-a; Layton/Guice-a; Sub-Mariner app. | .40 | 1.25 | 2.50 |
| Annual 11 ('90, $2.00, 68 pgs.) | .35 | 1.00 | 2.00 |
| King Size 4(8/77)-Newton-a(i) | .50 | 1.50 | 3.00 |

**IRON MAN & SUB-MARINER**
April, 1968 (One Shot) (Pre-dates Iron Man #1)
Marvel Comics Group

| | Good | Fine | N-Mint |
|---|---|---|---|
| 1-Colan/Craig-a-Iron Man; Colan/Everett-c | 11.50 | 34.50 | 80.00 |

# J

**JACE PEARSON OF THE TEXAS RANGERS** (4-Color #396 is titled Tales
  of the Texas Rangers; . . . 's Tales of . . . #11-on)
No. 396, 5/52 - No. 1021, 8-10/59 (No #10) (All-Photo-c)
Dell Publishing Co.

| | Good | Fine | N-Mint |
|---|---|---|---|
| 4-Color 396 (#1) | 5.50 | 16.50 | 38.00 |
| 2(5-7/53) - 9(2-4/55) | 3.50 | 10.50 | 24.00 |
| 4-Color 648(9/55) | 3.50 | 10.50 | 24.00 |
| 11(11-2/55/56) - 14,17-20(6-8/58) | 3.00 | 9.00 | 21.00 |
| 15,16-Toth-a | 4.00 | 12.00 | 28.00 |
| 4-Color 961-Spiegle-a | 3.50 | 10.50 | 24.00 |
| 4-Color 1021 | 3.00 | 9.00 | 21.00 |

**JACKIE GLEASON AND THE HONEYMOONERS** (TV)
June-July, 1956 - No. 12, Apr-May, 1958
National Periodical Publications

| | | | |
|---|---|---|---|
| 1 | 41.00 | 122.00 | 285.00 |
| 2 | 25.00 | 75.00 | 175.00 |
| 3-11 | 19.00 | 58.00 | 135.00 |
| 12 (Scarce) | 23.00 | 70.00 | 165.00 |

**JACKIE ROBINSON** (Famous Plays of . . .)
May, 1950 - No. 6, 1952 (Baseball hero) (All photo-c)
Fawcett Publications

| | | | |
|---|---|---|---|
| nn | 30.00 | 90.00 | 210.00 |
| 2 | 20.00 | 60.00 | 140.00 |
| 3-6 | 17.00 | 51.00 | 120.00 |

**JACKPOT COMICS**
Spring, 1941 - No. 9, Spring, 1943
MLJ Magazines

| | Good | Fine | N-Mint |
|---|---|---|---|
| 1-The Black Hood, Mr. Justice, Steel Sterling & Sgt. Boyle begin; Biro-c | | | |
| | 117.00 | 295.00 | 700.00 |
| 2 | 49.00 | 148.00 | 345.00 |
| 3 | 38.00 | 115.00 | 270.00 |
| 4-Archie begins (on sale 12/41)-(Also see Pep Comics No. 22); Montana-c | | | |
| | 114.00 | 342.00 | 800.00 |
| 5-Hitler-c | 49.00 | 148.00 | 345.00 |
| 6-9: 6,7-Bondage-c | 43.00 | 130.00 | 300.00 |

**JESSIE JAMES**
Aug, 1950 - No. 29, Aug-Sept, 1956
Avon Periodicals

| | Good | Fine | N-Mint |
|---|---|---|---|
| 1-Kubert Alabam r-/Cowpuncher #1 | 11.00 | 33.00 | 76.00 |
| 2-Kubert-a(3) | 8.50 | 25.50 | 60.00 |
| 3-Kubert Alabam r-/Cowpuncher #2 | 7.00 | 21.00 | 50.00 |
| 4,9,10-No Kubert | 2.85 | 8.50 | 20.00 |
| 5,6-Kubert Jesse James-a(3); one pg. Wood-a, #5 | | | |
| | 7.00 | 21.00 | 50.00 |
| 7-Kubert Jesse James-a(2) | 6.00 | 18.00 | 42.00 |
| 8-Kinstler-a(3) | 4.00 | 12.00 | 28.00 |
| 11-14 (Exist?) | 2.15 | 6.50 | 15.00 |
| 15-Kinstler r-/#3 | 2.15 | 6.50 | 15.00 |
| 16-Kinstler r-/#3 & Sheriff Bob Dixon's Chuck Wagon #1 with name changed to Sheriff Tom Wilson | 2.65 | 8.00 | 18.00 |
| 17-19,21: 17-Jesse James r-/#4; Kinstler-c idea from Kubert splash in #6. 18-Kubert Jesse James r-/#5. 19-Kubert Jesse James-r. 21-Two Jesse James r-/#4, Kinstler r-/#4 | 1.70 | 5.00 | 12.00 |
| 20-Williamson/Frazetta-a; r-Chief Vic. Apache Massacre; Kubert Jesse James r-/#6 | 8.50 | 25.50 | 60.00 |
| 22,23-No Kubert | 1.60 | 4.80 | 11.00 |
| 24-New McCarty strip by Kinstler plus Kinstler r-/#9 | | | |
| | 1.60 | 4.80 | 11.00 |
| 25-New McCarty Jesse James strip by Kinstler; Kinstler J. James r-/ #7,9 | | | |
| | 1.60 | 4.80 | 11.00 |
| 26,27-New McCarty J. James strip plus a Kinstler/McCann Jesse James-r | | | |
| | 1.60 | 4.80 | 11.00 |

|  | Good | Fine | N-Mint |
|---|---|---|---|

28,29: 28-Reprints most of Red Mountain, featuring Quantrells Raiders

|  | 1.60 | 4.80 | 11.00 |
|---|---|---|---|

Annual (nn; 1952; 25 cents)-". . . Brings Six-Gun Justice to the West" (100 pgs.)-3 earlier issues rebound; Kubert, Kinstler-a(3)

|  | 17.00 | 51.00 | 120.00 |
|---|---|---|---|

**JETSONS, THE** (TV)
Jan, 1963 - No. 36, Oct, 1970 (Hanna-Barbera)
Gold Key

| | Good | Fine | N-Mint |
|---|---|---|---|
| 1 | 9.30 | 28.00 | 65.00 |
| 2 | 5.70 | 17.00 | 40.00 |
| 3-10 | 4.00 | 12.00 | 28.00 |
| 11-20 | 3.50 | 10.50 | 24.00 |
| 21-36 | 2.85 | 8.50 | 20.00 |

**JETSONS, THE** (TV) (Hanna-Barbera)
Nov, 1970 - No. 20, Dec, 1973
Charlton Comics

| | Good | Fine | N-Mint |
|---|---|---|---|
| 1 | 3.70 | 11.00 | 26.00 |
| 2 | 2.15 | 6.50 | 15.00 |
| 3-10 | 1.60 | 4.80 | 11.00 |
| 11-20 | 1.15 | 3.50 | 8.00 |

**JIMMY WAKELY** (Cowboy movie star)
Sept-Oct, 1949 - No. 18, July-Aug, 1952 (1-13: 52 pgs.)
National Periodical Publications

1-Photo-c, 52 pgs. begin; Alex Toth-a; Kit Colby Girl Sheriff begins

|  | 32.00 | 95.00 | 225.00 |
|---|---|---|---|
| 2-Toth-a | 22.00 | 65.00 | 154.00 |

3,6,7-Frazetta-a in all, 3 pgs. each; Toth-a in all. 7-Last photo-c?

|  | 23.50 | 70.00 | 165.00 |
|---|---|---|---|

4-Frazetta-a, 3 pgs.; Kurtzman "Pot-Shot Pete," 1pg; Toth-a

|  | 23.50 | 70.00 | 165.00 |
|---|---|---|---|
| 5,8-15,18-Toth-a; 12,14-Kubert-a, 3 & 2 pgs. | 17.00 | 51.00 | 120.00 |
| 16,17 | 12.00 | 36.00 | 84.00 |

**JINGLE JANGLE COMICS**
Feb, 1942 - No. 42, Dec, 1949
Eastern Color Printing Co.

| | Good | Fine | N-Mint |
|---|---|---|---|
| 1-Pie-Face Prince of Old Pretzleburg, & Jingle Jangle Tales by George Carlson, Hortense, & Benny Bear begin | | | |
| | 22.00 | 65.00 | 154.00 |
| 2,3-No Pie-Face Prince | 10.00 | 30.00 | 70.00 |
| 4-Pie-Face Prince cover | 10.00 | 30.00 | 70.00 |
| 5 | 8.50 | 25.50 | 60.00 |
| 6-10: 8-No Pie-Face Prince | 8.00 | 24.00 | 56.00 |
| 11-15 | 5.00 | 15.00 | 35.00 |
| 16-30: 17,18-No Pie-Face Prince. 30-Xmas-c | 3.70 | 11.00 | 26.00 |
| 31-42: 36,42-Xmas-c | 2.65 | 8.00 | 18.00 |

**JOE PALOOKA** (1st Series) (Also see Feature Funnies)
1942 - No. 4, 1944
Columbia Comic Corp. (Publication Enterprises)

| | Good | Fine | N-Mint |
|---|---|---|---|
| 1-1st to portray American president; gov't permission required | | | |
| | 30.00 | 90.00 | 210.00 |
| 2 (1943)-Hitler-c | 17.00 | 51.00 | 120.00 |
| 3,4 | 12.00 | 36.00 | 84.00 |

**JOE PALOOKA** (2nd Series) (Battle Adv. #68-74; . . . Advs.
    #75,77-81,83-85,87; Champ of the Comics #76,82,86,89-93)
Nov, 1945 - No. 118, Mar, 1961
Harvey Publications

| | Good | Fine | N-Mint |
|---|---|---|---|
| 1 | 20.00 | 60.00 | 140.00 |
| 2 | 10.00 | 30.00 | 70.00 |
| 3,4,6 | 6.50 | 19.50 | 45.00 |
| 5-Boy Explorers by S&K (7-8/46) | 9.50 | 28.00 | 65.00 |
| 7-1st Powell Flyin' Fool, ends #25 | 5.70 | 17.00 | 40.00 |
| 8-10 | 5.00 | 15.00 | 35.00 |
| 11-14,16-20: 19-Freedom Train-c | 4.00 | 12.00 | 28.00 |

|  | Good | Fine | N-Mint |
|---|---|---|---|
| 15-Origin Humphrey; Super heroine Atoma app. by Powell | | | |
|  | 5.00 | 15.00 | 35.00 |
| 21-30: 30-Nude female painting | 3.00 | 9.00 | 21.00 |
| 31-61: 35-1st app. Little Max? 44-Joe Palooka marries Ann Howe | | | |
|  | 2.30 | 7.00 | 16.00 |
| 62-S&K Boy Explorers-r | 3.00 | 9.00 | 21.00 |
| 63-80: 66,67-'commie' torture story | 1.70 | 5.00 | 12.00 |
| 81-99,101-115 | 1.50 | 4.50 | 10.00 |
| 100 | 1.75 | 5.25 | 12.00 |
| 116-S&K Boy Explorers (r) (Giant, '60) | 2.85 | 8.50 | 20.00 |
| 117,118-Giants | 2.65 | 8.00 | 18.00 |

**JOHNNY MACK BROWN** (TV western star)
No. 269, Mar, 1950 - No. 963, Feb, 1959 (All Photo-c)
Dell Publishing Co.

|  | Good | Fine | N-Mint |
|---|---|---|---|
| 4-Color 269(#1)(3/50, 52 pgs.)-Johnny Mack Brown & his horse Rebel begin; photo front/back-c begin; Marsh-a begins, ends #9 | | | |
|  | 12.00 | 36.00 | 84.00 |
| 2(10-12/50, 52 pgs.) | 6.50 | 19.50 | 45.00 |
| 3(1-3/51, 52 pgs.) | 4.30 | 13.00 | 30.00 |
| 4-10 (9-11/52)(36 pgs.) | 3.50 | 10.50 | 24.00 |
| 4-Color 455,493,541,584,618 | 3.50 | 10.50 | 24.00 |
| 4-Color 645,685,722,776,834,963 | 3.50 | 10.50 | 24.00 |
| 4-Color 922-Manning-a | 4.00 | 12.00 | 28.00 |

**JOHN WAYNE ADVENTURE COMICS** (Movie star)
Winter, 1949 - No. 31, May, 1955 (Photo-c: 1-12,17,25-on)
Toby Press

|  | Good | Fine | N-Mint |
|---|---|---|---|
| 1 (36 pgs.)-Photo-c begin | 41.00 | 122.00 | 285.00 |
| 2 (36 pgs.)-Williamson/Frazetta-a(2) (one r-/Billy the Kid #1), 6 & 2 pgs.; photo back-c | | | |
|  | 41.00 | 125.00 | 290.00 |
| 3 (36 pgs.)-Williamson/Frazetta-a(2), 16 pgs. total; photo back-c | | | |
|  | 41.00 | 125.00 | 290.00 |
| 4 (52 pgs.)-Williamson/Frazetta-a(2), 16 pgs. total | | | |
|  | 41.00 | 125.00 | 290.00 |

| | Good | Fine | N-Mint |
|---|---|---|---|
| 5 (52 pgs.)-Kurtzman-a-(Alfred "L" Newman in Potshot Pete) | | | |
| | 28.50 | 85.00 | 200.00 |
| 6 (52 pgs.)-Williamson/Frazetta-a, 10 pgs.; Kurtzman a-'Pot-Shot Pete,' 5 | | | |
|     pgs.; & "Genius Jones," 1 pg. | 39.00 | 120.00 | 275.00 |
| 7 (52 pgs.)-Williamson/Frazetta-a, 10 pgs. | 32.00 | 95.00 | 225.00 |
| 8 (36 pgs.)-Williamson/Frazetta-a(2), 12 & 9 pgs. | | | |
| | 39.00 | 120.00 | 275.00 |
| 9-11: Photo western-c | 20.00 | 60.00 | 140.00 |
| 12-Photo war-c; Kurtzman-a, 2 pgs. "Genius" | | | |
| | 21.00 | 62.00 | 145.00 |
| 13-15: 13-Line-drawn-c begin, end #24 | 16.00 | 48.00 | 110.00 |
| 16-Williamson/Frazetta r-/Billy the Kid #1 | 22.00 | 65.00 | 155.00 |
| 17-Photo-c | 20.00 | 60.00 | 140.00 |
| 18-Williamson/Frazetta-a r-/#4 & 8, 19 pgs. | 27.00 | 81.00 | 190.00 |
| 19-24: 23-Evans-a? | 15.00 | 45.00 | 105.00 |
| 25-Photo-c return; end #31; Williamson/Frazetta-a r-/Billy the Kid #3 | | | |
| | 27.00 | 81.00 | 190.00 |
| 26-28,30-Photo-c | 18.00 | 54.00 | 125.00 |
| 29,31-Williamson/Frazetta-a in each, r-/#4,2 | 25.00 | 75.00 | 175.00 |

**JO-JO COMICS** ( . . . Congo King #7-29)
1945 - No. 29, July, 1949 (two No. 7's; no No. 13)
Fox Feature Syndicate

| | | | |
|---|---|---|---|
| nn(1945)-Funny animal, humor | 5.50 | 16.50 | 38.00 |
| 2(Sum,'46)-6: Funny animal; 2-Ten pg. Electro story | | | |
| | 2.85 | 8.50 | 20.00 |
| 7(7/47)-Jo-Jo, Congo King begins | 27.00 | 81.00 | 190.00 |
| 7(No. 8) (9/47) | 21.00 | 62.00 | 145.00 |
| 8-10(No. 9-11): 8-Tanee begins | 17.00 | 51.00 | 120.00 |
| 11,12(No. 12,13),14,16 | 14.00 | 42.00 | 100.00 |
| 15-Cited by Dr. Wertham in 5/47 Saturday Review of Literature | | | |
| | 16.00 | 48.00 | 110.00 |
| 17-Kamen bondage-c | 16.00 | 48.00 | 110.00 |
| 18-20 | 14.00 | 42.00 | 100.00 |
| 21-29 | 13.00 | 40.00 | 90.00 |

*The Joker #3, © DC Comics*

**JOKER, THE** (See Batman, Batman: The Killing Joke, Brave & the Bold,
    Detective & Justice League Annual #2)
May, 1975 - No. 9, Sept-Oct, 1976
National Periodical Publications

|  | Good | Fine | N-Mint |
|---|---|---|---|
| 1-Two-Face app. | 2.85 | 8.50 | 20.00 |
| 2,3 | 1.70 | 5.00 | 12.00 |
| 4-6 | 1.50 | 4.50 | 10.00 |
| 7,8 | 1.15 | 3.50 | 8.00 |
| 9 | 1.30 | 4.00 | 9.00 |

**JOKER COMICS**
April, 1942 - No. 42, August, 1950
Timely/Marvel Comics No. 36 on (TCI/CDS)

| | Good | Fine | N-Mint |
|---|---|---|---|
| 1-(Rare)-Powerhouse Pepper (1st app.) begins by Wolverton; Stuporman app. from Daring | 78.00 | 235.00 | 550.00 |
| 2-Wolverton-a; 1st app. Tessie the Typist | 33.00 | 100.00 | 230.00 |

|  | Good | Fine | N-Mint |
|---|---|---|---|
| 3-5-Wolverton-a | 23.00 | 70.00 | 160.00 |
| 6-10-Wolverton-a | 16.00 | 48.00 | 110.00 |
| 11-20-Wolverton-a | 13.00 | 40.00 | 90.00 |
| 21,22,24-27,29,30-Wolverton cont'd. & Kurtzman's "Hey Look" in #24-27 |  |  |  |
|  | 10.00 | 30.00 | 70.00 |
| 23-1st "Hey Look" by Kurtzman; Wolverton-a |  |  |  |
|  | 12.00 | 36.00 | 84.00 |
| 28,32,34,37-41 | 2.00 | 6.00 | 14.00 |
| 31-Last Powerhouse Pepper; not in #28 | 8.00 | 24.00 | 56.00 |
| 33,35,36-Kurtzman's "Hey Look" | 3.15 | 9.50 | 22.00 |
| 42-Only app. 'Patty Pinup,' a clone of Millie the Model |  |  |  |
|  | 2.30 | 7.00 | 16.00 |

**JONNY QUEST** (TV)
December, 1964 (Hanna-Barbera)
Gold Key

| | | | |
|---|---|---|---|
| 1 (10139-412) | 8.50 | 25.50 | 60.00 |

**JONNY QUEST** (TV)
June, 1986 - No. 31, Dec, 1988 (Hanna-Barbera)
Comico

| | | | |
|---|---|---|---|
| 1 | .70 | 2.00 | 4.00 |
| 2 | .45 | 1.30 | 2.60 |
| 3,5-Dave Stevens-c | .45 | 1.40 | 2.75 |
| 4,6-10 | .25 | .75 | 1.50 |
| 11-31: #15 on, $1.75. 30-Adapts TV episode |  | .60 | 1.25 |
| Special 1(9/88, $1.75), 2(10/88, $1.75) | .25 | .75 | 1.50 |

**JOURNEY INTO MYSTERY** (1st Series) (Thor No. 126 on)
6/52 - No. 48, 8/57; No. 49, 11/58 - No. 125, 2/66
Atlas (CPS No. 1-48/AMI No. 49-68/Marvel No. 69(6/61) on)

| | | | |
|---|---|---|---|
| 1 | 54.00 | 161.00 | 375.00 |
| 2 | 26.00 | 80.00 | 185.00 |
| 3,4 | 21.50 | 64.00 | 150.00 |
| 5-11 | 13.00 | 40.00 | 90.00 |

|  | Good | Fine | N-Mint |
|---|---|---|---|
| 12-20,22: 22-Davisesque-a; last pre-code issue (2/55) | | | |
| | 10.00 | 30.00 | 70.00 |
| 21-Kubert-a; Tothish-a by Andru | 11.00 | 32.00 | 75.00 |
| 23-32,35-38,40: 24-Torres?-a | 5.70 | 17.00 | 40.00 |
| 33-Williamson-a | 8.00 | 24.00 | 55.00 |
| 34,39: 34-Krigstein-a. 39-Wood-a | 7.00 | 21.00 | 50.00 |
| 41-Crandall-a; Frazettaesque-a by Morrow | 5.00 | 15.00 | 35.00 |
| 42,48-Torres-a | 5.00 | 15.00 | 35.00 |
| 43,44-Williamson/Mayo-a in both | 5.00 | 15.00 | 35.00 |
| 45,47,52,53 | 4.30 | 1300 | 30.00 |
| 46-Torres & Krigstein-a | 5.00 | 15.00 | 35.00 |
| 49-Matt Fox, Check-a | 5.00 | 15.00 | 35.00 |
| 50,54: 50-Davis-a. 54-Williamson-a | 4.50 | 14.00 | 32.00 |
| 51-Kirby/Wood-a | 4.50 | 14.00 | 32.00 |
| 55-61,63-73: 66-Return of Xemnu | 4.00 | 12.00 | 28.00 |
| 62-1st app. Xemnu (Titan) called "The Hulk" | 5.70 | 17.00 | 40.00 |
| 74-82-Fantasy content #74 on. 75-Last 10 cent issue. 80-Anti-communist | | | |
| propaganda story by Ditko | 3.50 | 10.50 | 24.00 |
| 83-Origin & 1st app. The Mighty Thor by Kirby (8/62) and begin series | | | |
| | 120.00 | 360.00 | 840.00 |
| 83-R-/from the Golden Record Comic Set | 5.70 | 17.00 | 40.00 |
| with the record. . . . | 10.70 | 32.00 | 75.00 |
| 84-2nd app. Thor | 34.00 | 102.00 | 240.00 |
| 85-1st app. Loki & Heimdall | 23.00 | 70.00 | 160.00 |
| 86-1st app. Odin | 17.00 | 51.00 | 120.00 |
| 87-89: 89-Origin Thor reprint/#83 | 14.00 | 42.00 | 100.00 |
| 90-No Kirby-a; Aunt May proto-type | 8.70 | 26.00 | 61.00 |
| 91,92,94-96-Sinnott-a | 7.15 | 21.50 | 50.00 |
| 93,97-Kirby-a; Tales of Asgard series begins #97 (Origin which concludes | | | |
| #99) | 9.50 | 28.50 | 66.00 |
| 98-100-Kirby/Heck-a. 98-Origin/1st app. The Human Cobra. 99-1st  app. | | | |
| Surtur & Mr. Hyde | 7.15 | 21.50 | 50.00 |
| 101-104,110: 102-Intro Sif | 4.00 | 12.00 | 28.00 |
| 105-109-Ten extra pages Kirby-a. 107-1st app. Grey Gargoyle | | | |
| | 4.00 | 12.00 | 28.00 |
| 111,113,114,116-125: 119-Intro Hogun, Fandrall, Volstagg | | | |
| | 3.15 | 9.50 | 22.00 |
| 112-Thor Vs. Hulk; origin Loki begins; ends #113 | | | |
| | 6.30 | 19.00 | 44.00 |

|  | Good | Fine | N-Mint |
|---|---|---|---|
| 115-Detailed origin Loki | 4.30 | 13.00 | 30.00 |
| Annual 1('65)-1st app. Hercules; Kirby-c/a | 9.30 | 28.00 | 65.00 |

**JOURNEY INTO UNKNOWN WORLDS**
No. 36, 9/50 - No. 38, 2/51; No. 4, 4/51 - No. 59, 8/57
Atlas Comics (WFP)

| | Good | Fine | N-Mint |
|---|---|---|---|
| 36(#1)-Science fiction/weird; 'End Of The Earth' c/story | | | |
| | 36.00 | 107.00 | 250.00 |
| 37(#2)-Science fiction; 'When Worlds Collide' c/story; Everett-c/a | | | |
| | 27.00 | 81.00 | 190.00 |
| 38(#3)-Science fiction | 21.50 | 64.00 | 150.00 |
| 4-6,8,10-Science fiction/weird | 14.00 | 42.00 | 100.00 |
| 7-Wolverton-a-"Planet of Terror," 6 pgs; electric chair c-inset/story | | | |
| | 25.00 | 75.00 | 175.00 |
| 9-Giant eyeball story | 14.00 | 42.00 | 100.00 |
| 11,12-Krigstein-a | 10.00 | 30.00 | 70.00 |
| 13,16,17,20 | 7.00 | 21.00 | 50.00 |
| 14-Wolverton-a-"One of Our Graveyards Is Missing," 4 pgs; Tuska-a | | | |
| | 21.50 | 64.00 | 150.00 |
| 15-Wolverton-a-"They Crawl By Night," 5 pgs. | | | |
| | 21.50 | 64.00 | 150.00 |
| 18,19-Matt Fox-a | 8.50 | 25.50 | 60.00 |
| 21-26,28-33-Last pre-code (2/55). 21-Decapitation-c. 24-Sci/fic story. | | | |
| 26-Atom bomb panel | 4.30 | 13.00 | 30.00 |
| 27-Sid Check-a | 4.50 | 14.00 | 32.00 |
| 34-Kubert, Torres-a | 4.50 | 14.00 | 32.00 |
| 35-Torres-a | 3.70 | 11.00 | 26.00 |
| 36-42 | 3.50 | 10.50 | 24.00 |
| 43,44: 43-Krigstein-a. 44-Davis-a | 4.00 | 12.00 | 28.00 |
| 45,55,59-Williamson-a in all; with Mayo #55,59. Crandall-a, #55,59 | | | |
| | 5.70 | 17.00 | 40.00 |
| 46,47,49,52,56-58 | 2.65 | 8.00 | 18.00 |
| 48,53-Crandall-a; Check-a, #48 | 5.50 | 16.50 | 38.00 |
| 50-Davis, Crandall-a | 5.00 | 15.00 | 35.00 |
| 51-Ditko, Wood-a | 4.30 | 13.00 | 30.00 |
| 54-Torres-a | 3.50 | 10.50 | 24.00 |

**JUMBO COMICS** (Created by S.M. Iger)
Sept, 1938 - No. 167, Apr, 1953 (No. 1-3: 68 pgs.; No. 4-8: 52 pgs.) (No. 1-8
  oversized-10½" × 14½"; black & white)
Fiction House Magazines (Real Adv. Publ. Co.)

|  | Good | Fine | N-Mint |
|---|---|---|---|
| 1-(Rare)-Sheena Queen of the Jungle by Meskin, The Hawk by Eisner, The Hunchback by Dick Briefer (ends #8) begin; 1st comic art by Jack Kirby (Count of Monte Cristo & Wilton of the West); Mickey Mouse appears (1 panel) with brief biography of Walt Disney. **Note:** Sheena was created by Iger for publication in England as a newspaper strip. The early issues of Jumbo contain Sheena strip-r | | | |
|  | 550.00 | 1375.00 | 3300.00 |
| 2-(Rare)-Origin Sheena. Diary of Dr. Hayward by Kirby (also #3) plus 2 other stories; contains strip from Universal Film featuring Edgar Bergen & Charlie McCarthy | 250.00 | 625.00 | 1500.00 |
| 3-Last Kirby issue | 200.00 | 500.00 | 1200.00 |
| 4-(Scarce)-Origin The Hawk by Eisner; Wilton of the West by Fine (ends #14) (1st comic work); Count of Monte Cristo by Fine (ends #15); The Diary of Dr. Hayward by Fine (cont'd. #8,9) | | | |
|  | 200.00 | 500.00 | 1200.00 |
| 5 | 125.00 | 315.00 | 750.00 |
| 6-8-Last B&W issue. #8 was a N. Y. World's Fair Special Edition | | | |
|  | 108.00 | 270.00 | 650.00 |
| 9-Stuart Taylor begins by Fine; Fine-c; 1st color issue(8-9/39)- 8¾" × 10¼"(oversized in width only) | 117.00 | 295.00 | 700.00 |
| 10-13: 10-Regular size 68 pg. issues begin; Sheena dons new costume #10 | | | |
|  | 58.00 | 145.00 | 350.00 |
| 14-Lightning begins (Intro.) | 43.00 | 130.00 | 300.00 |
| 15-20 | 28.50 | 86.00 | 200.00 |
| 21-30: 22-1st Tom, Dick & Harry; origin The Hawk retold | | | |
|  | 26.00 | 77.00 | 180.00 |
| 31-40: 35-Shows V2#11 (correct number does not appear) | | | |
|  | 23.00 | 70.00 | 160.00 |
| 41-50 | 19.00 | 58.00 | 135.00 |
| 51-60: 52-Last Tom, Dick & Harry | 16.50 | 50.00 | 115.00 |
| 61-70: 68-Sky Girl begins, ends #130; not in #79 | | | |
|  | 11.50 | 34.00 | 80.00 |
| 71-93,95-99: 89-ZX5 becomes a private eye | 10.00 | 30.00 | 70.00 |
| 94-Used in **Love and Death** by Legman | 10.00 | 30.00 | 70.00 |
| 100 | 11.50 | 34.00 | 80.00 |

|                                                    | Good   | Fine   | N-Mint |
|----------------------------------------------------|--------|--------|--------|
| 101-110: 103-Lingerie panel                        | 8.50   | 25.50  | 60.00  |
| 111-140                                            | 7.00   | 21.00  | 50.00  |
| 141-149-Two Sheena stories. 141-Long Bow, Indian Boy begins, ends #160 | 8.50 | 25.50 | 60.00 |
| 150-158: 155-Used in **POP**, pg. 98               | 7.00   | 21.00  | 50.00  |
| 159-163: Space Scouts serial in all; 163-Suicide Smith app. | 7.00 | 21.00 | 50.00 |
| 164-The Star Pirate begins, ends #165              | 7.00   | 21.00  | 50.00  |
| 165-167: 165,167-Space Rangers app.                | 7.00   | 21.00  | 50.00  |

**JUNGLE COMICS**
Jan, 1940 - No. 163, Summer, 1954
Fiction House Magazines

| | Good | Fine | N-Mint |
|---|---|---|---|
| 1-Origin The White Panther, Kaanga, Lord of the Jungle, Tabu, Wizard of the Jungle; Wambi, the Jungle Boy, Camilla & Capt. Terry Thunder begin | 142.00 | 355.00 | 850.00 |
| 2-Fantomah, Mystery Woman of the Jungle begins | 57.00 | 170.00 | 400.00 |
| 3,4 | 49.00 | 148.00 | 345.00 |
| 5 | 38.00 | 115.00 | 265.00 |
| 6-10: 7,8-Powell-c | 33.00 | 100.00 | 235.00 |
| 11-20: 13-Tuska-c | 23.00 | 70.00 | 165.00 |
| 21-30: 25-Shows V2#1 (correct number does not appear). #27-New origin Fantomah, Daughter of the Pharoahs; Camilla dons new costume | 19.00 | 60.00 | 135.00 |
| 31-40 | 16.00 | 48.00 | 110.00 |
| 41,43-50 | 12.00 | 36.00 | 85.00 |
| 42-Kaanga by Crandall, 12 pgs. | 15.00 | 45.00 | 105.00 |
| 51-60 | 11.00 | 32.00 | 75.00 |
| 61-70 | 9.30 | 28.00 | 65.00 |
| 71-80: 79-New origin Tabu | 8.50 | 25.50 | 60.00 |
| 81-97,99,101-110 | 7.00 | 21.00 | 50.00 |
| 98-Used in **SOTI**, pg. 185 & illo-"In ordinary comic books, there are pictures within pictures for children who know how to look"; used by N.Y. Legis. Comm. | 13.00 | 40.00 | 90.00 |
| 100 | 8.50 | 25.50 | 60.00 |
| 111-142,144,146-150: 118-Clyde Beatty app. 135-Desert Panther begins in Terry Thunder (origin), not in #137; ends (dies) #138 | 7.00 | 21.00 | 50.00 |

|                                          | Good  | Fine   | N-Mint |
|------------------------------------------|-------|--------|--------|
| 143,145-Used in **POP**, pg. 99          | 7.00  | 21.00  | 50.00  |
| 151-157,159-163: 152-Tiger Girl begins   | 7.00  | 21.00  | 50.00  |
| 158-Sheena app.                          | 8.50  | 25.50  | 60.00  |

**JUNGLE GIRL** (Nyoka, Jungle Girl No. 2 on)
Fall, 1942 (No month listed) (Based on film character)
Fawcett Publications

|                                                                        | Good  | Fine   | N-Mint |
|------------------------------------------------------------------------|-------|--------|--------|
| 1-Bondage-c; photo of Kay Aldridge who played Nyoka in movie serial app. on-c | 50.00 | 150.00 | 350.00 |

**JUNGLE JIM** (Also see Ace Comics)
No. 490, 8/53 - No. 1020, 8-10/59 (Painted-c)
Dell Publishing Co.

|                          | Good  | Fine  | N-Mint |
|--------------------------|-------|-------|--------|
| 4-Color 490(#1)          | 2.65  | 8.00  | 18.00  |
| 4-Color 565(#2, 6/54)    | 2.00  | 6.00  | 14.00  |
| 3(10-12/54)-5            | 1.70  | 5.00  | 12.00  |
| 6-19(1-3/59)             | 1.50  | 4.50  | 10.00  |
| 4-Color 1020(#20)        | 1.70  | 5.00  | 12.00  |

**JUSTICE LEAGUE** (. . . International #7-25; . . . America #26 on)
May, 1987 - Present (Also see Legends #6)
DC Comics

|                                                                              | Good  | Fine  | N-Mint |
|------------------------------------------------------------------------------|-------|-------|--------|
| 1-Batman, Green Lantern(Guy Gardner), Blue Beetle, Mr. Miracle, Capt. Marvel & Martian Manhunter begin | 1.50  | 4.50  | 9.00   |
| 2                                                                            | .90   | 2.75  | 5.50   |
| 3-Regular cover (white background)                                           | .75   | 2.25  | 4.50   |
| 3-Limited cover (yellow background, Superman logo)                           | 11.50 | 34.00 | 80.00  |
| 4-Booster Gold joins                                                         | .70   | 2.00  | 4.00   |
| 5,6: 5-Origin Gray Man; Batman vs. Guy Gardner; Creeper app.                 | .40   | 1.25  | 2.50   |
| 7-Double size ($1.25); Capt. Marvel & Dr. Fate resign; Capt. Atom, Rocket Red join | .50   | 1.50  | 3.00   |
| 8-10: 9,10-Millennium x-over                                                 | .35   | 1.00  | 2.00   |
| 11-23: 16-Bruce Wayne-c/story                                                |       | .60   | 1.20   |
| 24-($1.50)-Intro/1st app. Justice League Europe                              | .25   | .75   | 1.50   |

|                                                    | Good | Fine | N-Mint |
|----------------------------------------------------|------|------|--------|
| 25-45: 31,32-Justice League Europe x-over          |      | .50  | 1.00   |
| Annual 1 (9/87)                                    | .50  | 1.50 | 3.00   |
| Annual 2 ('88)-Joker-c/story                       | .70  | 2.00 | 4.00   |
| Annual 3 ('89, $1.75, 68 pgs.)                     | .30  | .90  | 1.75   |
| Annual 4 ('90, $2.00, 68 pgs.)                     | .35  | 1.00 | 2.00   |
| Special 1 ('90, $1.50, 52 pgs.)                    | .25  | .75  | 1.50   |

## JUSTICE LEAGUE EUROPE
April, 1989 - Present (75 cents, $1.00 #5 on, color)
DC Comics

|                                                    | Good | Fine | N-Mint |
|----------------------------------------------------|------|------|--------|
| 1-Giffen plots/breakdowns 1-8 (plots only 9-12)    | .35  | 1.10 | 2.20   |
| 2-20: 7-9-Batman app. 7,8-JLA x-over               |      | .50  | 1.00   |
| Annual 1 (1990, $2.00, 68 pgs.)-Giffen plots       | .35  | 1.00 | 2.00   |

## JUSTICE LEAGUE OF AMERICA (See Brave & the Bold #28-30)
Oct-Nov, 1960 - No. 261, Apr, 1987 (91-99,139-157: 52 pgs.)
National Periodical Publications/DC Comics

|                                                    | Good   | Fine   | N-Mint |
|----------------------------------------------------|--------|--------|--------|
| 1-Origin Despero; Aquaman, Batman, Flash, Green Lantern, J'onn J'onzz, Superman & Wonder Woman continue from Brave and the Bold | 138.00 | 414.00 | 965.00 |
| 2                                                  | 40.00  | 120.00 | 280.00 |
| 3-Origin/1st app. Kanjar Ro                        | 28.50  | 86.00  | 200.00 |
| 4-Green Arrow joins JLA                            | 24.00  | 72.00  | 165.00 |
| 5-Origin Dr. Destiny                               | 16.50  | 50.00  | 116.00 |
| 6-8,10: 6-Origin Prof. Amos Fortune. 7-Last 10 cent issue. 10-Origin Felix Faust; 1st app. Time Lord | 13.50  | 41.00  | 95.00  |
| 9-Origin J.L.A.                                    | 23.00  | 70.00  | 160.00 |
| 11-15: 12-Origin & 1st app. Dr. Light. 13-Speedy app. 14-Atom joins JLA | 8.30   | 25.00  | 58.00  |
| 16-20: 17-Adam Strange flashback                   | 6.00   | 18.00  | 42.00  |
| 21,22: 21-Re-intro. of JSA. 22-JSA x-over          | 14.00  | 42.00  | 100.00 |
| 23-28: 24-Adam Strange app. 28-Robin app.          | 3.70   | 11.00  | 26.00  |
| 29,30-JSA x-over; 1st Silver Age app. Starman      | 4.50   | 14.00  | 32.00  |
| 31-Hawkman joins JLA, Hawkgirl cameo               | 1.85   | 5.50   | 13.00  |
| 32-Intro & Origin Brain Storm                      | 1.85   | 5.50   | 13.00  |

*Justice League of America #102, © DC Comics*

| | Good | Fine | N-Mint |
|---|---|---|---|
| 33,35,36,40,41: 41-Intro & origin The Key | 1.60 | 4.80 | 11.00 |
| 34-Joker-c/story | 2.70 | 8.20 | 19.00 |
| 37,38-JSA x-over; 1st S.A. app. Mr. Terrific | 3.00 | 9.00 | 21.00 |
| 39-Giant G-16 | 2.30 | 7.00 | 16.00 |
| 42-45: 42-Metamorpho app. 43-Intro. Royal Flush Gang | | | |
| | 1.35 | 4.00 | 8.00 |
| 46-1st Silver-Age Sandman; JSA x-over | 2.15 | 6.50 | 15.00 |
| 47-JSA x-over | 1.50 | 4.50 | 10.00 |
| 48-Giant G-29 | 1.50 | 4.50 | 10.00 |
| 49-57,59,60: 55-Intro. Earth 2 Robin | 1.15 | 3.50 | 7.00 |
| 58-Giant G-41 | 1.35 | 4.00 | 8.00 |
| 61-66,68-72: 64-Intro/origin Red Tornado. 69-Wonder Woman quits; 71-Manhunter leaves. 72-Last 12 cent issue | | | |
| | .85 | 2.50 | 5.00 |
| 67-Giant G-53 | 1.00 | 3.00 | 6.00 |
| 73,74,77-80: 74-Black Canary joins. 78-Re-intro Vigilante | | | |
| | .70 | 2.00 | 4.00 |

|                                                                                              | **Good** | **Fine** | **N-Mint** |
|----------------------------------------------------------------------------------------------|---------|---------|-----------|
| 75-2nd app. Green Arrow in new costume                                                       | .90     | 2.75    | 5.50      |
| 76,85,93-(Giants G-65, G-77, G-89; 68 pgs.)                                                  | .85     | 2.50    | 5.00      |
| 81-84,86-92: 83-Death of Spectre                                                             | .70     | 2.00    | 4.00      |

94-Reprints origin/1st app. Sandman (Adv. #40) & origin/1st app. Starman (Adv. #61); Deadman x-over; N. Adams-a(4 pgs.); begin 25 cent, 52 pg. issues, ends #99 .......... 2.00  6.00  12.00

95-Origin Dr. Fate & Dr. Midnight reprint (More Fun #67, All-American #25) .......... .70  2.00  4.00

96-Origin Hourman (Adv. #48); Wildcat-r .......... .70  2.00  4.00

97-Origin JLA retold; Sargon, Starman-r .......... .70  2.00  4.00

98,99: 98-G.A. Sargon, Starman-r. 99-G.A. Sandman, Starman, Atom-r; last 52 pg. issue .......... .50  1.50  3.00

100-102: 102-Red Tornado dies .......... .85  2.50  5.00

103-106: 103-Phantom Stranger joins. 105-Elongated Man joins. 106-New Red Tornado joins .......... .50  1.50  3.00

107,108-G.A. Uncle Sam, Black Condor, The Ray, Dollman, Phantom Lady & The Human Bomb x-over .......... .85  2.50  5.00

109-116: 109-Hawkman resigns. 110-116: All 100 pg. issues. 111-Shining Knight, Green Arrow-r. 112-Crimson Avenger, Vigilante, origin Starman-r .......... .50  1.50  3.00

117-190: 117-Hawkman rejoins. 120,121,138-Adam Strange app. 128-Wonder Woman rejoins. 129-Death of Red Tornado. 135-137-G.A. Bulletman, Bulletgirl, Spy Smasher, Mr. Scarlet, Pinky & Ibis x-over. 137-Superman battles G.A. Capt. Marvel. 139-157-(52 pgs.). 144-Origin retold; origin J'onn J'onnz. 145-Red Tornado resurrected. 158-160-(44 pgs.). 161-Zatanna joins & new costume. 171-Mr. Terrific murdered. 178-Cover similar to #1; J'onn J'onzz app. 179-Firestorm joins. 181-Gr. Arrow leaves .......... .35  1.00  2.00

191-199: 192,193-Real origin Red Tornado. 193-1st app. All-Star Squadron as free 16 pg. insert .......... .25  .75  1.50

200-Anniversary issue (76 pgs., $1.50); origin retold; Green Arrow rejoins .......... .50  1.50  3.00

201-220: 203-Intro/origin new Royal Flush Gang. 208-All-Star Squadron app. 219,220-True origin Black Canary .......... .25  .75  1.50

221-250 (75 cents): 228-Re-intro Martian Manhunter. 233-New J.L.A. begins. 243-Aquaman leaves. 244,245-Crisis x-over. 250-Batman rejoins .......... .25  .75  1.50

251-260: 253-1st time origin Despero. 258-Death of Vibe. 258-261-Legends x-over. 260-Death of Steel .......... .50  1.00

| | Good | Fine | N-Mint |
|---|---|---|---|
| 261-Last issue | .60 | 1.75 | 3.50 |
| Annual 1(1983) | .40 | 1.25 | 2.50 |
| Annual 2(1984)-Intro new J.L.A. | .25 | .75 | 1.50 |
| Annual 3(1985)-Crisis x-over | .25 | .75 | 1.50 |

# K

**KA'A'NGA COMICS** (. . . Jungle King) (See Jungle Comics)
Spring, 1949 - No. 20, Summer, 1954
Fiction House Magazines (Glen-Kel Publ. Co.)

|  | Good | Fine | N-Mint |
|---|---|---|---|
| 1-Ka'a'nga, Lord of the Jungle begins | 24.00 | 73.00 | 170.00 |
| 2 (Wint., '49-'50) | 12.00 | 36.00 | 84.00 |
| 3,4 | 9.30 | 28.00 | 65.00 |
| 5-Camilla app. | 6.50 | 19.50 | 45.00 |
| 6-9: 7-Tuska-a. 9-Tabu, Wizard of the Jungle app. | | | |
|  | 4.50 | 14.00 | 32.00 |
| 10-Used in **POP**, pg. 99 | 4.85 | 14.50 | 34.00 |
| 11-15 | 3.70 | 11.00 | 26.00 |
| 16-Sheena app. | 4.00 | 12.00 | 28.00 |
| 17-20 | 3.15 | 9.50 | 22.00 |

**KATY KEENE** (Also see Laugh, Pep & Wilbur Comics)
1949 - No. 4, 1951; No. 5, 3/52 - No. 62, Oct, 1961
Archie Publ./Close-Up/Radio Comics

| | Good | Fine | N-Mint |
|---|---|---|---|
| 1-Bill Woggon-a begins | 65.00 | 195.00 | 455.00 |
| 2 | 32.00 | 95.00 | 225.00 |
| 3-5 | 27.00 | 81.00 | 190.00 |
| 6-10 | 22.00 | 65.00 | 154.00 |
| 11,13-20 | 19.00 | 57.00 | 132.00 |
| 12-(Scarce) | 21.00 | 62.00 | 146.00 |
| 21-40 | 13.00 | 40.00 | 90.00 |
| 41-62 | 10.00 | 30.00 | 70.00 |
| Annual 1('54) | 35.00 | 105.00 | 245.00 |
| Annual 2-6('55-59) | 18.00 | 54.00 | 125.00 |
| 3-D 1(1953-Large size) | 28.00 | 84.00 | 195.00 |
| Charm 1(9/58) | 16.00 | 48.00 | 110.00 |
| Glamour 1(1957) | 16.00 | 48.00 | 110.00 |
| Spectacular 1('56) | 16.00 | 48.00 | 110.00 |

**KEEN DETECTIVE FUNNIES**
No. 8, July, 1938 - No. 24, Sept, 1940
Centaur Publications

| | Good | Fine | N-Mint |
|---|---|---|---|
| V1#8-The Clock continues-r/Funny Picture Stories #1 | | | |
| | 83.00 | 210.00 | 500.00 |
| 9-Tex Martin by Eisner | 43.00 | 130.00 | 300.00 |
| 10,11: 11-Dean Denton story (begins?) | 37.00 | 110.00 | 260.00 |
| V2#1,2-The Eye Sees by Frank Thomas begins; ends #23 (Not in V2#3&5). | | | |
| 2-Jack Cole-a | 33.00 | 100.00 | 235.00 |
| 3-6,9-11: 3-TNT Todd begins. 4-Gabby Flynn begins. 5-Dean Denton | | | |
| story | 33.00 | 100.00 | 235.00 |
| 7-The Masked Marvel by Ben Thompson begins | | | |
| | 64.00 | 193.00 | 450.00 |
| 8-Nudist ranch panel w/four girls | 37.00 | 110.00 | 260.00 |
| 12(12/39)-Origin The Eye Sees by Frank Thomas; death of Masked | | | |
| Marvel's sidekick ZL | 43.00 | 130.00 | 300.00 |
| V3#1,2 | 37.00 | 110.00 | 260.00 |
| 18,19,21,22: 18-Bondage/torture-c | 37.00 | 110.00 | 260.00 |
| 20-Classic Eye Sees-c by Thomas | 43.00 | 130.00 | 300.00 |
| 23-Air Man begins (intro) | 43.00 | 130.00 | 300.00 |
| 24-Air Man-c | 43.00 | 130.00 | 300.00 |

**KERRY DRAKE DETECTIVE CASES** ( . . . Racket Buster No. 32,33) (Also
    see Chamber of Clues & Green Hornet Comics #42-47)
1944 - No. 5, 1944; No. 6, Jan, 1948 - No. 33, Aug, 1952
Life's Romances/Compix/Magazine Ent. No. 1-5/Harvey No. 6 on

| | Good | Fine | N-Mint |
|---|---|---|---|
| nn(1944)(A-1 Comics)(slightly oversize) | 12.00 | 36.00 | 84.00 |
| 2 | 8.00 | 24.00 | 56.00 |
| 3-5(1944) | 6.00 | 18.00 | 42.00 |
| 6,8(1948); 8-Bondage-c | 3.50 | 10.50 | 24.00 |
| 7-Kubert-a; biog of Andriola (artist) | 4.00 | 12.00 | 28.00 |
| 9,10-Two-part marijuana story; Kerry smokes marijuana in #10 | | | |
| | 6.75 | 20.00 | 47.00 |
| 11-15 | 3.00 | 9.00 | 21.00 |
| 16-33 | 2.35 | 7.00 | 16.00 |

**KID KOMICS**
Feb, 1943 - No. 10, Spring, 1946
Timely Comics (USA 1,2/FCI 3-10)

|  | Good | Fine | N-Mint |
|---|---|---|---|
| 1-Origin Captain Wonder & sidekick Tim Mullrooney & Subbie; intro the Sea-Going Lad, Pinto Pete, & Trixie Trouble; Knuckles & White-Wash Jones only app.; Wolverton art, 7 pgs. | 129.00 | 325.00 | 775.00 |
| 2-The Young Allies, Red Hawk, & Tommy Tyme begin; last Captain Wonder & Subbie | 73.00 | 185.00 | 440.00 |
| 3-The Vision & Daredevils app. | 50.00 | 125.00 | 300.00 |
| 4-The Destroyer begins; Sub-Mariner app.; Red Hawk & Tommy Tyme end | 43.00 | 110.00 | 260.00 |
| 5,6 | 31.00 | 78.00 | 185.00 |
| 7-10: The Whizzer app. 7; Destroyer not in #7,8; 10-Last Destroyer, Young Allies & Whizzer | 27.00 | 70.00 | 160.00 |

**KING COMICS** (Strip reprints)
Apr, 1936 - No. 159, Feb, 1952 (Winter on cover)
David McKay Publications/Standard No. 156-on

| | Good | Fine | N-Mint |
|---|---|---|---|
| 1-Flash Gordon by Alex Raymond; Brick Bradford, Mandrake the Magician, Popeye & Henry begin | 333.00 | 835.00 | 2000.00 |
| 2 | 150.00 | 375.00 | 900.00 |
| 3 | 108.00 | 270.00 | 650.00 |
| 4 | 66.00 | 200.00 | 465.00 |
| 5 | 50.00 | 150.00 | 350.00 |
| 6-10: 9-X-Mas-c | 33.00 | 100.00 | 230.00 |
| 11-20 | 25.00 | 75.00 | 175.00 |
| 21-30 | 21.00 | 62.00 | 145.00 |
| 31-40: 33-Last Segar Popeye | 18.50 | 56.00 | 130.00 |
| 41-50: 46-Little Lulu, Alvin & Tubby app. as text illos by Marge Buell 50-The Lone Ranger begins | 16.50 | 50.00 | 115.00 |
| 51-60: 52-Barney Baxter begins? | 12.00 | 36.00 | 85.00 |
| 61-The Phantom begins | 11.00 | 32.00 | 75.00 |
| 62-80: 76-Flag-c | 9.00 | 27.00 | 62.00 |
| 81-99: 82-Blondie begins? | 7.00 | 21.00 | 50.00 |
| 100 | 9.50 | 28.00 | 65.00 |
| 101-115-Last Raymond issue | 6.50 | 19.50 | 45.00 |
| 116-145: 117-Phantom origin retold | 5.00 | 15.00 | 35.00 |
| 146,147-Prince Valiant in both | 3.70 | 11.00 | 26.00 |

|  | Good | Fine | N-Mint |
|---|---|---|---|
| 148-155-Flash Gordon ends | 3.70 | 11.00 | 26.00 |
| 156-159 | 2.85 | 8.50 | 20.00 |

**KING OF THE ROYAL MOUNTED** (Zane Grey's)
No. 207, Dec, 1948 - No. 935, Sept-Nov, 1958
Dell Publishing Co.

| | Good | Fine | N-Mint |
|---|---|---|---|
| 4-Color 207('48) | 11.50 | 34.00 | 80.00 |
| 4-Color 265,283 | 8.00 | 24.00 | 56.00 |
| 4-Color 310,340 | 5.00 | 15.00 | 35.00 |
| 4-Color 363,384 | 4.00 | 12.00 | 28.00 |
| 8(6-8/52)-10 | 4.00 | 12.00 | 28.00 |
| 11-20 | 3.50 | 10.50 | 24.00 |
| 21-28(3-5/58) | 3.00 | 9.00 | 21.00 |
| 4-Color 935(9-11/58) | 3.00 | 9.00 | 21.00 |

**KORAK, SON OF TARZAN** (Edgar Rice Burroughs)
Jan, 1964 - No. 45, Jan, 1972 (Painted-c No. 1-?)
Gold Key

| | Good | Fine | N-Mint |
|---|---|---|---|
| 1-Russ Manning-a | 3.50 | 10.50 | 24.00 |
| 2-11-Russ Manning-a | 1.70 | 5.00 | 12.00 |
| 12-21: 14-Jon of the Kalahari ends. 15-Mabu, Jungle Boy begins. | | | |
| 21-Manning-a | 1.15 | 3.50 | 8.00 |
| 22-30 | .70 | 2.00 | 5.00 |
| 31-45 | .60 | 1.75 | 3.50 |

**KRAZY KOMICS** (1st Series)
July, 1942 - No. 26, Spr, 1947
Timely Comics (USA No. 1-21/JPC No. 22-26)

| | Good | Fine | N-Mint |
|---|---|---|---|
| 1-Ziggy Pig & Silly Seal begins | 19.00 | 58.00 | 135.00 |
| 2 | 9.30 | 28.00 | 65.00 |
| 3-10 | 5.00 | 15.00 | 35.00 |
| 11,13,14 | 3.70 | 11.00 | 26.00 |
| 12-Timely's entire art staff drew themselves into a Creeper story | | | |
| | 5.70 | 17.00 | 40.00 |
| 15-Has "Super Soldier" by Pfc. Stan Lee | 3.70 | 11.00 | 26.00 |
| 16-24,26 | 2.65 | 8.00 | 18.00 |
| 25-Kurtzman-a, 6 pgs. | 4.30 | 13.00 | 30.00 |

**KRAZY KOMICS** (2nd Series)
Aug, 1948 - No. 2, Nov, 1948
Timely/Marvel Comics

|  | Good | Fine | N-Mint |
|---|---|---|---|
| 1-Wolverton (10 pgs.) & Kurtzman (8 pgs.)-a; Eustice Hayseed begins, Li'l Abner swipe | 19.00 | 57.00 | 135.00 |
| 2-Wolverton-a, 10 pgs.; Powerhouse Pepper cameo | 11.50 | 34.00 | 80.00 |

# L

**LADY LUCK** (Formerly Smash #1-85)
No. 86, Dec, 1949 - No. 90, Aug, 1950
Quality Comics Group

|  | Good | Fine | N-Mint |
|---|---|---|---|
| 86(#1) | 35.00 | 105.00 | 245.00 |
| 87-90 | 27.00 | 81.00 | 190.00 |

**LASH LARUE WESTERN** (Movie star; king of the bullwhip)
Sum, 1949 - No. 46, Jan, 1954 (36 pgs., 1-7,9,13,16-on)
Fawcett Publications

| | Good | Fine | N-Mint |
|---|---|---|---|
| 1-Lash & his horse Black Diamond begin; photo front/back-c begin | | | |
| | 55.00 | 165.00 | 385.00 |
| 2(11/49) | 28.00 | 84.00 | 195.00 |
| 3-5 | 25.00 | 75.00 | 175.00 |
| 6,7,9: 6-Last photo back-c; intro. Frontier Phantom (Lash's twin | | | |
| brother) | 18.00 | 54.00 | 125.00 |
| 8,10 (52 pgs.) | 18.50 | 56.00 | 130.00 |
| 11,12,14,15 (52 pgs.) | 11.50 | 34.00 | 80.00 |
| 13,16-20 (36 pgs.) | 11.00 | 32.00 | 75.00 |
| 21-30: 21-The Frontier Phantom app. | 9.30 | 28.00 | 65.00 |
| 31-45 | 8.00 | 24.00 | 55.00 |
| 46-Last Fawcett issue & photo-c | 8.50 | 25.50 | 60.00 |

**LASH LARUE WESTERN** (Continues from Fawcett series)
No. 47, Mar-Apr, 1954 - No. 84, June, 1961
Charlton Comics

| | Good | Fine | N-Mint |
|---|---|---|---|
| 47-Photo-c | 7.00 | 21.00 | 50.00 |
| 48 | 5.70 | 17.00 | 40.00 |
| 49-60 | 4.50 | 14.00 | 32.00 |
| 61-66,69,70: 52-r/#8; 53-r/#22 | 4.00 | 12.00 | 28.00 |
| 67,68-(68 pgs.). 68-Check-a | 4.30 | 13.00 | 30.00 |
| 71-83 | 2.65 | 8.00 | 18.00 |
| 84-Last issue | 3.50 | 10.50 | 24.00 |

**LASSIE** (TV) (M-G-M's. . . No. 1-36)
June, 1950 - No. 70, July, 1969
Dell Publishing Co./Gold Key No. 59 (10/62) on

| | Good | Fine | N-Mint |
|---|---|---|---|
| 1 (52 pgs.)-Photo-c; inside lists One Shot #282 in error | | | |
| | 4.50 | 14.00 | 32.00 |
| 2-Painted-c begin | 2.65 | 8.00 | 18.00 |
| 3-10 | 2.00 | 6.00 | 14.00 |
| 11-19: 12-Rocky Langford (Lassie's master) marries Gerry Lawrence. | | | |
| 15-1st app. Timbu | 1.60 | 4.80 | 11.00 |
| 20-22-Matt Baker-a | 2.15 | 6.50 | 15.00 |
| 23-40: 33-Robinson-a. 39-1st app. Timmy as Lassie picks up her TV family | | | |
| | 1.00 | 3.00 | 7.00 |
| 41-70: 63-Last Timmy. 64-r-/#19. 65-Forest Ranger Corey Stuart begins, ends #69. 70-Forest Rangers Bob Ericson & Scott Turner app. (Lassie's new masters) | | | |
| | .75 | 2.25 | 4.50 |

**LAUGH COMICS** (Laugh #226 on)
No. 20, Fall, 1946 - No. 400, 1987
Archie Publications (Close-Up)

| | Good | Fine | N-Mint |
|---|---|---|---|
| 20-Archie begins; Katy Keene & Taffy begin by Woggon | | | |
| | 38.00 | 115.00 | 265.00 |
| 21-23,25 | 18.00 | 54.00 | 125.00 |
| 24-"Pipsy" by Kirby, 6 pgs. | 18.00 | 54.00 | 125.00 |
| 26-30 | 10.00 | 30.00 | 70.00 |
| 31-40 | 8.00 | 24.00 | 50.00 |
| 41-60: 41,54-Debbi by Woggon. 57-Spanking panel | | | |
| | 4.50 | 13.50 | 30.00 |
| 61-80: 67-Debbi by Woggon | 2.85 | 8.50 | 20.00 |
| 81-99 | 2.00 | 6.00 | 14.00 |
| 100 | 3.00 | 9.00 | 21.00 |
| 101-126: 125-Debbi app. | 1.35 | 4.00 | 9.00 |
| 127-144: Super-hero app. in all (see note) | 1.35 | 4.00 | 9.00 |
| 145-160: 157-Josie app. | .75 | 2.25 | 4.50 |
| 161-165,167-200 | .50 | 1.50 | 3.00 |
| 166-Beatles-c | .85 | 2.50 | 5.00 |

| | Good | Fine | N-Mint |
|---|---|---|---|
| 201-240 | .25 | .75 | 1.50 |
| 241-280 | | .40 | .80 |
| 281-400: 381-384-Katy Keene app.; by Woggon-381,382 | | | |
| | | .30 | .60 |

**LEADING COMICS** (. . . Screen Comics No. 42 on)
Winter, 1941-42 - No. 41, Feb-Mar, 1950
National Periodical Publications

| | Good | Fine | N-Mint |
|---|---|---|---|
| 1-Origin The Seven Soldiers of Victory; Crimson Avenger, Green Arrow & Speedy, Shining Knight, The Vigilante, Star Spangled Kid & Stripesy begin. The Dummy (Vigilante villain) app. | | | |
| | 175.00 | 440.00 | 1050.00 |
| 2-Meskin-a | 64.00 | 193.00 | 450.00 |
| 3 | 50.00 | 150.00 | 350.00 |
| 4,5 | 43.00 | 130.00 | 300.00 |
| 6-10 | 37.00 | 110.00 | 260.00 |
| 11-14(Spring, 1945) | 26.00 | 77.00 | 180.00 |
| 15-(Sum,'45)-Content change to funny animal | | | |
| | 11.00 | 32.00 | 75.00 |
| 16-22,24-30 | 4.50 | 14.00 | 32.00 |
| 23-1st app. Peter Porkchops by Otto Feur | 11.00 | 32.00 | 75.00 |
| 31,32,34-41 | 3.50 | 10.50 | 24.00 |
| 33-(Scarce) | 6.00 | 18.00 | 42.00 |

**LEADING SCREEN COMICS** (Formerly Leading Comics)
No. 42, Apr-May, 1950 - No. 77, Aug-Sept, 1955
National Periodical Publications

| | Good | Fine | N-Mint |
|---|---|---|---|
| 42 | 4.50 | 14.00 | 32.00 |
| 43-77 | 2.85 | 8.50 | 20.00 |

**LEAVE IT TO BINKY** (See Showcase #70)
2-3/48 - No. 60, 10/58; No. 61, 6-7/68 - No. 71, 2-3/70 (#1-22: 52 pgs.)
National Periodical Publications

| | Good | Fine | N-Mint |
|---|---|---|---|
| 1 | 14.00 | 42.00 | 100.00 |
| 2 | 7.00 | 21.00 | 50.00 |

|  | Good | Fine | N-Mint |
|---|---|---|---|
| 3-5: 5-Superman cameo | 5.00 | 15.00 | 35.00 |
| 6-10 | 4.00 | 12.00 | 28.00 |
| 11-20 | 3.00 | 9.00 | 21.00 |
| 21-28,30-45: 45-Last pre-code (2/55) | 2.00 | 6.00 | 14.00 |
| 29-Used in **POP**, pg. 78 | 2.00 | 6.00 | 14.00 |
| 46-60 | 1.00 | 3.00 | 7.00 |
| 61-71 | .70 | 2.00 | 4.00 |

## LEGENDS
Nov, 1986 - No. 6, Apr, 1987 (mini-series)
DC Comics

| | Good | Fine | N-Mint |
|---|---|---|---|
| 1-Byrne c/a(p) begins. 1st new Capt. Marvel | .35 | 1.00 | 2.00 |
| 2-5: 3-Intro new Suicide Squad; death of Blockbuster | | | |
| | .25 | .70 | 1.40 |
| 6-Intro/1st app. New Justice League | 1.00 | 3.00 | 6.00 |

## LEGENDS OF THE DARK KNIGHT (Batman)
Nov, 1989 - Present ($1.50, color)
DC Comics

| | Good | Fine | N-Mint |
|---|---|---|---|
| 1-"The Shaman of Gotham" begins, ends #5; outer cover has four different color variations, all worth same | .70 | 2.00 | 4.00 |
| 2 | .40 | 1.25 | 2.50 |
| 3-12: 6-10-"Gothic" parts 1-5 | .25 | .75 | 1.50 |

## LEGION OF SUPER-HEROES (See Action, Adventure & Superboy)
Feb, 1973 - No. 4, July-Aug, 1973
National Periodical Publications

| | Good | Fine | N-Mint |
|---|---|---|---|
| 1-Legion & Tommy Tomorrow reprints begin | | | |
| | .85 | 2.50 | 5.00 |
| 2-4: 2-Forte-r. 3-r/Adv. #340. Action #240. 4-r/Adv. #341, Action #233; Mooney-r | .50 | 1.50 | 3.00 |

*Legion of Super-Heroes #4 (1973), © DC Comics*

**LEGION OF SUPER-HEROES** (Also see Superman)
Aug, 1984 - No. 63, Aug, 1989 ($1.25-$1.75, deluxe format)
DC Comics

|  | Good | Fine | N-Mint |
|---|---|---|---|
| 1 | .35 | 1.00 | 2.00 |
| 2-10: 4-Death of Karate Kid. 5-Death of Nemesis Kid | .25 | .80 | 1.60 |
| 11-14: 12-Cosmic Boy, Lightning Lad, & Saturn Girl resign. 14-Intro new members: Tellus, Sensor Girl, Quislet |  | .60 | 1.20 |
| 15-18: 15-17-Crisis tie-ins. 18-Crisis x-over | .25 | .80 | 1.60 |
| 19-25: 25-Sensor Girl i.d. revealed as Princess Projectra |  | .60 | 1.20 |
| 26-36,39-44: 35-Saturn Girl rejoins. 40-$1.75 cover price begins. 42, 43-Millennium tie-ins. 44-Origin Quislet |  | .55 | 1.10 |
| 37,38-Death of Superboy | 1.35 | 4.00 | 8.00 |
| 45 ($2.95, 68 pgs.) | .40 | 1.20 | 2.40 |
| 46-49,51-62 |  | .55 | 1.10 |
| 50-Double size, $2.50 | .35 | 1.00 | 2.00 |

| | Good | Fine | N-Mint |
|---|---|---|---|
| 63-Final issue | .25 | .70 | 1.40 |
| Annual 1 (10/85, 52 pgs.)-Crisis tie-in | .30 | .90 | 1.80 |
| Annual 2 (10/86, 52 pgs.). 3 (10/87, 52 pgs.) | .25 | .80 | 1.60 |
| Annual 4(11/88, $2.50, 52 pgs.) | .35 | 1.00 | 2.00 |

**LEGION OF SUPER-HEROES**
Nov, 1989 - Present ($1.75, color)
DC Comics

| | Good | Fine | N-Mint |
|---|---|---|---|
| 1-Giffen-c/a(p), scripts begin | .40 | 1.25 | 2.50 |
| 2-14 | .30 | .90 | 1.80 |

**LITTLE ARCHIE** (The Adventures of . . .  #13-on)
1956 - No. 180, Feb, 1983 (Giants No. 3-84)
Archie Publications

| | Good | Fine | N-Mint |
|---|---|---|---|
| 1-(Scarce) | 26.50 | 80.00 | 185.00 |
| 2 | 13.00 | 42.00 | 90.00 |
| 3-5 | 8.50 | 25.50 | 60.00 |
| 6-10 | 5.50 | 16.50 | 38.00 |
| 11-20 | 3.50 | 10.50 | 24.00 |
| 21-30 | 2.15 | 6.50 | 15.00 |
| 31-40: Little Pureheart apps. #40-42,44 | 1.00 | 3.00 | 7.00 |
| 41-60: 42-Intro. The Little Archies. 59-Little Sabrina begins | | | |
| | .50 | 1.50 | 3.00 |
| 61-80 | .35 | 1.00 | 2.00 |
| 81-100 | | .50 | 1.00 |
| 101-180 | | .40 | .80 |
| . . . In Animal Land 1('57) | 9.20 | 27.50 | 64.00 |
| . . . In Animal Land 17(Winter, 1957-58)-19(Summer,'58)-Formerly Li'l Jinx | | | |
| | 4.50 | 13.50 | 31.00 |

**LITTLE DOT** (See Sad Sack Comics)
Sept, 1953 - No. 164, April, 1976
Harvey Publications

| | Good | Fine | N-Mint |
|---|---|---|---|
| 1-Intro./1st app. Richie Rich & Little Lotta | 45.00 | 135.00 | 320.00 |

|  | Good | Fine | N-Mint |
|---|---|---|---|
| 2-1st app. Freckles & Pee Wee (Richie Rich's poor friends) | | | |
|  | 21.00 | 64.00 | 150.00 |
| 3 | 15.00 | 45.00 | 105.00 |
| 4 | 11.00 | 32.50 | 75.00 |
| 5-Origin dots on Little Dot's dress | 12.50 | 37.50 | 85.00 |
| 6-Richie Rich, Little Lotta, & Little Dot all on cover; 1st Richie Rich | | | |
| cover featured | 12.50 | 37.50 | 85.00 |
| 7-10 | 5.00 | 15.00 | 35.00 |
| 11-20 | 4.00 | 12.00 | 28.00 |
| 21-40 | 2.00 | 6.00 | 14.00 |
| 41-60 | 1.00 | 3.00 | 7.00 |
| 61-80 | .70 | 2.00 | 4.00 |
| 81-100 | .50 | 1.50 | 3.00 |
| 101-141 | .35 | 1.00 | 2.00 |
| 142-145: All 52 pg. Giants | .40 | 1.20 | 2.40 |
| 146-164 | | .50 | 1.00 |

**LITTLE LOTTA**
11/55 - No. 110, 11/73; No. 111, 9/74 - No. 121, 5/76
Harvey Publications

|  | Good | Fine | N-Mint |
|---|---|---|---|
| 1-Richie Rich (r) & Little Dot begin | 17.00 | 51.00 | 120.00 |
| 2,3 | 8.00 | 24.00 | 56.00 |
| 4,5 | 4.35 | 13.00 | 30.00 |
| 6-10 | 3.00 | 9.00 | 21.00 |
| 11-20 | 1.70 | 5.00 | 12.00 |
| 21-40 | 1.15 | 3.50 | 8.00 |
| 41-60 | .85 | 2.50 | 6.00 |
| 61-80 | .50 | 1.50 | 3.00 |
| 81-99 | .35 | 1.00 | 2.00 |
| 100-103: All 52 pg. Giants | .40 | 1.20 | 2.40 |
| 104-121 | .25 | .75 | 1.50 |

**LONE RANGER, THE** (Movie, radio & TV; Clayton Moore starred as
    Lone Ranger in the movies; No. 1-37: strip reprints)
Jan-Feb, 1948 - No. 145, May-July, 1962
Dell Publishing Co.

|                                                                                          | Good  | Fine   | N-Mint |
|------------------------------------------------------------------------------------------|-------|--------|--------|
| 1 (36 pgs.)-The L. Ranger, his horse Silver, companion Tonto, & his horse Scout begin    | 49.00 | 148.00 | 345.00 |
| 2 (52 pgs. begin, end #41)                                                                | 24.00 | 73.00  | 170.00 |
| 3-5                                                                                       | 20.00 | 60.00  | 140.00 |
| 6,7,9,10                                                                                  | 17.00 | 51.00  | 120.00 |
| 8-Origin retold; Indian back-c begin, end #35                                            | 22.00 | 65.00  | 155.00 |
| 11-20: 11-"Young Hawk" Indian boy serial begins, ends #145                               | 11.50 | 34.00  | 80.00  |
| 21,22,24-31: 51-Reprint. 31-1st Mask logo                                                 | 9.30  | 28.00  | 65.00  |
| 23-Origin retold                                                                          | 13.00 | 40.00  | 90.00  |
| 32-37: 32-Painted-c begin. 36-Animal photo back-c begin, end #49. 37-Last newspaper-r issue; new outfit | 7.00  | 21.00  | 50.00  |
| 38-41 (All 52 pgs.)                                                                       | 5.00  | 15.00  | 35.00  |
| 42-50 (36 pgs.)                                                                           | 3.70  | 11.00  | 26.00  |
| 51-74 (52 pgs.): 71-Blank inside-c                                                         | 3.70  | 11.00  | 26.00  |
| 75-99: 76-Flag-c. 79-Xmas-c                                                               | 3.00  | 9.00   | 21.00  |
| 100                                                                                       | 4.50  | 14.00  | 32.00  |
| 101-111: Last painted-c                                                                   | 2.65  | 8.00   | 18.00  |
| 112-Clayton Moore photo-c begin, end #145                                                | 13.00 | 40.00  | 90.00  |
| 113-117                                                                                   | 7.00  | 21.00  | 50.00  |
| 118-Origin Lone Ranger, Tonto, & Silver retold; Special anniversary issue               | 12.00 | 36.00  | 85.00  |
| 119-145: 139-Last issue by Fran Striker                                                   | 5.70  | 17.00  | 40.00  |

**LONE RANGER, THE**
9/64 - No. 16, 12/69; No. 17, 11/72; No. 18, 9/74 - No. 28, 3/77
Gold Key (Reprints #13-20)

|                                                                                          | Good  | Fine  | N-Mint |
|------------------------------------------------------------------------------------------|-------|-------|--------|
| 1-Retells origin                                                                          | 2.85  | 8.50  | 20.00  |
| 2                                                                                         | 1.50  | 4.50  | 10.00  |
| 3-10: Small Bear-r in #6-10                                                                | 1.00  | 3.00  | 7.00   |
| 11-17: Small Bear-r in #11,12                                                             | .85   | 2.50  | 6.00   |
| 18-28                                                                                     | .55   | 1.65  | 4.00   |
| Golden West 1(30029-610)-Giant, 10/66-r/most Golden West #3-including Clayton Moore photo front/back-c | 5.00  | 15.00 | 35.00  |

*Lone Wolf and Cub #2, © First Comics*

## LONE WOLF AND CUB
May, 1987 - Present ($1.95-$2.50-$2.95, B&W, deluxe size)
First Comics

|  | Good | Fine | N-Mint |
|---|---|---|---|
| 1 | 2.00 | 6.00 | 12.00 |
| 1-2nd print, 3rd print | .35 | 1.00 | 2.00 |
| 2 | 1.10 | 3.25 | 6.50 |
| 2-2nd print | .35 | 1.00 | 2.00 |
| 3 | .70 | 2.00 | 4.00 |
| 4-12: 6-72 pg. origin issue. 8-$2.50-c begins | .45 | 1.30 | 2.60 |
| 13-25 | .40 | 1.25 | 2.50 |
| 26-30,33 ($2.95-c) | .50 | 1.50 | 3.00 |
| 31,32,34 ($3.25, 82 pgs.) | .55 | 1.65 | 3.25 |

## LONGSHOT
Sept, 1985 - No. 6, Feb, 1986 (Limited series)
Marvel Comics Group

| | | | |
|---|---|---|---|
| 1-Arthur Adams-c/a in all | 3.35 | 10.00 | 20.00 |

|  | Good | Fine | N-Mint |
|---|---|---|---|
| 2 | 2.50 | 7.50 | 15.00 |
| 3-5 | 2.00 | 6.00 | 12.00 |
| 6-Double size | 2.70 | 8.00 | 16.00 |

## LOONEY TUNES AND MERRIE MELODIES COMICS
1941 - No. 246, July-Sept, 1962
Dell Publishing Co.

|  | Good | Fine | N-Mint |
|---|---|---|---|
| 1-Porky Pig, Bugs Bunny, Daffy Duck, Elmer Fudd, Mary Jane & Sniffles, Pat, Patsy and Pete begin (1st comic book app. of each). Bugs Bunny story by Win Smith (early Mickey Mouse artist) | 121.00 | 365.00 | 850.00 |
| 2 (11/41) | 54.00 | 163.00 | 380.00 |
| 3-Kandi the Cave Kid begins by Walt Kelly; also in #4-6,8,11,15 | 48.00 | 145.00 | 340.00 |
| 4-Kelly-a | 43.00 | 130.00 | 300.00 |
| 5-Bugs Bunny The Super Rabbit app. (1st funny animal super hero?); Kelly-a | 32.00 | 95.00 | 225.00 |
| 6,8-Kelly-a | 24.00 | 70.00 | 165.00 |
| 7,9,10: 9-Painted-c. 10-Flag-c | 18.50 | 56.00 | 130.00 |
| 11,15-Kelly-a; 15-Xmas-c | 18.50 | 56.00 | 130.00 |
| 12-14,16-19 | 16.00 | 48.00 | 110.00 |
| 20-25: Pat, Patsy & Pete by Kelly in all | 16.00 | 48.00 | 110.00 |
| 26-30 | 11.00 | 32.00 | 75.00 |
| 31-40 | 8.00 | 24.00 | 56.00 |
| 41-50 | 5.50 | 16.50 | 38.00 |
| 51-60 | 3.60 | 11.00 | 25.00 |
| 61-80 | 2.15 | 7.00 | 16.00 |
| 81-99: 87-Xmas-c | 2.00 | 6.00 | 14.00 |
| 100 | 2.15 | 7.00 | 16.00 |
| 101-120 | 1.60 | 4.80 | 11.00 |
| 121-150 | 1.30 | 4.00 | 9.00 |
| 151-200 | 1.00 | 3.00 | 7.00 |
| 201-246 | .70 | 2.00 | 5.00 |

## LORNA THE JUNGLE GIRL (. . . Jungle Queen #1-5)
July, 1953 - No. 26, Aug, 1957
Atlas Comics (NPI 1/OMC 2-11/NPI 12-26)

|  | Good | Fine | N-Mint |
|---|---|---|---|
| 1-Origin | 11.00 | 32.00 | 75.00 |

| | Good | Fine | N-Mint |
|---|---|---|---|
| 2-Intro. & 1st app. Greg Knight | 6.00 | 18.00 | 42.00 |
| 3-5 | 5.00 | 15.00 | 35.00 |
| 6-11: 11-Last pre-code (1/55) | 3.70 | 11.00 | 26.00 |
| 12-17,19-26 | 2.85 | 8.50 | 20.00 |
| 18-Williamson/Colleta-c | 4.30 | 13.00 | 30.00 |

## LOVE LETTERS
11/49 - #6, 9/50; #7, 3/51 - #31, 6/53; #32, 2/54 - #51, 12/56
Quality Comics Group

| | Good | Fine | N-Mint |
|---|---|---|---|
| 1-Ward-c, Gustavson-a | 9.30 | 28.00 | 65.00 |
| 2-Ward-c, Gustavson-a | 8.50 | 25.50 | 60.00 |
| 3-Gustavson-a | 5.00 | 15.00 | 35.00 |
| 4-Ward-a, 9 pgs. | 8.50 | 25.50 | 60.00 |
| 5-8,10 | 1.70 | 5.00 | 12.00 |
| 9-One pg. Ward-"Be Popular with the Opposite Sex"; Robert Mitchum photo-c | 3.50 | 10.50 | 24.00 |
| 11-Ward-r/Broadway Romances #2 & retitled | 3.50 | 10.50 | 24.00 |
| 12-15,18-20 | 1.30 | 4.00 | 9.00 |
| 16,17-Ward-a; 16-Anthony Quinn photo-c. 17-Jane Russell photo-c | 4.60 | 14.00 | 32.00 |
| 21-29 | 1.15 | 3.50 | 8.00 |
| 30,31(6/53)-Ward-a | 2.65 | 8.00 | 18.00 |
| 32(2/54) - 39: Last precode (4/55) | 1.00 | 3.00 | 7.00 |
| 40-48 | .70 | 2.00 | 5.00 |
| 49,50-Baker-a | 2.65 | 8.00 | 18.00 |
| 51-Baker-c | 2.15 | 6.50 | 15.00 |

## LUCY SHOW, THE (TV) (Also see I Love Lucy)
June, 1963 - No. 5, June, 1964 (Photo-c: 1,2)
Gold Key

| | Good | Fine | N-Mint |
|---|---|---|---|
| 1 | 5.70 | 17.00 | 40.00 |
| 2 | 4.00 | 12.00 | 28.00 |
| 3-5: Photo back-c,1,2,4,5 | 3.50 | 10.50 | 24.00 |

# M

**MAD**
Oct-Nov, 1952 - Present (No. 24 on are magazine format) (Kurtzman
   editor No. 1-28, Feldstein No. 29 - No. ?)
E. C. Comics

|  | Good | Fine | N-Mint |
|---|---|---|---|
| 1-Wood, Davis, Elder start as regulars | 93.00 | 280.00 | 650.00 |
| 2-Davis-c | 42.00 | 125.00 | 295.00 |
| 3 | 27.00 | 81.00 | 190.00 |
| 4-Reefer mention story "Flob Was a Slob" by Davis | | | |
|  | 27.00 | 81.00 | 190.00 |
| 5-Low distribution; Elder-c | 52.00 | 155.00 | 365.00 |
| 6-10 | 19.00 | 57.00 | 135.00 |
| 11-Wolverton-a | 19.00 | 57.00 | 135.00 |
| 12-15 | 17.00 | 51.00 | 120.00 |
| 16-23(5/55): 21-1st app. Alfred E. Neuman on-c in fake ad. 22-all by Elder. | | | |
| 23-Special cancel announcement | 13.00 | 40.00 | 90.00 |
| 24(7/55)-1st magazine issue (25 cents); Kurtzman logo & border on-c | | | |
|  | 27.00 | 80.00 | 185.00 |
| 25-Jaffee starts as regular writer | 14.00 | 42.00 | 100.00 |
| 26 | 10.00 | 30.00 | 70.00 |
| 27-Davis-c; Jaffee starts as story artist; new logo | | | |
|  | 10.00 | 30.00 | 70.00 |
| 28-Elder-c; Heath back-c; last issue edited by Kurtzman; (three cover variations exist with different wording on contents banner on lower right of cover; value of each the same) | 8.00 | 24.00 | 56.00 |
| 29-Wood-c; Kamen-a; Don Martin starts as regular; Feldstein editing begins | 8.00 | 24.00 | 56.00 |
| 30-1st A. E. Neuman cover by Mingo; Crandall inside-c; last Elder-a; Bob Clarke starts as regular; Disneyland spoof | | | |
|  | 11.00 | 32.00 | 75.00 |
| 31-Freas starts as regular; last Davis art until #99 | | | |
|  | 7.00 | 21.00 | 50.00 |
| 32-Orlando, Drucker, Woodbridge start as regulars; Wood back-c | | | |
|  | 6.50 | 19.50 | 45.00 |
| 33-Orlando back-c | 6.50 | 19.50 | 45.00 |
| 34-Berg starts as regular | 5.50 | 16.50 | 38.00 |
| 35-Mingo wraparound-c; Crandall-a | 5.50 | 16.50 | 38.00 |

|  | Good | Fine | N-Mint |
|---|---|---|---|
| 36-40 | 3.70 | 11.00 | 26.00 |
| 41-50 | 2.85 | 8.50 | 20.00 |
| 51-60: 60-Two Clarke-c; Prohias starts as reg. | 1.70 | 5.00 | 12.00 |
| 61-70: 64-Rickard starts as regular. 68-Martin-c |  |  |  |
|  | 1.50 | 4.50 | 10.00 |
| 71-80: 76-Aragones starts as regular | 1.30 | 4.00 | 9.00 |
| 81-90: 86-1st Fold-in. 89-One strip by Walt Kelly. 90-Frazetta back-c |  |  |  |
|  | 1.15 | 3.50 | 8.00 |
| 91-100: 91-Jaffee starts as story artist. 99-Davis-a resumes |  |  |  |
|  | .85 | 2.60 | 6.00 |
| 101-120: 101-Infinity-c. 105-Batman TV show take-off. 106-Frazetta back-c |  |  |  |
|  | .70 | 2.00 | 4.00 |
| 121-140: 122-Drucker & Mingo-c. 128-Last Orlando. 130-Torres begins as regular. 135,139-Davis-c | .50 | 1.50 | 3.00 |
| 141-170: 165-Martin-c. 169-Drucker-c | .35 | 1.00 | 2.00 |
| 171-200: 173,178-Davis-c. 176-Drucker-c. 182-Bob Jones starts as regular. 186-Star Trek take-off. 187-Harry North starts as regular. 196-Star Wars take-off | .25 | .75 | 1.50 |
| 201-295: 203-Star Wars take-off. 204-Hulk TV show take-off. 208-Superman movie take-off. 286-Drucker-c. 289-Batman movie parody. 291-TMNT parody | .25 | .75 | 1.50 |

**MAGIC COMICS**
Aug, 1939 - No. 123, Nov-Dec, 1949
David McKay Publications

|  | Good | Fine | N-Mint |
|---|---|---|---|
| 1-Mandrake the Magician, Henry, Popeye (not by Segar), Blondie, Barney Baxter, Secret Agent X-9 (not by Raymond), Bunky by Billy DeBeck & Thornton Burgess text stories illustrated by Harrison Cady begin | 108.00 | 270.00 | 650.00 |
| 2 | 43.00 | 130.00 | 300.00 |
| 3 | 33.00 | 100.00 | 230.00 |
| 4 | 27.00 | 81.00 | 190.00 |
| 5 | 22.00 | 65.00 | 154.00 |
| 6-10 | 17.00 | 51.00 | 120.00 |
| 11-16,18-20 | 14.00 | 42.00 | 100.00 |
| 17-The Lone Ranger begins | 16.00 | 48.00 | 110.00 |
| 21-30 | 10.00 | 30.00 | 70.00 |
| 31-40 | 8.00 | 24.00 | 56.00 |
| 41-50 | 6.50 | 19.50 | 45.00 |

|  | Good | Fine | N-Mint |
|---|---|---|---|
| 51-60 | 5.00 | 15.00 | 35.00 |
| 61-70 | 3.70 | 11.00 | 26.00 |
| 71-99 | 3.00 | 9.00 | 21.00 |
| 100 | 3.70 | 11.00 | 26.00 |
| 101-106,109-123 | 2.30 | 7.00 | 16.00 |
| 107,108-Flash Gordon app; not by Raymond | 3.70 | 11.00 | 26.00 |

## MAGNUS, ROBOT FIGHTER (. . . 4000 A.D.)
Feb, 1963 - No. 46, Jan, 1977 (Painted covers)
Gold Key

| | | | |
|---|---|---|---|
| 1-Origin Magnus; Aliens series begins | 8.50 | 25.50 | 60.00 |
| 2,3 | 4.00 | 12.00 | 28.00 |
| 4-10 | 2.65 | 8.00 | 18.00 |
| 11-20 | 2.00 | 6.00 | 14.00 |
| 21,22,24-28: 22-Origin-r/#1. 28-Aliens ends | 1.30 | 4.00 | 9.00 |
| 23-12 cent and 15 cent editions exist | 1.30 | 4.00 | 9.00 |
| 29-46-Reprints | .70 | 2.00 | 5.00 |

## MAN-BAT (See Batman Family, Brave & the Bold, & Detective #400)
Dec-Jan, 1975-76 - No. 2, Feb-Mar, 1976; Dec, 1984
National Periodical Publications/DC Comics

| | | | |
|---|---|---|---|
| 1-Ditko-a(p); Aparo-c; Batman, She-Bat app. | 1.00 | 3.00 | 6.00 |
| 2-Aparo-c | .50 | 1.50 | 3.00 |
| 1 (12/84)-N. Adams-r(3)/Det.(Vs. Batman on-c) | | | |
| | .70 | 2.00 | 4.00 |

## MAN FROM U.N.C.L.E., THE (TV)
Feb, 1965 - No. 22, April, 1969 (All photo covers)
Gold Key

| | | | |
|---|---|---|---|
| 1 | 7.85 | 23.50 | 55.00 |
| 2-Photo back c-2-8 | 4.50 | 14.00 | 32.00 |
| 3-10: 7-Jet Dream begins (all new stories) | 2.85 | 8.50 | 20.00 |
| 11-22: 21,22-Reprint #10 & 7 | 2.30 | 7.00 | 16.00 |

**MANHUNT!**
Oct, 1947 - No. 14, 1953
Magazine Enterprises

| | Good | Fine | N-Mint |
|---|---|---|---|
| 1-Red Fox by L. B. Cole, Undercover Girl by Whitney, Space Ace begin; | | | |
| negligee panels | 19.00 | 57.00 | 132.00 |
| 2-Electrocution-c | 14.00 | 42.00 | 100.00 |
| 3-6 | 12.00 | 36.00 | 84.00 |
| 7-9: 7-Space Ace ends. 8-Trail Colt begins | 10.00 | 30.00 | 70.00 |
| 10-G. Ingels-a | 10.00 | 30.00 | 70.00 |
| 11(8/48)-Frazetta-a, 7 pgs.; The Duke, Scotland Yard begin | | | |
| | 19.00 | 57.00 | 132.00 |
| 12 | 7.00 | 21.00 | 50.00 |
| 13(A-1 #63)-Frazetta, r-/Trail Colt #1, 7 pgs. | 17.00 | 51.00 | 120.00 |
| 14(A-1 #77)-Bondage/hypo-c; last L. B. Cole Red Fox; Ingels-a | | | |
| | 11.00 | 32.00 | 75.00 |

**MAN-THING**
Jan, 1974 - No. 22, Oct, 1975; V2#1, Nov, 1979 - V2#11, July, 1980
Marvel Comics Group

| | | | |
|---|---|---|---|
| 1-2nd app. Howard the Duck | 1.35 | 4.00 | 8.00 |
| 2-4 | .35 | 1.00 | 2.00 |
| 5-11-Ploog-a | .25 | .75 | 1.50 |
| 12-22: 19-1st app. Scavenger. 21-Origin Scavenger & Man-Thing. | | | |
| 22-Howard the Duck cameo | | .50 | 1.00 |
| V2#1-11: 6-Golden-c | | .50 | 1.00 |
| Giant Size 1 (8/74)-Ploog-c/a | .35 | 1.00 | 2.00 |
| Giant Size 2 (1974), 3 (2/75) | | .50 | 1.00 |
| Giant Size 4 (5/75)-Howard the Duck by Brunner; Ditko-a(r) | | | |
| | .85 | 2.50 | 5.00 |
| Giant Size 5 (8/75)-Howard the Duck by Brunner (p) | | | |
| | .85 | 2.50 | 5.00 |

**MARGE'S LITTLE LULU** (Little Lulu #207 on)
No. 74, 6/45 - No. 164, 7-9/62; No. 165, 10/62 - No. 206, 8/72
Dell Publishing Co./Gold Key #165-206

| | | | |
|---|---|---|---|
| 4-Color 74('45)-Intro Lulu, Tubby & Alvin | 90.00 | 270.00 | 630.00 |
| 4-Color 97(2/46) | 47.00 | 140.00 | 330.00 |

|  | Good | Fine | N-Mint |
|---|---|---|---|

*(Above two books are all John Stanley—cover, pencils, and inks.)*

| | Good | Fine | N-Mint |
|---|---|---|---|
| 4-Color 110('46)-1st Alvin Story Telling Time; 1st app. Willy | | | |
| | 33.00 | 100.00 | 230.00 |
| 4-Color 115-1st app. Boys' Clubhouse | 33.00 | 100.00 | 230.00 |
| 4-Color 120, 131: 120-1st app. Eddie | 30.00 | 90.00 | 210.00 |
| 4-Color 139('47),146,158 | 27.00 | 81.00 | 190.00 |
| 4-Color 165 (10/47)-Smokes doll hair & has wild hallucinations. 1st | | | |
| Tubby detective story | 27.00 | 81.00 | 190.00 |
| 1(1-2/48)-Lulu's Diary feat. begins | 56.00 | 168.00 | 390.00 |
| 2-1st app. Gloria; 1st Tubby story in a L.L. comic; 1st app. Miss Feeny | | | |
| | 29.00 | 87.00 | 200.00 |
| 3-5 | 25.00 | 75.00 | 175.00 |
| 6-10: 7-1st app. Annie; Xmas-c | 18.00 | 54.00 | 125.00 |
| 11-20: 19-1st app. Wilbur. 20-1st app. Mr. McNabbem | | | |
| | 15.00 | 45.00 | 105.00 |
| 21-30: 26-r/F.C. 110. 30-Xmas-c | 11.50 | 34.00 | 80.00 |
| 31-38,40: 35-1st Mumday story | 10.00 | 30.00 | 70.00 |
| 39-Intro. Witch Hazel in "That Awful Witch Hazel" | | | |
| | 11.00 | 32.00 | 76.00 |
| 41-60: 42-Xmas-c. 45-2nd Witch Hazel app. 49-Gives Stanley & others | | | |
| credit | 8.50 | 25.50 | 60.00 |
| 61-80: 63-1st app. Chubby (Tubby's cousin). 68-1st app. Prof. Cleff. | | | |
| 78-Xmas-c. 80-Intro. Little Itch (2/55) | 6.50 | 19.50 | 45.00 |
| 81-99: 90-Xmas-c | 4.00 | 12.00 | 30.00 |
| 100 | 4.60 | 14.00 | 35.00 |
| 101-130: 123-1st app. Fifi | 3.50 | 10.50 | 24.00 |
| 131-164: 135-Last Stanley-p | 2.65 | 8.00 | 20.00 |
| 165-Giant; . . . In Paris ('62) | 4.00 | 12.00 | 32.00 |
| 166-Giant; . . . Christmas Diary ('62-'63) | 4.00 | 12.00 | 32.00 |
| 167-169 | 2.15 | 6.50 | 15.00 |
| 170,172,175,176,178-196,198-200-Stanley-r. 182-1st app. Little Scarecrow | | | |
| Boy | 1.30 | 4.00 | 9.00 |
| 171,173,174,177,197 | .85 | 2.50 | 6.00 |
| 201,203,206-Last issue to carry Marge's name | .55 | 1.65 | 4.00 |
| 202,204,205-Stanley-r | 1.00 | 3.00 | 7.00 |
| . . . & Tubby in Japan (12 cents)(5-7/62) 01476-207 | | | |
| | 5.70 | 17.00 | 40.00 |
| . . . Summer Camp 1(8/67-G.K.-Giant) '57-58-r | 4.65 | 14.00 | 32.00 |
| . . . Trick 'N' Treat 1(12–)(12/62-Gold Key) | 5.00 | 15.00 | 35.00 |

**MARGE'S TUBBY** (Little Lulu)
No. 381, Aug, 1952 - No. 49, Dec-Feb, 1961-62
Dell Publishing Co./Gold Key

|  | Good | Fine | N-Mint |
|---|---|---|---|
| 4-Color 381(#1)-Stanley script; Irving Tripp-a | | | |
|  | 12.00 | 36.00 | 84.00 |
| 4-Color 430,444-Stanley-a | 7.00 | 21.00 | 50.00 |
| 4-Color 461 (4/53)-1st Tubby & Men From Mars story; Stanley-a | | | |
|  | 6.50 | 19.50 | 45.00 |
| 5 (7-9/53)-Stanley-a | 5.00 | 15.00 | 35.00 |
| 6-10 | 3.50 | 10.50 | 24.00 |
| 11-20 | 2.85 | 8.50 | 20.00 |
| 21-30 | 2.35 | 7.00 | 16.00 |
| 31-49 | 2.00 | 6.00 | 14.00 |
| . . . & the Little Men From Mars No. 30020-410(10/64-G.K.)-25 cents; 68 | | | |
| pgs. | 5.00 | 15.00 | 40.00 |

**MARVEL AND DC PRESENT** (Featuring the Uncanny X-Men and the
    New Teen Titans)
Nov, 1982 (One Shot, 68 pgs, $2.00 cover, printed on Baxter paper)
Marvel Comics Group/DC Comics

| 1-Simonson/Austin-c/a; Perez-a(p) | 1.50 | 4.50 | 9.00 |
|---|---|---|---|

**MARVEL BOY** (Astonishing #3 on)
Dec, 1950 - No. 2, Feb, 1951
Marvel Comics (MPC)

| 1-Origin Marvel Boy by Russ Heath | 30.00 | 90.00 | 210.00 |
|---|---|---|---|
| 2-Everett-a | 25.00 | 75.00 | 175.00 |

**MARVEL COLLECTORS ITEM CLASSICS**
Feb, 1965 - No. 22, Aug, 1969 (68 pgs.) (Ditko, Kirby reprints in all)
Marvel Comics Group(ATF)

| 1-Fantastic Four, Spider-Man, Thor, Hulk, Iron Man-r begin; all are 25 | | | |
|---|---|---|---|
| cent cover price | 3.70 | 11.00 | 26.00 |
| 2 (4/66) - 4 | 2.00 | 6.00 | 14.00 |
| 5-22 | 1.00 | 3.00 | 6.00 |

*Marvel Mystery Comics #80, © Marvel Comics*

**MARVEL COMICS** (Marvel Mystery Comics #2 on)
October, November, 1939
Timely Comics (Funnies, Inc.)

|  | **Good** | **Fine** | **N-Mint** |
|---|---|---|---|
| 1-Origin Sub-Mariner by Bill Everett (1st newsstand app.); Human Torch by Carl Burgos, Kazar the Great, & Jungle Terror (only app.); intro. The Angel by Gustavson, The Masked Raider (ends #12) | 5000.00 | 12,600.00 | 27,500.00 |

*(Only one known copy exists in Mint condition which traded twice in 1986 for $69,000 & later for $82,000, & once in 1987 for $82,000. Two other copies are known in NM-M condition & their value would vary beyond the VF-NM price.)*

**MARVEL COMICS PRESENTS**
Early Sept, 1988 - Present ($1.25, color, bi-weekly)
Marvel Comics

| | | | |
|---|---|---|---|
| 1-Wolverine by Buscema in #1-10 | .75 | 2.25 | 4.50 |

|  | Good | Fine | N-Mint |
|---|---|---|---|
| 2-5 | .40 | 1.25 | 2.50 |
| 6-10: 6-Sub-Mariner app. 10-Colossus begins | .35 | 1.00 | 2.00 |

11-24,26-37: 17-Cyclops begins. 19-1st app. Damage Control. 24-Havok begins. 26-Hulk begins by Rogers. 29-Quasar app. 31- Excalibur begins by Austin (i). 33-Capt. America. 37-Devil-Slayer app. (1st?).

|  | Good | Fine | N-Mint |
|---|---|---|---|
|  |  | .60 | 1.25 |
| 25-Origin & 1st app. Nth Man | .35 | 1.00 | 2.00 |
| 38-Wolverine begins by Buscema; Hulk app. | .35 | 1.00 | 2.00 |
| 39-47,51-61: 54-61-Wolverine & Hulk app. | .25 | .75 | 1.50 |
| 48-50-Wolverine & Spider-Man team-up | .35 | 1.00 | 2.00 |
| 60-64 |  | .60 | 1.25 |

**MARVEL FAMILY** (Also see Captain Marvel Adventures No. 18)
Dec, 1945 - No. 89, Jan, 1954
Fawcett Publications

| | Good | Fine | N-Mint |
|---|---|---|---|
| 1-Origin Captain Marvel, Captain Marvel Jr., Mary Marvel, & Uncle Marvel retold; Origin/1st app. Black Adam | 65.00 | 195.00 | 455.00 |
| 2 | 35.00 | 105.00 | 245.00 |
| 3 | 25.00 | 75.00 | 175.00 |
| 4,5 | 19.00 | 57.00 | 135.00 |
| 6-10: 7-Shazam app. | 16.00 | 48.00 | 110.00 |
| 11-20 | 11.00 | 32.00 | 75.00 |
| 21-30 | 8.50 | 25.50 | 60.00 |
| 31-40 | 7.00 | 21.00 | 50.00 |
| 41-46,48-50 | 5.70 | 17.00 | 40.00 |
| 47-Flying Saucer-c/story | 7.00 | 21.00 | 50.00 |
| 51-76,79,80,82-89 | 5.00 | 15.00 | 35.00 |
| 77-Communist Threat-c | 7.00 | 21.00 | 50.00 |
| 78,81-Used in **POP**, pgs. 92,93 | 5.00 | 15.00 | 35.00 |

**MARVEL FEATURE**
Dec, 1971 - No. 12, Nov, 1973 (No. 1,2: 25 cents) (1-3: Quarterly)
Marvel Comics Group

| | Good | Fine | N-Mint |
|---|---|---|---|
| 1-Origin/1st app. The Defenders; Sub-Mariner, Hulk & Dr. Strange; '50s Sub-Mariner-r, Neal Adams-c | 2.15 | 6.50 | 15.00 |
| 2-G.A. 1950s Sub-Mariner-r | 1.50 | 4.50 | 9.00 |
| 3-Defender series ends | 1.50 | 4.50 | 9.00 |

|  | Good | Fine | N-Mint |
|---|---|---|---|

4-Re-intro Ant-Man(1st app. since '60s), begin series; brief origin.

|  | .85 | 2.50 | 5.00 |
|---|---|---|---|

5-12: 6-Wasp app. & begins team-up. 8-Origin Antman & Wasp. 9-Iron Man app. 10-Last Ant-Man. 11,12-Thing team-ups. 11-Origin Fantastic-4 retold

|  | .50 | 1.50 | 3.00 |
|---|---|---|---|

**MARVEL MYSTERY COMICS** (Formerly Marvel Comics) (Marvel Tales No. 93 on)
No. 2, Dec, 1939 - No. 92, June, 1949
Timely /Marvel Comics (TP 2-17/TCI 18-54/MCI 55-92)

2-American Ace begins, ends #3; Human Torch (blue costume) by Burgos, Sub-Mariner by Everett continues; 2 pg. origin recap of Human Torch

| | 750.00 | 1890.00 | 4500.00 |
|---|---|---|---|
| 3-New logo from Marvel pulp begins | 433.00 | 1085.00 | 2600.00 |

4-Intro. Electro, the Marvel of the Age (ends #19), The Ferret, Mystery Detective (ends #9)

| | 350.00 | 875.00 | 2100.00 |
|---|---|---|---|
| 5 (Scarce) | 533.00 | 1365.00 | 3200.00 |
| 6,7 | 217.00 | 545.00 | 1300.00 |
| 8-Human Torch & Sub-Mariner battle | 283.00 | 710.00 | 1700.00 |

9-(Scarce)-Human Torch & Sub-Mariner battle

| | 350.00 | 875.00 | 2100.00 |
|---|---|---|---|

10-Human Torch & Sub-Mariner battle, conclusion; Terry Vance, the Schoolboy Sleuth begins, ends #57

| | 190.00 | 475.00 | 1140.00 |
|---|---|---|---|
| 11 | 140.00 | 350.00 | 840.00 |
| 12-Classic Kirby-c | 140.00 | 350.00 | 840.00 |

13-Intro. & 1st app. The Vision by S&K; Sub-Mariner dons new costume, ends #15

| | 158.00 | 395.00 | 950.00 |
|---|---|---|---|
| 14-16 | 97.00 | 245.00 | 580.00 |

17-Human Torch/Sub-Mariner team-up by Everett/Burgos; pin-up on back-c

| | 112.00 | 280.00 | 670.00 |
|---|---|---|---|
| 18 | 92.00 | 230.00 | 550.00 |
| 19-Origin Toro in text | 94.00 | 235.00 | 565.00 |
| 20-Origin The Angel in text | 90.00 | 225.00 | 540.00 |

21-Intro. & 1st app. The Patriot; not in #46-48; pin-up on back-c

| | 81.00 | 205.00 | 485.00 |
|---|---|---|---|

22-25: 23-Last Gustavson Angel; origin The Vision in text. 24-Injury-to-eye story

| | 72.00 | 180.00 | 430.00 |
|---|---|---|---|

|  | Good | Fine | N-Mint |
|---|---|---|---|
| 26-30: 27-Ka-Zar ends; last S&K Vision who battles Satan. 28-Jimmy Jupiter in the Land of Nowhere begins, ends #48; Sub-Mariner vs. The Flying Dutchman | 63.00 | 160.00 | 380.00 |
| 31-Sub-Mariner by Everett ends, begins again #84 | 62.00 | 155.00 | 370.00 |
| 32-1st app. The Boboes | 62.00 | 155.00 | 370.00 |
| 33,35-40: 40-Zeppelin-c | 62.00 | 155.00 | 370.00 |
| 34-Everett, Burgos, Martin Goodman, Funnies, Inc. office appear in story & battles Hitler; last Burgos Human Torch | 72.00 | 180.00 | 430.00 |
| 41-43,45-48: 46-Hitler-c. 48-Last Vision; flag-c | 56.00 | 140.00 | 335.00 |
| 44-Classic Super Plane-c | 56.00 | 140.00 | 335.00 |
| 49-Origin Miss America | 72.00 | 180.00 | 430.00 |
| 50-Mary becomes Miss Patriot (origin) | 56.00 | 140.00 | 335.00 |
| 51-60: 53-Bondage-c | 50.00 | 125.00 | 300.00 |
| 61,62,64-Last German War-c | 47.00 | 120.00 | 280.00 |
| 63-Classic Hitler War-c; The Villainess Cat-Woman only app. | 50.00 | 125.00 | 300.00 |
| 65,66-Last Japanese War-c | 47.00 | 120.00 | 280.00 |
| 67-75: 74-Last Patriot. 75-Young Allies begin | 43.00 | 110.00 | 260.00 |
| 76-78: 76-Ten Chapter Miss America serial begins, ends #85 | 43.00 | 110.00 | 260.00 |
| 79-New cover format; Super Villains begin on cover; last Angel | 39.00 | 100.00 | 235.00 |
| 80-1st app. Capt. America in Marvel Comics | 50.00 | 125.00 | 300.00 |
| 81-Captain America app. | 39.00 | 100.00 | 235.00 |
| 82-Origin Namora; 1st Sub-Mariner/Namora team-up; Captain America app. | 67.00 | 170.00 | 400.00 |
| 83,85: 83-Last Young Allies. 85-Last Miss America; Blonde Phantom app. | 39.00 | 100.00 | 235.00 |
| 84-Blonde Phantom, Sub-Mariner by Everett begins; Captain America app. | 50.00 | 125.00 | 300.00 |
| 86-Blonde Phantom i.d. revealed; Captain America app.; last Bucky app. | 44.00 | 110.00 | 265.00 |
| 87-1st Capt. America/Golden Girl team-up | 50.00 | 125.00 | 300.00 |
| 88-Golden Girl, Namora, & Sun Girl (1st in Marvel Comics) x-over; Captain America, Blonde Phantom app.; last Toro | 44.00 | 110.00 | 265.00 |
| 89-1st Human Torch/Sun Girl team-up; 1st Captain America solo; Blonde Phantom app. | 47.00 | 120.00 | 280.00 |

|                                                                     | Good | Fine | N-Mint |
|---------------------------------------------------------------------|------|------|--------|
| 90-Blonde Phantom un-masked; Captain America app.                   |      |      |        |
|                                                                     | 47.00 | 120.00 | 280.00 |
| 91-Capt. America app.; intro Venus; Blonde Phantom & Sub-Mariner end |      |      |        |
|                                                                     | 47.00 | 120.00 | 280.00 |

92-Feature story on the birth of the Human Torch and the death of Professor Horton (his creator); 1st app. The Witness in Marvel Comics; Captain America app.     77.00     195.00     460.00

## MARVEL PREMIERE
April, 1972 - No. 61, Aug, 1981 (A tryout book for new characters)
Marvel Comics Group

1-Origin Warlock (pre #1) by Gil Kane/Adkins; origin Counter-Earth
                                                  1.40     4.25     8.50
2-Warlock ends; Kirby Yellow Claw-r               .90      2.75     5.50
3-Dr. Strange series begins (pre #1, 7/72), B. Smith-a(p); Smith-c?
                                                  1.35     4.00     8.00
4-Smith/Brunner-a                                 .70      2.00     4.00
5-10: 10-Death of the Ancient One                 .35      1.00     2.00
11-14: 11-Origin-r by Ditko. 14-Intro. God; last Dr. Strange(3/74), moves to
     own comic 3 months later                     .25      .80      1.60
15-Origin/1st app. Iron Fist(5/74), ends #25      1.70     5.00     10.00
16-20: Iron Fist in all                           .35      1.00     2.00
21-24,26-28: 26-Hercules. 27-Satana. 28-Legion of Monsters (Ghost Rider,
     Man-Thing, Morbius, Werewolf)                .25      .80      1.60
25-1st Byrne Iron Fist(moves to own title next)
                                                  1.00     3.00     6.00
29-49,51-56,61: 29,30-The Liberty Legion. 35-Origin/1st app. 3-D Man.
     44-Jack of Hearts. 47-Origin new Ant-Man. 49-The Falcon(1st solo
     book, 8/79). 51,52-Black Panther. 61-Star Lord     .40     .80
50-Alice Cooper                                   .70      2.00     4.00
57-Dr. Who (1st U.S. app.)                        .35      1.00     2.00
58-60-Dr. Who                                     .25      .75      1.50

## MARVEL SPOTLIGHT (A tryout book for new characters)
Nov, 1971 - No. 33, Apr, 1977; V2#1, July, 1979 - V2#11, Mar, 1981
Marvel Comics Group

|  | Good | Fine | N-Mint |
|---|---|---|---|
| 1-Origin Red Wolf (1st solo book); Wood inks, Neal Adams-c | .85 | 2.50 | 5.00 |
| 2-(Giant, 52 pgs.)-Venus-r by Everett; origin/1st app. Werewolf By Night (begins) by Ploog; N. Adams-c | .40 | 1.25 | 2.50 |
| 3,4: 4-Werewolf By Night ends (2/72) | .25 | .75 | 1.50 |
| 5-Origin/1st app. Ghost Rider (8/72) | 3.70 | 11.00 | 26.00 |
| 6-8-Last Ploog issue; Ghost Rider in all | 1.40 | 4.25 | 8.50 |
| 9-11-Last Ghost Rider(gets own title next mo.) | 1.40 | 4.25 | 8.50 |
| 12-27,30-33: 12-The Son of Satan begins (origin). 25-Sinbad. 26- Scarecrow. 27-Sub-Mariner. 30-The Warriors Three. 31-Nick Fury. 32-Intro/partial origin Spider-Woman(2/77); Nick Fury app. 33-Deathlok | .25 | .75 | 1.50 |
| 28,29: Moon Knight (28-1st solo app., 6/76) | .40 | 1.25 | 2.50 |
| V2#1-11: Capt. Marvel #1-4. 5-Dragon Lord. 6,7-StarLord; origin #6. 9-11-Capt. Universe app. | | .50 | 1.00 |

**MARVEL SUPER HEROES**
October, 1966 (25 cents, 68 pgs.) (1st Marvel One-shot)
Marvel Comics Group

|  | Good | Fine | N-Mint |
|---|---|---|---|
| 1-r-origin Daredevil from D.D. #1; r-Avengers #2; G.A. Sub-Mariner-r/ Marvel Mystery No. 8 (H. Torch app.) | 5.00 | 15.00 | 35.00 |

**MARVEL SUPER-HEROES** (Fantasy Masterpieces #1-11)
No. 12, 12/67 - No. 31, 11/71; No. 32, 9/72 - No. 105, 1/82
Marvel Comics Group

|  | Good | Fine | N-Mint |
|---|---|---|---|
| 12-Origin & 1st app. Capt. Marvel of the Kree | 5.70 | 17.00 | 40.00 |
| 13-2nd app. Capt. Marvel | 2.30 | 7.00 | 16.00 |
| 14-New Spider-Man story (5/68) | 2.85 | 8.50 | 20.00 |
| 15-17,19-31: 16-Origin & 1st app. Phantom Eagle. 17-Origin Black Knight. 31-Last giant size issue | .70 | 2.00 | 4.00 |
| 18-Origin/1st app. Guardians of the Galaxy | 1.60 | 4.80 | 11.00 |
| 32-105: 32-Hulk/Sub-Mariner-r begin | | .50 | 1.00 |

*Marvel Tales #104, © Marvel Comics*

**MARVEL TALES** (Formerly Marvel Mystery #1-92)
No. 93, Aug, 1949 - No. 159, Aug, 1957
Marvel/Atlas Comics (MCI)

| | Good | Fine | N-Mint |
|---|---|---|---|
| 93 | 34.00 | 103.00 | 240.00 |
| 94-Everett-a | 28.50 | 86.00 | 200.00 |
| 95,96,99,101,103,105 | 16.00 | 48.00 | 110.00 |
| 97-Sun Girl, 2 pgs; Kirbyish-a; one story used in N.Y. State Legislative document | 23.00 | 70.00 | 160.00 |
| 98-Krigstein-a | 17.00 | 51.00 | 120.00 |
| 100 | 17.00 | 51.00 | 120.00 |
| 102-Wolverton-a "The End of the World," 6 pgs. | 29.00 | 87.00 | 205.00 |
| 104-Wolverton-a "Gateway to Horror," 6 pgs; Heath-c | 26.50 | 80.00 | 185.00 |
| 106,107-Krigstein-a. 106-Decapitation story | 14.00 | 42.00 | 100.00 |

|  | Good | Fine | N-Mint |
|---|---|---|---|
| 108-120: 118-Hypo-c/panels in End of World story. 120-Jack Katz-a | | | |
|  | 8.50 | 25.50 | 60.00 |
| 121,123-131: 128-Flying Saucer-c. 131-Last precode (2/55) | | | |
|  | 7.00 | 20.00 | 48.00 |
| 122-Kubert-a | 7.50 | 22.00 | 52.00 |
| 132,133,135-141,143,145 | 4.00 | 12.00 | 28.00 |
| 134-Krigstein, Kubert-a; flying saucer-c | 5.00 | 15.00 | 35.00 |
| 142-Krigstein-a | 4.65 | 14.00 | 32.00 |
| 144-Williamson/Krenkel-a, 3 pgs. | 5.00 | 15.00 | 35.00 |
| 146,148-151,154,155,158 | 2.85 | 8.50 | 20.00 |
| 147-Ditko-a | 3.70 | 11.00 | 26.00 |
| 152-Wood, Morrow-a | 4.00 | 12.00 | 28.00 |
| 153-Everett End of World c/story | 4.00 | 12.00 | 28.00 |
| 156-Torres-a | 3.50 | 10.50 | 24.00 |
| 157,159-Krigstein-a | 4.65 | 14.00 | 32.00 |

**MARVEL TEAM-UP**
March, 1972 - No. 150, Feb, 1985 (Spider-Man team-ups most issues)
Marvel Comics Group

|  | Good | Fine | N-Mint |
|---|---|---|---|
| 1-Human Torch | 4.30 | 13.00 | 30.00 |
| 2,3-Human Torch | 1.50 | 4.50 | 9.00 |
| 4-X-Men | 2.40 | 7.20 | 17.00 |
| 5-10 | .85 | 2.50 | 5.00 |
| 11-14,16-20 | .65 | 1.90 | 3.80 |
| 15-Ghost Rider app. (early) | .85 | 2.50 | 5.00 |
| 21-30 | .50 | 1.50 | 3.00 |
| 31-50 | .35 | 1.00 | 2.00 |
| 51,52,56-58: 58-Ghost Rider app. | .25 | .75 | 1.50 |
| 53-Woodgod/Hulk; new X-Men app., 1st by Byrne (1/77) | | | |
|  | 1.15 | 3.50 | 7.00 |
| 54-Hulk/Woodgod; Byrne-a(p) | .70 | 2.00 | 4.00 |
| 55,59,60: 55-Warlock. 59-Yellowjacket/The Wasp. 60-The Wasp-All | | | |
| Byrne-a | .70 | 2.00 | 4.00 |
| 61-74,76-78,80: 61-70-All Byrne-a. 65-Capt. Britain (1st U.S. app.) | | | |
|  | .25 | .75 | 1.50 |
| 75,79-Byrne-a(p) | .40 | 1.25 | 2.50 |
| 81-88,90-99: 91-Ghost Rider app. |  | .50 | 1.00 |
| 89-Nightcrawler | .25 | .75 | 1.50 |

| | Good | Fine | N-Mint |
|---|---|---|---|
| 100-Fantastic-4(Double size); origin/1st app. Karma, one of the New Mutants; origin Storm; X-Men x-over; Miller-a/c(p); Byrne-a on new X-Men | 1.00 | 3.00 | 6.00 |
| 101-116 | | .50 | 1.00 |
| 117-Wolverine | .85 | 2.50 | 5.00 |
| 118-Professor X (Double-size); Wolverine (X-Men) cameo | | | |
| | .25 | .75 | 1.50 |
| 119-149: 135-Kitty Pryde; X-Men cameo | | .40 | .80 |
| 150-X-Men ($1.00); B. Smith-c | .50 | 1.50 | 3.00 |
| Annual 1(1976)-New X-Men app. | 1.35 | 4.00 | 8.00 |
| Annuals 2 (12/79) - #7 (10/84) | .25 | .75 | 1.50 |

**MARY MARVEL COMICS** (Monte Hale #29 on) (Also see Captain Marvel #18, Marvel Family & Wow)
Dec, 1945 - No. 28, Sept, 1948
Fawcett Publications

| 1-Captain Marvel intro. Mary on-c; intro/origin Georgia Sivana | | | |
|---|---|---|---|
| | 59.00 | 178.00 | 415.00 |
| 2 | 28.00 | 84.00 | 195.00 |
| 3 | 20.00 | 60.00 | 140.00 |
| 4 | 16.00 | 48.00 | 110.00 |
| 5-8: 8-Bulletgirl x-over in Mary Marvel | 13.00 | 40.00 | 90.00 |
| 9,10 | 10.00 | 30.00 | 70.00 |
| 11-20 | 7.50 | 22.00 | 52.00 |
| 21-28 | 6.50 | 19.50 | 45.00 |

**MASTER COMICS**
Mar, 1940 - No. 133, Apr, 1953 (No. 1-6: oversized issues) (#1-3: 15 cents, 52 pgs.; #4-6: 10 cents, 36 pgs.)
Fawcett Publications

| 1-Origin Master Man; The Devil's Dagger, El Carim, Master of Magic, Rick O'Say, Morton Murch, White Rajah, Shipwreck Roberts, Frontier Marshal, Streak Sloan, Mr. Clue begin (all features end #6) | | | |
|---|---|---|---|
| | 208.00 | 520.00 | 1250.00 |
| 2 | 100.00 | 250.00 | 600.00 |
| 3-5 | 67.00 | 170.00 | 400.00 |
| 6-Last Master Man | 75.00 | 190.00 | 450.00 |

|  | Good | Fine | N-Mint |
|---|---|---|---|

NOTE: #1-6 rarely found in near mint to mint condition due to large-size format.

| | Good | Fine | N-Mint |
|---|---|---|---|
| 7-(10/40)-Bulletman, Zoro, the Mystery Man (ends #22), Lee Granger, Jungle King, & Buck Jones begin; only app. The War Bird & Mark Swift & the Time Retarder | 125.00 | 315.00 | 750.00 |
| 8-The Red Gaucho (ends #13), Captain Venture (ends #22) & The Planet Princess begin | 50.00 | 150.00 | 350.00 |
| 9,10: 10-Lee Granger ends | 45.00 | 135.00 | 315.00 |
| 11-Origin Minute-Man | 100.00 | 300.00 | 600.00 |
| 12 | 53.00 | 160.00 | 375.00 |
| 13-Origin Bulletgirl | 92.00 | 275.00 | 550.00 |
| 14-16: 14-Companions Three begins, ends #31 | 45.00 | 135.00 | 315.00 |
| 17-20: 17-Raboy-a on Bulletman begins. 20-Captain Marvel cameo app. in Bulletman | 45.00 | 135.00 | 315.00 |
| 21-(Scarce)-Captain Marvel x-over in Bulletman; Capt. Nazi origin | 182.00 | 545.00 | 1275.00 |
| 22-Captain Marvel Jr. x-over in Bulletman; Capt. Nazi app; bondage-c | 150.00 | 450.00 | 1050.00 |
| 23-Capt. Marvel Jr. begins, vs. Capt. Nazi | 121.00 | 365.00 | 850.00 |
| 24,25,29 | 45.00 | 135.00 | 315.00 |
| 26-28,30-Captain Marvel Jr. vs. Capt. Nazi. 30-Flag-c | 45.00 | 135.00 | 315.00 |
| 31,32: 32-Last El Carim & Buck Jones; Balbo, the Boy Magician intro. in El Carim | 31.00 | 92.00 | 215.00 |
| 33-Balbo, the Boy Magician (ends #47), Hopalong Cassidy (ends #49) begins | 31.00 | 92.00 | 215.00 |
| 34-Capt. Marvel Jr. vs. Capt. Nazi | 31.00 | 92.00 | 215.00 |
| 35 | 31.00 | 92.00 | 215.00 |
| 36-40: 40-Flag-c | 27.00 | 81.00 | 190.00 |
| 41-Bulletman, Capt. Marvel Jr. & Bulletgirl x-over in Minute-Man; only app. Crime Crusaders Club (Capt. Marvel Jr., Minute-Man, Bulletman & Bulletgirl)-only team in Fawcett Comics | 31.00 | 92.00 | 215.00 |
| 42-47,49: 47-Hitler becomes Corpl. Hitler Jr. 49-Last Minute-Man | 17.00 | 51.00 | 120.00 |
| 48-Intro. Bulletboy; Capt. Marvel cameo in Minute-Man | 19.00 | 58.00 | 135.00 |

|                                                                                          | Good  | Fine  | N-Mint |
|------------------------------------------------------------------------------------------|-------|-------|--------|
| 50-Radar, Nyoka the Jungle Girl begin; Capt. Marvel x-over in Radar; origin Radar       | 13.00 | 40.00 | 90.00  |
| 51-58                                                                                     | 8.50  | 25.50 | 60.00  |
| 59-62: Nyoka serial "Terrible Tiara" in all; 61-Capt. Marvel Jr. 1st meets Uncle Marvel | 10.00 | 30.00 | 70.00  |
| 63-80                                                                                     | 6.50  | 19.50 | 45.00  |
| 81-92,94-99: 88-Hopalong Cassidy begins (ends #94). 95-Tom Mix begins (ends #133)        | 5.70  | 17.00 | 40.00  |
| 93-Krigstein-a                                                                            | 6.00  | 18.00 | 42.00  |
| 100                                                                                       | 6.50  | 19.50 | 45.00  |
| 101-106-Last Bulletman                                                                    | 4.30  | 13.00 | 30.00  |
| 107-131                                                                                   | 3.70  | 11.00 | 26.00  |
| 132-B&W and color illos in **POP**                                                       | 4.30  | 13.00 | 30.00  |
| 133-Bill Battle app.                                                                      | 5.70  | 17.00 | 40.00  |

**MAVERICK** (TV)
No. 892, 4/58 - No. 19, 4-6/62 (All have photo-c)
Dell Publishing Co.

|                                                     | Good | Fine  | N-Mint |
|-----------------------------------------------------|------|-------|--------|
| 4-Color 892 (#1): James Garner/Jack Kelly photo-c begin | 7.00 | 21.00 | 50.00  |
| 4-Color 930,945,962,980,1005 (6-8/59)               | 5.00 | 15.00 | 35.00  |
| 7 (10-12/59) - 14: Last Garner/Kelly-c              | 4.00 | 12.00 | 28.00  |
| 15-18: Jack Kelly/Roger Moore photo-c               | 4.00 | 12.00 | 28.00  |
| 19-Jack Kelly photo-c                               | 4.00 | 12.00 | 28.00  |

**METAL MEN** (See Brave & the Bold and Showcase)
4-5/63 - No. 41, 12-1/69-70; No. 42, 2-3/73 - No. 44, 7-8/73; No. 45, 4-5/76 - No. 56, 2-3/78
National Periodical Publications/DC Comics

|                                            | Good  | Fine  | N-Mint |
|--------------------------------------------|-------|-------|--------|
| 1                                          | 16.50 | 49.50 | 115.00 |
| 2                                          | 6.50  | 19.50 | 45.00  |
| 3-5                                        | 4.30  | 13.00 | 30.00  |
| 6-10                                       | 2.85  | 8.50  | 20.00  |
| 11-20                                      | 2.15  | 6.50  | 15.00  |
| 21-26,28-30                                | 1.50  | 4.50  | 9.00   |
| 27-Origin Metal Men                        | 2.15  | 6.50  | 15.00  |
| 31-38(1968-70): 38-Last 12 cent issue      | 1.15  | 3.50  | 7.00   |
| 39-44(1973)-Reprints                       | .70   | 2.00  | 4.00   |

|  | Good | Fine | N-Mint |
|---|---|---|---|
| 45('76) 49-Simonson-a in all | .70 | 2.00 | 4.00 |
| 50-56: 50-Part-r. 54,55-Green Lantern x-over | .70 | 2.00 | 4.00 |

**METAMORPHO** (See Action, Brave & the Bold, & World's Finest)
July-Aug, 1965 - No. 17, Mar-Apr, 1968 (All 12 cent issues)
National Periodical Publications

| 1 | 5.70 | 17.00 | 40.00 |
|---|---|---|---|
| 2,3 | 2.85 | 8.50 | 20.00 |
| 4-6 | 1.70 | 5.00 | 12.00 |
| 7-9 | 1.35 | 4.00 | 8.00 |
| 10-Origin & 1st app. Element Girl (1-2/67) | 1.85 | 5.50 | 13.00 |
| 11-17 | .85 | 2.50 | 5.00 |

**MICKEY AND DONALD** (Walt Disney's . . . #3 on)
Mar, 1988 - No. 18, May, 1990 (95 cents, color)
Gladstone Publishing

| 1-Don Rosa-a; r-/1949 Firestone giveaway | 1.00 | 3.00 | 6.00 |
|---|---|---|---|
| 2 | .40 | 1.25 | 2.50 |
| 3-Infinity-c | .35 | 1.00 | 2.00 |
| 4-8: Barks-r | | .60 | 1.20 |
| 9-15: 9-r/1948 Firestone giveaway; Xmas-c | | .50 | 1.00 |
| 16 ($1.50, 52 pgs.)-r/FC #157 | .25 | .75 | 1.50 |
| 17,18 ($1.95, 68 pgs.): 17-Barks M.M.-r/FC #79 plus Barks D.D.-r; Rosa-a; Xmas-c. 18-Barks-r; Kelly-c(r) | .35 | 1.00 | 2.00 |

**MICKEY MOUSE** ( . . . Secret Agent #107-109; Walt Disney's. . .
#148-205?) (See Walt Disney's Comics & Stories)
No. 16, 1941 - No. 84, 7-9/62; No. 85, 11/62 - No. 218, 7/84; No. 219, 10/86 -
No. 256, April, 1990
Dell Publ. Co./Gold Key No. 85-204/Whitman No. 205-218/ Gladstone No.
219 on

|  | Good | Fine | VF-NM |
|---|---|---|---|
| 4-Color 16(1941)-1st M.M. comic book-"vs. the Phantom Blot" by Gottfredson | 343.00 | 1030.00 | 2400.00 |

*(Prices vary widely on this book)*

|  | Good | Fine | N-Mint |
|---|---|---|---|
| 4-Color 27(1943)-"7 Colored Terror" | 50.00 | 150.00 | 350.00 |
| 4-Color 79(1945)-By Carl Barks (1 story) | 64.00 | 193.00 | 450.00 |

| | Good | Fine | N-Mint |
|---|---|---|---|
| 4-Color 116(1946) | 17.00 | 51.00 | 120.00 |
| 4-Color 141,157(1947) | 16.00 | 48.00 | 110.00 |
| 4-Color 170,181,194('48) | 13.00 | 40.00 | 90.00 |
| 4-Color 214('49),231,248,261 | 10.00 | 30.00 | 70.00 |
| 4-Color 268-Reprints/WDC&S #22-24 by Gottfredson ("Surprise Visitor") | | | |
| | 10.00 | 30.00 | 70.00 |
| 4-Color 279,286,296 | 8.50 | 25.50 | 60.00 |
| 4-Color 304,313(#1),325(#2),334 | 5.70 | 17.00 | 40.00 |
| 4-Color 343,352,362,371,387 | 4.30 | 13.00 | 30.00 |
| 4-Color 401,411,427(10-11/52) | 3.50 | 10.50 | 24.00 |
| 4-Color 819-Mickey Mouse in Magicland | 2.00 | 6.00 | 14.00 |
| 4-Color 1057,1151,1246(1959-61)-Album | 1.70 | 5.00 | 12.00 |
| 28(12-1/52-53)-32,34 | 1.70 | 5.00 | 12.00 |
| 33-(Exists with 2 dates, 10-11/53 & 12-1/54) | 1.70 | 5.00 | 12.00 |
| 35-50 | 1.15 | 3.50 | 8.00 |
| 51-73,75-80 | .85 | 2.50 | 6.00 |
| 74-Story swipe-"The Rare Stamp Search"/4-Color 422-"The Gilded Man" | | | |
| | 1.15 | 3.50 | 8.00 |
| 81-99: 93,95-titled "Mickey Mouse Club Album" | | | |
| | .85 | 2.50 | 6.00 |
| 100-105: Reprints 4-Color 427,194,279,170,343,214 in that order | | | |
| | 1.00 | 3.00 | 7.00 |
| 106-120 | .75 | 2.25 | 5.00 |
| 121-130 | .70 | 2.00 | 4.00 |
| 131-146 | .50 | 1.50 | 3.00 |
| 147,148: 147-Reprints "The Phantom Fires" from WDC&S 200-202. | | | |
| 148-Reprints "The Mystery of Lonely Valley" from WDC&S 208-210 | | | |
| | .85 | 3.50 | 5.00 |
| 149-158 | .35 | 1.00 | 2.00 |
| 159-Reprints "The Sunken City" from WDC&S 205-207 | | | |
| | .70 | 2.00 | 4.00 |
| 160-170: 162-170-r | .35 | 1.00 | 2.00 |
| 171-178,180-199 | | .50 | 1.00 |
| 179-(52 pgs.) | | .60 | 1.20 |
| 200-218: 200-r/Four Color #371 | | .40 | .80 |
| 219-1st Gladstone issue; The Seven Ghosts serial-r begins by Gottfredson | | | |
| | .85 | 2.50 | 5.00 |
| 220,221 | .50 | 1.50 | 3.00 |
| 222-225: 222-Editor-in-Grief strip-r | .40 | 1.25 | 2.50 |
| 226-230 | .25 | .75 | 1.50 |

|                                                    | Good | Fine | N-Mint |
|----------------------------------------------------|------|------|--------|
| 231-243,245-254: 240-r/March of Comics #27. 245-r/F.C. #279. 250-r/ F.C. #248 |      | .50  | 1.00   |
| 244 (1/89, $2.95, 100 pgs.)-60th anniversary; gives history of Mickey |      |      |        |
|                                                    | .60  | 1.75 | 3.50   |
| 255,256 ($1.95, 68 pgs.)                           | .35  | 1.00 | 2.00   |

**MIGHTY MOUSE** (1st Series)
Fall, 1946 - No. 4, Summer, 1947
Timely/Marvel Comics (20th Century Fox)

|        | Good  | Fine   | N-Mint |
|--------|-------|--------|--------|
| 1      | 50.00 | 150.00 | 350.00 |
| 2      | 24.00 | 73.00  | 170.00 |
| 3,4    | 17.00 | 51.00  | 120.00 |

**MIGHTY MOUSE** (2nd Series) (Paul Terry's . . . #62-71)
Aug, 1947 - No. 67, 11/55; No. 68, 3/56 - No. 83, 6/59
St. John Publishing Co./Pines No. 68 (3/56) on (TV issues #72 on)

|                                      | Good  | Fine  | N-Mint |
|--------------------------------------|-------|-------|--------|
| 5(#1)                                | 17.00 | 51.00 | 120.00 |
| 6-10                                 | 8.00  | 24.00 | 56.00  |
| 11-19                                | 5.00  | 15.00 | 35.00  |
| 20 (11/50) - 25-(52 pgs.)            | 4.00  | 12.00 | 28.00  |
| 20-25-(36 pg. editions)              | 3.70  | 11.00 | 26.00  |
| 26-37: 35-Flying saucer-c            | 2.85  | 8.50  | 20.00  |
| 38-45-(100 pgs.)                     | 6.50  | 19.50 | 45.00  |
| 46-83: 62,64,67-Painted-c. 82-Infinity-c | 2.00  | 6.00  | 14.00  |

**MILITARY COMICS** (Becomes Modern Comics #44 on)
Aug, 1941 - No. 43, Oct, 1945
Quality Comics Group

| | Good | Fine | N-Mint |
|---|---|---|---|
| 1-Origin/1st app. Blackhawk by C. Cuidera; Miss America, The Death Patrol by Jack Cole (also #2-7,27-30), & The Blue Tracer by Guardineer; X of the Underground, The Yankee Eagle, Q-Boat & Shot & Shell, Archie Atkins, Loops & Banks by Bud Ernest (Bob Powell) (ends #13) begin | 300.00 | 750.00 | 1800.00 |
| 2-Secret War News begins (by McWilliams #2-16); Cole-a | 125.00 | 375.00 | 875.00 |
| 3-Origin/1st app. Chop Chop | 94.00 | 282.00 | 660.00 |
| 4 | 86.00 | 257.00 | 600.00 |

|  | Good | Fine | N-Mint |
|---|---|---|---|
| 5-The Sniper begins; Miss America in costume #4-7 | | | |
| | 68.00 | 205.00 | 475.00 |
| 6-9: 8-X of the Underground begins (ends #13). 9-The Phantom Clipper | | | |
| begins (ends #16) | 55.00 | 165.00 | 385.00 |
| 10-Classic Eisner-c | 60.00 | 180.00 | 420.00 |
| 11-Flag-c | 43.00 | 130.00 | 305.00 |
| 12-Blackhawk by Crandall begins, ends #22 | 60.00 | 180.00 | 420.00 |
| 13-15: 14-Private Dogtag begins (ends #83) | 41.00 | 122.00 | 285.00 |
| 16-20: 16-Blue Tracer ends. 17-P.T. Boat begins | | | |
| | 33.00 | 100.00 | 230.00 |
| 21-31: 22-Last Crandall Blackhawk. 27-Death Patrol revived | | | |
| | 30.00 | 90.00 | 210.00 |
| 32-43 | 26.50 | 80.00 | 185.00 |

**MILLENNIUM**
Jan, 1988 - No. 8, Feb, 1988 (nd) (Weekly mini-series)
DC Comics

| | | | |
|---|---|---|---|
| 1-Staton c/a(p) begins | .40 | 1.25 | 2.50 |
| 2-8 | .25 | .80 | 1.60 |

**MISS FURY COMICS** (Newspaper strip reprints)
Winter, 1942-43 - No. 8, Winter, 1946
Timely Comics (NPI 1/CmPI 2/MPC 3-8)

| | | | |
|---|---|---|---|
| 1-Origin Miss Fury by Tarpé Mills (68 pgs.) in costume w/pin-ups | | | |
| | 167.00 | 420.00 | 1000.00 |
| 2-(60 pgs.)-In costume w/pin-ups | 64.00 | 193.00 | 450.00 |
| 3-(60 pgs.)-In costume w/pin-ups; Hitler-c | 54.00 | 160.00 | 375.00 |
| 4-(52 pgs.)-In costume, 2 pgs. w/pin-ups | 44.00 | 132.00 | 310.00 |
| 5-(52 pgs.)-In costume w/pin-ups | 39.00 | 118.00 | 275.00 |
| 6-(52 pgs.)-Not in costume in inside stories, w/pin-ups | | | |
| | 35.00 | 105.00 | 245.00 |
| 7,8-(36 pgs.)-In costume 1 pg. each, no pin-ups | | | |
| | 35.00 | 105.00 | 245.00 |

**MISSION IMPOSSIBLE** (TV)
May, 1967 - No. 4, Oct, 1968; No. 5, Oct, 1969 (All have photo-c)
Dell Publishing Co.

|  | Good | Fine | N-Mint |
|---|---|---|---|
| 1 | 4.00 | 12.00 | 28.00 |
| 2-5: 5-reprints #1 | 3.00 | 9.00 | 21.00 |

**MR. DISTRICT ATTORNEY** (Radio/TV)
Jan-Feb, 1948 - No. 67, Jan-Feb, 1959 (1-23: 52 pgs.)
National Periodical Publications

| 1 | 25.00 | 75.00 | 175.00 |
|---|---|---|---|
| 2 | 12.00 | 36.00 | 85.00 |
| 3-5 | 9.30 | 28.00 | 65.00 |
| 6-10 | 7.00 | 21.00 | 50.00 |
| 11-20 | 5.70 | 17.00 | 40.00 |
| 21-43: 43-Last pre-code (1-2/55) | 4.30 | 13.00 | 30.00 |
| 44-67 | 3.00 | 9.00 | 21.00 |

**MISTER MIRACLE** (See Brave & the Bold)
3-4/71 - V4#18, 2-3/74; V5#19, 9/77 - V6#25, 8-9/78; 1987
National Periodical Publications/DC Comics

| 1-(#1-3 are 15 cents) | .75 | 2.25 | 4.50 |
|---|---|---|---|
| 2-8: 4-Boy Commandos-r begin; begin 25 cent, 52 pg. issues, ends #8 | | | |
|  | .40 | 1.25 | 2.50 |
| 9,10: 9-Origin Mr. Miracle | .35 | 1.00 | 2.00 |
| 11-25: 15-Intro/1st app. Shilo Norman. 18-Barda & Scott Free wed; New | | | |
|     Gods app. | .25 | .75 | 1.50 |
| Special 1(1987, 52 pgs., $1.25) | .25 | .75 | 1.50 |

**MISTER MIRACLE**
Jan, 1989 - Present ($1.00, color)
DC Comics

| 1-Spin-off from Justice League International | .25 | .75 | 1.50 |
|---|---|---|---|
| 2-22: 9-Intro Maxi-Man |  | .50 | 1.00 |

**MISTER MYSTERY**
Sept, 1951 - No. 19, Oct, 1954
Mr. Publ. (Media Publ.) No. 1-3/SPM Publ./Stanmore (Aragon)

|                                                    | Good  | Fine   | N-Mint |
|----------------------------------------------------|-------|--------|--------|
| 1-Kurtzmanesque horror story                       | 19.00 | 57.00  | 135.00 |
| 2,3-Kurtzmanesque story                            | 13.00 | 40.00  | 90.00  |
| 4,6: Bondage-c; 6-Torture                          | 13.00 | 40.00  | 90.00  |
| 5,8,10                                             | 11.50 | 34.00  | 80.00  |
| 7-"The Brain Bats of Venus" by Wolverton; partially re-used in Weird |  |  |  |
|    Tales of the Future #7           | 41.00 | 122.00 | 285.00 |
| 9-Nostrand-a                                       | 12.00 | 36.00  | 84.00  |
| 11-Wolverton "Robot Woman" story/Weird Mysteries #2, cut up, rewrit- |  |  |  |
|    ten & partially redrawn          | 21.50 | 64.00  | 150.00 |
| 12-Classic injury to eye-c                         | 30.00 | 90.00  | 210.00 |
| 13,14,17,19                                        | 8.00  | 24.00  | 56.00  |
| 15-"Living Dead" junkie story                      | 11.00 | 32.00  | 75.00  |
| 16-Bondage-c                                       | 11.00 | 32.00  | 75.00  |
| 18-"Robot Woman" by Wolverton reprinted from Weird Mysteries #2; de- |  |  |  |
|    capitation, bondage-c            | 18.50 | 56.00  | 130.00 |

**MODERN COMICS** (Formerly Military Comics #1-43)
No. 44, Nov, 1945 - No. 102, Oct, 1950
Quality Comics Group

|                                                    | Good  | Fine  | N-Mint |
|----------------------------------------------------|-------|-------|--------|
| 44-Blackhawk continues                             | 26.00 | 77.00 | 180.00 |
| 45-52: 49-1st app. Fear, Lady Adventuress          | 16.00 | 48.00 | 110.00 |
| 53-Torchy by Ward begins (9/46)                    | 20.00 | 60.00 | 140.00 |
| 54-60: 55-J. Cole-a                                | 14.00 | 42.00 | 100.00 |
| 61-77,79,80: 73-J. Cole-a                          | 13.00 | 40.00 | 90.00  |
| 78 1st app. Madame Butterfly                       | 14.00 | 42.00 | 100.00 |
| 81-99,101: 82,83-One pg. J. Cole-a                 | 13.00 | 40.00 | 90.00  |
| 100                                                | 13.00 | 40.00 | 90.00  |
| 102-(Scarce)-J. Cole-a; Spirit by Eisner app.      | 16.00 | 48.00 | 110.00 |

**MONKEES, THE** (TV)
March, 1967 - No. 17, Oct, 1969 (#1-4,6,7,10 have photo-c)
Dell Publishing Co.

|                       | Good | Fine  | N-Mint |
|-----------------------|------|-------|--------|
| 1                     | 4.30 | 13.00 | 30.00  |
| 2-17: 17 reprints #1  | 2.15 | 6.50  | 15.00  |

**MONTE HALE WESTERN** (Movie star; Formerly Mary Marvel #1-28;
   also see Real Western Hero & Western Hero)
No. 29, Oct, 1948 - No. 88, Jan, 1956
Fawcett Publications/Charlton No. 83 on

|  | Good | Fine | N-Mint |
|---|---|---|---|
| 29-(#1, 52 pgs.)-Photo-c begin, end #82; Monte Hale & his horse Pardner | | | |
| begin | 21.50 | 64.00 | 150.00 |
| 30-(52 pgs.)-Big Bow and Little Arrow begin, end #34; Captain Tootsie by | | | |
| Beck | 13.00 | 40.00 | 90.00 |
| 31-36,38-40-(52 pgs.): 34-Gabby Hayes begins, ends #80. 39-Captain Toot- | | | |
| sie by Beck | 11.00 | 32.00 | 75.00 |
| 37,41,45,49-(36 pgs.) | 6.50 | 19.50 | 45.00 |
| 42-44,46-48,50-(52 pgs.): 47-Big Bow & Little Arrow app. | | | |
| | 7.00 | 21.00 | 50.00 |
| 51,52,54-56,58,59-(52 pgs.) | 5.70 | 17.00 | 40.00 |
| 53,57-(36 pgs.): 53-Slim Pickens app. | 4.30 | 13.00 | 30.00 |
| 60-81: 36 pgs. #60-on. 80-Gabby Hayes ends | 4.30 | 13.00 | 30.00 |
| 82-Last Fawcett issue (6/53) | 5.50 | 16.50 | 38.00 |
| 83-1st Charlton issue (2/55); B&W photo back-c begin. Gabby Hayes re- | | | |
| turns, ends #86 | 5.50 | 16.50 | 38.00 |
| 84 (4/55) | 4.30 | 13.00 | 30.00 |
| 85-86 | 4.00 | 12.00 | 28.00 |
| 87-Wolverton-r, 1/2 pg. | 4.30 | 13.00 | 30.00 |
| 88-Last issue | 4.30 | 13.00 | 30.00 |

**MOON KNIGHT** (Also see Marvel Spotlight #28, 29)
November, 1980 - No. 38, July, 1984 (Mando paper No. 33 on)
Marvel Comics Group

| | Good | Fine | N-Mint |
|---|---|---|---|
| 1-Origin resumed in #4; begin Sienkiewicz-c/a | .40 | 1.25 | 2.50 |
| 2-34,36-38: 4-Intro Midnight Man. 16-The Thing app. 25-Double size | | | |
| | | .50 | 1.00 |
| 35-($1.00, 52 pgs.)-X-men app.; F.F. cameo | .25 | .75 | 1.50 |

*More Fun Comics #9, © DC Comics*

**MORE FUN COMICS** (Formerly New Fun Comics #1-6)
No. 7, Jan, 1936 - No. 127, Nov-Dec, 1947 (No. 7,9-11: paper-c)
National Periodical Publications

|  | Good | Fine | VF-NM |
|---|---|---|---|
| 7(1/36)-Oversized, paper-c; 1 pg. Kelly-a | 300.00 | 750.00 | 1800.00 |
| 8(2/36)-Oversized (10″ × 12″), slick-c; 1 pg. Kelly-a | | | |
|  | 267.00 | 670.00 | 1600.00 |
| 9(3-4/36)(Very Rare)-Last Henri Duval by Siegel & Shuster | | | |
|  | 267.00 | 670.00 | 1600.00 |
| 10,11(7/36): 11-1st 'Calling All Cars' by Siegel & Shuster | | | |
|  | 175.00 | 440.00 | 1050.00 |
| 12(8/36)-Slick-c begin | 154.00 | 385.00 | 925.00 |
| V2#1(9/36, #13) | 154.00 | 385.00 | 925.00 |
| 2(10/36, #14)-Dr. Occult in costume (Superman prototype) begins, | | | |
| ends #17; see The Comics Magazine | 175.00 | 440.00 | 1050.00 |
| V2#3(11/36, #15), 16(V2#4), 17(V2#5)-Cover numbering begins #16. | | | |
| 16-Xmas-c | 114.00 | 285.00 | 685.00 |
| 18-20(V2#8, 5/37) | 87.00 | 220.00 | 525.00 |

|  | Good | Fine | N-Mint |
|---|---|---|---|
| 21(V2#9)-24(V2#12, 9/37) | 60.00 | 150.00 | 360.00 |
| 25(V3#1, 10/37)-27(V3#3, 12/37): 27-Xmas-c | 60.00 | 150.00 | 360.00 |
| 28-30: 30-1st non-funny cover | 60.00 | 150.00 | 360.00 |
| 31-35: 32-Last Dr. Occult | 51.00 | 130.00 | 305.00 |
| 36-40: 36-The Masked Ranger begins, ends #41. 39-Xmas-c | | | |
|  | 47.00 | 120.00 | 285.00 |
| 41-50 | 43.00 | 110.00 | 260.00 |
| 51-1st app. The Spectre (in costume) in one panel ad at end of Buccaneer story | 108.00 | 270.00 | 650.00 |
| 52-Origin The Spectre (in costume), Part 1 by Bernard Baily; last Wing Brady (Rare) | 1600.00 | 4000.00 | 9600.00 |
| 53-Origin The Spectre (in costume), Part 2; Capt. Desmo begins (Scarce) | | | |
|  | 1035.00 | 2600.00 | 6200.00 |

*(Prices vary widely on above two books)*

| 54-The Spectre in costume; last King Carter | | | |
|---|---|---|---|
|  | 417.00 | 1050.00 | 2500.00 |
| 55-(Scarce)-Dr. Fate begins (Intro & 1st app.); last Bulldog Martin | | | |
|  | 450.00 | 1125.00 | 2700.00 |
| 56-60: 56-Congo Bill begins | 192.00 | 480.00 | 1150.00 |
| 61-66: 63-Last St. Bob Neal. 64-Lance Larkin begins | | | |
|  | 133.00 | 335.00 | 800.00 |
| 67-(Scarce)-Origin Dr. Fate; last Congo Bill & Biff Bronson | | | |
|  | 200.00 | 500.00 | 1200.00 |
| 68-70: 68-Clip Carson begins. 70-Last Lance Larkin | | | |
|  | 118.00 | 295.00 | 710.00 |
| 71-(Scarce)-Origin & 1st app. Johnny Quick by Mort Wysinger | | | |
|  | 200.00 | 500.00 | 1200.00 |
| 72-Dr. Fate's new helmet; last Sgt. Carey, Sgt. O'Malley & Captain Desmo | | | |
|  | 102.00 | 255.00 | 615.00 |
| 73-(Rare)-Origin & 1st app. Aquaman; intro. Green Arrow & Speedy | | | |
|  | 300.00 | 750.00 | 1800.00 |
| 74-2nd Aquaman | 117.00 | 295.00 | 700.00 |
| 75-80: 76-Last Clip Carson; Johnny Quick by Meskin begins, ends #97. 80-1st small logo | 100.00 | 250.00 | 600.00 |
| 81-88: 87-Last Radio Squad | 73.00 | 185.00 | 440.00 |
| 89-Origin Green Arrow & Speedy Team-up | 83.00 | 210.00 | 500.00 |
| 90-99: 93-Dover & Clover begin. 97-Kubert-a. 98-Last Dr. Fate | | | |
|  | 46.00 | 115.00 | 275.00 |

|  | Good | Fine | N-Mint |
|---|---|---|---|
| 100 | 64.00 | 160.00 | 385.00 |
| 101-Origin & 1st app. Superboy (not by Siegel & Shuster); last Spectre issue | 300.00 | 750.00 | 1800.00 |
| 102-2nd Superboy | 79.00 | 200.00 | 475.00 |
| 103-3rd Superboy | 58.00 | 145.00 | 350.00 |
| 104-107: 104-1st Superboy-c. 105-Superboy-c. 107-Last J. Quick & Superboy | 48.00 | 120.00 | 290.00 |
| 108-120: 108-Genius Jones begins | 7.00 | 21.00 | 50.00 |
| 121-124,126: 121-123,126-Post-c | 5.70 | 17.00 | 40.00 |
| 125-Superman on cover | 30.00 | 90.00 | 210.00 |
| 127-(Scarce)-Post c/a | 14.00 | 42.00 | 100.00 |

## MUNSTERS, THE (TV)
Jan, 1965 - No. 16, Jan, 1968
Gold Key

|  | | | |
|---|---|---|---|
| 1 (10134-501)-Photo-c | 9.00 | 27.00 | 62.00 |
| 2 | 5.00 | 15.00 | 35.00 |
| 3-5: 4-Photo-c | 4.30 | 13.00 | 30.00 |
| 6-16 | 3.50 | 10.50 | 24.00 |

## MURDER, INCORPORATED
1/48 - No. 15, 12/49; (2 No. 9's); 6/50 - No. 3, 8/51
Fox Feature Syndicate

|  | | | |
|---|---|---|---|
| 1 (1st Series) | 16.00 | 48.00 | 110.00 |
| 2-Electrocution story; #1,2 have 'For Adults Only' on-c | 12.00 | 36.00 | 84.00 |
| 3-7,9(4/49),10(5/49),11-15 | 5.70 | 17.00 | 40.00 |
| 8-Used in SOTI, pg. 160 | 8.00 | 24.00 | 55.00 |
| 9(3/49)-Possible use in SOTI, pg. 145; r-Blue Beetle #56('48) | 7.00 | 21.00 | 50.00 |
| 5(#1, 6/50)(2nd Series)-Formerly My Desire | 4.30 | 13.00 | 30.00 |
| 2(8/50)-Morisi-a | 3.50 | 10.50 | 24.00 |
| 3(8/51)-Used in POP, pg. 81; Rico-a; lingerie-c/panels | 4.30 | 13.00 | 30.00 |

**MUTT AND JEFF** (See All-American Comics, All-Flash #18, Comic
    Cavalcade, The Funnies & Popular Comics)
Summer, 1939 (nd) - No. 148, Nov, 1965
All American/National 1-103(6/58)/Dell 104(10/58)-115
    (10-12/59)/Harvey 116(2/60)-148

|  | Good | Fine | N-Mint |
|---|---|---|---|
| 1(nn)-Lost Wheels | 78.00 | 235.00 | 550.00 |
| 2(nn)-Charging Bull (Summer 1940, nd; on sale 6/20/40) | | | |
| | 43.00 | 130.00 | 300.00 |
| 3(nn)-Bucking Broncos (Summer 1941, nd) | 30.00 | 90.00 | 210.00 |
| 4(Winter,'41), 5(Summer,'42) | 22.00 | 65.00 | 155.00 |
| 6-10 | 13.00 | 40.00 | 90.00 |
| 11-20 | 8.50 | 25.50 | 60.00 |
| 21-30 | 6.50 | 19.50 | 45.00 |
| 31-50 | 3.70 | 11.00 | 26.00 |
| 51-75-Last Fisher issue. 53-Last 52 pgs. | 2.30 | 7.00 | 16.00 |
| 76-99,101-103: 76-Last precode issue(1/55) | 1.50 | 4.50 | 10.00 |
| 100 | 1.70 | 5.00 | 12.00 |
| 104-148: 117,118,120-131-Richie Rich app. | .85 | 2.50 | 6.00 |

**MY FAVORITE MARTIAN** (TV)
1/64; No.2, 7/64 - No. 9, 10/66 (No. 1,3-9 have photo-c)
Gold Key

|  | | | |
|---|---|---|---|
| 1-Russ Manning-a | 5.00 | 15.00 | 35.00 |
| 2 | 2.65 | 8.00 | 18.00 |
| 3-9 | 2.30 | 7.00 | 16.00 |

**MY GREATEST ADVENTURE** (Doom Patrol #86 on)
Jan-Feb, 1955 - No. 85, Feb, 1964
National Periodical Publications

|  | | | |
|---|---|---|---|
| 1-Before CCA | 50.00 | 150.00 | 350.00 |
| 2 | 23.00 | 70.00 | 160.00 |
| 3-5 | 16.00 | 48.00 | 110.00 |
| 6-10 | 10.00 | 30.00 | 70.00 |
| 11-15,19 | 6.50 | 19.50 | 45.00 |
| 16-18,20,21,28-Kirby-a; 18-Kirby-c | 6.00 | 18.00 | 42.00 |
| 22-27,29,30 | 3.60 | 11.00 | 25.00 |
| 31-40 | 2.85 | 8.50 | 20.00 |

| | Good | Fine | N-Mint |
|---|---|---|---|
| 41-57,59 | 1.60 | 4.80 | 11.00 |
| 58,60,61-Toth-a; Last 10 cent issue | 2.30 | 7.00 | 16.00 |
| 62-76,78,79 | 1.25 | 3.75 | 7.50 |
| 77-Toth-a | 1.35 | 4.10 | 9.50 |
| 80-(6/63)-Intro/origin Doom Patrol and begin series; origin Robotman, Negative Man, & Elasti-Girl | 21.00 | 63.00 | 145.00 |
| 81-85: 81,85-Toth-a | 7.85 | 23.50 | 55.00 |

## MYSTERIES OF UNEXPLORED WORLDS
Aug, 1956 - No. 48, Sept, 1965
Charlton Comics

| | | | |
|---|---|---|---|
| 1 | 13.00 | 40.00 | 90.00 |
| 2-No Ditko | 5.00 | 15.00 | 35.00 |
| 3,4,6,8,9-Ditko-a | 7.00 | 21.00 | 50.00 |
| 5-Ditko-c/a (all) | 8.00 | 24.00 | 56.00 |
| 7-(68 pgs., 2/58); Ditko-a(4) | 8.50 | 25.50 | 60.00 |
| 10-Ditko-c/a(4) | 8.00 | 24.00 | 56.00 |
| 11-Ditko-c/a(3)-signed J. Kotdi | 8.00 | 24.00 | 56.00 |
| 12,19,21-24,26-Ditko-a | 5.70 | 17.00 | 40.00 |
| 13-18,20 | 1.70 | 5.00 | 12.00 |
| 25,27-30 | 1.15 | 3.50 | 8.00 |
| 31-45 | .70 | 2.00 | 4.00 |
| 46(5/65)-Son of Vulcan begins (origin) | .85 | 2.50 | 6.00 |
| 47,48 | .70 | 2.00 | 4.00 |

## MYSTERY IN SPACE
4-5/51 - No. 110, 9/66; No. 111, 9/80 - No. 117, 3/81 (#1-3· 52 pgs.)
National Periodical Publications

| | | | |
|---|---|---|---|
| 1-Frazetta-a, 8 pgs.; Knights of the Galaxy begins, ends #8 | | | |
| | 136.00 | 407.00 | 950.00 |
| 2 | 55.00 | 165.00 | 385.00 |
| 3 | 43.00 | 130.00 | 300.00 |
| 4,5 | 30.00 | 90.00 | 210.00 |
| 6-10: 7-Toth-a | 24.00 | 71.00 | 165.00 |
| 11-15: 13-Toth-a | 17.00 | 51.00 | 120.00 |
| 16-18,20-25: Interplanetary Insurance feature by Infantino in all. 24-Last precode issue | 16.00 | 48.00 | 110.00 |
| 19-Virgil Finlay-a | 17.00 | 51.00 | 120.00 |

|  | Good | Fine | N-Mint |
|---|---|---|---|
| 26-34,36-40: 26-Space Cabbie begins | 11.00 | 32.00 | 75.00 |
| 35-Kubert-a | 11.50 | 34.00 | 80.00 |
| 41-52: 47-Space Cabbie feature ends | 8.50 | 25.50 | 60.00 |
| 53-Adam Strange begins (8/59) (1st app. in Showcase) | | | |
| | 57.00 | 171.00 | 400.00 |
| 54 | 21.00 | 63.00 | 145.00 |
| 55 | 14.00 | 42.00 | 100.00 |
| 56-60 | 11.00 | 32.00 | 75.00 |
| 61-71: 61-1st app. Adam Strange foe Ulthoon. 62-1st app. A.S. foe Mortan. 63-Origin Vandor. 66-Star Rovers begin. 68-Dust Devils app. 71-Last 10 cent issue | 6.50 | 19.50 | 45.00 |
| 72-74,76-80 | 5.00 | 15.00 | 35.00 |
| 75-JLA x-over in Adam Strange (5/62) | 5.70 | 17.00 | 40.00 |
| 81-86 | 2.65 | 8.00 | 18.00 |
| 87-90: 87-89-Adam Strange & Hawkman stories. 90-Adam Strange & Hawkman team-up for 1st time | 2.85 | 8.50 | 20.00 |
| 91-102: 91-End Infantino art on Adam Strange. 92-Space Ranger begins. 94,98-Adam Strange/Space Ranger team-up. 102-Adam Strange ends (no space Ranger) | 1.00 | 3.00 | 6.00 |
| 103-110: 103-Origin Ultra, the Multi-Alien; Space Ranger ends. 110-(9/66)-Last 10 cent issue | .35 | 1.15 | 2.30 |
| V17#111(9/80)-117: 117-Newton-a(3 pgs.) | | .65 | 1.30 |

**MYSTERY MEN COMICS**
Aug, 1939 - No. 31, Feb, 1942
Fox Features Syndicate

| | Good | Fine | N-Mint |
|---|---|---|---|
| 1-Intro. & 1st app. The Blue Beetle, The Green Mask, Rex Dexter of Mars by Briefer, Zanzibar by Tuska, Lt. Drake, D-13-Secret Agent by Powell, Chen Chang, Wing Turner, & Captain Denny Scott | 162.00 | 405.00 | 975.00 |
| 2 | 64.00 | 193.00 | 450.00 |
| 3 (10/39) | 54.00 | 160.00 | 375.00 |
| 4-Capt. Savage begins | 48.00 | 145.00 | 340.00 |
| 5 | 38.00 | 115.00 | 265.00 |
| 6-8 | 32.00 | 95.00 | 225.00 |
| 9-The Moth begins | 28.00 | 84.00 | 195.00 |
| 10-Wing Turner by Kirby | 28.00 | 84.00 | 195.00 |
| 11-Intro. Domino | 22.00 | 65.00 | 155.00 |
| 12,14-18 | 20.00 | 60.00 | 140.00 |

| | Good | Fine | N-Mint |
|---|---|---|---|
| 13-Intro. Lynx & sidekick Blackie | 22.00 | 65.00 | 155.00 |
| 19-Intro. & 1st app. Miss X (ends #21) | 22.00 | 65.00 | 155.00 |
| 20-31: 26-The Wraith begins | 18.00 | 54.00 | 125.00 |

*Mystery Tales #44, © Marvel Comics*

**MYSTERY TALES**
March, 1952 - No. 54, Aug, 1957
Atlas Comics (20CC)

| | Good | Fine | N-Mint |
|---|---|---|---|
| 1 | 17.00 | 51.00 | 120.00 |
| 2-Krigstein-a | 9.30 | 28.00 | 65.00 |
| 3-9: 6-A-Bomb panel | 5.70 | 17.00 | 40.00 |
| 10-Story similar to 'The Assassin' from Shock SuspenStories | | | |
| | 6.50 | 19.50 | 45.00 |
| 11,13-17,19,20: 20-Electric chair issue | 4.30 | 13.00 | 30.00 |
| 12-Matt Fox-a | 5.00 | 15.00 | 35.00 |
| 18-Williamson-a | 5.70 | 17.00 | 40.00 |
| 21-Matt Fox-a; decapitation story | 5.00 | 15.00 | 35.00 |

|  | Good | Fine | N-Mint |
|---|---|---|---|
| 22-Forte/Matt Fox c; a(i) | 5.70 | 17.00 | 40.00 |
| 23-26 (2/55)-Last precode issue | 3.70 | 11.00 | 26.00 |
| 27,29-32,34,35,37,38,41-43,48,49 | 2.30 | 7.00 | 16.00 |
| 28-Jack Katz-a | 3.00 | 9.00 | 21.00 |
| 33-Crandall-a | 3.65 | 11.00 | 26.00 |
| 36,39-Krigstein-a | 3.65 | 11.00 | 26.00 |
| 40,45-Ditko-a | 3.65 | 11.00 | 26.00 |
| 44,51-Williamson/Krenkel-a | 4.65 | 14.00 | 32.00 |
| 46-Williamson/Krenkel-a; Crandall text illos | 4.65 | 14.00 | 32.00 |
| 47-Crandall, Ditko, Powell-a | 4.00 | 12.00 | 28.00 |
| 50-Torres, Morrow-a | 3.50 | 10.50 | 24.00 |
| 52,53 | 2.00 | 6.00 | 14.00 |
| 54-Crandall, Check-a | 3.00 | 9.00 | 21.00 |

**MYSTIC COMICS** (1st Series)
March, 1940 - No. 10, Aug, 1942
Timely Comics (TPI 1-5/TCI 8-10)

1-Origin The Blue Blaze, The Dynamic Man, & Flexo the Rubber Man;
   Zephyr Jones, 3X's & Deep Sea Demon app.; The Magician begins;
   c-from Spider pulp V18#1, 6/39          442.00    1105.00    2650.00
2-The Invisible Man & Master Mind Excello begin; Space Rangers, Zara
   of the Jungle, Taxi Taylor app.          177.00     443.00    1065.00
3-Origin Hercules, who last appears in #4  141.00     353.00     845.00
4-Origin The Thin Man & The Black Widow; Merzak the Mystic app.; last
   Flexo, Dynamic Man, Invisible Man & Blue Blaze (some issues have
   date sticker on cover; others have July w/August overprint in silver
   color); Roosevelt assassination-c        164.00     410.00     985.00
5-Origin The Black Marvel, The Blazing Skull, The Sub-Earth Man, Super
   Slave & The Terror; The Moon Man & Black Widow app.
                                            156.00     390.00     935.00
6-Origin The Challenger & The Destroyer   133.00     332.00     800.00
7-The Witness begins (origin); origin Davey & the Demon; last Black
   Widow; Simon & Kirby-c                   108.00     270.00     650.00
8                                            93.00     232.00     550.00
9-Gary Gaunt app.; last Black Marvel, Mystic & Blazing Skull; Hitler-c
                                             93.00     232.00     550.00
10-Father Time, World of Wonder, & Red Skeleton app.; last Challenger &
   Terror                                    93.00     232.00     550.00

**MYSTIC COMICS** (2nd Series)
Oct, 1944 - No. 4, Winter, 1944-45
Timely Comics (ANC)

|  | Good | Fine | N-Mint |
|---|---|---|---|
| 1-The Angel, The Destroyer, The Human Torch, Terry Vance the School- | | | |
| boy Sleuth, & Tommy Tyme begin | 79.00 | 198.00 | 475.00 |
| 2-Last Human Torch & Terry Vance; bondage-hypo-c | | | |
|  | 43.00 | 129.00 | 300.00 |
| 3-Last Angel (two stories) & Tommy Tyme | 39.00 | 118.00 | 275.00 |
| 4-The Young Allies app. | 34.00 | 103.00 | 240.00 |

# N

## 'NAM, THE
Dec, 1986 - Present
Marvel Comics Group

| | Good | Fine | N-Mint |
|---|---|---|---|
| 1-Golden a(p)/c begins, ends #13 | 2.00 | 6.00 | 12.00 |
| 1 (2nd printing) | .60 | 1.75 | 3.50 |
| 2 | 1.35 | 4.00 | 8.00 |
| 3,4 | .90 | 2.75 | 5.50 |
| 5-7 | .70 | 2.00 | 4.00 |
| 8-10 | .40 | 1.25 | 2.50 |
| 11-20: 12-Severin-a | .30 | .90 | 1.80 |
| 21-50: 25-begin $1.50-c. 32-Death R. Kennedy | .25 | .75 | 1.50 |

## NAMORA (See Marvel Mystery & Sub-Mariner Comics)
Fall, 1948 - No. 3, Dec, 1948
Marvel Comics (PrPI)

| | Good | Fine | N-Mint |
|---|---|---|---|
| 1-Sub-Mariner x-over in Namora; Everett, Rico-a | | | |
| | 63.00 | 190.00 | 440.00 |
| 2-The Blonde Phantom & Sub-Mariner story; Everett-a | | | |
| | 52.00 | 156.00 | 365.00 |
| 3-(Scarce)-Sub-Mariner app.; Everett-a | 46.00 | 139.00 | 325.00 |

## NAMOR, THE SUB-MARINER (See Prince Namor & Sub-Mariner)
Apr, 1990 - Present ($1.00, color)
Marvel Comics

| | Good | Fine | N-Mint |
|---|---|---|---|
| 1-Byrne-c/a(p)/scripts | .25 | .75 | 1.50 |
| 2-10 | | .50 | 1.00 |

## NATIONAL COMICS
July, 1940 - No. 75, Nov, 1949
Quality Comics Group

1-Uncle Sam begins; Origin sidekick Buddy by Eisner; origin Wonder

|  | Good | Fine | N-Mint |
|---|---|---|---|
| Boy & Kid Dixon; Merlin the Magician (ends #45); Cyclone, Kid Patrol, Sally O'Neil Policewoman, Pen Miller (ends #22), Prop Powers (ends #26), & Paul Bunyan (ends #22) begin | | | |
|  | 168.00 | 504.00 | 1175.00 |
| 2 | 78.00 | 235.00 | 550.00 |
| 3-Last Eisner Uncle Sam | 63.00 | 188.00 | 440.00 |
| 4-Last Cyclone | 45.00 | 135.00 | 315.00 |
| 5-(11/40)-Quicksilver begins (3rd w/lightning speed?); origin Uncle Sam | | | |
|  | 58.00 | 174.00 | 405.00 |
| 6-11: 8-Jack & Jill begins (ends #22). 9-Flag-c | | | |
|  | 43.00 | 130.00 | 300.00 |
| 12 | 31.50 | 94.00 | 220.00 |
| 13-16-Lou Fine-a | 39.00 | 118.00 | 275.00 |
| 17,19-22 | 28.50 | 86.00 | 200.00 |
| 18-(12/41)-Shows Orientals attacking Pearl Harbor; on stands one month before actual event | | | |
|  | 34.00 | 103.00 | 240.00 |
| 23-The Unknown & Destroyer 171 begin | 31.50 | 94.00 | 220.00 |
| 24-26,28,30: 26-Wonder Boy ends | 22.00 | 65.00 | 155.00 |
| 27-G-2 the Unknown begins (ends #46) | 22.00 | 65.00 | 155.00 |
| 29-Origin The Unknown | 22.00 | 65.00 | 155.00 |
| 31-33: 33-Chic Carter begins (ends #47) | 19.00 | 57.00 | 135.00 |
| 34-40: 35-Last Kid Patrol. 39-Hitler-c | 11.50 | 34.00 | 80.00 |
| 41-47,49,50: 42-The Barker begins (1st app?) | 9.00 | 27.00 | 62.00 |
| 48-Origin The Whistler | 9.00 | 27.00 | 62.00 |
| 51-Sally O'Neil by Ward, 8 pgs. (12/45) | 11.50 | 34.50 | 80.00 |
| 52-60 | 6.50 | 19.50 | 45.00 |
| 61-67: 67-Format change; Quicksilver app. | 4.65 | 14.00 | 32.00 |
| 68-75: The Barker ends | 3.00 | 9.00 | 21.00 |

**NEW ADVENTURE COMICS** (Formerly New Comics; becomes
    Adventure Comics #32 on)
V1#12, Jan, 1937 - No. 31, Oct, 1938
National Periodical Publications

|  | Good | Fine | VF-NM |
|---|---|---|---|
| V1#12-Federal Men by Siegel & Shuster continues; Jor-L mentioned | | | |
|  | 140.00 | 350.00 | 840.00 |
| V2#1(2/37, #13), V2#2 (#14) | 100.00 | 250.00 | 600.00 |

|  | Good | Fine | N-Mint |
|---|---|---|---|
| 15(V2#3)-20(V2#8): 15-1st Adventure logo. 16-1st Shuster-c; 1st nonfunny cover. 17-Nadir, Master of Magic begins, ends #30 | | | |
|  | 100.00 | 250.00 | 600.00 |
| 21(V2#9),22(V2#10, 2/37) | 83.00 | 208.00 | 500.00 |
| 23-31 | 67.00 | 168.00 | 400.00 |

**NEW COMICS** (New Adventure #12 on)
12/35 - No. 11, 12/36 (No. 1-6: paper cover) (No. 1-5: 84 pgs.)
National Periodical Publications

| V1#1-Billy the Kid, Sagebrush 'n' Cactus, Jibby Jones, Needles, The Vikings, Sir Loin of Beef, Now-When I Was a Boy, & other 1-2 pg. strips; 2 pgs. Kelly art(1st)-(Gulliver's Travels); Sheldon Mayer-a(1st) | | | |
|---|---|---|---|
|  | 500.00 | 1250.00 | 3000.00 |
| 2-Federal Men by Siegel & Shuster begins (Also see The Comics Magazine #2); Sheldon Mayer, Kelly-a (Rare) | | | |
|  | 267.00 | 670.00 | 1600.00 |
| 3-6: 3,4-Sheldon Mayer-a which continues in The Comics Magazine #1. 5-Kiefer-a | 154.00 | 385.00 | 925.00 |
| 7-11: 11-Christmas-c | 121.00 | 302.00 | 725.00 |

**NEW FUN COMICS** (More Fun #7 on)
Feb, 1935 - No. 6, Oct, 1935 (10″ × 15″, No. 1-4,6: slick covers)
(No. 1-5: 36 pgs; 68 pgs. No. 6-on)
National Periodical Publications

|  | Good | Fine | V. Fine |
|---|---|---|---|
| V1#1 (1st DC comic); 1st app. Oswald The Rabbit. Jack Woods (cowboy) begins | 1200.00 | 3000.00 | 7200.00 |
| 2(3/35)-(Very Rare) | 840.00 | 2100.00 | 5040.00 |
| 3-5(8/35): 5-Soft-c | 375.00 | 937.00 | 2250.00 |
| 6(10/35)-1st Dr. Occult (Superman prototype) by Siegel & Shuster (Leger & Reughts); last "New Fun" title. "New Comics #1 begins in Dec. which is reason for title change to More Fun; Henri Duval (ends #9) by Siegel & Shuster begins; paper-c | | | |
|  | 450.00 | 1125.00 | 2700.00 |

**NEW FUNNIES** (The Funnies #1-64; Walter Lantz. . .#109 on;
New TV . . . #259, 260, 272, 273; TV Funnies #261-271)
No. 65, July, 1942 - No. 288, Mar-Apr, 1962
Dell Publishing Co.

|                                                                                                                    | Good | Fine | N-Mint |
|--------------------------------------------------------------------------------------------------------------------|------|------|--------|
| 65(#1)-Andy Panda in a world of real people, Raggedy Ann & Andy, Oswald the Rabbit (with Woody Woodpecker x-overs), Li'l Eight Ball & Peter Rabbit begin | 37.00 | 110.00 | 260.00 |
| 66-70: 67-Billy & Bonnie Bee by Frank Thomas & Felix The Cat begin. 69-2 pg. Kelly-a; The Brownies begin (not by Kelly) | 17.00 | 51.00 | 120.00 |
| 71-75: 72-Kelly illos. 75-Brownies by Kelly?                                                                        | 11.00 | 32.00 | 75.00  |
| 76-Andy Panda (Carl Barks & Pabian-a); Woody Woodpecker x-over in Oswald ends | 57.00 | 171.00 | 400.00 |
| 77,78: 78-Andy Panda in a world with real people ends                                                              | 11.00 | 32.00 | 75.00  |
| 79-81                                                                                                              | 8.00 | 24.00 | 56.00  |
| 82-Brownies by Kelly begins; Homer Pigeon begins                                                                   | 9.50 | 28.50 | 65.00  |
| 83-85-Brownies by Kelly in ea. 83-Xmas-c. 85-Woody Woodpecker, 1 pg. strip begins | 9.50 | 28.50 | 65.00 |
| 86-90: 87-Woody Woodpecker stories begin                                                                           | 4.30 | 13.00 | 30.00  |
| 91-99                                                                                                              | 2.85 | 8.50 | 20.00  |
| 100 (6/45)                                                                                                          | 3.50 | 10.50 | 24.00  |
| 101-110                                                                                                            | 2.15 | 6.50 | 15.00  |
| 111-120: 119-Xmas-c                                                                                                | 1.60 | 4.80 | 11.00  |
| 121-150: 143-Xmas-c                                                                                                | 1.15 | 3.50 | 8.00   |
| 151-200: 155-Xmas-c. 168-Xmas-c, 182-Origin & 1st app. Knothead & Splinter. 191-Xmas-c | .85 | 2.50 | 6.00 |
| 201-240                                                                                                            | .70 | 2.00 | 5.00   |
| 241-288: 270-Walter Lantz c-app. 281-1st story swipe/WDC&S #100                                                    | .60 | 1.80 | 4.00   |

**NEW GODS, THE** (New Gods #12 on) (See Adventure Comics #459)
2-3/71 - V2#11, 10-11/72; V3#12, 7/77 - V3#19, 7-8/78
National Periodical Publications/DC Comics

| | Good | Fine | N-Mint |
|---|---|---|---|
| 1-Intro/1st app. Orion (#1-3 are 15 cents) | 1.00 | 3.00 | 6.00 |
| 2-11: 2-Darkseid app. 4-Origin Manhunter-r. 5,7,8-Young Gods feature. 7-Origin Orion. 9-1st app. Bug. | .50 | 1.50 | 3.00 |
| 12-19: 12-New costume Orion | | .60 | 1.20 |

**NEW GODS**
Feb, 1989 - Present ($1.50, color)
DC Comics

| | Good | Fine | N-Mint |
|---|---|---|---|
| 1-Russell-i | .35 | 1.00 | 2.00 |
| 2-22: 2-4-Starlin scripts | .25 | .75 | 1.50 |

**NEW MUTANTS, THE**
March, 1983 - Present
Marvel Comics Group

| | Good | Fine | N-Mint |
|---|---|---|---|
| 1 | 1.25 | 3.75 | 7.50 |
| 2,3 | .60 | 1.75 | 3.50 |
| 2-Limited test cover (75 cents) | 8.35 | 25.00 | 50.00 |
| 4-10: 10-1st app. Magma | .50 | 1.50 | 3.00 |
| 11-20: 13-Kitty Pryde app. 18-Intro. Warlock | .40 | 1.25 | 2.50 |
| 21-Double size; new Warlock origin | .50 | 1.50 | 3.00 |
| 22-30: 23-25-Cloak & Dagger app. | .40 | 1.25 | 2.50 |
| 31-40 | .35 | 1.00 | 2.00 |
| 41-49 | .25 | .75 | 1.50 |
| 50-58: 50-Double size | .35 | 1.00 | 2.00 |
| 59-Fall of The Mutants begins, ends #61 | .40 | 1.25 | 2.50 |
| 60-Double size, $1.25 | .30 | .90 | 1.80 |
| 61-Fall of The Mutants ends | .30 | .90 | 1.80 |
| 62,64-72,74-85,87-96: 68-Intro Spyder. 76-X-Factor & X-Terminator app. | | .50 | 1.00 |
| 63-X-Men & Wolverine app.; $1.00-c begins | .35 | 1.00 | 2.00 |
| 73-Double size, $1.50 | .25 | .75 | 1.50 |
| 86-McFarlane-c | .35 | 1.00 | 2.00 |
| Annual 1 (1984) | .85 | 2.50 | 5.00 |
| Annual 2 (10/86; $1.25) | .35 | 1.00 | 2.00 |
| Annual 3(9/87, $1.25) | .25 | .75 | 1.50 |
| Annual 4('88, $1.75) | .60 | 1.75 | 3.50 |
| Annual 5('89, $2.00, 68 pgs.)-Atlantis Attacks | .35 | 1.00 | 2.00 |
| Annual 6('90, $2.00, 68 pgs.) | .35 | 1.00 | 2.00 |
| Special 1-Special Edition ('85; 64 pgs.)-ties in with X-Men Alpha Flight mini-series; Art Adams/Austin-a | 1.00 | 3.00 | 6.00 |

*The New Teen Titans #24 (1st series), © DC Comics*

**NEW TEEN TITANS, THE** (See DC Comics Presents #26, Marvel and DC
    Present & Teen Titans; Tales of the Teen Titans #41 on)
November, 1980 - No. 40, March, 1984
DC Comics

|  | Good | Fine | N-Mint |
|---|---|---|---|
| 1-Robin, Kid Flash, Wonder Girl, The Changeling, Starfire, The Raven, | | | |
|     Cyborg begin; partial origin | 1.70 | 5.00 | 10.00 |
| 2 | 1.00 | 3.00 | 6.00 |
| 3-Origin Starfire; Intro The Fearsome 5 | .85 | 2.50 | 5.00 |
| 4-Origin continues; J.L.A. app. | .85 | 2.50 | 5.00 |
| 5-10: 6-Origin Raven. 7-Cyborg origin. 8-Origin Kid Flash retold. | | | |
|     10-Origin Changeling retold | .50 | 1.50 | 3.00 |
| 11-20: 13-Return of Madame Rouge & Capt. Zahl; Robotman revived. | | | |
|     14-Return of Mento; origin Doom Patrol. 15-Death of Madame Rouge | | | |

|  | Good | Fine | N-Mint |
|---|---|---|---|
| & Capt. Zahl; intro. new Brotherhood of Evil 16-1st app. Carrot (free 16 pg. preview). 18-Return of Starfire. 19-Hawkman teams-up | | | |
|  | .25 | .75 | 1.50 |
| 21-30: 21-Intro Night Force in free 16 pg. insert; intro Brother Blood. 23-1st app. Vigilante (not in costume), & Blackfire. 24-Omega Men app. 25-Omega Men cameo. 26-1st Terra. 29-The New Brotherhood of Evil & Speedy app. 30-Terra joins the Titans | | | |
|  | .60 | | 1.20 |
| 31-38,40: 38-Origin Wonder Girl | .40 | | .75 |
| 39-Last Dick Grayson as Robin; Kid Flash quits | | | |
|  | .35 | 1.00 | 2.00 |
| Annual 1(11/82)-Omega Men app. | .25 | .70 | 1.40 |
| Annual 2(9/83)-1st app. Vigilante in costume | | .45 | .90 |
| Annual 3(1984)-Death of Terra | | .45 | .90 |

**NEW TEEN TITANS, THE** (The New Titans #50 on)
Aug, 1984 - No. 49, Nov, 1988 ($1.25-$1.75; deluxe format)
DC Comics

| | Good | Fine | N-Mint |
|---|---|---|---|
| 1-New storyline; Perez-c/a begins | .85 | 2.50 | 5.00 |
| 2,3: 2-Re-intro Lilith | .50 | 1.50 | 3.00 |
| 4-10: 5-Death of Trigon. 7-9-Origin Lilith. 8-Intro Kole. 10-Kole joins | | | |
|  | .30 | .90 | 1.80 |
| 11-19: 13,14-Crisis x-over | | .60 | 1.20 |
| 20-Robin (Jason Todd) joins; original Teen Titans return | | | |
|  | .35 | 1.00 | 2.00 |
| 21-49: 37-Begin $1.75-c. 38-Infinity, Inc. x-over. 47-Origin all Titans. 48-1st app. Red Star | .25 | .70 | 1.40 |
| Annual 1 (9/85)-Intro. Vanguard | .35 | 1.00 | 2.00 |
| Annual 2 (8/86; $2.50): Byrne c/a(p); origin Brother Blood; intro new Dr. Light | .40 | 1.25 | 2.50 |
| Annual 3 (11/87)-Intro. Danny Chase | .35 | 1.00 | 2.00 |
| Annual 4 ('88, $2.50)-Perez-c | .40 | 1.15 | 2.30 |

**NEW TITANS, THE** (Formerly The New Teen Titans)
No. 50, Dec, 1988 - Present ($1.75, color)
DC Comics

| | Good | Fine | N-Mint |
|---|---|---|---|
| 50-Perez-c/a begins; new origin Wonder Girl | .75 | 2.25 | 4.50 |

|  | Good | Fine | N-Mint |
|---|---|---|---|
| 51-59: 50-55-Painted-c. 55-Nightwing (Dick Grayson) forces Danny Chase | | | |
| to resign; Batman app. in flashback | .40 | 1.25 | 2.50 |
| 60-A Lonely Place of Dying-Part 2/Batman | 1.10 | 3.25 | 6.50 |
| 61-A Lonely Place of Dying-Part 4/Batman | .70 | 2.00 | 4.00 |
| 62-72: 65-Timothy Drake (Robin) app. | .30 | .90 | 1.75 |
| Annual 5 (1989, $3.50, 68 pgs.) | .60 | 1.75 | 3.50 |
| Annual 6 ('90, $3.50, 68 pgs.) | .60 | 1.75 | 3.50 |

**NICKEL COMICS**
May, 1940 - No. 8, Aug, 1940 (36 pgs.; Bi-Weekly; 5 cents)
Fawcett Publications

|  | Good | Fine | N-Mint |
|---|---|---|---|
| 1-Origin/1st app. Bulletman | 100.00 | 300.00 | 700.00 |
| 2 | 45.00 | 135.00 | 315.00 |
| 3 | 40.00 | 120.00 | 280.00 |
| 4-The Red Gaucho begins | 34.00 | 102.00 | 235.00 |
| 5-7 | 30.00 | 90.00 | 210.00 |
| 8-World's Fair-c; Bulletman moved to Master Comics #7 in Oct. | | | |
|  | 30.00 | 90.00 | 210.00 |

**NICK FURY, AGENT OF SHIELD** (See Marv. Spotlight #31 & Shield)
6/68 - No. 15, 11/69; No. 16, 11/70 - No. 18, 3/71
Marvel Comics Group

|  | Good | Fine | N-Mint |
|---|---|---|---|
| 1 | 3.60 | 11.00 | 25.00 |
| 2-4: 4-Origin retold | 1.70 | 5.00 | 12.00 |
| 5-Classic-c | 2.15 | 6.50 | 15.00 |
| 6,7 | 1.15 | 3.50 | 8.00 |
| 8-11,13: 9-Hate Monger begins (ends #11). 11-Smith-c. 13-Last 12 cent | | | |
| issue | .70 | 2.00 | 4.00 |
| 12-Smith-c/a | .85 | 2.50 | 5.00 |
| 14 | .40 | 1.25 | 2.50 |
| 15-1st app. Bullseye (11/69) | 1.50 | 4.50 | 10.00 |
| 16-18-(All-r, 52 pgs.) | .30 | .90 | 1.80 |

**NICK FURY, AGENT OF S.H.I.E.L.D.** (See Strange Tales #135)
Sept, 1989 - Present ($1.50, color)
Marvel Comics

|  | Good | Fine | N-Mint |
|---|---|---|---|
| V2#1-18 | .25 | .75 | 1.50 |

## NICK FURY VS. SHIELD
June, 1988 - No. 6, Dec, 1988 ($3.50, 52 pgs, color, deluxe format)
Marvel Comics

|  | Good | Fine | N-Mint |
|---|---|---|---|
| 1-Steranko-c | 2.00 | 6.00 | 12.00 |
| 2 | 2.50 | 7.50 | 15.00 |
| 3 | 1.00 | 3.00 | 6.00 |
| 4-6 | .60 | 1.75 | 3.50 |

## NIGHTCRAWLER
Nov, 1985 - No. 4, Feb, 1986 (Mini-series from X-Men)
Marvel Comics Group

| | | | |
|---|---|---|---|
| 1-Cockrum-c/a | .50 | 1.50 | 3.00 |
| 2-4 | .35 | 1.00 | 2.00 |

## NYOKA, THE JUNGLE GIRL (Formerly Jungle Girl; see Master)
No. 2, Winter, 1945 - No. 77, June, 1953 (Movie serial)
Fawcett Publications

| | | | |
|---|---|---|---|
| 2 | 34.00 | 103.00 | 240.00 |
| 3 | 19.00 | 57.00 | 135.00 |
| 4,5 | 16.00 | 48.00 | 110.00 |
| 6-10 | 11.50 | 34.00 | 80.00 |
| 11,13,14,16-18-Krigstein-a | 11.50 | 34.00 | 80.00 |
| 12,15,19,20 | 9.30 | 28.00 | 65.00 |
| 21-30: 25-Clayton Moore photo-c? | 5.70 | 17.00 | 40.00 |
| 31-40 | 4.30 | 13.00 | 30.00 |
| 41-50 | 3.15 | 9.50 | 22.00 |
| 51-60 | 2.30 | 7.00 | 16.00 |
| 61-77 | 1.70 | 5.00 | 12.00 |

# O

**OFFICIAL HANDBOOK OF THE MARVEL UNIVERSE, THE**
Jan, 1983 - No. 15, May, 1984
Marvel Comics Group

| | Good | Fine | N-Mint |
|---|---|---|---|
| 1-Lists Marvel heroes & villains (letter A) | 1.00 | 3.00 | 6.00 |
| 2 (B-C) | .85 | 2.50 | 5.00 |
| 3-5: 3-(C-D). 4-(D-G). 5-(H-J) | .70 | 2.00 | 4.00 |
| 6-9: 6-(K-L). 7-(M). 8-(N-P); Punisher-c. 9-(Q-S) | | | |
| | .50 | 1.50 | 3.00 |
| 10-15: 10-(S). 11-(S-U). 12-(V-Z); Wolverine-c. 13,14-Book of the Dead. | | | |
| 15-Weaponry catalog | .40 | 1.25 | 2.50 |

**OUR ARMY AT WAR**
Aug, 1952 - No. 301, Feb, 1977
National Periodical Publications

| | | | |
|---|---|---|---|
| 1 | 40.00 | 120.00 | 280.00 |
| 2 | 19.00 | 58.00 | 135.00 |
| 3,4: 4-Krigstein-a | 18.50 | 56.00 | 130.00 |
| 5-7 | 9.30 | 28.00 | 65.00 |
| 8-11,14-Krigstein-a | 10.00 | 30.00 | 70.00 |
| 12,15-20 | 7.00 | 21.00 | 50.00 |
| 13-Krigstein c/a; flag-c | 9.30 | 28.00 | 65.00 |
| 21-31: Last precode (2/55) | 5.00 | 15.00 | 35.00 |
| 32-40 | 4.00 | 12.00 | 28.00 |
| 41-60 | 3.50 | 10.50 | 24.00 |
| 61-70 | 1.30 | 7.00 | 16.00 |
| 71-80 | 1.70 | 5.00 | 12.00 |
| 81-1st Sgt. Rock app. by Andru & Esposito in Easy Co. story | | | |
| | 42.00 | 126.00 | 295.00 |
| 82-Sgt. Rock cameo in Easy Co. story (6 panels) | | | |
| | 12.50 | 37.50 | 88.00 |
| 83-1st Kubert Sgt. Rock (6/59) | 14.00 | 42.00 | 100.00 |
| 84,86-90 | 5.00 | 15.00 | 35.00 |
| 85-1st app. & origin Ice Cream Soldier | 5.70 | 17.00 | 40.00 |
| 91-All Sgt. Rock issue | 9.50 | 28.50 | 66.00 |

|  | Good | Fine | N-Mint |
|---|---|---|---|
| 92-100: 92-1st app. Bulldozer. 95-1st app. Zack | | | |
| | 2.40 | 7.20 | 17.00 |
| 101-120: 101-1st app. Buster. 111-1st app. Wee Willie & Sunny. 113-1st app. Jackie Johnson. 118-Sunny dies. 120-1st app. Wildman | | | |
| | 1.25 | 3.75 | 7.50 |
| 121-127,129-150: 126-1st app. Canary. 139-1st app. Little Sure Shot | | | |
| | 1.05 | 3.15 | 6.30 |
| 128-Training & origin Sgt. Rock | 2.30 | 7.00 | 16.00 |
| 151-Intro. Enemy Ace by Kubert | 1.40 | 4.25 | 8.50 |
| 152-157,159-163,165-170: 153,155-Enemy Ace stories. 157-2 pg. pin-up. 162,163-Viking Prince x-over in Sgt. Rock | .90 | 2.65 | 5.30 |
| 158-1st app. & origin Iron Major (1965), formerly Iron Captain | | | |
| | 1.05 | 3.15 | 6.30 |
| 164-Giant G-19 | 1.05 | 3.15 | 6.30 |
| 171-176,178-181 | .55 | 1.60 | 3.20 |
| 177-(80 pg. Giant G-32) | .70 | 2.10 | 4.20 |
| 182,183,186-Neal Adams-a. 186-Origin retold | .90 | 2.65 | 5.30 |
| 184,185,187-189,191-199: 184-Wee Willie dies. 189-Intro. The Teen-age Underground Fighters of Unit 3 | .35 | 1.05 | 2.10 |
| 190-(80 pg. Giant G-44) | .55 | 1.60 | 3.20 |
| 200-12 pg. Rock story told in verse; Evans-a | .35 | 1.05 | 2.10 |
| 201-Krigstein-r/No. 14 | .35 | 1.05 | 2.10 |
| 202,206-215 | .30 | .90 | 1.80 |
| 203-(80 pg. Giant G-56)-All-r, no Sgt. Rock | .35 | 1.05 | 2.10 |
| 204,205-All-r, no Sgt. Rock | .25 | .80 | 1.60 |
| 216,229-(80 pg. Giants G-68, G-80) | .35 | 1.05 | 2.10 |
| 217-228,230-239,241,243-301: 249-Wood-a | .25 | .80 | 1.60 |
| 240-Neal Adams-a | .35 | 1.00 | 2.00 |
| 242-(50 cent issue DC-9)-Kubert-c | .30 | .90 | 1.80 |

**OUT OF THE NIGHT**
Feb-Mar, 1952 - No. 17, Oct-Nov, 1954
American Comics Group (Creston/Scope)

| | Good | Fine | N-Mint |
|---|---|---|---|
| 1-Williamson/LeDoux-a, 9 pgs | 21.50 | 64.00 | 150.00 |
| 2-Williamson-a, 5 pgs. | 18.00 | 54.00 | 125.00 |
| 3,5-10: 9-Sci/Fic story | 5.70 | 17.00 | 40.00 |
| 4-Williamson-a, 7 pgs. | 18.00 | 54.00 | 125.00 |
| 11,12,14-16 | 4.30 | 13.00 | 30.00 |
| 13-Nostrand-a; lingerie panels | 5.00 | 15.00 | 35.00 |
| 17-E.C. Wood swipe; lingerie panels | 4.50 | 14.00 | 32.00 |

**OUT OF THE SHADOWS**
No. 5, July, 1952 - No. 14, Aug, 1954
Standard Comics/Visual Editions

|  | Good | Fine | N-Mint |
|---|---|---|---|
| 5-Toth-p; Moreira, Tuska-a | 10.00 | 30.00 | 70.00 |
| 6-Toth/Celardo-a; Katz-a(2) | 8.50 | 25.50 | 60.00 |
| 7-Jack Katz-a(2) | 5.00 | 15.00 | 35.00 |
| 8,10: 10-Sekowsky-a | 3.70 | 11.00 | 26.00 |
| 9-Crandall-a(2) | 5.50 | 16.50 | 38.00 |
| 11-Toth-a, 2 pgs.; Katz-a | 4.50 | 14.00 | 32.00 |
| 12-Toth/Peppe-a(2); Katz-a | 8.50 | 25.50 | 60.00 |
| 13-Cannabalism story; Sekowsky-a | 5.50 | 16.50 | 38.00 |
| 14-Toth-a | 5.50 | 16.50 | 38.00 |

**OUT OF THIS WORLD**
Aug, 1956 - No. 16, Dec, 1959
Charlton Comics

|  | Good | Fine | N-Mint |
|---|---|---|---|
| 1 | 7.00 | 21.00 | 50.00 |
| 2 | 3.50 | 10.50 | 24.00 |
| 3-6-Ditko-a(4) each | 9.50 | 28.50 | 65.00 |
| 7-(68 pgs., 2/58; 15 cents)-Ditko-c/a(4) | 9.50 | 28.50 | 65.00 |
| 8-(68 pgs., 5/58)-Ditko-a(2) | 7.00 | 21.00 | 50.00 |
| 9-12,16-Ditko-a | 5.70 | 17.00 | 40.00 |
| 13-15 | 2.00 | 6.00 | 14.00 |

# P

**PARTRIDGE FAMILY, THE** (TV)
March, 1971 - No. 21, Dec, 1973
Charlton Comics

| | Good | Fine | N-Mint |
|---|---|---|---|
| 1 | 1.15 | 3.50 | 8.00 |
| 2-4,6-21 | .70 | 2.00 | 4.00 |
| 5-Partridge Family Summer Special (52 pgs.); The Shadow, Lone Ranger, Charlie McCarthy, Flash Gordon, Hopalong Cassidy, Gene Autry & others app. | 1.50 | 4.50 | 10.00 |

**PEANUTS** (Charlie Brown) (See Tip Top Comics)
No. 878, 2/58 - No. 13, 5-7/62; 5/63 - No. 4, 2/64
Dell Publishing Co./Gold Key

| | | | |
|---|---|---|---|
| 4-Color 878(#1) | 5.70 | 17.00 | 40.00 |
| 4-Color 969,1015('59) | 5.00 | 15.00 | 35.00 |
| 4(2-4/60) | 3.50 | 10.50 | 24.00 |
| 5-13 | 2.30 | 7.00 | 16.00 |
| 1(Gold Key, 5/63) | 2.85 | 8.50 | 20.00 |
| 2-4 | 2.00 | 6.00 | 14.00 |

**PEP COMICS**
Jan, 1940 - No. 411?, 1987
MLJ Magazines/Archie Publications No. 56 (3/46) on

| | | | |
|---|---|---|---|
| 1-Intro. The Shield by Irving Novick (1st patriotic hero); origin The Comet by Jack Cole, The Queen of Diamonds & Kayo Ward; The Rocket, The Press Guardian (The Falcon #1 only), Sergeant Boyle, Fu Chang, & Bentley of Scotland Yard | 200.00 | 500.00 | 1200.00 |
| 2-Origin The Rocket | 75.00 | 225.00 | 525.00 |
| 3 | 59.00 | 175.00 | 410.00 |
| 4-Wizard cameo | 50.00 | 150.00 | 350.00 |
| 5-Wizard cameo in Shield story | 50.00 | 150.00 | 350.00 |
| 6-10: 8-Last Cole Comet, no Cole-a in #6,7 | 37.00 | 110.00 | 260.00 |

318

|  | Good | Fine | N-Mint |
|---|---|---|---|
| 11-Dusty, Shield's sidekick begins; last Press Guardian, Fu Chang | | | |
|  | 37.00 | 110.00 | 260.00 |
| 12-Origin Fireball; last Rocket & Queen of Diamonds | | | |
|  | 50.00 | 150.00 | 350.00 |
| 13-15 | 34.00 | 103.00 | 240.00 |
| 16-Origin Madam Satan; blood drainage-c | 50.00 | 150.00 | 350.00 |
| 17-Origin The Hangman; death of The Comet | | | |
|  | 100.00 | 300.00 | 700.00 |
| 18-20-Last Fireball | 32.00 | 95.00 | 225.00 |
| 21-Last Madam Satan | 32.00 | 95.00 | 225.00 |
| 22-Intro. & 1st app. Archie, Betty, & Jughead(12/41); (also see Jackpot) | | | |
|  | 221.00 | 665.00 | 1550.00 |

*(Prices vary widely on this book)*

|  | Good | Fine | N-Mint |
|---|---|---|---|
| 23 | 61.00 | 182.00 | 425.00 |
| 24,25 | 51.00 | 152.00 | 355.00 |
| 26-1st app. Veronica Lodge | 59.00 | 175.00 | 410.00 |
| 27-30: 30-Capt. Commando begins | 41.00 | 122.00 | 285.00 |
| 31-35: 34-Bondage/Hypo-c | 30.00 | 90.00 | 210.00 |
| 36-1st Archie-c | 50.00 | 150.00 | 350.00 |
| 37-40 | 23.50 | 71.00 | 165.00 |
| 41-50: 41-Archie-c begin. 47-Last Hangman issue; infinity-c. 48-Black Hood begins (5/44); ends #51,59,60 | 17.00 | 51.00 | 120.00 |
| 51-60: 52-Suzie begins. 56-Last Capt. Commando. 59-Black Hood not in costume; spanking & lingerie panels; Archie dresses as his aunt; Suzie ends. 60-Katy Keene begins, ends #154 | | | |
|  | 12.00 | 36.00 | 84.00 |
| 61-65-Last Shield. 62-1st app. Li'l Jinx | 9.30 | 28.00 | 65.00 |
| 66-80: 66-G-Man Club becomes Archie Club (2/48) | | | |
|  | 6.50 | 19.50 | 45.00 |
| 81-99 | 4.35 | 13.00 | 30.00 |
| 100 | 5.00 | 15.00 | 35.00 |
| 101-130 | 2.00 | 6.00 | 14.00 |
| 131-149 | 1.00 | 3.00 | 7.00 |
| 150-160-Super-heroes app. in each (see note). 150 (10/61?)-2nd or 3rd app. The Jaguar? 157-Li'l Jinx story | .85 | 2.60 | 6.00 |
| 161-167,169-200 | .35 | 1.00 | 2.50 |
| 168-Jaguar app. | .70 | 2.00 | 5.00 |
| 201-260 | .25 | .75 | 1.50 |

|  | Good | Fine | N-Mint |
|---|---|---|---|
| 261-411: 383-Marvelous Maureen begins (Sci/fi). 393-Thunderbunny begins | | .35 | .70 |

NOTE: The Fly app. in 151, 154, 160. Flygirl app. in 153, 155, 156, 158. Jaguar app. in 150, 152, 157, 159, 168. Katy Keene by Bill Woggon in many later issues.

**PETER PORKCHOPS** (See Leading Comics #23)
11-12/49 - No. 61, 9-11/59; No. 62, 10-12/60 (1-5: 52 pgs.)
National Periodical Publications

| | Good | Fine | N-Mint |
|---|---|---|---|
| 1 | 16.00 | 48.00 | 110.00 |
| 2 | 8.00 | 24.00 | 56.00 |
| 3-10 | 5.50 | 16.50 | 38.00 |
| 11-30 | 3.70 | 11.00 | 26.00 |
| 31-62 | 2.30 | 7.00 | 16.00 |

*The Phantom #18, © King Features Syndicate*

**PHANTOM, THE** (nn 29-Published overseas only; see Ace Comics)
Nov, 1962 - No. 17, July, 1966; No. 18, Sept, 1966 - No. 28, Dec, 1967;
   No. 30, Feb, 1969 - No. 74, Jan, 1977
Gold Key (No. 1-17)/King (No. 18-28)/Charlton (No. 30 on)

| | Good | Fine | N-Mint |
|---|---|---|---|
| 1-Manning-a | 5.00 | 15.00 | 35.00 |
| 2-King, Queen & Jack begins, ends #11 | 2.30 | 7.00 | 16.00 |
| 3-10 | 1.70 | 5.00 | 12.00 |
| 11-17: 12-Track Hunter begins | 1.15 | 3.50 | 8.00 |
| 18-Flash Gordon begins; Wood-a | 1.50 | 4.50 | 10.00 |
| 19,20-Flash Gordon ends | 1.00 | 3.00 | 7.00 |
| 21-24,26,27: 21-Mandrake begins. 20,24-Girl Phantom app. 26-Brick Bradford app. | .85 | 2.60 | 6.00 |
| 25-Jeff Jones-a; 1 pg. Williamson ad | 1.30 | 4.00 | 9.00 |
| 28(nn)-Brick Bradford app. | .85 | 2.60 | 6.00 |
| 30-40: 36,39-Ditko-a | .55 | 1.65 | 4.00 |
| 41-66: 46-Intro. The Piranha. 62-Bolle-c | .35 | 1.00 | 2.00 |
| 67-71,73-Newton-c/a; 67-Origin retold | .35 | 1.00 | 2.00 |
| 72 | .25 | .75 | 1.50 |
| 74-Newton Flag-c; Newton-a | .35 | 1.00 | 2.00 |

**PHANTOM, THE**
May, 1988 - No. 4, Aug, 1988 ($1.25, color)
DC Comics

| | | | |
|---|---|---|---|
| 1-Orlando-c/a in all | .35 | 1.00 | 2.00 |
| 2-4 | .25 | .75 | 1.50 |

**PHANTOM, THE**
Mar, 1989 - No. 13, Mar, 1990 ($1.50, color)
DC Comics

| | | | |
|---|---|---|---|
| 1-Brief origin | .35 | 1.00 | 2.00 |
| 2-13 | .25 | .75 | 1.50 |

**PHANTOM LADY** (1st Series) (Also see All Top)
No. 13, Aug, 1947 - No. 23 April, 1949
Fox Features Syndicate

|  | Good | Fine | N-Mint |
|---|---|---|---|
| 13(#1)-Phantom Lady by Matt Baker begins; The Blue Beetle app. | | | |
|  | 115.00 | 345.00 | 800.00 |
| 14(#2) | 72.00 | 215.00 | 500.00 |
| 15-P.L. injected with experimental drug | 61.00 | 182.00 | 425.00 |
| 16-Negligee-c, panels | 61.00 | 182.00 | 425.00 |

17-Classic bondage cover; used in **SOTI**, illo-"Sexual stimulation by combining 'headlights' with the sadist's dream of tying up a woman"

|  | Good | Fine | N-Mint |
|---|---|---|---|
|  | 145.00 | 435.00 | 1015.00 |
| 18,19 | 55.00 | 165.00 | 385.00 |
| 20-23: 23-Bondage-c | 46.00 | 140.00 | 325.00 |

**PHANTOM STRANGER, THE** (1st Series) (See Saga of Swamp Thing)
Aug-Sept, 1952 - No. 6, June-July, 1953
National Periodical Publications

| 1 (Scarce) | 57.00 | 171.00 | 400.00 |
|---|---|---|---|
| 2 (Scarce) | 43.00 | 130.00 | 300.00 |
| 3-6 (Scarce) | 34.00 | 103.00 | 240.00 |

**PHANTOM STRANGER, THE** (2nd Series) (See Showcase #80)
May-June, 1969 - No. 41, Feb-Mar, 1976
National Periodical Publications

| 1-Only 12 cent issue | 2.30 | 7.00 | 16.00 |
|---|---|---|---|
| 2,3: 2-? are 15 cents | 1.00 | 3.00 | 7.00 |
| 4-Neal Adams-a | 1.15 | 3.50 | 8.00 |
| 5-10 | .70 | 2.00 | 4.00 |
| 11-20 | .35 | 1.00 | 2.00 |

21-41: 22-Dark Circle begins. 23-Spawn of Frankenstein begins by Kaluta; series ends #30. 31-The Black Orchid begins. 39-41-Deadman app.

|  | .25 | .75 | 1.50 |
|---|---|---|---|

**PHANTOM STRANGER** (See Justice League of America #103)
Oct, 1987 - No. 4, Jan, 1988 (mini-series, 75 cents, color)
DC Comics

| 1-Mignola/Russell-c/a in all | .25 | .75 | 1.50 |
|---|---|---|---|
| 2-4 |  | .50 | 1.00 |

**PHANTOM ZONE, THE** (See Adventure #283 & Superboy #100, 104)
Jan, 1982 - No. 4, April, 1982
DC Comics

|  | Good | Fine | N-Mint |
|---|---|---|---|
| 1-Superman App. in all |  | .50 | 1.00 |
| 2-4: Batman, Green Lantern app. |  | .60 | 1.25 |

**PINK PANTHER, THE** (TV)
April, 1971 - No. 87, 1984
Gold Key

|  | Good | Fine | N-Mint |
|---|---|---|---|
| 1-The Inspector begins | 1.20 | 3.50 | 8.00 |
| 2-10 | .70 | 2.00 | 4.00 |
| 11-30: Warren Tufts-a #16-on | .40 | 1.20 | 2.50 |
| 31-60 | .25 | .75 | 1.50 |
| 61-87 |  | .50 | 1.00 |

**PLANET COMICS**
Jan, 1940 - No. 73, Winter, 1953
Fiction House Magazines

| | Good | Fine | N-Mint |
|---|---|---|---|
| 1-Origin Auro, Lord of Jupiter; Flint Baker & The Red Comet begin; Eisner/Fine-c | 433.00 | 1085.00 | 2600.00 |
| 2-(Scarce) | 217.00 | 545.00 | 1300.00 |
| 3-Eisner-c | 174.00 | 435.00 | 1045.00 |
| 4-Gale Allen and the Girl Squadron begins | 150.00 | 375.00 | 900.00 |
| 5,6-(Scarce) | 135.00 | 340.00 | 810.00 |
| 7-12: 12-The Star Pirate begins | 100.00 | 300.00 | 700.00 |
| 13-14: 13-Reff Ryan begins | 75.00 | 225.00 | 525.00 |
| 15-(Scarce)-Mars, God of War begins | 80.00 | 240.00 | 560.00 |
| 16-20,22 | 71.00 | 215.00 | 500.00 |
| 21-The Lost World & Hunt Bowman begin | 75.00 | 225.00 | 525.00 |
| 23-26: 26-The Space Rangers begin | 71.00 | 215.00 | 500.00 |
| 27-30 | 52.00 | 156.00 | 365.00 |
| 31-35: 33-Origin Star Pirates Wonder Boots, reprinted in #52. 35-Mysta of the Moon begins | 44.00 | 133.00 | 310.00 |
| 36-45: 41-New origin of "Auro, Lord of Jupiter." 42-Last Gale Allen. 43-Futura begins | 37.00 | 112.00 | 260.00 |
| 46-60: 53-Used in **SOTI**, pg. 32 | 28.50 | 86.00 | 200.00 |
| 61-64 | 19.00 | 57.00 | 135.00 |

| | Good | Fine | N-Mint |
|---|---|---|---|
| 65-68,70: 65-70-All partial-r of earlier issues | 19.00 | 57.00 | 135.00 |
| 69-Used in **POP**, pgs. 101, 102 | 19.00 | 57.00 | 135.00 |
| 71-73-No series stories | 16.00 | 48.00 | 110.00 |

**PLASTIC MAN** (Also see Police Comics & Smash Comics #17)
Sum, 1943 - No. 64, Nov, 1956
Vital Publ. No. 1,2/Quality Comics No. 3 on

| | Good | Fine | N-Mint |
|---|---|---|---|
| nn(#1)-'In The Game of Death'; Jack Cole-c/a begins; ends-#64? | 129.00 | 385.00 | 900.00 |
| nn(#2, 2/44)-'The Gay Nineties Nightmare' | 79.00 | 235.00 | 550.00 |
| 3 (Spr, '46) | 51.00 | 152.00 | 355.00 |
| 4 (Sum, '46) | 45.00 | 135.00 | 315.00 |
| 5 (Aut, '46) | 37.00 | 110.00 | 260.00 |
| 6-10 | 26.00 | 79.00 | 185.00 |
| 11-20 | 24.00 | 71.00 | 165.00 |
| 21-30: 26-Last non-r issue? | 19.00 | 58.00 | 135.00 |
| 31-40: 40-Used in **POP**, pg. 91 | 14.00 | 42.00 | 100.00 |
| 41-64: 53-Last precode issue | 11.50 | 34.00 | 80.00 |

**PLASTIC MAN**
11-12/66 - No. 10, 5-6/68; V4#11, 2-3/76 - No. 20, 10-11/77
National Periodical Publications/DC Comics

| | Good | Fine | N-Mint |
|---|---|---|---|
| 1-Gil Kane-c/a; 12 cent issues begin | 2.15 | 6.50 | 15.00 |
| 2-5: 4-Infantino-c; Mortimer-a | 1.00 | 3.00 | 6.00 |
| 6-10('68): 10-Sparling-a; last 12 cent issue | .85 | 2.50 | 5.00 |
| V4#11('76)-20: 11-20-Fraden-p. 17-Origin retold | | | |
| | .25 | .75 | 1.50 |

**POLICE COMICS**
Aug, 1941 - No. 127, Oct, 1953
Quality Comics Group (Comic Magazines)

1-Origin Plastic Man (1st app.) by Jack Cole, The Human Bomb by
  Gustavson, & No. 711; intro. Chic Carter by Eisner, The Firebrand by
  Reed Crandall, The Mouthpiece, Phantom Lady, & The Sword

| | Good | Fine | N-Mint |
|---|---|---|---|
| | 308.00 | 770.00 | 1850.00 |
| 2-Plastic Man smuggles opium | 130.00 | 390.00 | 910.00 |
| 3 | 108.00 | 325.00 | 755.00 |

|  | Good | Fine | N-Mint |
|---|---|---|---|
| 4 | 93.00 | 280.00 | 650.00 |
| 5-Plastic Man forced to smoke marijuana | 93.00 | 280.00 | 650.00 |
| 6,7 | 83.00 | 250.00 | 580.00 |
| 8-Manhunter begins (origin) | 98.00 | 295.00 | 685.00 |
| 9,10 | 77.00 | 230.00 | 540.00 |
| 11-The Spirit strip-r begin by Eisner(Origin-strip #1) | | | |
| | 125.00 | 375.00 | 875.00 |
| 12-Intro. Ebony | 80.00 | 240.00 | 560.00 |
| 13-Intro. Woozy Winks; last Firebrand | 80.00 | 240.00 | 560.00 |
| 14-19: 15-Last No. 711; Destiny begins | 52.00 | 155.00 | 365.00 |
| 20-The Raven x-over in Phantom Lady; features Jack Cole himself | | | |
| | 52.00 | 155.00 | 365.00 |
| 21,22-Raven & Spider Widow x-over in Phantom Lady #21; cameo in | | | |
|    Phantom Lady #22 | 39.00 | 118.00 | 275.00 |
| 23-30: 23-Last Phantom Lady. 24-Chic Carter becomes The Sword, only issue. 24-26-Flatfoot Burns by Kurtzman in all | | | |
| | 35.00 | 105.00 | 245.00 |
| 31-41-Last Spirit-r by Eisner | 25.00 | 75.00 | 175.00 |
| 42,43-Spirit-r by Eisner/Fine | 21.50 | 64.00 | 150.00 |
| 44-Fine Spirit-r begin, end #88,90,92 | 18.00 | 54.00 | 125.00 |
| 45-50-(#50 on-c, #49 on inside)(1/46) | 18.00 | 54.00 | 125.00 |
| 51-60: 58-Last Human Bomb | 14.00 | 42.00 | 100.00 |
| 61-88: 63-(Some issues have #65 printed on cover, but #63 on inside) | | | |
|    Kurtzman-a, 6 pgs. | 12.00 | 36.00 | 84.00 |
| 89,91,93-No Spirit | 11.00 | 32.00 | 75.00 |
| 90,92-Spirit by Fine | 12.00 | 36.00 | 84.00 |
| 94-99,101,102: Spirit by Eisner in all; 101-Last Manhunter. 102-Last Spirit & Plastic Man by Jack Cole | 16.50 | 49.00 | 115.00 |
| 100 | 18.50 | 56.00 | 130.00 |
| 103-Content change to crime - Ken Shannon begins (1st app.) | | | |
| | 8.50 | 25.50 | 60.00 |
| 104-111,114-127-Crandall-a most issues | 6.00 | 18.00 | 42.00 |
| 112-Crandall-a | 6.00 | 18.00 | 42.00 |
| 113-Crandall-c/a(2), 9 pgs. each | 6.50 | 19.50 | 45.00 |

**POPEYE** (See King Comics & Magic Comics)
2-4/48 - #65, 7-9/62; #66, 10/62 - #80, 5/66; #81, 8/66 - #92, 12/67; #94, 2/69 - #138, 1/77; #139, 5/78 - #171, 7/84 (no #93,160,161)
Dell #1-65/Gold Key #66-80/King #81-92/Charlton #94-138/Gold Key #139-155/Whitman #156 on

|  | Good | Fine | N-Mint |
|---|---|---|---|
| 1 | 21.50 | 64.00 | 150.00 |
| 2 | 11.00 | 32.00 | 75.00 |
| 3-10 | 9.30 | 28.00 | 65.00 |
| 11-20 | 7.00 | 21.00 | 50.00 |
| 21-40 | 5.00 | 15.00 | 35.00 |
| 41-45,47-50 | 3.70 | 11.00 | 26.00 |
| 46-Origin Swee' Pee | 5.50 | 16.50 | 38.00 |
| 51-60 | 2.85 | 8.50 | 20.00 |
| 61-65 (Last Dell issue) | 2.30 | 7.00 | 16.00 |
| 66,67-Both 84 pgs. (Gold Key) | 4.00 | 12.00 | 32.00 |
| 68-80 | 1.85 | 5.50 | 13.00 |
| 81-92,94-100 | 1.00 | 3.00 | 7.00 |
| 101-130 | .70 | 2.00 | 5.00 |
| 131-159,162-171: 144-50th Anniversary issue | .55 | 1.65 | 4.00 |

**POPULAR COMICS**
Feb, 1936 - No. 145, July-Sept, 1948
Dell Publishing Co.

| | Good | Fine | N-Mint |
|---|---|---|---|
| 1-Dick Tracy, Little Orphan Annie, Terry & the Pirates, Gasoline Alley, Don Winslow, Harold Teen, Little Joe, Skippy, Moon Mullins, Mutt & Jeff, Tailspin Tommy, Smitty, Smokey Stover, Winnie Winkle & The Gumps begin (all strip-r) | 167.00 | 420.00 | 1000.00 |
| 2 | 70.00 | 210.00 | 490.00 |
| 3 | 54.00 | 163.00 | 380.00 |
| 4,5: 5-Tom Mix begins | 43.00 | 130.00 | 300.00 |
| 6-10: 8,9-Scribbly, Reglar Fellers app. | 35.00 | 105.00 | 245.00 |
| 11-20: 12-Xmas-c | 27.00 | 81.00 | 190.00 |
| 21-27-Last Terry & the Pirates, Little Orphan Annie, & Dick Tracy | 19.00 | 58.00 | 135.00 |
| 28-37: 28-Gene Autry app. 31,32-Tim McCoy app. 35-Christmas-c; Tex Ritter app. | 16.50 | 50.00 | 115.00 |
| 38-43-Tarzan in text only. 38-Gang Busters (radio) & Zane Grey's Tex Thorne begins? 43-1st non-funny-c? | 18.50 | 55.00 | 130.00 |
| 44,45: 45-Tarzan-c | 13.00 | 40.00 | 90.00 |
| 46-Origin Martan, the Marvel Man | 17.00 | 51.00 | 120.00 |
| 47-50 | 12.00 | 36.00 | 84.00 |
| 51-Origin The Voice (The Invisible Detective) strip begins | 13.00 | 40.00 | 90.00 |
| 52-59: 55-End of World story | 11.00 | 32.00 | 75.00 |

| | Good | Fine | N-Mint |
|---|---|---|---|
| 60-Origin Professor Supermind and Son | 11.50 | 34.00 | 80.00 |
| 61-71: 63-Smilin' Jack begins | 9.30 | 28.00 | 65.00 |
| 72-The Owl & Terry & the Pirates begin; Smokey Stover reprints begin | | | |
| | 14.00 | 42.00 | 100.00 |
| 73-75 | 11.50 | 34.00 | 80.00 |
| 76-78-Capt. Midnight in all | 13.00 | 40.00 | 90.00 |
| 79-85-Last Owl | 10.00 | 30.00 | 70.00 |
| 86-99: 98-Felix the Cat, Smokey Stover-r begin | | | |
| | 8.00 | 24.00 | 56.00 |
| 100 | 9.30 | 28.00 | 65.00 |
| 101-130: 114-Last Dick Tracy-r? | 5.00 | 15.00 | 35.00 |
| 131-145: 142-Last Terry & the Pirates | 4.30 | 13.00 | 30.00 |

**PORKY PIG** (. . . & Bugs Bunny #40-69)
No. 16, 1942 - No. 81, Mar-Apr, 1962; Jan, 1965 - No. 109, July, 1984
Dell Publishing Co./Gold Key No. 1-93/Whitman No. 94 on

| | Good | Fine | N-Mint |
|---|---|---|---|
| 4-Color 16(#1, 1942) | 38.00 | 114.00 | 265.00 |
| 4-Color 48(1944)-Carl Barks-a | 70.00 | 210.00 | 490.00 |
| 4-Color 78(1945) | 14.00 | 42.00 | 100.00 |
| 4-Color 112(7/46) | 8.50 | 25.50 | 60.00 |
| 4-Color 156,182,191('49) | 6.50 | 19.50 | 45.00 |
| 4-Color 226,241('49),260,271,277,284,295 | 4.30 | 13.00 | 30.00 |
| 4-Color 303,311,322,330 | 3.00 | 9.00 | 21.00 |
| 4-Color 342,351,360,370,385,399,410,426 | 2.30 | 7.00 | 16.00 |
| 25 (11-12/52)-30 | 1.30 | 4.00 | 9.00 |
| 31-50 | .70 | 2.00 | 4.50 |
| 51-81(3-4/62) | .45 | 1.35 | 3.00 |
| 1(1/65-Gold Key)(2nd Series) | .75 | 2.25 | 5.00 |
| 2,4,5-R/4-Color 226,284 & 271 in that order | .45 | 1.35 | 3.00 |
| 3,6-10 | .35 | 1.00 | 2.00 |
| 11-50 | | .50 | 1.00 |
| 51-109 | | .30 | .60 |

**POWERHOUSE PEPPER COMICS** (See Joker Comics)
No. 1, 1943; No. 2, May, 1948 - No. 5, Nov, 1948
Marvel Comics (20CC)

| | Good | Fine | N-Mint |
|---|---|---|---|
| 1-(60 pgs.)-Wolverton-c/a in all | 57.00 | 170.00 | 400.00 |
| 2 | 35.00 | 105.00 | 245.00 |

|  | Good | Fine | N-Mint |
|---|---|---|---|
| 3,4 | 34.00 | 100.00 | 235.00 |
| 5-(Scarce) | 39.00 | 118.00 | 275.00 |

**POWER MAN** (Formerly Hero for Hire; . . . & Iron Fist #68 on)
No. 17, Feb, 1974 - No. 125, Sept, 1986
Marvel Comics Group

| | | | |
|---|---|---|---|
| 17-20: 17-Luke Cage continues; Iron Man app. | .50 | 1.50 | 3.00 |
| 21-31: 31-Part Neal Adams-i | .25 | .75 | 1.50 |
| 32-47: 36-Reprint. 45-Starlin-c | | .50 | 1.00 |
| 48-Byrne-a; Powerman/Iron Fist 1st meet | .50 | 1.50 | 3.00 |
| 49,50-Byrne-a(p); 50-Iron Fist joins Cage | .50 | 1.50 | 3.00 |
| 51-56,58-60: 58-Intro El Aguila | | .40 | .80 |
| 57-New X-Men app. | .85 | 2.50 | 5.00 |
| 61-65,67-83,85-125: 75-Double size. 77-Daredevil app. 87-Moon Knight app. 90-Unus app. 109-The Reaper app. 100-Double size; origin K'un L'un. 125-Double size | | .40 | .80 |
| 66,84-Sabretooth app. | .35 | 1.00 | 2.00 |
| Giant-Size 1('75) | .25 | .80 | 1.60 |
| Annual 1(1976)-Punisher cameo in flashback | | .50 | 1.00 |

**POWER PACK**
Aug, 1984 - Present
Marvel Comics Group

| | | | |
|---|---|---|---|
| 1-($1.00) | .70 | 2.00 | 4.00 |
| 2-5 | .45 | 1.35 | 2.70 |
| 6-8-Cloak & Dagger app. | .35 | 1.00 | 2.00 |
| 9-18 | .25 | .75 | 1.50 |
| 19-Dbl. size; Cloak & Dagger, Wolverine app. | 1.00 | 3.00 | 6.00 |
| 20-24 | | .60 | 1.25 |
| 25-Double size | .30 | .90 | 1.80 |
| 26-Begin direct sale; Cloak & Dagger app. | | .60 | 1.25 |
| 27-Mutant massacre, Wolverine app. | 1.00 | 3.00 | 6.00 |
| 28-43: 42-1st Inferno tie-in | | .60 | 1.25 |
| 44,45,47-49,51-60: 44-Begin $1.50-c | .25 | .75 | 1.50 |
| 46-Punisher app. | .40 | 1.25 | 2.50 |
| 50-Double size ($1.95) | .35 | 1.00 | 2.00 |

**PRISONER, THE** (TV)
1988 - No. 4, Jan, 1989 ($3.50, mini-series, squarebound)
DC Comics

|  | Good | Fine | N-Mint |
|---|---|---|---|
| 1-Book A | .75 | 2.25 | 4.50 |
| 2-4: Book B-D | .60 | 1.75 | 3.50 |

**PRIZE COMICS** ( . . . Western #69 on)
March, 1940 - No. 68, Feb-Mar, 1948
Prize Publications

| | Good | Fine | N-Mint |
|---|---|---|---|
| 1-Origin Power Nelson, The Futureman & Jupiter, Master Magician; Ted O'Neil, Secret Agent M-11, Jaxon of the Jungle, Bucky Brady & Storm Curtis begin | 78.00 | 235.00 | 550.00 |
| 2-The Black Owl begins | 37.00 | 110.00 | 260.00 |
| 3,4 | 30.00 | 90.00 | 210.00 |
| 5,6: Dr. Dekkar, Master of Monsters app. in each | 27.00 | 81.00 | 190.00 |
| 7-(Scarce)-Black Owl by S&K; origin/1st app. Dr. Frost & Frankenstein; The Green Lama, Capt. Gallant, The Great Voodini & Twist Turner begin; Kirby-c | 58.00 | 175.00 | 410.00 |
| 8,9-Black Owl & Ted O'Neil by S&K | 32.00 | 95.00 | 225.00 |
| 10-12,14-20: 11-Origin Bulldog Denny. 16-Spike Mason begins | 27.00 | 81.00 | 190.00 |
| 13-Yank & Doodle begin (origin) | 32.00 | 95.00 | 225.00 |
| 21-24 | 18.00 | 54.00 | 125.00 |
| 25-30 | 12.00 | 36.00 | 84.00 |
| 31-33 | 9.00 | 27.00 | 62.00 |
| 34-Origin Airmale, Yank & Doodle; The Black Owl joins army, Yank & Doodle's father assumes Black Owl's role | 10.00 | 30.00 | 70.00 |
| 35-40: 35-Flying Fist & Bingo begin. 37-Intro. Stampy, Airmale's sidekick; Hitler-c | 8.00 | 24.00 | 56.00 |
| 41-50: 45-Yank & Doodle learn Black Owl's I.D. (their father). 48- Prince Ra begins | 5.70 | 17.00 | 40.00 |
| 51-62,64-68: 53-Transvestism story. 55-No Frankenstein. 64-Black Owl retires. 65,66-Frankenstein-c by Briefer | 5.00 | 15.00 | 35.00 |
| 63-Simon & Kirby c/a | 7.00 | 21.00 | 50.00 |

*Prize Comics Western #82, © Prize Publications*

**PRIZE COMICS WESTERN** (Formerly Prize Comics #1-68)
No. 69 (V7#2), Apr-May, 1948 - No. 119, Nov-Dec, 1956
Prize Publications (Feature) (No. 69-84: 52 pgs.)

|  | Good | Fine | N-Mint |
|---|---|---|---|
| 69(V7#2) | 7.00 | 21.00 | 50.00 |
| 70-75 | 5.00 | 15.00 | 35.00 |
| 76-Randolph Scott photo-c; "Canadian Pacific" movie adaptation | | | |
|  | 7.00 | 21.00 | 50.00 |
| 77-Photo-c; Severin, Mart Bailey-a; "Streets of Laredo" movie adapt. | | | |
|  | 5.70 | 17.00 | 40.00 |
| 78-Photo-c; Kurtzman-a, 10 pgs.; Severin, Mart Bailey-a; "Bullet Code," & | | | |
| "Roughshod" movie adapt. | 9.00 | 27.00 | 62.00 |
| 79-Photo-c; Kurtzman-a, 8 pgs.; Severin & Elder, Severin, Mart Bailey-a; | | | |
| "Stage To Chino" movie adapt. | 9.00 | 27.00 | 62.00 |
| 80,81-Photo-c; Severin/Elder-a(2) | 5.70 | 17.00 | 40.00 |
| 82-Photo-c; 1st app. The Preacher by Mart Bailey; Severin/Elder-a(3) | | | |
|  | 5.70 | 17.00 | 40.00 |

|  | Good | Fine | N-Mint |
|---|---|---|---|
| 83,84 | 4.30 | 13.00 | 30.00 |
| 85-American Eagle by John Severin begins (1-2/50) | | | |
|  | 12.00 | 36.00 | 84.00 |
| 86,92,95,101-105 | 5.50 | 16.50 | 38.00 |
| 87-91,93,94,96-99,110,111-Severin/Elder a(2-3) each | | | |
|  | 5.70 | 17.00 | 40.00 |
| 100 | 7.00 | 21.00 | 50.00 |
| 106-108,112 | 3.70 | 11.00 | 26.00 |
| 109-Severin/Williamson-a | 6.00 | 18.00 | 42.00 |
| 113-Williamson/Severin-a(2) | 6.50 | 19.50 | 45.00 |
| 114-119: Drifter series in all; by Mort Meskin 114-118 | | | |
|  | 2.65 | 8.00 | 18.00 |

**PUNISHER** (See Amazing Spider-Man #129, Captain America #241,
    Daredevil #182-184, 257, Power Pack #46, Spectacular Spider-Man)
Jan, 1986 - No. 5, May, 1986 (mini-series)
Marvel Comics Group

|  | Good | Fine | N-Mint |
|---|---|---|---|
| 1-Double size | 5.70 | 17.00 | 40.00 |
| 2 | 3.35 | 10.00 | 20.00 |
| 3-Has 2 cover prices, 75 & 95(w/UPC) cents | 1.70 | 5.00 | 10.00 |
| 4,5 | 1.35 | 4.00 | 8.00 |

**PUNISHER**
July, 1987 - Present
Marvel Comics Group

|  | Good | Fine | N-Mint |
|---|---|---|---|
| V2#1 | 2.70 | 8.00 | 16.00 |
| 2 | 1.50 | 4.50 | 9.00 |
| 3-5 | .90 | 2.75 | 5.50 |
| 6-8 | .85 | 2.50 | 5.00 |
| 9 | 1.15 | 3.50 | 7.00 |
| 10-Daredevil app. | 2.15 | 6.50 | 13.00 |
| 11-15 | .75 | 2.25 | 4.50 |
| 16-20: 13-18-Kingpin app. | .50 | 1.50 | 3.00 |
| 21-24,26-30: 24-1st app. Shadowmasters | .35 | 1.00 | 2.00 |
| 25-Double size ($1.50)-Shadowmasters app. | .50 | 1.50 | 3.00 |
| 31-44 |  | .60 | 1.25 |
| Annual 1(8/88)-Evolutionary War app. | 1.35 | 4.00 | 8.00 |

|                                              | Good | Fine | N-Mint |
|----------------------------------------------|------|------|--------|
| Annual 2('89, $2.00, 68 pgs.)-Atlantis Attacks x-over; Moon Knight app. |      |      |        |
|                                              | .60  | 1.75 | 3.50   |
| Annual 3(1990, $2.00, 68 pgs.)               | .35  | 1.00 | 2.00   |

**PUNISHER WAR JOURNAL**
Nov, 1988 - Present ($1.50, color)
Marvel Comics

|                                              | Good | Fine | N-Mint |
|----------------------------------------------|------|------|--------|
| 1-Origin The Punisher; Matt Murdock cameo    |      |      |        |
|                                              | 1.70 | 5.00 | 10.00  |
| 2-Daredevil x-over                           | 1.15 | 3.50 | 7.00   |
| 3-5: 3-Daredevil x-over                      | 1.00 | 3.00 | 6.00   |
| 6-Two part Wolverine story begins            | 1.70 | 5.00 | 10.00  |
| 7-Wolverine story ends                       | .85  | 2.50 | 5.00   |
| 8-10                                         | .60  | 1.75 | 3.50   |
| 11-13                                        | .40  | 1.25 | 2.50   |
| 14-25                                        | .30  | .90  | 1.80   |

# Q

**QUASAR** (See Avengers #302 & Marvel Team-Up #113)
Oct, 1989 - Present ($1.00, color)
Marvel Comics

|  | Good | Fine | N-Mint |
|---|---|---|---|
| 1-Origin; formerly Marvel Boy; Ryan-c/a in all | .35 | 1.00 | 2.00 |
| 2-5: 3-Human Torch app. | .25 | .75 | 1.50 |
| 6-16: 7-Cosmic Spidey app. |  | .50 | 1.00 |

**QUEEN OF THE WEST, DALE EVANS** (TV)
No. 479, 7/53 - No. 22, 1-3/59 (All photo-c; photo back c-4-8, 15)
Dell Publishing Co.

| | | | |
|---|---|---|---|
| 4-Color 479(#1, '53) | 7.00 | 21.00 | 50.00 |
| 4-Color 528(#2, '54) | 5.00 | 15.00 | 35.00 |
| 3(4-6/54)-Toth-a | 5.70 | 17.00 | 40.00 |
| 4-Toth, Manning-a | 5.70 | 17.00 | 40.00 |
| 5-10-Manning-a. 5-Marsh-a | 4.00 | 12.00 | 28.00 |
| 11,19,21-No Manning 21-Tufts-a | 3.00 | 9.00 | 21.00 |
| 12-18,20,22-Manning-a | 3.50 | 10.50 | 24.00 |

**QUESTION, THE** (Also see Blue Beetle & Crisis on Infinite Earths)
Feb, 1987 - No. 36, Mar, 1990 ($1.50-$1.75, color, mature readers)
DC Comics

| | | | |
|---|---|---|---|
| 1-Sienkiewicz painted-c | .70 | 2.00 | 4.00 |
| 2-Sienkiewicz c-2-19i, 21-23i, Annual 1i | .50 | 1.50 | 3.00 |
| 3-5 | .40 | 1.25 | 2.50 |
| 6-36: 8-Intro. The Mikado. 16-Begin $1.75-c | .35 | 1.00 | 2.00 |
| Annual 1(9/88) | .45 | 1.40 | 2.75 |
| Annual 2('89, $3.50, 68 pgs.)-Green Arrow app. | .60 | 1.75 | 3.50 |

# R

**RAGGEDY ANN AND ANDY** (Also see New Funnies)
No. 5, 1942 - No. 533, 2/54; 10-12/64 - No. 4, 3/66
Dell Publishing Co.

|  | Good | Fine | N-Mint |
|---|---|---|---|
| 4-Color 5(1942) | 34.00 | 100.00 | 235.00 |
| 4-Color 23(1943) | 24.00 | 73.00 | 170.00 |
| 4-Color 45(1943) | 20.00 | 60.00 | 140.00 |
| 4-Color 72(1945) | 16.50 | 50.00 | 115.00 |
| 1(6/46)-Billy & Bonnie Bee by Frank Thomas | | | |
|  | 16.50 | 50.00 | 115.00 |
| 2,3: 3-Egbert Elephant by Dan Noonan begins | | | |
|  | 8.00 | 24.00 | 56.00 |
| 4-Kelly-a, 16 pgs. | 8.50 | 25.50 | 60.00 |
| 5-10: 7-Little Black Sambo, Black Mumbo & Black Jumbo only app; | | | |
| Christmas-c | 6.50 | 19.50 | 45.00 |
| 11-20 | 5.00 | 15.00 | 35.00 |
| 21-Alice In Wonderland cover/story | 5.00 | 15.00 | 35.00 |
| 22-27,29-39(8/49), 4-Color 262(1/50) | 3.70 | 11.00 | 26.00 |
| 28-Kelly-c | 4.30 | 13.00 | 30.00 |
| 4-Color 306,354,380,452,533 | 3.00 | 9.00 | 21.00 |
| 1(10-12/64-Dell) | 1.15 | 3.50 | 8.00 |
| 2,3(10-12/65), 4(3/66) | .75 | 2.25 | 5.00 |

**RANGERS COMICS** (. . . of Freedom #1-7)
Oct, 1941 - No. 69, Winter, 1952-53
Fiction House Magazines (Flying stories)

| 1-Intro. Ranger Girl & The Rangers of Freedom; ends #7, cover app. | | | |
|---|---|---|---|
| only-#5 | 92.00 | 230.00 | 550.00 |
| 2 | 36.00 | 107.00 | 250.00 |
| 3 | 30.00 | 90.00 | 210.00 |
| 4,5 | 26.00 | 77.00 | 180.00 |
| 6-10: 8-U.S. Rangers begin | 21.50 | 64.00 | 150.00 |
| 11,12-Commando Rangers app. | 19.00 | 57.00 | 135.00 |
| 13-Commando Ranger begins-not same as Commando Rangers | | | |
|  | 19.00 | 57.00 | 135.00 |
| 14-20 | 14.00 | 42.00 | 100.00 |

| | Good | Fine | N-Mint |
|---|---|---|---|
| 21-Intro/origin Firehair (begins) | 18.50 | 56.00 | 130.00 |
| 22-30: 23-Kazanda begins, ends #28. 28-Tiger Man begins (origin). | | | |
| 30-Crusoe Island begins, ends #40 | 13.00 | 40.00 | 90.00 |
| 31-40: 33-Hypodermic panels | 11.50 | 34.00 | 80.00 |
| 41-46 | 8.50 | 25.50 | 60.00 |
| 47-56-"Eisnerish" Dr. Drew by Grandenetti | 9.50 | 28.50 | 65.00 |
| 57-60-Straight Dr. Drew by Grandenetti | 6.50 | 19.50 | 45.00 |
| 61,62,64-66: 64-Suicide Smith begins | 5.70 | 17.00 | 40.00 |
| 63-Used in **POP**, pgs. 85, 99 | 5.70 | 17.00 | 40.00 |
| 67-69: 67-Space Rangers begin, end #69 | 5.70 | 17.00 | 40.00 |

**RAWHIDE KID**
3/55 - No. 16, 9/57; No. 17, 8/60 - No. 151, 5/79
Atlas/Marvel Comics (CnPC No. 1-16/AMI No. 17-30)

| | Good | Fine | N-Mint |
|---|---|---|---|
| 1-Rawhide Kid, his horse Apache & sidekick Randy begin; Wyatt Earp app. | 22.50 | 67.00 | 158.00 |
| 2 | 10.50 | 31.00 | 74.00 |
| 3-5 | 6.00 | 18.00 | 42.00 |
| 6,8-10 | 4.85 | 14.50 | 34.00 |
| 7-Williamson-a, 4 pgs. | 6.00 | 18.00 | 42.00 |
| 11-15 | 3.00 | 9.00 | 21.00 |
| 16-Torres-a | 3.30 | 10.00 | 23.00 |
| 17-Origin by Jack Kirby | 5.30 | 16.00 | 37.00 |
| 18-22,24-30 | 2.40 | 7.20 | 17.00 |
| 23-Origin retold by Jack Kirby | 4.50 | 14.00 | 32.00 |
| 31,32,36-44: 40-Two-Gun Kid x-over. 42-1st Larry Lieber issue | 1.85 | 5.50 | 13.00 |
| 33-35-Davis-a. 35-Intro & death of The Raven | 2.40 | 7.20 | 17.00 |
| 45,46: 45-Origin retold. 46-Toth-a | 2.40 | 7.20 | 17.00 |
| 47-70: 50-Kid Colt x-over. 64-Kid Colt story. 66-Two-Gun Kid story. 67-Kid Colt story | 1.25 | 3.70 | 7.40 |
| 71-86: 79-Williamson-a(r). 86-Origin-r; Williamson-a r-/Ringo Kid #13 (4 pgs.) | .70 | 2.10 | 4.20 |
| 87-99,101-151: 115-Last new story | .45 | 1.30 | 2.60 |
| 100-Origin retold & expanded | .55 | 1.60 | 3.20 |
| Special 1(9/71)-All Kirby/Ayers reprints | .45 | 1.30 | 2.60 |

*Real Screen Comics #3, © DC Comics*

**REAL SCREEN COMICS** (#1 titled Real Screen Funnies; TV Screen
   Cartoons #129-138)
Spring, 1945 - No. 128, May-June, 1959 (#1-40: 52 pgs.)
National Periodical Publications

|  | Good | Fine | N-Mint |
|---|---|---|---|
| 1-The Fox & the Crow, Flippity & Flop, Tito & His Burro begin | | | |
|  | 55.00 | 165.00 | 385.00 |
| 2 | 26.50 | 79.00 | 185.00 |
| 3-5 | 14.00 | 42.00 | 100.00 |
| 6-10 (2-3/47) | 10.00 | 30.00 | 70.00 |
| 11-20 (10-11/48): 13-The Crow x-over in Flippity & Flop | | | |
|  | 8.00 | 24.00 | 55.00 |
| 21-30 (6-7/50) | 5.50 | 16.50 | 38.00 |
| 31-50 | 3.70 | 11.00 | 26.00 |
| 51-99 | 2.65 | 8.00 | 18.00 |

| | Good | Fine | N-Mint |
|---|---|---|---|
| 100 | 3.50 | 10.50 | 24.00 |
| 101-128 | 2.00 | 6.00 | 14.00 |

**REAL WESTERN HERO** (Formerly Wow #1-69; becomes Western Hero
    #76 on)
No. 70, Sept, 1948 - No. 75, Feb, 1949 (All 52 pgs.)
Fawcett Publications

70(#1)-Tom Mix, Monte Hale, Hopalong Cassidy, Young Falcon begin
| | 18.50 | 56.00 | 130.00 |
|---|---|---|---|

71-Gabby Hayes begins; Captain Tootsie by Beck
| | 11.50 | 34.00 | 80.00 |
|---|---|---|---|

72-75: 72-Captain Tootsie by Beck. 75-Big Bow and Little Arrow app.
| | 11.50 | 34.00 | 80.00 |
|---|---|---|---|

**RED MASK** (Formerly Tim Holt)
No. 42, 6-7/1954 - No. 53, 5/56; No. 54, 9/57
Magazine Enterprises No. 42-53/Sussex No. 54 (M.E. on-c)

42-Ghost Rider by Ayers continues, ends #50; Black Phantom continues;
    3-D effect c/stories begin       13.00   40.00   90.00
43-3-D effect-c/stories              11.00   32.00   75.00
44-50: 3-D effect stories only. 50-Last Ghost Rider
                                     10.00   30.00   70.00
51-The Presto Kid begins by Ayers (1st app.); Presto Kid-c begins, ends
    #54; last 3-D effect story       10.00   30.00   70.00
52-Origin The Presto Kid            10.00   30.00   70.00
53,54-Last Black Phantom             7.00   21.00   50.00

**RED RAVEN COMICS** (Human Torch #2 on)
August, 1940    (Also see Sub-Mariner #26, 2nd series)
Timely Comics

1-Origin Red Raven; Comet Pierce & Mercury by Kirby, The Human Top
    & The Eternal Brain; intro. Magar, the Mystic & only app.; Kirby-c
                                    457.00  1150.00  3200.00
            *(Prices vary widely on this book)*

**RED RYDER COMICS** (Hi Spot #2) (Movies, radio) (Also see Crackajack
    Funnies)
9/40; No. 3, 8/41 - No. 5, 12/41; No. 6, 4/42 - No. 151, 4-6/57
Hawley Publ. No. 1-5/Dell Publishing Co. (K.K.) No. 6 on

|  | Good | Fine | N-Mint |
|---|---|---|---|
| 1-Red Ryder, his horse Thunder, Little Beaver & his horse Papoose strip reprints begin by Fred Harman; 1st meeting of Red & Little Beaver; Harman line-drawn-c #1-85 | 84.00 | 253.00 | 590.00 |
| 3-(Scarce)-Alley Oop, King of the Royal Mtd., Capt. Easy, Freckles & His Friends, Myra North & Dan Dunn strip-r begin | 53.00 | 160.00 | 370.00 |
| 4,5 | 28.50 | 86.00 | 200.00 |
| 6-1st Dell issue | 28.50 | 86.00 | 200.00 |
| 7-10 | 21.50 | 64.00 | 150.00 |
| 11-20 | 16.00 | 48.00 | 110.00 |
| 21-32-Last Alley Oop, Dan Dunn, Capt. Easy, Freckles | 10.00 | 30.00 | 70.00 |
| 33-40 (52 pgs.) | 6.50 | 19.50 | 45.00 |
| 41 (52 pgs.)-Rocky Lane photo back-c; photo back-c begin, end #57 | 7.00 | 21.00 | 50.00 |
| 42-46 (52 pgs.): 46-Last Red Ryder strip-r | 5.70 | 17.00 | 40.00 |
| 47-53 (52 pgs.): 47-New stories on Red Ryder begin | 4.30 | 13.00 | 30.00 |
| 54-57 (36 pgs.) | 3.70 | 11.00 | 26.00 |
| 58-73 (36 pgs.): 73-Last King of the Royal Mtd. strip-r by Jim Gary | 3.50 | 10.50 | 24.00 |
| 74-85,93 (52 pgs.)-Harman line-drawn-c | 3.70 | 11.00 | 26.00 |
| 86-92 (52 pgs.)-Harman painted-c | 3.70 | 11.00 | 26.00 |
| 94-96 (36 pgs.)-Harman painted-c | 2.65 | 8.00 | 18.00 |
| 97,98,107,108 (36 pgs.)-Harman line-drawn-c | 2.65 | 8.00 | 18.00 |
| 99,101-106 (36 pgs.)-Jim Bannon Photo-c | 2.65 | 8.00 | 18.00 |
| 100 (36 pgs.)-Bannon photo-c | 3.00 | 9.00 | 21.00 |
| 109-118 (52 pgs.)-Harman line-drawn-c | 2.00 | 6.00 | 14.00 |
| 119-129 (52 pgs.): 119-Painted-c begin, not by Harman, end #151 | 1.70 | 5.00 | 12.00 |
| 130-144 (36 pgs., #130-on) | 1.50 | 4.50 | 10.00 |
| 145-148: 145-Title change to Red Ryder Ranch Magazine with photos | 1.30 | 4.00 | 9.00 |

|                                  | Good  | Fine  | N-Mint |
|----------------------------------|-------|-------|--------|
| 149-151: 149-Title changed to Red Ryder Ranch Comics | | | |
|                                  | 1.30  | 4.00  | 9.00   |
| 4-Color 916 (7/58)               | 1.60  | 4.80  | 11.00  |

**RED SONJA** (Also see Conan #23)
1/77 - No. 15, 5/79; V1#1, 2/83 - V2#2, 3/83; V3#1, 8/83 - V3#4, 2/84; V3#5,
    1/85 - V3#13, 1986
Marvel Comics Group

|                                  | Good  | Fine  | N-Mint |
|----------------------------------|-------|-------|--------|
| 1-Created by Robert E. Howard    | .50   | 1.50  | 3.00   |
| 2-5                              | .35   | 1.00  | 2.00   |
| 6-15, V1#1,2                     |       | 50    | 1.00   |
| V3#1-4 ($1.00, 52 pgs.)          |       | .60   | 1.20   |
| 5-13 (65-75 cents)               |       | .50   | 1.00   |

**REX ALLEN COMICS** (Movie star)
No. 316, Feb, 1951 - No. 31, Dec-Feb, 1958-59 (All-photo-c)
Dell Publishing Co.

|                                  | Good  | Fine  | N-Mint |
|----------------------------------|-------|-------|--------|
| 4-Color 316(#1)(52 pgs.)-Rex Allen & his horse Koko begin; Marsh-a | | | |
|                                  | 11.50 | 34.00 | 80.00  |
| 2 (9-11/51, 36 pgs.)             | 5.70  | 17.00 | 40.00  |
| 3-10                             | 4.65  | 14.00 | 32.00  |
| 11-20                            | 3.70  | 11.00 | 26.00  |
| 21-23,25-31                      | 3.50  | 10.50 | 24.00  |
| 24-Toth-a                        | 4.30  | 13.00 | 30.00  |

**REX HART** (Whip Wilson #9 on)
No. 6, Aug, 1949 - No. 8, Feb, 1950 (All photo-c)
Timely/Marvel Comics (USA)

|                                  | Good  | Fine  | N-Mint |
|----------------------------------|-------|-------|--------|
| 6-Rex Hart & his horse Warrior begin; Black Rider app; Captain Tootsie | | | |
| by Beck                          | 9.30  | 28.00 | 65.00  |
| 7,8: 18 pg. Thriller in each. 8-Blaze the Wonder Collie app. in text | | | |
|                                  | 7.00  | 21.00 | 50.00  |

**RICHIE RICH** (. . . the Poor Little Rich Boy)
Nov, 1960 - No. 218, Oct, 1982; No. 219, Oct, 1986 - Present
Harvey Publications

| | Good | Fine | N-Mint |
|---|---|---|---|
| 1-(See Little Dot for 1st app.) | 90.00 | 250.00 | 440.00 |
| 2 | 40.00 | 100.00 | 180.00 |
| 3-5 | 20.00 | 60.00 | 120.00 |
| 6-10: 8-Christmas-c | 12.50 | 37.50 | 75.00 |
| 11-20 | 5.35 | 16.00 | 32.00 |
| 21-40 | 3.00 | 9.00 | 18.00 |
| 41-60 | 2.00 | 6.00 | 12.00 |
| 61-80: 65-1st app. Dollar the Dog | 1.20 | 3.50 | 7.00 |
| 81-100 | .70 | 2.00 | 4.00 |
| 101-111,117-120 | .50 | 1.50 | 3.00 |
| 112-116: All 52 pg. Giants | .60 | 1.80 | 3.60 |
| 121-140 | .40 | 1.25 | 2.50 |
| 141-160: 145-Infinity-c | .35 | 1.00 | 2.00 |
| 161-180 | .25 | .75 | 1.50 |
| 181-254 | | .50 | 1.00 |

**RIFLEMAN, THE** (TV)
No. 1009, 7-9/59 - No. 12, 7-9/62; No. 13, 11/62 - No. 20, 10/64
Dell Publ. Co./Gold Key No. 13 on

| | | | |
|---|---|---|---|
| 4-Color 1009 (#1) | 8.50 | 25.50 | 60.00 |
| 2 (1-3/60)-All have Chuck Conners photo-c | 6.50 | 19.50 | 45.00 |
| 3-Toth-a, 4 pgs. | 7.00 | 21.00 | 50.00 |
| 4,5,7-10 | 5.00 | 15.00 | 35.00 |
| 6-Toth-a, 4 pgs. | 5.70 | 17.00 | 40.00 |
| 11-20 | 4.30 | 13.00 | 30.00 |

**RINGO KID WESTERN, THE** (See Wild Western)
Aug, 1954 - No. 21, Sept, 1957
Atlas Comics (HPC)/Marvel Comics

| | | | |
|---|---|---|---|
| 1-Origin; The Ringo Kid & his horse Arab begin | | | |
| | 9.30 | 28.00 | 65.00 |
| 2-Black Rider app.; origin Arab | 4.50 | 14.00 | 32.00 |
| 3-5 | 2.85 | 8.50 | 20.00 |
| 6-8-Severin-a(3) each | 3.70 | 11.00 | 26.00 |
| 9,11,14-21 | 2.00 | 6.00 | 14.00 |
| 10,13-Williamson-a, 4 pgs. | 3.70 | 11.00 | 26.00 |
| 12-Orlando-a, 4 pgs. | 2.30 | 7.00 | 16.00 |

**RIN TIN TIN** (TV) ( . . . & Rusty #21 on)
Nov, 1952 - No. 38, May-July, 1961; Nov, 1963 (All Photo-c)
Dell Publishing Co./Gold Key

|  | Good | Fine | N-Mint |
|---|---|---|---|
| 4-Color 434 (#1) | 5.00 | 15.00 | 35.00 |
| 4-Color 476,523 | 3.70 | 11.00 | 26.00 |
| 4(3-5/54)-10 | 3.00 | 9.00 | 21.00 |
| 11-20 | 2.30 | 7.00 | 16.00 |
| 21-38 | 2.00 | 6.00 | 14.00 |
| . . . & Rusty 1 (11/63-Gold Key) | 2.00 | 6.00 | 14.00 |

*Rip Hunter Time Master #17, © DC Comics*

**RIP HUNTER TIME MASTER** (See Showcase #20, 21, 25, 26)
Mar-Apr, 1961 - No. 29, Nov-Dec, 1965
National Periodical Publications

|  | Good | Fine | N-Mint |
|---|---|---|---|
| 1 | 20.00 | 60.00 | 140.00 |
| 2 | 10.30 | 31.00 | 72.00 |
| 3-5: 5-Last 10 cent issue | 6.30 | 19.00 | 44.00 |
| 6,7-Toth-a in each | 5.50 | 16.50 | 39.00 |
| 8-15 | 4.00 | 12.00 | 28.00 |
| 16-29: 29-G. Kane-c | 2.40 | 7.20 | 17.00 |

**ROBOTECH MASTERS** (TV)
July, 1985 - No. 23, Apr, 1988 ($1.50, color)
Comico

|  |  |  |  |
|---|---|---|---|
| 1 | .60 | 1.75 | 3.50 |
| 2,3 | .40 | 1.25 | 2.50 |
| 4-23 (#23, $1.75) | .35 | 1.00 | 2.00 |

**ROBOTECH: THE MACROSS SAGA** (TV) (Formerly Macross)
No. 2, Feb, 1985 - No. 36, Feb, 1989 ($1.50, color)
Comico

|  |  |  |  |
|---|---|---|---|
| 2 | .85 | 2.50 | 5.00 |
| 3-5 | .50 | 1.50 | 3.00 |
| 6,7 | .40 | 1.25 | 2.50 |
| 8-25: 12,17-Ken Steacy painted-c | .35 | 1.00 | 2.00 |
| 26-36: 26-34-$1.75. 35,36-$1.95-c | .30 | .90 | 1.75 |

**ROBOTECH: THE NEW GENERATION** (TV)
July, 1985 - No. 25, July, 1988 ($1.50, color)
Comico

|  |  |  |  |
|---|---|---|---|
| 1 | .50 | 1.50 | 3.00 |
| 2-4 | .40 | 1.25 | 2.50 |
| 5-21: 9,13-Ken Steacy painted-c | .35 | 1.00 | 2.00 |
| 22-25 ($1.75) | .35 | 1.00 | 2.00 |

**ROCKY AND HIS FIENDISH FRIENDS** (TV) (Bullwinkle)
Oct, 1962 - No. 5, Sept, 1963 (Jay Ward)
Gold Key

|  |  |  |  |
|---|---|---|---|
| 1 (84 pgs., 25 cents) | 9.50 | 28.50 | 76.00 |

| | Good | Fine | N-Mint |
|---|---|---|---|
| 2,3 (84 pgs., 25 cents) | 7.50 | 22.50 | 60.00 |
| 4,5 (Regular size, 12 cents) | 5.00 | 15.00 | 35.00 |

## ROCKY LANE WESTERN (Movie star, TV)
May, 1949 - No. 87, Nov, 1959
Fawcett Publications/Charlton No. 56 on

| | Good | Fine | N-Mint |
|---|---|---|---|
| 1 (36 pgs.)-Rocky, his stallion Black Jack, & Slim Pickens begin; photo-c begin, end #57; photo back-c | 44.00 | 133.00 | 310.00 |
| 2 (36 pgs.)-Last photo back-c | 16.50 | 50.00 | 115.00 |
| 3-5 (52 pgs.): 4-Captain Tootsie by Beck | 13.00 | 40.00 | 90.00 |
| 6,10 (36 pgs.) | 10.00 | 30.00 | 70.00 |
| 7-9 (52 pgs.) | 11.50 | 34.00 | 80.00 |
| 11-13,15-17 (52 pgs.): 15-Black Jack's Hitching Post begins, ends #25 | 8.50 | 25.50 | 60.00 |
| 14,18 (36 pgs.) | 7.00 | 21.00 | 50.00 |
| 19-21,23,24 (52 pgs.): 20-Last Slim Pickens. 21-Dee Dickens begins, ends #55,57,65-68 | 7.00 | 21.00 | 50.00 |
| 22,25-28,30 (36 pgs. begin) | 6.50 | 19.50 | 45.00 |
| 29-Classic complete novel "The Land of Missing Men,"-hidden land of ancient temple ruins (r-in #65) | 8.00 | 24.00 | 56.00 |
| 31-40 | 6.00 | 18.00 | 42.00 |
| 41-54 | 5.00 | 15.00 | 35.00 |
| 55-Last Fawcett issue (1/54) | 5.50 | 16.50 | 38.00 |
| 56-1st Charlton issue (2/54)-Photo-c | 6.50 | 19.50 | 45.00 |
| 57,60-Photo-c | 4.30 | 13.00 | 30.00 |
| 58,59,61-64: 59-61-Young Falcon app. 64-Slim Pickens app. | 3.50 | 10.50 | 24.00 |
| 65-R-/#29, "The Land of Missing Men" | 3.70 | 11.00 | 26.00 |
| 66-68: Reprints #30,31,32 | 2.65 | 8.00 | 18.00 |
| 69-78,80-86 | 2.65 | 8.00 | 18.00 |
| 79-Giant Edition, 68 pgs. | 3.70 | 11.00 | 26.00 |
| 87-Last issue | 3.50 | 10.50 | 24.00 |

## ROD CAMERON WESTERN (Movie star)
Feb, 1950 - No. 20, April, 1953
Fawcett Publications

| | Good | Fine | N-Mint |
|---|---|---|---|
| 1-Rod Cameron, his horse War Paint, & Sam The Sheriff begin; photo front/back-c begin | 28.50 | 86.00 | 200.00 |

| | Good | Fine | N-Mint |
|---|---|---|---|
| 2 | 14.00 | 42.00 | 100.00 |
| 3-Novel length story "The Mystery of the Seven Cities of Cibola" | | | |
| | 12.00 | 36.00 | 84.00 |
| 4-10: 9-Last photo back-c | 10.00 | 30.00 | 70.00 |
| 11-19 | 8.50 | 25.50 | 60.00 |
| 20-Last issue & photo-c | 9.30 | 28.00 | 65.00 |

**ROMANTIC STORY**
11/49 - #22, Sum, 1953; #23, 5/54 - #27, 12/54; #28, 8/55 - #130, 11/73
Fawcett/Charlton Comics No. 23 on

| | Good | Fine | N-Mint |
|---|---|---|---|
| 1-Photo-c begin, end #22,24 | 5.00 | 15.00 | 35.00 |
| 2 | 2.30 | 7.00 | 16.00 |
| 3-5 | 2.00 | 6.00 | 14.00 |
| 6-14 | 1.70 | 5.00 | 12.00 |
| 15-Evans-a | 2.65 | 8.00 | 18.00 |
| 16-22(Sum, '53; last Fawcett issue). 21-Toth-a? | | | |
| | 1.30 | 4.00 | 9.00 |
| 23-39: 26,29-Wood swipes | 1.30 | 4.00 | 9.00 |
| 40-(100 pgs.) | 3.50 | 10.50 | 24.00 |
| 41-50 | .85 | 2.60 | 6.00 |
| 51-56,58-80 | .45 | 1.35 | 3.00 |
| 57-Hypo needle story | .70 | 2.00 | 4.00 |
| 81-100 | | .60 | 1.20 |
| 101-130 | | .40 | .80 |

**RONIN**
July, 1983 - No. 6, Apr, 1984 ($2.50, mini-series, 52 pgs.)
DC Comics

| | Good | Fine | N-Mint |
|---|---|---|---|
| 1-Miller script, c/a in all | 1.00 | 3.00 | 6.00 |
| 2 | .85 | 2.50 | 5.00 |
| 3-5 | .70 | 2.00 | 4.00 |
| 6-Scarcer | 1.35 | 4.00 | 8.00 |

**ROOTS OF THE SWAMPTHING**
July, 1986 - No. 5, Nov, 1986 ($2.00, Baxter paper, 52 pgs.)
DC Comics

|  | Good | Fine | N-Mint |
|---|---|---|---|
| 1-5: R/Swamp Thing #1-10 by Wrightson & House of Myst.-r; 1-new Wrightson-c(2-5-r). 4-Batman-c/story-r/S.T. #7 | | | |
|  | .40 | 1.25 | 2.50 |

**ROY ROGERS COMICS** (. . . & Trigger #92(8/55)-on) (Roy starred in
Republic movies, radio & TV) (Singing cowboy) (See Dale Evans)
Jan, 1948 - No. 145, Sept-Oct, 1961 (#1-19: 36 pgs.)
Dell Publishing Co.

| | Good | Fine | N-Mint |
|---|---|---|---|
| 1-Roy, his horse Trigger, & Chuck Wagon Charley's Tales begin; photo-c begin, end #145 | 39.00 | 118.00 | 275.00 |
| 2 | 19.00 | 58.00 | 135.00 |
| 3-5 | 16.00 | 48.00 | 110.00 |
| 6-10 | 11.50 | 34.00 | 80.00 |
| 11-19: 19-. . . Charley's Tales ends | 8.00 | 24.00 | 55.00 |
| 20 (52 pgs.)-Trigger feature begins, ends #46 | 8.00 | 24.00 | 55.00 |
| 21-30 (52 pgs.) | 6.50 | 19.50 | 45.00 |
| 31-46 (52 pgs.): 37-Xmas-c | 5.00 | 15.00 | 35.00 |
| 47-56 (36 pgs.): 47-Chuck Wagon Charley's Tales returns, ends #133 | | | |
| 49-Xmas-c. 55-Last photo back-c | 4.00 | 12.00 | 28.00 |
| 57 (52 pgs.)-Heroin drug propaganda story | 4.60 | 14.00 | 32.00 |
| 58-70 (52 pgs.): 61-Xmas-c | 3.50 | 10.50 | 24.00 |
| 71-80 (52 pgs.): 73-Xmas-c | 2.85 | 8.50 | 20.00 |
| 81-91 (36 pgs. #81-on): 85-Xmas-c | 2.65 | 8.00 | 18.00 |
| 92-99,101-110,112-118: 92-Title changed to Roy Rogers and Trigger (8/55) | | | |
|  | 2.65 | 8.00 | 18.00 |
| 100-Trigger feature returns, ends #133? | 4.00 | 12.00 | 28.00 |
| 111,119-124-Toth-a | 4.35 | 13.00 | 30.00 |
| 125-131 | 3.00 | 9.00 | 21.00 |
| 132-144-Manning-a. 144-Dale Evans feat. | 3.50 | 10.50 | 24.00 |
| 145-Last issue | 4.00 | 12.00 | 28.00 |

**RULAH JUNGLE GODDESS** (Formerly Zoot; see All Top Comics)
No. 17, Aug, 1948 - No. 27, June, 1949
Fox Features Syndicate

|  | Good | Fine | N-Mint |
|---|---|---|---|
| 17 | 30.00 | 90.00 | 210.00 |
| 18-Classic girl-fight interior splash | 26.00 | 79.00 | 185.00 |
| 19,20 | 23.50 | 70.00 | 165.00 |
| 21-Used in **SOTI**, pg. 388,389 | 26.00 | 78.00 | 180.00 |
| 22-Used in **SOTI**, pg. 22,23 | 23.50 | 70.00 | 165.00 |
| 23-27 | 17.00 | 51.00 | 120.00 |

# S

## SAD SACK COMICS
Sept, 1949 - No. 287, Oct, 1982
Harvey Publications

|  | Good | Fine | N-Mint |
|---|---|---|---|
| 1-Infinity-c; Little Dot begins (1st app.); civilian issues begin, end #21 | | | |
|  | 20.00 | 60.00 | 140.00 |
| 2-Flying Fool by Powell | 9.50 | 28.50 | 65.00 |
| 3 | 5.70 | 17.00 | 40.00 |
| 4-10 | 3.50 | 10.50 | 24.00 |
| 11-21 | 2.35 | 7.00 | 16.00 |
| 22-("Back In The Army Again" on covers #22-36). "The Specialist" story about Sad Sack's return to Army | 1.35 | 4.00 | 8.00 |
| 23-50 | .85 | 2.50 | 5.00 |
| 51-100 | .50 | 1.50 | 3.00 |
| 101-150 | .25 | .75 | 1.50 |
| 151-222 |  | .40 | .80 |
| 223-228 (25 cent Giants, 52 pgs.) | .25 | .75 | 1.50 |
| 229-287: 286,287 had limited distribution |  | .40 | .80 |
| 3-D 1 (1/54-titled "Harvey 3-D Hits") | 10.00 | 30.00 | 70.00 |

## SAGA OF RA'S AL GHUL, THE (See Batman #232)
Jan, 1988 - No. 4, Apr, 1988 ($2.50, color, mini-series)
DC Comics

|  | Good | Fine | N-Mint |
|---|---|---|---|
| 1-Batman reprints; Neal Adams-a(r) in all | .75 | 2.25 | 4.50 |
| 2-4: 4-New N. Adams/Nebres-c | .65 | 1.90 | 3.75 |

## SAGA OF SWAMP THING, THE (Swamp Thing #39-41,46 on)
May, 1982 - Present (Later issues for mature readers; #86 on: $1.50)
DC Comics

|  | Good | Fine | N-Mint |
|---|---|---|---|
| 1-Origin retold; Phantom Stranger series begins; ends #13; movie adaptation; Yeates-c/a begins | .25 | .75 | 1.50 |
| 2-15: 2-Photo-c from movie |  | .50 | 1.00 |
| 16-19: Bissette-a. 13-Last Yeates-a | .35 | 1.00 | 2.00 |
| 20-1st Alan Moore issue | 3.15 | 9.50 | 22.00 |
| 21-New origin | 2.85 | 8.50 | 20.00 |

| | Good | Fine | N-Mint |
|---|---|---|---|
| 22-25: 24-JLA x-over; Last Yeates-c | 1.30 | 4.00 | 8.00 |
| 26-30 | .90 | 2.75 | 5.50 |
| 31-33 | .50 | 1.50 | 3.00 |
| 34 | 1.50 | 4.50 | 9.00 |
| 35,36 | .35 | 1.10 | 2.25 |
| 37-1st app. John Constantine, apps. thru #40 | 1.25 | 3.75 | 7.50 |
| 38-40: John Constantine app. | .70 | 2.00 | 4.00 |
| 41-45: 44-Batman cameo | .30 | .90 | 1.75 |
| 46-51: 46-Crisis x-over; Batman cameo & John Constantine app. 50-($1.25, 52 pgs.)-Deadman, Dr. Fate, Demon | .25 | .75 | 1.50 |
| 52: Two part Arkham Asylum-c/story begins; Joker-c/cameo | .50 | 1.50 | 3.00 |
| 53-($1.25, 52 pgs.)-Batman-c/story (Arkham) | .70 | 2.00 | 4.00 |
| 54-64: 58-Spectre preview. 64-Last Moore issue | | .60 | 1.25 |
| 65,66: Direct only begins | | .50 | 1.00 |
| 67-99: 79-Superman app. 85-Jonah Hex app. | .25 | .75 | 1.50 |
| 100 ($2.50, 52 pgs.) | .40 | 1.25 | 2.50 |
| Annual 1(11/82)-Movie Adaptation | | .50 | 1.00 |
| Annual 2(1/85)-Alan Moore scripts, Bissette-a(p) | .50 | 1.50 | 3.00 |
| Annual 3(10/87, $2.00) | .35 | 1.00 | 2.00 |
| Annual 4(10/88)-Batman-c/story | .50 | 1.50 | 3.00 |
| Annual 5('89, $2.95, 68 pgs.)-Batman cameo; re-intro Brother Power, 1st app. since 1968 | .50 | 1.50 | 3.00 |

**SAINT, THE** (Also see Silver Streak #18)
Aug, 1947 - No. 12, Mar, 1952
Avon Periodicals

| | Good | Fine | N-Mint |
|---|---|---|---|
| 1-Kamen bondage-c/a | 28.00 | 84.00 | 195.00 |
| 2 | 15.00 | 45.00 | 105.00 |
| 3,4: 4-Lingerie panels | 12.00 | 36.00 | 84.00 |
| 5-Spanking panel | 18.00 | 54.00 | 125.00 |
| 6-Miss Fury app., 14 pgs. | 20.00 | 60.00 | 140.00 |
| 7-c-/Avon paperback #118 | 11.00 | 32.00 | 76.00 |
| 8,9(12/50): Saint strip-r in #8-12; 9-Kinstler-c | 9.00 | 27.00 | 62.00 |
| 10-Wood-a, 1 pg; c-/Avon paperback #289 | 9.00 | 27.00 | 62.00 |

|                                  | Good  | Fine   | N-Mint |
|----------------------------------|-------|--------|--------|
| 11                               | 6.50  | 19.50  | 45.00  |
| 12-c-/Avon paperback #123        | 8.50  | 25.50  | 60.00  |

**SAMSON** (See Fantastic Comics)
Fall, 1940 - No. 6, Sept, 1941
Fox Features Syndicate

| 1-Powell-a, signed 'Rensie'; Wing Turner by Tuska app; Fine-c? | | | |
|----------------------------------|-------|--------|--------|
|                                  | 59.00 | 178.00 | 415.00 |
| 2-Dr. Fung by Powell; Fine-c?    | 28.00 | 84.00  | 195.00 |
| 3-Navy Jones app.; Simon-c       | 23.00 | 70.00  | 160.00 |
| 4-Yarko the Great, Master Magician by Eisner begins; Fine-c? | | | |
|                                  | 18.50 | 56.00  | 130.00 |
| 5,6: 6-Origin The Topper         | 18.50 | 56.00  | 130.00 |

**SANDMAN, THE** (See Adventure Comics #40 & World's Finest #3)
Winter, 1974; No. 2, Apr-May, 1975 - No. 6, Dec-Jan, 1975-76
DC Comics

|                                  | Good  | Fine   | N-Mint |
|----------------------------------|-------|--------|--------|
| 1-Kirby-a(p) in 1,4-6; c-1-5     | .70   | 2.00   | 4.00   |
| 2-6: 6-Kirby/Wood-c/a            | .40   | 1.25   | 2.50   |

**SANDMAN**
Jan, 1989 - Present ($1.50, color, mature readers)
DC Comics

|                                  | Good  | Fine   | N-Mint |
|----------------------------------|-------|--------|--------|
| 1 ($2.00, 52 pgs.)               | 1.70  | 5.00   | 10.00  |
| 2                                | 1.15  | 3.50   | 7.00   |
| 3-5: 3-John Constantine app.     | 1.00  | 3.00   | 6.00   |
| 6-8: 8-Regular edition; no indicia | .75 | 2.25   | 4.50   |
| 8-Limited edition (only 600+ copies); has Karen Berger editorial | | | |
|                                  | 6.70  | 20.00  | 40.00  |
| 9-14: 14-Double size ($2.50, 52 pgs.) | .50 | 1.50 | 3.00   |
| 15-22                            | .25   | .75    | 1.50   |

**SCOOBY DOO** (. . . Where are you? #1-16,26)
March, 1970 - No. 30, Feb, 1975 (Hanna-Barbera)
Gold Key

|                                  | Good  | Fine   | N-Mint |
|----------------------------------|-------|--------|--------|
| 1                                | 2.85  | 8.50   | 20.00  |

|                                    | Good  | Fine   | N-Mint |
|------------------------------------|-------|--------|--------|
| 2-5                                | 1.50  | 4.50   | 10.00  |
| 6-10                               | 1.00  | 3.00   | 7.00   |
| 11-20: 11-Tufts-a                  | .70   | 2.00   | 5.00   |
| 21-30                              | .50   | 1.50   | 3.00   |

### SCOOBY DOO (TV)
April, 1975 - No. 11, Dec, 1976 (Hanna Barbera)
Charlton Comics

|        |       |      |      |
|--------|-------|------|------|
| 1      | 1.15  | 3.50 | 8.00 |
| 2-5    | .70   | 2.00 | 4.00 |
| 6-11   | .50   | 1.50 | 3.00 |

### SCRIBBLY (See All-American Comics, The Funnies & Popular)
8-9/48 - No. 13, 8-9/50; No. 14, 10-11/51 - No. 15, 12-1/51-52
National Periodical Publications

|                                      | Good  | Fine   | N-Mint |
|--------------------------------------|-------|--------|--------|
| 1-Sheldon Mayer-a in all; 52pgs. begin | 48.00 | 144.00 | 335.00 |
| 2                                    | 28.00 | 85.00  | 200.00 |
| 3-5                                  | 24.00 | 73.00  | 170.00 |
| 6-10                                 | 17.00 | 51.00  | 120.00 |
| 11-15: 13-Last 52 pgs.               | 13.00 | 40.00  | 90.00  |

### SEA DEVILS (See Showcase #27-29)
Sept-Oct, 1961 - No. 35, May-June, 1967
National Periodical Publications

|                                             | Good  | Fine  | N-Mint |
|---------------------------------------------|-------|-------|--------|
| 1                                           | 19.00 | 57.00 | 135.00 |
| 2-Last 10 cent issue                        | 7.85  | 23.50 | 55.00  |
| 3-5: 3-Begin 12 cent issues thru #35        | 5.00  | 15.00 | 35.00  |
| 6-10                                        | 2.85  | 8.50  | 20.00  |
| 11,12,14-20                                 | 1.85  | 5.50  | 13.00  |
| 13-Kubert, Colan-a                          | 2.15  | 6.50  | 15.00  |
| 21,23-35                                    | 1.50  | 4.50  | 10.00  |
| 22-Intro. International Sea Devils; origin & 1st app. Capt. X & Man Fish |       |       |        |
|                                             | 1.50  | 4.50  | 10.00  |

### SECRET ORIGINS (See 80 Page Giant #8)
Aug-Oct, 1961 (Annual) (Reprints)
National Periodical Publications

|  | Good | Fine | N-Mint |
|---|---|---|---|
| 1('61)-Origin Adam Strange (Showcase #17), Green Lantern (G.L. #1), Challs (partial/Showcase #6, 6 pgs. Kirby-a). J'onn J'onzz (Det. #225), The Flash (Showcase #4). Green Arrow (1pg. text). Superman-Batman team (W. Finest #94). Wonder Woman (W. Woman #105) | | | |
|  | 18.00 | 54.00 | 125.00 |

## SECRET ORIGINS
April, 1986 - No. 50, Aug, 1990 (All origins) (52 pgs. #6 on)
DC Comics

| | | | |
|---|---|---|---|
| 1-Origin Superman | .60 | 1.75 | 3.50 |
| 2-Blue Beetle | .50 | 1.50 | 3.00 |
| 3-5 | .40 | 1.25 | 2.50 |
| 6-G.A. Batman | .70 | 2.00 | 4.00 |
| 7-10: 7-Green Lantern(Guy Gardner) | .40 | 1.15 | 2.25 |
| 11,12,14-26: 20-Batgirl/G.A. Dr. Mid-Nite | .35 | 1.00 | 2.00 |
| 13-Origin Nightwing; Johnny Thunder app. | .70 | 2.00 | 4.00 |
| 27-38,40-44: 33-Art Adams part inks | .30 | .90 | 1.80 |
| 39-Animal Man-c/story | .40 | 1.25 | 2.50 |
| 45-49: 46-JLA/LSH/New Titans. 47-LSH | .25 | .75 | 1.50 |
| 50 ($3.95, 100 pgs.) | .70 | 2.00 | 4.00 |
| Annual 1 (8/87)-Capt. Comet/Doom Patrol | .35 | 1.00 | 2.00 |
| Annual 2 ('88, $2.00)-Origin Flash II & Flash III | .35 | 1.00 | 2.00 |
| Annual 3 ('89, $2.95, 84 pgs.)-Teen Titans | .50 | 1.50 | 2.95 |
| Special 1 (10/89, $2.00)-Batman villains: Penguin, Riddler, & Two-Face; Bolland-c | .40 | 1.25 | 2.50 |

## SENSATIONAL SHE-HULK, THE
May, 1989 - Present ($1.50, color, deluxe format)
Marvel Comics

| | | | |
|---|---|---|---|
| 1-Byrne-c/a(p)/scripts begin, end #8 | .35 | 1.00 | 2.00 |
| 2-8: 4-Reintro G.A. Blonde Phantom | .30 | .90 | 1.75 |
| 9-22: 14,15-Howard the Duck app. | .25 | .75 | 1.50 |

*Sensation Comics #81, © DC Comics*

**SENSATION COMICS**
Jan, 1942 - No. 109, May-June, 1952
National Periodical Publ./All-American

| | Good | Fine | N-Mint |
|---|---|---|---|
| 1-Origin Mr. Terrific, Wildcat, The Gay Ghost, & Little Boy Blue; Wonder Woman (cont'd from All Star #8), The Black Pirate begin; intro. Justice & Fair Play Club | 383.00 | 960.00 | 2300.00 |
| 2 | 135.00 | 407.00 | 950.00 |
| 3-W. Woman gets secretary's job | 80.00 | 240.00 | 560.00 |
| 4-1st app. Stretch Skinner in Wildcat | 71.00 | 215.00 | 500.00 |
| 5-Intro. Justin, Black Pirate's son | 54.00 | 160.00 | 375.00 |
| 6-Origin/1st app. Wonder Woman's magic lasso | 46.00 | 137.00 | 320.00 |
| 7-10 | 43.00 | 130.00 | 300.00 |
| 11-20: 13-Hitler, Tojo, Mussolini-c | 37.00 | 110.00 | 260.00 |
| 21-30 | 27.00 | 81.00 | 190.00 |
| 31-33 | 21.00 | 62.00 | 145.00 |

|  | Good | Fine | N-Mint |
|---|---|---|---|
| 34-Sargon, the Sorcerer begins, ends #36; begins again #52 | | | |
|  | 21.00 | 62.00 | 145.00 |
| 35-40: 38-Xmas-c | 17.00 | 51.00 | 120.00 |
| 41-50: 43-The Whip app. | 14.00 | 42.00 | 100.00 |
| 51-60: 51-Last Black Pirate. 56,57-Sargon by Kubert | | | |
|  | 13.00 | 40.00 | 90.00 |
| 61-80: 63-Last Mr. Terrific. 65,66-Wildcat by Kubert. 68-Origin Huntress | | | |
|  | 13.00 | 40.00 | 90.00 |
| 81-Used in **SOTI**, pg. 33,34; Krigstein-a | 15.00 | 45.00 | 105.00 |
| 82-90: 83-Last Sargon. 86-The Atom app. 90-Last Wildcat | | | |
|  | 11.00 | 32.00 | 75.00 |
| 91-Streak begins by Alex Toth | 11.00 | 32.00 | 75.00 |
| 92,93: 92-Toth-a, 2 pgs. | 10.00 | 30.00 | 70.00 |
| 94-1st all girl issue | 12.00 | 36.00 | 84.00 |
| 95-99,101-106: Wonder Woman ends. 99-1st app. Astra, Girl of the Future, | | | |
| ends 106. 105-Last 52 pgs. | 12.00 | 36.00 | 84.00 |
| 100 | 16.00 | 48.00 | 110.00 |
| 107-(Scarce)-1st mystery issue; Toth-a | 24.00 | 70.00 | 165.00 |
| 108-(Scarce)-Johnny Peril by Toth(p) | 21.00 | 62.00 | 145.00 |
| 109-(Scarce)-Johnny Peril by Toth(p) | 24.00 | 70.00 | 165.00 |

**SERGEANT BILKO** (Phil Silvers) (TV)
May-June, 1957 - No. 18, Mar-Apr, 1960
National Periodical Publications

| 1 | 17.00 | 51.00 | 120.00 |
|---|---|---|---|
| 2 | 12.00 | 36.00 | 84.00 |
| 3-5 | 10.00 | 30.00 | 70.00 |
| 6-18: 11,12,15-Photo-c | 8.00 | 24.00 | 56.00 |

**SGT. BILKO'S PVT. DOBERMAN** (TV)
June-July, 1958 - No. 11, Feb-Mar, 1960
National Periodical Publications

| 1 | 13.50 | 40.00 | 95.00 |
|---|---|---|---|
| 2 | 8.50 | 25.50 | 60.00 |
| 3-5: 5-Photo-c | 6.50 | 19.50 | 45.00 |
| 6-11: 6,9-Photo-c | 5.00 | 15.00 | 35.00 |

**SGT. FURY** (& His Howling Commandos)
May, 1963 - No. 167, Dec, 1981
Marvel Comics Group (BPC earlier issues)

|  | Good | Fine | N-Mint |
|---|---|---|---|
| 1-1st app. Sgt. Fury; Kirby/Ayers-c/a | 32.00 | 96.00 | 225.00 |
| 2-Kirby-a | 11.50 | 34.00 | 80.00 |
| 3-5: 3-Reed Richards x-over. 4-Death of Junior Juniper. 5-1st Baron Strucker app.; Kirby-a | 7.00 | 21.00 | 50.00 |
| 6-10: 8-Baron Zemo, 1st Percival Pinkerton app. 10-1st app. Capt. Savage (the Skipper) | 5.00 | 15.00 | 35.00 |
| 11,12,14-20: 14-1st Blitz Squad. 18-Death of Pamela Hawley | 2.15 | 6.50 | 15.00 |
| 13-Capt. America & Bucky app. (12/64); Kirby-a | 7.00 | 21.00 | 50.00 |
| 21-30: 25-Red Skull app. 27-1st Eric Koenig app., origin Fury's eye patch. | 1.40 | 4.25 | 8.50 |
| 31-50: 34-Origin Howling Commandos | 1.05 | 3.15 | 7.50 |
| 51-100: 100-Capt. America, Fantastic-4 cameos | .75 | 2.25 | 4.50 |
| 101-167: 101-Origin retold. 167-reprints #1 | .55 | 1.65 | 3.30 |
| Annual 1 ('65, 25 cents, 72 pgs.)-r/#4,5 & new-a | 2.35 | 7.00 | 16.50 |
| Special 2-7 ('66-11/71) | .75 | 2.25 | 4.50 |

**SERGEANT PRESTON OF THE YUKON** (TV)
No. 344, Aug, 1951 - No. 29, Nov-Jan, 1958-59
Dell Publishing Co.

|  | Good | Fine | N-Mint |
|---|---|---|---|
| 4-Color 344(#1)-Sergeant Preston & his dog Yukon King begin; painted-c begin, end #18 | 5.70 | 17.00 | 40.00 |
| 4-Color 373,397,419('52) | 3.70 | 11.00 | 26.00 |
| 5(11-1/52-53)-10(2-4/54) | 3.00 | 9.00 | 21.00 |
| 11,12,14-17 | 2.30 | 7.00 | 16.00 |
| 13-Origin S. Preston | 3.00 | 9.00 | 21.00 |
| 18-Origin Yukon King; last painted-c | 3.00 | 9.00 | 21.00 |
| 19-29: All photo-c | 3.00 | 9.00 | 21.00 |

**SHADOW, THE**
Oct-Nov, 1973 - No. 12, Aug-Sept, 1975
National Periodical Publications

|                                         | Good  | Fine  | N-Mint |
|-----------------------------------------|-------|-------|--------|
| 1-Kaluta-a begins                       | 1.50  | 4.50  | 9.00   |
| 2                                       | .85   | 2.50  | 5.00   |
| 3-Kaluta/Wrightson-a                    | .90   | 2.75  | 5.50   |
| 4,6-Kaluta-a ends                       | .60   | 1.75  | 3.50   |
| 5,7-12: 11-The Avenger (pulp character) x-over |       |       |        |
|                                         | .35   | 1.00  | 2.00   |

## SHADOW, THE
May, 1986 - No. 4, Aug, 1986 (Mini-series, mature readers)
DC Comics

|                     | Good | Fine | N-Mint |
|---------------------|------|------|--------|
| 1-Chaykin-a in all  | 1.15 | 3.50 | 7.00   |
| 2-4                 | .75  | 2.25 | 4.50   |

## SHADOW, THE
Aug, 1987 - No. 19, Jan, 1989 ($1.50, mature readers)
DC Comics

|                                              | Good | Fine | N-Mint |
|----------------------------------------------|------|------|--------|
| 1                                            | .50  | 1.50 | 3.00   |
| 2-19: 13-Death of Shadow. 18-E.C.-c swipe    | .35  | 1.00 | 2.00   |
| Annual 1 (12/87, $2.25)-Orlando-a            | .40  | 1.25 | 2.50   |
| Annual 2 (12/88, $2.50)                      | .40  | 1.25 | 2.50   |

## SHADOW COMICS (Pulp, radio)
March, 1940 - V9#5, Aug, 1949
Street & Smith Publications

V1#1-Shadow, Doc Savage, Bill Barnes, Nick Carter, Frank Merriwell, Iron
    Munro, the Astonishing Man begin   167.00   420.00   1000.00
  2-The Avenger begins, ends #6; Capt. Fury only app.
        62.00   185.00   435.00
    3(nn-5/40)-Norgil the Magician app. (also #9)
        48.00   145.00   335.00
    4,5: 4-The Three Musketeers begins, ends #8. 5-Doc Savage ends
        39.00   118.00   275.00
  6,8,9       30.00   90.00   210.00
    7-Origin & 1st app. Hooded Wasp & Wasplet; series ends V3#8
        34.00   100.00   235.00
    10-Origin The Iron Ghost, ends #11; The Dead End Kids begins, ends
    #14       30.00   90.00   210.00

|  | Good | Fine | N-Mint |
|---|---|---|---|
| 11-Origin The Hooded Wasp & Wasplet retold | | | |
| | 30.00 | 90.00 | 210.00 |
| 12-Dead End Kids app. | 26.00 | 77.00 | 180.00 |
| V2#1,2(11/41): 2-Dead End Kids story | 24.00 | 73.00 | 170.00 |
| 3-Origin & 1st app. Supersnipe; series begins; Little Nemo story | | | |
| | 30.00 | 90.00 | 210.00 |
| 4,5: 4-Little Nemo story | 21.50 | 64.00 | 150.00 |
| 6-9: 6-Blackstone the Magician app. | 20.00 | 60.00 | 140.00 |
| 10-12: 10-Supersnipe app. | 20.00 | 60.00 | 140.00 |
| V3#1-12: 10-Doc Savage begins, not in V5#5, V6#10-12, V8#4 | | | |
| | 18.50 | 56.00 | 130.00 |
| V4#1-12 | 17.00 | 51.00 | 120.00 |
| V5#1-12 | 16.00 | 47.00 | 110.00 |
| V6#1-11: 9-Intro. Shadow, Jr. | 14.00 | 42.00 | 100.00 |
| 12-Powell-c/a; atom bomb panels | 16.00 | 48.00 | 110.00 |
| V7#1,2,5,7-9,12: 2,5-Shadow, Jr. app.; Powell-a | | | |
| | 16.00 | 48.00 | 110.00 |
| 3,6,11-Powell-c/a | 17.00 | 51.00 | 120.00 |
| 4-Powell-c/a; Atom bomb panels | 18.50 | 56.00 | 130.00 |
| 10(1/48)-Flying Saucer issue; Powell-c/a (2nd of this theme; see The | | | |
| Spirit 9/28/47) | 21.50 | 64.00 | 150.00 |
| V8#1-12-Powell-a | 17.00 | 51.00 | 120.00 |
| V9#1,5-Powell-a | 16.00 | 48.00 | 110.00 |
| 2-4-Powell-c/a | 17.00 | 51.00 | 120.00 |

**SHADOW OF THE BATMAN**
Dec, 1985 - No. 5, Apr, 1986 ($1.75 cover; mini-series)
DC Comics

| 1-Detective-r (all have wraparound-c) | 1.85 | 5.50 | 11.00 |
|---|---|---|---|
| 2,3,5 | 1.15 | 3.50 | 7.00 |
| 4-Joker-c/story | 1.70 | 5.00 | 10.00 |

**SHEENA, QUEEN OF THE JUNGLE** (See Jumbo Comics & 3-D . . . )
Spring, 1942 - No. 18, Winter, 1952-53 (#1,2: 68 pgs.)
Fiction House Magazines

| 1-Sheena begins | 107.00 | 321.00 | 750.00 |
|---|---|---|---|
| 2 (Winter, 1942/43) | 54.00 | 160.00 | 375.00 |
| 3 (Spring, 1943) | 37.00 | 110.00 | 260.00 |

|                                      | Good  | Fine  | N-Mint |
|--------------------------------------|-------|-------|--------|
| 4, 5 (Fall, 1948 - Sum., '49)        | 21.50 | 64.00 | 150.00 |
| 6,7 (Spring, '50 - '50, 52 pgs.)     | 19.00 | 58.00 | 135.00 |
| 8-10('50, 36 pgs.)                   | 17.00 | 51.00 | 120.00 |
| 11-17                                | 14.00 | 42.00 | 100.00 |
| 18-Used in **POP**, pg. 98           | 14.00 | 42.00 | 100.00 |

**SHIELD** (Nick Fury & His Agents of . . . ) (Also see Nick Fury)
Feb, 1973 - No. 5, Oct, 1973 (All 20 cents)
Marvel Comics Group

|                                      | Good | Fine | N-Mint |
|--------------------------------------|------|------|--------|
| 1-Steranko-c                         | .70  | 2.00 | 4.00   |
| 2-Steranko flag-c                    | .35  | 1.00 | 2.00   |
| 3-5: 1-5 all contain-r from Strange Tales #146-155. 3-5-are cover-r; | | | |
|    3-Kirby/Steranko-c(r). 4-Steranko-c(r) | .35 | 1.00 | 2.00 |

**SHIELD WIZARD COMICS** (Also see Pep & Top-Notch Comics)
Summer, 1940 - No. 13, Spring, 1944
MLJ Magazines

|                                      | Good   | Fine   | N-Mint |
|--------------------------------------|--------|--------|--------|
| 1-(V1#5 on inside)-Origin The Shield by Irving Novick & The Wizard by | | | |
|    Ed Ashe, Jr; Flag-c | 125.00 | 375.00 | 875.00 |
| 2-Origin The Shield retold; intro. Wizard's sidekick, Roy | | | |
|                                      | 57.00  | 171.00 | 400.00 |
| 3,4                                  | 37.00  | 110.00 | 260.00 |
| 5-Dusty, the Boy Detective begins    | 33.00  | 100.00 | 230.00 |
| 6-8: 6-Roy the Super Boy begins      | 28.50  | 86.00  | 200.00 |
| 9,10                                 | 25.00  | 75.00  | 175.00 |
| 11-13: 13-Bondage-c                  | 23.50  | 70.00  | 165.00 |

**SHOCK SUSPENSTORIES**
Feb-Mar, 1952 - No. 18, Dec-Jan, 1954-55
E. C. Comics

|                                      | Good  | Fine   | N-Mint |
|--------------------------------------|-------|--------|--------|
| 1-Classic Feldstein electrocution-c; Ray Bradbury adaptation | | | |
|                                      | 45.00 | 135.00 | 315.00 |
| 2                                    | 27.00 | 81.00  | 190.00 |
| 3                                    | 18.50 | 56.00  | 130.00 |
| 4-Used in **SOTI**, pg. 387,388      | 18.50 | 56.00  | 130.00 |
| 5-Hanging-c                          | 17.00 | 51.00  | 120.00 |

|  | Good | Fine | N-Mint |
|---|---|---|---|
| 6,7: 6-Classic bondage-c. 7-Classic face melting-c | | | |
| | 21.50 | 64.00 | 150.00 |
| 8-Williamson-a | 18.50 | 56.00 | 130.00 |
| 9-11: 9-Injury to eye panel. 10-Junkie story | 14.00 | 42.00 | 100.00 |
| 12-"The Monkey"-classic junkie cover/story; drug propaganda issue | | | |
| | 18.00 | 54.00 | 125.00 |
| 13-Frazetta's only solo story for E.C., 7 pgs. | 23.00 | 70.00 | 160.00 |
| 14-Used in Senate Investigation hearings | 11.00 | 32.00 | 75.00 |
| 15-Used in 1954 Reader's Digest article, "For the Kiddies to Read" | | | |
| | 11.00 | 32.00 | 75.00 |
| 16-"Red Dupe" editorial; rape story | 11.00 | 32.00 | 75.00 |
| 17,18 | 11.00 | 32.00 | 75.00 |

*Showcase #23, © DC Comics*

**SHOWCASE**
3-4/56 - No. 93, 9/70; No. 94, 8-9/77 - No. 104, 9/78
National Periodical Publications/DC Comics

| | Good | Fine | N-Mint |
|---|---|---|---|
| 1-Fire Fighters | 70.00 | 210.00 | 485.00 |
| 2-King of the Wild; Kubert-a (animal stories) | | | |
| | 27.00 | 81.00 | 185.00 |
| 3-The Frogmen | 22.00 | 65.00 | 155.00 |
| 4-Origin The Flash (1st DC Silver Age Hero, Sept-Oct, 1956) & The Turtle; Kubert-a; r-in Secret Origins #1 | 340.00 | 1360.00 | 3400.00 |
| 5-Manhunters | 24.00 | 72.00 | 165.00 |
| 6-Origin Challengers (1st app.) by Kirby, partly r-/in Secret Origins #1 & Challengers of the Unknown #64,65 | 86.00 | 258.00 | 600.00 |
| 7-Challengers by Kirby r-in/Challengers of the Unknown #75 | | | |
| | 47.00 | 140.00 | 330.00 |
| 8-The Flash; intro/origin Capt. Cold | 150.00 | 450.00 | 1050.00 |
| 9,10-Lois Lane. 9-(Pre#1, 7-8/57). 10-Jor-el cameo | | | |
| | 43.00 | 130.00 | 300.00 |
| 11,12-Challengers by Kirby | 36.00 | 108.00 | 250.00 |
| 13-The Flash; origin Mr. Element | 105.00 | 315.00 | 735.00 |
| 14-The Flash; origin Dr. Alchemy, former Mr. Element | | | |
| | 105.00 | 315.00 | 735.00 |
| 15-Space Ranger (1st app.) | 23.00 | 70.00 | 160.00 |
| 16-Space Ranger | 18.00 | 54.00 | 125.00 |
| 17-Adventures on Other Worlds; origin/1st app. Adam Strange (11-12/58) | | | |
| | 54.00 | 162.00 | 375.00 |
| 18-Adventures on Other Worlds (A. Strange) | 30.00 | 90.00 | 210.00 |
| 19-Adam Strange | 30.00 | 90.00 | 210.00 |
| 20-1st app/origin Rip Hunter (5-6/59); Moriera-a | | | |
| | 23.00 | 70.00 | 160.00 |
| 21-Rip Hunter; Sekowsky-c/a | 12.00 | 36.00 | 85.00 |
| 22-Origin & 1st app. Silver Age Green Lantern by Gil Kane (9-10/59) | | | |
| | 132.00 | 396.00 | 925.00 |
| 23,24-Green Lantern. 23-Nuclear explosion-c | | | |
| | 50.00 | 150.00 | 350.00 |
| 25,26-Rip Hunter by Kubert | 7.00 | 21.00 | 50.00 |
| 27-1st app. Sea Devils (7-8/60); Heath-c/a | 21.00 | 63.00 | 150.00 |
| 28,29-Sea Devils; Heath-c/a | 13.00 | 40.00 | 90.00 |
| 30-Origin Silver Age Aquaman (see Adventure #260 for 1st app.) | | | |
| | 20.00 | 60.00 | 140.00 |
| 31-33-Aquaman | 8.00 | 24.00 | 55.00 |
| 34-Origin & 1st app. Silver Age Atom by Kane & Anderson (9-10/61) | | | |
| | 44.00 | 132.00 | 310.00 |
| 35-The Atom by Gil Kane; last 10 cent issue | 14.00 | 42.00 | 100.00 |

| | Good | Fine | N-Mint |
|---|---|---|---|
| 36-The Atom by Gil Kane | 8.50 | 25.50 | 60.00 |
| 37-1st app. Metal Men (3-4/62) | 22.00 | 66.00 | 155.00 |
| 38-40-Metal Men | 9.30 | 28.00 | 65.00 |
| 41,42-Tommy Tomorrow | 2.65 | 8.00 | 18.00 |
| 43-Dr. No (James Bond) | 22.00 | 66.00 | 155.00 |
| 44-Tommy Tomorrow | 2.15 | 6.50 | 15.00 |
| 45-Sgt. Rock; origin retold; Heath-c | 4.30 | 13.00 | 30.00 |
| 46,47-Tommy Tomorrow | 1.15 | 3.50 | 8.00 |
| 48,49-Cave Carson | 1.15 | 3.50 | 8.00 |
| 50,51-I Spy (Danger Trail-r by Infantino), King Farady story (#50 is not a | | | |
| reprint) | 1.15 | 3.50 | 8.00 |
| 52-Cave Carson | 1.15 | 3.50 | 8.00 |
| 53,54-G.I. Joe; Heath-a | 1.15 | 3.50 | 8.00 |
| 55,56-Dr. Fate & Hourman | 1.15 | 3.50 | 8.00 |
| 57,58-Enemy Ace by Kubert | 1.60 | 4.80 | 11.00 |
| 59-Teen Titans (3rd app., 11-12/65) | 4.70 | 14.00 | 33.00 |
| 60-1st Silver Age app. The Spectre; Anderson-a (1-2/66)-origin in text | | | |
| | 5.00 | 15.00 | 35.00 |
| 61,64-The Spectre by Anderson | 1.15 | 3.50 | 8.00 |
| 62-Origin/1st app. Inferior Five (5-6/66) | 2.30 | 7.00 | 16.00 |
| 63,65-Inferior Five | 1.15 | 3.50 | 8.00 |
| 66,67-B'wana Beast | .70 | 2.00 | 4.00 |
| 68,69,71-Maniaks | .70 | 2.00 | 4.00 |
| 70-Binky | .70 | 2.00 | 4.00 |
| 72-Top Gun (Johnny Thunder-r)-Toth-a | .70 | 2.00 | 4.00 |
| 73-Origin/1st app. Creeper; Ditko-c/a (3-4/67) | 2.15 | 6.50 | 15.00 |
| 74-Intro/1st app. Anthro; Post-c/a (5-6/67) | 2.15 | 6.50 | 15.00 |
| 75-1st app/origin Hawk & the Dove; Ditko-c/a | | | |
| | 2.15 | 6.50 | 15.00 |
| 76-1st app. Bat Lash | 1.15 | 3.50 | 8.00 |
| 77-1st app. Angel & the Ape | 1.50 | 4.50 | 10.00 |
| 78-Jonny Double | .50 | 1.50 | 3.00 |
| 79-Dolphin; Aqualad origin-r | .85 | 2.50 | 5.00 |
| 80-Phantom Stranger-r; Neal Adams-c | .85 | 2.50 | 5.00 |
| 81-Windy & Willy | .50 | 1.50 | 3.00 |
| 82-Nightmaster by Grandenetti & Giordano; Kubert-c | | | |
| | 1.00 | 3.00 | 6.00 |
| 83,84-Nightmaster by Wrightson/Jones/Kaluta in each; Kubert-c. | | | |
| 84-Origin retold | 2.65 | 8.00 | 18.00 |
| 85-87-Firehair; Kubert-a | .85 | 2.50 | 5.00 |

|  | Good | Fine | N-Mint |
|---|---|---|---|
| 88-90-Jason's Quest: 90-Manhunter 2070 app. | .35 | 1.00 | 2.00 |
| 91-93-Manhunter 2070; origin-92 | .35 | 1.00 | 2.00 |
| 94-Intro/origin new Doom Patrol & Robotman | .50 | 1.50 | 3.00 |
| 95,96-The Doom Patrol. 95-Origin Celsius | .35 | 1.00 | 2.00 |
| 97-99-Power Girl; origin-97,98; JSA cameos | .35 | 1.00 | 2.00 |
| 100-(52 pgs.)-Most Showcase characters feat. | .35 | 1.00 | 2.00 |
| 101-103-Hawkman; Adam Strange x-over | .35 | 1.00 | 2.00 |
| 104-(52 pgs.)-O.S.S. Spies at War | .35 | 1.00 | 2.00 |

**SILVER STREAK COMICS** (Crime Does Not Pay #22 on)
Dec, 1939 - May, 1942; 1946 (Silver logo-#1-5)
Your Guide Publs. No. 1-7/New Friday Publs. No. 8-17/Comic House
    Publ./Newsbook Publ.

| | Good | Fine | N-Mint |
|---|---|---|---|
| 1-(Scarce)-Intro. The Claw by Cole (r-/in Daredevil #21), Red Reeves, Boy Magician, & Captain Fearless; The Wasp, Mister Midnight begin; Spirit Man app. Silver metallic-c begin, end #5 | 329.00 | 985.00 | 2300.00 |
| 2-The Claw by Cole; Simon c/a | 143.00 | 430.00 | 1000.00 |
| 3-1st app. & origin Silver Streak (2nd with lightning speed); Dickie Dean the Boy Inventor, Lance Hale, Ace Powers, Bill Wayne, & The Planet Patrol begin | 129.00 | 385.00 | 900.00 |
| 4-Sky Wolf begins; Silver Streak by Jack Cole (new costume); intro. Jackie, Lance Hale's sidekick | 68.00 | 204.00 | 475.00 |
| 5-Jack Cole c/a(2) | 79.00 | 235.00 | 550.00 |
| 6-(Scarce)-Origin & 1st app. Daredevil (blue & yellow costume) by Jack Binder; The Claw returns; classic Cole Claw-c | 271.00 | 815.00 | 1900.00 |
| *(Prices vary widely on this book)* | | | |
| 7-Claw vs. Daredevil (new costume-blue & red) by Jack Cole & 3 other Cole stories (38 pgs.) | 179.00 | 535.00 | 1250.00 |
| 8-Claw vs. Daredevil by Cole; last Cole Silver Streak | 107.00 | 321.00 | 750.00 |
| 9-Claw vs. Daredevil by Cole | 76.00 | 230.00 | 535.00 |
| 10-Origin Captain Battle; Claw vs. Daredevil by Cole | 71.00 | 212.00 | 495.00 |
| 11-Intro. Mercury by Bob Wood, Silver Streak's sidekick; conclusion Claw vs. Daredevil by Rico | 49.00 | 147.00 | 340.00 |
| 12-14: 13-Origin Thun-Dohr | 40.00 | 120.00 | 280.00 |
| 15-17-Last Daredevil issue | 37.00 | 110.00 | 260.00 |

| | Good | Fine | N-Mint |
|---|---|---|---|
| 18-The Saint begins; by Leslie Charteris | 31.00 | 92.00 | 215.00 |
| 19-21(1942): 20,21 have Wolverton's Scoop Scuttle | | | |
| | 19.00 | 58.00 | 135.00 |
| 22,24(1946)-Reprints | 13.00 | 40.00 | 90.00 |
| 23-Reprints?; bondage-c | 13.00 | 40.00 | 90.00 |
| nn(11/46)(Newsbook Publ.)-R-/S.S. story from #4-7 plus 2 Captain Fear- | | | |
| less stories, all in color | 24.00 | 70.00 | 170.00 |

**SILVER SURFER, THE** (See Fantastic Four & Fantasy Masterpieces)
Aug, 1968 - No. 18, Sept, 1970; June, 1982 (No. 1-7: 68 pgs.)
Marvel Comics Group

| | Good | Fine | N-Mint |
|---|---|---|---|
| 1-Origin by John Buscema (p); Watcher begins (origin), ends #7 | | | |
| | 21.00 | 63.00 | 150.00 |
| 2 | 6.30 | 19.00 | 44.00 |
| 3-1st app. Mephisto | 5.70 | 17.00 | 40.00 |
| 4-Low distribution; Thor app. | 13.50 | 41.00 | 95.00 |
| 5-7-Last giant size. 5-The Stranger app. 6-Brunner inks. 7- Brunner-c | | | |
| | 4.30 | 13.00 | 30.00 |
| 8-10 | 2.85 | 8.50 | 20.00 |
| 11-13,15-18: 18-Kirby-c/a | 1.85 | 5.50 | 13.00 |
| 14-Spider-Man x-over | 2.65 | 8.00 | 18.00 |
| V2#1 (6/82, 52 pgs.)-Byrne-c/a | 1.00 | 3.00 | 6.00 |

**SILVER SURFER, THE**
July, 1987 - Present
Marvel Comics Group

| | Good | Fine | N-Mint |
|---|---|---|---|
| 1-Double size ($1.25) | .70 | 2.00 | 4.00 |
| 2 | .40 | 1.25 | 2.50 |
| 3-10 | .30 | .90 | 1.80 |
| 11-20: 19-Rogers-a | | .60 | 1.20 |
| 21-24,26-30,32-44: 34-Starlin scripts begin. 34,35-Thanos returns. 36- | | | |
| Capt. Marvel & Warlock app. | | .50 | 1.00 |
| 25,31 ($1.50, 52 pgs.): 25-Skrulls app. | .25 | .75 | 1.50 |
| Annual 1 (8/88, $1.75)-Evolutionary War app. | .40 | 1.25 | 2.50 |
| Annual 2 ('89, $2.00, 68 pgs.)-Atlantis Attacks | .35 | 1.00 | 2.00 |
| Annual 3 (1990, $2.00, 68 pgs.) | .35 | 1.00 | 2.00 |

**SILVER SURFER, THE**
Dec, 1988 - No. 2, Jan, 1989 ($1.00, limited series)
Epic Comics (Marvel)

| | Good | Fine | N-Mint |
|---|---|---|---|
| 1,2: By Stan Lee & Moebius | .30 | .90 | 1.75 |

**SLAM BANG COMICS**
March, 1940 - No. 7, Sept, 1940 (Combined with Master Comics #7)
Fawcett Publications

| | | | |
|---|---|---|---|
| 1-Diamond Jack, Mark Swift & The Time Retarder, Lee Granger, Jungle King begin | 57.00 | 171.00 | 400.00 |
| 2 | 28.50 | 86.00 | 200.00 |
| 3-Classic-c | 28.50 | 86.00 | 200.00 |
| 4-7: 7-Bondage-c | 21.50 | 64.00 | 150.00 |

**SMASH COMICS** (Lady Luck #86 on)
Aug, 1939 - No. 85, Oct, 1949
Quality Comics Group

| | | | |
|---|---|---|---|
| 1-Origin Hugh Hazard & His Iron Man, Bozo the Robot, Espionage, Starring Black X by Eisner, & Invisible Justice; Chic Carter & Wings Wendall begin | 71.00 | 215.00 | 500.00 |
| 2-The Lone Star Rider app; Invisible Hood gains power of invisibility | 34.00 | 100.00 | 235.00 |
| 3-Captain Cook & John Law begin | 23.00 | 70.00 | 160.00 |
| 4,5: 4-Flash Fulton begins | 21.00 | 62.00 | 145.00 |
| 6-12: 12-One pg. Fine-a | 16.00 | 48.00 | 115.00 |
| 13-Magno begins; last Eisner issue; The Ray app. in full page ad; The Purple Trio begins | 16.00 | 48.00 | 115.00 |
| 14-Intro. The Ray by Lou Fine & others | 110.00 | 330.00 | 770.00 |
| 15,16 | 55.00 | 165.00 | 385.00 |
| 17-Wun Cloo becomes plastic super-hero by Jack Cole (9 months before Plastic Man) | 55.00 | 165.00 | 385.00 |
| 18-Midnight by Jack Cole begins (origin) | 65.00 | 195.00 | 455.00 |
| 19-22: Last Fine Ray; The Jester begins-#22 | 38.00 | 115.00 | 265.00 |
| 23,24: 24-The Sword app.; last Chic Carter; Wings Wendall dons new costume #24,25 | 30.00 | 90.00 | 210.00 |
| 25-Origin Wildfire | 35.00 | 105.00 | 245.00 |
| 26-30: 28-Midnight-c begin | 26.00 | 77.00 | 180.00 |

|  | Good | Fine | N-Mint |
|---|---|---|---|
| 31,32,34: Ray by Rudy Palais; also #33 | 20.00 | 60.00 | 140.00 |
| 33-Origin The Marksman | 24.00 | 73.00 | 170.00 |
| 35-37 | 20.00 | 60.00 | 140.00 |
| 38-The Yankee Eagle begins; last Midnight by Jack Cole | | | |
| | 20.00 | 60.00 | 140.00 |
| 39,40-Last Ray issue | 16.00 | 48.00 | 110.00 |
| 41,43-50 | 7.00 | 21.00 | 50.00 |
| 42-Lady Luck begins by Klaus Nordling | 9.50 | 28.50 | 65.00 |
| 51-60 | 6.00 | 18.00 | 42.00 |
| 61-70 | 5.00 | 15.00 | 35.00 |
| 71-85 | 4.65 | 14.00 | 32.00 |

**SMILIN' JACK** (See Popular Comics & Super Comics)
No. 5, 1940 - No. 8, Oct-Dec, 1949
Dell Publishing Co.

|  | Good | Fine | N-Mint |
|---|---|---|---|
| 4-Color 5 | 42.00 | 125.00 | 290.00 |
| 4-Color 10 (1940) | 39.00 | 116.00 | 270.00 |
| Large Feature Comic 12,14,25 (1941) | 27.00 | 81.00 | 190.00 |
| 4-Color 4 (1942) | 31.00 | 92.00 | 215.00 |
| 4-Color 14 (1943) | 25.00 | 75.00 | 175.00 |
| 4-Color 36,58 (1943-44) | 14.00 | 42.00 | 100.00 |
| 4-Color 80 (1945) | 11.50 | 34.00 | 80.00 |
| 4-Color 149 (1947) | 8.50 | 25.50 | 60.00 |
| 1 (1-3/48) | 8.50 | 25.50 | 60.00 |
| 2 | 4.65 | 14.00 | 32.00 |
| 3-8 | 3.50 | 10.50 | 24.00 |

**SMITTY** (See Popular Comics & Super Comics)
No. 11, 1940 - No. 7, Aug-Oct, 1949; Apr, 1958
Dell Publishing Co.

|  | Good | Fine | N-Mint |
|---|---|---|---|
| 4-Color 11 (1940) | 24.00 | 71.00 | 165.00 |
| Large Feature Comic 26 (1941) | 16.00 | 48.00 | 110.00 |
| 4-Color 6 (1942) | 13.00 | 40.00 | 90.00 |
| 4-Color 32 (1943) | 11.00 | 32.00 | 76.00 |
| 4-Color 65 (1945) | 8.50 | 25.50 | 60.00 |
| 4-Color 99 (1946) | 7.00 | 21.00 | 50.00 |
| 4-Color 138 (1947) | 6.50 | 19.50 | 45.00 |
| 1 (11-1/47-48) | 6.50 | 19.50 | 45.00 |

|  | Good | Fine | N-Mint |
|---|---|---|---|
| 2 | 3.50 | 10.50 | 24.00 |
| 3 (8-10/48), 4 (1949) | 2.30 | 7.00 | 16.00 |
| 5-7 | 1.70 | 5.00 | 12.00 |
| 4-Color 909 (4/58) | 1.50 | 4.50 | 10.00 |

**SOLO AVENGERS** (Becomes Avengers Spotlight #21 on)
Dec, 1987 - No. 20, July, 1989
Marvel Comics

|  | | | |
|---|---|---|---|
| 1 | .35 | 1.10 | 2.20 |
| 2-5 | .25 | .70 | 1.40 |
| 6-20: 11-Intro Bobcat | | .50 | 1.00 |

**SPACE ADVENTURES**
7/52 - No. 21, 5/56; No. 23, 5/58 - No. 59, 11/64; V3#60, 10/67; V1#2, 7/68 -
    V1#8, 7/69; No. 9, 5/78 - No. 13, 3/79
Capitol Stories/Charlton Comics

|  | | | |
|---|---|---|---|
| 1 | 14.00 | 42.00 | 100.00 |
| 2 | 7.00 | 21.00 | 50.00 |
| 3-5 | 5.70 | 17.00 | 40.00 |
| 6-9 | 5.00 | 15.00 | 35.00 |
| 10,11-Ditko-c/a; 11-Two Ditko stories | 17.00 | 51.00 | 120.00 |
| 12-Ditko-c (classic) | 20.00 | 60.00 | 140.00 |
| 13-(Fox-r, 10-11/54); Blue Beetle story | 5.70 | 17.00 | 40.00 |
| 14-Blue Beetle story (Fox-r, 12-1/54-55) | 4.65 | 14.00 | 32.00 |
| 15-18-Rocky Jones app.(TV); 15-Part photo-c | 5.00 | 15.00 | 35.00 |
| 16-Krigstein-a | 9.50 | 28.50 | 65.00 |
| 19 | 4.00 | 12.00 | 28.00 |
| 20-Reprints Fawcett's "Destination Moon" | 11.00 | 32.00 | 76.00 |
| 21-(8/56) (no #22) | 5.00 | 15.00 | 35.00 |
| 23-(5/58)-Reprints "Destination Moon" | 9.50 | 28.50 | 65.00 |
| 24,25,31,32-Ditko-a | 6.50 | 19.50 | 45.00 |
| 26,27-Ditko-a(4) each | 8.00 | 24.00 | 56.00 |
| 28-30 | 2.30 | 7.00 | 16.00 |
| 33-Origin/1st app. Capt. Atom by Ditko (3/60) | | | |
| | 18.50 | 56.00 | 130.00 |
| 34-40,42-All Captain Atom by Ditko | 7.00 | 21.00 | 50.00 |
| 41,43-59: 44,45-Mercury Man in each | .85 | 2.60 | 6.00 |

|  | Good | Fine | N-Mint |
|---|---|---|---|

V3#60(10/67)-Origin Paul Mann & The Saucers From the Future

|  | .85 | 2.50 | 5.00 |
|---|---|---|---|
| 2-8('68-'69)-1,2,5,6,8-Ditko-a; 2,4-Aparo-c/a | .40 | 1.25 | 2.50 |
| 9-13('78-'79)-Capt. Atom-r/Space Adventures by Ditko; 9-Reprints origin/1st app. from #33 |  | .50 | 1.00 |

## SPACE DETECTIVE
July, 1951 - No. 4, July, 1952
Avon Periodicals

| 1-Rod Hathway, Space Det. begins, ends #4; Wood-c/a(3)-23 pgs.; "Opium Smugglers of Venus" drug story; Lucky Dale-r/Saint #4 |  |  |  |
|---|---|---|---|
|  | 62.00 | 185.00 | 435.00 |
| 2-Tales from the Shadow Squad story; Wood/Orlando-c; Wood inside layouts |  |  |  |
|  | 30.00 | 90.00 | 210.00 |
| 3-Kinstler-c | 19.00 | 57.00 | 132.00 |
| 4-Kinstler-a | 19.00 | 57.00 | 132.00 |

## SPACE FAMILY ROBINSON (TV) (. . . Lost in Space #15-36)
Dec, 1962 - No. 36, Oct, 1969 (All painted covers)
Gold Key

| 1-(low distr.); Spiegle-a in all | 8.50 | 25.50 | 60.00 |
|---|---|---|---|
| 2(3/63)-Family becomes lost in space | 4.50 | 14.00 | 32.00 |
| 3-10: 6-Captain Venture begins | 2.30 | 7.00 | 16.00 |
| 11-20 | 1.50 | 4.50 | 10.00 |
| 21-36 | .85 | 2.60 | 6.00 |

## SPACE GHOST (TV)
March, 1967 (Hanna-Barbera) (TV debut was 9/10/66)
Gold Key

| 1 (10199-703)-Spiegle-a | 12.50 | 37.50 | 88.00 |
|---|---|---|---|

## SPACE GHOST (TV) (Graphic Novel)
Dec, 1987 (One Shot) (52 pgs.; deluxe format; $3.50) (Hanna-Barbera)
Comico

| 1-Steve Rude-c/a(p) | .85 | 2.50 | 5.00 |
|---|---|---|---|

**SPACEMAN** (Speed Carter . . . )
Sept, 1953 - No. 6, July, 1954
Atlas Comics (CnPC)

|   | Good | Fine | N-Mint |
|---|------|------|--------|
| 1 | 21.50 | 64.00 | 150.00 |
| 2 | 14.00 | 42.00 | 100.00 |
| 3-6: 4-A-Bomb-c | 11.50 | 34.00 | 80.00 |

**SPACE MAN**
No. 1253, 1-3/62 - No. 8, 3-5/64; No. 9, 7/72 - No. 10, 10/72
Dell Publishing Co.

|   | | | |
|---|------|------|--------|
| 4-Color 1253 (#1)(1-3/62) | 3.50 | 10.50 | 24.00 |
| 2,3 | 1.70 | 5.00 | 12.00 |
| 4-8 | 1.00 | 3.00 | 7.00 |
| 9-Reprints #1253 | .40 | 1.25 | 2.80 |
| 10-Reprints #2 | .35 | 1.00 | 2.00 |

**SPARKLER COMICS** (Cover title becomes Nancy & Sluggo 101? on)
July, 1941 - No. 120, Jan, 1955
United Features Syndicate

1-Origin Sparkman; Tarzan (by Hogarth in all issues), Captain & the
    Kids, Ella Cinders, Danny Dingle, Dynamite Dunn, Nancy, Abbie &
    Slats, Frankie Doodle, Broncho Bill begin; Sparkman c-#1-12

|   | | | |
|---|------|------|--------|
|   | 71.00 | 215.00 | 500.00 |
| 2 | 31.50 | 94.00 | 220.00 |
| 3,4 | 27.00 | 81.00 | 190.00 |
| 5-10: 9-Sparkman's new costume | 22.00 | 65.00 | 154.00 |

11-13,15-20: 12-Sparkman new costume-color change. 19-1st Race Riley

|   | | | |
|---|------|------|--------|
|   | 18.50 | 56.00 | 130.00 |
| 14-Tarzan-c by Hogarth | 21.50 | 64.00 | 150.00 |

21-24,26,27,29,30: 22-Race Riley & the Commandos strips begin, ends #44

|   | | | |
|---|------|------|--------|
|   | 14.00 | 42.00 | 100.00 |
| 25,28,31,34,37,39-Tarzan-c by Hogarth | 18.00 | 54.00 | 125.00 |
| 32,33,35,36,38,40 | 8.50 | 25.50 | 60.00 |
| 41,43,45,46,48,49 | 6.00 | 18.00 | 42.00 |
| 42,44,47,50-Tarzan-c | 11.00 | 32.00 | 75.00 |

51,52,54-70: 57-Li'l Abner begins (not in #58); Fearless Fosdick app.-#58

|   | | | |
|---|------|------|--------|
|   | 4.30 | 13.00 | 30.00 |

|  | Good | Fine | N-Mint |
|---|---|---|---|
| 53-Tarzan-c by Hogarth | 9.30 | 28.00 | 65.00 |
| 71-80 | 3.50 | 10.50 | 24.00 |
| 81,82,84-90: 85-Li'l Abner ends. 86-Lingerie panels | | | |
|  | 2.65 | 8.00 | 18.00 |
| 83-Tarzan-c | 4.65 | 14.00 | 32.00 |
| 91-96,98-99 | 2.30 | 7.00 | 16.00 |
| 97-Origin Casey Ruggles by Warren Tufts | 5.00 | 15.00 | 35.00 |
| 100 | 2.85 | 8.50 | 20.00 |
| 101-107,109-112,114-120 | 1.70 | 5.00 | 12.00 |
| 108,113-Toth-a | 5.00 | 15.00 | 35.00 |

**SPECIAL EDITION COMICS**
1940 (August) (One Shot, 68 pgs.)
Fawcett Publications

| | Good | Fine | N-Mint |
|---|---|---|---|
| 1-1st book devoted entirely to Captain Marvel; C.C. Beck-c/a; only app. of Capt. Marvel with belt buckle; Capt. Marvel appears with button-down flap, 1st story (came out before Captain Marvel #1) | | | |
| | 271.00 | 815.00 | 1900.00 |

**SPECIAL EDITION X-MEN**
Feb, 1983 (One Shot) (Baxter paper, $2.00)
Marvel Comics Group

| | Good | Fine | N-Mint |
|---|---|---|---|
| 1-R/Giant-Size X-Men #1 plus one new story | 1.35 | 4.00 | 8.00 |

**SPECTACULAR SPIDER-MAN, THE** (Peter Parker . . . #54-132,134)
Dec, 1976 - Present
Marvel Comics Group

| | Good | Fine | N-Mint |
|---|---|---|---|
| 1-Origin retold; Tarantula app. | 3.35 | 10.00 | 20.00 |
| 2-5: 2-Kraven the Hunter app. 4-Vulture app. | 1.15 | 3.50 | 7.00 |
| 6-10: 6-8-Morbius app. 9,10-White Tiger app. | .75 | 2.25 | 4.50 |
| 11-20: 17,18-Champions x-over | .70 | 2.00 | 4.00 |
| 21,24-26: 21-Scorpion app. 26-Daredevil app. | .50 | 1.50 | 3.00 |
| 22,23-Moon Knight app. | .60 | 1.75 | 3.50 |
| 27-Miller's 1st art on Daredevil | 2.00 | 6.00 | 12.00 |
| 28-Miller Daredevil (p) | 1.70 | 5.00 | 10.00 |

*The Spectacular Spider-Man #141,*
*© Marvel Comics*

|  | Good | Fine | N-Mint |
|---|---|---|---|
| 29-57,59: 33-Origin Iguana. 38-Morbius app. | .40 | 1.25 | 2.50 |
| 58-Byrne-a(p) | .70 | 2.00 | 4.00 |
| 60-Double size; origin retold with new facts revealed | .45 | 1.30 | 2.60 |
| 61-63,65-68,71-74: 65-Kraven the Hunter app. | .35 | 1.00 | 2.00 |
| 64-1st app. Cloak & Dagger (3/82) | 1.85 | 5.50 | 11.00 |
| 69,70-Cloak & Dagger app. | 1.00 | 3.00 | 6.00 |
| 75-Double size | .40 | 1.25 | 2.50 |
| 76-80 | .35 | 1.00 | 2.00 |
| 81,82-Punisher, Cloak & Dagger app. | 1.35 | 4.00 | 8.00 |
| 83-Origin Punisher retold | 1.50 | 4.50 | 9.00 |
| 84-93,97-99: 90-Spider-man's new black costume, last panel (ties w/ Amaz. Spider-Man #252). 98-Intro The Spot | .35 | 1.00 | 2.00 |
| 94-96-Cloak & Dagger app. | .35 | 1.00 | 2.00 |
| 100-Double size | .40 | 1.25 | 2.50 |

|  | Good | Fine | N-Mint |
|---|---|---|---|
| 101-130: 107-Death of Jean DeWolff. 111-Secret Wars II tie-in. 128-Black Cat new costume. 130-Hobgoblin app. | .25 | .75 | 1.50 |
| 131-Six part Kraven tie-in | .85 | -2.50 | 5.00 |
| 132-Kraven tie-in | .70 | 2.00 | 4.00 |
| 133-139: 139-Origin Tombstone | .35 | 1.00 | 2.00 |
| 140-Punisher cameo app. | .40 | 1.25 | 2.50 |
| 141-Punisher app. | .75 | 2.25 | 4.50 |
| 142,143-Punisher app. | .50 | 1.50 | 3.00 |
| 144-157: 147-Hobgoblin app. 151-Tombstone returns | .35 | 1.00 | 2.00 |
| 158-Spider-Man gets new powers (1st Cosmic Spidey, continued in Web of Spider-Man #59) | .35 | 1.00 | 2.00 |
| 159-170: 161-163-Hobgoblin app. |  | .50 | 1.00 |
| Annuals 1-7: 1(1979). 2(1980)-Origin/1st app. Rapier. 3(1981)-Last Manwolf. 4(1984). 5(1985). 6(1985). 7(1987) | .35 | 1.00 | 2.00 |
| Annual 8 ('88, $1.75)-Evolutionary War x-over | .45 | 1.30 | 2.60 |
| Annual 9 ('89, $2.00, 68 pgs.)-Atlantis Attacks | .35 | 1.00 | 2.00 |
| Annual 10 ('90, $2.00, 68 pgs.) | .35 | 1.00 | 2.00 |

**SPECTRE, THE** (See Adventure Comics 431, More Fun & Showcase)
Nov-Dec, 1967 - No. 10, May-June, 1969 (All 12 cents)
National Periodical Publications

| | | | |
|---|---|---|---|
| 1-Anderson-c/a | 2.85 | 8.50 | 20.00 |
| 2-5-Neal Adams-c/a; 3-Wildcat x-over | 2.15 | 6.50 | 15.00 |
| 6-8,10: 6-8-Anderson inks. 7-Hourman app. | 1.00 | 3.00 | 7.00 |
| 9-Wrightson-a | 1.15 | 3.50 | 8.00 |

**SPECTRE, THE** (See Saga of Swamp Thing #58 & Wrath of the. . . )
Apr, 1987 - No. 31, Oct, 1989 ($1.00, new format)
DC Comics

| | | | |
|---|---|---|---|
| 1-Colan-a(p) begins; Kaluta-c | .35 | 1.10 | 2.25 |
| 2-10: 3-Kaluta-c. 10-Morrow-a | .25 | .75 | 1.50 |
| 11-31: 10-Batman cameo. 10,11-Millennium tie-ins | .60 | .1.25 | |
| Annual 1 (1988, $2.00)-Deadman app. | .35 | 1.00 | 2.00 |

**SPEED COMICS** (New Speed)
Oct, 1939 - No. 44, Jan-Feb, 1947 (No. 14-16: pocket size, 100 pgs.)
Brookwood Publ./Speed Publ./Harvey Publications No. 14 on

|  | Good | Fine | N-Mint |
|---|---|---|---|
| 1-Origin Shock Gibson; Ted Parrish, the Man with 1000 Faces begins; | | | |
|    Powell-a | 79.00 | 235.00 | 550.00 |
| 2-Powell-a | 38.00 | 115.00 | 270.00 |
| 3 | 24.00 | 72.00 | 170.00 |
| 4-Powell-a? | 21.00 | 62.00 | 145.00 |
| 5 | 19.00 | 57.00 | 135.00 |
| 6-11: 7-Mars Mason begins, ends #11 | 16.50 | 50.00 | 115.00 |
| 12 (3/41; shows #11 in indicia)-The Wasp begins; Major Colt app. (Capt. | | | |
|    Colt #12) | 20.00 | 60.00 | 140.00 |
| 13-Intro. Captain Freedom & Young Defenders; Girl Commandos, Pat | | | |
|    Parker, War Nurse begins; Major Colt app. | | | |
| | 24.00 | 73.00 | 170.00 |
| 14-16 (100 pg. pocket size, 1941): 14-2nd Harvey comic (See Pocket). | | | |
|    15-Pat Parker dons costume, last in costume #23; no Girl Comman- | | | |
|    dos | 18.50 | 56.00 | 130.00 |
| 17-Black Cat begins (origin), r-/Pocket #1; not in #40,41 | | | |
| | 30.00 | 90.00 | 210.00 |
| 18-20 | 16.50 | 50.00 | 115.00 |
| 21,22,25-30: 26-Flag-c | 14.00 | 42.00 | 100.00 |
| 23-Origin Girl Commandos | 21.00 | 62.00 | 145.00 |
| 24-Pat Parker team-up with Girl Commandos | | | |
| | 14.00 | 42.00 | 100.00 |
| 31-44: 38-Flag-c | 11.50 | 34.00 | 80.00 |

**SPIDER-MAN** (See Amazing . . . , Spectacular . . . , & Web Of . . . )

**SPIDER-MAN**
Aug. 1990-Present
Marvel Comics

|  | Good | Fine | N-Mint |
|---|---|---|---|
| 1-Silver edition, direct sale only | .35 | 1.00 | 2.00 |
| 1-Silver bagged edition, still sealed | 2.50 | 7.50 | 15.00 |
| 1-Regular edition w/ Spidy face in UPC area | .30 | .90 | 1.75 |
| 1-Regular bagged edition w/ Spidy face in UPC area price is for still | | | |
|    sealed only | 1.70 | 5.00 | 10.00 |

| | Good | Fine | N-Mint |
|---|---|---|---|
| 1-Newstand bagged edition w/ UPC lines in UPC area | | | |
| | .35 | 1.00 | 2.00 |
| 1-Gold edition, 2nd print | .35 | 1.00 | 2.00 |
| 2-5 | .30 | .90 | 1.75 |

**SPIDER-MAN VS. WOLVERINE**
Feb, 1987 (One-shot, 68 pgs.)
Marvel Comics Group

| | Good | Fine | N-Mint |
|---|---|---|---|
| 1-Williamson-i; intro Charlemagne | 1.35 | 4.00 | 8.00 |

**SPIRIT, THE** (1st Series) (Also see Police Comics #11)
1944 - No. 22, Aug, 1950
Quality Comics Group (Vital)

| | Good | Fine | N-Mint |
|---|---|---|---|
| nn(#1)-"Wanted Dead or Alive" | 41.00 | 122.00 | 285.00 |
| nn(#2)-"Crime Doesn't Pay" | 26.00 | 77.00 | 180.00 |
| nn(#3)-"Murder Runs Wild" | 19.00 | 57.00 | 135.00 |
| 4,5 | 14.00 | 42.00 | 100.00 |
| 6-10 | 13.00 | 40.00 | 90.00 |
| 11 | 11.50 | 34.00 | 80.00 |
| 12-17-Eisner-c | 20.00 | 60.00 | 140.00 |
| 18-21-Strip-r by Eisner; Eisner-c | 28.50 | 86.00 | 200.00 |
| 22-Used by N.Y. Legis. Comm; Classic Eisner-c | | | |
| | 44.00 | 133.00 | 310.00 |

**SPIRIT, THE** (2nd Series)
Spring, 1952 - No. 5, 1954
Fiction House Magazines

| | Good | Fine | N-Mint |
|---|---|---|---|
| 1-Not Eisner | 19.00 | 57.00 | 135.00 |
| 2-Eisner-c/a(2) | 21.50 | 64.00 | 150.00 |
| 3-Eisner/Grandenetti-c | 14.00 | 42.00 | 100.00 |
| 4-Eisner/Grandenetti-c; Eisner-a | 17.00 | 51.00 | 120.00 |
| 5-Eisner-c/a(4) | 22.00 | 65.00 | 154.00 |

**SPY SMASHER** (See Whiz Comics)
Fall, 1941 - No. 11, Feb, 1943 (Also see Crime Smasher)
Fawcett Publications

|                                                          | Good   | Fine   | N-Mint  |
|----------------------------------------------------------|--------|--------|---------|
| 1-Spy Smasher begins; silver metallic-c                  | 121.00 | 362.00 | 845.00  |
| 2-Raboy-c                                                | 60.00  | 180.00 | 420.00  |
| 3,4: 3-Bondage-c                                         | 50.00  | 150.00 | 350.00  |
| 5-7: Raboy-a; 6-Raboy-c/a. 7-Part photo-c                | 43.00  | 130.00 | 300.00  |
| 8-11: 9-Hitler, Tojo, Mussolini-c. 10-Hitler-c           | 38.00  | 115.00 | 265.00  |

**STAR SPANGLED COMICS** (. . . War Stories #131 on)
Oct, 1941 - No. 130, July, 1952
National Periodical Publications

| | Good | Fine | N-Mint |
|---|---|---|---|
| 1-Origin Tarantula; Captain X of the R.A.F., Star Spangled Kid & Armstrong of the Army begin | 158.00 | 395.00 | 950.00 |
| 2 | 61.00 | 182.00 | 425.00 |
| 3-5 | 41.00 | 122.00 | 285.00 |
| 6-Last Armstrong of the Army | 27.00 | 81.00 | 190.00 |
| 7-Origin/1st app. The Guardian by S&K, & Robotman by Paul Cassidy; The Newsboy Legion & TNT begin; last Captain X | 192.00 | 480.00 | 1150.00 |
| 8-Origin TNT & Dan the Dyna-Mite | 82.00 | 245.00 | 575.00 |
| 9,10 | 71.00 | 215.00 | 500.00 |
| 11-17 | 57.00 | 171.00 | 400.00 |
| 18-Origin Star Spangled Kid | 71.00 | 215.00 | 500.00 |
| 19-Last Tarantula | 57.00 | 171.00 | 400.00 |
| 20-Liberty Belle begins | 57.00 | 171.00 | 400.00 |
| 21-29-Last S&K issue; 23-Last TNT. 25-Robotman by Jimmy Thompson begins | 43.00 | 130.00 | 300.00 |
| 30-40 | 20.00 | 60.00 | 140.00 |
| 41-50 | 16.50 | 50.00 | 115.00 |
| 51-64: Last Newsboy Legion & The Guardian; #53 by S&K | 16.00 | 48.00 | 110.00 |
| 65-Robin begins with cover app. | 40.00 | 120.00 | 280.00 |
| 66-68,70-80 | 18.50 | 55.00 | 130.00 |
| 69-Origin Tomahawk | 22.00 | 65.00 | 154.00 |
| 81-Origin Merry, Girl of 1000 Gimmicks | 16.00 | 48.00 | 110.00 |
| 82,83,85,86: 83-Capt. Compass begins, ends #130 | 16.00 | 48.00 | 110.00 |
| 84,87 (Rare) | 20.00 | 60.00 | 140.00 |
| 88-94: Batman-c/stories in all. 88-Last Star Spangled Kid. 91-Federal Men begin, end #93. 94-Manhunters Around the World begin, end #121 | 20.00 | 60.00 | 140.00 |

|  | Good | Fine | N-Mint |
|---|---|---|---|
| 95-99 | 12.00 | 36.00 | 84.00 |
| 100 | 15.00 | 45.00 | 105.00 |
| 101-112,114,115,117-121: 114-Retells Robin's origin. 120-Last 52 pgs. |  |  |  |
|  | 10.00 | 30.00 | 70.00 |
| 113-Frazetta-a, 10 pgs. | 26.50 | 80.00 | 185.00 |
| 116-Flag-c | 10.00 | 30.00 | 70.00 |
| 122-Ghost Breaker begins (origin), ends #130 |  |  |  |
|  | 9.00 | 27.00 | 62.00 |
| 123-129 | 7.00 | 21.00 | 50.00 |
| 130 | 11.50 | 34.00 | 80.00 |

**STAR SPANGLED WAR STORIES** (Star Spangled Comics #1-130)
No. 131, 8/52 - No. 133, 10/52; No. 3, 11/52 - No. 204, 2-3/77
National Periodical Publications

|  | Good | Fine | N-Mint |
|---|---|---|---|
| 131(#1) | 24.00 | 72.00 | 170.00 |
| 132,133: 133-Used in **POP**, Pg. 94 | 16.00 | 48.00 | 110.00 |
| 3-5: 4-Devil Dog Dugan app. | 11.50 | 34.00 | 80.00 |
| 6-Evans-a | 9.30 | 28.00 | 65.00 |
| 7-10 | 7.00 | 21.00 | 50.00 |
| 11-20 | 5.70 | 17.00 | 40.00 |
| 21-30: Last precode (2/55) | 4.30 | 13.00 | 30.00 |
| 31-33,35-40 | 3.15 | 9.50 | 22.00 |
| 34-Krigstein-a | 5.00 | 15.00 | 35.00 |
| 41-50 | 2.85 | 8.50 | 20.00 |
| 51-83: 67-Easy Co. story w/o Sgt. Rock | 2.30 | 7.00 | 16.00 |
| 84-Origin Mlle. Marie | 5.00 | 15.00 | 35.00 |
| 85-89-Mlle. Marie in all | 2.85 | 8.50 | 20.00 |
| 90-1st Dinosaur issue & begin series | 12.00 | 36.00 | 85.00 |
| 91-No dinosaur story | 2.15 | 6.50 | 15.00 |
| 92-100: All Dinosaur issues | 5.00 | 15.00 | 35.00 |
| 101-133,135-137-Last Dinosaur story; Heath Birdman-#129,131 |  |  |  |
|  | 3.60 | 11.00 | 25.00 |
| 134-Neal Adams-a | 4.30 | 13.00 | 30.00 |
| 138-Enemy Ace begins by Joe Kubert | 1.00 | 3.00 | 6.00 |
| 139-143,145: 145-Last 12 cent issue (6-7/69) | .75 | 2.25 | 4.50 |
| 144-Neal Adams & Kubert-a | 1.10 | 3.25 | 6.50 |
| 146-148,152,153,155 | .75 | 2.25 | 4.50 |
| 149,150-Viking Prince by Kubert | .75 | 2.25 | 4.50 |
| 151-1st Unknown Soldier (6-7/70) | 1.10 | 3.25 | 6.50 |

| | | | |
|---|---|---|---|
| 154-Origin Unknown Soldier | .90 | 2.75 | 5.50 |
| 156-1st Battle Album | .35 | 1.00 | 2.00 |
| 157-161-Last Enemy Ace | .30 | .90 | 1.80 |
| 162-204: 181-183-Enemy Ace vs. Balloon Buster serial app. | | | |
| | | .50 | 1.00 |

**STARTLING COMICS**
June, 1940 - No. 53, May, 1948
Better Publications (Nedor)

| | | | |
|---|---|---|---|
| 1-Origin Captain Future-Man Of Tomorrow, Mystico (By Eisner/Fine), The Wonder Man; The Masked Rider begins; drug use story | | | |
| | 71.00 | 212.00 | 495.00 |
| 2 | 30.00 | 90.00 | 210.00 |
| 3 | 23.00 | 70.00 | 160.00 |
| 4 | 17.00 | 51.00 | 120.00 |
| 5-9 | 13.00 | 40.00 | 90.00 |
| 10-The Fighting Yank begins (origin & 1st app.) | | | |
| | 55.00 | 165.00 | 385.00 |
| 11-15: 12-Hitler, Hirohito, Mussolini-c | 16.50 | 50.00 | 115.00 |
| 16-Origin The Four Comrades; not in #32,35 | 18.50 | 56.00 | 130.00 |
| 17-Last Masked Rider & Mystico | 12.00 | 36.00 | 84.00 |
| 18-Pyroman begins (origin) | 30.00 | 90.00 | 210.00 |
| 19 | 13.00 | 40.00 | 90.00 |
| 20-The Oracle begins; not in #26,28,33,34 | 13.00 | 40.00 | 90.00 |
| 21-Origin The Ape, Oracle's enemy | 12.00 | 36.00 | 84.00 |
| 22-33 | 11.00 | 32.00 | 75.00 |
| 34-Origin The Scarab & only app. | 11.50 | 34.00 | 80.00 |
| 35-Hypodermic syringe attacks Fighting Yank in drug story | | | |
| | 11.50 | 34.00 | 80.00 |
| 36-43: 36-Last Four Comrades. 40-Last Capt. Future & Oracle. 41-Front Page Peggy begins. 43-Last Pyroman | 11.00 | 32.00 | 75.00 |
| 44-Lance Lewis, Space Detective begins; Ingels-c | | | |
| | 17.00 | 51.00 | 120.00 |
| 45-Tygra begins (Intro/origin) | 17.00 | 51.00 | 120.00 |
| 46-Ingels-c/a | 17.00 | 51.00 | 120.00 |
| 47-53: 49-Last Fighting Yank. 50,51-Sea-Eagle app. | | | |
| | 13.00 | 40.00 | 90.00 |

**STAR TREK** (TV)
7/67; No. 2, 6/68; No. 3, 12/68; No. 4, 6/69 - No. 61, 3/79
Gold Key

|  | Good | Fine | N-Mint |
|---|---|---|---|
| 1-Photo-c begin, end #9 | 21.50 | 64.00 | 150.00 |
| 2-5 | 11.00 | 33.00 | 77.00 |
| 6-9 | 7.50 | 22.50 | 53.00 |
| 10-20 | 5.00 | 15.00 | 35.00 |
| 21-30 | 3.50 | 10.50 | 24.00 |
| 31-40 | 1.85 | 5.50 | 13.00 |
| 41-61: 52-Drug propaganda story | 1.30 | 4.00 | 9.00 |

**STAR TREK**
April, 1980 - No. 18, Feb, 1982
Marvel Comics Group

|  | | | |
|---|---|---|---|
| 1-r/Marvel Super Special; movie adapt. | .60 | 1.75 | 3.50 |
| 2-18: 5-Miller-c | .35 | 1.00 | 2.00 |

**STAR TREK**
Feb, 1984 - No. 56, Nov, 1988 (Mando paper, 75 cents)
DC Comics

|  | | | |
|---|---|---|---|
| 1-Sutton-a(p) begin | 1.15 | 3.50 | 7.00 |
| 2-5 | .70 | 2.10 | 4.20 |
| 6-10: 7-Origin Saavik | .55 | 1.60 | 3.20 |
| 11-20, 33: 33 ($1.25, 52 pg.)-20th Anniversary | .35 | 1.05 | 2.10 |
| 21-32,50: 50-($1.50, 52 pgs.) | .25 | .80 | 1.60 |
| 34-49,51-56: 37-Painted-c. 49-Begin $1.00-c | | .55 | 1.10 |
| Annual 1-3: 1(1985). 2(1986). 3(1988, $1.50) | .35 | 1.05 | 2.10 |

**STAR TREK**
Oct, 1989 - Present ($1.50, color)
DC Comics

|  | | | |
|---|---|---|---|
| 1-Capt. Kirk and crew | .40 | 1.25 | 2.50 |
| 2,3 | .35 | 1.00 | 2.00 |
| 4-14 | .25 | .75 | 1.50 |

**STAR TREK: THE NEXT GENERATION** (TV)
Feb, 1988 - No. 6, July, 1988 (Mini series, based on TV show)
DC Comics

|  | Good | Fine | N-Mint |
|---|---|---|---|
| 1 (52 pgs.)-Sienkiewicz painted-c | .75 | 2.25 | 4.50 |
| 2-6 ($1.00) | .55 | 1.60 | 3.20 |

**STAR TREK: THE NEXT GENERATION** (TV)
Oct, 1989 - Present ($1.50, color)
DC Comics

|  | | | |
|---|---|---|---|
| 1-Capt. Picard and crew from TV show | .40 | 1.25 | 2.50 |
| 2,3 | .35 | 1.00 | 2.00 |
| 4-14 | .25 | .75 | 1.50 |

**STAR WARS** (Movie)
July, 1977 - No. 107, Sept, 1986
Marvel Comics Group

1-(Regular 30 cent edition)-Price in square w/UPC code

|  | | | |
|---|---|---|---|
|  | 2.00 | 6.00 | 12.00 |

1-(35 cent cover; limited distribution - 1500 copies?)-Price in square
w/UPC code

|  | | | |
|---|---|---|---|
|  | 45.00 | 135.00 | 315.00 |
| 2-4: 4-Battle with Darth Vader | .85 | 2.50 | 5.00 |
| 5-10 | .50 | 1.50 | 3.00 |
| 11-20 | .35 | 1.00 | 2.00 |
| 21-38 | .25 | .75 | 1.50 |

39-44-The Empire Strikes Back-r by Al Williamson in all

|  | | | |
|---|---|---|---|
|  | .35 | 1.00 | 2.00 |
| 45-107: 92,100-($1.00, 52 pgs.) | | .50 | 1.00 |

1-9-Reprints; has "reprint" in upper lefthand corner of cover or on inside or price and number inside a diamond with no date or UPC on
cover; 30 cent and 35 cent issues published

|  | | | |
|---|---|---|---|
|  | | .25 | .50 |
| Annual 1 (12/79) | .35 | 1.00 | 2.00 |
| Annual 2 (11/82), 3 (12/83) | | .60 | 1.20 |

**STRAIGHT ARROW** (Radio)
Feb-Mar, 1950 - No. 55, Mar, 1956 (All 36 pgs.)
Magazine Enterprises

| | Good | Fine | N-Mint |
|---|---|---|---|
| 1-Straight Arrow (alias Steve Adams) & his palomino Fury begin; 1st mention of Sundown Valley & the Secret Cave; Whitney-a | 21.50 | 64.00 | 150.00 |
| 2-Red Hawk begins (1st app?) by Powell (Origin), ends #55 | 10.00 | 30.00 | 70.00 |
| 3-Frazetta-c | 14.00 | 42.00 | 100.00 |
| 4,5: 4-Secret Cave-c | 6.00 | 18.00 | 42.00 |
| 6-10 | 4.65 | 14.00 | 32.00 |
| 11-Classic story "The Valley of Time," with an ancient civilization made of gold | 5.00 | 15.00 | 35.00 |
| 12-19 | 3.50 | 10.50 | 24.00 |
| 20-Origin Straight Arrow's Shield | 5.00 | 15.00 | 35.00 |
| 21-Origin Fury | 5.70 | 17.00 | 40.00 |
| 22-Frazetta-c | 10.00 | 30.00 | 70.00 |
| 23,25-30: 25-Secret Cave-c. 28-Red Hawk meets The Vikings | 3.00 | 9.00 | 21.00 |
| 24-Classic story "The Dragons of Doom!" with prehistoric pterodactyls | 4.65 | 14.00 | 32.00 |
| 31-38 | 2.65 | 8.00 | 18.00 |
| 39-Classic story "The Canyon Beast," with a dinosaur egg hatching a Tyranosaurus Rex | 3.50 | 10.50 | 24.00 |
| 40-Classic story "Secret of The Spanish Specters," with Conquistadors' lost treasure | 3.50 | 10.50 | 24.00 |
| 41,42,44-54: 45-Secret Cave-c | 2.15 | 6.50 | 15.00 |
| 43-Intro & 1st app. Blaze, Straight Arrow's Warrior dog | 2.65 | 8.00 | 18.00 |
| 55-Last issue | 3.00 | 9.00 | 21.00 |

**STRANGE ADVENTURES**
Aug-Sept, 1950 - No. 244, Oct-Nov, 1973 (No. 1-12: 52 pgs.)
National Periodical Publications

| | Good | Fine | N-Mint |
|---|---|---|---|
| 1-Adaptation of "Destination Moon"; Kris KL-99 & Darwin Jones begin; photo-c | 115.00 | 345.00 | 800.00 |
| 2 | 54.00 | 161.00 | 375.00 |
| 3,4 | 34.00 | 100.00 | 235.00 |

*Strange Adventures #124, © DC Comics*

|  | Good | Fine | N-Mint |
|---|---|---|---|
| 5-8,10: 7-Origin Kris KL-99 | 30.00 | 90.00 | 210.00 |
| 9-Captain Comet begins (6/51, Intro/origin) | | | |
|  | 81.00 | 242.00 | 565.00 |
| 11,14,15 | 25.00 | 75.00 | 175.00 |
| 12,13,17-Toth-a | 27.00 | 81.00 | 190.00 |
| 16,18-20 | 18.00 | 54.00 | 125.00 |
| 21-30 | 15.00 | 45.00 | 105.00 |
| 31,34-38 | 13.00 | 40.00 | 90.00 |
| 32,33-Krigstein-a | 14.00 | 42.00 | 100.00 |
| 39-Ill. in **SOTI**-"Treating police contemptuously" (top right) | | | |
|  | 20.00 | 60.00 | 140.00 |
| 40-49-Last Capt. Comet; not in 45,47,48 | 11.50 | 34.00 | 80.00 |
| 50-53-Last precode issue (2/55) | 8.50 | 25.50 | 60.00 |
| 54-70 | 5.00 | 15.00 | 35.00 |
| 71-99 | 3.70 | 11.00 | 26.00 |
| 100 | 5.70 | 17.00 | 40.00 |

|  | Good | Fine | N-Mint |
|---|---|---|---|
| 101-110: 104-Space Museum begins by Sekowsky | | | |
| | 2.85 | 8.50 | 20.00 |
| 111-116: 114-Star Hawkins begins, ends #185; Heath-a in Wood E.C. style | | | |
| | 2.30 | 7.00 | 16.00 |
| 117-1st app./Origin Atomic Knights & begins | | | |
| | 16.00 | 48.00 | 110.00 |
| 118-120 | 3.60 | 11.00 | 25.00 |
| 121-134: 124-Origin Faceless Creature. 134-Last 10 cent issue | | | |
| | 2.85 | 8.50 | 20.00 |
| 135-160: 159-Star Rovers app. 160-Last Atomic Knights | | | |
| | 1.70 | 5.00 | 12.00 |
| 161-179: 161-Last Space Museum. 163-Star Rovers app. 170-Infinity-c. | | | |
| 177-Origin Immortal Man | .70 | 2.00 | 4.00 |
| 180-Origin Animal Man | 14.00 | 42.00 | 100.00 |
| 181-183,185-189: 187-Origin The Enchantress | .40 | 1.25 | 2.50 |
| 184-2nd app. Animal Man | 7.00 | 21.00 | 50.00 |
| 190-1st Animal Man in costume | 5.70 | 17.00 | 40.00 |
| 191-194,196-200,202-204 | .40 | 1.25 | 2.50 |
| 195-1st full length Animal Man story | 5.00 | 15.00 | 35.00 |
| 201-2nd full length Animal Man story | 2.85 | 8.50 | 20.00 |
| 205-Intro/origin Deadman by Infantino (10/67) | | | |
| | 4.50 | 14.00 | 32.00 |
| 206-Neal Adams-a begins | 2.65 | 8.00 | 18.00 |
| 207-210 | 1.70 | 5.00 | 12.00 |
| 211-216: 211-Space Museum-r. 216-Last Deadman | | | |
| | 1.50 | 4.50 | 10.00 |
| 217-230: 217-Adam Strange & Atomic Knights-r begin. 218-Last 12 cent issue? 226-236-(68-52 pgs.) | .50 | 1.50 | 3.00 |
| 231-244: 231-Last Atomic Knights-r | | .50 | 1.00 |

### STRANGE STORIES OF SUSPENSE
No. 5, Oct, 1955 - No. 16, Aug, 1957
Atlas Comics (CSI)

| | | | |
|---|---|---|---|
| 5(#1) | 8.50 | 25.50 | 60.00 |
| 6,9 | 5.00 | 15.00 | 35.00 |
| 7-E. C. swipe cover/Vault of Horror #32 | 5.50 | 16.50 | 38.00 |
| 8-Williamson/Mayo-a; Pakula-a | 6.00 | 18.00 | 42.00 |
| 10-Crandall, Torres, Meskin-a | 6.00 | 18.00 | 42.00 |
| 11 | 3.00 | 9.00 | 21.00 |
| 12-Torres, Pakula-a | 3.50 | 10.50 | 24.00 |

| | Good | Fine | N-Mint |
|---|---|---|---|
| 13-E.C. art swipes | 3.00 | 9.00 | 21.00 |
| 14-Williamson-a | 4.30 | 13.00 | 30.00 |
| 15-Krigstein-a | 3.70 | 11.00 | 26.00 |
| 16-Fox, Powell-a | 4.30 | 13.00 | 30.00 |

**STRANGE SUSPENSE STORIES** (Lawbreakers Suspense Stories #10-15;
    This Is Suspense #23-26)
6/52 - No. 5, 2/53; No. 16, 1/54 - No. 22, 11/54; No. 27, 10/55 - No. 77,
    10/65; V3#1, 10/67 - V1#9, 9/69
Fawcett Publications/Charlton Comics No. 16 on

| | Good | Fine | N-Mint |
|---|---|---|---|
| 1-(Fawcett)-Powell, Sekowsky-a | 20.00 | 60.00 | 140.00 |
| 2-George Evans horror story | 13.00 | 40.00 | 90.00 |
| 3-5 (2/53)-George Evans horror stories | 11.00 | 32.00 | 75.00 |
| 16(1-2/54) | 6.50 | 19.50 | 45.00 |
| 17,21 | 5.00 | 15.00 | 35.00 |
| 18-E.C. swipe/HOF 7; Ditko-c/a(2) | 11.00 | 32.00 | 75.00 |
| 19-Ditko electric chair-c; Ditko-a | 13.00 | 40.00 | 90.00 |
| 20-Ditko-c/a(2) | 11.00 | 32.00 | 75.00 |
| 22(11/54)-Ditko-c, Shuster-a; last pre-code issue; becomes This Is Suspense | 8.50 | 25.50 | 60.00 |
| 27(10/55)-(Formerly This Is Suspense #26) | 2.00 | 6.00 | 14.00 |
| 28-30,38 | 1.70 | 5.00 | 12.00 |
| 31-33,35,37,40,51-Ditko-c/a(2-3 each) | 5.70 | 17.00 | 40.00 |
| 34-Story of ruthless business man, Wm. B. Gaines; Ditko-c/a | 8.00 | 24.00 | 56.00 |
| 36-(68 pgs.); Ditko-a | 7.00 | 21.00 | 50.00 |
| 39,41,52,53-Ditko-a | 5.00 | 15.00 | 35.00 |
| 42-44,46,49,54-60 | 1.50 | 4.50 | 10.00 |
| 45,47,48,50-Ditko-c/a | 4.00 | 12.00 | 28.00 |
| 61-74 | .50 | 1.50 | 3.00 |
| 75(6/65)-Reprints origin/1st app. Captain Atom by Ditko from Space Adventures #33 (75-77: 12 cent issues) | 8.50 | 25.50 | 60.00 |
| 76,77-Captain Atom-r by Ditko/Space Advs. | 3.50 | 10.50 | 24.00 |
| V3#1(10/67)-4: All 12 cent issues | .50 | 1.50 | 3.00 |
| V1#2-9: 2-Ditko-a, atom bomb-c (all 12 cents) | .35 | 1.00 | 2.00 |

**STRANGE TALES** (Becomes Doctor Strange #169 on)
June, 1951 - #168, May, 1968; #169, Sept, 1973 - #188, Nov, 1976
Atlas (CCPC #1-67/ZPC #68-79/VPI #80-85)/Marvel #86(7/61) on

| | Good | Fine | N-Mint |
|---|---|---|---|
| 1 | 80.00 | 240.00 | 560.00 |
| 2 | 36.00 | 107.00 | 250.00 |
| 3,5: 3-Atom bomb panels | 26.00 | 80.00 | 185.00 |
| 4-"The Evil Eye," cosmic eyeball story | 28.50 | 86.00 | 200.00 |
| 6-9 | 18.50 | 56.00 | 130.00 |
| 10-Krigstein-a | 20.00 | 60.00 | 140.00 |
| 11-14,16-20 | 10.00 | 30.00 | 70.00 |
| 15-Krigstein-a | 11.00 | 32.00 | 75.00 |
| 21,23-27,29-32,34-Last precode issue(2/55): 27-Atom bomb panels | | | |
| | 8.00 | 24.00 | 56.00 |
| 22-Krigstein, Forte/Fox-a | 8.50 | 25.50 | 60.00 |
| 28-Jack Katz story used in Senate Investigation report, pgs. 7 & 169 | | | |
| | 8.50 | 25.50 | 60.00 |
| 33-Davis-a | 8.00 | 24.00 | 56.00 |
| 35-41,43,44 | 5.00 | 15.00 | 35.00 |
| 42,45,59,61-Krigstein-a; #61 (2/58) | 5.70 | 17.00 | 40.00 |
| 46-52,54,55,57,60: 60 (8/57) | 4.30 | 13.00 | 30.00 |
| 53-Torres, Crandall-a | 5.70 | 17.00 | 40.00 |
| 56-Crandall-a | 5.00 | 15.00 | 35.00 |
| 58,64-Williamson-a in each, with Mayo-#58 | 5.70 | 17.00 | 40.00 |
| 62-Torres-a | 4.50 | 14.00 | 32.00 |
| 63,65 | 4.30 | 13.00 | 30.00 |
| 66-Crandall-a | 4.50 | 14.00 | 32.00 |
| 67-80-Ditko/Kirby-a. 79-Dr. Strange prototype app. | | | |
| | 4.00 | 12.00 | 28.00 |
| 81-92-Last 10 cent issue. Ditko/Kirby-a | 3.70 | 11.00 | 26.00 |
| 93-100-Kirby-a | 3.50 | 10.50 | 24.00 |
| 101-Human Torch begins by Kirby (10/62) | 43.00 | 130.00 | 300.00 |
| 102 | 16.70 | 50.00 | 116.00 |
| 103-105 | 13.50 | 41.00 | 95.00 |
| 106,108,109 | 9.00 | 27.00 | 63.00 |
| 107-Human Torch/Sub-Mariner battle | 11.50 | 34.00 | 80.00 |
| 110-Intro Dr. Strange, Ancient One & Wong by Ditko | | | |
| | 32.00 | 96.00 | 225.00 |
| 111-2nd Dr. Strange | 7.85 | 23.50 | 55.00 |
| 112,113 | 5.30 | 16.00 | 37.00 |
| 114-Acrobat disguised as Captain America, 1st app. since the G.A.; intro. & 1st app. Victoria Bentley | 12.00 | 36.00 | 84.00 |
| 115-Origin Dr. Strange+ begin series; Sandman (villain) app. | | | |
| | 18.00 | 54.00 | 125.00 |

| | Good | Fine | N-Mint |
|---|---|---|---|
| 116-120: 116-Thing/Torch battle | 4.30 | 13.00 | 30.00 |
| 121-129,131-134: Thing/Torch team-up in all; 126-Intro Clea. 134-Last Human Torch; Wood-a(i) | 2.30 | 7.00 | 16.00 |
| 130-The Beatles cameo | 3.00 | 9.00 | 21.00 |
| 135-Nick Fury, Agent of Shield begins (origin) by Kirby, ends #167 | 4.30 | 13.00 | 30.00 |
| 136-147,149: 146-Last Ditko Dr. Strange who is in consecutive stories since No. 113 | 1.60 | 4.80 | 11.00 |
| 148-Origin Ancient One | 1.85 | 5.50 | 13.00 |
| 150(11/66)-John Buscema's 1st work at Marvel | 1.60 | 4.80 | 11.00 |
| 151-1st Marvel work by Steranko (w/Kirby) | 1.85 | 5.50 | 13.00 |
| 152,153-Kirby/Steranko-a | 1.60 | 4.80 | 11.00 |
| 154-158-Steranko-a/script | 1.60 | 4.80 | 11.00 |
| 159-Origin Nick Fury; Intro Val; Captain America app; Steranko-a | 1.85 | 5.50 | 13.00 |
| 160-162-Steranko-a/scripts; Cap. America app. | 1.60 | 4.80 | 11.00 |
| 163-166,168-Steranko-a(p) | 1.60 | 4.80 | 11.00 |
| 167-Steranko pen/script; classic flag-c | 2.15 | 6.50 | 15.00 |
| 169-177: 169,170-Brother Voodoo origin in each; series ends #173. 174-Origin Golem. 177-Brunner-c | .25 | .75 | 1.50 |
| 178-Warlock by Starlin with covers; origin Warlock & Him; Starlin scripts in 178-181 | 1.50 | 4.50 | 9.00 |
| 179-181-Warlock by Starlin with covers. 179-Intro/1st app. Pip the Troll. 180-Intro Gamora | .85 | 2.50 | 5.00 |
| 182-188 | .25 | .75 | 1.50 |
| Annual 1(1962)-Reprints from Strange Tales #73,76,78, Tales of Suspense #7,9, Tales to Astonish #1,6,7, & Journey Into Mystery #53, 55,59 | 21.50 | 64.00 | 150.00 |
| Annual 2(1963)-r-/from Strange Tales #67, Strange Worlds (Atlas) #1-3, World of Fantasy #16, Human Torch vs. Spider-Man by Kirby/Ditko; Kirby-c (early Spider-Man app.) | 22.00 | 66.00 | 155.00 |

**STRANGE TERRORS**
June, 1952 - No. 7, Mar, 1953
St. John Publishing Co.

| | | | |
|---|---|---|---|
| 1-Bondage-c; Zombies spelled Zoombies on-c; Fineesque-a | 13.00 | 40.00 | 90.00 |

|                                                                                                  | Good  | Fine   | N-Mint |
|--------------------------------------------------------------------------------------------------|-------|--------|--------|
| 2                                                                                                | 7.00  | 21.00  | 50.00  |
| 3-Kubert-a; painted-c                                                                            | 10.00 | 30.00  | 70.00  |
| 4-Kubert-a(reprinted in Mystery Tales #18); Ekgren-c; Fineesque-a; Jerry Iger caricature         | 18.00 | 54.00  | 125.00 |
| 5-Kubert-a; painted-c                                                                            | 10.00 | 30.00  | 70.00  |
| 6-Giant, 100 pgs.(1/53); bondage-c                                                               | 14.00 | 42.00  | 100.00 |
| 7-Giant, 100 pgs.; Kubert-c/a                                                                     | 18.50 | 56.00  | 130.00 |

**STRANGE WORLDS** (#18 continued from Avon's Eerie #1-17)
Nov, 1950 - No. 22, Sept-Oct, 1955 (No #11-17)
Avon Periodicals

|                                                                                                              | Good  | Fine   | N-Mint |
|--------------------------------------------------------------------------------------------------------------|-------|--------|--------|
| 1-Kenton of the Star Patrol by Kubert (r-/Eerie #1-'47); Crom the Barbarian by John Giunta                   | 38.00 | 115.00 | 265.00 |
| 2-Wood-a; Crom the Barbarian by Giunta; Dara of the Vikings app.; used in **SOTI**, pg. 112; injury to eye panel | 33.00 | 100.00 | 230.00 |
| 3-Wood/Orlando-a(Kenton),     Wood/Williamson/Frazetta/Krenkel/ Orlando-a (7 pgs.); Malu Slave Girl Princess app.; Kinstler-c | 68.00 | 205.00 | 485.00 |
| 4-Wood-c/a (Kenton); Orlando-a; origin The Enchanted Daggar; Sultan-a | 32.00 | 95.00  | 225.00 |
| 5-Orlando/Wood-a (Kenton); Wood-c                                                                            | 27.00 | 81.00  | 190.00 |
| 6-Kinstler-a(2); Orlando/Wood-c; Check-a                                                                     | 17.00 | 51.00  | 120.00 |
| 7-Kinstler, Fawcette & Becker/Alascia-a                                                                      | 13.00 | 40.00  | 90.00  |
| 8-Kubert, Kinstler, Hollingsworth & Lazarus-a; Lazarus-c                                                     | 14.00 | 42.00  | 100.00 |
| 9-Kinstler, Fawcette, Alascia-a                                                                              | 13.00 | 40.00  | 90.00  |
| 10-Exist?                                                                                                    | 12.00 | 36.00  | 84.00  |
| 18-R/"Attack on Planet Mars" by Kubert                                                                       | 13.50 | 40.00  | 95.00  |
| 19-R/Avon's "Robotmen of the Lost Planet"                                                                    | 13.50 | 40.00  | 95.00  |
| 20-War stories; Wood-c(r)/U.S. Paratroops #1                                                                 | 3.65  | 11.00  | 25.00  |
| 21,22-War stories                                                                                            | 3.35  | 10.00  | 23.00  |

**STRANGE WORLDS**
Dec, 1958 - No. 5, Aug, 1959
Marvel Comics (MPI No. 1,2/Male No. 3,5)

|                                            | Good  | Fine  | N-Mint |
|--------------------------------------------|-------|-------|--------|
| 1-Kirby & Ditko-a; flying saucer issue     | 20.00 | 60.00 | 140.00 |
| 2-Ditko-c/a                                | 12.15 | 36.50 | 85.00  |

|  | Good | Fine | N-Mint |
|---|---|---|---|
| 3-Kirby-a(2) | 9.15 | 27.50 | 64.00 |
| 4-Williamson-a | 10.70 | 32.00 | 75.00 |
| 5-Ditko-a | 8.50 | 25.50 | 60.00 |

**SUB-MARINER, THE** (2nd Series) (Sub-Mariner #31 on)
May, 1968 - No. 72, Sept, 1974 (No. 43: 52 pgs.)
Marvel Comics Group

| | Good | Fine | N-Mint |
|---|---|---|---|
| 1-Origin Sub-Mariner | 11.00 | 32.00 | 75.00 |
| 2-Triton app. | 2.85 | 8.50 | 20.00 |
| 3-10: 5-1st Tiger Shark. 7-Photo-c | 1.50 | 4.50 | 10.00 |
| 11-13 | 1.15 | 3.50 | 7.00 |
| 14-Sub-Mariner vs. G.A. Human Torch; death of Toro | | | |
| | 1.70 | 5.00 | 12.00 |
| 15-20: 19-1st Sting Ray | 1.00 | 3.00 | 6.00 |
| 21-40: 37-Death of Lady Dorma. 35-Ties into 1st Defenders story; | | | |
| 38-Origin | .70 | 2.00 | 4.00 |
| 41-72: 44,45-Sub-Mariner vs. H. Torch. 50-1st app. Nita, Namor's niece. | | | |
| 61-Last artwork by Everett; 1st 4 pgs. completed by Mortimer; pgs. | | | |
| 5-20 by Mooney. 62-1st Tales of Atlantis, ends #66 | | | |
| | .50 | 1.50 | 3.00 |
| Special 1 (1/71), Special 2 (1/72)-Everett-a | .50 | 1.50 | 3.00 |

**SUB-MARINER COMICS** (1st Series) (The Sub-Mariner #1,2,33-42)
Spring, 1941 - No. 23, Sum, '47; No. 24, Wint, '47 - No. 31, 4/49; No. 32,
7/49; No. 33, 4/54 - No. 42, 10/55
Timely/Marvel Comics (TCI 1-7/SePI 8/MPI 9-32/Atlas Comics (CCC
33-42))

| | Good | Fine | N-Mint |
|---|---|---|---|
| 1-The Sub-Mariner by Everett & The Angel begin | | | |
| | 467.00 | 1170.00 | 2800.00 |
| 2-Everett-a | 220.00 | 550.00 | 1320.00 |
| 3-Churchill assassination-c; 40 pg. Sub-Mariner story | | | |
| | 150.00 | 375.00 | 900.00 |
| 4-Everett-a, 40 pgs.; 1 pg. Wolverton-a | 138.00 | 345.00 | 830.00 |
| 5 | 100.00 | 250.00 | 600.00 |
| 6-10: 9-Wolverton-a, 3 pgs.; flag-c | 75.00 | 190.00 | 450.00 |

*Sub-Mariner Comics #15, © Marvel Comics*

|  | Good | Fine | N-Mint |
|---|---|---|---|
| 11-15 | 52.00 | 130.00 | 315.00 |
| 16-20 | 47.00 | 120.00 | 280.00 |
| 21-Last Angel; Everett-a | 36.00 | 90.00 | 215.00 |
| 22-Young Allies app. | 36.00 | 90.00 | 215.00 |
| 23-The Human Torch, Namora x-over | 36.00 | 90.00 | 215.00 |
| 24-Namora x-over | 36.00 | 90.00 | 215.00 |
| 25-The Blonde Phantom begins, ends No. 31; Kurtzman-a; Namora x-over | | | |
|  | 43.00 | 110.00 | 260.00 |
| 26,27 | 40.00 | 100.00 | 240.00 |
| 28-Namora cover; Everett-a | 40.00 | 100.00 | 240.00 |
| 29-31 (4/49): 29-The Human Torch app. 31-Capt. America app. | | | |
|  | 40.00 | 100.00 | 240.00 |
| 32 (7/49, Scarce)-Origin Sub-Mariner | 62.00 | 155.00 | 370.00 |
| 33 (4/54)-Origin Sub-Mariner; The Human Torch app.; Namora x-over in | | | |
| Sub-Mariner #33-42 | 36.00 | 90.00 | 215.00 |
| 34,35-Human Torch in each | 25.00 | 62.00 | 150.00 |
| 36,37,39-41: 36,39-41-Namora app. | 25.00 | 62.00 | 150.00 |

| | Good | Fine | N-Mint |
|---|---|---|---|
| 38-Origin Sub-Mariner's wings; Namora app. | 32.00 | 80.00 | 195.00 |
| 42-Last issue | 28.00 | 70.00 | 170.00 |

## SUGAR & SPIKE
Apr-May, 1956 - No. 98, Oct-Nov, 1971
National Periodical Publications

| | Good | Fine | N-Mint |
|---|---|---|---|
| 1 (Scarce) | 61.00 | 182.00 | 425.00 |
| 2 | 30.00 | 90.00 | 210.00 |
| 3-5 | 27.00 | 81.00 | 190.00 |
| 6-10 | 17.00 | 51.00 | 120.00 |
| 11-20 | 13.00 | 40.00 | 90.00 |
| 21-29,31-40: 26-Xmas-c | 7.00 | 21.00 | 50.00 |
| 30-Scribbly x-over | 8.50 | 25.50 | 60.00 |
| 41-60 | 3.50 | 10.50 | 24.00 |
| 61-80: 72-Origin & 1st app. Bernie the Brain | 2.30 | 7.00 | 16.00 |
| 81-98: 85-(68 pgs.); r-#72. #96-(68 pgs.). #97,98-(52 pgs.) | | | |
| | 1.70 | 5.00 | 12.00 |

## SUICIDE SQUAD (See Brave & the Bold & Legends #3)
May, 1987 - Present (Direct sale only #32 on)
DC Comics

| | Good | Fine | N-Mint |
|---|---|---|---|
| 1-39,44-48: 9-Millennium x-over. 10-Batman-c/story. 13-JLI app. (Batman). 16-Re-intro Shade The Changing Man | | | |
| | | .50 | 1.00 |
| 40-43-"The Phoenix Gambit" Batman storyline. 40-Free Batman/Suicide Squad poster | | | |
| | | .50 | 1.00 |
| Annual 1 (1988, $1.50)-Manhunter x-over | .25 | .75 | 1.50 |

## SUNSET CARSON
Feb, 1951 - No. 4, 1951
Charlton Comics

| | Good | Fine | N-Mint |
|---|---|---|---|
| 1-Photo/retouched-c (Scarce, all issues) | 62.00 | 185.00 | 435.00 |
| 2 | 41.00 | 122.00 | 285.00 |
| 3,4 | 30.00 | 90.00 | 210.00 |

**SUPERBOY** (. . . & the Legion of Super-Heroes with #231)
Mar-Apr, 1949 - No. 258, Dec, 1979 (#1-16: 52 pgs.)
National Periodical Publications/DC Comics

| | Good | Fine | N-Mint |
|---|---|---|---|
| 1-Superman cover | 250.00 | 750.00 | 1750.00 |
| 2-Used in **SOTI**, pg. 35-36,226 | 96.00 | 290.00 | 675.00 |
| 3 | 70.00 | 210.00 | 490.00 |
| 4,5: 5-Pre-Supergirl tryout | 59.00 | 178.00 | 415.00 |
| 6-10: 8-1st Superbaby. 10-1st app. Lana Lang | | | |
| | 43.00 | 130.00 | 300.00 |
| 11-15 | 32.00 | 95.00 | 225.00 |
| 16-20 | 22.00 | 65.00 | 155.00 |
| 21-26,28-30 | 17.00 | 51.00 | 120.00 |
| 27-Low distribution | 18.00 | 54.00 | 125.00 |
| 31-38: 38-Last pre-code issue | 12.00 | 36.00 | 84.00 |
| 39-48,50 (7/56) | 8.30 | 28.00 | 65.00 |
| 49 (6/56)-1st app. Metallo (Jor-El's robot) | 11.00 | 32.00 | 75.00 |
| 51-60: 55-Spanking-c | 6.50 | 19.50 | 45.00 |
| 61-67 | 5.00 | 15.00 | 35.00 |
| 68-Origin/1st app. original Bizarro (10-11/58) | | | |
| | 19.30 | 58.00 | 135.00 |
| 69-77,79: 75-Spanking-c. 76-1st Supermonkey. 77-Pre-Pete Ross tryout | | | |
| | 4.30 | 13.00 | 30.00 |
| 78-Origin Mr. Mxyzptlk & Superboy's costume | | | |
| | 8.00 | 24.00 | 55.00 |
| 80-1st meeting Superboy/Supergirl (4/60) | 4.30 | 13.00 | 30.00 |
| 81-85,87,88: 82-1st Bizarro Krypto. 83-Origin & 1st app. Kryptonite Kid | | | |
| | 3.15 | 9.50 | 22.00 |
| 86(1/61)-4th Legion app; Intro Pete Ross | 9.30 | 28.00 | 65.00 |
| 89(6/61)-Mon-el 1st app. | 13.00 | 40.00 | 90.00 |
| 90-92: 90-Pete Ross learns Superboy's I.D. 92-Last 10 cent issue | | | |
| | 2.85 | 8.50 | 20.00 |
| 93(12/61)-10th Legion app; Chameleon Boy app. | | | |
| | 3.50 | 10.50 | 24.00 |
| 94-97,99 | 1.70 | 5.00 | 12.00 |
| 98(7/62)-19th Legion app; Origin & intro. Ultra Boy; Pete Ross joins Legion | 2.85 | 8.50 | 20.00 |
| 100(10/62)-Ultra Boy app; 1st app. Phantom Zone villains, Dr. Xadu & Erndine. 2 pg. map of Krypton; origin Superboy retold; r-cover of Superman #1; Pete Ross joins Legion | 11.50 | 34.50 | 80.00 |

|                                                                      | Good | Fine | N-Mint |
|----------------------------------------------------------------------|------|------|--------|
| 101-120: 104-Origin Phantom Zone. 115-Atomic bomb-c. 117-Legion app. |      |      |        |
|                                                                      | 1.00 | 3.00 | 6.00   |

121-128: 124(10/65)-1st app. Insect Queen (Lana Lang). 125-Legion cameo. 126-Origin Krypto the Super Dog retold with new facts

|                                                             |      |      |      |
|-------------------------------------------------------------|------|------|------|
|                                                             | .50  | 1.50 | 3.00 |
| 129 (80-pg. Giant G-22)-Reprints origin Mon-el             | .70  | 2.00 | 4.00 |
| 138 (80-pg. Giant G-35)                                     | .70  | 2.00 | 4.00 |

130-137,139,140: 131-Legion statues cameo in Dog Legionnaires story. 132-1st app. Supremo

|       |      |      |      |
|-------|------|------|------|
|       | .40  | 1.25 | 2.50 |

141-146,148-155,157-164,166-173,175,176: 145-Superboy's parents regain their youth. 172,173,176-Legion app.; 172-Origin Yango (Super Ape)

|       |      |      |      |
|-------|------|------|------|
|       | .35  | 1.00 | 2.00 |

147(6/68)-Giant G-47; origin Saturn Girl, Lightning Lad, Cosmic Boy; origin Legion of Super-Pets-r/Adv. 293?

|       |      |      |      |
|-------|------|------|------|
|       | .85  | 2.50 | 5.00 |
| 156,165,174 (Giants G-59,71,83) | .50  | 1.50 | 3.00 |

177-184,186,187 (All 52 pgs.): 184-Origin Dial H for Hero-r

|       |      |      |
|-------|------|------|
|       | .50  | 1.00 |

185-DC 100 Pg. Super Spectacular #12; Legion-c/story; Teen Titans, Kid Eternity, Star Spangled Kid-r

|       |      |      |      |
|-------|------|------|------|
|       | .25  | .75  | 1.50 |
| 188-196: 191-Origin Sunboy retold; Legion app. | | .50 | 1.00 |

197-Legion begins; Lightning Lad's new costume

|       |      |      |      |
|-------|------|------|------|
|       | .75  | 2.25 | 4.50 |

198,199: 198-Element Lad & Princess Projectra get new costumes

|       |      |      |      |
|-------|------|------|------|
|       | .35  | 1.00 | 2.00 |

200-Bouncing Boy & Duo Damsel marry; Jonn' Jonzz' cameo

|       |      |      |      |
|-------|------|------|------|
|       | .75  | 2.25 | 4.50 |

201,204,206,207,209: 204-Supergirl resigns from Legion. 209-Karate Kid new costume

|       |      |      |      |
|-------|------|------|------|
|       | .35  | 1.00 | 2.00 |

202,205-(100 pgs.): 202-Light Lass gets new costume

|                          |      |      |      |
|--------------------------|------|------|------|
|                          | .45  | 1.25 | 2.50 |
| 203-Invisible Kid dies   | .50  | 1.50 | 3.00 |
| 208-(68 pgs.)            | .45  | 1.25 | 2.50 |
| 210-Origin Karate Kid    | .45  | 1.25 | 2.50 |

211-220: 212-Matter-Eater Lad resigns. 216-1st app. Tyroc who joins Legion in #218

|       |      |      |      |
|-------|------|------|------|
|       | .30  | .90  | 1.80 |

221-249: 226-Intro. Dawnstar. 228-Death of Chemical King. 240-Origin Dawnstar. 242-(52 pgs.). 243-Legion of Substitute Heroes app. 243-245-(44 pgs.)

|       |      |      |
|-------|------|------|
|       | .60  | 1.20 |

|  | Good | Fine | N-Mint |
|---|---|---|---|
| 250-258: 253-Intro Blok. 257-Return of Bouncing Boy & Duo Damsel by | | | |
|    Ditko | | .50 | 1.00 |
| Annual 1(Sum/64, 84 pgs.)-Origin Krypto-r | 6.50 | 19.50 | 45.00 |

**SUPERBOY** (TV)
Feb, 1990 - Present ($1.00, color)
DC Comics

|  | Good | Fine | N-Mint |
|---|---|---|---|
| 1-10: Mooney-a(p); 1-Photo-c from TV show | | .50 | 1.00 |

**SUPER COMICS**
May, 1938 - No. 121, Feb-Mar, 1949
Dell Publishing Co.

| | Good | Fine | N-Mint |
|---|---|---|---|
| 1-Terry & The Pirates, The Gumps, Dick Tracy, Little Orphan Annie, Gasoline Alley, Little Joe, Smilin' Jack, Smokey Stover, Smitty, Tiny Tim, Moon Mullins, Harold Teen, Winnie Winkle begin | | | |
| | 103.00 | 260.00 | 615.00 |
| 2 | 43.00 | 130.00 | 300.00 |
| 3 | 38.00 | 115.00 | 270.00 |
| 4,5 | 30.00 | 90.00 | 210.00 |
| 6-10 | 24.00 | 73.00 | 170.00 |
| 11-20 | 19.00 | 57.00 | 135.00 |
| 21-29: 21-Magic Morro begins (Origin, 2/40). 22-Ken Ernst-c | | | |
| | 16.00 | 48.00 | 115.00 |
| 30-"Sea Hawk" movie adaptation-c/story with Errol Flynn | | | |
| | 16.00 | 48.00 | 115.00 |
| 31-40 | 13.00 | 40.00 | 90.00 |
| 41-50: 43-Terry & The Pirates ends | 11.00 | 32.00 | 75.00 |
| 51-60 | 8.00 | 24.00 | 56.00 |
| 61-70: 65-Brenda Starr-r begin? 67-Xmas-c | 6.50 | 19.50 | 45.00 |
| 71-80 | 5.50 | 16.50 | 40.00 |
| 81-99 | 4.50 | 14.00 | 32.00 |
| 100 | 5.50 | 16.50 | 40.00 |
| 101-115-Last Dick Tracy (moves to own title) | 3.70 | 11.00 | 26.00 |
| 116,118-All Smokey Stover | 3.00 | 9.00 | 21.00 |
| 117-All Gasoline Alley | 3.00 | 9.00 | 21.00 |
| 119-121-Terry & The Pirates app. in all | 3.00 | 9.00 | 21.00 |

**SUPER DUCK COMICS** (The Cockeyed Wonder)
Fall, 1944 - No. 94, Dec, 1960
MLJ Mag. No. 1-4(9/45)/Close-Up No. 5 on (Archie)

|  | Good | Fine | N-Mint |
|---|---|---|---|
| 1-Origin | 19.00 | 58.00 | 135.00 |
| 2 | 8.50 | 25.50 | 60.00 |
| 3-5: 3-1st Mr. Monster | 6.50 | 19.50 | 45.00 |
| 6-10 | 4.50 | 14.00 | 32.00 |
| 11-20 | 2.85 | 8.50 | 20.00 |
| 21,23-40 | 2.30 | 7.00 | 16.00 |
| 22-Used in **SOTI**, pg. 35,307,308 | 3.50 | 10.50 | 24.00 |
| 41-60 | 1.50 | 4.50 | 10.00 |
| 61-94 | 1.15 | 3.50 | 8.00 |

**SUPER MAGIC** (Super Magician Comics #2 on)
May, 1941
Street & Smith Publications

| | Good | Fine | N-Mint |
|---|---|---|---|
| V1#1-Blackstone the Magician app.; origin & 1st app. Rex King (Black Fury); not Eisner-c | 38.00 | 115.00 | 265.00 |

**SUPER MAGICIAN COMICS** (Super Magic #1)
No. 2, Sept, 1941 - V5#8, Feb-Mar, 1947
Street & Smith Publications

| | Good | Fine | N-Mint |
|---|---|---|---|
| V1#2-Rex King, Man of Adventure app. | 16.00 | 48.00 | 110.00 |
| 3-Tao-Anwar, Boy Magician begins | 9.30 | 28.00 | 65.00 |
| 4-Origin Transo | 8.50 | 25.50 | 60.00 |
| 5-7,9-12: 8-Abbott & Costello story. 11-Supersnipe app. | 8.50 | 25.50 | 60.00 |
| 8-Abbott & Costello story | 10.00 | 30.00 | 70.00 |
| V2#1-The Shadow app. | 11.50 | 34.00 | 80.00 |
| 2-12: 5-Origin Tigerman. 8-Red Dragon begins | 4.50 | 14.00 | 32.00 |
| V3#1-12: 5-Origin Mr. Twilight | 4.50 | 14.00 | 32.00 |
| V4#1-12: 11-Nigel Elliman begins | 4.00 | 12.00 | 28.00 |
| V5#1-6 | 4.00 | 12.00 | 28.00 |
| 7,8-Red Dragon by Cartier | 12.00 | 36.00 | 84.00 |

*Superman #146, © DC Comics*

**SUPERMAN** (Adventures Of . . . #424 on; see Action Comics)
Summer, 1939 - No. 423, Sept, 1986
National Periodical Publications/DC Comics

|  | **Good** | **Fine** | **VF-NM** |
|---|---|---|---|
| 1(nn)-1st four Action stories reprinted; origin Superman by Siegel & Shuster; has a new 2 pg. origin plus 4 pgs. omitted in Action story | 4000.00 | 11,000.00 | 26,000.00 |

*(No known copy exists beyond Vf-NM condition)*

|  | **Good** | **Fine** | **N-Mint** |
|---|---|---|---|
| 2-All daily strip-r | 567.00 | 1420.00 | 3400.00 |
| 3-2nd story-r from Action #5; 3rd story-r from Action #6 | 417.00 | 1050.00 | 2500.00 |
| 4-1st mention of Daily Planet? (Spr/40)-Also see Action #23 | 300.00 | 750.00 | 1800.00 |
| 5 | 242.00 | 605.00 | 1450.00 |
| 6,7: 7-1st Perry White? | 175.00 | 440.00 | 1050.00 |
| 8-10: 10-1st bald Luthor | 142.00 | 355.00 | 850.00 |

|  | Good | Fine | N-Mint |
|---|---|---|---|
| 11-13,15: 13-Jimmy Olsen app. | 108.00 | 270.00 | 650.00 |
| 14-Patriotic Shield-c by Fred Ray | 129.00 | 325.00 | 775.00 |
| 16-20: 17-Hitler, Hirohito-c | 92.00 | 230.00 | 550.00 |
| 21-23,25 | 72.00 | 180.00 | 430.00 |
| 24-Flag-c | 83.00 | 210.00 | 500.00 |
| 26-29: 28-Lois Lane Girl Reporter series begins, ends #40,42 | | | |
|  | 65.00 | 165.00 | 390.00 |
| 28-Overseas edition for Armed Forces; same as reg. #28 | | | |
|  | 65.00 | 165.00 | 390.00 |
| 30-Origin & 1st app. Mr. Mxyztplk; name later became Mxyzptlk | | | |
|  | 91.00 | 275.00 | 640.00 |
| 31-40: 33-(3-4/45)-3rd app. Mxyztplk | 48.00 | 145.00 | 340.00 |
| 41-50: 45-Lois Lane as Superwoman (see Action #60 for 1st app.) | | | |
|  | 36.00 | 108.00 | 250.00 |
| 51,52 | 29.00 | 87.00 | 205.00 |
| 53-Origin Superman retold | 71.00 | 215.00 | 500.00 |
| 54,56-60 | 30.00 | 90.00 | 210.00 |
| 55-Used in SOTI, pg. 33 | 32.00 | 95.00 | 225.00 |
| 61-Origin Superman retold; origin Green Kryptonite (1st Kryptonite story) | 54.00 | 160.00 | 375.00 |
| 62-65,67-70: 62-Orson Welles app. 65-1st Krypton Foes: Mala, K120, & U-Ban | 30.00 | 90.00 | 210.00 |
| 66-2nd Superbaby story | 31.00 | 92.00 | 215.00 |
| 71-75: 75-Some have #74 on-c | 27.00 | 81.00 | 190.00 |
| 72-Giveaway(9-10/51)-(Rare)-Price blackened out; came with banner wrapped around book | 35.00 | 105.00 | 245.00 |
| 76-Batman x-over; Superman & Batman learn each other's I.D. | | | |
|  | 71.00 | 215.00 | 500.00 |
| 77-80: 78-Last 52 pgs. | 24.00 | 73.00 | 170.00 |
| 81-Used in POP, pg. 88 | 24.00 | 73.00 | 170.00 |
| 82-90 | 22.00 | 65.00 | 155.00 |
| 91-95: 95-Last precode issue | 21.00 | 62.00 | 145.00 |
| 96-99 | 17.00 | 51.00 | 120.00 |
| 100 (9-10/55) | 60.00 | 180.00 | 420.00 |
| 101-110 | 14.00 | 42.00 | 100.00 |
| 111-120 | 12.00 | 36.00 | 85.00 |
| 121-130: 123-Pre-Supergirl tryout. 127-Origin/1st app. Titano. 128-Red Kryptonite used (4/59). 129-Intro/origin Lori Lemaris, The Mermaid | | | |
|  | 10.00 | 30.00 | 70.00 |
| 131-139: 139-Lori Lemaris app. | 7.00 | 21.00 | 50.00 |

| | Good | Fine | N-Mint |
|---|---|---|---|
| 140-1st Blue Kryptonite & Bizarro Supergirl; origin Bizarro Jr. #1 | | | |
| | 7.00 | 21.00 | 50.00 |
| 141-145,148: 142-2nd Batman x-over | 5.00 | 15.00 | 35.00 |
| 146-Superman's life story | 6.50 | 19.50 | 45.00 |
| 147(8/61)-7th Legion app; 1st app. Legion of Super-Villains; intro. Adult Legion | | | |
| | 7.00 | 21.00 | 50.00 |
| 149(11/61)-9th Legion app. (cameo); last 10 cent issue | | | |
| | 7.00 | 21.00 | 50.00 |
| 150-162: 152(4/62)-15th Legion app. 155(8/62)-20th Legion app; Lightning Man & Cosmic Man, & Adult Legion app. 156,162-Legion app. 157-Gold Kryptonite used (see Adv. 299); Mon-el app.; Lightning Lad cameo (11/62). 158-1st app. Flamebird & Nightwing & Nor-Kan of Kandor. 161-1st told death of Ma and Pa Kent | | | |
| | 3.15 | 9.50 | 22.00 |
| 163-166,168-180: 166-Xmas-c. 168-All Luthor issue. 169-Last Sally Selwyn. 172,173-Legion cameos | 2.15 | 6.50 | 15.00 |
| 167-New origin Brainiac & Brainiac 5; intro Tixarla (Later Luthor's wife) | | | |
| | 4.30 | 13.00 | 30.00 |
| 181,182,184-186,188-192,194-196,198-200: 181-1st 2965 story/series 189-Origin/destruction of Krypton II. 199-1st Superman/Flash race (8/67) | 1.30 | 4.00 | 9.00 |
| 183,187,193,197 (Giants G-18,G-23,G-31,G-36) | 1.60 | 4.80 | 11.00 |
| 201,203-206,208-211,213-216,218-221,223-226,228-231,234-238: 213-Brainiac-5 app. | 1.00 | 3.00 | 6.00 |
| 202 (80-pg. Giant G-42)-All Bizarro issue | 1.25 | 3.75 | 7.50 |
| 207,212,217,222,227,239 (Giants G-48,G-54,G-60,G-66,G-72,G-84): 207-Legion app.; 30th anniversary Superman | | | |
| | 1.25 | 3.75 | 7.50 |
| 232(Giant, G-78)-All Krypton issue | 1.25 | 3.75 | 7.50 |
| 233-1st app. Morgan Edge, Clark Kent switch from newspaper reporter to TV newscaster | 1.00 | 3.00 | 6.00 |
| 240-Kaluta-a | .45 | 1.40 | 2.75 |
| 241-244 (52 pgs.). 243-G.A.-r/#38 | .40 | 1.25 | 2.50 |
| 245-DC 100 Pg. Super Spectacular #7; reprints | .50 | 1.50 | 3.00 |
| 246-248,250,251,253 (All 52 pgs.) | | .55 | 1.10 |
| 249,254-Neal Adams-a. 249-(52 pgs.); origin & 1st app. Terra-Man by Neal Adams (inks) | .90 | 2.75 | 5.50 |
| 252-DC 100 Pg. Super Spect. #13; N. Adams-c | .75 | 2.20 | 4.40 |
| 255-263: 263-Photo-c | | .55 | 1.10 |
| 264-1st app. Steve Lombard | .30 | .85 | 1.65 |

| | Good | Fine | N-Mint |
|---|---|---|---|
| 265-271,273-277,279-283,285-299: 276-Intro Capt. Thunder. 289-Photo-c. | | | |
| 292-Origin Lex Luthor retold | | .55 | 1.10 |
| 272,278,284-All 100 pgs. G.A.-r in all | .30 | .85 | 1.65 |
| 300-Retells origin | .55 | 1.65 | 3.30 |
| 301-399: 323-Intro. Atomic Skull | | .55 | 1.10 |
| 400 (10/84, $1.50, 68 pgs.)-Many top artists featured; Chaykin painted | | | |
| cover, Miller back-c | .35 | 1.10 | 2.20 |
| 401-422: 405-Super-Batman story. 408-Nuclear Holocaust-c/story. | | | |
| 411-Special Julius Schwartz tribute issue. 414,415-Crisis x-over. | | | |
| 422-Horror-c | | .55 | 1.10 |
| 423-Alan Moore scripts; Perez-a(i) | 1.00 | 3.00 | 6.00 |

**SUPERMAN** (2nd series)
Jan, 1987 - Present ($.75-$1.00, bi-weekly #19-?)
DC Comics

| | Good | Fine | N-Mint |
|---|---|---|---|
| 1-Byrne-c/a begins; intro Metallo | .35 | 1.00 | 2.00 |
| 2-8,10: 3-Legends x-over. 7-Origin/1st app. Rampage. 8-Legion app. | | | |
| | | .60 | 1.20 |
| 9-Joker-c | .50 | 1.50 | 3.00 |
| 11-43,47,48: 11-1st app. Mr. Mxyzptlk. 12-Lori Lemaris revived. 13-1st | | | |
| app. Toyman. 13,14-Millennium x-over. 20-Doom Patrol app.; | | | |
| Supergirl revived in cameo. 28-Steranko-c(p). 31-Mr. Mxyzptlk app. | | | |
| 37-Kirby-c(p); Newsboy Legion app. | | .40 | .80 |
| 44-46-"Dark Knight Over Metropolis" Batman storyline | | | |
| | | .40 | .80 |
| Annual 1,2: 1(8/87)-No Byrne-a. 2('88)-Byrne-a .25 | | .75 | 1.50 |

**SUPERMAN'S GIRLFRIEND LOIS LANE** (See Action Comics #1, 80 Page
Giant #3,14, Showcase #9,10, & Superman #28)
Mar-Apr, 1958 - No. 136, Jan-Feb, 1974; No. 137, Sept-Oct, 1974
National Periodical Publications

| | Good | Fine | N-Mint |
|---|---|---|---|
| 1 | 63.00 | 190.00 | 440.00 |
| 2 | 25.00 | 75.00 | 175.00 |
| 3 | 18.00 | 54.00 | 125.00 |
| 4,5 | 14.00 | 42.00 | 100.00 |
| 6-10: 9-Pat Boone app. | 9.30 | 28.00 | 65.00 |
| 11-20: 14-Supergirl x-over | 5.70 | 17.00 | 40.00 |
| 21-29: 23-1st app. Lena Thorul, Lex Luthor's sister. 29-Aquaman, Batman, | | | |

|  | Good | Fine | N-Mint |
|---|---|---|---|
| Green Arrow cameo; last 10 cent issue | 3.15 | 9.50 | 22.00 |
| 30-32,34-49: 47-Legion app. | 1.15 | 3.50 | 8.00 |
| 33(5/62)-Mon-el app. | 1.70 | 5.00 | 12.00 |
| 50(7/64)-Triplicate Girl, Phantom Girl & Shrinking Violet app. | | | |
| | 1.30 | 4.00 | 9.00 |
| 51-55,57-67,69,70: 59-Jor-el app.; Batman back-up story. 70-Penguin & | | | |
| Catwoman app.; Batman & Robin cameo | .50 | 1.50 | 3.00 |
| 56-Saturn Girl app. | .85 | 2.50 | 5.00 |
| 68-(Giant G-26) | 1.10 | 3.25 | 6.50 |
| 71-76,78: 74-1st Bizarro Flash; JLA cameo | .35 | 1.00 | 2.00 |
| 77-(Giant G-39) | .50 | 1.50 | 3.00 |
| 79-Neal Adams-c begin, end No. 95,108 | .35 | 1.00 | 2.00 |
| 80-85,87-94: 89-Batman x-over; all N. Adams-c | .35 | 1.00 | 2.00 |
| 86-(Giant G-51)-Neal Adams-c | .50 | 1.50 | 3.00 |
| 95-(Giant G-63)-Wonder Woman x-over; N. Adams-c | | | |
| | .50 | 1.50 | 3.00 |
| 96-103,105-111: 105-Origin/1st app. The Rose & the Thorn. 108-Neal | | | |
| Adams-c. 111-Morrow-a | .35 | 1.00 | 2.00 |
| 104,113-(Giants G-75,87) | .50 | 1.50 | 3.00 |
| 112,114-123 (52 pgs.): 122-G.A.-r/Superman #30. 123-G.A. Batman-r | | | |
| | .35 | 1.00 | 2.00 |
| 124-137: 130-Last Rose & the Thorn. 132-New Zatanna story. 136- Wonder | | | |
| Woman x-over | .35 | 1.00 | 2.00 |
| Annual 1(Sum,'62) | 5.30 | 16.00 | 17.00 |
| Annual 2(Sum,'63) | 3.15 | 9.50 | 22.00 |

**SUPERMAN'S PAL JIMMY OLSEN** (See Action #6 & 80 Page Giant)
Sept-Oct, 1954 - No. 163, Feb-Mar, 1974
National Periodical Publications

| | | | |
|---|---|---|---|
| 1 | 95.00 | 285.00 | 665.00 |
| 2 | 40.00 | 120.00 | 275.00 |
| 3-Last pre-code issue | 25.00 | 75.00 | 175.00 |
| 4,5 | 18.00 | 54.00 | 125.00 |
| 6-10 | 13.00 | 40.00 | 90.00 |
| 11-20 | 8.50 | 26.00 | 60.00 |
| 21-30: 29-1st app. Krypto in Jimmy Olsen | 4.50 | 14.00 | 32.00 |
| 31-40: 31-Origin Elastic Lad. 33-One pg. biography of Jack Larson (TV | | | |
| Jimmy Olsen). 36-Intro Lucy Lane | 2.85 | 8.50 | 20.00 |
| 41-47,49,50: 41-1st J.O. Robot | 1.85 | 5.50 | 13.00 |

|                                                                                              | Good | Fine | N-Mint |
|----------------------------------------------------------------------------------------------|------|------|--------|
| 48-Intro/origin Superman Emergency Squad                                                     | 1.85 | 5.50 | 13.00  |
| 51-56: 56-Last 10 cent issue                                                                 | 1.35 | 4.00 | 8.00   |
| 57-62,64-70: 57-Olsen marries Supergirl. 70-Element Lad app.                                 |      |      |        |
|                                                                                              | .70  | 2.00 | 4.00   |
| 63(9/62)-Legion of Super-Villains app.                                                       | .85  | 2.50 | 5.00   |
| 71,74,75,78,80-84,86,89,90: 86-J.O. Robot becomes Congorilla                                 |      |      |        |
|                                                                                              | .50  | 1.50 | 3.00   |
| 72(10/63)-Legion app; Elastic Lad (Olsen) joins                                              |      |      |        |
|                                                                                              | .70  | 2.00 | 4.00   |
| 73-Ultra Boy app.                                                                            | .70  | 2.00 | 4.00   |
| 76,85-Legion app.                                                                            | .70  | 2.00 | 4.00   |
| 77-Olsen with Colossal Boy's powers & costume; origin Titano retold                          |      |      |        |
|                                                                                              | .50  | 1.50 | 3.00   |
| 79(9/64)-Titled The Red-headed Beatle of 1000 B.C.                                           |      |      |        |
|                                                                                              | .50  | 1.50 | 3.00   |
| 87-Legion of Super-Villains app.                                                             | .70  | 2.00 | 4.00   |
| 88-Star Boy app.                                                                             | .50  | 1.50 | 3.00   |
| 91-94,96-99,101-103,105-110: 99-Legion app. 106-Legion app. 110-Infinity-c                   |      |      |        |
|                                                                                              | .35  | 1.00 | 2.00   |
| 95,104 (Giants G-25,G-38)                                                                    | .70  | 2.00 | 4.00   |
| 100-Legion cameo                                                                             | .50  | 1.50 | 3.00   |
| 111,112,114-121,123-130,132                                                                  | .35  | 1.00 | 2.00   |
| 113,122,131 (Giants G-50,G-62,G-74)                                                          | .35  | 1.00 | 2.00   |
| 133-Re-intro Newsboy Legion & begins by Kirby                                                |      |      |        |
|                                                                                              | .50  | 1.50 | 3.00   |
| 134-163: 135-G.A. Guardian app. 136-Origin new Guardian. 139-Last 15                         |      |      |        |
|     cent issue. 140-(Giant G-86). 141-Newsboy Legion reprints by S&K     |      |      |        |
|     begin (52 pg. issues begin). 149,150-G.A. Plastic Man reprint in both;|      |      |        |
|     last 52 pg. issue. 150-Newsboy Legion app.                           |      |      |        |
|                                                                                              | .35  | 1.00 | 2.00   |

**SUPERMOUSE** (. . . the Big Cheese)
Dec, 1948 - No. 34, Sept, 1955; No. 35, Apr, 1956 - No. 45, Fall, 1958
Standard Comics/Pines No. 35 on (Literary Ent.)

|                                   | Good  | Fine  | N-Mint |
|-----------------------------------|-------|-------|--------|
| 1-Frazetta text illos (3)         | 16.00 | 48.00 | 110.00 |
| 2-Frazetta text illos             | 8.50  | 25.50 | 60.00  |
| 3,5,6-Text illos by Frazetta in all | 6.50 | 19.50 | 45.00  |
| 4-Two pg. text illos by Frazetta  | 7.00  | 21.00 | 50.00  |
| 7-10                              | 2.30  | 7.00  | 16.00  |

|  | Good | Fine | N-Mint |
|---|---|---|---|
| 11-20: 13-Racist humor (Indians) | 1.70 | 5.00 | 12.00 |
| 21-45 | 1.15 | 3.50 | 8.00 |
| 1-Summer Holiday issue (Summer,'56-Pines)-100 pgs. | | | |
| | 5.00 | 15.00 | 35.00 |
| 2-Giant Summer issue (Summer,'58-Pines)-100 pgs. | | | |
| | 4.00 | 12.00 | 28.00 |

**SUPER-MYSTERY COMICS**
July, 1940 - V8#6, July, 1949
Ace Magazines (Periodical House)

| | Good | Fine | N-Mint |
|---|---|---|---|
| V1#1-Magno, the Magnetic Man & Vulcan begin | | | |
| | 71.00 | 215.00 | 500.00 |
| 2 | 34.00 | 100.00 | 240.00 |
| 3-The Black Spider begins | 27.00 | 81.00 | 190.00 |
| 4-Origin Davy | 24.00 | 73.00 | 170.00 |
| 5-Intro. The Clown; begin series | 24.00 | 73.00 | 170.00 |
| 6(2/41) | 21.00 | 62.00 | 145.00 |
| V2#1(4/41)-Origin Buckskin | 21.00 | 62.00 | 145.00 |
| 2-6(2/42) | 18.50 | 56.00 | 130.00 |
| V3#1(4/42),2: 1-Vulcan & Black Ace begin | 16.00 | 48.00 | 115.00 |
| 3-Intro. The Lancer; Dr. Nemesis & The Sword begin; Kurtzman-c/a(2) | | | |
| (Mr. Risk & Paul Revere Jr.) | 23.00 | 70.00 | 160.00 |
| 4-Kurtzman-a | 18.50 | 56.00 | 130.00 |
| 5-Kurtzman-a(2); L.B. Cole-a; Mr. Risk app. | | | |
| | 19.00 | 57.00 | 135.00 |
| 6(10/43)-Mr. Risk app.; Kurtzman's Paul Revere Jr.; L.B. Cole-a | | | |
| | 19.00 | 57.00 | 135.00 |
| V4#1(1/44)-L.B. Cole-a | 14.00 | 42.00 | 100.00 |
| 2-6(4/45): 2,5,6-Mr. Risk app. | 11.50 | 34.00 | 80.00 |
| V5#1(7/45)-6 | 9.30 | 28.00 | 65.00 |
| V6#1-6: 3-Torture story. 4-Last Magno. Mr. Risk app. in #2,4-6 | | | |
| | 8.00 | 24.00 | 56.00 |
| V7#1-6, V8#1-4,6 | 8.00 | 24.00 | 56.00 |
| V8#5-Meskin, Tuska, Sid Greene-a | 9.30 | 28.00 | 65.00 |

**SUPER RABBIT**
Fall, 1944 - No. 14, Nov, 1948
Timely Comics (CmPI)

|  | Good | Fine | N-Mint |
|---|---|---|---|
| 1-Hitler-c | 32.00 | 95.00 | 225.00 |
| 2 | 16.00 | 48.00 | 115.00 |
| 3-5 | 9.00 | 27.00 | 62.00 |
| 6-Origin | 7.00 | 21.00 | 50.00 |
| 7-10; 9-Infinity-c | 5.00 | 15.00 | 35.00 |
| 11-Kurtzman's "Hey Look" | 5.70 | 17.00 | 40.00 |
| 12-14 | 4.00 | 12.00 | 28.00 |

**SUPERSNIPE COMICS** (Formerly Army & Navy #1-5)
V1#6, Oct, 1942 - V5#1, Aug-Sept, 1949 (See Shadow Comics V2#3)
Street & Smith Publications

| | Good | Fine | N-Mint |
|---|---|---|---|
| V1#6-Rex King Man of Adventure (costumed hero) by Jack Binder begins; Supersnipe by George Marcoux continues from Army & Navy #5; Bill Ward-a | 34.00 | 100.00 | 235.00 |
| 7,8,10-12: 8-Hitler, Tojo, Mussolini-c. 11-Little Nemo app. | 19.00 | 56.00 | 130.00 |
| 9-Doc Savage x-over in Supersnipe; Hitler-c | 22.00 | 65.00 | 155.00 |
| V2#1-12: 1-Huck Finn by Clare Dwiggins begins, ends V3#5 | 13.00 | 40.00 | 90.00 |
| V3#1-12: 8-Bobby Crusoe by Dwiggins begins, ends V3#12 | 10.00 | 30.00 | 70.00 |
| V4#1-12, V5#1: V4#10-Xmas-c | 7.00 | 21.00 | 50.00 |

**SUSPENSE** (Radio/TV; Real Life Tales of . . . #1-4)
Dec, 1949 - No. 29, Apr, 1953 (#1-8,17-23: 52 pgs.)
Marvel/Atlas Comics (CnPC No. 1-10/BFP No. 11-29)

| | Good | Fine | N-Mint |
|---|---|---|---|
| 1-Powell-a; Peter Lorre, Sidney Greenstreet photo-c from Hammett's 'The Maltese Falcon' | 18.00 | 54.00 | 125.00 |
| 2-Crime stories; photo-c | 9.30 | 28.00 | 65.00 |
| 3-Change to horror | 9.30 | 28.00 | 65.00 |
| 4,7-10 | 6.00 | 18.00 | 42.00 |
| 5-Krigstein, Tuska, Everett-a | 7.00 | 21.00 | 50.00 |
| 6-Tuska, Everett, Morisi-a | 6.50 | 19.50 | 45.00 |

|  | Good | Fine | N-Mint |
|---|---|---|---|
| 11-17,19,20: 14-Hypo-c; A-Bomb panels | 5.00 | 15.00 | 35.00 |
| 18,22-Krigstein-a | 5.70 | 17.00 | 40.00 |
| 21,23,26-29 | 4.00 | 12.00 | 28.00 |
| 24-Tuska-a | 4.50 | 14.00 | 32.00 |
| 25-Electric chair-c/story | 7.00 | 21.00 | 50.00 |

**SWAMP THING** (See Roots of the . . . , & The Saga of . . . )
Oct-Nov, 1972 - No. 24, Aug-Sept, 1976
National Periodical Publications/DC Comics

| 1-Wrightson-c/a begins | 2.00 | 6.00 | 14.00 |
|---|---|---|---|
| 2 | 1.35 | 4.00 | 8.00 |
| 3-Intro. Patchworkman | 1.00 | 3.00 | 6.00 |
| 4-6,8-10: 10-Last Wrightson issue | .70 | 2.00 | 4.00 |
| 7-Batman-c/story | 1.15 | 3.50 | 7.00 |
| 11-24-Redondo-a; 23-Swamp Thing reverts back to Dr. Holland | | | |
| | | .50 | 1.00 |

# T

**TALES FROM THE CRYPT** (Formerly The Crypt Of Terror)
No. 20, Oct-Nov, 1950 - No. 46, Feb-Mar, 1955
E.C. Comics

|  | Good | Fine | N-Mint |
|---|---|---|---|
| 20 | 55.00 | 165.00 | 385.00 |
| 21-Kurtzman-r/Haunt of Fear #15(#1) | 45.00 | 135.00 | 315.00 |
| 22-Moon Girl costume at costume party, one panel | | | |
|  | 36.00 | 107.00 | 250.00 |
| 23-25 | 27.00 | 81.00 | 190.00 |
| 26-30 | 21.00 | 64.00 | 150.00 |
| 31-Williamson-a(1st at E.C.); B&W and color illos. in **POP**; Kamen draws himself, Gaines & Feldstein; Ingels, Craig & Davis draw themselves in his story | 24.00 | 73.00 | 170.00 |
| 32,35-39 | 17.00 | 51.00 | 120.00 |
| 33-Origin The Crypt Keeper | 30.00 | 90.00 | 210.00 |
| 34-Used in **POP**, pg. 83; lingerie panels | 17.00 | 51.00 | 120.00 |
| 40-Used in Senate hearings & in Hartford Cournat anti-comics editorials-1954 | 17.00 | 51.00 | 120.00 |
| 41-45: 45-2 pgs. showing E.C. staff | 16.00 | 48.00 | 110.00 |
| 46-Low distribution; pre-advertised cover for unpublished 4th horror title 'Crypt of Terror' used on this book | 20.00 | 60.00 | 140.00 |

**TALES OF ASGARD**
Oct, 1968 (25 cents, 68 pages); Feb, 1984 ($1.25, 52 pgs.)
Marvel Comics Group

| | | | |
|---|---|---|---|
| 1-Thor r-/from Journey into Mystery #97-106; new Kirby-c | | | |
|  | 1.70 | 5.00 | 12.00 |
| V2#1 (2/84)-Thor-r; Simonson-c | | .50 | 1.00 |

**TALES OF SUSPENSE** (Captain America #100 on)
Jan, 1959 - No. 99, March, 1968
Atlas (WPI No. 1,2/Male No. 3-12/VPI No. 13-18)/Marvel No. 19 on

| | | | |
|---|---|---|---|
| 1-Williamson-a, 5 pgs. | 47.50 | 142.00 | 330.00 |

*Tales of Suspense #43, © Marvel Comics*

|  | Good | Fine | N-Mint |
|---|---|---|---|
| 2-3 | 21.00 | 64.00 | 150.00 |
| 4-Williamson-a, 4 pgs.; Kirby/Everett-c/a | 22.00 | 65.00 | 155.00 |
| 5-10 | 13.00 | 40.00 | 90.00 |
| 11,13-20: 14-Intro. Colossus. 16-Intro Metallo (Pre-Iron Man prototype) | | | |
|  | 8.50 | 25.50 | 60.00 |
| 12-Crandall-a | 9.30 | 28.00 | 65.00 |
| 21-25: 25-Last 10 cent issue | 5.70 | 17.00 | 40.00 |
| 26-38: 32-Sazzik The Sorcerer app. (Dr. Strange prototype) | | | |
|  | 4.30 | 13.00 | 30.00 |
| 39 (3/63)-Origin & 1st app. Iron Man & begin series; 1st Iron Man story | | | |
| has Kirby layouts | 105.00 | 420.00 | 1050.00 |
| 40-Iron Man in new armor | 72.00 | 216.00 | 500.00 |
| 41 | 40.00 | 120.00 | 275.00 |
| 42-45: 45-Intro. & 1st app. Happy & Pepper | 16.50 | 50.00 | 115.00 |
| 46,47 | 8.50 | 25.00 | 60.00 |
| 48-New Iron Man armor | 10.30 | 31.00 | 72.00 |
| 49-X-Men x-over; 1st Tales of the Watcher back-up story. | | | |
|  | 6.70 | 20.00 | 45.00 |

| | Good | Fine | N-Mint |
|---|---|---|---|
| 50-51: 50-1st app. Mandarin | 5.15 | 15.50 | 36.00 |
| 52-1st app. The Black Widow | 7.70 | 23.00 | 54.00 |
| 53-Origin The Watcher (5/64; 2nd app.); Black Widow app. | | | |
| | 5.70 | 17.00 | 20.00 |
| 54-56 | 3.50 | 10.50 | 24.00 |
| 57-1st app./Origin Hawkeye (9/64) | 9.30 | 28.00 | 65.00 |
| 58-Captain America battles Iron Man (10/64)-Classic-c; 2nd Kraven app. | | | |
| | 10.00 | 30.00 | 70.00 |
| 59-Iron Man plus Captain America double feature begins (11/64); intro Jarvis, Avenger's butler; classic-c | 12.00 | 36.00 | 85.00 |
| 60 | 5.00 | 15.00 | 35.00 |
| 61-62,64: 62-Origin Mandarin (2/65) | 3.70 | 11.00 | 26.00 |
| 63-1st Silver Age origin Captain America(3/65) | | | |
| | 7.85 | 23.50 | 55.00 |
| 65-1st Silver-Age Red Skull (6/65) | 5.15 | 15.50 | 36.00 |
| 66-Origin Red Skull | 5.15 | 15.50 | 36.00 |
| 67-98: 69-1st app. Titanium Man. 75-Intro/1st app. Agent 13 later named Sharon Carter. 76-Intro Batroc & Sharon Carter, Agent 13 of Shield. 79-Intro Cosmic Cube. 94-Intro Modok. 95-Capt. America's i.d. revealed | 2.15 | 6.50 | 15.00 |
| 99-Becomes Captain America with #100 | 3.50 | 10.50 | 24.00 |

**TALES OF THE MYSTERIOUS TRAVELER**
Aug, 1956 - No. 13, June, 1959; V2#14, Oct, 1985 - No. 15, Dec, 1985
Charlton Comics

| | Good | Fine | N-Mint |
|---|---|---|---|
| 1-No Ditko-a | 14.00 | 42.00 | 100.00 |
| 2-Ditko-a(1) | 12.00 | 36.00 | 84.00 |
| 3-Ditko-c/a(1) | 11.00 | 32.00 | 75.00 |
| 4-6-Ditko-c/a(3-4 stories each) | 15.00 | 45.00 | 105.00 |
| 7-9-Ditko-a(1-2 each) | 11.00 | 32.00 | 75.00 |
| 10,11-Ditko-c/a(3-4 each) | 12.00 | 36.00 | 84.00 |
| 12,13 | 4.50 | 14.00 | 32.00 |
| V2#14,15 (1985)-Ditko-c/a | | .40 | .80 |

**TALES OF THE TEEN TITANS** (Formerly The New Teen Titans)
No. 41, April, 1984 - No. 91, July, 1988 (75 cents)
DC Comics

41-43,45-59: 43-1st app. Terminator. 46-Aqualad & Aquagirl join.

|  | Good | Fine | N-Mint |
|---|---|---|---|
| 50-Double size. 53-Intro Azreal. 56-Intro Jinx. 57-Neutron app. | | | |
| 59-r/DC Comics Presents #26 | | .40 | .80 |
| 44-Dick Grayson becomes Nightwing & joins Titans; Jericho joins also; | | | |
| origin Terminator | .60 | 1.75 | 3.50 |
| 60-91: r/New Teen Titans Baxter series. 68-B. Smith-c. 70-Origin Kole. | | | |
| #83-91 are $1.00 cover | | .40 | .80 |
| Annual 3('84; $1.25)-Death of Terra | | .60 | 1.20 |
| Annual 4(11/86, reprints), 5('87) | | .60 | 1.20 |

**TALES TO ASTONISH** (Becomes The Incredible Hulk #102 on)
Jan, 1959 - No. 101, March, 1968
Atlas (MAP No. 1/ZPC No. 2-14/VPI No. 15-21/Marvel No. 22 on)

| | Good | Fine | N-Mint |
|---|---|---|---|
| 1-Jack Davis-a | 50.00 | 150.00 | 350.00 |
| 2-Ditko-c | 21.00 | 64.00 | 150.00 |
| 3-5: 5-Williamson-a, 4 pgs. | 16.50 | 50.00 | 115.00 |
| 6-10 | 12.00 | 36.00 | 80.00 |
| 11-20 | 7.00 | 21.00 | 50.00 |
| 21-26,28-34 | 4.30 | 13.00 | 30.00 |
| 27-1st Antman app. (1/62); last 10 cent issue | | | |
| | 124.00 | 372.00 | 865.00 |
| 35-(9/62)-2nd Antman, 1st in costume; begin series | | | |
| | 84.00 | 252.00 | 585.00 |
| 36 | 34.00 | 102.00 | 235.00 |
| 37-40 | 15.00 | 45.00 | 105.00 |
| 41-43 | 9.30 | 28.00 | 65.00 |
| 44-Origin & 1st app. The Wasp | 10.70 | 32.00 | 75.00 |
| 45-48: 46-1st Crimson Dynamo | 6.50 | 19.00 | 46.00 |
| 49-Antman becomes Giant Man | 10.70 | 32.00 | 75.00 |
| 50-56,58: 50-Origin/1st app. Human Top. 52-Origin/1st app. Black Knight | | | |
| | 3.60 | 11.00 | 25.00 |
| 57-Spider-Man app. | 5.70 | 17.00 | 40.00 |
| 59-Giant Man vs. Hulk feature story | 7.85 | 23.50 | 55.00 |
| 60-Giant Man/Hulk double feature begins | 10.00 | 30.00 | 70.00 |
| 61-69: 62-1st app./origin The Leader; new Wasp costume. 65-New Giant | | | |
| Man costume. 68-New Human Top costume. 69-Last Giant Man | | | |
| | 3.30 | 10.00 | 23.00 |
| 70-Sub-Mariner & Incredible Hulk begins | 5.70 | 17.00 | 40.00 |

|                                                              | **Good** | **Fine** | **N-Mint** |
|--------------------------------------------------------------|----------|----------|------------|
| 71-101: 90-1st app. The Abomination. 92,93-Silver Surfer app. 100-Hulk |          |          |            |
| battles Sub-Mariner                                          | 2.85     | 8.50     | 20.00      |

## TARGET COMICS
Feb, 1940 - V10#3 (#105), Aug-Sept, 1949
Funnies, Inc./Novelty Publications/Star Publications

V1#1-Origin & 1st app. Manowar, The White Streak by Burgos, & Bulls-
Eye Bill by Everett; City Editor (ends #5), High Grass Twins by Jack
Cole (ends #4), T-Men by Joe Simon (ends #9), Rip Rory (ends #4),
Fantastic Feature Films by Tarpe Mills (ends #39), & Calling 2-R
(ends #14) begin; Marijuana use story

|                                                              |          |          |            |
|--------------------------------------------------------------|----------|----------|------------|
|                                                              | 168.00   | 505.00   | 1175.00    |
| 2                                                            | 79.00    | 235.00   | 550.00     |
| 3,4                                                          | 58.00    | 174.00   | 405.00     |
| 5-Origin The White Streak in text; Space Hawk by Wolverton begins |          |          |            |
| (See Blue Bolt & Circus)                                     | 131.00   | 395.00   | 920.00     |
| 6-The Chameleon by Everett begins; White Streak origin cont'd. in text |          |          |            |
|                                                              | 74.00    | 220.00   | 515.00     |
| 7-Wolverton Spacehawk-c (Scarce)                             | 171.00   | 515.00   | 1200.00    |
| 8,9,12                                                       | 55.00    | 165.00   | 385.00     |
| 10-Intro. & 1st app. The Target; Kirby-c                     | 74.00    | 220.00   | 515.00     |
| 11-Origin The Target & The Targeteers                        | 74.00    | 220.00   | 515.00     |
| V2#1-Target by Bob Wood; flag-c                              | 39.00    | 118.00   | 275.00     |
| 2-10-part Treasure Island serial begins                      | 39.00    | 118.00   | 275.00     |
| 3-5: 4-Kit Carter, The Cadet begins                          | 29.00    | 86.00    | 200.00     |
| 6-9:Red Seal with White Streak in 6-10                       | 29.00    | 86.00    | 200.00     |
| 10-Classic-c                                                 | 32.00    | 95.00    | 225.00     |
| 11,12: 12-10-part Last of the Mohicans serial begins; Delay-a |          |          |            |
|                                                              | 29.00    | 86.00    | 200.00     |
| V3#1-10-Last Wolverton issue. 8-Flag-c; 6-part Gulliver Travels serial be- |      |          |            |
| gins; Delay-a                                                | 29.00    | 86.00    | 200.00     |
| 11,12                                                        | 5.00     | 15.00    | 35.00      |
| V4#1-5,7-12                                                  | 3.00     | 9.00     | 21.00      |
| 6-Targetoons by Wolverton, 1 pg.                             | 3.00     | 9.00     | 21.00      |
| V5#1-8                                                       | 2.30     | 7.00     | 16.00      |
| V6#1-10, V7#1-12                                             | 2.00     | 6.00     | 14.00      |
| V8#1,3-5,8,9,11,12                                           | 1.70     | 5.00     | 12.00      |
| 2,6,7-Krigstein-a                                            | 2.30     | 7.00     | 16.00      |
| 10-L.B. Cole-c                                               | 5.00     | 15.00    | 35.00      |

| | Good | Fine | N-Mint |
|---|---|---|---|
| V9#1,3,6,8,10,12, V10#2-L.B. Cole-c | 5.00 | 15.00 | 35.00 |
| V9#2,4,5,7,9,11, V10#1,3 | 1.70 | 5.00 | 12.00 |

**TARZAN** (. . . of the Apes #138 on) (Also see Crackajack Funnies,
    Popular Comics, Sparkler Comics & Tip Top Comics)
1-2/48 - No. 131, 7-8/62; No. 132, 11/62 - No. 206, 2/72
Dell Publishing Co./Gold Key No. 132 on

| | Good | Fine | N-Mint |
|---|---|---|---|
| 1-Jesse Marsh-a begins | 71.00 | 215.00 | 500.00 |
| 2 | 41.00 | 125.00 | 290.00 |
| 3-5 | 30.00 | 90.00 | 210.00 |
| 6-10: 6-1st Tantor the Elephant. 7-1st Valley of the Monsters | | | |
| | 25.00 | 75.00 | 175.00 |
| 11-15: 11-Two Against the Jungle begins, ends #24. 13-Lex Barker photo-c | | | |
|     begin | 21.00 | 62.00 | 145.00 |
| 16-20 | 16.00 | 48.00 | 110.00 |
| 21-24,26-30 | 12.00 | 36.00 | 84.00 |
| 25-1st "Brothers of the Spear" episode; series ends #156,160,161, 196-206 | | | |
| | 14.00 | 42.00 | 100.00 |
| 31-40 | 7.00 | 21.00 | 50.00 |
| 41-54: Last Barker photo-c | 5.70 | 17.00 | 40.00 |
| 55-60: 56-Eight pg. Boy story | 4.50 | 14.00 | 32.00 |
| 61,62,64-70 | 3.50 | 10.50 | 24.00 |
| 63-Two Tarzan stories, 1 by Manning | 3.70 | 11.00 | 26.00 |
| 71-79 | 2.85 | 8.50 | 20.00 |
| 80-99: 80-Gordon Scott photo-c begin | 3.15 | 9.50 | 22.00 |
| 100 | 4.00 | 12.00 | 28.00 |
| 101-109 | 2.65 | 8.00 | 18.00 |
| 110 (Scarce)-Last photo-c | 3.15 | 9.50 | 22.00 |
| 111-120 | 2.00 | 6.00 | 14.00 |
| 121-131: Last Dell issue | 1.50 | 4.50 | 10.00 |
| 132-154: Gold Key issues | 1.15 | 3.50 | 8.00 |
| 155-Origin Tarzan | 1.50 | 4.50 | 10.00 |
| 156-161: 157-Banlu, Dog of the Arande begins, ends #159, 195. | | | |
|     169-Leopard Girl app. | .85 | 2.60 | 6.00 |
| 162,165,168,171 (TV)-Ron Ely photo covers | 1.00 | 3.00 | 7.00 |
| 163,164,166-167,169-170: 169-Leopard Girl app. | | | |
| | .70 | 2.00 | 5.00 |
| 172-199,201-206: 178-Tarzan origin r-/#155; Leopard Girl app, also in #179, | | | |
|     190-193 | .60 | 1.80 | 4.00 |

|  | Good | Fine | N-Mint |
|---|---|---|---|
| 200 (Scarce) | .70 | 2.00 | 5.00 |
| Story Digest 1(6/70)-G.K. | .70 | 2.00 | 5.00 |

**TARZAN** (Continuation of Gold Key series)
No. 207, April, 1972 - No. 258, Feb, 1977
National Periodical Publications

| | Good | Fine | N-Mint |
|---|---|---|---|
| 207-Origin Tarzan by Joe Kubert, part 1; John Carter begins (origin); 52 pg. issues thru #209 | .60 | 1.75 | 3.50 |
| 208-210: Origin, parts 2-4. 209-Last John Carter. 210-Kubert-a | .25 | .75 | 1.50 |
| 211-Hogarth, Kubert-a | | .50 | 1.00 |
| 212-214: Adaptations from "Jungle Tales of Tarzan." 213-Beyond the Farthest Star begins, ends #218 | | .50 | 1.00 |
| 215-218,224,225-All by Kubert. 215-part Foster-r | | .50 | 1.00 |
| 219-223: Adapts "The Return of Tarzan" by Kubert | | .50 | 1.00 |
| 226-229: 226-Manning-a | | .50 | 1.00 |
| 230-100 pgs.; Kubert, Kaluta-a(p); Korak begins, ends #234; Carson of Venus app. | .25 | .75 | 1.50 |
| 231-234: Adapts "Tarzan and the Lion Man"; all 100 pgs.; Rex, the Wonder Dog r-#232, 233 | | .50 | 1.00 |
| 235-Last Kubert issue; 100 pgs. | | .50 | 1.00 |
| 236-258: 238-(68 pgs.). 240-243 adapts "Tarzan & the Castaways." 250-256 adapts "Tarzan the Untamed." 252,253-r/#213 | | .50 | 1.00 |

**TEENAGE MUTANT NINJA TURTLES**
1984 - Present ($1.50-$1.75, B&W; all 44-52 pgs.)
Mirage Studios

| | Good | Fine | N-Mint |
|---|---|---|---|
| 1-1st printing (3000 copies)-Only printing to have ad for Gobbledygook #1 & 2 | 50.00 | 150.00 | 300.00 |
| 1-2nd printing (6/84)(15,000 copies) | 12.00 | 35.00 | 70.00 |
| 1-3rd printing (2/85)(36,000 copies) | 5.00 | 15.00 | 30.00 |
| 1-4th printing, new-c (50,000 copies) | 2.50 | 7.50 | 15.00 |
| 1-5th printing, new-c (8/88-c, 11/88 inside) | .70 | 2.00 | 4.00 |
| 2-1st printing (15,000 copies) | 15.00 | 45.00 | 90.00 |
| 2-2nd printing | 2.00 | 6.00 | 12.00 |

*Teenage Mutant Ninja Turtles #1 (5th printing),*
*© Mirage Studios*

|  | Good | Fine | N-Mint |
|---|---|---|---|
| 2-3rd printing; new Corben-c/a (2/85) | .85 | 2.50 | 5.00 |
| 3-1st printing | 6.70 | 20.00 | 40.00 |
| 3-Variant, 500 copies, given away in NYC. Has 'Laird's Photo' in white rather than light blue | 13.30 | 40.00 | 80.00 |
| 3-2nd printing | 1.00 | 3.00 | 6.00 |
| 4-1st printing | 3.35 | 10.00 | 20.00 |
| 4-2nd printing (5/87) | .70 | 2.00 | 4.00 |
| 5-1st printing; Fugitoid begins, ends #7 | 2.50 | 7.50 | 15.00 |
| 5-2nd printing (11/87) | .50 | 1.50 | 3.00 |
| 6-1st printing (4/87-c, 5/87 inside) | 2.00 | 6.00 | 12.00 |
| 6-2nd printing | .40 | 1.25 | 2.50 |
| 7-4 pg. Corben color insert; 1st color TMNT | 2.00 | 6.00 | 12.00 |
| 7-2nd printing (1/89) | .40 | 1.25 | 2.50 |
| 8 | 1.50 | 4.50 | 9.00 |
| 9,10: 9 (9/86)-Rip In Time by Corben | 1.00 | 3.00 | 6.00 |
| 11-15 | .75 | 2.25 | 4.50 |

|  | Good | Fine | N-Mint |
|---|---|---|---|
| 16-18 | .70 | 2.00 | 4.00 |
| 19-34: 19-Begin $1.75-c. 24,25-Veitch-c/a | .35 | 1.00 | 2.00 |

## TEENAGE MUTANT NINJA TURTLES ADVENTURES (TV)
8/88 - No. 3, 12/88; 3/89 - Present ($1.00, color, mini-series)
Archie Comics

| | | | |
|---|---|---|---|
| 1-Adapts TV cartoon; not by Eastman/Laird | .70 | 2.00 | 4.00 |
| 2,3 (mini-series) | .50 | 1.50 | 3.00 |
| 1 (2nd on-going series) | .50 | 1.50 | 3.00 |
| 2-5: 5-Begins original stories not based on TV | .35 | 1.00 | 2.00 |
| 6-14 | | .60 | 1.20 |

## TEEN TITANS (See Brave & the Bold, Marvel & DC Present, New Teen
Titans and Showcase)
1-2/66 - No. 43, 1-2/73; No. 44, 11/76 - No. 53, 2/78
National Periodical Publications/DC Comics

| | | | |
|---|---|---|---|
| 1-Titans join Peace Corps; Batman, Flash, Aquaman, Wonder Woman cameos | 13.50 | 41.00 | 95.00 |
| 2 | 6.50 | 19.00 | 45.00 |
| 3-5: 4-Speedy app. | 3.15 | 9.50 | 22.00 |
| 6-10: 6-Doom Patrol app. | 2.00 | 6.00 | 14.00 |
| 11-18: 11-Speedy app. 18-1st app. Starfire | 1.60 | 4.80 | 11.00 |
| 19-Wood-i; Speedy begins as regular | 1.60 | 4.80 | 11.00 |
| 20-22: All Neal Adams-a. 21-Hawk & Dove app. 22-Origin Wonder Girl | 1.85 | 5.50 | 13.00 |
| 23-30: 23-Wonder Girl dons new costume. 25-Flash, Aquaman, Batman, Green Arrow, Green Lantern, Superman, & Hawk & Dove guests; 1st app. Lilith who joins T.T. West in #50. 29-Hawk & Dove & Ocean Master app. 30-Aquagirl app. | 1.15 | 3.50 | 7.00 |
| 31-43: 31-Hawk & Dove app. 36,37-Superboy-r. 38-Green Arrow/ Speedy-r; Aquaman/Aqualad story. 39-Hawk & Dove-r. (36-39: 52 pgs.) | 1.00 | 3.00 | 6.00 |
| 44,45,47,49,51,52: 44-Mal becomes the Guardian | .70 | 2.00 | 4.00 |
| 46-Joker's daughter begins | 1.35 | 4.00 | 8.00 |
| 48-Intro Bumblebee; Joker's daughter becomes Harlequin | 1.35 | 4.00 | 8.00 |

| | Good | Fine | N-Mint |
|---|---|---|---|
| 50-1st revival original Bat-Girl; intro. Teen Titans West | | | |
| | 1.00 | 3.00 | 6.00 |
| 53-Origin retold | .85 | 2.50 | 5.00 |

**TERRORS OF THE JUNGLE**
No. 17, May, 1952 - No. 10, Sept, 1954
Star Publications

| | Good | Fine | N-Mint |
|---|---|---|---|
| 17-Reprints Rulah #21, used in **SOTI**; L.B. Cole bondage-c | | | |
| | 16.50 | 50.00 | 115.00 |
| 18-Jo-Jo-r | 11.00 | 32.00 | 75.00 |
| 19,20(1952)-Jo-Jo-r; Disbrow-a | 9.30 | 28.00 | 65.00 |
| 21-Jungle Jo, Tangi-r; used in **POP**, pg. 100 & color illos. | | | |
| | 11.50 | 34.00 | 80.00 |
| 4,6,7-Disbrow-a | 9.30 | 28.00 | 65.00 |
| 5,8,10: All Disbrow-a. 5-Jo-Jo-r. 8-Rulah, Jo-Jo-r. 10-Rulah-r | | | |
| | 9.30 | 28.00 | 65.00 |
| 9-Jo-Jo-r; Disbrow-a; Tangi by Orlando | 9.30 | 28.00 | 65.00 |

**TERRY AND THE PIRATES** (See Popular Comics & Super Comics)
No. 3, 4/47 - No. 26, 4/51; No. 26, 6/55 - No. 28, 10/55
Harvey Publications/Charlton No. 26-28 (Two #26's exist)

| | Good | Fine | N-Mint |
|---|---|---|---|
| 3(#1)-Boy Explorers by S&K; Terry & the Pirates begin by Caniff | | | |
| | 20.00 | 60.00 | 140.00 |
| 4-S&K Boy Explorers | 13.00 | 40.00 | 90.00 |
| 5-10 | 7.00 | 21.00 | 50.00 |
| 11-Man in Black app. by Powell | 7.00 | 21.00 | 50.00 |
| 12-20: 16-Girl threatened with red hot poker | 5.35 | 16.00 | 37.00 |
| 21-26(4/51)-Last Caniff issue | 4.75 | 14.00 | 33.00 |
| 26-28('55)(Formerly This Is Suspense)-Not by Caniff | | | |
| | 3.70 | 11.00 | 26.00 |

**TERRY-TOONS COMICS** (Later issues titled "Paul Terry's . . . )
Oct, 1942 - No. 86, May, 1951 (Two #60's exist)
Timely/Marvel No. 1-60 (8/47)/St. John No. 60 (9/47) on

| | Good | Fine | N-Mint |
|---|---|---|---|
| 1 (Scarce)-Features characters that 1st app. on movie screen; Gandy Goose begins | | | |
| | 50.00 | 150.00 | 350.00 |
| 2 | 25.00 | 75.00 | 175.00 |

|            | Good  | Fine   | N-Mint |
|------------|-------|--------|--------|
| 3-5        | 15.00 | 45.00  | 105.00 |
| 6-10       | 10.00 | 30.00  | 70.00  |
| 11-20      | 6.50  | 19.50  | 45.00  |
| 21-37      | 4.30  | 13.00  | 30.00  |
| 38-Mighty Mouse begins (1st app.)(11/45) | 38.00 | 115.00 | 270.00 |
| 39-2nd Mighty Mouse app. | 13.00 | 40.00 | 90.00 |
| 40-49: 43-Infinity-c | 5.50 | 16.50 | 38.00 |
| 50-1st app. Heckle & Jeckle | 12.00 | 36.00 | 84.00 |
| 51-60(8/47): 55-Infinity-c. 60(9/47)-Atomic explosion panel | | | |
|            | 4.00  | 12.00  | 28.00  |
| 61-84      | 2.65  | 8.00   | 18.00  |
| 85,86-Same book as Paul Terry's Comics #85,86 with only a title change; published at same time? | 2.65 | 8.00 | 18.00 |

**TEX RITTER WESTERN** (Movie star; singing cowboy)
Oct, 1950 - No. 46, May, 1959 (Photo-c: 1-21) (See Western Hero)
Fawcett No. 1-20 (1/54)/Charlton No. 21 on

| 1-Tex Ritter, his stallion White Flash & dog Fury begin; photo front/ back-c begin | 30.00 | 90.00 | 210.00 |
|------------|-------|--------|--------|
| 2          | 15.00 | 45.00  | 105.00 |
| 3-5: 5-Last photo back-c | 13.00 | 40.00 | 90.00 |
| 6-10       | 11.00 | 32.00  | 75.00  |
| 11-19      | 7.00  | 21.00  | 50.00  |
| 20-Last Fawcett issue (1/54) | 8.00 | 24.00 | 56.00 |
| 21-1st Charlton issue; photo-c (3/54) | 8.00 | 24.00 | 56.00 |
| 22         | 4.50  | 14.00  | 32.00  |
| 23-30: 23-25-Young Falcon app. | 3.50 | 10.50 | 24.00 |
| 31-38,40-45 | 2.85 | 8.50   | 20.00  |
| 39-Williamson-c/a (1/58) | 4.35 | 13.00 | 30.00 |
| 46-Last issue | 3.15 | 9.50 | 22.00 |

**THING!, THE**
Feb, 1952 - No. 17, Nov, 1954
Song Hits No. 1,2/Capitol Stories/Charlton

| 1          | 25.00 | 75.00  | 175.00 |
|------------|-------|--------|--------|
| 2,3: 3-Drug mention (several panels) | 18.00 | 54.00 | 125.00 |
| 4-6,8,10   | 13.00 | 40.00  | 90.00  |

|  | Good | Fine | N-Mint |
|---|---|---|---|
| 7-Injury to eye-c & inside panel. E.C. swipes from Vault of Horror #28 | 26.00 | 77.00 | 180.00 |
| 9-Used in **SOTI**, pg. 388 & illo-"Stomping on the face is a form of brutality which modern children learn early" | 29.00 | 86.00 | 200.00 |
| 11-Necronomicon story; Hansel & Gretel parody; Injury-to-eye panel; Check-a | 23.00 | 70.00 | 160.00 |
| 12-"Cinderella" parody; Ditko-c/a; lingerie panels | 35.00 | 105.00 | 245.00 |
| 13,15-Ditko c/a(3 & 5); 13-Ditko E.C. swipe/Haunt of Fear #15(#1)-"House of Horror" | 35.00 | 105.00 | 245.00 |
| 14-Extreme violence/torture; Rumpelstiltskin story; Ditko-c/a(4) | 35.00 | 105.00 | 245.00 |
| 16-Injury to eye panel | 17.00 | 51.00 | 120.00 |
| 17-Ditko-c; classic parody-"Through the Looking Glass"; Powell-a(r) | 27.00 | 81.00 | 190.00 |

**THIS MAGAZINE IS HAUNTED**
Oct, 1951 - No. 14, 12/53; No. 15, 2/54 - V3 #21, Nov, 1954
Fawcett Publications/Charlton No. 15 (2/54) on

| | Good | Fine | N-Mint |
|---|---|---|---|
| 1-Evans-a(i?) | 18.00 | 54.00 | 125.00 |
| 2,5-Evans-a | 12.00 | 36.00 | 84.00 |
| 3,4 | 6.50 | 19.50 | 45.00 |
| 6-9,11,12,14 | 5.00 | 15.00 | 35.00 |
| 10-Severed head-c | 8.00 | 24.00 | 56.00 |
| 13-Severed head-c/story | 7.00 | 21.00 | 50.00 |
| 15,20 | 4.30 | 13.00 | 30.00 |
| 16,19-Ditko-c. 19-Injury-to-eye panel; story r-/#1 | 9.50 | 28.50 | 65.00 |
| 17-Ditko-c/a(3); blood drainage story | 13.00 | 40.00 | 100.00 |
| 18-Ditko-c/a; E.C. swipe/Haunt of Fear 5; injury-to-eye panel | 12.00 | 36.00 | 84.00 |
| 21-Ditko-c, Evans-a | 9.50 | 28.50 | 65.00 |

**THOR** (Formerly Journey Into Mystery) (The Mighty Thor #? on)
March, 1966 - Present (See The Avengers #1 & Tales of Asgard)
Marvel Comics Group

| | Good | Fine | N-Mint |
|---|---|---|---|
| 126 | 7.00 | 21.00 | 50.00 |
| 127-133,135-140 | 2.65 | 8.00 | 18.00 |

|                                                                      | Good | Fine  | N-Mint |
|----------------------------------------------------------------------|------|-------|--------|
| 134-Intro High Evolutionary                                          | 3.85 | 11.50 | 27.00  |
| 141-145,150: 146-Inhumans begin, end #151                            | 1.70 | 5.00  | 12.00  |
| 146,147-Origin The Inhumans                                          | 1.70 | 5.00  | 12.00  |
| 148,149-Origin Black Bolt in each; 149-Origin Medusa, Crystal, Maximus, Gorgon, Kornak | 1.70 | 5.00  | 12.00  |
| 151-157,159,160                                                      | 1.70 | 5.00  | 12.00  |
| 158-Origin-r/No. 83. 158,159-Origin Dr. Blake                        | 5.00 | 15.00 | 35.00  |
| 161,163,164,167,170-179-Last Kirby issue                             | 1.30 | 4.00  | 9.00   |
| 162,168,169-Origin Galactus                                          | 2.30 | 7.00  | 16.00  |
| 165,166-Warlock (Him) app.                                           | 1.15 | 3.50  | 8.00   |
| 180,181-Neal Adams-a                                                 | 1.15 | 3.50  | 8.00   |
| 182-192,194-200                                                      | .70  | 2.00  | 4.00   |
| 193-(52 pgs.); Silver Surfer x-over                                  | 2.00 | 6.00  | 14.00  |
| 201-299: 225-Intro. Firelord. 271-Iron Man x-over. 274-Death of Balder the Brave. 294-Origin Asgard & Odin | .25  | .75   | 1.50   |
| 300-End of Asgard; origin of Odin & The Destroyer                    | .40  | 1.25  | 2.50   |
| 301-336: 316-Iron Man x-over                                         |      | .50   | 1.00   |
| 337-Simonson-c/a begins; Beta Ray Bill becomes new Thor              | 1.15 | 3.50  | 7.00   |
| 338                                                                  | .50  | 1.50  | 3.00   |
| 339,340: 340-Donald Blake returns as Thor                            | .25  | .75   | 1.50   |
| 341-373,375-381,383: 373-X-Factor tie-in                             |      | .50   | 1.00   |
| 374-Mutant massacre; X-Factor app.                                   | 1.00 | 3.00  | 6.00   |
| 382-Anniversary issue ($1.25)                                        | .35  | 1.00  | 2.00   |
| 384-Intro. new Thor                                                  | .35  | 1.00  | 2.00   |
| 385-399,401-428: 390-Avengers x-over. 395-Intro Earth Force. 411-New Warriors cameo. 412-Intro New Warriors |      | .50   | 1.00   |
| 400 ($1.75, 68 pgs.)-Origin Loki                                     | .40  | 1.25  | 2.50   |
| Giant-Size 1('75)                                                    | .35  | 1.00  | 2.00   |
| Special 2(9/66)-See Journey Into Mystery for 1st annual              | 2.65 | 8.50  | 18.00  |
| King Size Special 3(1/71)                                            | .85  | 2.50  | 5.00   |
| Special 4(12/71)                                                     | .50  | 1.50  | 3.00   |
| Annual 5(11/76), 6(10/77), 7(1978), 8(1979)                          | .50  | 1.50  | 3.00   |
| Annual 9(1981), 10(1982), 11(1983), 12(1984)                         | .50  | 1.50  | 3.00   |
| Annual 13(1985)                                                      | .35  | 1.00  | 2.00   |
| Annual 14(1989, $2.00, 68 pgs.)-Atlantis Attacks                     | .35  | 1.00  | 2.00   |
| Annual 15(1990, $2.00, 68 pgs.)                                      | .35  | 1.00  | 2.00   |

### 3-D BATMAN
1953, Reprinted in 1966 (Price includes glasses)
National Periodical Publications

|  | Good | Fine | N-Mint |
|---|---|---|---|
| 1953-Reprints Batman #42 & 48; Tommy Tomorrow app. (25 cents) | | | |
|  | 71.00 | 215.00 | 500.00 |
| 1966-Tommy Tomorrow app. | 22.00 | 65.00 | 150.00 |

### 3-D DOLLY
December, 1953 (2 pairs glasses included)
Harvey Publications

| 1-Richie Rich story redrawn from his 1st app. in Little Dot #1 | | | |
|---|---|---|---|
|  | 12.00 | 36.00 | 84.00 |

### 3-D SHEENA, JUNGLE QUEEN
1953
Fiction House Magazines

| 1 | 38.00 | 115.00 | 265.00 |
|---|---|---|---|

### THREE STOOGES
No. 1043, Oct-Dec, 1959 - No. 55, June, 1972
Dell Publishing Co./Gold Key No. 10 (10/62) on

| 4-Color 1043 (#1) | 7.00 | 21.00 | 50.00 |
|---|---|---|---|
| 4-Color 1078,1127,1170,1187 | 5.00 | 15.00 | 35.00 |
| 6(9-11/61) - 10: 6-Professor Putter begins; ends #16 | | | |
|  | 3.70 | 11.00 | 26.00 |
| 11-14,16-20: 17-The Little Monsters begin (5/64)(1st app.?) | | | |
|  | 3.50 | 10.50 | 24.00 |
| 15-Go Around the World in a Daze (movie scenes) | | | |
|  | 3.70 | 11.00 | 26.00 |
| 21,23-30 | 2.65 | 8.00 | 18.00 |
| 22-Movie scenes/'The Outlaws Is Coming' | 3.70 | 11.00 | 26.00 |
| 31-55 | 2.00 | 6.00 | 14.00 |

*Thrilling Comics #10, © Standard Comics*

**THRILLING COMICS**
Feb, 1940 - No. 80, April, 1951
Better Publ./Nedor/Standard Comics

|  | Good | Fine | N-Mint |
|---|---|---|---|
| 1-Origin Doc Strange (37 pgs.); Nickie Norton of the Secret Service begins | 64.00 | 193.00 | 450.00 |
| 2-The Rio Kid, The Woman in Red, Pinocchio begins | 29.00 | 86.00 | 200.00 |
| 3-The Ghost & Lone Eagle begin | 26.00 | 79.00 | 185.00 |
| 4-10 | 17.00 | 51.00 | 120.00 |
| 11-18,20 | 13.00 | 40.00 | 90.00 |
| 19-Origin The American Crusader, ends #39,41 | 19.00 | 56.00 | 130.00 |
| 21-30: 24-Intro. Mike, Doc Strange's sidekick. 29-Last Rio Kid | 11.50 | 34.00 | 80.00 |
| 31-40: 36-Commando Cubs begin | 9.30 | 28.00 | 65.00 |

41-52: 41-Hitler bondage-c. 44-Hitler-c. 52-The Ghost ends

|  | Good | Fine | N-Mint |
|---|---|---|---|
|  | 7.00 | 21.00 | 50.00 |
| 53-The Phantom Detective begins; The Cavalier app.; no Commando | | | |
| Cubs | 7.00 | 21.00 | 50.00 |
| 54-The Cavalier app.; no Commando Cubs | 7.00 | 21.00 | 50.00 |
| 55-Lone Eagle ends | 7.00 | 21.00 | 50.00 |
| 56-Princess Pantha begins | 14.00 | 42.00 | 100.00 |
| 57-60 | 13.00 | 40.00 | 90.00 |
| 61-66: 61-Ingels-a; The Lone Eagle app. 65-Last Phantom Detective & | | | |
| Commando Cubs. 66-Frazetta text illo | 13.00 | 40.00 | 90.00 |
| 67,70-73: Frazetta-a(5-7 pgs.) in each. 72-Sea Eagle app. | | | |
|  | 18.00 | 54.00 | 125.00 |
| 68,69-Frazetta-a(2), 8 & 6 pgs.; 9 & 7 pgs. | 19.00 | 57.00 | 132.00 |
| 74-Last Princess Pantha; Tara app. Buck Ranger, Cowboy Detective be- | | | |
| gins | 6.50 | 19.50 | 45.00 |
| 75-78: 75-Western format begins | 3.70 | 11.00 | 26.00 |
| 79-Krigstein-a | 5.00 | 15.00 | 35.00 |
| 80-Severin & Elder, Celardo, Moreira-a | 5.00 | 15.00 | 35.00 |

**THUNDER AGENTS**
11/65 - No. 17, 12/67; No. 18, 9/68, No. 19, 11/68, No. 20, 11/69
Tower Comics

| 1-Origin & 1st app. Dynamo, Noman, Menthor, & The Thunder Squad; | | | |
|---|---|---|---|
| 1st app. The Iron Maiden | 7.00 | 21.00 | 50.00 |
| 2-Death of Egghead | 3.60 | 11.00 | 25.00 |
| 3-5: 4-Guy Gilbert becomes Lightning who joins Thunder Squad; Iron | | | |
| Maiden app. | 2.85 | 8.50 | 20.00 |
| 6-10: 7-Death of Menthor. 8-Origin & 1st app. The Raven | | | |
|  | 1.70 | 5.00 | 12.00 |
| 11-15: 13-Undersea Agent app.; no Raven story | | | |
|  | 1.15 | 3.50 | 8.00 |
| 16-19 | 1.00 | 3.00 | 6.00 |
| 20-Special Collectors Edition; all reprints | .70 | 2.00 | 4.00 |

**THUNDERCATS** (TV)
Dec, 1985 - No. 24, June, 1988
Star Comics/Marvel #22 on

| | Good | Fine | N-Mint |
|---|---|---|---|
| 1-Mooney c/a begins | .35 | 1.00 | 2.00 |
| 2-24: 12-Begin $1.00-c; 20-Williamson-i | | .50 | 1.00 |

**TIM HOLT** (Movie star) (Red Mask #42 on; see Crack Western)
1948 - No. 41, April-May, 1954 (All 36 pgs.)
Magazine Enterprises

| | Good | Fine | N-Mint |
|---|---|---|---|
| 1-(A-1 #14)-Photo-c begin, end No. 18, 29; Tim Holt, His horse Lightning & sidekick Chito begin | 35.00 | 105.00 | 245.00 |
| 2-(A-1 #17)(9-10/48) | 22.00 | 65.00 | 155.00 |
| 3-(A-1 #19)-Photo back-c | 15.00 | 45.00 | 105.00 |
| 4(1-2/49),5: 5-Photo back-c | 11.50 | 34.00 | 80.00 |
| 6-1st app. The Calico Kid (alias Rex Fury), his horse Ebony & Sidekick Sing-Song (begin series); photo back-c | 13.00 | 40.00 | 90.00 |
| 7-10: 7-Calico Kid by Ayers. 8-Calico Kid by Guardineer (r-/in Great Western 10). 9-Map of Tim's Home Range | 9.30 | 28.00 | 65.00 |
| 11-The Calico Kid becomes The Ghost Rider (Origin & 1st app.) by Dick Ayers (r-/in Great Western 8); his horse Spectre & sidekick Sing-Song begin series | 25.00 | 75.00 | 175.00 |
| 12-16,18-Last photo-c | 6.50 | 19.50 | 45.00 |
| 17-Frazetta Ghost Rider-c | 25.00 | 75.00 | 175.00 |
| 19,22,24: 19-Last Tim Holt-c; Bolle line-drawn-c begin | 5.00 | 15.00 | 35.00 |
| 20-Tim Holt becomes Redmask (Origin); begin series; Redmask-c #20-on | 9.50 | 28.50 | 65.00 |
| 21-Frazetta Ghost Rider/Redmask-c | 21.50 | 65.00 | 150.00 |
| 23-Frazetta Redmask-c | 17.00 | 51.00 | 120.00 |
| 25-1st app. Black Phantom | 10.00 | 30.00 | 70.00 |
| 26-30: 28-Wild Bill Hickok, Bat Masterson team up with Redmask. 29-B&W photo-c | 5.00 | 15.00 | 35.00 |
| 31-33-Ghost Rider ends | 4.30 | 13.00 | 30.00 |
| 34-Tales of the Ghost Rider begins (horror)-Classic "The Flower Women" & "Hard Boiled Harry!" | 5.00 | 15.00 | 35.00 |
| 35-Last Tales of the Ghost Rider | 4.30 | 13.00 | 30.00 |
| 36-The Ghost Rider returns, ends No. 41; liquid hallucinogenic drug story | 5.50 | 16.50 | 38.00 |
| 37-Ghost Rider classic "To Touch Is to Die!," about Inca treasure | 5.50 | 16.50 | 38.00 |

|  | Good | Fine | N-Mint |
|---|---|---|---|
| 38-The Black Phantom begins; classic Ghost Rider "The Phantom Guns of Feather Gap!" | 5.50 | 16.50 | 38.00 |
| 39-41: All 3-D effect c/stories | 12.00 | 36.00 | 84.00 |

**TIP TOP COMICS**
4/36 - No. 210, 1957; No. 211, 11-1/57-58 - No. 225, 5-7/61
United Features #1-187/St. John #188-210/Dell Publishing Co. #211 on

|  | Good | Fine | N-Mint |
|---|---|---|---|
| 1-Tarzan by Hal Foster, Li'l Abner, Broncho Bill, Fritzi Ritz, Ella Cinders, Capt. & The Kids begin; strip-r | 180.00 | 450.00 | 1080.00 |
| 2 | 82.00 | 205.00 | 490.00 |
| 3 | 55.00 | 165.00 | 385.00 |
| 4 | 41.00 | 125.00 | 290.00 |
| 5-10: 7-Photo & biography of Edgar Rice Burroughs. 8-Christmas-c | 33.00 | 100.00 | 230.00 |
| 11-20: 20-Christmas-c | 24.00 | 73.00 | 170.00 |
| 21-40: 36-Kurtzman panel (1st published comic work) | 22.00 | 65.00 | 155.00 |
| 41-Has 1st Tarzan Sunday | 22.00 | 65.00 | 155.00 |
| 42-50: 43-Mort Walker panel | 19.00 | 56.00 | 130.00 |
| 51-53 | 16.00 | 48.00 | 110.00 |
| 54-Origin Mirror Man & Triple Terror, also featured on cover | 20.00 | 60.00 | 140.00 |
| 55,56,58,60: Last Tarzan by Foster | 13.00 | 40.00 | 90.00 |
| 57,59,61,62-Tarzan by Hogarth | 17.00 | 51.00 | 120.00 |
| 63-80: 65,67-70,72-74,77,78-No Tarzan | 9.00 | 27.00 | 62.00 |
| 81-90 | 8.00 | 24.00 | 56.00 |
| 91-99 | 5.70 | 17.00 | 40.00 |
| 100 | 6.50 | 19.50 | 45.00 |
| 101-140: 110-Gordo story. 111-Li'l Abner app. 118, 132-no Tarzan | 3.70 | 11.00 | 26.00 |
| 141-170: 145,151-Gordo stories. 157-Last Li'l Abner; lingerie panels | 2.65 | 8.00 | 18.00 |
| 171-188-Tarzan reprints by B. Lubbers in all. #177?-Peanuts by Schulz begins; no Peanuts in #178,179,181-183 | 2.85 | 8.50 | 20.00 |
| 189-225 | 1.70 | 5.00 | 12.00 |

**T-MAN**
Sept., 1951 - No. 38, Dec, 1956
Quality Comics Group

| | Good | Fine | N-Mint |
|---|---|---|---|
| 1-Jack Cole-a | 12.00 | 36.00 | 84.00 |
| 2-Crandall-c | 7.00 | 21.00 | 50.00 |
| 3,6-8: Crandall-c | 5.70 | 17.00 | 40.00 |
| 4,5-Crandall-c/a each; 5-Drug test | 6.50 | 19.50 | 45.00 |
| 9-Crandall-c | 5.00 | 15.00 | 35.00 |
| 10,12 | 2.85 | 8.50 | 20.00 |
| 11-Used in **POP**, pg. 95 & color illo. | 5.00 | 15.00 | 35.00 |
| 13-19,21-24,26 | 2.65 | 8.00 | 18.00 |
| 20-H-Bomb explosion-c/story | 5.50 | 16.50 | 38.00 |
| 25-All Crandall-a | 4.65 | 14.00 | 32.00 |
| 27-38 | 2.00 | 6.00 | 14.00 |

**TOMAHAWK** (Son of . . . on-c of #131-140; see Star Spangled Comics &
World's Finest Comics #65)
Sept-Oct, 1950 - No. 140, May-June, 1972
National Periodical Publications

| | Good | Fine | N-Mint |
|---|---|---|---|
| 1 | 46.00 | 137.00 | 320.00 |
| 2-Frazetta/Williamson-a, 4 pgs. | 26.00 | 77.00 | 180.00 |
| 3-5 | 13.00 | 40.00 | 90.00 |
| 6-10: 7-Last 52 pgs. | 10.00 | 30.00 | 70.00 |
| 11-20 | 6.50 | 19.50 | 45.00 |
| 21-27,30: Last precode (2/55) | 5.00 | 15.00 | 35.00 |
| 28-1st app. Lord Shilling (arch-foe) | 6.50 | 19.50 | 45.00 |
| 29-Frazetta-r/Jimmy Wakely #3 (3 pgs.) | 12.00 | 36.00 | 84.00 |
| 31-40 | 3.50 | 10.50 | 24.00 |
| 41-50 | 2.65 | 8.00 | 18.00 |
| 51-56,58-60 | 2.00 | 6.00 | 14.00 |
| 57-Frazetta-r/Jimmy Wakely #6 (3 pgs.) | 6.50 | 19.50 | 45.00 |
| 61-77: 77-Last 10 cent issue | 1.15 | 3.50 | 8.00 |
| 78-85: 81-1st app. Miss Liberty. 83-Origin Tomahawk's Rangers | | | |
| | .60 | 1.80 | 4.00 |
| 86-100: 96-Origin/1st app. The Hood, alias Lady Shilling | | | |
| | .35 | 1.00 | 2.00 |
| 101-110: 107-Origin/1st app. Thunder-Man | | .60 | 1.20 |
| 111-130,132-138,140 | | .50 | 1.00 |
| 131-Frazetta-r/Jimmy Wakely #7 (3 pgs.); origin Firehair retold | | | |
| | .35 | 1.00 | 2.00 |
| 139-Frazetta-r/Star Spangled #113 | | .60 | 1.20 |

**TOMB OF DRACULA**
April, 1972 - No. 70, Aug, 1979
Marvel Comics Group

|  | Good | Fine | N-Mint |
|---|---|---|---|
| 1-Colan-p in all | 1.70 | 5.00 | 10.00 |
| 2-10: 3-Intro. Dr. Rachel Van Helsing & Inspector Chelm. 10-1st app. | | | |
| Blade the Vampire Slayer | .70 | 2.00 | 4.00 |
| 11,12,14-20: 12-Brunner-c(p) | .40 | 1.25 | 2.50 |
| 13-Origin Blade the Vampire Slayer | .40 | 1.25 | 2.50 |
| 21-70: 50-Silver Surfer app. 70-Double size | .35 | 1.00 | 2.00 |

**TOM MIX WESTERN** (Movie, radio star) (Also see The Comics,
    Crackajack Funnies, Master Comics, Popular Comics, Real Western
    Hero & Western Hero)
Jan, 1948 - No. 61, May, 1953 (1-17: 52 pgs.)
Fawcett Publications

|  | Good | Fine | N-Mint |
|---|---|---|---|
| 1 (Photo-c, 52 pgs.)-Tom Mix & his horse Tony begin; Tumbleweed Jr. | | | |
| begins, ends #52,54,55 | 43.00 | 130.00 | 300.00 |
| 2 (Photo-c) | 24.00 | 73.00 | 170.00 |
| 3-5 (Painted/photo-c): 5-Billy the Kid & Oscar app. | | | |
|  | 19.00 | 57.00 | 135.00 |
| 6,7 (Painted/photo-c) | 16.00 | 48.00 | 110.00 |
| 8-Kinstler tempera-c | 16.00 | 48.00 | 110.00 |
| 9,10 (Painted/photo-c)-Used in **SOTI**, pgs. 323-325 | | | |
|  | 14.00 | 42.00 | 100.00 |
| 11-Kinstler oil-c | 13.00 | 40.00 | 90.00 |
| 12 (Painted/photo-c) | 11.50 | 34.00 | 80.00 |
| 13-17 (Painted-c, 52 pgs.) | 11.50 | 34.00 | 80.00 |
| 18,22 (Painted-c, 36 pgs.) | 9.30 | 28.00 | 65.00 |
| 19 (Photo-c, 52 pgs.) | 11.50 | 34.00 | 80.00 |
| 20,21,23 (Painted-c, 52 pgs.) | 9.30 | 28.00 | 65.00 |
| 24,25,27-29 (52 pgs.): 24-Photo-c begin, end #61. 29-Slim Pickens app. | | | |
|  | 9.30 | 28.00 | 65.00 |
| 26,30 (36 pgs.) | 8.50 | 25.50 | 60.00 |
| 31-33,35-37,39,40,42 (52 pgs.): 39-Red Eagle app. | | | |
|  | 8.00 | 24.00 | 56.00 |
| 34,38 (36 pgs. begin) | 6.50 | 19.50 | 45.00 |
| 41,43-60 | 4.50 | 14.00 | 32.00 |
| 61-Last issue | 5.70 | 17.00 | 40.00 |

**TOP-NOTCH COMICS** (. . . Laugh #28-45)
Dec, 1939 - No. 45, June, 1944
MLJ Magazines

|  | Good | Fine | N-Mint |
|---|---|---|---|
| 1-Origin The Wizard; Kardak the Mystic Magician, Swift of the Secret Service (ends No. 3), Air Patrol, The Westpointer, Manhunters (by J. Cole), Mystic (ends #2) & Scott Rand (ends #3) begin | 100.00 | 300.00 | 700.00 |
| 2-Dick Storm (ends #8), Stacy Knight M.D. (ends #4) begin; Jack Cole-a | 49.00 | 148.00 | 345.00 |
| 3-Bob Phantom, Scott Rand on Mars begin; J. Cole-a | 39.00 | 115.00 | 270.00 |
| 4-Origin/1st app. Streak Chandler on Mars; Moore of the Mounted only app.; J. Cole-a | 34.00 | 100.00 | 235.00 |
| 5-Flag-c; origin/1st app. Galahad; Shanghai Sheridan begins (ends #8); Shield cameo | 27.00 | 81.00 | 190.00 |
| 6-Meskin-a | 24.00 | 73.00 | 170.00 |
| 7-The Shield x-over in Wizard; The Wizard dons new costume | 36.00 | 107.00 | 250.00 |
| 8-Origin The Firefly & Roy, the Super Boy | 40.00 | 120.00 | 280.00 |
| 9-Origin & 1st app. The Black Hood; Fran Frazier begins | 100.00 | 300.00 | 700.00 |
| 10 | 41.00 | 125.00 | 290.00 |
| 11-20 | 27.00 | 81.00 | 185.00 |
| 21-30: 23,24-No Wizard, Roy app. in each. 25-Last Bob Phantom, Roy app. 26-Roy app. 27-Last Firefly. 28-Suzie begins. 29-Last Kardak | 23.00 | 70.00 | 160.00 |
| 31-44: 33-Dotty & Ditto by Woggon begins. 44-Black Hood series ends | 12.00 | 36.00 | 84.00 |
| 45-Last issue | 7.00 | 21.00 | 50.00 |

**TRANSFORMERS, THE** (TV) (Also see G.I. Joe and . . . )
Sept, 1984 - Present (75 cents, $1.00) (Prices are for 1st printings)
Marvel Comics Group

|  | Good | Fine | N-Mint |
|---|---|---|---|
| 1-Based on Hasbro toys | .60 | 1.75 | 3.50 |
| 2,3 | .35 | 1.00 | 2.00 |

|  | Good | Fine | N-Mint |
|---|---|---|---|
| 4-10 | .25 | .75 | 1.50 |
| 11-72: 21-Intro Aerialbots. 54-Intro Micromasters |  |  |  |
|  |  | .50 | 1.00 |

## TRANSFORMERS: HEADMASTERS, THE
July, 1987 - No. 4, Jan, 1988 (mini-series)
Marvel Comics Group

| 1-4 | .25 | .75 | 1.50 |
|---|---|---|---|

## TRANSFORMERS UNIVERSE, THE
Dec, 1986 - No. 4, March, 1987 ($1.25, mini-series)
Marvel Comics Group

| 1-4-A guide to all characters | .25 | .75 | 1.50 |
|---|---|---|---|

## TRUE CRIME COMICS
No. 2, May, 1947; No. 3, July-Aug, 1948 - No. 6, June-July, 1949; V2 #1,
    Aug-Sept, 1949 (52 pgs.)
Magazine Village

2-Jack Cole-c/a; used in **SOTI**, pg. 81,82 plus illo.-"A sample of the injury-
  to-eye motif" & illo.-"Dragging living people to death"; used in **POP**,
  pg. 105; "Murder, Morphine and Me" classic drug propaganda story
  used by N.Y. Legis. Comm.          75.00     225.00     525.00
3-Classic Cole-c/a; drug story with hypo, opium den & withdrawing ad-
  dict          50.00     150.00     350.00
4-Jack Cole-c/a; c-taken from a story panel in #3; r-(2) **SOTI** & **POP**
  stories/#2          45.00     135.00     315.00
5-Jack Cole-c; Marijuana racket story     21.50     65.00     150.00
6          10.00     30.00     70.00
V2#1-Used in **SOTI**, pgs. 81,82 & illo.-"Dragging living people to death";
  Toth, Wood (3 pgs.), Roussos-a; Cole-r from #2
          32.00     95.00     225.00

## TUROK, SON OF STONE
No. 596, 12/54 - No. 29, 9/62; No. 30, 12/62 - No. 91, 7/74; No. 92, 9/74 -
　　No. 125, 1/80; No. 126, 3/81 - No. 130, 4/82
Dell Publ. Co. No. 1-29/Gold Key No. 30-91/Gold Key or Whitman No.
　　92-125/Whitman No. 126 on

|  | Good | Fine | N-Mint |
|---|---|---|---|
| 4-Color 596 (12/54)(#1)-1st app./origin Turok & Andar | | | |
|  | 24.00 | 73.00 | 170.00 |
| 4-Color 656 (10/55)(#2)-1st mention of Lanok | | | |
|  | 17.00 | 50.00 | 120.00 |
| 3(3-5/56)-5 | 12.00 | 36.00 | 84.00 |
| 6-10 | 8.00 | 24.00 | 56.00 |
| 11-20: 17-Prehistoric pygmies | 4.00 | 12.00 | 28.00 |
| 21-30: 30-Back-c pin-ups begin. 30-33-Painted back-c pin-ups | | | |
|  | 2.30 | 7.00 | 16.00 |
| 31-50: 31-Drug use story | 1.15 | 3.50 | 8.00 |
| 51-60: 58-Flying Saucer c/story | .70 | 2.00 | 5.00 |
| 61-83: 62-12 & 15 cent-c. 63-Only line drawn-c | .35 | 1.00 | 2.00 |
| 84-Origin & 1st app. Hutec | .35 | 1.00 | 2.00 |
| 85-130: 114,115-(52 pgs.) | | .50 | 1.00 |
| Giant 1(30031-611) (11/66) | 4.50 | 13.50 | 36.00 |

## TWILIGHT ZONE, THE (TV)
No. 1173, 3-5/61 - No. 91, 4/79; No. 92, 5/82
Dell Publishing Co./Gold Key/Whitman No. 92

| | Good | Fine | N-Mint |
|---|---|---|---|
| 4-Color 1173-Crandall/Evans-c/a | 5.70 | 17.00 | 40.00 |
| 4-Color 1288-Crandall/Evans-c/a | 4.50 | 14.00 | 32.00 |
| 01-860-207 (5-7/62-Dell) | 3.70 | 11.00 | 26.00 |
| 12-860-210 on-c; 01-860-210 on inside(8-10/62-Dell)-Evans-c/a; Crandall/ | | | |
| 　　Frazetta-a(2) | 3.70 | 11.00 | 26.00 |
| 1(11/62-Gold Key)-Crandall, Evans-a | 3.50 | 10.50 | 24.00 |
| 2 | 1.70 | 5.00 | 12.00 |
| 3,4,9-Toth-a, 11,10 & 15 pgs. | 2.00 | 6.00 | 14.00 |
| 5-8,10,11 | 1.30 | 4.00 | 9.00 |

*The Twilight Zone #16, © Cayuga Productions*

|  | Good | Fine | N-Mint |
|---|---|---|---|
| 12,13,15: 12-Williamson-a. 13,15-Crandall-a | 1.70 | 5.00 | 12.00 |
| 14-Williamson/Orlando/Crandall/Torres-a | 2.00 | 6.00 | 14.00 |
| 16-20 | 1.00 | 3.00 | 7.00 |
| 21-Crandall-a(r) | .70 | 2.00 | 5.00 |
| 22-27: 25-Evans/Crandall-a(r). 26-Crandall, Evans-a(r). 27-Evans-r(2) | | | |
|  | .60 | 1.80 | 4.00 |
| 28-32: 32-Evans-a(r) | .35 | 1.00 | 2.00 |
| 33-42,44-50,52-70 | .25 | .75 | 1.50 |
| 43,51: 43-Crandall-a. 51-Williamson-a | .30 | .90 | 1.80 |
| 71-92: 71-Reprint. 83,84-(52 pgs.) |  | .50 | 1.00 |

# U

**UNCLE SAM QUARTERLY** (Blackhawk #9 on) (See National Comics)
Autumn, 1941 - No. 8, Fall, 1943
Quality Comics Group

|  | Good | Fine | N-Mint |
|---|---|---|---|
| 1-Origin Uncle Sam; Fine/Eisner-c, chapter headings, 2 pgs. by Eisner. (2 versions: dark cover, no price; light cover with price); Jack Cole-a | 112.00 | 335.00 | 785.00 |
| 2-Cameos by The Ray, Black Condor, Quicksilver, The Red Bee, Alias the Spider, Hercules & Neon the Unknown; Eisner, Fine-c/a | 54.00 | 160.00 | 375.00 |
| 3-Tuska-c/a | 39.00 | 115.00 | 270.00 |
| 4 | 33.00 | 100.00 | 230.00 |
| 5-8 | 27.00 | 81.00 | 190.00 |

**UNCLE SCROOGE** (Disney) (See Walt Disney's Comics & Stories)
No. 386, 3/52 - No. 39, 8-10/62; No. 40, 12/62 - No. 209, 1984; No. 210,
10/86 - No. 242, April, 1990
Dell #1-39/Gold Key #40-173/Whitman #174-209/Gladstone #210 on

| | Good | Fine | N-Mint |
|---|---|---|---|
| 4-Color 386(#1)-in "Only a Poor Old Man" by Carl Barks | 60.00 | 180.00 | 420.00 |
| 4-Color 456(#2)-in "Back to the Klondike" by Carl Barks | 29.00 | 86.00 | 200.00 |
| 4-Color 495(No.3)-r-in #105 | 26.00 | 77.00 | 180.00 |
| 4(12-2/53-54) | 20.00 | 60.00 | 140.00 |
| 5 | 16.00 | 48.00 | 110.00 |
| 6-r-in U.S. #106,165,233 | 15.00 | 45.00 | 105.00 |
| 7-The Seven Cities of Cibola by Barks | 11.50 | 34.00 | 80.00 |
| 8-10: 8-r-in #111,222. 9-r-in #104,214. 10-r-in #67 | 9.30 | 28.00 | 65.00 |
| 11-20: 11-r-in #237. 17-r-in #215. 20-r-in #213 | 8.00 | 24.00 | 56.00 |
| 21-30: 26-r-in #211 | 6.50 | 19.50 | 45.00 |
| 31-40: 34-r-in #228 | 5.50 | 16.50 | 38.00 |
| 41-50 | 4.00 | 12.00 | 28.00 |
| 51-60 | 3.70 | 11.00 | 26.00 |
| 61-66,68-70: 70-Last Barks issue with original story | 2.85 | 8.50 | 20.00 |

| | Good | Fine | N-Mint |
|---|---|---|---|
| 67,72,73-Barks-r | 1.85 | 5.50 | 13.00 |
| 71-Written by Barks only | 1.85 | 5.50 | 13.00 |
| 74-One pg. Barks-r | 1.15 | 3.50 | 8.00 |
| 75-81,83-Not by Barks | 1.15 | 3.50 | 8.00 |
| 82,84-Barks-r begin | 1.15 | 3.50 | 8.00 |
| 85-100 | 1.00 | 3.00 | 6.00 |
| 101-110 | .85 | 2.50 | 5.00 |
| 111-120 | .70 | 2.00 | 4.00 |
| 121-141,143-152,154-157 | .60 | 1.75 | 3.50 |
| 142-Reprints 4-Color #456 with-c | .70 | 2.00 | 4.00 |
| 153,158,162-164,166,168-170,178,180: No Barks | | .50 | 1.00 |
| 159-160,165,167,172-176-Barks-a | .25 | .75 | 1.50 |
| 161(r-#14), 171(r-#11), 177(r-#16), 179(r-#9), 183(r-#6)-Barks-r | | | |
| | .25 | .75 | 1.50 |
| 181(r-4-Color #495), 195(r-4-Color #386) | .25 | .70 | 1.40 |
| 182,186,191-194,197-202,204-206: No Barks | | .40 | .80 |
| 184,185,187,188-Barks-a | | .50 | 1.00 |
| 189(r-#5), 190(r-#4), 196(r-#13), 203(r-#12), 207(r-#93,92), 208(r-U.S. #18), 209(r-U.S. #21)-Barks-r | | .60 | 1.20 |
| 210-1st Gladstone issue; r-WDC&S #134 (1st Beagle Boys) | | | |
| | .85 | 2.50 | 5.00 |
| 211-218: 217-R-U.S. #7(Seven Cities of Cibola) | .40 | 1.25 | 2.50 |
| 219-Son Of The Sun by Rosa | 1.70 | 5.00 | 10.00 |
| 220-Don Rosa story/a | .50 | 1.50 | 3.00 |
| 221-230: 224-Rosa-c/a. 226,227-Rosa-a | .25 | .75 | 1.50 |
| 231-240: 235-Rosa story/art | | .50 | 1.00 |
| 241-($1.95, 68 pgs.)-Rosa finishes over Barks-r | | | |
| | .35 | 1.00 | 2.00 |
| 242-($1.95, 68 pgs.)-Barks-r; Rosa-a(1 pg.) | .35 | 1.00 | 2.00 |
| Uncle Scrooge & Money(G.K.)-Barks-r/from WDC&S #130 (3/67) | | | |
| | 4.00 | 12.00 | 24.00 |

**UNCLE SCROOGE ADVENTURES** (Walt Disney's . . . #4 on)
Nov, 1987 - No. 21, May, 1990
Gladstone Publishing

| | Good | Fine | N-Mint |
|---|---|---|---|
| 1-Barks-r begin | .70 | 2.00 | 4.00 |
| 2-5: 5-Rosa-c/a | .25 | .75 | 1.50 |
| 6-19: 9,14-Rosa-a. 10-r/U.S. #18(all Barks) | | .50 | 1.00 |
| 20,21 ($1.95, 68 pgs.) 20-Rosa-c/a. 21-Rosa-a | .35 | 1.00 | 1.95 |

**UNDERDOG** (TV)
July, 1970 - No. 10, Jan, 1972; Mar, 1975 - No. 23, Feb, 1979
Charlton Comics/Gold Key

|  | Good | Fine | N-Mint |
|---|---|---|---|
| 1 (1st series) | 2.30 | 7.00 | 16.00 |
| 2-10 | .85 | 2.60 | 6.00 |
| 1 (Gold Key)(2nd series) | 1.50 | 4.50 | 10.00 |
| 2-10 | .60 | 1.80 | 4.00 |
| 11-23: 13-1st app. Shack of Solitude | .50 | 1.50 | 3.00 |

**UNTOLD LEGEND OF THE BATMAN, THE**
July, 1980 - No. 3, Sept, 1980 (Mini-series)
DC Comics

|  | Good | Fine | N-Mint |
|---|---|---|---|
| 1-Origin; Joker-c; Byrne-a | .70 | 2.00 | 4.00 |
| 2,3 | .50 | 1.50 | 3.00 |

**USA COMICS**
Aug, 1941 - No. 17, Fall, 1945
Timely Comics (USA)

1-Origin Major Liberty (called Mr. Liberty #1), Rockman by Wolverton, & The Whizzer by Avison; The Defender with sidekick Rusty & Jack Frost begin; The Young Avenger only app.; S&K-c plus 1 pg. art
350.00    875.00    2100.00

2-Origin Captain Terror & The Vagabond; last Wolverton Rockman
183.00    460.00    1100.00

3-No Whizzer
142.00    355.00    850.00

4-Last Rockman, Major Liberty, Defender, Jack Frost, & Capt. Terror; Corporal Dix app.
117.00    295.00    700.00

5-Origin American Avenger & Roko the Amazing; The Blue Blade, The Black Widow & Victory Boys, Gypo the Gypsy Giant & Hills of Horror only app.; Sergeant Dix begins; no Whizzer. Hitler-c
97.00    245.00    580.00

6-Captain America, The Destroyer, Jap Buster Johnson, Jeep Jones begin; Terror Squad only app.
108.00    270.00    650.00

7-Captain Daring, Disk-Eyes the Detective by Wolverton app.; origin & only app. Marvel Boy; Secret Stamp begins; no Whizzer, Sergeant Dix
90.00    225.00    540.00

| | Good | Fine | N-Mint |
|---|---|---|---|
| 8-10: 9-Last Secret Stamp. 10-The Thunderbird only app. | | | |
| | 65.00 | 165.00 | 390.00 |
| 11,12: 11-No Jeep Jones | 53.00 | 135.00 | 320.00 |
| 13-17: 13-No Whizzer; Jeep Jones ends. 15-No Destroyer; Jap Buster Johnson ends | | | |
| | 39.00 | 98.00 | 235.00 |

**U.S. AIR FORCE COMICS**
Oct, 1958 - No. 37, Mar-Apr, 1965
Charlton Comics

| | Good | Fine | N-Mint |
|---|---|---|---|
| 1 | 1.30 | 4.00 | 9.00 |
| 2 | .65 | 1.90 | 4.50 |
| 3-10 | .50 | 1.50 | 3.00 |
| 11-20 | .35 | 1.00 | 2.00 |
| 21-37 | .25 | .75 | 1.50 |

# V

## VAULT OF HORROR
No. 12, Apr-May, 1950 - No. 40, Dec-Jan, 1954-55
E. C. Comics

|  | Good | Fine | N-Mint |
|---|---|---|---|
| 12 | 116.00 | 348.00 | 810.00 |
| 13-Morphine story | 54.00 | 160.00 | 375.00 |
| 14 | 46.00 | 140.00 | 325.00 |
| 15 | 39.00 | 118.00 | 275.00 |
| 16 | 30.00 | 90.00 | 210.00 |
| 17-19 | 23.00 | 70.00 | 160.00 |
| 20-22,24,25 | 17.00 | 51.00 | 120.00 |
| 23-Used in **POP**, pg. 84 | 17.00 | 51.00 | 120.00 |
| 26-B&W & color illos in **POP** | 17.00 | 51.00 | 120.00 |
| 27-35: 35-Xmas-c | 13.00 | 40.00 | 90.00 |
| 36-"Pipe Dream"-classic opium addict story by Krigstein; 'Twin Bill' cited in articles by T.E. Murphy, Wertham | 13.00 | 40.00 | 90.00 |
| 37-Williamson-a | 13.00 | 40.00 | 90.00 |
| 38-39: 39-Bondage-c | 11.00 | 32.00 | 75.00 |
| 40-Low distribution | 13.00 | 40.00 | 90.00 |

## VENUS (See Marvel Mystery #91 & Marvel Spotlight #2)
August, 1948 - No. 19, April, 1952
Marvel/Atlas Comics (CMC 1-9/LCC 10-19)

| | Good | Fine | N-Mint |
|---|---|---|---|
| 1-Venus & Hedy Devine begin; Kurtzman's "Hey Look" | 43.00 | 130.00 | 300.00 |
| 2 | 25.00 | 75.00 | 175.00 |
| 3,5 | 22.00 | 65.00 | 150.00 |
| 4-Kurtzman's "Hey Look" | 23.00 | 70.00 | 160.00 |
| 6-9: 6-Loki app. 7,8-Painted-c | 20.00 | 60.00 | 140.00 |
| 10-S/F-horror issues begin (7/50) | 22.00 | 65.00 | 150.00 |
| 11-S/F end of the world(11/50) | 26.00 | 77.00 | 180.00 |
| 12 | 19.00 | 58.00 | 135.00 |
| 13-19-Venus by Everett, 2-3 stories each; covers-#13,15-19; 14-Everett part cover (Venus) | 29.00 | 86.00 | 200.00 |

**V FOR VENDETTA**
Sept, 1988 - No. 10, May, 1989 ($2.00, maxi-series, mature readers)
DC Comics

|  | Good | Fine | N-Mint |
|---|---|---|---|
| 1-Alan Moore scripts in all | .75 | 2.25 | 4.50 |
| 2-5 | .40 | 1.25 | 2.50 |
| 6-10 | .35 | 1.00 | 2.00 |

**VIGILANTE, THE** (Also see Action Comics #42 & Leading Comics)
Oct, 1983 - No. 50, Feb, 1988 ($1.25; Baxter paper)
DC Comics

| | Good | Fine | N-Mint |
|---|---|---|---|
| 1-Origin | .85 | 2.50 | 5.00 |
| 2 | .50 | 1.50 | 3.00 |
| 3-10: 3-Cyborg app. 4-1st app. The Exterminator; Newton-a(p). 6,7-Origin | .35 | 1.00 | 2.00 |
| 11-50: 20,21-Nightwing app. 35-Origin Mad Bomber. 47-Batman-c/ story. 50-Ken Steacy painted-c | .30 | .90 | 1.75 |
| Annual 1 (1985) | .40 | 1.25 | 2.50 |
| Annual 2 (1986) | .35 | 1.10 | 2.25 |

# W

**WAGON TRAIN** (1st Series) (TV)
No. 895, Mar, 1958 - No. 13, Apr-June, 1962 (All photo-c)
Dell Publishing Co.

|  | Good | Fine | N-Mint |
|---|---|---|---|
| 4-Color 895 (#1) | 5.70 | 17.00 | 40.00 |
| 4-Color 971,1019 | 3.70 | 11.00 | 26.00 |
| 4(1-3/60),6-13 | 3.00 | 9.00 | 21.00 |
| 5-Toth-a | 3.50 | 10.50 | 24.00 |

**WAGON TRAIN** (2nd Series) (TV)
Jan, 1964 - No. 4, Oct, 1964 (All photo-c)
Gold Key

|  | Good | Fine | N-Mint |
|---|---|---|---|
| 1 | 3.00 | 9.00 | 21.00 |
| 2-4: 3,4-Tufts-a | 2.00 | 6.00 | 14.00 |

**WALT DISNEY'S COMICS AND STORIES** (Cont. of Mickey Mouse
Magazine) (#1-30 contain Donald Duck newspaper reprints) (Titled
'Comics And Stories' #264 on)
10/40 - #263, 8/62; #264, 10/62 - #510, 1984; #511, 10/86 - #547, 4/90
Dell Publishing Co./Gold Key #264-473/Whitman #474-510/Gladstone
#511 on

**NOTE:** The whole number can always be found at the bottom of the title
page in the lower left-hand or right-hand panel.

|  | Good | Fine | VF-NM |
|---|---|---|---|
| 1(V1#1-c; V2#1-indicia)-Donald Duck strip-r by Al Taliaferro & Gott-<br>fredson's Mickey Mouse begin | 370.00 | 1480.00 | 3700.00 |
| *(Prices vary widely on this book)* | | | |
| 2 | 220.00 | 660.00 | 1760.00 |

|  | Good | Fine | N-Mint |
|---|---|---|---|
| 3 | 107.00 | 320.00 | 750.00 |
| 4-Xmas-c | 77.00 | 231.00 | 540.00 |

*Walt Disney's Comics and Stories #15,*
*© The Disney Company*

|  | Good | Fine | N-Mint |
|---|---|---|---|
| 4-Special promotional, complimentary issue; cover same except one corner was blanked out & boxed in to identify the giveaway (not a paste-over). This special pressing was probably sent out to former subscribers to Mickey Mouse Mag. whose subscriptions had expired. (Very rare-5 known copies) | 115.00 | 345.00 | 800.00 |
| 5 | 64.00 | 190.00 | 445.00 |
| 6-10 | 50.00 | 150.00 | 350.00 |
| 11-14 | 43.00 | 130.00 | 300.00 |
| 15-17: 15-The 3 Little Kittens (17 pgs.). 16-The 3 Little Pigs (29 pgs.); Xmas-c. 17-The Ugly Duckling (4 pgs.) | 38.00 | 115.00 | 265.00 |
| 18-21 | 30.00 | 90.00 | 210.00 |
| 22-30: 22-Flag-c | 27.00 | 80.00 | 185.00 |
| 31-Donald Duck by Carl Barks begins; see Four Color #9 for first Barks Donald Duck | 157.00 | 470.00 | 1100.00 |
| 32-Barks-a | 90.00 | 270.00 | 630.00 |
| 33-Barks-a (infinity-c) | 64.00 | 190.00 | 445.00 |

| | Good | Fine | N-Mint |
|---|---|---|---|
| 34-Gremlins by Walt Kelly begin, end #41; Barks-a | | | |
| | 52.00 | 156.00 | 365.00 |
| 35,36-Barks-a | 45.00 | 135.00 | 315.00 |
| 37-Donald Duck by Jack Hannah | 21.00 | 64.00 | 150.00 |
| 38-40-Barks-a. 39-Christmas-c. 40-Gremlins by Kelly | | | |
| | 32.00 | 95.00 | 220.00 |
| 41-50-Barks-a; 41-Gremlins by Kelly | 26.00 | 77.00 | 180.00 |
| 51-60-Barks-a; 51-Christmas-c. 52-Li'l Bad Wolf begins, ends #203 (not in #55). 58-Kelly flag-c | 19.00 | 58.00 | 135.00 |
| 61-70: Barks-a. 61-Dumbo story. 63,64-Pinocchio stories. 63-c-swipe from New Funnies #94. 64-Xmas-c. 65-Pluto story. 66-Infinity-c. 67,68-M. Mouse Sunday-r by Bill Wright | 16.00 | 48.00 | 110.00 |
| 71-80: Barks-a. 75-77-Brer Rabbit stories, no Mickey Mouse. 76- Xmas-c | | | |
| | 11.50 | 34.00 | 80.00 |
| 81-87,89,90: Barks-a. 82-84-Bongo stories. 86-90-Goofy & Agnes app. 89-Chip 'n' Dale story | 9.50 | 28.50 | 65.00 |
| 88-1st app. Gladstone Gander by Barks | 11.50 | 34.00 | 80.00 |
| 91-97,99: Barks-a. 95-1st WDC&S Barks-c. 96-No Mickey Mouse; Little Toot begins, ends #97. 99-Xmas-c | 7.50 | 22.50 | 52.00 |
| 98-1st Uncle Scrooge app. in WDC&S | 16.00 | 48.00 | 110.00 |
| 100-Barks-a | 8.50 | 25.50 | 60.00 |
| 101-106,108-110-Barks-a | 6.50 | 19.50 | 45.00 |
| 107-Barks-a; Taliaferro-c. Donald acquires super powers | | | |
| | 6.50 | 19.50 | 45.00 |
| 111,114,117-All Barks | 5.00 | 15.00 | 35.00 |
| 112-Drug (ether) issue (Donald Duck) | 5.50 | 16.50 | 38.00 |
| 113,115,116,118-123: Not by Barks. 116-Dumbo x-over. 121-Grandma Duck begins, ends #168; not in #135,142,146,155 | | | |
| | 2.15 | 6.50 | 15.00 |
| 124,126-130-All Barks. 124-Xmas-c | 4.35 | 13.00 | 30.00 |
| 125-Intro. & 1st app. Junior Woodchucks; Barks-a | | | |
| | 7.00 | 21.00 | 50.00 |
| 131,133,135-139-All Barks | 4.35 | 13.00 | 30.00 |
| 132-Barks-a(2) (D. Duck & Grandma Duck) | 5.15 | 15.50 | 36.00 |
| 134-Intro. & 1st app. The Beagle Boys | 8.50 | 25.50 | 60.00 |
| 140-1st app. Gyro Gearloose by Barks | 8.50 | 25.50 | 60.00 |
| 141-150-All Barks. 143-Little Hiawatha begins, ends #151,159 | | | |
| | 2.65 | 8.00 | 18.00 |

|  | Good | Fine | N-Mint |
|---|---|---|---|
| 151-170-All Barks | 2.35 | 7.00 | 16.00 |
| 171-200-All Barks | 2.00 | 6.00 | 14.00 |
| 201-240: All Barks. 204-Chip 'n' Dale & Scamp begin | | | |
|  | 1.70 | 5.00 | 12.00 |
| 241-283: Barks-a. 241-Dumbo x-over. 247-Gyro Gearloose begins, ends #274. 256-Ludwig Von Drake begins, ends #274 | | | |
|  | 1.50 | 4.50 | 9.00 |
| 284,285,287,290,295,296,309-311-Not by Barks | .85 | 2.50 | 5.00 |
| 286,288,289,291-294,297,298,308-All Barks stories; 293-Grandma Duck's Farm Friends. 297-Gyro Gearloose. 298-Daisy Duck's Diary-r | | | |
|  | 1.35 | 4.00 | 8.00 |
| 299-307-All contain early Barks-r (#43-117). 305-Gyro Gearloose | | | |
|  | 1.50 | 4.50 | 9.00 |
| 312-Last Barks issue with original story | 1.35 | 4.00 | 8.00 |
| 313-315,317-327,329-334,336-341 | .70 | 2.00 | 4.00 |
| 316-Last issue published during life of Walt Disney | | | |
|  | .70 | 2.00 | 4.00 |
| 328,335,342-350-Barks-r | .85 | 2.50 | 5.00 |
| 351-360-w/posters inside; Barks reprints (2 versions of each with & without posters)-without posters . . . | .75 | 2.25 | 4.50 |
| 351-360-With posters | 1.15 | 3.50 | 8.00 |
| 361-400-Barks-r | .75 | 2.25 | 4.50 |
| 401-429-Barks-r. 410-Annette Funicello photo-c | | | |
|  | .50 | 1.50 | 3.00 |
| 430,433,437,438,441,444,445,466,506,509,510-No Barks | | | |
|  |  | .35 | .70 |
| 431,432,434-436,439,440,442,443-Barks-r | .25 | .75 | 1.50 |
| 446-465,467-505,507,508-510: All Barks-r. 494-r/WDC&S #98 (1st Uncle Scrooge) | | .50 | 1.00 |
| 511-Wuzzles by Disney studio | .85 | 2.50 | 5.00 |
| 512 | .50 | 1.50 | 3.00 |
| 513-520: 518-Infinity-c | .30 | .90 | 1.80 |
| 521-540: 522-r/1st app. Huey, Dewey & Louie from D. Duck Sunday page. 535-546-Barks-r | |  .60 | 1.20 |
| 541-545: (All $1.50, 52 pgs.) | .25 | .75 | 1.50 |
| 546 ($1.95, 68 pgs.)-Kelly-r | .35 | 1.00 | 2.00 |
| 547 ($1.95, 68 pgs.)-Rosa-a | .35 | 1.00 | 2.00 |

**WAMBI, JUNGLE BOY** (See Jungle Comics)
Spring, 1942 - No. 3, Spring, 1943; No. 4, Fall, 1948 - No. 18, Winter,
    1952-53 (#1-3: 68 pgs.)
Fiction House Magazines

|  | Good | Fine | N-Mint |
|---|---|---|---|
| 1-Wambi, the Jungle Boy begins | 30.00 | 90.00 | 210.00 |
| 2 (1942)-Kiefer-c | 16.00 | 48.00 | 110.00 |
| 3 (1943)-Kiefer-c/a | 11.50 | 34.00 | 80.00 |
| 4 (1948)-Origin in text | 7.00 | 21.00 | 50.00 |
| 5 (Fall, '49, 36 pgs.)-Kiefer-c/a | 6.00 | 18.00 | 42.00 |
| 6-10: 7-52 pgs. | 5.00 | 15.00 | 35.00 |
| 11-18 | 3.70 | 11.00 | 26.00 |

**WANTED, THE WORLD'S MOST DANGEROUS VILLAINS**
July-Aug, 1972 - No. 9, Aug-Sept, 1973 (All reprints)
National Periodical Publications

1-Batman, Green Lantern (story r-from G.L. #1), & Green Arrow
|  | Good | Fine | N-Mint |
|---|---|---|---|
|  | .35 | 1.00 | 2.00 |

2-Batman/Joker/Penguin-c/story r-from Batman #25; plus Flash story
    r-from Flash #121
|  |  |  |  |
|---|---|---|---|
|  | .50 | 1.50 | 3.00 |

3-9: 3-Dr. Fate, Hawkman(r/Flash #100), & Vigilante. 4-Gr. Lantern & Kid
    Eternity. 5-Dollman/Green Lantern. 6-Burnley Starman; Wildcat/
    Sargon. 7-Johnny Quick/Hawkman/Hourman by Baily. 8-Dr. Fate/
    Flash(r/Flash #114). 9-S&K Sandman/Superman
|  |  |  |  |
|---|---|---|---|
|  | .50 | | 1.00 |

**WAR COMICS**
Dec, 1950 - No. 49, Sept, 1957
Marvel/Atlas (USA No. 1-41/JPI No. 42-49)

|  | Good | Fine | N-Mint |
|---|---|---|---|
| 1 | 6.50 | 19.50 | 45.00 |
| 2 | 3.00 | 9.00 | 21.00 |
| 3-10 | 2.30 | 7.00 | 16.00 |
| 11-20 | 1.50 | 4.50 | 10.00 |
| 21,23-32: Last precode (2/55). 26-Valley Forge story | | | |
|  | 1.30 | 4.00 | 9.00 |
| 22-Krigstein-a | 3.00 | 9.00 | 21.00 |
| 33-37,39-42,44,45,47,48 | 1.15 | 3.50 | 8.00 |
| 38-Kubert/Moskowitz-a | 2.30 | 7.00 | 16.00 |

| | Good | Fine | N-Mint |
|---|---|---|---|
| 43,49-Torres-a. 43-Davis E.C. swipe | 2.00 | 6.00 | 14.00 |
| 46-Crandall-a | 2.30 | 7.00 | 16.00 |

## WATCHMEN
Sept, 1986 - No. 12, Oct, 1987 (12 issue maxi-series)
DC Comics

| | Good | Fine | N-Mint |
|---|---|---|---|
| 1-Alan Moore scripts in all | 1.15 | 3.50 | 7.00 |
| 2,3 | .85 | 2.50 | 5.00 |
| 4-10 | .65 | 1.90 | 3.75 |
| 11,12 | .50 | 1.50 | 3.00 |

## WEB OF EVIL
Nov, 1952 - No. 21, Dec, 1954
Comic Magazines/Quality Comics Group

| | Good | Fine | N-Mint |
|---|---|---|---|
| 1-Used in **SOTI**, pg. 388. Jack Cole-a; morphine use story | | | |
| | 18.00 | 54.00 | 125.00 |
| 2,3-Jack Cole-a | 10.00 | 30.00 | 70.00 |
| 4,6,7-Jack Cole-c/a | 11.00 | 32.00 | 75.00 |
| 5-Electrocution-c; Jack Cole-c/a | 13.00 | 40.00 | 90.00 |
| 8-11-Jack Cole-a | 7.00 | 21.00 | 50.00 |
| 12,13,15,16,19-21 | 3.70 | 11.00 | 26.00 |
| 14-Part Crandall-c; Old Witch swipe | 4.65 | 14.00 | 32.00 |
| 17-Opium drug propaganda story | 4.00 | 12.00 | 28.00 |
| 18-Acid-in-face story | 5.00 | 15.00 | 35.00 |

## WEB OF SPIDER-MAN, THE
Apr, 1985 - Present
Marvel Comics Group

| | Good | Fine | N-Mint |
|---|---|---|---|
| 1-Painted-c (3rd app. black costume?) | 1.70 | 5.50 | 10.00 |
| 2,3 | .85 | 2.50 | 5.00 |
| 4-8: 7-Hulk x-over; Wolverine splash | .55 | 1.65 | 3.30 |
| 9-13: Dominic Fortune guest stars; painted-c | .50 | 1.55 | 3.10 |
| 14-28: 19-Intro Humbug & Solo | .40 | 1.20 | 2.40 |
| 29-Wolverine app. | 1.35 | 4.00 | 8.00 |
| 30-Origin The Rose & Hobgoblin; Punisher & Wolverine cameo in flashback | .60 | 1.75 | 3.50 |
| 31-Six part Kraven storyline | .90 | 2.75 | 5.50 |

| | Good | Fine | N-Mint |
|---|---|---|---|
| 32-Kraven storyline continues | .85 | 2.50 | 5.00 |
| 33,34 | .25 | .75 | 1.50 |
| 35-49: 38-Hobgoblin app.; begin $1.00-c. 48-Hobgoblin, Kingpin app. | | | |
| | | .60 | 1.20 |
| 50-($1.50, 52 pgs.) | .35 | 1.00 | 2.00 |
| 51-58 | | .55 | 1.10 |
| 59-Cosmic Spidey cont./Spect. Spider-Man | .35 | 1.00 | 2.00 |
| 60-70 | | .50 | 1.00 |
| Annual 1 (9/85) | .45 | 1.30 | 2.60 |
| Annual 2 (9/86)-New Mutants; Art Adams-a | .90 | 2.75 | 5.50 |
| Annual 3 (10/87) | .35 | 1.10 | 2.20 |
| Annual 4 (10/88, $1.75)-Evolutionary War x-over | | | |
| | .55 | 1.65 | 3.30 |
| Annual 5 (1989, $2.00, 68 pgs.)-Atlantis Attacks; Captain Universe by | | | |
|     Ditko (p) & Silver Sable stories; F.F. app. | .35 | 1.10 | 2.20 |
| Annual 6 (1990, $2.00, 68 pgs.) | .35 | 1.00 | 2.00 |

**WEIRD, THE**
Apr, 1988 - No. 4, July, 1988 ($1.50, color, mini-series)
DC Comics

| | Good | Fine | N-Mint |
|---|---|---|---|
| 1-Wrightson-c/a in all | .40 | 1.25 | 2.50 |
| 2-4 | .35 | 1.00 | 2.00 |

**WEIRD COMICS**
April, 1940 - No. 20, Jan, 1942
Fox Features Syndicate

| | Good | Fine | N-Mint |
|---|---|---|---|
| 1-The Birdman, Thor, God of Thunder (ends #5), The Sorceress of | | | |
|     Zoom, Blast Bennett, Typhon, Voodoo Man, & Dr. Mortal begin; Fine | | | |
|     bondage-c | 107.00 | 321.00 | 750.00 |
| 2-Lou Fine-c | 52.00 | 156.00 | 365.00 |
| 3,4: 3-Simon-c. 4-Torture-c | 36.00 | 107.00 | 250.00 |
| 5-Intro. Dart & sidekick Ace (ends #20); bondage/hypo-c | | | |
| | 38.00 | 115.00 | 265.00 |
| 6,7-Dynamite Thor app. in each | 35.00 | 105.00 | 245.00 |
| 8-Dynamo, the Eagle (1st app.) & sidekick Buddy & Marga, the Panther | | | |
|     Woman begin | 35.00 | 105.00 | 245.00 |
| 9 | 28.00 | 85.00 | 200.00 |
| 10-Navy Jones app. | 28.00 | 85.00 | 200.00 |

|  | Good | Fine | N-Mint |
|---|---|---|---|
| 11-16: 16-Flag-c | 24.00 | 70.00 | 165.00 |
| 17-Origin The Black Rider | 24.00 | 70.00 | 165.00 |
| 18-20: 20-Origin The Rapier; Swoop Curtis app; Churchill, Hitler-c | | | |
|  | 24.00 | 70.00 | 165.00 |

**WEIRD FANTASY** (Becomes Weird Science-Fantasy #23 on)
No. 13, May-June, 1950 - No. 22, Nov-Dec, 1953
E. C. Comics

| 13(#1) (1950) | 84.00 | 250.00 | 585.00 |
|---|---|---|---|
| 14-Necronomicon story; atomic explosion-c | 46.00 | 137.00 | 320.00 |
| 15,16: 16-Used in **SOTI**, pg. 144 | 37.00 | 110.00 | 260.00 |
| 17 (1951) | 31.00 | 92.00 | 215.00 |
| 6-10 | 23.00 | 70.00 | 160.00 |
| 11-13 (1952) | 17.00 | 51.00 | 120.00 |
| 14-Frazetta/Williamson(1st team-up at E.C.)/Krenkel-a, 7 pgs.; Orlando draws E.C. staff | 30.00 | 90.00 | 210.00 |
| 15-Williamson/Evans-a(3), 4,3,&7 pgs. | 19.00 | 57.00 | 135.00 |
| 16-19-Williamson/Krenkel-a in all. 18-Williamson/Feldstein-c | | | |
|  | 17.00 | 51.00 | 120.00 |
| 20-Frazetta/Williamson-a, 7 pgs. | 19.00 | 57.00 | 135.00 |
| 21-Frazetta/Williamson-c & Williamson/Krenkel-a | | | |
|  | 30.00 | 90.00 | 210.00 |
| 22-Bradbury adaptation | 13.00 | 40.00 | 90.00 |

**WEIRD MYSTERIES**
Oct, 1952 - No. 14, Jan, 1955
Gillmore Publications

| 1-Partial Wolverton-c swiped from splash page "Flight to the Future" in Weird Tales of the Future #2; "Eternity" has an Ingels swipe | | | |
|---|---|---|---|
|  | 20.00 | 60.00 | 140.00 |
| 2-"Robot Woman" by Wolverton; Bernard Baily-c-reprinted in Mister Mystery #18; acid in face panel | 38.00 | 115.00 | 265.00 |
| 3,6: Both have decapitation-c | 13.00 | 40.00 | 90.00 |
| 4-"The Man Who Never Smiled" (3 pgs.) by Wolverton; B. Baily skull-c | | | |
|  | 29.00 | 90.00 | 205.00 |
| 5-Wolverton story "Swamp Monster," 6 pgs. | | | |
|  | 34.00 | 100.00 | 235.00 |

|  | Good | Fine | N-Mint |
|---|---|---|---|
| 7-Used in **SOTI**, illo-"Indeed" & illo-"Sex and Blood" | | | |
| | 21.50 | 65.00 | 150.00 |
| 8-Wolverton-c panel reprint/No. 5; used in a 1954 Reader's Digest anti-comics article by T. E. Murphy entitled "For the Kiddies to Read" | | | |
| | 12.00 | 36.00 | 85.00 |
| 9-Excessive violence, gore & torture | 11.00 | 32.00 | 75.00 |
| 10-Silhouetted nudity panel | 10.00 | 30.00 | 70.00 |
| 11-14 (#13,14-Exist?) | 7.00 | 21.00 | 50.00 |

*Weird Science #15, © William M. Gaines*

**WEIRD SCIENCE** (Becomes Weird Science-Fantasy #23 on)
No. 12, May-June, 1950 - No. 22, Nov-Dec, 1953
E. C. Comics

| | | | |
|---|---|---|---|
| 12(#1) (1950) | 86.00 | 257.00 | 600.00 |
| 13 | 49.00 | 146.00 | 340.00 |
| 14,15 (1950) | 43.00 | 130.00 | 305.00 |

|                                                                      | Good   | Fine   | N-Mint |
|----------------------------------------------------------------------|--------|--------|--------|
| 5-10: 5-Atomic explosion-c                                           | 27.00  | 81.00  | 185.00 |
| 11-14 (1952)                                                         | 17.00  | 51.00  | 120.00 |
| 15-18-Williamson/Krenkel-a in each; 15-Williamson-a. 17-Used in **POP**, pgs. 81,82 | 20.00  | 60.00  | 140.00 |
| 19,20-Williamson/Frazetta-a, 7 pgs each. 19-Used in **SOTI**, illo-"A young girl on her wedding night stabs her sleeping husband to death with a hatpin . . . " | 27.00  | 80.00  | 185.00 |
| 21-Williamson/Frazetta-a, 6 pgs.; Wood draws E.C. staff; Gaines & Feldstein app. in story | 27.00  | 80.00  | 185.00 |
| 22-Williamson/Frazetta/Krenkel-a, 8 pgs.; Wood draws himself in his story - last pg. & panel | 27.00  | 80.00  | 185.00 |

**WEIRD SCIENCE-FANTASY** (Formerly Weird Science & Weird Fantasy)
No. 23 Mar, 1954 - No. 29, May-June, 1955
E. C. Comics

|                                                                      | Good   | Fine   | N-Mint |
|----------------------------------------------------------------------|--------|--------|--------|
| 23-Williamson & Wood-a                                               | 19.00  | 57.00  | 135.00 |
| 24-Williamson & Wood-a; Harlan Ellison's 1st professional story, 'Up-heaval!,' later adapted into a short story as 'Mealtime,' and then into a TV episode of Voyage to the Bottom of the Sea as 'The Price of Doom' | 19.00  | 57.00  | 135.00 |
| 25-Williamson-c; Williamson/Torres/Krenkel-a plus Wood-a             | 23.00  | 70.00  | 165.00 |
| 26-Flying Saucer Report; Wood, Crandall, Orlando-a                   | 18.50  | 56.00  | 130.00 |
| 27                                                                   | 19.00  | 57.00  | 135.00 |
| 28-Williamson/Krenkel/Torres-a; Wood-a                               | 22.00  | 65.00  | 154.00 |
| 29-Frazetta-c; Williamson/Krenkel & Wood-a                           | 42.00  | 125.00 | 295.00 |

**WEIRD TALES OF THE FUTURE**
March, 1952 - No. 8, July, 1953
S.P.M. Publ. No. 1-4/Aragon Publ. No. 5-8

|                                                                      | Good   | Fine   | N-Mint |
|----------------------------------------------------------------------|--------|--------|--------|
| 1-Andru-a(2)                                                         | 26.00  | 77.00  | 180.00 |
| 2,3-Wolverton-c/a(3) each. 2-"Jumpin Jupiter" satire by Wolverton begins, ends #5 | 48.00  | 145.00 | 335.00 |
| 4-"Jumpin Jupiter" satire by Wolverton; partial Wolverton-c          | 24.00  | 73.00  | 170.00 |
| 5-Wolverton-c/a(2)                                                   | 48.00  | 145.00 | 335.00 |
| 6-Bernard Baily-c                                                   | 13.00  | 40.00  | 90.00  |

|  | Good | Fine | N-Mint |
|---|---|---|---|
| 7-"The Mind Movers" from the art to Wolverton's "Brain Bats of Venus" from Mr. Mystery #7 which was cut apart, pasted up, partially redrawn, and rewritten by Harry Kantor, the editor; Bernard Baily-c | 24.00 | 72.00 | 170.00 |
| 8-Reprints Weird Mysteries #1(10/52) minus cover; gory cover showing heart ripped out | 12.00 | 36.00 | 84.00 |

**WEIRD TERROR**
Sept, 1952 - No. 13, Sept, 1954
Allen Hardy Associates (Comic Media)

| | Good | Fine | N-Mint |
|---|---|---|---|
| 1-"Portrait of Death," adapted from Lovecraft's "Pickman's Model"; lingerie panels, Hitler story | 12.00 | 36.00 | 84.00 |
| 2-Text on Marquis DeSade, Torture, Demonology, & St. Elmo's Fire | 6.50 | 19.50 | 45.00 |
| 3-Extreme violence, whipping, torture; article on sin eating, dowsing | 5.70 | 17.00 | 40.00 |
| 4-Dismemberment, decapitation, article on human flesh for sale, Devil, whipping | 9.30 | 28.00 | 65.00 |
| 5-Article on body snatching, mutilation; cannibalism story | 5.70 | 17.00 | 40.00 |
| 6-Dismemberment, decapitation, man hit by lightning | 9.30 | 28.00 | 65.00 |
| 7,9,10 | 5.70 | 17.00 | 40.00 |
| 8-Decapitation story; Ambrose Bierce adapt. | 8.00 | 24.00 | 56.00 |
| 11-End of the world story with atomic blast panels; Tothish-a by Bill Discount | 8.00 | 24.00 | 56.00 |
| 12-Discount-a | 5.00 | 15.00 | 35.00 |
| 13-Severed head panels | 5.70 | 17.00 | 40.00 |

**WEREWOLF BY NIGHT** (See Marvel Spotlight #2-4)
Sept, 1972 - No. 43, Mar, 1977
Marvel Comics Group

| | Good | Fine | N-Mint |
|---|---|---|---|
| 1-Ploog-a-cont'd./Marvel Spotlight #4 | 1.00 | 3.00 | 6.00 |
| 2-31: 15-New origin Werewolf | | .50 | 1.00 |
| 32-Origin & 1st app. Moon Knight | 2.00 | 6.00 | 12.00 |
| 33-2nd app. Moon Knight | 1.15 | 3.50 | 7.00 |
| 34-36,38-43: 35-Starlin/Wrightson-c | | .50 | 1.00 |
| 37-Moon Knight app; part Wrightson-c | .50 | 1.50 | 3.00 |

| | Good | Fine | N-Mint |
|---|---|---|---|
| Giant Size 2(10/74, 68 pgs.)(Formerly G-S Creatures)-Frankenstein app; | | | |
| Ditko-a(r) | | .50 | 1.00 |
| Giant Size 3-5(7/75, 68 pgs.); 4-Morbius the Living Vampire app. | | | |
| | | .50 | 1.00 |

## WEST COAST AVENGERS
Sept, 1984 - No. 4, Dec, 1984 (mini-series; Mando paper)
Marvel Comics Group

| | Good | Fine | N-Mint |
|---|---|---|---|
| 1-Hawkeye, Iron Man, Mockingbird, Tigra | 1.15 | 3.50 | 7.00 |
| 2-4 | .75 | 2.25 | 4.50 |

## WEST COAST AVENGERS (Becomes Avengers West Coast #48 on)
Oct, 1985 - No. 47, Aug, 1989 (On-going series)
Marvel Comics Group

| | Good | Fine | N-Mint |
|---|---|---|---|
| V2#1 | .90 | 2.75 | 5.50 |
| 2,3 | .70 | 2.00 | 4.00 |
| 4-6 | .50 | 1.50 | 3.00 |
| 7-10 | .40 | 1.25 | 2.50 |
| 11-20 | .35 | 1.10 | 2.20 |
| 21-30 | .25 | .70 | 1.40 |
| 31-41 | | .55 | 1.10 |
| 42-Byrne-a(p)/scripts begin | .35 | 1.10 | 2.20 |
| 43-47: 46,46-Byrne-c. 46-1st app. Great Lakes Avengers | | | |
| | | .55 | 1.10 |
| Annual 1 (10/86) | .35 | 1.10 | 2.20 |
| Annual 2 (9/87) | .35 | 1.00 | 2.00 |
| Annual 3 (10/88, $1.75)-Evolutionary War app. | .45 | 1.40 | 2.80 |
| Annual V2#4 ('89, $2.00, 68 pgs.)-Atlantis Attacks; Byrne/Austin-a | | | |
| | | .35 | 1.10 | 2.20 |

## WESTERN COMICS
Jan-Feb, 1948 - No. 85, Jan-Feb, 1961 (1-27: 52 pgs.)
National Periodical Publications

| | Good | Fine | N-Mint |
|---|---|---|---|
| 1-The Wyoming Kid & his horse Racer, The Vigilante (Meskin-a), The | | | |
| Cowboy Marshal, Rodeo Rick begin | 29.00 | 86.00 | 200.00 |
| 2 | 16.50 | 50.00 | 115.00 |
| 3,4-Last Vigilante | 13.00 | 40.00 | 90.00 |

|  | Good | Fine | N-Mint |
|---|---|---|---|
| 5-Nighthawk & his horse Nightwind begin (not in #6); Captain Tootsie | | | |
|    by Beck | 11.50 | 34.00 | 80.00 |
| 6,7,9,10 | 9.30 | 28.00 | 65.00 |
| 8-Origin Wyoming Kid; 2 pg. pin-ups of rodeo queens | | | |
| | 11.50 | 34.00 | 80.00 |
| 11-20 | 6.50 | 19.50 | 45.00 |
| 21-40: 27-Last 52 pgs. | 5.00 | 15.00 | 35.00 |
| 41-49: Last precode (2/55). 43-Pow Wow Smith begins, ends #85 | | | |
| | 4.00 | 12.00 | 28.00 |
| 50-60 | 4.00 | 12.00 | 28.00 |
| 61-85-Last Wyoming Kid. 77-Origin Matt Savage Trail Boss. 82-1st app. | | | |
|    Fleetfoot, Pow Wow's girlfriend | 2.30 | 7.00 | 16.00 |

**WESTERN HERO** (Wow Comics #1-69; Real Western Hero #70-75)
No. 76, Mar, 1949 - No. 112, Mar, 1952
Fawcett Publications

| | Good | Fine | N-Mint |
|---|---|---|---|
| 76(#1, 52 pgs.)-Tom Mix, Hopalong Cassidy, Monte Hale, Gabby Hayes, | | | |
|    Young Falcon (ends #78,80), & Big Bow and Little Arrow (ends | | | |
|    #102,105) begin; painted-c begin | 14.00 | 42.00 | 100.00 |
| 77 (52 pgs.) | 10.00 | 30.00 | 70.00 |
| 78,80-82 (52 pgs.): 81-Capt. Tootsie by Beck | 10.00 | 30.00 | 70.00 |
| 79,83 (36 pgs.): 83-Last painted-c | 7.00 | 21.00 | 50.00 |
| 84-86,88-90 (52 pgs.): 84-Photo-c begin, end #112. 86-Last Hopalong | | | |
|    Cassidy | 8.00 | 24.00 | 56.00 |
| 87,91,95,99 (36 pgs.): 87-Bill Boyd begins, ends #95 | | | |
| | 6.50 | 19.50 | 45.00 |
| 92,94,96,98,101 (52 pgs.): 96-Tex Ritter begins. 101-Red Eagle app. | | | |
| | 7.00 | 21.00 | 50.00 |
| 100 (52 pgs.) | 8.00 | 24.00 | 56.00 |
| 102-111 (36 pgs. begin) | 6.50 | 19.50 | 45.00 |
| 112-Last issue | 7.00 | 21.00 | 50.00 |

**WESTERN OUTLAWS**
Feb, 1954 - No. 21, Aug, 1957
Atlas Comics (ACI No. 1-14/WPI No. 15-21)

| | Good | Fine | N-Mint |
|---|---|---|---|
| 1-Heath, Powell-a; Maneely hanging-c | 6.50 | 19.50 | 45.00 |
| 2 | 3.00 | 9.00 | 21.00 |
| 3-10: 7-Violent-a by R.Q. Sale | 2.65 | 8.00 | 18.00 |

|                                                    | Good  | Fine  | N-Mint |
|----------------------------------------------------|-------|-------|--------|
| 11,14-Williamson-a in both, 6 pgs. each            | 4.00  | 12.00 | 28.00  |
| 12,18,20,21: Severin covers                        | 2.00  | 6.00  | 14.00  |
| 13-Baker-a                                          | 2.65  | 8.00  | 18.00  |
| 15-Torres-a                                         | 2.85  | 8.50  | 20.00  |
| 16-Williamson text illo                            | 2.00  | 6.00  | 14.00  |
| 17-Crandall-a, Williamson text illo                | 3.00  | 9.00  | 21.00  |
| 19-Crandall-a                                       | 2.65  | 8.00  | 18.00  |

**WESTERN WINNERS** (Formerly All-West. Winners; Black Rider #8)
No. 5, June, 1949 - No. 7, Dec, 1949
Marvel Comics (CDS)

|                                                                              | Good  | Fine  | N-Mint |
|------------------------------------------------------------------------------|-------|-------|--------|
| 5-Two-Gun Kid, Kid Colt, Black Rider                                         | 12.00 | 36.00 | 85.00  |
| 6-Two-Gun Kid, Black Rider, Heath Kid Colt story; Captain Tootsie By         |       |       |        |
|   C.C. Beck                                                                   | 10.00 | 30.00 | 70.00  |
| 7-Randolph Scott Photo-c w/true stories about the West                       |       |       |        |
|                                                                              | 10.00 | 30.00 | 70.00  |

**WHAT IF . . . ?** (1st series)
Feb, 1977 - No. 47, Oct, 1985; June, 1988 (All 52 pgs.)
Marvel Comics Group

|                                                                              | Good  | Fine  | N-Mint |
|------------------------------------------------------------------------------|-------|-------|--------|
| 1-Brief origin Spider-Man, Fantastic Four                                    | 1.70  | 5.00  | 10.00  |
| 2-Origin The Hulk retold                                                     | 1.00  | 3.00  | 6.00   |
| 3-5                                                                          | .75   | 2.20  | 4.40   |
| 6-10: 9-Origins Venus, Marvel Boy, Human Robot, 3-D Man                      |       |       |        |
|                                                                              | .55   | 1.65  | 3.30   |
| 11,12                                                                        | .45   | 1.40  | 2.80   |
| 13-Conan app.                                                                | .75   | 2.20  | 4.40   |
| 14-26,29,30: 22-Origin Dr. Doom retold                                       | .35   | 1.10  | 2.20   |
| 27-X-Men app.; Miller-c                                                      | 1.10  | 3.30  | 6.60   |
| 28-Daredevil by Miller                                                       | 1.10  | 3.30  | 6.60   |
| 31-X-Men app.; death of Hulk, Wolverine & Magneto                           |       |       |        |
|                                                                              | 1.10  | 3.30  | 6.60   |
| 32-47: 32,36-Byrne-a. 34-Marvel crew each draw themselves. 35-What if        |       |       |        |
|   Elektra had lived?; Miller/Austin-a. 37-Old X-Men & Silver Surfer app.     |       |       |        |
|                                                                              | .30   | .85   | 1.70   |
| Special 1 ($1.50, 6/88)-Iron Man, F.F., Thor app.                           |       |       |        |
|                                                                              | .30   | .85   | 1.70   |

**WHAT IF . . . ?** (2nd series)
July, 1989 - Present ($1.25 color)
Marvel Comics

| | Good | Fine | N-Mint |
|---|---|---|---|
| V2#1-. . . The Avengers Had Lost the Evol. War | | | |
| | .50 | 1.50 | 3.00 |
| 2-5: 2-Daredevil, Punisher app. | .25 | .70 | 1.40 |
| 6-X-Men app. | .40 | 1.25 | 2.50 |
| 7-Wolverine app. | .35 | 1.00 | 2.00 |
| 8-12: 9,12-X-Men. 10-Punisher. 11-F.F. 13-Prof. X | | | |
| | .25 | .75 | 1.50 |
| 13-20 | | .60 | 1:25 |

**WHAT THE-?!**
Aug, 1988 - Present ($1.25-$1.50, semi-annually #5 on; #6-$1.00)
Marvel Comics

| | | | |
|---|---|---|---|
| 1 | .35 | 1.00 | 2.00 |
| 2,4,5-Punisher/Wolverine parody | .25 | .75 | 1.50 |
| 3-X-Men parody; McFarlane-a | .50 | 1.50 | 3.00 |
| 6-8 | | .50 | 1.00 |

**WHIP WILSON** (Movie star) (Formerly Rex Hart)
No. 9, April, 1950 - No. 11, Sept, 1950 (9,10: 52 pgs., 11: 36 pgs.)
Marvel Comics

| | | | |
|---|---|---|---|
| 9-Photo-c; Whip Wilson & his horse Bullet begin; origin Bullet; issue #23 listed on splash page; cover changed to #9 | | | |
| | 19.50 | 60.00 | 135.00 |
| 10,11-Photo-c | 16.00 | 48.00 | 110.00 |

**WHITE PRINCESS OF THE JUNGLE**
July, 1951 - No. 5, Nov, 1952
Avon Periodicals

| | | | |
|---|---|---|---|
| 1-Origin of White Princess (Taanda) & Capt'n Courage (r); Kinstler-c | | | |
| | 23.00 | 70.00 | 160.00 |
| 2-Reprints origin of Malu, Slave Girl Princess from Avon's Slave Girl Comics #1 w/Malu changed to Zora; Kinstler-c/a(2) | | | |
| | 17.00 | 51.00 | 120.00 |
| 3-Origin Blue Gorilla; Kinstler-c/a | 13.00 | 40.00 | 90.00 |

|                                                      | Good  | Fine  | N-Mint |
|------------------------------------------------------|-------|-------|--------|
| 4-Jack Barnum, White Hunter app.; r-/Sheena #9       | 11.00 | 32.00 | 75.00  |
| 5-Blue Gorilla by Kinstler                           | 11.00 | 32.00 | 75.00  |

## WHIZ COMICS
No. 2, Feb, 1940 - No. 155, June, 1953
Fawcett Publications

|                                                                                                                                                                                   | Good     | Fine     | VF-NM     |
|-----------------------------------------------------------------------------------------------------------------------------------------------------------------------------------|----------|----------|-----------|
| 1-(nn on cover, #2 inside)-Origin & 1st newsstand app. Captain Marvel (formerly Captain Thunder) by C. C. Beck (created by Bill Parker), Spy Smasher, Golden Arrow, Ibis the Invincible, Dan Dare, Scoop Smith, Sivana, & Lance O'Casey begin | 3,000.00 | 8,400.00 | 18,200.00 |

*(Only one known copy exists in Mint condition which has not sold)*

|                                                                                                                           | Good   | Fine   | N-Mint  |
|---------------------------------------------------------------------------------------------------------------------------|--------|--------|---------|
| 2-(nn on cover, #3 inside); cover to Flash #1 redrawn, pg. 12, panel 4; Spy Smasher reveals I.D. to Eve                    | 300.00 | 900.00 | 2100.00 |
| 3-(#3 on cover, #4 inside)-1st app. Beautia                                                                                | 185.00 | 557.00 | 1300.00 |
| 4-(#4 on cover, #5 inside)                                                                                                 | 153.00 | 460.00 | 1070.00 |
| 5-Captain Marvel wears button-down flap on splash page only                                                               | 114.00 | 343.00 | 800.00  |
| 6-10: 7-Dr. Voodoo begins (by Raboy-#9-22)                                                                                 | 93.00  | 280.00 | 650.00  |
| 11-14                                                                                                                      | 61.00  | 182.00 | 425.00  |
| 15-Origin Sivana; Dr. Voodoo by Raboy                                                                                      | 78.00  | 232.00 | 545.00  |
| 16-18-Spy Smasher battles Captain Marvel                                                                                   | 78.00  | 232.00 | 545.00  |
| 19,20                                                                                                                      | 43.00  | 130.00 | 300.00  |
| 21-Origin & 1st app. Lt. Marvels                                                                                           | 45.00  | 135.00 | 315.00  |
| 22-24: 23-Only Dr. Voodoo by Tuska                                                                                         | 35.00  | 105.00 | 245.00  |
| 25-Origin/1st app. Captain Marvel Jr. (x-over in Capt. Marvel); Capt. Nazi app; origin Old Shazam in text                  | 104.00 | 312.00 | 730.00  |
| 26-30                                                                                                                      | 29.00  | 86.00  | 200.00  |
| 31,32: 32-1st app. The Trolls                                                                                              | 21.50  | 64.00  | 150.00  |
| 33-Spy Smasher, Captain Marvel x-over on cover and inside                                                                  | 26.50  | 79.00  | 185.00  |
| 34,36-40: 37-The Trolls app.                                                                                               | 19.00  | 57.00  | 135.00  |
| 35-Captain Marvel & Spy Smasher-c                                                                                          | 21.50  | 64.00  | 150.00  |
| 41-50: 43-Spy Smasher, Ibis, Golden Arrow x-over in Capt. Marvel. 44-Flag-c. 47-Origin recap (1 pg.)                       | 12.00  | 36.00  | 84.00   |
| 51-60: 52-Capt. Marvel x-over in Ibis. 57-Spy Smasher, Golden Arrow, Ibis cameo                                           | 9.30   | 28.00  | 65.00   |

|                                                      | Good  | Fine   | N-Mint |
|------------------------------------------------------|-------|--------|--------|
| 61-70                                                | 8.00  | 24.00  | 56.00  |
| 71,77-80                                             | 6.00  | 18.00  | 42.00  |

72-76-Two Captain Marvel stories in each; 76-Spy Smasher becomes

| Crime Smasher                                        | 6.50  | 19.50  | 45.00  |

81-99: 86-Captain Marvel battles Sivana Family. 91-Infinity-c

|                                                      | 6.00  | 18.00  | 42.00  |
| 100                                                  | 8.50  | 25.50  | 60.00  |
| 101,103-105                                          | 5.00  | 15.00  | 35.00  |
| 102-Commando Yank app.                               | 5.00  | 15.00  | 35.00  |
| 106-Bulletman app.                                   | 5.00  | 15.00  | 35.00  |

107-141,143-152: 107-White House photo-c. 108-Brooklyn Bridge photo-c.

| 112-photo-c. 139-Infinity-c                          | 4.30  | 13.00  | 30.00  |
| 142-Used in **POP**, pg. 89                          | 4.35  | 13.00  | 30.00  |
| 153-155-(Scarce)                                     | 8.50  | 25.50  | 60.00  |

**WILBUR COMICS** (Teen-age) (Also see Zip Comics)
Sum', 1944 - No. 87, 11/59; No. 88, 9/63; No. 89, 10/64; No. 90, 10/65 (No.
1-46: 52 pgs.)
MLJ Magazines/Archie Publ. No. 8, Spr. '46 on

| 1                                                    | 24.00 | 73.00  | 170.00 |
| 2(Fall,'44)                                          | 12.00 | 36.00  | 84.00  |
| 3,4(Wint,'44-'5; Spr,'45)                            | 10.00 | 30.00  | 70.00  |

5-1st app. Katy Keene-begin series; Wilbur story same as Archie story in
Archie #1 except that Wilbur replaces Archie

|                                                      | 37.00 | 110.00 | 260.00 |
| 6-10(Fall,'46)                                       | 9.50  | 28.50  | 65.00  |
| 11-20                                                | 5.00  | 15.00  | 35.00  |
| 21-30(1949)                                          | 4.00  | 12.00  | 28.00  |
| 31-50                                                | 2.00  | 6.00   | 14.00  |
| 51-69: 59-Last 10 cent issue?                        | 1.15  | 3.50   | 8.00   |
| 70-90                                                | .85   | 2.50   | 5.00   |

**WILD BOY OF THE CONGO**
No. 10, Feb-Mar, 1951 - No. 15, June, 1955
Ziff-Davis No. 10-12,4-6/St. John No. 7? on

10(#1)(2-3/51)-Origin; bondage-c by Saunders; used in **SOTI**, pg. 189

|                                                      | 8.00  | 24.00  | 56.00  |
| 11(4-5/51),12(8-9/51)-Norman Saunders-c              | 4.30  | 13.00  | 30.00  |

|  | Good | Fine | N-Mint |
|---|---|---|---|
| 4(10-11/51)-Saunders bondage-c | 4.30 | 13.00 | 30.00 |
| 5(Winter,'51)-Saunders-c | 3.70 | 11.00 | 26.00 |
| 6,8,9(10/53),10: 6-Saunders-c | 3.50 | 10.50 | 24.00 |
| 7(8-9/52)-Baker-c; Kinstler-a | 4.00 | 12.00 | 28.00 |
| 11-13-Baker-c(St. John) | 4.00 | 12.00 | 28.00 |
| 14(4/55)-Baker-c; r-#12('51) | 4.00 | 12.00 | 28.00 |
| 15(6/55) | 2.65 | 8.00 | 18.00 |

**WILD WEST** (Wild Western #3 on)
Spring, 1948 - No. 2, July, 1948
Marvel Comics (WFP)

| | Good | Fine | N-Mint |
|---|---|---|---|
| 1-Two-Gun Kid, Arizona Annie, & Tex Taylor begin; Shores-c | | | |
| | 10.00 | 30.00 | 70.00 |
| 2-Captain Tootsie by Beck; Shores-c | 8.50 | 25.50 | 60.00 |

**WILD WESTERN** (Wild West #1, 2)
No. 3, 9/48 - No. 57, 9/57 (3-11: 52 pgs; 12-on: 36 pgs)
Marvel/Atlas Comics (WFP)

| | Good | Fine | N-Mint |
|---|---|---|---|
| 3(#1)-Tex Morgan begins; Two-Gun Kid, Tex Taylor, & Arizona Annie continue from Wild West | 11.00 | 32.00 | 75.00 |
| 4-Last Arizona Annie; Captain Tootsie by Beck; Kid Colt app. | 8.00 | 24.00 | 56.00 |
| 5-2nd app. Black Rider (1/49); Blaze Carson, Captain Tootsie by Beck app. | 8.50 | 25.50 | 60.00 |
| 6-8: 6-Blaze Carson app; Anti-Wertham editorial | 6.00 | 18.00 | 42.00 |
| 9-Photo-c; Black Rider begins, ends #19 | 7.00 | 21.00 | 50.00 |
| 10-Charles Starrett photo-c | 8.50 | 25.50 | 60.00 |
| 11-(Last 52 pg. issue) | 4.70 | 17.00 | 40.00 |
| 12-14,16-19: All Black Rider-c/stories. 12-14-The Prairie Kid & his horse Fury app. | 4.30 | 13.00 | 30.00 |
| 15-Red Larabee, Gunhawk (Origin), his horse Blaze, & Apache Kid begin, end #22; Black Rider c/story | 5.70 | 17.00 | 40.00 |
| 20-29: 20-Kid Colt-c begin | 3.70 | 11.00 | 26.00 |
| 30-Katz-a | 4.30 | 13.00 | 30.00 |
| 31-40 | 2.65 | 8.00 | 18.00 |
| 41-47,49-51,53,57 | 1.70 | 5.00 | 12.00 |
| 48-Williamson/Torres-a, 4 pgs; Drucker-a | 4.00 | 12.00 | 28.00 |

| | Good | Fine | N-Mint |
|---|---|---|---|
| 52-Crandall-a | 3.00 | 9.00 | 21.00 |
| 54,55-Williamson-a in both, 5 & 4 pgs., #54 with Mayo plus 2 text illos | | | |
| | 3.50 | 10.50 | 24.00 |
| 56-Baker-a? | 2.00 | 6.00 | 14.00 |

## WINGS COMICS
Sept, 1940 - No. 124, 1954
Fiction House Magazines

| | Good | Fine | N-Mint |
|---|---|---|---|
| 1-Skull Squad, Clipper Kirk, Suicide Smith, Jane Martin, War Nurse, Phantom Falcons, Greasemonkey Griffin, Parachute Patrol & Powder Burns begin | 72.00 | 215.00 | 500.00 |
| 2 | 35.00 | 105.00 | 245.00 |
| 3-5 | 27.00 | 80.00 | 185.00 |
| 6-10 | 22.00 | 65.00 | 154.00 |
| 11-15 | 19.00 | 57.00 | 135.00 |
| 16-Origin Captain Wings | 21.00 | 62.00 | 145.00 |
| 17-20 | 14.00 | 42.00 | 100.00 |
| 21-30 | 13.00 | 40.00 | 90.00 |
| 31-40 | 11.00 | 32.00 | 75.00 |
| 41-50 | 8.50 | 25.50 | 60.00 |
| 51-60: 60-Last Skull Squad | 7.00 | 21.00 | 50.00 |
| 61-67: 66-Ghost Patrol begins (becomes Ghost Squadron #71) | | | |
| | 7.00 | 21.00 | 50.00 |
| 68,69: 68-Clipper Kirk becomes The Phantom Falcon-origin, Part 1; Part 2-#69 | 7.00 | 21.00 | 50.00 |
| 70-72: 70-1st app. The Phantom Falcon in costume, origin-Part 3; Capt. Wings battles Col. Kamikaze in all | 5.50 | 16.50 | 38.00 |
| 73-99 | 5.50 | 16.50 | 38.00 |
| 100 | 6.50 | 19.50 | 45.00 |
| 101-114,116-124: 111-Last Jane Martin. 112-Flying Saucer c/story | | | |
| | 4.00 | 12.00 | 28.00 |
| 115-Used in **POP**, pg. 89 | 4.60 | 14.00 | 32.00 |

## WITCHING HOUR (The Witching Hour later issues)
Feb-Mar, 1969 - No. 85, Oct, 1978
National Periodical Publications/DC Comics

| | Good | Fine | N-Mint |
|---|---|---|---|
| 1-Toth plus Neal Adams-a, 3 pgs. | .70 | 2.00 | 4.00 |
| 2,6 | .35 | 1.00 | 2.00 |

|  | Good | Fine | N-Mint |
|---|---|---|---|
| 3,5-Wrightson-a; Toth-p. 3-Last 12 cent issue | .40 | 1.25 | 2.50 |
| 4,7,9-12: Toth-a in all | .25 | .75 | 1.50 |
| 8-Neal Adams-a | .50 | 1.50 | 3.00 |
| 13-Neal Adams-c/a, 2 pgs. | .35 | 1.00 | 2.00 |
| 14-Williamson/Garzon, Jones-a; N. Adams-c | .35 | 1.00 | 2.00 |
| 15-20 |  | .50 | 1.00 |
| 21-85: 38-(100 pgs.). 84-(44 pgs.) |  | .25 | .50 |

*Wolverine #2 (1982), © Marvel Comics*

**WOLVERINE** (See Alpha Flight, Daredevil #196, 249, Havok & . . . ,
   Incredible Hulk #180, Incredible Hulk & . . . , Marvel Comics
   Presents, Power Pack, Spider-Man vs. . . . & X-Men #94)
Sept, 1982 - No. 4, Dec, 1982 (Mini-series)
Marvel Comics Group

|  | Good | Fine | N-Mint |
|---|---|---|---|
| 1-Frank Miller-c/a(p) | 2.70 | 8.00 | 16.00 |

| | Good | Fine | N-Mint |
|---|---|---|---|
| 2,3-Miller-c/a(p) | 1.85 | 5.50 | 11.00 |
| 4-Miller-c/a(p) | 2.15 | 6.50 | 13.00 |

**WOLVERINE**
Nov, 1988 - Present ($1.50, color, Baxter paper)
Marvel Comics

| | | | |
|---|---|---|---|
| 1-Buscema a-1-16, c-1-10; Williamson i-1,4-8 | 1.70 | 5.00 | 10.00 |
| 2 | 1.00 | 3.00 | 6.00 |
| 3-5 | .75 | 2.25 | 4.50 |
| 6-9: 6-McFarlane back-c. 7,8-Hulk app. | .70 | 2.00 | 4.00 |
| 10-1st battle with Sabertooth | 1.50 | 4.50 | 9.00 |
| 11-16: 11-New Costume | .50 | 1.50 | 3.00 |
| 17-20: 17-Byrne-c/a(p) begins, ends #23 | .35 | 1.00 | 2.00 |
| 21-30 | .25 | .75 | 1.50 |

**WOLVERINE SAGA**
Sept, 1989 - No. 4, Mid-Dec, 1989 ($3.95, color, mini-series, 52 pgs.)
Marvel Comics

| | | | |
|---|---|---|---|
| 1-Austin-c(i); art w/text; gives history | .85 | 2.50 | 5.00 |
| 2-4: 4-Kaluta-c; Austin back-c | .70 | 2.00 | 4.00 |

**WOMEN OUTLAWS**
July, 1948 - No. 8, Sept, 1949
Fox Features Syndicate

| | | | |
|---|---|---|---|
| 1-Used in **SOTI**, illo-"Giving children an image of American woman- hood"; negligee panels | 27.00 | 81.00 | 190.00 |
| 2-Spanking panel | 23.00 | 70.00 | 160.00 |
| 3-Kamen-a | 20.00 | 60.00 | 140.00 |
| 4-8 | 14.00 | 42.00 | 100.00 |
| nn(nd)-Contains Cody of the Pony Express; same cover as #7 | 11.00 | 32.00 | 75.00 |

**WONDER COMICS** (Wonderworld #3 on)
May, 1939 - No. 2, June, 1939
Fox Features Syndicate

| | | | |
|---|---|---|---|
| 1-(Scarce)-Wonder Man only app. by Will Eisner; Dr. Fung (by Powell), K-51 begins; Bob Kane-a; Eisner-c | 358.00 | 900.00 | 2150.00 |

|                                                                                                                | Good   | Fine   | N-Mint  |
|----------------------------------------------------------------------------------------------------------------|--------|--------|---------|
| 2-(Scarce)-Yarko the Great, Master Magician by Eisner begins; 'Spark' Stevens by Bob Kane, Patty O'Day, Tex Mason app. Lou Fine's 1st-c; a (2 pgs.) | 200.00 | 500.00 | 1200.00 |

**WONDER WOMAN** (See All-Star, Sensation & World's Finest)
Summer, 1942 - No. 329, Feb, 1986
National Periodical Publications/All-American Publ./DC Comics

| | Good | Fine | N-Mint |
|---|---|---|---|
| 1-Origin Wonder Woman retold (see All-Star #8); H. G. Peter-a begins | 307.00 | 921.00 | 2150.00 |
| 2-Origin & 1st app. Mars; Duke of Deception app. | 100.00 | 300.00 | 700.00 |
| 3 | 74.00 | 220.00 | 515.00 |
| 4,5: 5-1st Dr. Psycho app. | 55.00 | 165.00 | 385.00 |
| 6-10: 6-1st Cheetah app. | 43.00 | 130.00 | 300.00 |
| 11-20 | 33.00 | 100.00 | 230.00 |
| 21-30 | 24.00 | 73.00 | 170.00 |
| 31-40 | 18.00 | 54.00 | 125.00 |
| 41-44,46-48 | 14.00 | 42.00 | 100.00 |
| 45-Origin retold | 24.00 | 73.00 | 170.00 |
| 49-Used in **SOTI**, pgs. 234,236; Last 52 pg. issue | 14.00 | 42.00 | 100.00 |
| 50-(44 pgs.)-Used in **POP**, pg. 97 | 13.00 | 40.00 | 90.00 |
| 51-60 | 10.00 | 30.00 | 70.00 |
| 61-72: 62-Origin of W.W. i.d. 64-Story about 3-D movies. 70-1st Angle Man app. 72-Last pre-code | 8.50 | 25.50 | 60.00 |
| 73-90: 80-Origin The Invisible Plane | 6.50 | 19.50 | 45.00 |
| 91-94,96-99: 97-Last H. G. Peter-a. 98-Origin W.W. i.d. with new facts | 4.30 | 13.00 | 30.00 |
| 95-A-Bomb-c | 5.00 | 15.00 | 35.00 |
| 100 | 5.50 | 16.50 | 38.00 |
| 101-104,106-110: 107-1st advs. of Wonder Girl; 1st Merboy; tells how Wonder Woman won her costume | 3.60 | 11.00 | 25.00 |
| 105-(Scarce)-Wonder Woman's secret origin; W. Woman appears as a girl (not Wonder Girl) | 8.50 | 25.00 | 60.00 |
| 111-120 | 2.00 | 6.00 | 14.00 |
| 121-126: 122-1st app. Wonder Tot. 124-1st app. Wonder Woman Family. 126-Last 10 cent issue | 1.30 | 4.00 | 9.00 |
| 127-130: 128-Origin The Invisible Plane retold | 1.15 | 3.50 | 8.00 |

|  | Good | Fine | N-Mint |
|---|---|---|---|
| 131-150 | .85 | 2.50 | 5.00 |
| 151-158,160-170 (1967) | .70 | 2.00 | 4.00 |
| 159-Origin retold | .85 | 2.50 | 5.00 |
| 171-178 | .50 | 1.50 | 3.00 |
| 179-195: 179-Wears no costume to issue #203. 180-Death of Steve Trevor. | | | |
| 195-Wood inks? | .45 | 1.25 | 2.50 |
| 196 (52 pgs.)-Origin r-/All Star 8 | .50 | 1.50 | 3.00 |
| 197,198 (52 pgs.)-Reprints | .50 | 1.50 | 3.00 |
| 199,200-Jones-c; 52 pgs. | .85 | 2.50 | 5.00 |
| 201-210: 204-Return to old costume; death of I Ching. 202-Fafhrd & The | | | |
| Grey Mouser debut | | .60 | 1.20 |
| 211-240: 211,214-(100 pgs.), 217-(68 pgs.). 220-N. Adams assist. 223-Steve | | | |
| Trevor revived as Steve Howard & learns W.W.'s I.D. 228- Both W. | | | |
| Women team up & new World War II stories begin, end #243. | | | |
| 237-Origin retold | | .50 | 1.00 |
| 241-266,269-280,284-286: 241-Intro Bouncer. 247-249-(44 pgs.). 248-Steve | | | |
| Trevor Howard dies. 249-Hawkgirl app. 250-Intro/origin Orana, the | | | |
| new W. Woman. 251-Orana dies. 269-Last Wood a(i) for DC? (7/80). | | | |
| 271-Huntress & 3rd Life of Steve Trevor begin | | | |
|  | | .50 | 1.00 |
| 267,268-Re-intro Animal Man (5 & 6/80) | 2.50 | 7.50 | 15.00 |
| 281-283-Joker covers & stories | .35 | 1.00 | 2.00 |
| 287-New Teen Titans x-over | .25 | .75 | 1.50 |
| 288-299: 288-New costume & logo. 291-293-Three part epic with Super- | | | |
| Heroines | | .50 | 1.00 |
| 300-($1.50, 76 pgs.)-Anniversary issue; Giffen-a; New Teen Titans, JLA | | | |
| app. | .25 | .75 | 1.50 |
| 301-328: 308-Huntress begins | | .50 | 1.00 |
| 329-Double size | .25 | .75 | 1.50 |

**WONDER WOMAN**
Feb, 1987 - Present
DC Comics

| 1-New origin; Perez-c/a begins | .50 | 1.50 | 3.00 |
|---|---|---|---|
| 2-10: 8-Origin Cheetah | | .65 | 1.30 |
| 11-20: 12,13-Millennium x-over. 18,26-Free 16 pg. story | | | |
|  | | .65 | 1.30 |
| 21-48: 24-Last Perez-a; c/scripts continue | | .50 | 1.00 |
| Annual 1 ('88, $1.50)-Art Adams-a(p&i) | .25 | .75 | 1.50 |

|  | Good | Fine | N-Mint |
|---|---|---|---|
| Annual 2 ('89, $2.00, 68 pgs.)-All women artists issue; Perez-c(i) | | | |
|  | .35 | 1.00 | 2.00 |

## WONDERWORLD COMICS (Formerly Wonder Comics)
No. 3, July, 1939 - No. 33, Jan, 1942
Fox Features Syndicate

| | Good | Fine | N-Mint |
|---|---|---|---|
| 3-Intro The Flame by Fine; Dr. Fung (Powell-a), K-51 (Powell-a?), & Yarko the Great, Master Magician (Eisner-a) continues; Eisner/ Fine-c | | | |
| | 130.00 | 325.00 | 780.00 |
| 4 | 55.00 | 165.00 | 385.00 |
| 5-10 | 50.00 | 150.00 | 350.00 |
| 11-Origin The Flame | 59.00 | 175.00 | 410.00 |
| 12-20: 13-Dr. Fung ends | 30.00 | 90.00 | 210.00 |
| 21-Origin The Black Lion & Cub | 27.00 | 81.00 | 190.00 |
| 22-27: 22,25-Dr. Fung app. | 21.50 | 64.00 | 150.00 |
| 28-1st app/origin U.S. Jones; Lu-Nar, the Moon Man begins | | | |
| | 26.00 | 77.00 | 180.00 |
| 29,31-33: 32-Hitler-c | 16.50 | 50.00 | 115.00 |
| 30-Origin Flame Girl | 30.00 | 90.00 | 210.00 |

## WORLD'S BEST COMICS (World's Finest Comics #2 on)
Spring, 1941 (Cardboard-c) (DC's 6th annual format comic)
National Periodical Publications (100 pgs.)

| | Good | Fine | N-Mint |
|---|---|---|---|
| 1-The Batman, Superman, Crimson Avenger, Johnny Thunder, The King, Young Dr. Davis, Zatara, Lando, Man of Magic, & Red, White & Blue begin; Superman, Batman & Robin covers begin (inside-c blank) | | | |
| | 415.00 | 1040.00 | 2500.00 |

## WORLD'S FINEST COMICS (Formerly World's Best Comics #1)
No. 2, Sum, 1941 - No. 323, Jan, 1986 (early issues have 100 pgs.)
National Periodical Publ./DC Comics (#1-17 have cardboard covers)

| | Good | Fine | N-Mint |
|---|---|---|---|
| 2 (100 pgs.)-Superman, Batman & Robin covers continue | | | |
| | 196.00 | 490.00 | 1175.00 |
| 3-The Sandman begins; last Johnny Thunder; origin & 1st app. The Scarecrow | 167.00 | 420.00 | 1000.00 |
| 4-Hop Harrigan app.; last Young Dr. Davis | 117.00 | 295.00 | 700.00 |

| | Good | Fine | N-Mint |
|---|---|---|---|
| 5-Intro. TNT & Dan the Dyna-Mite; last King & Crimson Avenger | 117.00 | 295.00 | 700.00 |
| 6-Star Spangled Kid begins; Aquaman app.; S&K Sandman with Sandy in new costume begins, ends #7 | 92.00 | 230.00 | 550.00 |
| 7-Green Arrow begins; last Lando, King, & Red, White & Blue; S&K art | 92.00 | 230.00 | 550.00 |
| 8-Boy Commandos begin | 83.00 | 210.00 | 500.00 |
| 9-Batman cameo in Star Spangled Kid; S&K-a; last 100 pg. issue; Hitler, Mussolini, Tojo-c | 75.00 | 190.00 | 450.00 |
| 10-S&K-a | 75.00 | 190.00 | 450.00 |
| 11-17-Last cardboard cover issue | 65.00 | 165.00 | 390.00 |
| 18-20: 18-Paper covers begin; last Star Spangled Kid | 59.00 | 150.00 | 355.00 |
| 21-30: 30-Johnny Peril app. | 43.00 | 110.00 | 260.00 |
| 31-40: 33-35-Tomahawk app. | 37.00 | 95.00 | 225.00 |
| 41-50: 41-Boy Commandos end. 42-Wyoming Kid begins, ends #63. 43-Full Steam Foley begins, ends #48. 48-Last square binding. 49-Tom Sparks, Boy Inventor begins | 29.00 | 75.00 | 175.00 |
| 51-60: 51-Zatara ends. 59-Manhunters Around the World begins, ends #62 | 29.00 | 75.00 | 175.00 |
| 61-64: 63-Capt. Compass app. | 25.00 | 65.00 | 150.00 |
| 65-Origin Superman; Tomahawk begins, ends #101 | 32.00 | 80.00 | 190.00 |
| 66-70-(15 cent issues)(Scarce)-Last 68 pg. issue | 24.00 | 65.00 | 165.00 |
| 71-(10 cent issue)(Scarce)-Superman & Batman begin as team | 30.00 | 90.00 | 210.00 |
| 72,73-(10 cent issues)(Scarce) | 21.50 | 64.00 | 150.00 |
| 74-80: 74-Last pre-code issue | 11.50 | 34.00 | 80.00 |
| 81-90: 88-1st Joker/Luthor team-up. 90-Batwoman's 1st app. in World's Finest | 8.00 | 24.00 | 55.00 |
| 91-93,95-99: 96-99-Kirby Green Arrow | 5.00 | 15.00 | 35.00 |
| 94-Origin Superman/Batman team retold | 22.00 | 65.00 | 155.00 |
| 100 | 12.00 | 36.00 | 85.00 |
| 101-121: 102-Tommy Tomorrow begins, ends. #124. 113-Intro. Miss Arrowette in Green Arrow; 1st Batmite/Mr. Mxyzptlk team-up. 121-Last 10 cent issue | 3.60 | 11.00 | 25.00 |
| 122-128,130-142: 125-Aquaman begins, ends #139. 140-Last Green Arrow. 142-Origin The Composite Superman (villain); Legion app. | 1.70 | 5.00 | 12.00 |

|                                                                          | Good | Fine | N-Mint |
|--------------------------------------------------------------------------|------|------|--------|
| 129-Joker-c/story                                                        | 2.85 | 8.50 | 20.00  |
| 143-150: 143-1st Mailbag                                                 | 1.15 | 3.50 | 8.00   |
| 151-155,157-160                                                          | 1.00 | 3.00 | 6.00   |
| 156-1st Bizarro Batman; Joker-c/story                                    | 3.60 | 11.00| 25.00  |
| 161,170 (80-Pg. Giants G-28,G-40)                                        | 1.00 | 3.00 | 7.00   |
| 162-165,167-169,171-174: 168,172-Adult Legion app.                       |      |      |        |
|                                                                          | .70  | 2.00 | 4.00   |
| 166-Joker-c/story                                                        | 1.15 | 3.50 | 8.00   |
| 175,176-Neal Adams-a; both r-J'onn J'onzz origin/Detective #225,226      |      |      |        |
|                                                                          | .85  | 2.50 | 5.00   |
| 177,178,180-187,189-196,198-204: 182-Silent Knight-r/Brave & Bold #6. 186-Johnny Quick-r. 187-Green Arrow origin-r/Adv. #256. 190-193-Robin-r. 198,199-3rd Superman/Flash race | .35 | 1.00 | 2.00 |
| 179,188,197 (80-Pg. Giant G-52,G-64,G-76)                                | .50  | 1.50 | 3.00   |
| 205-6 pgs. Shining Knight by Frazetta/Adv. #153; 52 pgs.; Teen Titans x-over | .35 | 1.00 | 2.00 |
| 206 (80-Pg. Giant G-88)                                                  | .35  | 1.00 | 2.00   |
| 207-212 (52 pgs.)                                                        | .25  | .75  | 1.50   |
| 213-222: 215-Intro. Batman Jr. & Superman Jr. 217-Metamorpho begins, ends #220; Batman/Superman team-ups begin |      |      |        |
|                                                                          | .25  | .75  | 1.50   |
| 223,226-N. Adams-r; 100 pgs.; 223-Deadman origin; 226-S&K, Toth-r; Manhunter part origin-r/Detective #225,226 | .25 | .75 | 1.50 |
| 224,225,227,228-(100 pgs.)                                               | .25  | .75  | 1.50   |
| 229-243: 229-r-/origin Superman-Batman team                              | .25  | .75  | 1.50   |
| 244-248: 244-Green Arrow, Black Canary, Wonder Woman, Vigilante begin; $1.00, 84 pg. issues begin. 246-Death of Stuff in Vigilante; origin Vigilante retold. 248-Last Vigilante | .25 | .75 | 1.50 |
| 249-The Creeper begins by Ditko, ends #255                               | .70  | 2.00 | 4.00   |
| 250-282: 250-The Creeper origin retold by Ditko. 252-Last 84 pg. issue. 253-Capt. Marvel begins; 68 pgs. begin, end #265. 256- Hawkman begins. 257-Black Lightning begins. 266-282-(52 pgs.). 268-Capt. Marvel Jr. origin retold. 271-Origin Superman/Batman team retold. 274-Zatanna begins. 279,280-Capt. Marvel Jr. & Kid Eternity learn they are brothers | .25 | .75 | 1.50 |
| 283-297 (36 pgs.). 284-Legion app.                                       | .25  | .75  | 1.50   |
| 298,299 (75 cent issues begin)                                           | .25  | .75  | 1.50   |
| 300-($1.25, 52 pgs.)-Justice League of America, New Teen Titans & The Outsiders app.; Perez-a(3 pgs.) | .35 | 1.00 | 2.00 |

| | Good | Fine | N-Mint |
|---|---|---|---|

301-323: 304-Origin Null and Void. 309,319-Free 16 pg. story in each (309-Flash Force 2000, 319-Mask preview)

| | .25 | .75 | 1.50 |
|---|---|---|---|

**WOW COMICS** (Real Western Hero #70 on)
Winter, 1940-41; No. 2, Summer, 1941 - No. 69, Fall, 1948
Fawcett Publications

nn(#1)-Origin Mr. Scarlet by S&K; Atom Blake, Boy Wizard, Jim Dolan, & Rick O'Shay begin; Diamond Jack, The White Rajah, & Shipwreck Roberts, only app.; the cover was printed on unstable paper stock and is rarely found in fine or mint condition; blank inside-c; bondage-c by Beck (Rare) 625.00 1875.00 5000.00
*(Prices vary widely on this book)*

| | Good | Fine | N-Mint |
|---|---|---|---|
| 2 (Scarce)-The Hunchback begins | 64.00 | 193.00 | 450.00 |
| 3 (Fall, 1941) | 40.00 | 120.00 | 280.00 |
| 4-Origin Pinky | 46.00 | 137.00 | 320.00 |
| 5 | 33.00 | 100.00 | 230.00 |
| 6-Origin The Phantom Eagle; Commando Yank begins | 27.00 | 81.00 | 190.00 |
| 7,8,10 | 25.00 | 75.00 | 175.00 |
| 9 (1/6/43)-Capt. Marvel, Capt. Marvel Jr., Shazam app.; Scarlet & Pinky x-over; Mary Marvel c/stories begin (cameo #9) | 36.00 | 107.00 | 250.00 |
| 11-17,19,20: 15-Flag-c | 16.00 | 48.00 | 110.00 |
| 18-1st app. Uncle Marvel (10/43); infinity-c | 17.00 | 51.00 | 120.00 |
| 21-30: 28-Pinky x-over in Mary Marvel | 9.30 | 28.00 | 65.00 |
| 31-40 | 6.50 | 19.50 | 45.00 |
| 41-50 | 5.00 | 15.00 | 35.00 |
| 51-58: Last Mary Marvel | 4.00 | 12.00 | 28.00 |
| 59-69: 59-Ozzie begins. 62-Flying Saucer gag-c (1/48). 65-69-Tom Mix stories | 3.50 | 10.50 | 24.00 |

# X

**X-FACTOR** (Also see The Avengers #263 & Fantastic Four #286)
Feb, 1986 - Present
Marvel Comics Group

|  | Good | Fine | N-Mint |
|---|---|---|---|
| 1-($1.25, 52 pgs)-Story recaps 1st app. from Avengers #263; original X-Men app.; Layton/Guice-a | 1.35 | 4.00 | 8.00 |
| 2,3 | .85 | 2.50 | 5.00 |
| 4,5 | .75 | 2.25 | 4.50 |
| 6-10 | .60 | 1.75 | 3.50 |
| 11-20 | .50 | 1.50 | 3.00 |
| 21-23 | .40 | 1.25 | 2.50 |
| 24-26: Fall Of The Mutants. 26-New outfits | .70 | 2.00 | 4.00 |
| 27-30 | .35 | 1.00 | 2.00 |
| 31-37,39-49: 35-Origin Cyclops. 41,42-Art Adams-a(p). 44-P. Smith-a begins | .25 | .75 | 1.50 |
| 38,50-Double size ($1.50); 50-McFarlane-c(i) | .35 | 1.00 | 2.00 |
| 51-60: 52,53-Sabertooth app. 54-Intro Crimson |  | .50 | 1.00 |
| Annual 1 (10/86), 2 (10/87) | .40 | 1.25 | 2.50 |
| Annual 3 ('88, $1.75)-Evolutionary War app. | .50 | 1.50 | 3.00 |
| Annual 4 ('89, $2.00, 68 pgs.)-Atlantis Attacks; Byrne/Simonson-a, Byrne-c | .40 | 1.25 | 2.50 |
| Annual 5 ('90, $2.00, 68 pgs.) | .35 | 1.00 | 2.00 |

**X-MEN, THE** (X-Men #94-141; The Uncanny . . . #142 on; see Classic X-Men, Marvel & DC Present, Marvel Team-up, Nightcrawler, Special Edition . . . , X-Factor & X-Terminators)
Sept, 1963 - Present
Marvel Comics Group

| | Good | Fine | N-Mint |
|---|---|---|---|
| 1-Origin/1st app. X-Men; 1st app. Magneto | | | |
| | 130.00 | 520.00 | 1150.00 |
| 2-1st app. The Vanisher | 54.00 | 162.00 | 380.00 |
| 3-1st app. The Blob | 28.00 | 84.00 | 200.00 |
| 4-1st Quick Silver & Scarlet Witch & Brotherhood of the Evil Mutants | | | |
| | 23.00 | 70.00 | 160.00 |
| 5 | 19.00 | 57.00 | 130.00 |

458

*X-Men #13, © Marvel Comics*

|  | Good | Fine | N-Mint |
|---|---|---|---|
| 6-10: 6-Sub-Mariner app. 8-1st Unus the Untouchable. 9-Avengers app. | | | |
| 10-1st Silver-Age app. Ka-Zar | 14.00 | 42.00 | 100.00 |
| 11,13-15: 11-1st app. The Stranger. 14-1st app. Sentinels. 15-Origin Beast | | | |
|  | 9.30 | 28.00 | 65.00 |
| 12-Origin Prof. X | 11.00 | 32.00 | 75.00 |
| 16-20: 19-1st app. The Mimic | 6.50 | 19.50 | 45.00 |
| 21-27,29,30 | 5.00 | 15.00 | 35.00 |
| 28-1st app. The Banshee (r-in #76) | 5.70 | 17.00 | 40.00 |
| 31-34,36,37,39,40: 39-New costumes | 3.60 | 11.00 | 25.00 |
| 35-Spider-Man app. | 5.00 | 15.00 | 35.00 |
| 38-Origin The X-Men feat. begins, ends #57 | 4.30 | 13.00 | 30.00 |
| 41-49: 42-Death of Prof. X (Changeling disguised as). 44-Red Raven app. | | | |
| (G.A.). 49-Steranko-c; 1st Polaris | 2.85 | 8.50 | 20.00 |
| 50,51-Steranko-c/a | 3.60 | 11.00 | 25.00 |
| 52 | 2.30 | 7.00 | 16.00 |
| 53-Barry Smith-c/a (1st comic book work) | 3.60 | 11.00 | 25.00 |
| 54,55-Barry Smith-c | 2.85 | 8.50 | 20.00 |

|  | Good | Fine | N-Mint |
|---|---|---|---|
| 56-63,65-Neal Adams-a(p). 56-Intro Havoc without costume. 65- Return of | | | |
| Professor X. 58-1st app. Havoil | 4.00 | 12.00 | 28.00 |
| 64-1st Sunfire app. | 2.85 | 8.50 | 20.00 |
| 66-Last new story | 2.00 | 6.00 | 14.00 |
| 67-86: 67-Reprints begin, end #93 | 1.70 | 5.00 | 12.00 |
| 87-93-r-#39-45 with-c | 1.70 | 5.00 | 12.00 |
| 94(8/75)-New X-Men begin; Colossus, Nightcrawler, Thunderbird, Storm, | | | |
| Wolverine, & Banshee join; Angel, Marvel Girl, & Iceman resign | | | |
|  | 19.00 | 57.00 | 130.00 |
| 95-Death Thunderbird | 5.70 | 17.00 | 40.00 |
| 96-99 (regular 25 cent cover) | 4.00 | 12.00 | 28.00 |
| 98,99 (30 cent cover) | 4.50 | 14.00 | 32.00 |
| 100-Old vs. New X-Men; part origin Phoenix | 4.30 | 13.00 | 30.00 |
| 101-Phoenix origin concludes | 4.00 | 12.00 | 28.00 |
| 102-107: 102-Origin Storm. 104-Intro. Star Jammers. 106-Old vs. New | | | |
| X-Men | 1.85 | 5.50 | 13.00 |
| 108-Byrne-a begins (See Marvel Team-Up 53) | 4.35 | 13.00 | 30.00 |
| 109-1st Vindicator | 3.70 | 11.00 | 25.00 |
| 110,111: 110-Phoenix joins | 2.15 | 6.50 | 15.00 |
| 112-119: 117-Origin Professor X | 1.70 | 5.00 | 12.00 |
| 120-1st app. Alpha Flight (cameo), story line begins | | | |
|  | 4.00 | 12.00 | 28.00 |
| 121-1st Alpha Flight (full story) | 4.35 | 13.00 | 30.00 |
| 122-128: 124-Colossus becomes Proletarian | 1.85 | 5.50 | 11.00 |
| 129-Intro Kitty Pryde | 2.15 | 6.50 | 13.00 |
| 130-1st app. The Dazzler by Byrne | 2.35 | 7.00 | 14.00 |
| 131-135: 131-Dazzler app. 133-Wolverine app. 134-Phoenix becomes Dark | | | |
| Phoenix | 1.70 | 5.00 | 10.00 |
| 136,138: 138-Dazzler app.; Cyclops leaves | 1.45 | 4.25 | 8.50 |
| 137-Giant; death of Phoenix | 1.85 | 5.50 | 11.00 |
| 139-Alpha Flight app.; Kitty Pryde joins | 2.50 | 7.50 | 15.00 |
| 140-Alpha Flight app. | 3.00 | 9.00 | 18.00 |
| 141-Intro Future X-Men & The New Brotherhood of Evil Mutants; death of | | | |
| Frank Richards | 1.75 | 5.25 | 10.50 |
| 142,143: 142-Deaths of Wolverine, Storm & Colossus. 143-Last Byrne is- | | | |
| sue | 1.05 | 3.15 | 6.30 |
| 144-150: 144-Man-Thing app. 145-Old X-Men app. 148-Spider-Woman, | | | |
| Dazzler app. 150-Double size | .90 | 2.65 | 5.30 |
| 151-157,159-161,163,164: 161-Origin Magneto. 163-Origin Binary. 164-1st | | | |
| app. Binary as Carol Danvers | .60 | 1.85 | 3.70 |

| | Good | Fine | N-Mint |
|---|---|---|---|
| 158-1st app. Rogue in X-Men (See Avengers Annual #10) | | | |
| | .70 | 2.10 | 4.20 |
| 162-Wolverine solo story | .85 | 2.50 | 5.00 |
| 165-Paul Smith-a begins | .90 | 2.65 | 5.30 |
| 166-Double size; Paul Smith-a | .70 | 2.10 | 4.20 |
| 167-170: 167-New Mutants x-over. 168-1st app. Madelyne Pryor in X-Men | | | |
| (See Avengers Annual #10) | .55 | 1.60 | 3.20 |
| 171-Rogue joins X-Men; Simonson-c/a | 1.00 | 3.00 | 6.00 |
| 172-174: 172,173-Two part Wolverine solo story. 173-Two cover varia- | | | |
| tions, blue & black. 174-Phoenix cameo | .55 | 1.60 | 3.20 |
| 175-Double size; anniversary issue; Phoenix returns. Last Paul Smith-c/a | | | |
| | .70 | 2.00 | 4.00 |
| 176-185: 181-Sunfire app. 182-Rogue solo story | | | |
| | .45 | 1.30 | 2.60 |
| 186-Double-size; Barry Smith/Austin-a | .60 | 1.75 | 3.50 |
| 187-192,194-199: 190,191-Spider-Man & Avengers x-over. 195-Power Pack | | | |
| x-over | .40 | 1.25 | 2.50 |
| 193-Double size; 100th app. New X-Men | .70 | 2.00 | 4.00 |
| 200-Double size | .85 | 2.50 | 5.00 |
| 201-209: 204-Nightcrawler solo story. 207-Wolverine/Phoenix story | | | |
| | .50 | 1.50 | 3.00 |
| 210-213-Mutant Massacre. 212-Wolverine vs. Sabertooth | | | |
| | 1.85 | 5.50 | 11.00 |
| 214-224: 219-Havok joins | .35 | 1.00 | 2.00 |
| 225-227: Fall Of The Mutants. 226-Double size | | | |
| | 1.00 | 3.00 | 6.00 |
| 228-241: 229-$1.00 begin | .30 | .90 | 1.75 |
| 242-Double size, X-Factor app., Inferno tie-in | .35 | 1.00 | 2.00 |
| 243-252,254-270: 258-Wolverine solo story | | .50 | 1.00 |
| 253-All new X-men begin | .25 | .75 | 1.50 |
| Annual 3(2/80) | 1.25 | 3.75 | 7.50 |
| Annual 4(11/80)-Dr. Strange app. | 1.00 | 3.00 | 6.00 |
| Annual 5(10/81) | .70 | 2.10 | 4.25 |
| Annual 6(11/82) | .50 | 1.50 | 3.00 |
| Annual 7(1/84), 8(12/84) | .40 | 1.25 | 2.50 |
| Annual 9(1985)-New Mutants; Art Adams-a | 1.50 | 4.50 | 9.00 |
| Annual 10(1/87)-Art Adams-a | 1.50 | 4.50 | 9.00 |
| Annual 11(11/87) | .35 | 1.00 | 2.00 |
| Annual 12('88, $1.75)-Evolutionary War app. | .50 | 1.50 | 3.00 |
| Annual 13('89, $2.00, 68 pgs.)-Atlantis Attacks | .35 | 1.00 | 2.00 |

| | Good | Fine | N-Mint |
|---|---|---|---|
| Annual 14('90, $2.00, 68 pgs.) | .35 | 1.00 | 2.00 |
| Giant-Size 1(Summer,'75, 50 cents)-1st app. new X-Men; Intro Night-crawler, Storm, Colossus & Thunderbird; Wolverine app. | | | |
| | 13.50 | 34.00 | 95.00 |
| Giant-Size 2(11/75)-51 pgs. Neal Adams-a(r) | 2.85 | 9.00 | 20.00 |
| Special 1(12/70)-Kirby-c/a; origin The Stranger | | | |
| | 2.85 | 9.00 | 20.00 |
| Special 2(11/71) | 2.85 | 9.00 | 20.00 |

**X-MEN/ALPHA FLIGHT**
Jan, 1986 - No. 2, Jan, 1986 ($1.50, mini-series)
Marvel Comics Group

| | Good | Fine | N-Mint |
|---|---|---|---|
| 1,2: 1-Intro The Berserkers; Paul Smith-a | .60 | 1.75 | 3.50 |

**X-MEN AND THE MICRONAUTS, THE**
Jan, 1984 - No. 4, April, 1984 (Mini-series)
Marvel Comics Group

| | Good | Fine | N-Mint |
|---|---|---|---|
| 1-4: Guice-c/a(p) in all | .25 | .75 | 1.50 |

**X-MEN CLASSIC** (Formerly Classic X-Men)
No. 46, Apr, 1990 - Present ($1.25, color)
Marvel Comics

| | Good | Fine | N-Mint |
|---|---|---|---|
| 46-54: New X-Men reprints continue | | .65 | 1.30 |

**X-MEN CLASSICS** (Also see Classic X-Men)
Dec, 1983 - No. 3, Feb, 1984 ($2.00; Baxter paper)
Marvel Comics Group

| | Good | Fine | N-Mint |
|---|---|---|---|
| 1-3: X-Men-r by Neal Adams | .50 | 1.50 | 3.00 |

**X-MEN VS. THE AVENGERS**
Apr, 1987 - No. 4, July, 1987 ($1.50, mini-series, Baxter paper)
Marvel Comics Group

| | Good | Fine | N-Mint |
|---|---|---|---|
| 1 | .60 | 1.75 | 3.50 |
| 2-4 | .40 | 1.25 | 2.50 |

**X-TERMINATORS**
Oct, 1988 - No. 4, Jan, 1989 ($1.00, color, mini-series)
Marvel Comics

|                                            | Good | Fine | N-Mint |
|--------------------------------------------|------|------|--------|
| 1-X-Men/X-Factor tie-in; Williamson-i      | .50  | 1.50 | 3.00   |
| 2                                          | .30  | .90  | 1.75   |
| 3,4                                        |      | .60  | 1.25   |

# Y

## YELLOW CLAW
Oct, 1956 - No. 4, April, 1957
Atlas Comics (MjMC)

|  | Good | Fine | N-Mint |
|---|---|---|---|
| 1-Origin by Joe Maneely | 29.00 | 86.00 | 200.00 |
| 2-Kirby-a | 23.00 | 70.00 | 160.00 |
| 3,4-Kirby-a; 4-Kirby/Severin-a | 20.00 | 60.00 | 140.00 |

## YOUNG ALLIES COMICS (All-Winners #21)
Summer, 1941 - No. 20, Oct, 1946
Timely Comics (USA 1-7/NPI 8,9/YAI 10-20)

| | Good | Fine | N-Mint |
|---|---|---|---|
| 1-Origin/1st app. The Young Allies; 1st meeting of Captain America & Human Torch; Red Skull app.; S&K c/splash; Hitler-c | 250.00 | 625.00 | 1500.00 |
| 2-Captain America & Human Torch app.; Simon & Kirby-c | 117.00 | 290.00 | 700.00 |
| 3-Fathertime, Captain America & Human Torch app. | 92.00 | 230.00 | 550.00 |
| 4-The Vagabond & Red Skull, Capt. America, Human Torch app. | 88.00 | 220.00 | 525.00 |
| 5-Captain America & Human Torch app. | 53.00 | 130.00 | 315.00 |
| 6-10: 9-Hitler, Tojo, Mussolini-c. 10-Origin Tommy Tyme & Clock of Ages; ends #19 | 41.00 | 105.00 | 245.00 |
| 11-20: 12-Classic decapitation story | 32.00 | 80.00 | 190.00 |

## YOUNG ALL-STARS
June, 1987 - No. 31, Nov, 1989 ($1.00, deluxe format, color)
DC Comics

| | Good | Fine | N-Mint |
|---|---|---|---|
| 1-1st app. Iron Munro & The Flying Fox | .70 | 2.00 | 4.00 |
| 2,3 | .35 | 1.00 | 2.00 |
| 4-31: 7-18-$1.25. 8,9-Millennium tie-ins. 19-23-$1.50. 24-Begin $1.75-c | .30 | .90 | 1.75 |
| Annual 1 ('88, $2.00) | .35 | 1.00 | 2.00 |

# Z

## ZANE GREY'S STORIES OF THE WEST
No. 197, 9/48 - No. 996, 5-7/59; 11/64 (All painted-c)
Dell Publishing Co./Gold Key 11/64

|  | Good | Fine | N-Mint |
|---|---|---|---|
| 4-Color 197(#1)(9/48) | 6.00 | 18.00 | 42.00 |
| 4-Color 222,230,236('49) | 5.00 | 15.00 | 35.00 |
| 4-Color 246,255,270,301,314,333,346 | 3.70 | 11.00 | 26.00 |
| 4-Color 357,372,395,412,433,449,467,484 | 3.00 | 9.00 | 21.00 |
| 4-Color 511-Kinstler-a | 3.50 | 10.50 | 24.00 |
| 4-Color 532,555,583,604,616,632(5/55) | 3.00 | 9.00 | 21.00 |
| 27(9-11/55) - 39(9-11/58) | 2.30 | 7.00 | 16.00 |
| 4-Color 996(5-7/59) | 2.30 | 7.00 | 16.00 |
| 10131-411-(11/64-G.K.)-Nevada; r-4-Color #996 | | | |
|  | 1.30 | 4.00 | 9.00 |

## ZIP COMICS
Feb, 1940 - No. 47, Summer, 1944
MLJ Magazines

| | Good | Fine | N-Mint |
|---|---|---|---|
| 1-Origin Kalathar the Giant Man, The Scarlet Avenger, & Steel Sterling; Mr. Satan, Nevada Jones & Zambini, the Miracle Man, War Eagle, Captain Valor begins | 117.00 | 295.00 | 700.00 |
| 2 | 50.00 | 150.00 | 350.00 |
| 3 | 39.00 | 115.00 | 270.00 |
| 4,5 | 33.00 | 100.00 | 230.00 |
| 6-9: 9-Last Kalathar & Mr. Satan | 29.00 | 86.00 | 200.00 |
| 10-Inferno, the Flame Breather begins, ends #13 | | | |
|  | 26.00 | 77.00 | 180.00 |
| 11,12: 11-Inferno without costume | 24.00 | 73.00 | 170.00 |
| 13-17,19: 17-Last Scarlet Avenger | 24.00 | 73.00 | 170.00 |
| 18-Wilbur begins (1st app.) | 27.00 | 81.00 | 190.00 |
| 20-Origin Black Jack (1st app.) | 36.00 | 107.00 | 250.00 |
| 21-26: 25-Last Nevada Jones. 26-Black Witch begins; last Captain Valor | | | |
|  | 23.00 | 70.00 | 160.00 |
| 27-Intro. Web | 35.00 | 105.00 | 245.00 |
| 28-Origin Web | 35.00 | 105.00 | 245.00 |
| 29,30 | 19.00 | 57.00 | 135.00 |

| | Good | Fine | N-Mint |
|---|---|---|---|
| 31-38: 34-1st Applejack app. 35-Last Zambini, Black Jack. 38-Last Web issue | 14.00 | 42.00 | 100.00 |
| 39-Red Rube begins (origin, 8/43) | 14.00 | 42.00 | 100.00 |
| 40-47: 45-Wilbur ends | 10.00 | 30.00 | 70.00 |

**ZOOT** (Rulah Jungle Goddess #17 on)
nd (1946) - No. 16, July, 1948 (Two #13s & 14s)
Fox Features Syndicate

| | Good | Fine | N-Mint |
|---|---|---|---|
| nn-Funny animal only | 8.50 | 25.50 | 60.00 |
| 2-The Jaguar app. | 7.00 | 21.00 | 50.00 |
| 3(Fall,'46) - 6-Funny animals & teen-age | 4.00 | 12.00 | 28.00 |
| 7-Rulah, Jungle Goddess begins (6/47); origin & 1st app. | | | |
| | 33.00 | 100.00 | 230.00 |
| 8-10 | 24.00 | 72.00 | 165.00 |
| 11-Kamen bondage-c | 25.00 | 75.00 | 175.00 |
| 12-Injury-to-eye panels | 16.00 | 48.00 | 110.00 |
| 13(2/48) | 16.00 | 48.00 | 110.00 |
| 14(3/48)-Used in **SOTI**, pg. 104, "One picture showing a girl nailed by her wrists to trees with blood flowing from the wounds, might be taken straight from an ill. ed. of the Marquis deSade" | | | |
| | 19.00 | 57.00 | 135.00 |
| 13(4/48), 14(5/48) | 16.00 | 48.00 | 110.00 |
| 15,16 | 16.00 | 48.00 | 110.00 |

**ZORRO** (Walt Disney with #882)(TV)
May, 1949 - No. 15, Sept-Nov, 1961 (Photo-c 882 on)
Dell Publishing Co.

| | Good | Fine | N-Mint |
|---|---|---|---|
| 4-Color 228 | 16.00 | 48.00 | 110.00 |
| 4-Color 425,497 | 8.50 | 25.50 | 60.00 |
| 4-Color 538-Kinstler-a | 9.30 | 28.00 | 65.00 |
| 4-Color 574,617,732 | 8.50 | 25.50 | 60.00 |
| 4-Color 882-Photo-c begin; Toth-a | 7.00 | 21.00 | 50.00 |
| 4-Color 920,933,960,976-Toth-a in all | 7.00 | 21.00 | 50.00 |
| 4-Color 1003('59) | 5.70 | 17.00 | 40.00 |
| 4-Color 1037-Annette Funicello photo-c | 8.00 | 24.00 | 56.00 |
| 8(12-2/59-60) | 4.00 | 12.00 | 28.00 |
| 9,12-Toth-a | 4.30 | 13.00 | 30.00 |
| 10,11,13-15-Last photo-c | 3.00 | 9.00 | 21.00 |

**ZORRO** (Walt Disney) (TV)
Jan, 1966 - No. 9, March, 1968 (All photo-c)
Gold Key

|  | Good | Fine | N-Mint |
|---|---|---|---|
| 1-Toth-a | 3.00 | 9.00 | 21.00 |
| 2,4,5,7-9-Toth-a | 2.30 | 7.00 | 16.00 |
| 3,6-Tufts-a | 2.00 | 6.00 | 14.00 |

# Big Little Books

# INTRODUCTION

Big Little Books first appeared in 1933 in the heart of the Depression, the same year that the first comic books were being tested. The idea for Big Little Books came about through a series of circumstances set in motion by a young Samuel Lowe, who headed the creative marketing and sales staff at Whitman. Sam frequently went into the shop to get a first-hand view of what the equipment could do. On one such trip through the bindery, he saw strips or blocks of paper falling from lifts of printed sheets on the cutter. It seemed to him that this paper was being wasted, and he picked up a handful. Holding it between thumb and middle finger, he walked around the office for several days asking people, "Don't you think this would make a nice book? It just fits a small hand. But what should go into it?"

The rest is history. They decided upon *Dick Tracy, Orphan Annie,* and *Mickey Mouse* for the first books. The first shipments went into nearby Milwaukee stores late in the year and before Christmas the phones were ringing like mad. Of course, the paper at the end of the sheets was not used except for the initial dummies—it was simply the source of the idea which created Big Little Books. Over the next three decades, after a title change to Better Little Books in 1938, hundreds of Big Little Books were produced.

In the beginning, famous newspaper strips were adapted to the Big Little Book format, followed by popular movies, classic novels and some original material. The colorful covers and spines of these fat little books were eye-catching and caught on instantly. Other companies followed Whitman's lead and began their series of similarly formated books. The largest of these was the Saalfield Publishing Co., who latched onto exclusive rights to publishing *Shirley Temple* books. Saalfield also published several collectible *movie* books as well as a few popular strip characters such as *Brick Bradford, Just Kids* and *Popeye*. However, most of their books were original western, crime and sport oriented themes. No other publisher ever came close to competing with the avalanche of Whitman titles satisfying consumer demand. Whitman had all the best syndicated stars wrapped up early-on, including *Tarzan, Dick Tracy, Buck Rogers, Flash Gordon, Disney,* and a host of others, and never lost their hold on the market.

The public recognized from the beginning the uniqueness of these colorful children's books, and many collectors began saving them. Although the paper drives of the '40s consumed untold thousands, many survived and show up at flea markets, antique shows and comic book conventions for sale.

The name Big Little Book has now become a generic term in describing books of this type. It is believed that the name Big Little Book was changed to Better Little Book because the term had previously been used by another publisher. It is known that Little Big Book had been used in the late 1920s.

Today the collector's market for Big Little Books is very healthy and growing. These books are rare in mint condition and sell rapidly whenever they turn up in this grade.

Big Little Books are collected in many ways. Some collectors only want Whitman books. Others collect special characters or genres such as *Dick Tracy, Tarzan, Popeye*, westerns or Disney. Still others want them all.

The most popular titles, of course, correspond with the most popular characters. *Flash Gordon, Buck Rogers, Donald Duck, Mickey Mouse, Dick Tracy, Popeye, Tarzan, The Shadow, Captain Midnight, The Green Hornet*, etc., are high on everyone's list. Whatever your collecting interest, most Big Little Books are under $50.00 and are affordable to most budgets.

As supplies dry up with an ever-increasing demand, the future growth should continue to be good. No time is better than now to begin your collection. The following listing was completely compiled from several large private collections. It is not complete, but is nearly so, and will be expanded and improved with each new future edition.

Many popular titles were republished as giveaways or premiums and are listed alphabetically under the original version listing in most cases. The most common giveaways were distributed by Cocomalt. Other variants of the Big Little Book are also listed, such as Big Big Books, Fast-Action Books, Penny Books, Pop-Up Books and Wee Little Books. The author would be grateful to know of any omissions or errors in the listings.

# HOW TO USE THE LISTINGS

All titles are listed alphabetically, regardless of publisher, with the following exception. When more than one book was published of a given character, they are listed numerically within that grouping. For instance, to look up a *Dick Tracy* book, you would go to the *Dick Tracy* listing first and then find the book listed numerically. If it is a giveaway with no number, you will usually find it listed under the original book and title it reprints. Generally, the earlier the date, the closer to the beginning of the listing the book will appear. The information is listed in this order: Issue number, title, date, publisher, page count (which includes covers and end sheets), special information, artists, etc.

# GRADING

Before a Big Little Book's value can be assessed, its condition or state of preservation must be determined. A book in **Mint** condition will bring many times the price of the same book in **Poor** condition. Many variables influence the grading of a Big Little Book and all must be considered in the final evaluation. Due to the way they are constructed, damage occurs with very little use—usually to the spine, book edges and binding. Consequently, books in near mint to mint condition are scarce. More important defects that affect grading are: split spines, pages missing, page browning or brittleness, writing, crayoning, loose pages, color fading, chunks missing, and rolling or out of square. The following grading guide is given to aid the novice.

**Mint:** Absolutely perfect in every way, regardless of age; white pages; original printing luster retained on covers and spine; no color fading; no wear on edges or corners of book; virtually an unread copy with binding still square and tight.

**Near Mint:** Almost perfect; full cover gloss and white pages with only very slight wear on book corners and edges; binding still square and tight with no pages missing.

**Very Fine:** Most of cover gloss retained with minor wear appearing at corners and around edges; paper quality still fresh from white to off-white; spine tight with no pages missing.

**Fine:** Slight wear beginning to show; cover gloss reduced but still clean; pages still relatively fresh and white; very minor splits and wear at spine and book edges; relatively flat and square with no pages missing.

**Very Good:** Obviously a read copy with original printing luster almost gone; some fading and discoloration, but not soiled; some signs of wear such as minor corner splits, rolling and page yellowing with possibly one of the blank inside pages missing; no chunks missing.

**Good:** An average used copy complete with only minor pieces missing from spine, which may be partially split; slightly soiled or marked with rolling, color flaking and wear around edges, but perfectly sound and legible; could have minor tape repairs or one or more of blank inside pages missing, but otherwise complete.

**Fair:** Very heavily read and soiled with small chunks missing from cover; most or all of spine could be missing; multiple splits in spine and loose pages, but still sound and legible, bringing 50 to 70 percent of good price.

**Poor:** Damaged, heavily weathered, soiled or otherwise unsuited for collecting purposes.

# A WORD ON PRICING

The prices are given for good, fine and near-mint condition. A book in fair would be 50–70% of the good price. Very good would be halfway between the good and fine price, and very fine would be halfway between the fine and near-mint price. The prices listed were averaged from convention sales, dealers' lists, adzines, auctions, and by special contact with dealers and collectors from coast to coast. The prices and the spreads were determined from sales of copies in available condition or the highest grade known. Since most available copies are in the good to fine range, neither dealers nor collectors should let the mint column influence the prices they are willing to charge or pay for books in less than perfect condition.

In the past, the BLB market has lacked a point of focus due to the absence of an annual price guide that accurately reports sales and growth in the market. Due to this, current prices for BLBs still vary considerably from region to region. It is our hope that this book will contribute to the stability of the BLB market. The prices listed reflect a six times spread from good to near-mint (1 - 3 - 6). We feel this spread accurately reflects the current market, especially when you consider the scarcity of books in NM-Mint condition. When one or both end sheets are missing, the book's value would drop about a half grade.

**Abbreviations:** *a*-art; *c*-cover; *nn*-no number; *p*-pages; *r*-reprint.

**Publisher Codes:** *BRP*-Blue Ribbon Press; *ERB*-Edgar Rice Burroughs; *EVW*-Engel van Wiseman; *Faw*-Fawcett Publishing Co.; *Gold*-Goldsmith Publishing Co.; *Lynn*-Lynn Publishing Co.; *McKay*-David McKay Co.; *Whit*-Whitman Publishing Co.; *World*-World Syndicate Publishing Co.

**Terminology:** *All Pictures Comics*-no text, all drawings; *Flip Pictures*-upper right corner of interior pages contain drawings that are put into motion when riffled; *Movie Scenes*-book illustrated with scenes from the movie.

"Big Little Book" is a registered trademark of Whitman Publishing Co. "Pop-Up" is a registered trademark of Blue Ribbon Press.

# BIG LITTLE BOOK
# LISTINGS

|                                                                                                   | Good  | Fine   | N-Mint |
| ------------------------------------------------------------------------------------------------- | ----- | ------ | ------ |
| **1175-Abbie an' Slats**, 1940, Sal, 400p                                                         | 7.00  | 21.00  | 40.00  |
| **1182-Abbie an' Slats and Becky**, 1940, Sal, 400p                                               | 7.00  | 21.00  | 40.00  |
| **1177-Ace Drummond**, 1935, Whit, 432p                                                           | 5.00  | 15.00  | 30.00  |
| **Admiral Byrd** (See Paramount Newsreel . . . )                                                  |       |        |        |
| **nn-Adventures of Charlie McCarthy and Edgar Bergen, The**, 1938, Dell, 194p, Fast-Action Story, soft-c | 13.00 | 40.00  | 80.00  |
| **1422-Adventures of Huckleberry Finn, The**, 1939, Whit, 432p, Henry E. Vallely-a                | 6.00  | 18.00  | 36.00  |
| **1648-Adventures of Jim Bowie** (TV Series), 1958, Whit, 280p                                    | 3.00  | 9.00   | 18.00  |
| **1056-Adventures of Krazy Kat and Ignatz Mouse in Koko Land**, 1934, Sal, 160p, oblong size, hard-c, Herriman c/a | 43.00 | 130.00 | 260.00 |
| **1306-Adventures of Krazy Kat and Ignatz Mouse in Koko Land**, 1934, Sal, 164p, oblong size, soft-c, Herriman c/a | 43.00 | 130.00 | 260.00 |
| **1082-Adventures of Pete the Tramp, The**, 1935, Sal, hard-c, by C. D. Russell                   | 8.50  | 25.00  | 50.00  |
| **1312-Adventures of Pete the Tramp, The**, 1935, Sal, soft-c, by C. D. Russell                   | 8.50  | 25.00  | 50.00  |

*The Adventures of Huckleberry Finn #1422,*
*© Harper & Brothers, 1939*

|  | Good | Fine | N-Mint |
|---|---|---|---|
| **1053-Adventure of Tim Tyler**, 1934, Sal, hard-c, oblong size, by Lyman Young | 15.00 | 45.00 | 90.00 |
| **1303-Adventures of Tim Tyler**, 1934, Sal, soft-c, oblong size, by Lyman Young | 15.00 | 45.00 | 90.00 |
| **1058-Adventures of Tom Sawyer, The**, 1934, Sal, 160p, hard-c, Park Sumner-a | 6.00 | 18.00 | 36.00 |
| **1308-Adventures of Tom Sawyer, The**, 1934, Sal, 160p, soft-c, Park Sumner-a | 6.00 | 18.00 | 36.00 |
| **1448-Air Fighters of America**, 1941, Whit, 432p, flip pictures | 5.50 | 16.50 | 33.00 |
| **Alexander Smart, ESQ**. (See Top-Line Comics) |  |  |  |
| **759-Alice in Wonderland**, 1933, Whit, 160p, hard photo-c, movie scenes | 17.00 | 50.00 | 100.00 |
| **1481-Allen Pike of the Parachute Squad U.S.A.**, 1941, Whit, 432p | 5.50 | 16.50 | 33.00 |
| **763-Alley Oop and Dinny**, 1935, Whit, 384p, V. T. Hamlin-a | 10.00 | 30.00 | 60.00 |

|  | Good | Fine | N-Mint |
|---|---|---|---|

**1473-Alley Oop and Dinny in the Jungles of Moo,** 1938, Whit, 432p,
V. T. Hamlin-a                               9.00        27.00        54.00
   **nn-Alley Oop and the Missing King of Moo**, 1938, Whit, 36p,
   2½″ × 3½″, Penny Book              5.00        15.00        30.00
   **nn-Alley Oop in the Kingdom of Foo**, 1938, Whit, 68p, 3¾″ × 3½″,
   Pan-Am premium                     10.00        30.00        60.00
   **nn-Alley Oop the Invasion of Moo**, 1935, Whit, 260p, Cocomalt
   premium, soft-c; V. T. Hamlin-a   12.00        35.00        70.00
   **Andy Burnette** (See Walt Disney's . . . )
   **Andy Panda** (See Walter Lantz . . . )
 **531-Andy Panda**, 1943, Whit. 3¾″ × 8½″, Tall Comic Book, All Pictures Comics                              17.00        50.00      100.00
**1425-Andy Panda and Tiny Tom**, 1944, Whit, All Pictures Comics
                                              7.50        22.50        45.00
**1431-Andy Panda and the Mad Dog Mystery**, 1947, Whit, 288p, by
   Walter Lantz                             5.50        16.50        33.00
**1441-Andy Panda in the City of Ice**, 1948, Whit, All Pictures Comics,
   by Walter Lantz                         7.00        21.00        42.00
**1459-Andy Panda and the Pirate Ghosts**, 1949, Whit, 288p, by Walter
   Lantz                                    5.50        16.50        33.00
**1485-Andy Panda's Vacation**, 1946, Whit, All Pictures Comics, by
   Walter Lantz                             7.00        21.00        42.00
   **15-Andy Panda (The Adventures of)**, 1942, Dell, Fast-Action Story
                                             13.00        40.00        80.00
**707-10-Andy Panda and Presto the Pup**, 1949, Whit
                                              5.00        15.00        30.00
**1130-Apple Mary and Dennie Foil the Swindlers**, 1936, Whit, 432p
   (Forerunner to Mary Worth)         7.00        21.00        42.00
**1403-Apple Mary and Dennie's Lucky Apples**, 1939, Whit, 432p
                                              5.50        16.50        33.00
**2017-(#17)-Aquaman-Scourge of the Sea**, 1968, Whit, 260p, 39 cents,
   hard-c, color illos                      2.50         7.50        15.00
**1192-Arizona Kid on the Bandit Trail, The**, 1936, Whit, 432p
                                              5.00        15.00        30.00
**1469-Bambi (Walt Disney's)**, 1942, Whit, 432p
                                             14.00        42.00        84.00
**1497-Bambi's Children** (Disney), 1943, Whit, 432p, Disney Studio-a
                                             13.00        40.00        80.00
**1138-Bandits at Bay**, 1938, Sal, 400p    5.00        15.00        30.00

*Barney Baxter in the Air with the Eagle Squadron #1459,*
*© King Features Syndicate, 1938*

|  | Good | Fine | N-Mint |
|---|---|---|---|
| **1459-Barney Baxter in the Air with the Eagle Squadron**, 1938, Whit, 432p | 7.00 | 21.00 | 42.00 |
| **1083-Barney Google**, 1935, Sal, hard-c | 6.00 | 35.00 | 70.00 |
| **1313-Barney Google**, 1935, Sal, soft-c | 10.00 | 30.00 | 60.00 |
| **2031-Batman and Robin in the Cheetah Caper**, 1969, Whit, 258p | 2.50 | 7.50 | 15.00 |
| **5771-2-Batman and Robin in the Cheetah Caper**, 1975?, Whit, 258p | .50 | 1.50 | 3.00 |
| **nn-Beauty and the Beast**, nd (1930s), np (Whit), 36p, 3″ × 3½″ Penny Book | 1.50 | 4.50 | 9.00 |
| **760-Believe It or Not!**, 1931, Whit, 160p, by Ripley | 7.00 | 20.00 | 40.00 |
| **Betty Bear's Lesson** (See Wee Little Books) |  |  |  |
| **1119-Betty Boop in Snow White**, 1934, Whit, 240p, hard-c; adapted from Max Fleischer Paramount Talkartoon | 28.00 | 85.00 | 170.00 |
| **1158-Betty Boop in "Miss Gullivers Travels,"** 1935, Whit, 288p, hard-c | 27.00 | 80.00 | 160.00 |

|                                                                                                                      | Good  | Fine   | N-Mint |
|----------------------------------------------------------------------------------------------------------------------|-------|--------|--------|
| **1432-Big Chief Wahoo and the Lost Pioneers**, 1942, Whit, 432p, Elmer Woggon-a                                     | 6.00  | 18.00  | 36.00  |
| **1443-Big Chief Wahoo and the Great Gusto**, 1938, Whit, 432p, Elmer Woggon-a                                       | 6.00  | 18.00  | 36.00  |
| **1483-Big Chief Wahoo and the Magic Lamp**, 1940, Whit, 432p, flip pictures, Woggon-c/a                             | 6.00  | 18.00  | 36.00  |
| **725-Big Little Mother Goose, The**, 1934, Whit, 580p                                                               | 60.00 | 180.00 | 360.00 |
| **1006-Big Little Nickel Book**, 1935, Whit, 144p, Blackie Bear stories, folk tales in primer style                  | 5.00  | 15.00  | 30.00  |
| **1007-Big Little Nickel Book**, 1935, Whit, 144p, Wee Wee Woman, etc.                                               | 5.00  | 15.00  | 30.00  |
| **1008-Big Little Nickel Book**, 1935, Whit, 144p, Peter Rabbit, etc.                                                | 5.00  | 15.00  | 30.00  |
| **721-Big Little Paint Book, The**, 1933, Whit, 336p, 3¾″ × 8½″, for crayoning                                       | 60.00 | 180.00 | 360.00 |
| **1178-Billy of Bar-Zero**, 1940, Sal, 400p                                                                          | 5.00  | 15.00  | 30.00  |
| **773-Billy the Kid**, 1935, Whit, 432p, Hal Arbo-a                                                                  | 7.00  | 21.00  | 40.00  |
| **1159-Billy the Kid on Tall Butte**, 1939, Sal, 400p                                                                | 5.00  | 15.00  | 30.00  |
| **1174-Billy the Kid's Pledge**, 1940, Sal, 400p                                                                     | 5.00  | 15.00  | 30.00  |
| **nn-Billy the Kid, Western Outlaw**, 1935, Whit, 260p, Cocomalt premium, Hal Arbo-a, soft-c                         | 8.00  | 24.00  | 48.00  |
| **1057-Black Beauty**, 1934, Sal, hard-c                                                                             | 5.00  | 15.00  | 30.00  |
| **1307-Black Beauty**, 1934, Sal, soft-c                                                                             | 5.00  | 15.00  | 30.00  |
| **1414-Black Silver and His Pirate Crew**, 1937, Whit, 300p                                                          | 5.50  | 16.50  | 33.00  |
| **1447-Blaze Brandon with the Foreign Legion**, 1938, Whit, 432p                                                     | 5.50  | 16.50  | 33.00  |
| **1410-Blondie and Dagwood in Hot Water**, 1946, Whit, 352p, by Chic Young                                           | 6.00  | 18.00  | 36.00  |
| **1415-Blondie and Baby Dumpling**, 1937, Whit, 432p, by Chic Young                                                  | 7.50  | 22.50  | 45.00  |
| **1419-Oh, Blondie the Bumsteads Carry On**, 1941, Whit, 432p, flip pictures, by Young                               | 7.50  | 22.50  | 45.00  |
| **1423-Blondie Who's Boss?**, 1942, Whit, 432p, flip pictures, by Chic Young                                         | 7.50  | 22.50  | 45.00  |

|                                                                                | Good | Fine  | N-Mint |
|--------------------------------------------------------------------------------|------|-------|--------|
| **1429-Blondie with Baby Dumpling and Daisy**, 1939, Whit, 432p, by Chic Young | 7.50 | 22.50 | 45.00  |
| **1430-Blondie Count Cookie in Too!**, 1947, Whit, 288p, by Chic Young         | 6.00 | 18.00 | 36.00  |
| **1438-Blondie and Dagwood Everybody's Happy**, 1948, Whit, 288p, by Chic Young | 6.00 | 18.00 | 36.00  |

*Blondie, No Dull Moments #1450,*
*© King Features Syndicate, 1948*

|                                                                                | Good | Fine  | N-Mint |
|--------------------------------------------------------------------------------|------|-------|--------|
| **1450-Blondie No Dull Moments**, 1948, Whit, 288p, by Chic Young              | 6.00 | 18.00 | 36.00  |
| **1463-Blondie Fun for All!**, 1949, Whit, 288p, by Chic Young                 | 6.00 | 18.00 | 36.00  |
| **1466-Blondie or Life Among the Bumsteads**, 1944, Whit, 352p, by Chic Young  | 7.50 | 22.50 | 45.00  |
| **1476-Blondie and Bouncing Baby Dumpling**, 1940, Whit, 432p, by Chic Young   | 7.50 | 22.50 | 45.00  |
| **1487-Blondie Baby Dumpling and All!**, 1941, Whit, 432p, flip pictures, by Young | 7.50 | 22.50 | 45.00  |
| **1490-Blondie Papa Knows Best**, 1945, Whit, 352p, by Chic Young              | 6.00 | 18.00 | 36.00  |

|  | Good | Fine | N-Mint |
|---|---|---|---|
| **1491-Blondie-Cookie and Daisy's Pups**, 1943, Whit, 432p | | | |
|  | 7.50 | 22.50 | 45.00 |
| **703-10-Blondie and Dagwood Some Fun!**, 1949, Whit, by Chic Young | | | |
|  | 5.00 | 15.00 | 30.00 |
| **21-Blondie and Dagwood**, 194?, Lynn, by Chic Young | | | |
|  | 12.00 | 35.00 | 70.00 |
| **1108-Bobby Benson on the H-Bar-O Ranch**, 1934, Whit, 300p, based on radio serial | 7.00 | 20.00 | 40.00 |
| **Bobby Thatcher and the Samarang Emerald** (See Top-Line Comics) | | | |
| **1432-Bob Stone the Young Detective**, 1937, Whit, 240p, movie scenes | 8.00 | 24.00 | 48.00 |
| **2002-(#2)-Bonanza-the Bubble Gum Kid**, 1967, Whit, 260p, 39 cents, hard-c, color illos | 3.00 | 9.00 | 18.00 |
| **1139-Border Eagle, The**, 1938, Sal, 400p | 5.00 | 15.00 | 30.00 |
| **1153-Boss of the Chisholm Trail**, 1939, Sal, 400p | | | |
|  | 5.00 | 15.00 | 30.00 |
| **1425-Brad Turner in Transatlantic Flight**, 1939, Whit, 432p | | | |
|  | 5.50 | 16.50 | 33.00 |
| **1058-Brave Little Tailor, The** (Disney), 1939, Whit, 5″ × 5½″, 68p, hard-c (Mickey Mouse) | 7.00 | 20.00 | 40.00 |
| **1427-Brenda Starr and the Masked Impostor**, 1943, Whit, 352p, Dale Messick-a | 8.50 | 25.00 | 50.00 |
| **1426-Brer Rabbit (Walt Disney's . . . )**, 1947, Whit, All Pict, Comics, from *Song Of The South* movie | 13.00 | 40.00 | 80.00 |
| **704-10-Brer Rabbit**, 1949?, Whit | 12.00 | 35.00 | 70.00 |
| **1059-Brick Bradford in the City Beneath the Sea**, 1934, Sal, hard-c, by William Ritt & Clarence Gray | 10.00 | 30.00 | 60.00 |
| **1309-Brick Bradford in the City Beneath the Sea**, 1934, Sal, soft-c, by Ritt & Gray | 10.00 | 30.00 | 60.00 |
| **1468-Brick Bradford with Brocco the Modern Buccaneer**, 1938, Whit, 432p, by Wm. Ritt & Clarence Gray | | | |
|  | 7.00 | 21.00 | 42.00 |
| **1133-Bringing Up Father**, 1936, Whit, 432p, by George McManus | | | |
|  | 11.00 | 32.50 | 65.00 |
| **1100-Broadway Bill**, 1935, Sal, photo-c, 4½″ × 5¼″, movie scenes (Columbia Pictures, horse racing) | 8.00 | 24.00 | 48.00 |
| **1580-Broadway Bill**, 1935, Sal, soft-c, photo-c, movie scenes | | | |
|  | 8.00 | 24.00 | 48.00 |
| **1181-Broncho Bill**, 1940, Sal, 400p | 5.00 | 15.00 | 30.00 |

|  | Good | Fine | N-Mint |
|---|---|---|---|

**nn-Broncho Bill in Suicide Canyon** (See Top-Line Comics)

**1417-Bronc Peeler the Lone Cowboy**, 1937, Whit, 432p, by Fred Harman, forerunner of Red Ryder          7.00     21.00     42.00

**1470-Buccaneer, The**, 1938, Whit, 240p, photo-c, movie scenes
                                                     7.00     21.00     42.00

**1646-Buccaneers, The** (TV Series), 1958, Whit, 4½″ × 5¾″, 280p, Russ Manning-a          2.50     7.50     15.00

**1104-Buck Jones in the Fighting Code**, 1934, Whit, 160p, hard-c, movie scenes          11.00     35.00     70.00

**1116-Buck Jones in Ride 'Em Cowboy (Universal Presents)**, 1935, Whit, 240p, photo-c, movie scenes     11.00     35.00     70.00

**1174-Buck Jones in the Roaring West (Universal Presents)**, 1935, Whit, 240p, movie scenes     11.00     35.00     70.00

*Buck Jones in the Fighting Rangers #1188,*
*© Whitman Publishing Co., 1936*

**1188-Buck Jones in the Fighting Rangers (Universal Presents)**, 1936, Whit, 240p, photo-c, movie scenes
                                              11.00     35.00     70.00

**1404-Buck Jones and the Two-Gun Kid**, 1937, Whit, 432p
                                               6.00     18.00     36.00

|  | Good | Fine | N-Mint |
|---|---|---|---|

**1451-Buck Jones and the Killers of Crooked Butte**, 1940, Whit, 432p
|  | 6.00 | 18.00 | 36.00 |

**1461-Buck Jones and the Rock Creek Cattle War**, 1938, Whit, 432p
|  | 6.00 | 18.00 | 36.00 |

**1486-Buck Jones and the Rough Riders in Forbidden Trails**, 1943, Whit, flip pictures, based on movie; Tim McCoy app.
|  | 8.00 | 24.00 | 48.00 |

**3-Buck Jones in the Red Ryder**, 1934, EVW, 160p, movie scenes
|  | 12.00 | 35.00 | 70.00 |

**15-Buck Jones in Rocky Rhodes**, 1935, EVW, 160p, photo-c, movie scenes
|  | 12.00 | 35.00 | 70.00 |

**4069-Buck Jones and the Night Riders**, 1937, Whit, 7″ × 9½″, 320p, Big Big Book
|  | 32.00 | 95.00 | 190.00 |

**nn-Buck Jones on the Six-Gun Trail**, 1939, Whit, 36p, 2½″ × 3½″, Penny Book
|  | 4.00 | 12.00 | 24.00 |

**742-Buck Rogers in the 25th Century A.D.**, 1933, Whit, 320p, Dick Calkins-a
|  | 25.00 | 75.00 | 150.00 |

**nn-Buck Rogers in the 25th Century A.D.**, 1933, Whit, 204p, Cocomalt premium, Calkins-a
|  | 15.00 | 45.00 | 90.00 |

**765-Buck Rogers in the City Below the Sea**, 1934, Whit, 320p, Dick Calkins-a
|  | 18.00 | 55.00 | 110.00 |

**765-Buck Rogers in the City Below the Sea**, 1934, Whit, 324p, soft-c, Dick Calkins c/a
|  | 30.00 | 90.00 | 180.00 |

**1143-Buck Rogers on the Moons of Saturn**, 1934, Whit, 320p, Dick Calkins-a
|  | 18.00 | 55.00 | 110.00 |

**nn-Buck Rogers on the Moons of Saturn**, 1934, Whit, 324p, premium w/no ads, soft 3-color-c, Dick Calkins-a
|  | 30.00 | 90.00 | 180.00 |

**1169-Buck Rogers and the Depth Men of Jupiter**, 1935, Whit, 432p, Calkins-a
|  | 18.00 | 55.00 | 110.00 |

**1178-Buck Rogers and the Doom Comet**, 1935, Whit, 432p, Calkins-a
|  | 17.00 | 50.00 | 100.00 |

**1197-Buck Rogers and the Planetoid Plot**, 1936, Whit, 432p, Calkins-a
|  | 17.00 | 50.00 | 100.00 |

**1409-Buck Rogers Vs. the Fiend of Space**, 1940, Whit, 432p, Calkins-a
|  | 17.00 | 50.00 | 100.00 |

**1437-Buck Rogers in the War with the Planet Venus**, 1938, Whit, 432p, Calkins-a
|  | 17.00 | 50.00 | 100.00 |

**1474-Buck Rogers and the Overturned World**, 1941, Whit, 432p, flip pictures, Calkins-a
|  | 17.00 | 50.00 | 100.00 |

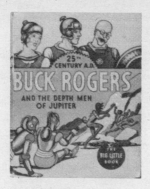

*Buck Rogers and the Depth Men of Jupiter #1169,*
*© John F. Dille, 1935*

|  | Good | Fine | N-Mint |
|---|---|---|---|
| **1490-Buck Rogers and the Super-Dwarf of Space**, 1943, Whit, All Pictures Comics, Calkins-a | 17.00 | 50.00 | 100.00 |
| **4057-Buck Rogers, The Adventures of**, 1934, Whit, 7″ × 9½″, 320p, Big Big Book, "The Story of Buck Rogers on the Planet Eros"; Calkins-c/a | 63.00 | 190.00 | 380.00 |
| **nn-Buck Rogers**, 1935, Whit, 4″ × 3½″, Tarzan Ice Cream cup premium (Rare) | 53.00 | 160.00 | 320.00 |
| **nn-Buck Rogers in the City of Floating Globes**, 1935, Whit, 258p, Cocomalt premium, soft-c, Dick Calkins-a | 43.00 | 130.00 | 260.00 |
| **1135-Buckskin and Bullets**, 1938, Sal, 400p | 5.00 | 15.00 | 30.00 |
| **Buffalo Bill** (See Wild West Adventures of . . . ) |  |  |  |
| **nn-Buffalo Bill**, 1934, World, All pictures, by J. Carroll Mansfield | 5.50 | 16.50 | 33.00 |
| **713-Buffalo Bill and the Pony Express**, 1934, Whit, 384p, Hal Arbo-a | 7.00 | 21.00 | 42.00 |
| **1194-Buffalo Bill Plays a Lone Hand**, 1936, Whit, 432p, Hal Arbo-a | 5.50 | 16.50 | 33.00 |

|                                                                                 | Good  | Fine  | N-Mint |
|---------------------------------------------------------------------------------|-------|-------|--------|
| **530-Bugs Bunny**, 1943, Whit, All Pictures Comics, Tall Comic Book, 3¾" × 8¾", reprints/Looney Tunes 1 & 5 | 17.00 | 50.00 | 100.00 |
| **1403-Bugs Bunny and the Pirate Loot**, 1947, Whit, All Pictures Comics | 7.00 | 21.00 | 42.00 |
| **1435-Bugs Bunny**, 1944, Whit, All Pictures Comics | 8.00 | 24.00 | 48.00 |
| **1440-Bugs Bunny in Risky Business**, 1948, Whit, All Pictures Comics | 7.00 | 21.00 | 42.00 |
| **1455-Bugs Bunny and Klondike Gold**, 1948, Whit, 288p | 7.00 | 21.00 | 42.00 |
| **1465-Bugs Bunny the Masked Marvel**, 1949, Whit, 288p | 7.00 | 21.00 | 42.00 |
| **1496-Bugs Bunny and His Pals**, 1945, Whit, All Pictures Comics; r/4-Color 33 | 8.00 | 24.00 | 48.00 |
| **706-10-Bugs Bunny and the Giant Brothers**, 1949, Whit | 4.50 | 13.50 | 27.00 |
| **2007-(#7)-Bugs Bunny-Double Trouble on Diamond Fountain,** 1967, Whit, 260p, 39 cents, hard-c, color illos | 2.00 | 6.00 | 12.00 |
| **2952-Bugs Bunny's Mistake**, 1949, Whit, 3¼" × 4", 24p, Tiny Tales, full color (5 cents) | 4.00 | 12.00 | 24.00 |
| **5757-2-Bugs Bunny in Double Trouble on Diamond Island**, 1967, (1980-reprints #2007), Whit, 260p, soft-c, 79 cents, B&W | .50 | 1.50 | 3.00 |
| **5772-2-Bugs Bunny the Last Crusader**, 1975, Whit, 79 cents, flip-it book | .50 | 1.50 | 3.00 |
| **13-Bugs Bunny and the Secret of Storm Island**, 1942, Dell, 194p, Fast-Action Story | 15.00 | 45.00 | 90.00 |
| **1169-Bullet Benton**, 1939, Sal, 400p | 5.00 | 15.00 | 30.00 |
| **nn-Bulletman and the Return of Mr. Murder**, 1941, Faw, 196p, Dime Action Book | 22.00 | 65.00 | 130.00 |
| **1142-Bullets Across the Border** (A Billy the Kid story), 1938, Sal, 400p | 5.00 | 15.00 | 30.00 |
| **Bunky** (See Top-Line Comics) | | | |
| **837-Bunty** (Punch and Judy), 1935, Whit, 28p, Magic-Action with 3 Pop-Ups | 10.00 | 30.00 | 60.00 |

|  | Good | Fine | N-Mint |
|---|---|---|---|

**1091-Burn 'Em Up Barnes**, 1935, Sal, Hard-c, movie scenes
                                       7.00     21.00     42.00

**1321-Burn 'Em Up Barnes**, 1935, Sal, Soft-c, movie scenes
      7.00     21.00     42.00

**1415-Buz Sawyer and Bomber 13**, 1946, Whit, 352p, Roy Crane-a
      7.00     21.00     42.00

**1412-Calling W-I-X-Y-Z, Jimmy Kean and the Radio Spies**, 1939,
Whit, 300p      7.00     21.00     42.00

**Call of the Wild** (See Jack London's . . . )

**1107-Camels Are Coming**, 1935, Sal, movie scenes
      6.00     18.00     36.00

**1587-Camels Are Coming**, 1935, Sal, movie scenes
      6.00     18.00     36.00

**nn-Captain and the Kids, Boys Will Be Boys, The**, 1938, 68p,
Pan-Am Oil premium, soft-c     7.50     22.50     45.00

*Captain Easy, Soldier of Fortune #1128,*
*© NEA Service, 1934*

**1128-Captain Easy Soldier of Fortune**, 1934, Whit, 432p, Roy Crane-a
      9.00     27.00     54.00

| | Good | Fine | N-Mint |
|---|---|---|---|

**nn-Captain Easy Soldier of Fortune**, 1934, Whit, 436p, Premium-no
ads, soft 3-color-c, Roy Crane-a     13.00     40.00     80.00

**1474-Captain Easy Behind Enemy Lines**, 1943, Whit, 352p, Roy
Crane-a     8.00     24.00     48.00

**nn-Captain Easy and Wash Tubbs**, 1935, 260p, Cocomalt premium,
Roy Crane-a     8.00     24.00     48.00

**1444-Captain Frank Hawks Air Ace and the League of Twelve**, 1938,
Whit, 432p     6.00     18.00     36.00

**nn-Captain Marvel**, 1941, Faw, 196p, Dime Action Book
22.00     65.00     130.00

**1402-Captain Midnight and Sheik Jomak Khan**, 1946, Whit, 352p
11.00     32.50     65.00

**1452-Captain Midnight and the Moon Woman**, 1943, Whit, 352p
11.00     32.50     65.00

**1458-Captain Midnight Vs. the Terror of the Orient**, 1942, Whit,
432p, flip pictures, Hess-a     11.00     32.50     65.00

**1488-Captain Midnight and the Secret Squadron**, 1941, Whit, 432p
11.00     32.50     65.00

**Captain Robb of . . .** (See Dirigible ZR90. . )

**L20-Ceiling Zero**, 1936, Lynn, 128p, 7½" × 5", hard-c, James Cagney,
Pat O'Brien photos on-c, movie scenes, Warner Bros. Pictures
6.00     18.00     42.00

**1093-Chandu the Magician**, 1935, Sal, 5" × 5¼", 160p, hard-c, Bela
Lugosi photo-c, movie scenes     8.00     24.00     48.00

**1323-Chandu the Magician**, 1935, Sal, 5" × 5¼", 160p, soft-c, Bela
Lugosi photo-c     8.00     24.00     48.00

**Charlie Chan** (See Inspector . . . )

**1459-Charlie Chan Solves a New Mystery** (See Inspector. . . ), 1940,
Whit, 432p, Alfred Andriola-a     9.00     27.00     54.00

**1478-Charlie Chan of the Honolulu Police, Inspector**, 1939, Whit,
432p, Andriola-a     9.00     27.00     54.00

**Charlie McCarthy** (See Story of . . . )

**734-Chester Gump at Silver Creek Ranch**, 1933, Whit, 320p, Sidney
Smith-a     10.00     30.00     60.00

|  | Good | Fine | N-Mint |
|---|---|---|---|

**nn-Chester Gump at Silver Creek Ranch**, 1933, Whit, 204p, Cocomalt premium, soft-c, Sidney Smith-a
| | 10.00 | 30.00 | 60.00 |

**nn-Chester Gump at Silver Creek Ranch**, 1933, Whit, 52p, 4″ × 5½″, premium-no ads, soft-c, Sidney Smith-a
| | 13.00 | 40.00 | 80.00 |

**766-Chester Gump Finds the Hidden Treasure**, 1934, Whit, 320p, Sidney Smith-a
| | 10.00 | 30.00 | 60.00 |

**nn-Chester Gump Finds the Hidden Treasure**, 1934, Whit, 52p, 3½″ × 5¾″, premium-no ads, soft-c, Sidney Smith-a
| | 13.00 | 40.00 | 80.00 |

**nn-Chester Gump Finds the Hidden Treasure**, 1934, Whit, 52p, 4″ × 5½″, premium-no ads, Sidney Smith-a
| | 13.00 | 40.00 | 80.00 |

**1146-Chester Gump in the City of Gold**, 1935, Whit, 432p, Sidney Smith-a
| | 10.00 | 30.00 | 60.00 |

**nn-Chester Gump in the City of Gold**, 1935, Whit, 436p, premium-no ads, 3-color, soft-c, Sidney Smith-a
| | 15.00 | 45.00 | 90.00 |

**1402-Chester Gump in the Pole to Pole Flight**, 1937, Whit, 432p
| | 8.50 | 25.00 | 50.00 |

**5-Chester Gump and His Friends**, 1934, Whit, 132p, 3½″ × 3½″, soft-c, Tarzan Ice Cream cup lid premium
| | 15.00 | 45.00 | 90.00 |

**nn-Chester Gump at the North Pole**, 1938, Whit, 68p, soft-c, 3½″ × 3½″, Pan-Am giveaway
| | 9.00 | 27.00 | 54.00 |

**nn-Chicken Greedy**, nd (1930s), np (Whit), 36p, 3″ × 2½″, Penny Book
| | 1.50 | 4.50 | 9.00 |

**nn-Chicken Licken**, nd (1930s), np (Whit), 36p, 3″ × 2½″, Penny Book
| | 1.50 | 4.50 | 9.00 |

**1101-Chief of the Rangers**, 1935, Sal, hard-c, Tom Mix photo-c, movie scenes
| | 12.00 | 35.00 | 70.00 |

**1581-Chief of the Rangers**, 1935, Sal, soft-c, Tom Mix photo-c, movie scenes
| | 12.00 | 35.00 | 70.00 |

**Child's Garden of Verses** (See Wee Little Books)

*Chip Collins' Adventures on Bat Island #L14,*
*© King Features Syndicate, 1935*

|  | Good | Fine | N-Mint |
|---|---|---|---|
| **L14-Chip Collins' Adventures on Bat Island**, 1935, Lynn, 192p | | | |
|  | 8.50 | 25.00 | 50.00 |
| **2025-Chitty Chitty Bang Bang**, 1968, Whit, movie photos | | | |
|  | 2.50 | 7.50 | 15.00 |
| **Chubby Little Books**, 1935, Whit, 3″ × 2½″, 200p | | | |
| W803-Golden Hours Story Book, The | | | |
|  | 4.00 | 12.00 | 24.00 |
| W803-Story Hours Story Book, The | | | |
|  | 4.00 | 12.00 | 24.00 |
| W804-Gay Book of Little Stories, The | | | |
|  | 4.00 | 12.00 | 24.00 |
| W804-Glad Book of Little Stories, The | | | |
|  | 4.00 | 12.00 | 24.00 |
| W804-Joy Book of Little Stories, The | | | |
|  | 4.00 | 12.00 | 24.00 |
| W804-Sunny Book of Little Stories, The | | | |
|  | 4.00 | 12.00 | 24.00 |
| **1453-Chuck Malloy Railroad Detective on the Streamliner**, 1938, Whit, 300p | | | |
| Whit, 300p | 5.50 | 16.50 | 33.00 |

|  | Good | Fine | N-Mint |
|---|---|---|---|

Cinderella (See Walt Disney's . . . )

Clyde Beatty (See The Steel Arena)

1410-Clyde Beatty Daredevil Lion and Tiger Tamer, 1939, Whit, 300p
   7.00   21.00   42.00

1480-Coach Bernie Bierman's Brick Barton and the Winning Eleven, 1938, 300p
   5.50   16.50   33.00

1446-Convoy Patrol (A Thrilling U.S. Navy Story), 1942, Whit, 432p, flip pictures
   5.50   16.50   33.00

1127-Corley of the Wilderness Trail, 1937, Sal, hard-c
   6.00   18.00   36.00

1607-Corley of the Wilderness Trail, 1937, Sal, soft-c
   6.00   18.00   36.00

1-Count of Monte Cristo, 1934, EVW, 160p (Five Star Library), movie scenes, hard-c
   10.00   30.00   60.00

1457-Cowboy Lingo Boys' Book of Western Facts, 1938, Whit, 300p, Fred Harman-a
   6.00   18.00   36.00

1171-Cowboy Malloy, 1940, Sal, 400p
   5.00   15.00   30.00

1106-Cowboy Millionaire, 1935, Sal, movie scenes with George O'Brien, photo-c, hard-c
   10.00   30.00   60.00

1586-Cowboy Millionaire, 1935, Sal, movie scenes with George O'Brien, photo-c, soft-c
   10.00   30.00   60.00

724-Cowboy Stories, 1933, Whit, 300p, Hal Arbo-a
   9.00   27.00   54.00

nn-Cowboy Stories, 1933, Whit, 52p, soft-c, premium-no ads, 4" × 5½", Hal Arbo-a
   10.00   30.00   60.00

1161-Crimson Cloak, The, 1939, Sal, 400p
   5.00   15.00   30.00

L19-Curley Harper at Lakespur, 1935, Lynn, 192p
   6.00   18.00   36.00

5785-2-Daffy Duck in Twice the Trouble, 1980, Whit, 260p, 79 cents, soft-c
   .50   1.50   3.00

2018-(#18)-Daktari-Night of Terror, 1968, Whit, 260p, 39 cents, hard-c, color illos
   2.50   7.50   15.00

1010-Dan Dunn and the Gangsters' Frame-Up, 1937, Whit, 7¼" × 5½", 64p, Nickle Book
   7.00   21.00   42.00

1116-Dan Dunn "Crime Never Pays," 1934, Whit, 320p, by Norman Marsh
   8.50   25.00   50.00

|  | Good | Fine | N-Mint |
|---|---|---|---|

**1125-Dan Dunn on the Trail of the Counterfeiters**, 1936, Whit, 432p,
   by Norman Marsh       8.50    25.00    50.00

**1171-Dan Dunn and the Crime Master**, 1937, Whit, 432p, by Norman
   Marsh       8.50    25.00    50.00

**1417-Dan Dunn and the Underworld Gorillas**, 1941, Whit, All Pictures Comics, flip pictures, by Norman Marsh
      8.50    25.00    50.00

**1454-Dan Dunn on the Trail of Wu Fang**, 1938, Whit, 432p, by Norman Marsh       10.00    30.00    60.00

**1481-Dan Dunn and the Border Smugglers**, 1938, Whit, 432p, by
   Norman Marsh       8.50    25.00    50.00

*Dan Dunn and the Dope Ring #1492,*
*© Publishers' Syndicate, Inc., 1940*

**1492-Dan Dunn and the Dope Ring**, 1940, Whit, 432p, by Norman
   Marsh       8.50    25.00    50.00

**nn-Dan Dunn and the Bank Hold-Up**, 1938, Whit, 36p, 2½″ × 3½″,
   Penny Book       4.50    14.00    28.00

|  | Good | Fine | N-Mint |
|---|---|---|---|
| **nn-Dan Dunn and the Zeppelin of Doom**, 1938, Dell, 196p, Fast-Action Story, soft-c | 17.00 | 50.00 | 100.00 |
| **nn-Dan Dunn Meets Chang Loo**, 1938, Whit, 66p, Pan-Am premium, by Norman Marsh | 7.00 | 21.00 | 42.00 |
| **nn-Dan Dunn Plays a Lone Hand**, 1938, Whit, 36p, 2½″ × 3½″, Penny Book | 4.50 | 14.00 | 28.00 |
| **6-Dan Dunn and the Counterfeiter Ring**, 1938, Whit, 132p, 3¾″ × 3½″, Buddy book | 15.00 | 45.00 | 90.00 |
| **9-Dan Dunn's Mysterious Ruse**, 1936, Whit, 132p, soft-c, 3½″ × 3½″, Tarzan Ice Cream cup lid premium | 15.00 | 45.00 | 90.00 |
| **1177-Danger Trail North**, 1940, Sal, 400p | 5.00 | 15.00 | 30.00 |
| **1151-Danger Trails in Africa**, 1935, Whit, 432p | 6.00 | 18.00 | 42.00 |
| **nn-Daniel Boone**, 1934, World, High Lights of History Series, hard-c, All in Pictures | 5.50 | 16.50 | 33.00 |
| **1160-Dan of the Lazy L**, 1939, Sal, 400p | 5.00 | 15.00 | 30.00 |
| **1148-David Copperfield**, 1934, Whit, hard-c, 160p, photo-c, movie scenes (W. C. Fields) | 10.00 | 30.00 | 60.00 |
| **nn-David Copperfield**, 1934, Whit, soft-c, 164p, movie scenes | 10.00 | 30.00 | 60.00 |
| **1151-Death by Short Wave**, 1938, Sal | 8.00 | 24.00 | 48.00 |
| **1156-Denny the Ace Detective**, 1938, Sal, 400p | 5.00 | 15.00 | 30.00 |
| **1431-Desert Eagle and the Hidden Fortress, The**, 1941, Whit, 432p, flip pictures | 6.00 | 18.00 | 36.00 |
| **1458-Desert Eagle Rides Again, The**, 1939, Whit, 300p | 6.00 | 18.00 | 36.00 |
| **1136-Desert Justice**, 1938, Sal, 400p | 5.00 | 15.00 | 30.00 |
| **1484-Detective Higgins of the Racket Squad**, 1938, Whit, 432p | 6.00 | 18.00 | 36.00 |
| **1124-Dickie Moore in the Little Red School House**, 1936, Whit, 240p, photo-c, movie scenes (Chesterfield Motion Picts. Corp) | 8.50 | 25.00 | 50.00 |
| **W-707-Dick Tracy the Detective, The Adventures of**, 1933, Whit, 320p (The 1st Big Little Book), by Chester Gould | 50.00 | 150.00 | 300.00 |

|  | Good | Fine | N-Mint |
|---|---|---|---|

**nn-Dick Tracy Detective, The Adventures of**, 1933, Whit, 52p, 4″ × 5½″, premium-no ads, soft-c, by Chester Gould

33.00     100.00     200.00

*Dick Tracy and Dick Tracy, Jr. #710,*
*© Chester Gould, 1933*

**710-Dick Tracy and Dick Tracy, Jr.** (The Advs. of . . . ), 1933, Whit, 320p, by Gould          30.00     90.00     180.00

**nn-Dick Tracy and Dick Tracy, Jr.** (The Advs. of . . . ), 1933, Whit, 52p, premium-no ads, soft-c, 4″ × 5½″, by Chester Gould
30.00     90.00     180.00

**nn-Dick Tracy the Detective and Dick Tracy, Jr.**, 1933, Whit, 52p, premium-no ads, 3½″ × 5¾″, soft-c, by Chester Gould
30.00     90.00     180.00

**723-Dick Tracy Out West**, 1933, Whit, 300p by Chester Gould
25.00     75.00     150.00

**749-Dick Tracy from Colorado to Nova Scotia**, 1933, Whit, 320p, by Chester Gould          18.00     55.00     110.00

|  | Good | Fine | N-Mint |
|---|---|---|---|

**nn-Dick Tracy from Colorado to Nova Scotia**, 1933, Whit, 204p, premium-no ads, soft-c, by Chester Gould

|  | 18.00 | 55.00 | 110.00 |
|---|---|---|---|

**1105-Dick Tracy and the Stolen Bonds**, 1934, Whit, 320p, by Chester Gould

|  | 16.00 | 48.00 | 96.00 |
|---|---|---|---|

**1112-Dick Tracy and the Racketeer Gang**, 1936, Whit, 432p, by Chester Gould

|  | 12.50 | 37.50 | 75.00 |
|---|---|---|---|

**1137-Dick Tracy Solves the Penfield Mystery**, 1934, Whit, 320p, by Chester Gould

|  | 15.00 | 45.00 | 90.00 |
|---|---|---|---|

**nn-Dick Tracy Solves the Penfield Mystery**, 1934, Whit, 324p, premium-no ads, 3-color, soft-c, by Chester Gould

|  | 20.00 | 60.00 | 120.00 |
|---|---|---|---|

**1163-Dick Tracy and the Boris Arson Gang**, 1935, Whit, 432p, by Chester Gould

|  | 12.00 | 36.00 | 72.00 |
|---|---|---|---|

**1170-Dick Tracy on the Trail of Larceny Lu**, 1935, Whit, 432p, by Chester Gould

|  | 12.00 | 36.00 | 72.00 |
|---|---|---|---|

**1185-Dick Tracy in Chains of Crime**, 1936, Whit, 432p, by Chester Gould

|  | 12.00 | 36.00 | 72.00 |
|---|---|---|---|

**1412-Dick Tracy and Yogee Yamma**, 1946, Whit, 352p, by Chester Gould

|  | 10.00 | 30.00 | 60.00 |
|---|---|---|---|

**1420-Dick Tracy and the Hotel Murders**, 1937, Whit, 432p, by Chester Gould

|  | 12.00 | 36.00 | 72.00 |
|---|---|---|---|

**1434-Dick Tracy and the Phantom Ship**, 1940, Whit, 432p, by Chester Gould

|  | 12.00 | 36.00 | 72.00 |
|---|---|---|---|

**1436-Dick Tracy and the Mad Killer**, 1947, Whit, 288p, by Chester Gould

|  | 10.00 | 30.00 | 60.00 |
|---|---|---|---|

**1439-Dick Tracy and His G-Men**, 1941, Whit, 432p, Flip pictures, by Chester Gould

|  | 12.00 | 36.00 | 72.00 |
|---|---|---|---|

**1445-Dick Tracy and the Bicycle Gang**, 1948, Whit, 288p, by Chester Gould

|  | 10.00 | 30.00 | 60.00 |
|---|---|---|---|

**1446-Detective Dick Tracy and the Spider Gang**, 1937, Whit, 240p, movie scenes (Republic Motion Pictures)

|  | 15.00 | 45.00 | 90.00 |
|---|---|---|---|

**1449-Dick Tracy Special F.B.I. Operative**, 1943, Whit, 432p, by Chester Gould

|  | 12.00 | 36.00 | 72.00 |
|---|---|---|---|

**1454-Dick Tracy on the High Seas**, 1939, Whit, 432p, by Chester Gould

|  | 12.00 | 36.00 | 72.00 |
|---|---|---|---|

|  | Good | Fine | N-Mint |
|---|---|---|---|

**1460-Dick Tracy and the Tiger Lilly Gang**, 1949, Whit, 288p, by Chester Gould
                          10.00     30.00     60.00

**1478-Dick Tracy on Voodoo Island**, 1944, Whit, 352p, by Chester Gould
                          10.00     30.00     60.00

**1479-Detective Dick Tracy VS. Crooks in Disguise**, 1939, Whit, 432p, flip pictures, by Chester Gould     12.00     36.00     72.00

**1482-Dick Tracy and the Wreath Kidnaping Case**, 1945, Whit, 352p
                          10.00     30.00     60.00

**1488-Dick Tracy the Super-Detective**, 1939, Whit, 432p, by Chester Gould     12.00     36.00     72.00

**1491-Dick Tracy the Man with No Face**, 1938, Whit, 432p
                          12.00     36.00     72.00

**1495-Dick Tracy Returns**, 1939, Whit, 432p, based on Republic Motion Picture serial, Chester Gould-a
                          12.00     36.00     72.00

**2001-(#1)-Dick Tracy-Encounters Facey**, 1967, Whit, 260p, 39 cents, hard-c, color illos     2.50     7.50     15.00

**4055-Dick Tracy, The Adventures of**, 1934, Whit, 7″ × 9½″, 320p, Big Big Book, by Chester Gould     53.00     160.00     320.00

**4071-Dick Tracy and the Mystery of the Purple Cross**, 1938, 7″ × 9½″, 320p, Big Big Book, by Chester Gould
                          80.00     240.00     480.00

**nn-Dick Tracy and the Invisible Man**, 1939, Whit, 3¾″ × 3¾″, 132p, stapled, soft-c, Quaker Oats premium; NBC radio play script, Chester Gould-a     17.00     50.00     100.00

**Vol. 2-Dick Tracy's Ghost Ship**, 1939, Whit, 3½″ × 3½″, 132p, soft-c, stapled, Quaker Oats premium; NBC radio play script episode from actual radio show; Gould-a     17.00     50.00     100.00

**3-Dick Tracy Meets a New Gang**, 1934, Whit, 3½″ × 3½″, 132p, soft-c, Tarzan Ice Cream cup lid premium
                          30.00     90.00     180.00

**11-Dick Tracy in Smashing the Famon Racket**, 1938, Whit, 3¾″ × 3½″, Buddy Book ice cream premium, by Chester Gould
                          30.00     90.00     180.00

**nn-Dick Tracy Gets His Man**, 1938, Whit, 36p, 2½″ × 3½″, Penny Book     5.35     16.00     32.00

**nn-Dick Tracy the Detective**, 1938, Whit, 36p, 2½″ × 3½″, Penny Book     5.35     16.00     32.00

|  | Good | Fine | N-Mint |
|---|---|---|---|

**9-Dick Tracy and the Frozen Bullet Murders**, 1941, Dell, 196p, Fast-Action Story, soft-c, by Gould    23.00    70.00    140.00

**6833-Dick Tracy Detective and Federal Agent**, 1936, Dell, 244p, Cartoon Story Books, hard-c, by Chester Gould
25.00    75.00    150.00

**nn-Dick Tracy Detective and Federal Agent**, 1936, Dell, 244p, Fast-Action Story, soft-c, by Gould    23.00    70.00    140.00

**nn-Dick Tracy and the Blackmailers**, 1939, Dell, 196p, Fast-Action Story, soft-c, by Gould    23.00    70.00    140.00

**nn-Dick Tracy and the Chain of Evidence, Detective**, 1938, Whit, 196p, Fast-Action Story, soft-c, by Chester Gould
23.00    70.00    140.00

**nn-Dick Tracy and the Crook without a Face**, 1938, Whit, 68p, 3¾" × 3¾", Pan-Am giveaway, Gould c/a
14.00    42.00    84.00

**nn-Dick Tracy and the Maroon Mask Gang**, 1938, Dell, 196p, Fast-Action Story, soft-c, by Gould    23.00    70.00    140.00

**nn-Dick Tracy Cross-Country Race**, 1934, Whit, 8p, 2½" × 3", Big Thrill chewing gum premium    7.00    21.00    42.00

**nn-Dick Whittington and His Cat**, nd (1930s), np (Whit), 36p, Penny Book    1.50    4.50    9.00

**Dinglehoofer und His Dog Adolph** (See Top-Line Comics)

**Dinky** (See Jackie Cooper in . . . )

**1464-Dirigible ZR90 and the Disappearing Zeppelin** (Captain Robb of . . . ), 1941, Whit, 300p, Al Lewin-a
13.00    40.00    80.00

**1167-Dixie Dugan Among the Cowboys**, 1939, Sal, 400p
6.00    18.00    36.00

**1188-Dixie Dugan and Cuddles**, 1940, Sal, 400p, by Striebel & McEvoy    6.00    18.00    36.00

**Doctor Doom** (See Foreign Spies . . . & International Spy . . )

**Dog of Flanders, A** (See Frankie Thomas in . . . )

**1114-Dog Stars of Hollywood**, 1936, Sal, photo-c, photo-illos
10.00    30.00    60.00

**1594-Dog Stars of Hollywood**, 1936, Sal, photo-c, soft-c, photo-illos
10.00    30.00    60.00

**Donald Duck** (See Silly Symphony . . . & Walt Disney's . . . )

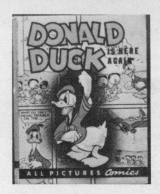

*Donald Duck Is Here Again! #1484,*
*© The Disney Company, 1944*

|  | Good | Fine | N-Mint |
|---|---|---|---|
| **1404-Donald Duck (Says Such a Life)** (Disney), 1939, Whit, 432p, Taliaferro-a | 12.00 | 35.00 | 70.00 |
| **1411-Donald Duck and Ghost Morgan's Treasure** (Disney), 1946, Whit, All Pictures Comics, Barks-a; R/4-Color 9 | 14.00 | 42.00 | 84.00 |
| **1422-Donald Duck Sees Stars** (Disney), 1941, Whit, 432p, flip pictures, Taliaferro-a | 12.00 | 35.00 | 70.00 |
| **1424-Donald Duck Says Such Luck** (Disney), 1941, Whit, 432p, flip pictures, Taliaferro-a | 12.00 | 35.00 | 70.00 |
| **1430-Donald Duck Headed for Trouble** (Disney), 1942, Whit, 432p, flip pictures, Taliaferro-a | 12.00 | 35.00 | 70.00 |
| **1432-Donald Duck and the Green Serpent** (Disney), 1947, Whit, All Pictures Comics, Barks-a; R/4-Color 108 | 14.00 | 42.00 | 84.00 |

|  | Good | Fine | N-Mint |
|---|---|---|---|
| **1434-Donald Duck Forgets to Duck** (Disney), 1939, Whit, 432p, Taliaferro-a | 12.00 | 35.00 | 70.00 |
| **1438-Donald Duck Off the Beam** (Disney), 1943, Whit, 352p, flip pictures, Taliaferro-a | 12.00 | 35.00 | 70.00 |
| **1438-Donald Duck Off the Beam** (Disney), 1943, Whit, 432p, flip pictures, Taliaferro-a | 12.00 | 35.00 | 70.00 |
| **1449-Donald Duck Lays Down the Law**, 1948, Whit, 288p, Barks-a | 14.00 | 42.00 | 84.00 |
| **1457-Donald Duck in Volcano Valley** (Disney), 1949, Whit, 288p, Barks-a | 14.00 | 42.00 | 84.00 |
| **1462-Donald Duck Gets Fed Up** (Disney), 1940, Whit, 432p, Taliaferro-a | 12.00 | 35.00 | 70.00 |
| **1478-Donald Duck-Hunting for Trouble** (Disney), 1938, Whit, 432p, Taliaferro-a | 12.00 | 35.00 | 70.00 |
| **1484-Donald Duck Is Here Again!**, 1944, Whit, All Pictures Comics, Taliaferro-a | 12.00 | 35.00 | 70.00 |
| **1486-Donald Duck Up in the Air** (Disney), 1945, Whit, 352p, Barks-a | 14.00 | 42.00 | 84.00 |
| **705-10-Donald Duck and the Mystery of the Double X** (Disney), 1949, Whit, Barks-a | 7.50 | 22.50 | 45.00 |
| **2009-(#9)-Donald Duck-The Fabulous Diamond Fountain** (Walt Disney), 1967, Whit, 260p, 39 cents, hard-c, color illos | 1.70 | 5.00 | 10.00 |
| **nn-Donald Duck and the Ducklings**, 1938, Whit, 194p, Fast-Action Story, soft-c, Taliaferro-a | 20.00 | 60.00 | 120.00 |
| **nn-Donald Duck Out of Luck** (Disney), 1940, Dell, 196p, Fast-Action Story, has 4-Color No. 4 on back-c, Taliaferro-a | 20.00 | 60.00 | 120.00 |
| **8-Donald Duck Takes It on the Chin** (Disney), 1941, Dell, 196p, Fast-Action Story, soft-c, Taliaferro-a | 20.00 | 60.00 | 120.00 |
| **5760-2-Donald Duck in Volcano Valley** (Disney), 1973, Whit, 79 cents, flip-it book | .50 | 1.50 | 3.00 |
| **L13-Donnie and the Pirates**, 1935, Lynn, 192p | 8.00 | 24.00 | 48.00 |
| **1438-Don O'Dare Finds War**, 1940, Whit, 432p | 5.50 | 16.50 | 33.00 |

|  | Good | Fine | N-Mint |
|---|---|---|---|
| **1107-Don Winslow, U.S.N.**, 1935, Whit, 432p | | | |
| | 10.00 | 30.00 | 60.00 |
| **nn-Don Winslow, U.S.N.**, 1935, Whit, 436p, premium-no ads, 3-color, soft-c | 13.00 | 40.00 | 80.00 |
| **1408-Don Winslow and the Giant Girl Spy**, 1946, Whit, 352p | | | |
| | 7.50 | 22.50 | 45.00 |
| **1418-Don Winslow Navy Intelligence Ace**, 1942, Whit, 432p, flip pictures | 10.00 | 30.00 | 60.00 |

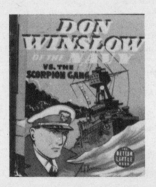

*Don Winslow of the Navy Vs. the Scorpion Gang #1419,*
*© Frank V. Martinek, 1938*

| | Good | Fine | N-Mint |
|---|---|---|---|
| **1419-Don Winslow of the Navy Vs. the Scorpion Gang**, 1938, Whit, 432p | 10.00 | 30.00 | 60.00 |
| **1453-Don Winslow of the Navy and the Secret Enemy Base**, 1943, Whit, 352p | 10.00 | 30.00 | 60.00 |

|                                                          | Good  | Fine  | N-Mint |
|----------------------------------------------------------|-------|-------|--------|
| **1489-Don Winslow of the Navy and the Great War Plot**, 1940, Whit, | | | |
| 432p                                                     | 10.00 | 30.00 | 60.00  |
| **nn-Don Winslow U.S. Navy and the Missing Admiral**, 1938, Whit, | | | |
| 36p, 2½″ × 3½″, Penny Book                                | 4.50  | 14.00 | 28.00  |
| **1137-Doomed to Die,** 1938, Sal, 400p                  | 5.00  | 15.00 | 30.00  |
| **1140-Down Cartridge Creek**, 1938, Sal, 400p           |       |       |        |
|                                                          | 5.00  | 15.00 | 30.00  |
| **1416-Draftie of the U.S. Army**, 1943, Whit, All Pictures Comics | | | |
|                                                          | 6.00  | 18.00 | 36.00  |
| **1100B-Dreams** (Your dreams & what they mean), 1938, Whit, 36p, | | | |
| 2½″ × 3½″, Penny Book                                     | 2.00  | 6.00  | 12.00  |
| **L24-Dumb Dora and Bing Brown**, 1936, Lynn             |       |       |        |
|                                                          | 10.00 | 30.00 | 60.00  |
| **1400-Dumbo of the Circus-Only His Ears Grew!** (Disney), 1941, | | | |
| Whit, 432p, based on Disney movie                        |       |       |        |
|                                                          | 13.00 | 40.00 | 80.00  |
| **10-Dumbo the Flying Elephant** (Disney), 1944, Dell, 194p, Fast- | | | |
| Action Story, soft-c                                     | 17.00 | 50.00 | 100.00 |
| **nn-East O' the Sun and West O' the Moon**, nd (1930s), np (Whit), | | | |
| 36p, 3″ × 2½″, Penny Book                                 | 1.50  | 4.50  | 9.00   |
| **774-Eddie Cantor in an Hour with You**, 1934, Whit, 154p, 4¾″ × 5¼″, | | | |
| photo-c, movie scenes                                    | 11.00 | 32.50 | 65.00  |
| **nn-Eddie Cantor in Laughland**, 1934, Gold, 132p, soft, photo-c, | | | |
| Vallely-a                                                | 10.00 | 30.00 | 60.00  |
| **1106-Ella Cinders and the Mysterious House**, 1934, Whit, 432p | | | |
|                                                          | 9.00  | 27.00 | 54.00  |
| **nn-Ella Cinders and the Mysterious House**, 1934, Whit, 52p, | | | |
| premium-no ads, soft-c, 3½″ × 5¾″                         | 12.00 | 35.00 | 70.00  |
| **nn-Ella Cinders**, 1935, Whit, 148p, 3¾″ × 4″, Tarzan Ice Cream cup | | | |
| lid premium                                              | 14.00 | 42.00 | 84.00  |
| **nn-Ella Cinders Plays Duchess**, 1938, Whit, 68p, 3¾″ × 3½″, Pan-Am | | | |
| Oil premium                                              | 10.00 | 30.00 | 60.00  |
| **nn-Ella Cinders Solves a Mystery**, 1938, Whit, 68p, Pan-Am Oil pre- | | | |
| mium, soft-c                                             | 10.00 | 30.00 | 60.00  |
| **11-Ella Cinders' Exciting Experience**, 1934, Whit, 3½″ × 3½″, 132p, | | | |
| Tarzan Ice Cream cup lid giveaway                        |       |       |        |
|                                                          | 14.00 | 42.00 | 84.00  |

*Ellery Queen, the Adventure of the Last Man Club #1406,*
*© Ellery Queen, 1940*

|  | Good | Fine | N-Mint |
|---|---|---|---|
| **1406-Ellery Queen the Adventure of the Last Man Club**, 1940, Whit, 432p | 8.50 | 25.00 | 50.00 |
| **1472-Ellery Queen the Master Detective**, 1942, Whit, 432p, flip pictures | 8.50 | 25.00 | 50.00 |
| **1081-Elmer and His Dog Spot**, 1935, Sal, hard-c | 6.00 | 18.00 | 36.00 |
| **1311-Elmer and His Dog Spot**, 1935, Sal, soft-c | 6.00 | 18.00 | 36.00 |
| **722-Erik Noble and the Forty-Niners**, 1934, Whit, 384p | 7.00 | 21.00 | 42.00 |

|  | Good | Fine | N-Mint |
|---|---|---|---|
| **nn-Erik Noble and the Forty-Niners**, 1934, Whit, 386p, 3-color, soft-c | 12.00 | 35.00 | 70.00 |
| **1058-Farmyard Symphony, The** (Disney), 1939, 5″ × 5½″, 68p, hard-c | 7.00 | 21.00 | 42.00 |
| **1129-Felix the Cat**, 1936, Whit, 432p, Messmer-a | 17.00 | 50.00 | 100.00 |
| **1439-Felix the Cat**, 1943, Whit, All Pictures Comics, Messmer-a | 15.00 | 45.00 | 90.00 |
| **1465-Felix the Cat**, 1945, Whit, All Pictures Comics, Messmer-a | 13.00 | 40.00 | 80.00 |
| **nn-Felix** (Flip book), 1967, World Retrospective of Animation Cinema, 188p, 2½″ × 4″, by Otto Messmer | 2.50 | 7.50 | 15.00 |
| **nn-Fighting Cowboy of Nugget Gulch, The**, 1939, Whit, 36p, 2½″ × 3½″, Penny Book | 4.00 | 12.00 | 24.00 |
| **1401-Fighting Heroes Battle for Freedom**, 1943, Whit, All Pictures Comics, from "Heroes of Democracy" strip, by Stookie Allen | 5.50 | 16.50 | 33.00 |
| **6-Fighting President, The**, 1934, EVW (Five Star Library), 160p, photo-c, photo ill., F. D. Roosevelt | 8.00 | 24.00 | 48.00 |
| **nn-Fire Chief Ed Wynn and "His Old Fire Horse,"** 1934, Gold, 132p, H. Vallely-a, photo, soft-c | 8.00 | 24.00 | 48.00 |
| **1464-Flame Boy and the Indians' Secret**, 1938, Whit, 300p, Sekakuku-a (Hopi Indian) | 5.50 | 16.50 | 33.00 |
| **22-Flaming Guns** 1935, EVW, with Tom Mix, movie scenes | 12.00 | 35.00 | 70.00 |
| **1110-Flash Gordon on the Planet Mongo**, 1934, Whit, 320p, by Alex Raymond | 21.00 | 62.50 | 125.00 |
| **1166-Flash Gordon and the Monsters of Mongo**, 1935, Whit, 432p, by Alex Raymond | 17.00 | 50.00 | 100.00 |
| **nn-Flash Gordon and the Monsters of Mongo**, 1935, Whit, 436p, premium-no ads, 3-color, soft-c, by Alex Raymond | 27.00 | 80.00 | 160.00 |

*Flash Gordon and the Tournaments of Mongo #1171,*
*© King Features Syndicate, 1935*

|  | Good | Fine | N-Mint |
|---|---|---|---|
| **1171-Flash Gordon and the Tournaments of Mongo**, 1935, Whit, 432p, by Alex Raymond | 17.00 | 50.00 | 100.00 |
| **1190-Flash Gordon and the Witch Queen of Mongo**, 1936, Whit, 432p, by Alex Raymond | 15.00 | 45.00 | 90.00 |
| **1407-Flash Gordon in the Water World of Mongo**, 1937, Whit, 432p, by Alex Raymond | 15.00 | 45.00 | 90.00 |
| **1423-Flash Gordon and the Perils of Mongo**, 1940, Whit, 432p, by Alex Raymond | 14.00 | 42.00 | 84.00 |
| **1424-Flash Gordon in the Jungles of Mongo**, 1947, Whit, 352p, by Alex Raymond | 12.50 | 37.50 | 75.00 |
| **1443-Flash Gordon in the Ice World of Mongo**, 1942, Whit, 432p, flip pictures, by Alex Raymond | 14.00 | 42.00 | 84.00 |
| **1447-Flash Gordon and the Fiery Desert of Mongo**, 1948, Whit, 288p, Raymond-a | 12.50 | 37.50 | 75.00 |

|  | Good | Fine | N-Mint |
|---|---|---|---|
| **1469-Flash Gordon and the Power Men of Mongo**, 1943, Whit, 352p, by Alex Raymond | 14.00 | 42.00 | 84.00 |
| **1479-Flash Gordon and the Red Sword Invaders**, 1945, Whit, 352p, by Alex Raymond | 12.50 | 37.50 | 75.00 |
| **1484-Flash Gordon and the Tyrant of Mongo**, 1941, Whit, 432p, flip pictures, by Alex Raymond | 14.00 | 42.00 | 84.00 |
| **1492-Flash Gordon in the Forest Kingdom of Mongo**, 1938, Whit, 432p, by Alex Raymond | 15.00 | 45.00 | 90.00 |
| **12-Flash Gordon and the Ape Men of Mor**, 1942, Dell, 196p, Fast-Action Story, by Raymond | 25.00 | 75.00 | 150.00 |
| **6833-Flash Gordon Vs. the Emperor of Mongo**, 1936, Dell, 244p, Cartoon Story Books, hard-c, Alex Raymond c/a | 28.00 | 85.00 | 170.00 |
| **nn-Flash Gordon Vs. the Emperor of Mongo**, 1936, Dell, 244p, Fast-Action Story, soft-c, Alex Raymond c/a | 25.00 | 75.00 | 150.00 |
| **1467-Flint Roper and the Six-Gun Showdown**, 1941, Whit, 300p | 5.50 | 16.50 | 33.00 |
| **2014-(#14)-Flintstones-The Case of the Many Missing Things**, 1968, Whit, 260p, 39 cents, hard-c, color illos | 2.00 | 6.00 | 12.00 |
| **2003-(#3)-Flipper-Killer Whale Trouble**, 1967, Whit, 260p, hard-c, 39 cents, color illos | 1.70 | 5.00 | 10.00 |
| **1108-Flying the Sky Clipper with Winsie Atkins**, 1936, Whit, 432p | 5.50 | 16.50 | 33.00 |
| **1460-Foreign Spies Doctor Doom and the Ghost Submarine**, 1939, Whit, 432p, Al McWilliams-a | 7.50 | 22.50 | 45.00 |
| **1100B-Fortune Teller**, 1938, Whit, 36p, 2½″ × 3½″ Penny Book | 2.00 | 6.00 | 12.00 |
| **1175-Frank Buck Presents Ted Towers Animal Master**, 1935, Whit, 432p | 6.00 | 18.00 | 36.00 |
| **2015-(#15)-Frankenstein, Jr.-The Menace of the Heartless Monster**, 1968, Whit, 260p, 39 cents, hard-c, color illos | 2.00 | 6.00 | 12.00 |
| **16-Frankie Thomas in a Dog of Flanders**, 1935, EVW, movie scenes | 10.00 | 30.00 | 60.00 |
| **1121-Frank Merriwell at Yale**, 1935, 432p | 6.00 | 18.00 | 36.00 |

|  | Good | Fine | N-Mint |
|---|---|---|---|

**Freckles and His Friends in the North Woods** (See Top-Line Comics)

**nn-Freckles and His Friends Stage a Play**, 1938, Whit, 36p, 2½″ × 3½″, Penny Book            4.50    14.00    28.00

**1164-Freckles and the Lost Diamond Mine**, 1937, Whit, 432p, Merrill Blosser-a            7.50    22.50    45.00

**nn-Freckles and the Mystery Ship**, 1935, Whit, 66p, Pan-Am premium            8.50    25.00    50.00

**1100B-Fun, Puzzles, Riddles**, 1938, Whit, 36p, 2½″ × 3½″, Penny Book            2.00    6.00    12.00

**1433-Gang Busters Step In**, 1939, Whit, 432p, Henry E. Vallely-a            7.00    21.00    42.00

**1437-Gang Busters Smash Through**, 1942, Whit, 432p            7.00    21.00    42.00

*Gang Busters in Action! #1451,*
*© Whitman Publishing Co., 1938*

|  | Good | Fine | N-Mint |
|---|---|---|---|
| **1451-Gang Busters in Action!**, 1938, Whit, 432p | 7.00 | 21.00 | 42.00 |
| **nn-Gangbusters and Guns of the Law**, 1940, Dell, 4″ × 5″, 194p, Fast-Action Story, soft-c | 15.00 | 45.00 | 90.00 |
| **nn-Gang Busters and the Radio Clues**, 1938, Whit, 36p, 2½″ × 3½″, Penny Book | 4.00 | 12.00 | 24.00 |
| **1409-Gene Autry and Raiders of the Range**, 1946, Whit, 352p | 8.00 | 24.00 | 48.00 |
| **1425-Gene Autry and the Mystery of Paint Rock Canyon**, 1947, Whit, 288p | 8.00 | 24.00 | 48.00 |
| **1428-Gene Autry Special Ranger**, 1941, Whit, 432p, Erwin Hess-a | 9.00 | 27.00 | 54.00 |
| **1430-Gene Autry and the Land Grab Mystery**, 1948, Whit, 288p | 7.00 | 21.00 | 42.00 |
| **1433-Gene Autry in Public Cowboy No. 1**, 1938, Whit, 240p, photo-c, movie scenes (1st) | 12.50 | 37.50 | 75.00 |
| **1434-Gene Autry and the Gun-Smoke Reckoning**, 1943, Whit, 352p | 9.00 | 27.00 | 54.00 |
| **1456-Gene Autry in Special Ranger Rule**, 1945, Whit, 352p, Henry E. Vallely-a | 9.00 | 27.00 | 54.00 |
| **1461-Gene Autry and the Red Bandit's Ghost**, 1949, Whit, 288p | 7.00 | 21.00 | 42.00 |
| **1483-Gene Autry in Law of the Range**, 1939, Whit, 432p | 9.00 | 27.00 | 54.00 |
| **1493-Gene Autry and the Hawk of the Hills**, 1942, Whit, 428p, flip pictures, Vallely-a | 9.00 | 27.00 | 54.00 |
| **1494-Gene Autry Cowboy Detective**, 1940, Whit, 432p, Erwin Hess-a | 9.00 | 27.00 | 54.00 |
| **700-10-Gene Autry and the Bandits of Silver Tip**, 1949, Whit | 5.00 | 15.00 | 30.00 |
| **714-10-Gene Autry and the Range War**, 1950, Whit | 5.00 | 15.00 | 30.00 |
| **nn-Gene Autry in Gun Smoke**, 1938, Whit, 196p, Fast-Action Story, soft-c | 17.00 | 50.00 | 100.00 |
| **1176-Gentleman Joe Palooka**, 1940, Sal, 400p | 10.00 | 30.00 | 60.00 |
| **George O'Brien** (See The Cowboy Millionaire) | | | |
| **1101-George O'Brien and the Arizona Badman**, 1936?, Whit | 10.00 | 30.00 | 60.00 |

|  | Good | Fine | N-Mint |
|---|---|---|---|
| **1418-George O'Brien in Gun Law**, 1938, Whit, 240p, photo-c, movie scenes, RKO Radio Pictures | 10.00 | 30.00 | 60.00 |
| **1457-George O'Brien and the Hooded Riders**, 1940, Whit, 432p, Erwin Hess-a | 6.00 | 18.00 | 36.00 |
| **nn-George O'Brien and the Arizona Bad Man**, 1939, Whit, 36p, 2½" × 3½", Penny Book | 4.50 | 14.00 | 28.00 |
| **1462-Ghost Avenger**, 1943, Whit, 432p, flip pictures, Henry Vallely-a | 6.00 | 18.00 | 36.00 |
| **nn-Ghost Gun Gang Meet Their Match, The**, 1939, Whit, 36p, 2½" × 3½", Penny Book | 4.00 | 12.00 | 24.00 |
| **nn-Gingerbread Boy, The**, nd (1930s), np (Whit), 36p, Penny Book | 1.50 | 4.50 | 9.00 |
| **1173-G-Man in Action, A**, 1940, Sal, 400p, J. R. White-a | 5.00 | 15.00 | 30.00 |
| **1118-G-Man on the Crime Trail**, 1936, Whit, 432p | 7.00 | 21.00 | 42.00 |
| **1147-G-Man Vs. the Red X** , 1936, Whit, 432p | 7.00 | 21.00 | 42.00 |
| **1162-G-Man Allen**, 1939, Sal, 400p | 5.00 | 15.00 | 30.00 |
| **1173-G-Man in Action, A**, 1940, Sal, 400p | 5.00 | 15.00 | 30.00 |
| **1434-G-Man and the Radio Bank Robberies**, 1937, Whit, 432p | 7.00 | 21.00 | 42.00 |
| **1469-G-Man and the Gun Runners, The**, 1940, Whit, 432p | 7.00 | 21.00 | 42.00 |
| **1470-G-Man Vs. the Fifth Column**, 1941, Whit, 432p, flip pictures | 7.00 | 21.00 | 42.00 |
| **1493-G-Man Breaking the Gambling Ring**, 1938, Whit, 432p, James Gary-a | 7.00 | 21.00 | 42.00 |
| **4-G-Men Foil the Kidnappers**, 1936, Whit, 132p, 3½" × 3½", soft-c, Tarzan Ice Cream cup lid premium | 14.00 | 42.00 | 84.00 |
| **nn-G-Man on Lightning Island**, 1936, Dell, 244p, Fast-Action Story, soft-c, Henry E. Vallely-a | 12.00 | 35.00 | 70.00 |
| **6833-G-Man on Lightning Island**, 1936, Dell, 244p, Cartoon Story Book, hard-c, Henry E. Vallely-a | 12.00 | 35.00 | 70.00 |
| **1157-G-Men on the Trail**, 1938, Sal, 400p | 5.00 | 15.00 | 30.00 |
| **1168-G-Men on the Job**, 1935, Whit, 432p | 7.00 | 21.00 | 42.00 |
| **nn-G-Men on the Job Again**, 1938, Whit, 36p, 2½" × 3½", Penny Book | 4.00 | 12.00 | 24.00 |
| **nn-G-Men and the Missing Clues**, 1938, Whit, 36p, 2½" × 3½", Penny Book | 4.00 | 12.00 | 24.00 |

*G-Man on Lightning Island, nn,*
© *Whitman Publishing Co., 1936*

|  | Good | Fine | N-Mint |
|---|---|---|---|
| **1097-Go into Your Dance**, 1935, Sal, 160p, photo-c, movie scenes with Al Jolson & Ruby Keeler | 7.50 | 22.50 | 45.00 |
| **1577-Go into Your Dance**, 1935, Sal, 160p, photo-c, soft-c | 7.50 | 22.50 | 45.00 |
| **5751-Goofy in Giant Trouble** (Walt Disney's . . . ), 1968, Whit, 260p, 39 cents, soft-c, color illos | 1.70 | 5.00 | 10.00 |
| **5751-2-Goofy in Giant Trouble**, 1968 (1980-reprint of '67 version), Whit, 260p, 79 cents, soft-c, B&W | .50 | 1.50 | 3.00 |
| **8-Great Expectations**, 1934, EVW (Five Star Library), 160p, photo-c, movie scenes | 12.00 | 35.00 | 70.00 |
| **1453-Green Hornet Strikes!, The**, 1940, Whit, 432p, Robert Weisman-a | 20.00 | 60.00 | 120.00 |
| **1480-Green Hornet Cracks Down, The**, 1942, Whit, 432p, flip pictures, Henry Vallely-a | 18.00 | 55.00 | 110.00 |
| **1496-Green Hornet Returns, The**, 1941, Whit, 432p, flip pictures | 18.00 | 55.00 | 110.00 |

|  | Good | Fine | N-Mint |
|---|---|---|---|

**1172-Gulliver's Travels**, 1939, Sal, 320p, adapted from Paramount
    Pict. Cartoons                 12.00     35.00     70.00

**nn-Gumps in Radio Land, The** (Andy Gump and The Chest of
    Gold), 1937, Lehn & Fink Prod. Corp., 100p, 3¼″ × 5½″, Pebeco
    Tooth Paste giveaway, by Gus Edson
                              14.00     42.00     84.00

**nn-Gunmen of Rustlers' Gulch, The**, 1939, Whit, 36p, 2½″ × 3½″,
    Penny Book            4.00     12.00     24.00

**1426-Guns in the Roaring West**, 1937, Whit, 300p
                              5.50     16.50     33.00

**1647-Gunsmoke** (TV Series), 1958, Whit, 280p, 4½″ × 5¾″
                              4.50     13.50     27.00

**1101-Hairbreath Harry in Department QT**, 1935, Whit, 384p, by J. M.
    Alexander            7.50     22.50     45.00

**1413-Hal Hardy in the Lost Land of Giants**, 1938, Whit, 300p, "The
    World 1,000,000 Years Ago"     6.00     18.00     36.00

**1159-Hall of Fame of the Air**, 1936, Whit, 432p, by Capt. Eddie
    Rickenbacker          5.50     16.50     33.00

**nn-Hansel and Gretel, The Story of**, nd (1930s), no publ., 36p,
    Penny Book            1.50     4.50     9.00

**1145-Hap Lee's Selection of Movie Gags**, 1935, Whit, 160p, photos of
    stars                 8.50     25.00     50.00

**Happy Prince, The** (See Wee Little Books)

**1111-Hard Rock Harrigan-A Story of Boulder Dam**, 1935, Sal,
    photo-c, photo illus.     5.50     16.50     33.00

**1591-Hard Rock Harrigan-A Story of Boulder Dam**, 1935, Sal,
    photo-c, photo illus.     5.50     16.50     33.00

**1418-Harold Teen Swinging at the Sugar Bowl**, 1939, Whit, 432p, by
    Carl Ed            7.00     21.00     42.00

**1100B-Hobbies**, 1938, Whit, 36p, 2½″ × 3½″, Penny Book
                              2.00     6.00     12.00

**1125-Hockey Spare, The**, 1937, Sal, sports book
                              4.50     13.50     27.00

**1605-Hockey Spare, The**, 1937, Sal, soft-c
                              4.50     13.50     27.00

**728-Homeless Homer**, 1934, Whit, by Dee Dobbin, for young kids
                            2.00     6.00     12.00

*Harold Teen Swinging at the Sugar Bowl #1418,*
*© Carl Ed, 1939*

|  | Good | Fine | N-Mint |
|---|---|---|---|
| **17-Hoosier Schoolmaster, The**, 1935, EVW, movie scenes | | | |
| | 10.00 | 30.00 | 60.00 |
| **715-Houdini's Big Little Book of Magic**, 1927 (1933), Whit, 300p | | | |
| | 11.00 | 32.50 | 65.00 |
| **nn-Houdini's Big Little Book of Magic**, 1927 (1933), Whit, 196p, | | | |
| American Oil Co. premium, soft-c | 8.50 | 25.00 | 50.00 |
| **nn-Houdini's Big Little Book of Magic**, 1927 (1933), Whit, 204p, | | | |
| Cocomalt premium, soft-c | 8.50 | 25.00 | 50.00 |
| **Huckleberry Finn** (See The Adventures of . . . ) | | | |
| **1644-Hugh O'Brian TV's Wyatt Earp** (TV Series), 1958, Whit, 280p | | | |
| | 4.00 | 12.00 | 24.00 |
| **1424-Inspector Charlie Chan Villainy on the High Seas**, 1942, Whit, | | | |
| 432p, flip pictures | 9.00 | 27.00 | 54.00 |
| **1186-Inspector Wade of Scotland Yard**, 1940, Sal, 400p | | | |
| | 6.00 | 18.00 | 36.00 |
| **1448-Inspector Wade Solves the Mystery of the Red Aces**, 1937, | | | |
| Whit, 432p | 6.00 | 18.00 | 36.00 |
| **1148-International Spy Doctor Doom Faces Death at Dawn**, 1937, | | | |
| Whit, 432p, Arbo-a | 7.50 | 22.50 | 45.00 |

|  | Good | Fine | N-Mint |
|---|---|---|---|

**1155-In the Name of the Law**, 1937, Whit, 432p, Henry E. Vallely-a
    7.00    21.00    42.00

**2012-(#12)-Invaders, The-Alien Missile Threat** (TV Series), 1967, Whit, 260p, hard-c, 39 cents, color illos
    2.35    7.00    14.00

**1403-Invisible Scarlet O'Neil**, 1942, Whit, All Pictures Comics, flip pictures
    7.00    21.00    42.00

**1406-Invisible Scarlet O'Neil Versus the King of the Slums**, 1946, Whit, 352p
    6.00    18.00    36.00

**1098-It Happened One Night**, 1935, Sal, 160p, Little Big Book, Clark Gable, Claudette Colbert photo-c, movie scenes
    12.00    35.00    70.00

**1578-It Happened One Night**, 1935, Sal, 160p, soft-c
    12.00    35.00    70.00

**Jack and Jill** (See Wee Little Books)

**1432-Jack Armstrong and the Mystery of the Iron Key**, 1939, Whit, 432p, Henry E. Vallely-a
    7.50    22.50    45.00

**1435-Jack Armstrong and the Ivory Treasure**, 1937, Whit, 432p, Henry Vallely-a
    7.50    22.50    45.00

**Jackie Cooper** (See Story of . . . )

**1084-Jackie Cooper in Peck's Bad Boy**, 1934, Sal, 160p, hard, photo-c, movie scenes
    10.00    30.00    60.00

**1314-Jackie Cooper in Peck's Bad Boy**, 1934, Sal, 160p, soft, photo-c, movie scenes
    10.00    30.00    60.00

**1402-Jackie Cooper in "Gangster's Boy,"** 1939, Whit, 240p, photo-c, movie scenes
    8.50    25.00    50.00

**13-Jackie Cooper in Dinky**, 1935, EVW, 160p, movie scenes
    10.00    30.00    60.00

**nn-Jack King of the Secret Service and the Counterfeiters**, 1939, Whit, 36p, 2½" × 3½", Penny Book, by John G. Gray
    4.00    12.00    24.00

**L11-Jack London's Call of the Wild**, 1935, Lynn, 20th Cent. Pic., movie scenes with Clark Gable
    10.00    30.00    60.00

**nn-Jack Pearl as Detective Baron Munchausen**, 1934, Gold, 132p, soft-c
    8.00    24.00    48.00

**1102-Jack Swift and His Rocket Ship**, 1934, Whit, 320p
    12.00    35.00    70.00

*Jane Arden the Vanished Princess #1498,*
*© Des Moines Register & Tribune Syndicate, 1938*

|  | Good | Fine | N-Mint |
|---|---|---|---|
| **1498-Jane Arden the Vanished Princess**, Whit, 300p | | | |
| | 7.00 | 21.00 | 42.00 |
| **1179-Jane Withers in This Is the Life** (20th Century-Fox Presents . . . ), 1935, Whit, 240p, photo-c, movie scenes | | | |
| | 9.00 | 27.00 | 54.00 |
| **1463-Jane Withers in Keep Smiling**, 1938, Whit, 240p, photo-c, movie scenes | 9.00 | 27.00 | 54.00 |
| **Jaragu of the Jungle** (See Rex Beach's . . . ) | | | |
| **1447-Jerry Parker Police Reporter and the Candid Camera Clue**, 1941, Whit, 300p | 5.50 | 16.50 | 33.00 |
| **Jim Bowie** (See Adventures of . . . ) | | | |
| **nn-Jim Bryant of the Highway Patrol and the Mysterious Accident**, 1939, Whit, 36p, 2½″ × 3½″, Penny Book | | | |
| | 4.50 | 14.00 | 28.00 |
| **1466-Jim Craig State Trooper and the Kidnapped Governor**, 1938, Whit, 432p | 5.50 | 16.50 | 33.00 |
| **nn-Jim Doyle Private Detective and the Train Hold-Up**, 1939, Whit, 36p, 2½″ × 3½″, Penny Book | 4.00 | 12.00 | 24.00 |

|  | Good | Fine | N-Mint |
|---|---|---|---|
| **1180-Jim Hardy Ace Reporter**, 1940, Sal, 400p, Dick Moores-a | 6.00 | 18.00 | 36.00 |
| **1143-Jimmy Allen in the Air Mail Robbery**, 1936, Whit, 432p | 5.50 | 16.50 | 33.00 |
| **L15-Jimmy and the Tiger**, 1935, Lynn, 192p | 6.00 | 18.00 | 36.00 |
| **Jimmy Skunk's Justice** (See Wee Little Books) | | | |
| **1428-Jim Starr of the Border Patrol**, 1937, Whit, 432p | 5.50 | 16.50 | 33.00 |
| **Joan of Arc** (See Wee Little Books) | | | |
| **1105-Joe Louis the Brown Bomber**, 1936, Whit, 240p, photo-c, photo-illus. | 10.00 | 30.00 | 60.00 |
| **Joe Palooka** (See Gentleman . . . ) | | | |
| **1123-Joe Palooka the Heavyweight Boxing Champ**, 1934, Whit, 320p, Ham Fisher-a | 10.00 | 30.00 | 60.00 |
| **1168-Joe Palooka's Greatest Adventure**, 1939, Sal | 10.00 | 30.00 | 60.00 |
| **nn-Joe Penner's Duck Farm**, 1935, Gold, Henry Vallely-a | 8.00 | 24.00 | 48.00 |
| **1402-John Carter of Mars**, 1940, Whit, 432p, John Coleman Burroughs-a | 27.00 | 80.00 | 160.00 |
| **nn-John Carter of Mars**, 1940, Dell, 194p, Fast-Action Story, soft-c | 27.00 | 80.00 | 160.00 |
| **1164-Johnny Forty Five,** 1938, Sal, 400p | 5.00 | 15.00 | 30.00 |
| **John Wayne** (See Westward Ho!) | | | |
| **1100B-Jokes** (A book of laughs galore), 1938, Whit, 36p, 2½″ × 3½″, Penny Book | 2.00 | 6.00 | 12.00 |
| **1100B-Jokes** (A book of side-splitting funny stories), 1938, Whit, 36p, 2½″ × 3½″ Penny Book | 2.00 | 6.00 | 12.00 |
| **2026-Journey to the Center of the Earth, The Fiery Foe**, 1968, Whit | 2.00 | 6.00 | 12.00 |
| **Jungle Jim** (See Top-Line Comics) | | | |
| **1138-Jungle Jim**, 1936, Whit, 432p, Alex Raymond-a | 12.00 | 35.00 | 70.00 |
| **1139-Jungle Jim and the Vampire Woman**, 1937, Whit, 432p, Alex Raymond-a | 13.00 | 40.00 | 80.00 |
| **1442-Junior G-Men**, 1937, Whit, 432p, Henry E. Vallely-a | 6.00 | 18.00 | 36.00 |

*Jungle Jim and the Vampire Woman #1139,*
*© King Features Syndicate, 1937*

|  | Good | Fine | N-Mint |
|---|---|---|---|
| **nn-Junior G-Men Solve a Crime**, 1939, Whit, 36p, 2½″ × 3½″, Penny Book | 4.00 | 12.00 | 24.00 |
| **1422-Junior Nebb on the Diamond Bar Ranch**, 1938, Whit, 300p, by Sol Hess | 6.00 | 18.00 | 36.00 |
| **1470-Junior Nebb Joins the Circus**, 1939, Whit, 300p, by Sol Hess | 6.00 | 18.00 | 36.00 |
| **nn-Junior Nebb Elephant Trainer**, 1939, Whit, 68p, Pan-Am Oil premium, soft-c | 7.50 | 22.50 | 45.00 |
| **1052-"Just Kids"** (Adventures of . . . ), 1934, Sal, oblong size, by Ad Carter | 15.00 | 45.00 | 90.00 |
| **1094-Just Kids and the Mysterious Stranger**, 1935, Sal, 160p, by Ad Carter | 9.00 | 27.00 | 54.00 |
| **1184-Just Kids and Deep-Sea Dan**, 1940, Sal, 400p, by Ad Carter | 7.00 | 21.00 | 42.00 |
| **1302-Just Kids, The Adventures of**, 1934, Sal, oblong size, soft-c, by Ad Carter | 15.00 | 45.00 | 90.00 |
| **1324-Just Kids and the Mysterious Stranger**, 1935, Sal, 160p, soft-c, by Ad Carter | 9.00 | 27.00 | 54.00 |

| | Good | Fine | N-Mint |
|---|---|---|---|

**1401-Just Kids**, 1937, Whit, 432p, by Ad Carter
          8.00     24.00     48.00

**1055-Katzenjammer Kids in the Mountains**, 1934, Sal, Oblong, H. H. Knerr-a     14.00     42.00     84.00

**14-Katzenjammer Kids, The**, 1942, Dell, 194p, Fast-Action Story, H. H. Knerr-a     14.00     42.00     84.00

**1411-Kay Darcy and the Mystery Hideout**, 1937, Whit, 300p, Charles Mueller-a     7.00     21.00     42.00

**1180-Kayo in the Land of Sunshine** (With Moon Mullins), 1937, Whit, 432p, by Willard     8.00     24.00     48.00

**1415-Kayo and Moon Mullins and the One Man Gang**, 1939, Whit, 432p, by Frank Willard     8.00     24.00     48.00

**7-Kayo and Moon Mullins 'Way Down South**, 1938, Whit, 132p, 3½″ × 3½″, Buddy Book     15.00     45.00     90.00

**1105-Kazan in Revenge of the North** (James Oliver Curwood's . . . ), 1937, Whit, 432p, Henry E. Vallely-a
          5.50     16.50     33.00

**1471-Kazan, King of the Pack** (James Oliver Curwood's . . . ), 1940, Whit, 432p     5.00     15.00     30.00

**1420-Keep 'Em Flying! U.S.A. for America's Defense**, 1943, Whit, 432p, Henry E. Vallely-a, flip pictures
          5.50     16.50     33.00

**1133-Kelly King at Yale Hall**, 1937, Sal     5.00     15.00     30.00

**Ken Maynard** (See Strawberry Roan, Western Frontier, & Wheels of Destiny)

**776-Ken Maynard in "Gun Justice,"** 1934, Whit, 160p, movie scenes (Universal Pic.)     12.00     35.00     70.00

**1430-Ken Maynard in Western Justice**, 1938, Whit, 432p, Irwin Myers-a     7.00     21.00     42.00

**1442-Ken Maynard and the Gun Wolves of the Gila**, 1939, Whit, 432p     7.00     21.00     42.00

**nn-Ken Maynard in Six-Gun Law**, 1938, Whit, 36p, 2½″ × 3½″, Penny Book     4.50     14.00     28.00

**1134-King of Crime**, 1938, Sal, 400p     5.00     15.00     30.00

**King of the Royal Mounted** (See Zane Grey)

**1010-King of the Royal Mounted in Arctic Law**, 1937, Whit, 7¼″ × 5½″, 64p, Nickle Book     7.00     21.00     42.00

*Ken Maynard in Western Justice #1430,*
*© Ken Maynard, 1938*

|  | Good | Fine | N-Mint |
|---|---|---|---|
| **nn-Kit Carson**, 1933, World, by J. Carroll Mansfield, High Lights Of History Series, hard-c | 5.50 | 16.50 | 33.00 |
| **nn-Kit Carson**, 1933, World, same as hard-c above but with a black cloth-c | 5.50 | 16.50 | 33.00 |
| **1105-Kit Carson and the Mystery Riders**, 1935, Sal, hard-c, Johnny Mack Brown photo-c, movie scenes | 12.00 | 35.00 | 70.00 |
| **1585-Kit Carson and the Mystery Riders**, 1935, Sal, soft-c, Johnny Mack Brown photo-c, movie scenes | 12.00 | 35.00 | 70.00 |
| **Krazy Kat** (See Advs. of . . . ) | | | |
| **2004-(#4)-Lassie-Adventure in Alaska** (TV Series), 1967, Whit, 260p, 39 cents, hard-c, color illos | 2.00 | 6.00 | 12.00 |
| **2027-Lassie and the Shabby Sheik** (TV Series), 1968, Whit | 2.00 | 6.00 | 12.00 |
| **1132-Last Days of Pompeii, The**, 1935, Whit, 5¼″ × 6¼″, 260p, photo-c, movie scenes | 8.50 | 25.00 | 50.00 |
| **1128-Last Man Out** (Baseball), 1937, Sal, hard-c | 4.50 | 13.50 | 27.00 |

|  | Good | Fine | N-Mint |
|---|---|---|---|

**L30-Last of the Mohicans, The**, 1936, Lynn, 192p, movie scenes with Randolph Scott, United Artists Pictures

|  | 10.00 | 30.00 | 60.00 |
|---|---|---|---|

**1126-Laughing Dragon of Oz, The**, 1934, Whit, 432p, by Frank Baum

|  | 43.00 | 130.00 | 260.00 |
|---|---|---|---|

**1086-Laurel and Hardy**, 1934, Sal, 160p, hard-c, photo-c, movie scenes

|  | 8.50 | 25.00 | 50.00 |
|---|---|---|---|

**1316-Laurel and Hardy**, 1934, Sal, 160p, soft-c, photo-c, movie scenes

|  | 8.50 | 25.00 | 50.00 |
|---|---|---|---|

**1092-Law of the Wild, The**, 1935, Sal, 160p, photo-c, movie scenes of Rex, The Wild Horse & Rin-Tin-Tin Jr.

|  | 5.50 | 16.50 | 33.00 |
|---|---|---|---|

**1322-Law of the Wild, The**, 1935, Sal, 160p, photo-c, movie scenes, soft-c

|  | 5.50 | 16.50 | 33.00 |
|---|---|---|---|

**1100B-Learn to Be a Ventriloquist**, 1938, Whit, 36p, 2½″ × 3½″, Penny Book

|  | 2.00 | 6.00 | 12.00 |
|---|---|---|---|

**1149-Lee Brady Range Detective**, 1938, Sal, 400p

|  | 5.00 | 15.00 | 30.00 |
|---|---|---|---|

**L10-Les Miserables** (Victor Hugo's . . . ), 1935, Lynn, 192p, movie scenes

|  | 9.00 | 27.00 | 54.00 |
|---|---|---|---|

**1441-Lightning Jim U.S. Marshal Brings Law to the West**, 1940, Whit, 432p, based on radio program

|  | 5.50 | 16.50 | 33.00 |
|---|---|---|---|

**nn-Lightning Jim Whipple U.S. Marshal in Indian Territory**, 1939, Whit, 36p, 2½″ × 3½″, Penny Book

|  | 4.00 | 12.00 | 24.00 |
|---|---|---|---|

**653-Lions and Tigers** (With Clyde Beatty), 1934, Whit, 160p, photo-c, movie scenes

|  | 9.00 | 27.00 | 54.00 |
|---|---|---|---|

**1187-Li'l Abner and the Ratfields**, 1940, Sal, 400p, by Al Capp

|  | 12.00 | 35.00 | 70.00 |
|---|---|---|---|

**1193-Li'l Abner and Sadie Hawkins Day**, 1940, Sal, 400p, by Al Capp

|  | 12.00 | 35.00 | 70.00 |
|---|---|---|---|

**1198-Li'l Abner in New York**, 1936, Whit, 432p, by Al Capp

|  | 12.00 | 35.00 | 70.00 |
|---|---|---|---|

**1401-Li'l Abner among the Millionaires**, 1939, Whit, 432p, by Al Capp

|  | 12.00 | 35.00 | 70.00 |
|---|---|---|---|

**1054-Little Annie Rooney**, 1934, Sal, Oblong-4″ × 8″, All Pictures Comics, hard-c

|  | 13.00 | 40.00 | 80.00 |
|---|---|---|---|

**1304-Little Annie Rooney**, 1934, Sal, Oblong-4″ × 8″, All Pictures, soft-c

|  | 13.00 | 40.00 | 80.00 |
|---|---|---|---|

**1117-Little Annie Rooney and the Orphan House**, 1936, Whit, 432p

|  | 7.00 | 21.00 | 42.00 |
|---|---|---|---|

|                                                                                 | Good  | Fine  | N-Mint |
|---------------------------------------------------------------------------------|-------|-------|--------|
| **1406-Little Annie Rooney on the Highway to Adventure**, 1938, Whit, 432p       | 7.00  | 21.00 | 42.00  |
| **1149-Little Big Shot** (With Sybil Jason), 1935, Whit, 240p, photo-c, movie scenes | 7.00  | 21.00 | 42.00  |
| **nn-Little Black Sambo**, nd (1930s), np (Whit), 36p, 3″ × 2½″, Penny Book       | 5.00  | 15.00 | 30.00  |
| **Little Bo-Peep** (See Wee Little Books)                                         |       |       |        |
| **Little Colonel, The** (See Shirley Temple)                                      |       |       |        |
| **1148-Little Green Door, The**, 1938, Sal, 400p                                  | 5.00  | 15.00 | 30.00  |
| **1112-Little Hollywood Stars**, 1935, Sal, movie scenes (Little Rascals, etc.), hard-c | 8.50  | 25.00 | 50.00  |
| **1592-Little Hollywood Stars**, 1935, Sal, movie scenes, soft-c                  | 8.50  | 25.00 | 50.00  |
| **1087-Little Jimmy's Gold Hunt**, 1935, Sal, 160p, hard-c, Little Big Book, by Swinnerton | 7.50  | 22.50 | 45.00  |
| **1317-Little Jimmy's Gold Hunt**, 1935, Sal, 160p, 4¼″ × 5¾″, soft-c, by Swinnerton | 7.50  | 22.50 | 45.00  |
| **Little Joe and the City Gangsters** (See Top-Line Comics)                       |       |       |        |
| **Little Joe Otter's Slide** (See Wee Little Books)                               |       |       |        |
| **1118-Little Lord Fauntleroy**, 1936, Sal, movie scenes, photo-c, 4½″ × 5¼″, starring Mickey Rooney & Freddie Bartholomew, hard-c | 7.00  | 21.00 | 42.00  |
| **1598-Little Lord Fauntleroy**, 1936, Sal, photo-c, movie scenes, soft-c         | 7.00  | 21.00 | 42.00  |
| **1192-Little Mary Mixup and the Grocery Robberies**, 1940, Sal                   | 6.00  | 18.00 | 36.00  |
| **8-Little Mary Mixup Wins a Prize**, 1936, Whit, 132p, 3½″ × 3½″, soft-c, Tarzan Ice Cream cup lid premium | 14.00 | 42.00 | 84.00  |
| **1150-Little Men**, 1934, Whit, 4¾″ × 5¼″, movie scenes (Mascot Prod.), photo-c, hard-c | 7.00  | 21.00 | 42.00  |
| **9-Little Minister, The Katharine Hepburn**, 1935, 160p, 4¼″ × 5½″, EVW (Five Star Library), movie scenes (RKO) | 8.50  | 25.00 | 50.00  |
| **1120-Little Miss Muffet**, 1936, Whit, 432p, by Fanny Y. Cory                   | 7.00  | 21.00 | 42.00  |
| **708-Little Orphan Annie**, 1933, Whit, 320p, by Harold Gray, the 2nd Big Little Book | 30.00 | 90.00 | 180.00 |

| | Good | Fine | N-Mint |
|---|---|---|---|

**nn-Little Orphan Annie**, 1928 ('33), Whit, 52p, 4″ × 5½″, premium-no ads, soft-c, by Harold Gray

|  | 20.00 | 60.00 | 120.00 |
|---|---|---|---|

*Little Orphan Annie and Sandy #716,*
*© Harold Gray, 1933*

**716-Little Orphan Annie and Sandy**, 1933, Whit, 320p, by Harold Gray     17.00    50.00    100.00

**nn-Little Orphan Annie and Sandy**, 1933, Whit, 52p, premium-no ads, 4″ × 5½″, soft-c, by Harold Gray

    20.00    60.00    120.00

**748-Little Orphan Annie and Chizzler**, 1933, Whit, 320p, by Harold Gray     14.00    42.00    84.00

**1010-Little Orphan Annie and the Big Town Gunmen**, 1937, 7¼″ × 5½″, 64p, Nickle Book     7.00    21.00    42.00

**1103-Little Orphan Annie with the Circus**, 1934, Whit, 320p, by Harold Gray     12.00    35.00    70.00

**1140-Little Orphan Annie and the Big Train Robbery**, 1934, Whit, 300p, by Gray     12.00    35.00    70.00

|  | Good | Fine | N-Mint |
|---|---|---|---|
| **1140-Little Orphan Annie and the Big Train Robbery**, 1934, Whit, 300p, premium-no ads, soft-c, by Harold Gray | 17.00 | 50.00 | 100.00 |
| **1154-Little Orphan Annie and the Ghost Gang**, 1935, Whit, 432p, by Harold Gray | 12.00 | 32.50 | 65.00 |
| **nn-Little Orphan Annie and the Ghost Gang**, 1935, Whit, 436p, premium-no ads, 3-color, soft-c, by Harold Gray | 17.00 | 50.00 | 100.00 |
| **1162-Little Orphan Annie and Punjab the Wizard**, 1935, Whit, 432p, by Harold Gray | 12.00 | 32.50 | 65.00 |
| **1186-Little Orphan Annie and the $1,000,000 Formula**, 1936, Whit, 432p, by Gray | 10.00 | 30.00 | 60.00 |
| **1414-Little Orphan Annie and the Ancient Treasure of Am**, 1939, Whit, 432p, by Gray | 8.50 | 25.00 | 50.00 |
| **1416-Little Orphan Annie in the Movies**, 1937, Whit, 432p, by Harold Gray | 8.50 | 25.00 | 50.00 |
| **1417-Little Orphan Annie and the Secret of the Well**, 1947, Whit, 352p, by Gray | 7.50 | 22.50 | 45.00 |
| **1435-Little Orphan Annie and the Gooneyville Mystery**, 1947, Whit, 288p, by Gray | 7.50 | 22.50 | 45.00 |
| **1446-Little Orphan Annie in the Thieves' Den**, 1948, Whit, 288p, by Harold Gray | 7.50 | 22.50 | 45.00 |
| **1449-Little Orphan Annie and the Mysterious Shoemaker**, 1938, Whit, 432p, by Harold Gray | 8.50 | 25.00 | 50.00 |
| **1457-Little Orphan Annie and Her Junior Commandos**, 1943, Whit, 352p, by H. Gray | 7.50 | 22.50 | 45.00 |
| **1461-Little Orphan Annie and the Underground Hide-Out**, 1945, Whit, 352p, by Gray | 7.50 | 22.50 | 45.00 |
| **1468-Little Orphan Annie and the Ancient Treasure of Am**, 1949 (Misdated 1939), 288p, by Gray | 8.00 | 24.00 | 48.00 |
| **1482-Little Orphan Annie and the Haunted Mansion**, 1941, Whit, 432p, flip pictures, by Harold Gray | 8.50 | 25.00 | 50.00 |
| **4054-Little Orphan Annie, The Story of**, 1934, 7" × 9½", 320p, Big Big Book, Harold Gray c/a | 43.00 | 130.00 | 260.00 |
| **nn-Little Orphan Annie Gets into Trouble**, 1938, Whit, 36p, 2½" × 3½", Penny Book | 4.50 | 14.00 | 28.00 |
| **nn-Little Orphan Annie in Hollywood**, 1937, Whit, 3½" × 3¾", Pan-Am premium, soft-c | 9.00 | 27.00 | 54.00 |

|                                                                 | Good  | Fine   | N-Mint |
|-----------------------------------------------------------------|-------|--------|--------|
| **nn-Little Orphan Annie in Rags to Riches**, 1938, Dell, 194p, Fast-Action Story, soft-c | 18.00 | 55.00  | 110.00 |
| **nn-Little Orphan Annie Saves Sandy**, 1938, Whit, 36p, 2½″ × 3½″, Penny Book | 4.50  | 14.00  | 28.00  |
| **nn-Little Orphan Annie under the Big Top**, 1938, Dell, 194p, Fast-Action Story, soft-c | 18.00 | 55.00  | 110.00 |

**nn-Little Orphan Annie Wee Little Books** (In open box) nn, 1934, Whit, 44p, by H. Gray

|                                  | Good  | Fine   | N-Mint |
|----------------------------------|-------|--------|--------|
| L.O.A. and Daddy Warbucks        | 4.50  | 14.00  | 28.00  |
| L.O.A. and Her Dog Sandy         | 4.50  | 14.00  | 28.00  |
| L.O.A. and the Lucky Knife       | 4.50  | 14.00  | 28.00  |
| L.O.A. and the Pinch-Pennys      | 4.50  | 14.00  | 28.00  |
| L.O.A. at Happy Home             | 4.50  | 14.00  | 28.00  |
| L.O.A. Finds Mickey              | 4.50  | 14.00  | 28.00  |
| Complete set with box            | 37.00 | 110.00 | 220.00 |

|                                                                 | Good  | Fine   | N-Mint |
|-----------------------------------------------------------------|-------|--------|--------|
| **nn-Little Polly Flinders, The Story of**, nd (1930s), no publ., 36p, 2½″ × 3″, Penny Book | 1.50  | 4.50   | 9.00   |
| **nn-Little Red Hen, The**, nd (1930s), np (Whit), 36p, Penny Book | 1.50  | 4.50   | 9.00   |
| **nn-Little Red Riding Hood**, nd (1930s), np (Whit), 36p, 3″ × 2½″, Penny Book | 1.50  | 4.50   | 9.00   |
| **nn-Little Red Riding Hood and the Big Bad Wolf** (Disney), 1934, McKay, 36p, stiff-c, Disney Studio-a | 18.00 | 55.00  | 110.00 |
| **757-Little Women**, 1934, Whit, 4¾″ × 5¼″, 160p, photo-c, movie scenes, starring Katharine Hepburn | 10.00 | 30.00  | 60.00  |
| **Littlest Rebel, The** (See Shirley Temple) | | | |
| **1181-Lone Ranger and His Horse Silver**, 1935, Whit, 432p, Hal Arbo-a | 15.00 | 45.00  | 90.00  |
| **1196-Lone Ranger and the Vanishing Herd**, 1936, Whit, 432p | 12.00 | 35.00  | 70.00  |
| **1407-Lone Ranger and Dead Men's Mine, The**, 1939, Whit, 432p | 11.00 | 32.50  | 65.00  |
| **1421-Lone Ranger on the Barbary Coast, The**, 1944, Whit, 352p, Henry Vallely-a | 9.00  | 27.00  | 54.00  |
| **1428-Lone Ranger and the Secret Weapon, The**, 1943, Whit, 352p | 9.00  | 27.00  | 54.00  |

*The Lone Ranger and the Secret Killer #1431,*
*© The Lone Ranger, Inc., 1937*

|  | Good | Fine | N-Mint |
|---|---|---|---|
| **1431-Lone Ranger and the Secret Killer, The**, 1937, Whit, 432p, II. Anderson-a | 11.00 | 35.00 | 70.00 |
| **1450-Lone Ranger and the Black Shirt Highwayman, The**, 1939, Whit, 432p | 11.00 | 32.50 | 65.00 |
| **1465-Lone Ranger and the Menace of Murder Valley, The**, 1938, Whit, 432p, Robert Wiseman-a | 11.00 | 32.50 | 65.00 |
| **1468-Lone Ranger Follows Through, The**, 1941, Whit, 432p, H. E. Vallely-a | 11.00 | 32.50 | 65.00 |
| **1477-Lone Ranger and the Great Western Span, The**, 1942, Whit, 424p, H. E. Vallely-a | 9.00 | 27.00 | 54.00 |
| **1489-Lone Ranger and the Red Renegades, The**, 1939, Whit, 432p | 11.00 | 32.50 | 65.00 |
| **1498-Lone Ranger and the Silver Bullets**, 1946, Whit, 352p, Henry E. Vallely-a | 9.00 | 27.00 | 54.00 |
| **712-10-Lone Ranger and the Secret of Somber Cavern, The**, 1950, Whit | 5.00 | 15.00 | 30.00 |
| **2013-(#13)-Lone Ranger Outwits Crazy Cougar, The**, 1968, Whit, 260p, 39 cents, hard-c, color illos | 2.00 | 6.00 | 12.00 |

|  | Good | Fine | N-Mint |
|---|---|---|---|
| **nn-Lone Ranger and the Lost Valley, The**, 1938, Dell, 196p, Fast-Action Story, soft-c | 17.00 | 50.00 | 100.00 |
| **1405-Lone Star Martin of the Texas Rangers**, 1939, Whit, 432p | 5.00 | 15.00 | 30.00 |
| **19-Lost City, The**, 1935, EVW, movie scenes | 10.00 | 30.00 | 60.00 |
| **1103-Lost Jungle, The** (With Clyde Beatty), 1936, Sal, movie scenes, hard-c | 9.00 | 27.00 | 54.00 |
| **1583-Lost Jungle, The** (With Clyde Beatty), 1936, Sal, movie scenes, soft-c | 9.00 | 27.00 | 54.00 |
| **753-Lost Patrol, The**, 1934, Whit, 160p, photo-c, movie scenes | 8.00 | 24.00 | 48.00 |
| **1189-Mac of the Marines in Africa**, 1936, Whit, 432p | 7.00 | 21.00 | 42.00 |
| **1400-Mac of the Marines in China**, 1938, Whit, 432p | 7.00 | 21.00 | 42.00 |
| **1100B-Magic Tricks** (With explanations), 1938, Whit, 36p, 2½″ × 3½″, Penny Book | 2.00 | 6.00 | 12.00 |
| **1100B-Magic Tricks** (How to do them), 1938, Whit, 36p, 2½″ × 3½″, Penny Book | 2.00 | 6.00 | 12.00 |
| **Major Hoople** (See Our Boarding House) | | | |
| **1167-Mandrake the Magician**, 1935, Whit, 432p, by Lee Falk & Phil Davis | 12.00 | 35.00 | 70.00 |
| **1418-Mandrake the Magician and the Flame Pearls**, 1946, Whit, 352p, by Lee Falk & Phil Davis | 8.00 | 24.00 | 48.00 |
| **1431-Mandrake the Magician and the Midnight Monster**, 1939, Whit, 432p, by Lee Falk & Phil Davis | 9.00 | 27.00 | 54.00 |
| **1454-Mandrake the Magician Mighty Solver of Mysteries**, 1941, Whit, 432p, by Lee Falk & Phil Davis, flip pictures | 9.00 | 27.00 | 54.00 |
| **2011-(#11)-Man From U.N.C.L.E., The-The Calcutta Affair** (TV Series), 1967, Whit, 260p, 39 cents, hard-c, color illos | 2.50 | 8.00 | 16.00 |
| **1429-Marge's Little Lulu Alvin and Tubby**, 1947, Whit, All Pictures Comics, Stanley-a | 13.00 | 40.00 | 80.00 |
| **1438-Mary Lee and the Mystery of the Indian Beads**, 1937, Whit, 300p | 5.50 | 16.50 | 33.00 |
| **1165-Masked Man of the Mesa, The**, 1939, Sal, 400p | 5.00 | 15.00 | 30.00 |

*Mandrake the Magician #1167,*
*© King Features Syndicate, 1935*

|  | Good | Fine | N-Mint |
|---|---|---|---|
| **1436-Maximo the Amazing Superman**, 1940, Whit, 432p, Henry E. Vallely-a | 8.50 | 25.00 | 50.00 |
| **1444-Maximo the Amazing Superman and the Crystals of Doom**, 1941, Whit, 432p, Henry E. Vallely-a | 8.50 | 25.00 | 50.00 |
| **1445-Maximo the Amazing Superman and the Supermachine**, 1941, Whit, 432p | 8.50 | 25.00 | 50.00 |
| **755-Men of the Mounted**, 1934, Whit, 320p | 8.50 | 25.00 | 50.00 |
| **nn-Men of the Mounted**, 1933, Whit, 52p, 3½″ × 5¾″, premium-no ads; another version with Poll Parrot & Perkins ad; soft-c | 12.00 | 35.00 | 70.00 |
| **nn-Men of the Mounted**, 1934, Whit, Cocomalt premium, soft-c, by Ted McCall | 7.50 | 22.50 | 45.00 |
| **1475-Men with Wings**, 1938, Whit, 240p, photo-c, movie scenes (Paramount Pics.) | 7.00 | 21.00 | 42.00 |
| **1170-Mickey Finn**, 1940, Sal, 400p, by Frank Leonard | 7.00 | 21.00 | 42.00 |
| **717-Mickey Mouse** (Disney), 1933, Whit, 320p, Gottfredson-a (Two diff. covers printed) | 75.00 | 225.00 | 450.00 |

*Mickey Mouse in Blaggard Castle #726,*
*© The Disney Company, 1934*

|  | Good | Fine | N-Mint |
|---|---|---|---|
| **726-Mickey Mouse in Blaggard Castle** (Disney), 1934, Whit, 320p, Gottfredson-a | 17.00 | 50.00 | 100.00 |
| **731-Mickey Mouse the Mail Pilot** (Disney), 1933, Whit, 300p, Gottfredson-a | 18.00 | 55.00 | 110.00 |
| **nn-Mickey Mouse the Mail Pilot** (Disney), 1933, Whit, 292p, American Oil Co. premium, soft-c, Gottfredson-a; another version 3½″ × 4¾″ | 15.00 | 45.00 | 90.00 |
| **750-Mickey Mouse Sails for Treasure Island** (Disney), 1933, Whit, 320p, Gottfredson-a | 18.00 | 55.00 | 110.00 |
| **nn-Mickey Mouse Sails for Treasure Island** (Disney), 1935, Whit, 196p, premium-no ads, soft-c, Gottfredson-a | 18.00 | 55.00 | 110.00 |
| **nn-Mickey Mouse Sails for Treasure Island** (Disney), 1935, hit, 196p, Kolynos Dental Cream premium | 18.00 | 55.00 | 110.00 |
| **756-Mickey Mouse Presents a Walt Disney Silly Symphony** (Disney), 1934, Whit, 240p, Buckey Bug app. | 16.00 | 48.00 | 96.00 |

|                                                                                  | Good | Fine | N-Mint |
|----------------------------------------------------------------------------------|------|------|--------|
| **1111-Mickey Mouse Presents Walt Disney's Silly Symphonies Stories**, 1936, Whit, 432p, Donald Duck, Bucky Bug app. | 16.00 | 48.00 | 96.00 |
| **1128-Mickey Mouse and Pluto the Racer** (Disney), 1936, Whit, 432p, Gottfredson-a | 14.00 | 42.00 | 84.00 |
| **1139-Mickey Mouse the Detective** (Disney), 1934, Whit, 300p, Gottfredson-a | 16.00 | 48.00 | 96.00 |
| **1139-Mickey Mouse the Detective** (Disney), 1934, Whit, 304p, premium-no ads, soft-c, Gottfredson-a | 21.50 | 65.00 | 130.00 |
| **1153-Mickey Mouse and the Bat Bandit** (Disney), 1935, Whit, 432p, Gottfredson-a | 15.00 | 45.00 | 90.00 |
| **nn-Mickey Mouse and the Bat Bandit** (Disney), 1935, Whit, 436p, premium-no ads, 3-color, soft-c, Gottfredson-a | 21.50 | 65.00 | 130.00 |
| **1160-Mickey Mouse and Bobo the Elephant** (Disney), 1935, Whit, 432p, Gottfredson-a | 15.00 | 45.00 | 90.00 |
| **1187-Mickey Mouse and the Sacred Jewel** (Disney), 1936, Whit, 432p, Gottfredson-a | 13.00 | 40.00 | 80.00 |
| **1401-Mickey Mouse in the Treasure Hunt** (Disney), 1941, Whit, 430p, flip pictures with Pluto, Gottfredson-a | 12.00 | 35.00 | 70.00 |
| **1409-Mickey Mouse Runs His Own Newspaper** (Disney), 1937, Whit, 432p, Gottfredson-a | 12.00 | 35.00 | 70.00 |
| **1413-Mickey Mouse and the 'Lectro Box** (Disney), 1946, Whit, 352p, Gottfredson-a | 10.00 | 30.00 | 60.00 |
| **1417-Mickey Mouse on Sky Island** (Disney), 1941, Whit, 432p, flip pictures, Gottfredson-a; considered by Gottfredson to be his best Mickey story | 12.00 | 35.00 | 70.00 |
| **1428-Mickey Mouse in the Foreign Legion** (Disney), 1940, Whit, 432p, Gottfredson-a | 12.00 | 35.00 | 70.00 |
| **1429-Mickey Mouse and the Magic Lamp** (Disney), 1942, Whit, 432p, flip pictures | 12.00 | 35.00 | 70.00 |
| **1433-Mickey Mouse and the Lazy Daisy Mystery** (Disney), 1947, Whit, 288p | 10.00 | 30.00 | 60.00 |
| **1444-Mickey Mouse in the World of Tomorrow** (Disney), 1948, Whit, 288p, Gottfredson-a | 13.00 | 40.00 | 80.00 |
| **1451-Mickey Mouse and the Desert Palace** (Disney),1948, Whit, 288p | 10.00 | 30.00 | 60.00 |

*Mickey Mouse and the Pirate Submarine #1463,*
*© The Disney Company, 1939*

|  | Good | Fine | N-Mint |
|---|---|---|---|
| **1463-Mickey Mouse and the Pirate Submarine** (Disney), 1939, Whit, 432p, Gottfredson-a | 12.00 | 35.00 | 70.00 |
| **1464-Mickey Mouse and the Stolen Jewels** (Disney), 1949, Whit, 288p | 11.00 | 32.50 | 65.00 |
| **1471-Mickey Mouse and the Dude Ranch Bandit** (Disney), 1943, Whit, 432p, flip pictures | 12.00 | 35.00 | 70.00 |
| **1475-Mickey Mouse and the 7 Ghosts** (Disney), 1940, Whit, 432p, Gottfredson-a | 12.00 | 35.00 | 70.00 |
| **1476-Mickey Mouse in the Race for Riches** (Disney), 1938, Whit, 432p, Gottfredson-a | 12.00 | 35.00 | 70.00 |
| **1483-Mickey Mouse Bell Boy Detective** (Disney), 1945, Whit, 352p | 11.00 | 32.50 | 65.00 |
| **1499-Mickey Mouse on the Cave-Man Island** (Disney), 1944, Whit, 352p | 11.00 | 32.50 | 65.00 |
| **4062-Mickey Mouse, The Story of**, 1935, Whit, 7″ × 9½″, 320p, Big Big Book, Gottfredson-a | 53.00 | 160.00 | 320.00 |

|  | Good | Fine | N-Mint |
|---|---|---|---|

**4062-Mickey Mouse and the Smugglers, The Story of** (Scarce), 1935, Whit, 7″ × 9½″, 320p, Big Big Book, same contents as above version; Gottfredson-a

|  | 75.00 | 225.00 | 450.00 |
|---|---|---|---|

**708-10-Mickey Mouse on the Haunted Island** (Disney), 1950, Whit, Gottfredson-a

|  | 7.00 | 20.00 | 40.00 |
|---|---|---|---|

**nn-Mickey Mouse and Minnie at Macy's**, 1934, Whit, 148p, 3¼″ × 3½″, soft-c, R. H. Macy & Co. Xmas giveaway

|  | 50.00 | 150.00 | 300.00 |
|---|---|---|---|

**nn-Mickey Mouse and Minnie March to Macy's**, 1935, Whit, 148p, 3½″ × 3½″, soft-c, R. H. Macy & Co. Xmas giveaway

|  | 50.00 | 150.00 | 300.00 |
|---|---|---|---|

**nn-Mickey Mouse and the Magic Carpet**, 1935, Whit, 148p, 3½″ × 4″, soft-c, giveaway, Gottfredson-a, Donald Duck app.

|  | 43.00 | 130.00 | 260.00 |
|---|---|---|---|

**nn-Mickey Mouse Silly Symphonies**, 1934, Dean & Son, Ltd. (England), 48p, with 4 pop-ups, Babes In The Woods, King Neptune, with dust jacket

|  | 58.00 | 175.00 | 350.00 |
|---|---|---|---|
| Without dust jacket | 42.00 | 125.00 | 250.00 |

**3061-Mickey Mouse to Draw and Color** (The Big Little Set), nd (early 1930s), Whit, with crayons; box contains 320 loose pages to color, reprinted from early Mickey Mouse BLBs

|  | 58.00 | 175.00 | 350.00 |
|---|---|---|---|

**16-Mickey Mouse and Pluto** (Disney), Dell, 196p, Fast-Action Story

|  | 21.00 | 62.50 | 125.00 |
|---|---|---|---|

**nn-Mickey Mouse the Sheriff of Nugget Gulch** (Disney), 1938, Dell, 196p, Fast-Action Story, soft-c, Gottfredson-a

|  | 21.00 | 62.50 | 125.00 |
|---|---|---|---|

**nn-Mickey Mouse with Goofy and Mickey's Nephews**, 1938, Dell, 196p, Fast-Action Story, Gottfredson-a

|  | 21.00 | 62.50 | 125.00 |
|---|---|---|---|

**Series A-Mickey Mouse** (In actual Motion Pictures), nd (1932?), Moviescope Corp., 50p, stapled, 1¾″ × 2½″ flip book. Earliest known M. Mouse flip book.

|  | 7.00 | 20.00 | 40.00 |
|---|---|---|---|

**512-Mickey Mouse Wee Little Books** (In open box), nn, 1934, 44p, small size, soft-c

| M. Mouse and Tanglefoot | 6.00 | 18.00 | 36.00 |
|---|---|---|---|
| M. Mouse at the Carnival | 6.00 | 18.00 | 36.00 |
| M. Mouse Will not Quit! | 6.00 | 18.00 | 36.00 |
| M. Mouse Wins the Race! | 6.00 | 18.00 | 36.00 |
| M. Mouse's Misfortune | 6.00 | 18.00 | 36.00 |

|  | Good | Fine | N-Mint |
|---|---|---|---|
| M. Mouse's Uphill Fight | 6.00 | 18.00 | 36.00 |
| Complete set with box | 43.00 | 130.00 | 260.00 |

**1493-Mickey Rooney and Judy Garland and How They Got Into the Movies**, 1941, Whit, 432p, photo-c

|  | 8.50 | 25.00 | 50.00 |
|---|---|---|---|

**1427-Mickey Rooney Himself**, 1939, Whit, 240p, photo-c, movie scenes, life story

|  | 8.50 | 25.00 | 50.00 |
|---|---|---|---|

**532-Mickey's Dog Pluto** (Disney), 1943, Whit, All Picture Comics, Tall Comic Book, 3¾" × 8¾"

|  | 17.00 | 50.00 | 100.00 |
|---|---|---|---|

**2113-Midget Jumbo Coloring Book**, 1935, Sal

|  | 20.00 | 60.00 | 120.00 |
|---|---|---|---|

**21-Midsummer Night's Dream**, 1935, EVW, movie scenes

|  | 10.00 | 30.00 | 60.00 |
|---|---|---|---|

**nn-Minute-Man** (Mystery of the Spy Ring), 1941, Faw, Dime Action Book

|  | 22.00 | 65.00 | 130.00 |
|---|---|---|---|

**710-Moby Dick the Great White Whale, The Story of**, 1934, Whit, 160p, photo-c, movie scenes from "The Sea Beast"

|  | 8.50 | 25.00 | 50.00 |
|---|---|---|---|

**746-Moon Mullins and Kayo** (Kayo and Moon Mullins-inside), 1933, Whit, 320p, Frank Willard c/a

|  | 11.00 | 32.50 | 65.00 |
|---|---|---|---|

**nn-Moon Mullins and Kayo**, 1933, Whit, Cocomalt premium, soft-c, by Willard

|  | 10.00 | 30.00 | 60.00 |
|---|---|---|---|

**1134-Moon Mullins and the Plushbottom Twins**, 1935, Whit, 432p, Willard c/a

|  | 10.00 | 30.00 | 60.00 |
|---|---|---|---|

**nn-Moon Mullins and the Plushbottom Twins**, 1935, Whit, 436p, premium-no ads, 3-color, soft-c, by Frank Willard

|  | 15.00 | 45.00 | 90.00 |
|---|---|---|---|

**1058-Mother Pluto** (Disney), 1939, Whit, 68p, hard-c

|  | 7.00 | 21.00 | 42.00 |
|---|---|---|---|

**1100B-Movie Jokes** (From the talkies), 1938, Whit, 36p, 2½" × 3½", Penny Book

|  | 2.00 | 6.00 | 12.00 |
|---|---|---|---|

**1408-Mr. District Attorney on the Job**, 1941, Whit, 432p, flip pictures

|  | 5.50 | 16.50 | 33.00 |
|---|---|---|---|

**nn-Musicians of Bremen, The**, nd (1930s), np (Whit), 36p, 3" × 2½", Penny Book

|  | 1.50 | 4.50 | 9.00 |
|---|---|---|---|

**1113-Mutt and Jeff**, 1936, Whit, 300p, by Bud Fisher

|  | 12.00 | 35.00 | 70.00 |
|---|---|---|---|

**1116-My Life and Times** (By Shirley Temple), 1936, Sal, Little Big Book, hard-c, photo-c/illos

|  | 8.50 | 25.00 | 50.00 |
|---|---|---|---|

*Mr. District Attorney on the Job #1408,*
*© Phillips H. Lord, Inc., 1941*

|  | Good | Fine | N-Mint |
|---|---|---|---|
| **1596-My Life and Times** (By Shirley Temple), 1936, Sal, Little Big Book, soft-c, photo-c/illos | 8.50 | 25.00 | 50.00 |
| **1497-Myra North Special Nurse and Foreign Spies**, 1938, Whit, 432p | 6.00 | 18.00 | 36.00 |
| **1400-Nancy and Sluggo**, 1946, Whit, All Pictures Comics, Ernie Bushmiller-a | 7.00 | 21.00 | 42.00 |
| **1487-Nancy Has Fun**, 1944, Whit, All Pictures Comics | 7.00 | 21.00 | 42.00 |
| **1150-Napoleon and Uncle Elby**, 1938, Sal, 400p, by Clifford McBride | 7.00 | 21.00 | 42.00 |
| **1166-Napoleon, Uncle Elby, and Little Mary**, 1939, Sal, 400p, by Clifford McBride | 7.00 | 21.00 | 42.00 |
| **1179-Ned Brant Adventure Bound**, 1940, Sal, 400p | 6.00 | 18.00 | 36.00 |
| **1146-Nevada Rides the Danger Trail**, 1938, Sal, 400p, J. R. White-a | 5.00 | 15.00 | 30.00 |
| **1147-Nevada Whalen, Avenger**, 1938, Sal, 400p | 5.00 | 15.00 | 30.00 |

|  | Good | Fine | N-Mint |
|---|---|---|---|
| **Nicodemus O'Malley** (See Top-Line Comics) | | | |
| **1115-Og Son of Fire**, 1936, Whit, 432p | 5.00 | 15.00 | 30.00 |
| **1419-Oh, Blondie the Bumsteads** (See Blondie) | | | |
| **11-Oliver Twist**, 1935, EVW (Five Star Library), movie scenes, starring Dickie Moore (Monogram Pictures) | | | |
|  | 10.00 | 30.00 | 60.00 |
| **718-"Once Upon a Time . . ,"** 1933, Whit, 364p, soft-c | | | |
|  | 10.00 | 30.00 | 60.00 |
| **712-100 Fairy Tales for Children, The**, 1933, Whit, 288p, Circle Library | | | |
|  | 4.50 | 14.00 | 28.00 |
| **1099-One Night of Love**, 1935, Sal, 160p, hard-c, photo-c, movie scenes, Columbia Pictures, starring Grace Moore | | | |
|  | 8.50 | 25.00 | 50.00 |
| **1579-One Night of Love**, 1935, Sal, 160p, soft-c, photo-c, movie scenes, Columbia Pictures, starring Grace Moore | | | |
|  | 8.50 | 25.00 | 50.00 |
| **1155-$1000 Reward**, 1938, Sal, 400p | 5.00 | 15.00 | 30.00 |
| **Orphan Annie** (See Little Orphan . . . ) | | | |
| **L17-O'Shaughnessy's Boy**, 1935, Lynn, 192p, movie scenes, w/Wallace Beery & Jackie Cooper (Metro-Goldwyn-Mayer) | | | |
|  | 7.50 | 22.50 | 45.00 |
| **1109-Oswald the Lucky Rabbit**, 1934, Whit, 288p | | | |
|  | 11.00 | 32.50 | 65.00 |
| **1403-Oswald Rabbit Plays G Man**, 1937, Whit, 240p, movie scenes by Walter Lantz | | | |
|  | 12.00 | 35.00 | 70.00 |
| **1190-Our Boarding House, Major Hoople and His Horse**, 1940, Sal, 400p | | | |
|  | 8.00 | 24.00 | 48.00 |
| **1085-Our Gang**, 1934, Sal, 160p, photo-c movie scenes, hard-c | | | |
|  | 8.50 | 25.00 | 50.00 |
| **1315-Our Gang**, 1934, Sal, 160p, photo-c movie scenes, soft-c | | | |
|  | 8.50 | 25.00 | 50.00 |
| **1451-"Our Gang" on the March**, 1942, Whit, 432p, flip pictures, Vallely-a | | | |
|  | 8.50 | 25.00 | 50.00 |
| **1456-Our Gang Adventures**, 1948, Whit, 288p | | | |
|  | 7.00 | 21.00 | 42.00 |
| **nn-Paramount Newsreel Men with Admiral Byrd in Little America**, 1934, Whit, 96p, 6¼" × 6¾", photo-c, photo ill. | | | |
|  | 7.00 | 21.00 | 42.00 |
| **nn-Patch**, nd (1930s), np (Whit), 36p, 3" × 2½", Penny Book | | | |
|  | 1.50 | 4.50 | 9.00 |

*"Our Gang" on the March #1451, © Loew's Inc., 1942*

|  | Good | Fine | N-Mint |
|---|---|---|---|
| **1445-Pat Nelson Ace of Test Pilots**, 1937, Whit, 432p | | | |
| | 5.00 | 15.00 | 30.00 |
| **1411-Peggy Brown and the Mystery Basket**, 1941, Whit, 432p, flip pictures, Henry E. Vallely-a | | | |
| | 6.00 | 18.00 | 36.00 |
| **1423-Peggy Brown and the Secet Treasure**, 1947, Whit, 288p, Henry E. Vallely-a | | | |
| | 6.00 | 18.00 | 36.00 |
| **1427-Peggy Brown and the Runaway Auto Trailer**, 1937, Whit, 300p, Henry E. Vallely-a | | | |
| | 6.00 | 18.00 | 36.00 |
| **1463-Peggy Brown and the Jewel of Fire**, 1943, Whit, 352p, Henry E. Vallely-a | | | |
| | 6.00 | 18.00 | 36.00 |
| **1491-Peggy Brown in the Big Haunted House**, 1940, Whit, 432p, Vallely-a | | | |
| | 6.00 | 18.00 | 36.00 |
| **1143-Peril Afloat**, 1938, Sal, 400p | 5.00 | 15.00 | 30.00 |
| **1199-Perry Winkle and the Rinkeydinks**, 1937, Whit, 432p, by Martin Branner | | | |
| | 8.50 | 25.00 | 50.00 |
| **1487-Perry Winkle and the Rinkeydinks Get a Horse**, 1938, Whit, 432p, by Martin Branner | | | |
| | 8.50 | 25.00 | 50.00 |
| **Peter Pan** (See Wee Little Books) | | | |

|  | Good | Fine | N-Mint |
|---|---|---|---|
| **nn-Peter Rabbit**, nd (1930s), np (Whit), 36p, Penny Book, 3″ × 2½″ | 2.00 | 6.00 | 12.00 |
| **Peter Rabbit's Carrots** (See Wee Little Books) | | | |
| **1100-Phantom, The**, 1936, Whit, 432p, by Lee Falk & Ray Moore | 20.00 | 60.00 | 120.00 |
| **1416-Phantom and the Girl of Mystery, The**, 1947, Whit, 352p, by Falk & Moore | 10.00 | 30.00 | 60.00 |
| **1421-Phantom and Desert Justice, The**, 1941, Whit, 432p, flip pictures, by Falk & Moore | 12.50 | 37.50 | 75.00 |
| **1468-Phantom and the Sky Pirates, The**, 1945, Whit, 352p, by Falk & Moore | 10.00 | 30.00 | 60.00 |
| **1474-Phantom and the Sign of the Skull, The**, 1939, Whit, 432p, by Falk & Moore | 14.00 | 42.00 | 84.00 |
| **1489-Phantom, Return of the . . .** , 1942, Whit, 432p, flip pictures, by Falk & Moore | 12.50 | 37.50 | 75.00 |
| **1130-Phil Barton, Sleuth** (Scout Book), 1937, Sal, hard-c | 4.50 | 13.50 | 27.00 |
| **Pied Piper of Hamlin** (See Wee Little Books) | | | |
| **1466-Pilot Pete Dive Bomber**, 1941, Whit, 432p, flip pictures | 5.50 | 16.50 | 33.00 |
| **5783-2-Pink Panther at Castle Kreep, The**, 1980, Whit, 260p, soft-c, 79 cents, B&W | .50 | 1.50 | 3.00 |
| **Pinocchio and Jiminy Cricket** (See Walt Disney's . . . ) | | | |
| **nn-Pioneers of the Wild West** (Blue-c), 1933, World, High Lights of History Series | 5.50 | 16.50 | 33.00 |
| **nn-Pioneers of the Wild West** (Red-c), 1933, World, High Lights of History Series | 5.50 | 16.50 | 33.00 |
| **1123-Plainsman, The**, 1936, Whit, 240p, photo-c, movie scenes (Paramount Pics.) | 7.00 | 21.00 | 42.00 |
| **Pluto** (See Mickey's Dog . . . & Walt Disney's . . . ) | | | |
| **2114-Pocket Coloring Book**, 1935, Sal | 20.00 | 60.00 | 120.00 |
| **1060-Polly and Her Pals on the Farm**, 1934, Sal, 164p, hard-c, by Cliff Sterrett | 10.00 | 30.00 | 60.00 |
| **1310-Polly and Her Pals on the Farm**, 1934, Sal, soft-c | 10.00 | 30.00 | 60.00 |
| **1051-Popeye, Adventures of . . .** , 1934, Sal, oblong size, E. C. Segar-a, hard-c | 25.00 | 75.00 | 150.00 |
| **1088-Popeye in Puddleburg**, 1934, Sal, 160p, hard-c, E. C. Segar-a | 12.00 | 35.00 | 70.00 |

|                                                                          | Good  | Fine  | N-Mint |
|--------------------------------------------------------------------------|-------|-------|--------|
| **1113-Popeye Starring in Choose Your Weppins**, 1936, Sal, 160p, hard-c, Segar-a | 12.00 | 35.00 | 70.00 |
| **1117-Popeye's Ark**, 1936, Sal, 4½″ × 5½″, hard-c, Segar-a             | 12.00 | 35.00 | 70.00 |
| **1163-Popeye Sees the Sea**, 1936, Whit, 432p, Segar-a                  | 13.00 | 40.00 | 80.00 |
| **1301-Popeye, Adventures of . . .** , 1934, Sal, oblong size, Segar-a   | 25.00 | 75.00 | 150.00 |
| **1318-Popeye in Puddleburg**, 1934, Sal, 160p, soft-c, Segar-a          | 12.00 | 35.00 | 70.00 |
| **1405-Popeye and the Jeep**, 1937, Whit, 432p, Segar-a                  | 13.00 | 40.00 | 80.00 |
| **1406-Popeye the Super-Fighter**, 1939, Whit, All Pictures Comics, flip pictures, Segar-a | 12.50 | 37.50 | 75.00 |
| **1422-Popeye the Sailor Man**, 1947, Whit, All Pictures Comics          | 9.00  | 27.00 | 54.00 |

*Popeye in Quest of His Poopdeck Pappy #1450,*
*© King Features Syndicate, 1937*

| | Good | Fine | N-Mint |
|---|---|---|---|
| **1450-Popeye in Quest of His Poopdeck Pappy**, 1937, Whit, 432p, Segar c/a | 13.00 | 40.00 | 80.00 |

|                                                                                                   | Good | Fine | N-Mint |
|---------------------------------------------------------------------------------------------------|------|------|--------|

**1458-Popeye and Queen Olive Oyl**, 1949, Whit, 288p, Sagendorf-a
| | 8.50 | 25.00 | 50.00 |

**1459-Popeye and the Quest for the Rainbird**, 1943, Whit, Winner & Zaboly-a
| | 10.00 | 30.00 | 60.00 |

**1480-Popeye the Spinach Eater**, 1945, Whit, All Pictures Comics
| | 9.00 | 27.00 | 54.00 |

**1485-Popeye in a Sock for Susan's Sake**, 1940, Whit, 432p, flip pictures
| | 10.00 | 30.00 | 60.00 |

**1497-Popeye and Caster Oyl the Detective**, 1941, Whit, 432p, flip pictures, Segar-a
| | 12.00 | 35.00 | 70.00 |

**1499-Popeye and the Deep Sea Mystery**, 1939, Whit, 432p, Segar c/a
| | 12.00 | 35.00 | 70.00 |

**1593-Popeye Starring in Choose Your Weppins**, 1936, Sal, 160p, soft-c, Segar-a
| | 12.00 | 35.00 | 70.00 |

**1597-Popeye's Ark**, 1936, Sal, 4½″ × 5½″, soft-c, Segar-a
| | 12.00 | 35.00 | 70.00 |

**2008-(#8)-Popeye-Ghost Ship to Treasure Island**, 1967, Whit, 260p, 39 cents, hard-c, color illos
| | 2.00 | 6.00 | 12.00 |

**4063-Popeye, Thimble Theatre Starring**, 1935, Whit, 7″ × 9½″, 320p, Big Big Book, Segar c/a (Cactus cover w/yellow logo)
| | 38.00 | 115.00 | 230.00 |

**4063-Popeye, Thimble Theatre Starring**, 1935, Whit, 7″ × 9½″, 320p, Big Big Book, Segar c/a (Big Balloon-c w/red logo), (2nd printing w/same contents as above)
| | 43.00 | 130.00 | 260.00 |

**5761-2-Popeye and Queen Olive Oyl**, 1973 (1980 reprint of 1973 version), 260p, 79 cents, B&W, soft-c
| | .50 | 1.50 | 3.00 |

**103-"Pop-Up" Buck Rogers in the Dangerous Mission** (with Pop-Up picture), 1934, BRP, 62p, The Midget Pop-Up Book w/Pop-Up in center of book, Calkins-a
| | 47.00 | 140.00 | 280.00 |

**206-"Pop-Up" Buck Rogers-Strange Adventures in the Spider-Ship, The**, 1935, BRP, 24p, 8″ × 9″, 3 Pop-Ups, hard-c, by Dick Calkins
| | 68.00 | 205.00 | 410.00 |

**nn-"Pop-Up" Cinderella**, 1933, BRP, 7½″ × 9¾″, 4 Pop-Ups, hard-c w/dust jacket ($2.00)
| | 57.00 | 170.00 | 340.00 |
| Without dust jacket | 47.00 | 140.00 | 280.00 |

**207-"Pop-Up" Dick Tracy-Capture of Boris Arson**, 1935, BRP, 24p, 8″ × 9″, 3 Pop-Ups, hard-c, by Gould
| | 58.00 | 175.00 | 350.00 |

|  | Good | Fine | N-Mint |
|---|---|---|---|

**210-"Pop-Up" Flash Gordon Tournament of Death, The**, 1935, BRP, 24p, 8″ × 9″, 3 Pop-Ups, hard-c, by Alex Raymond

|  | 58.00 | 175.00 | 350.00 |
|---|---|---|---|

**202-"Pop-Up" Goldilocks and the Three Bears, The**, 1934, BRP, 24p, 8″ × 9″, 3 Pop-Ups, hard-c

|  | 18.00 | 55.00 | 110.00 |
|---|---|---|---|

**nn-"Pop-Up" Jack and the Beanstalk**, 1933, BRP, hard-c (50 cents), 1 Pop-Up

|  | 12.50 | 37.50 | 75.00 |
|---|---|---|---|

**nn-"Pop-Up" Jack the Giant Killer**, 1933, BRP, hard-c (50 cents), 1 Pop-Up

|  | 12.50 | 37.50 | 75.00 |
|---|---|---|---|

**nn-"Pop-Up" Jack the Giant Killer**, 1933, BRP, 4 Pop-Ups, hard-c w/dust jacket ($2.00)

|  | 57.00 | 170.00 | 340.00 |
|---|---|---|---|
| Without dust jacket | 47.00 | 140.00 | 280.00 |

**nn-"Pop-Up" Little Black Sambo** (with Pop-Up picture), 1934, BRP, 62p, The Midget Pop-Up Book, one Pop-Up in center of book

|  | 33.00 | 100.00 | 200.00 |
|---|---|---|---|

**208-"Pop-Up" Little Orphan Annie and Jumbo the Circus Elephant**, 1935, BRP, 24p, 8″ × 9″, 3 Pop-Ups, hard-c, by H. Gray

|  | 43.00 | 130.00 | 260.00 |
|---|---|---|---|

**nn-"Pop-Up" Little Red Ridinghood**, 1933, BRP, hard-c (50 cents), 1 Pop-Up

|  | 12.50 | 37.50 | 75.00 |
|---|---|---|---|

**nn-"Pop-Up" Mickey Mouse, The**, 1933, BRP, 34p, 6½″ × 9″, 3 Pop-Ups, hard-c, Gottfredson-a (75 cents)

|  | 68.00 | 205.00 | 410.00 |
|---|---|---|---|

**nn-"Pop-Up" Mickey Mouse in King Arthur's Court, The**, 1933, BRP, 56p, 7½″ × 9¾″, 4 Pop-Ups, hard-c w/dust jacket, Gottfredson-a ($2.00)

|  | 88.00 | 265.00 | 530.00 |
|---|---|---|---|
| Without dust jacket | 70.00 | 200.00 | 400.00 |

**101-"Pop-Up" Mickey Mouse in "Ye Olden Days"** (with Pop-Up picture), 1934, 62p, BRP, The Midget Pop-Up Book, one Pop-Up in center of book, Gottfredson-a

|  | 47.00 | 140.00 | 280.00 |
|---|---|---|---|

**nn-"Pop-Up" Minnie Mouse, The**, 1933, BRP, 36p, 6½″ × 9″, 3 Pop-Ups, hard-c (75 cents), Gottfredson-a

|  | 68.00 | 205.00 | 410.00 |
|---|---|---|---|

**203-"Pop-Up" Mother Goose, The**, 1934, BRP, 24p, 8″ × 9¼″, 3 Pop-Ups, hard-c

|  | 33.00 | 100.00 | 200.00 |
|---|---|---|---|

**nn-"Pop-Up" Mother Goose Rhymes, The**, 1933, BRP, 96p, 7½″ × 9¾″, 4 Pop-Ups, hard-c w/dust jacket ($2.00)

|  | 57.00 | 170.00 | 340.00 |
|---|---|---|---|
| Without dust jacket | 47.00 | 140.00 | 280.00 |

|                                                                                                                                    | Good  | Fine   | N-Mint |
|------------------------------------------------------------------------------------------------------------------------------------|-------|--------|--------|
| **209-"Pop-Up" New Adventures of Tarzan**, 1935, BRP, 24p, 8″ × 9″, 3 Pop-Ups, hard-c                                               | 57.00 | 170.00 | 340.00 |
| **104-"Pop-Up" Peter Rabbit, The** (with Pop-Up picture), 1934, BRP, 62p, The Midget Pop-Up Book, one Pop-Up in center of book      | 27.00 | 80.00  | 160.00 |
| **nn-"Pop-Up" Pinocchio**, 1933, BRP, 7½″ × 9¾″, 4 Pop-Ups, hard-c                                                                  |       |        |        |
| w/dust jacket ($2.00)                                                                                                               | 73.00 | 220.00 | 440.00 |
| Without dust jacket                                                                                                                 | 62.00 | 185.00 | 370.00 |

*"Pop-Up" Popeye Among the White Savages #102,*
© *King Features Syndicate, 1934*

**102-"Pop-Up" Popeye among the White Savages** (with Pop-Up picture), 1934, BRP, 62p, The Midget Pop-Up Book, one Pop-Up in center of book, E. C. Segar-a    43.00    130.00    260.00

**205-"Pop-Up" Popeye with the Hag of the Seven Seas, The**, 1935, BRP, 24p, 8″ × 9″, 3 Pop-Ups, hard-c, Segar-a    43.00    130.00    260.00

**201-"Pop-Up" Puss in Boots, The**, 1934, BRP, 24p, 3 Pop-Ups, hard-c    18.00    55.00    110.00

|  | Good | Fine | N-Mint |
|---|---|---|---|
| **nn-"Pop-Up" Silly Symphonies, The** (Mickey Mouse Presents His . . .), 1933, BRP, 56p, 9¾″ × 7½″, 4 Pop-Ups, hard-c w/dust jacket ($2.00) | 83.00 | 250.00 | 500.00 |
| Without dust jacket | 70.00 | 200.00 | 400.00 |
| **nn-"Pop-Up" Sleeping Beauty**, 1933, BRP, hard-c (50 cents), 1 Pop-Up | 26.00 | 77.50 | 155.00 |
| **212-"Pop-Up" Terry and the Pirates in Shipwrecked, The**, 1935, BRP, 24p, 8″ × 9″, 3 Pop-Ups, hard-c | 43.00 | 130.00 | 260.00 |
| **211-"Pop-Up" Tim Tyler in the Jungle, The**, 1935, BRP, 24p, 8″ × 9″, 3 Pop-Ups, hard-c | 26.00 | 77.50 | 155.00 |
| **1404-Porky Pig and His Gang**, 1946, Whit, All Pictures Comics, Barks-a r/4-Color 48 | 13.00 | 40.00 | 80.00 |
| **1408-Porky Pig and Petunia**, 1942, Whit, All Pictures Comics, flip pictures, r/4-Color 16 & Famous Gang Book of Comics | 8.50 | 25.00 | 50.00 |
| **1176-Powder Smoke Range**, 1935, Whit, 240p, photo-c, movie scenes, Hoot Gibson, Harey Carey app. (RKO Radio Pict.) | 8.50 | 25.00 | 50.00 |
| **1058-Practical Pig!, The** (Disney), 1939, Whit, 68p, 5″ × 5½″, hard-c | 7.00 | 21.00 | 42.00 |
| **758-Prairie Bill and the Covered Wagon**, 1934, Whit, 384p, Hal Arbo-a | 7.00 | 21.00 | 42.00 |
| **nn-Prairie Bill and the Covered Wagon**, 1934, Whit, 390p, premium-no ads, 3-color, soft-c, Hal Arbo-a | 12.00 | 35.00 | 70.00 |
| **1440-Punch Davis of the U.S. Aircraft Carrier**, 1945, Whit, 352p | 5.00 | 15.00 | 30.00 |
| **nn-Puss in Boots**, nd (1930s), np (Whit), 36p, Penny Book | 1.50 | 4.50 | 9.00 |
| **1100B-Puzzle Book**, 1938, Whit, 36p, 2½″ × 3½″, Penny Book | 2.00 | 6.00 | 12.00 |
| **1100B-Puzzles**, 1938, Whit, 36p, 2½″ × 3½″, Penny Book | 2.00 | 6.00 | 12.00 |
| **1100B-Quiz Book, The**, 1938, Whit, 36p, 2½″ × 3½″, Penny Book | 2.00 | 6.00 | 12.00 |
| **1142-Radio Patrol**, 1935, Whit, 432p, by Eddie Sullivan & Charlie Schmidt (#1) | 7.50 | 22.50 | 45.00 |
| **1173-Radio Patrol Trailing the Safeblowers**, 1937, Whit, 432p | 6.00 | 18.00 | 36.00 |

|  | Good | Fine | N-Mint |
|---|---|---|---|
| **1496-Radio Patrol Outwitting the Gang Chief**, 1939, Whit, 432p | | | |
| | 6.00 | 18.00 | 36.00 |
| **1498-Radio Patrol and Big Dan's Mobsters**, 1937, Whit, 432p | | | |
| | 6.00 | 18.00 | 36.00 |
| **1441-Range Busters, The**, 1942, Whit, 432p, Henry E. Vallely-a | | | |
| | 6.00 | 18.00 | 36.00 |
| **1163-Ranger and the Cowboy, The**, 1939, Sal, 400p | | | |
| | 5.00 | 15.00 | 30.00 |
| **1154-Rangers on the Rio Grande**, 1938, Sal, 400p | | | |
| | 5.00 | 15.00 | 30.00 |
| **1447-Ray Land of the Tank Corps, U.S.A.**, 1942, Whit, 432p, flip pictures, Hess-a | 5.00 | 15.00 | 30.00 |
| **1157-Red Barry Ace-Detective**, 1935, Whit, 432p, by Will Gould | | | |
| | 7.00 | 21.00 | 42.00 |
| **1426-Red Barry Undercover Man**, 1939, Whit, 432p, by Will Gould | | | |
| | 6.00 | 18.00 | 36.00 |
| **20-Red Davis**, 1935, EVW, 160p | 8.00 | 24.00 | 48.00 |
| **1449-Red Death on the Range, The**, 1940, Whit, 432p, Fred Harman-a | | | |
| (Bronc Peeler) | 7.00 | 21.00 | 42.00 |
| **nn-Red Hen and the Fox, The**, nd (1930s), np (Whit), 36p, 3″ × 2½″, Penny Book | 1.50 | 4.50 | 9.00 |
| **1145-Red Hot Holsters**, 1938, Sal, 400p | 5.00 | 15.00 | 30.00 |
| **1400-Red Ryder and Little Beaver on Hoofs of Thunder**, 1939, Whit, 432p, Harman c/a | 10.00 | 30.00 | 60.00 |
| **1414-Red Ryder and the Squaw-Tooth Rustlers**, 1946, Whit, 352p, Fred Harman-a | 7.00 | 21.00 | 42.00 |
| **1427-Red Ryder and the Code of the West**, 1941, Whit, 432p, flip pictures, by Harman | 9.00 | 27.00 | 54.00 |
| **1440-Red Ryder the Fighting Westerner**, 1940, Whit, Harman-a | | | |
| | 9.00 | 27.00 | 54.00 |
| **1443-Red Ryder and the Rimrock Killer**, 1948, Whit, 288p, Harman-a | | | |
| | 6.00 | 18.00 | 36.00 |
| **1450-Red Ryder and Western Border Guns**, 1942, Whit, 432p, flip pictures, by Harman | 9.00 | 27.00 | 54.00 |
| **1454-Red Ryder and the Secret Canyon**, 1948, Whit, 288p, Harman-a | | | |
| | 6.00 | 18.00 | 36.00 |
| **1466-Red Ryder and Circus Luck**, 1947, Whit, 288p, by Fred Harman | | | |
| | 6.00 | 18.00 | 36.00 |
| **1473-Red Ryder in War on the Range**, 1945, Whit, 352p, by Fred Harman | 7.00 | 21.00 | 42.00 |

*Red Ryder and Little Beaver on Hoofs of Thunder #1400,*
*© NEA Service, 1939*

|  | Good | Fine | N-Mint |
|---|---|---|---|
| **1475-Red Ryder and the Outlaws of Painted Valley**, 1943, Whit, 352p, by Harman | 7.50 | 22.50 | 45.00 |
| **702-10-Red Ryder Acting Sheriff**, 1949, Whit, by Fred Harman | 5.00 | 15.00 | 30.00 |
| **nn-Red Ryder Brings Law to Devil's Hole**, 1939, Dell, 196p, Fast-Action Story, Harman c/a | 15.00 | 45.00 | 90.00 |
| **nn-Red Ryder and the Highway Robbers**, 1938, Whit, 36p, 2½″ × 3½″, Penny Book | 4.50 | 14.00 | 28.00 |
| **754-Reg'lar Fellers**, 1933, Whit, 320p, by Gene Byrnes | 9.00 | 27.00 | 54.00 |
| **nn-Reg'lar Fellers**, 1933, Whit, 202p, Cocomalt premium, by Gene Byrnes | 9.00 | 27.00 | 54.00 |
| **1424-Rex Beach's Jaragu of the Jungle**, 1937, Whit, 432p | 5.50 | 16.50 | 33.00 |
| **12-Rex, King of Wild Horses in "Stampede,"** 1935, EVW, 160p, movie scenes, Columbia Pictures | 7.00 | 21.00 | 42.00 |
| **1100B-Riddles for Fun**, 1938, Whit, 36p, 2½″ × 3½″, Penny Book | 2.00 | 6.00 | 12.00 |

| | Good | Fine | N-Mint |
|---|---|---|---|
| **1100B-Riddles to Guess**, 1938, Whit, 36p, 2½″ × 3½″, Penny Book | | | |
| | 2.00 | 6.00 | 12.00 |
| **1425-Riders of Lone Trails**, 1937, Whit, 300p | | | |
| | 5.00 | 15.00 | 30.00 |
| **1141-Rio Raiders** (A Billy the Kid Story), 1938, Sal, 400p | | | |
| | 5.00 | 15.00 | 30.00 |
| **5767-2-Road Runner, The Lost Road Runner Mine, The**, 1974 (1980), | | | |
| 260p, 79 cents, B&W, soft-c | .50 | 1.50 | 3.00 |
| **Robin Hood** (See Wee Little Books) | | | |
| **10-Robin Hood**, 1935, EVW, 160p, movie scenes w/Douglas | | | |
| Fairbanks (United Artists), hard-c | 12.00 | 35.00 | 70.00 |
| **719-Robinson Crusoe** (The Story of . . . ), nd (1933), Whit, 364p, | | | |
| soft-c | 9.00 | 27.00 | 54.00 |
| **1421-Roy Rogers and the Dwarf-Cattle Ranch**, 1947, Whit, 352p, | | | |
| Henry E. Vallely-a | 8.00 | 24.00 | 48.00 |
| **1437-Roy Rogers and the Deadly Treasure**, 1947, Whit, 288p | | | |
| | 7.00 | 21.00 | 42.00 |
| **1448-Roy Rogers and the Mystery of the Howling Mesa**, 1948, Whit, | | | |
| 288p | 7.00 | 21.00 | 42.00 |
| **1452-Roy Rogers in Robbers' Roost**, 1948, Whit, 288p | | | |
| | 7.00 | 21.00 | 42.00 |
| **1460-Roy Rogers Robinhood of the Range**, 1942, Whit, 432p, Hess-a | | | |
| (1st) | 8.00 | 24.00 | 48.00 |
| **1462-Roy Rogers and the Mystery of the Lazy M**, 1949, Whit | | | |
| | 6.00 | 18.00 | 36.00 |
| **1476-Roy Rogers King of the Cowboys**, 1943, Whit, 352p, Irwin | | | |
| Myers-a, based on movie | 9.00 | 27.00 | 54.00 |
| **1494-Roy Rogers at Crossed Feathers Ranch**, 1945, Whit, 320p, | | | |
| Erwin Hess-a | 7.00 | 21.00 | 42.00 |
| **701-10-Roy Rogers and the Snowbound Outlaws**, 1949, 3¼″ × 5½″ | | | |
| | 4.50 | 14.00 | 28.00 |
| **715-10-Roy Rogers Range Detective**, 1950, Whit, 2½″ × 5″ | | | |
| | 4.50 | 14.00 | 28.00 |
| **nn-Sandy Gregg Federal Agent on Special Assignment**, 1939, | | | |
| Whit, 36p, 2½″ × 3½″ Penny Book | 4.00 | 12.00 | 24.00 |
| **Sappo** (See Top-Line Comics) | | | |
| **1122-Scrappy**, 1934, Whit, 288p | 12.00 | 35.00 | 70.00 |
| **L12-Scrappy** (The Adventures of . . . ), 1935, Lynn, 192p, movie | | | |
| scenes | 12.00 | 35.00 | 70.00 |

|                          | Good  | Fine  | N-Mint |
|--------------------------|-------|-------|--------|

**1191-Secret Agent K-7**, 1940, Sal, 400p, based on radio show
|       | 5.00  | 15.00 | 30.00  |

*Secret Agent X-9 #1144, © King Features Syndicate, 1936*

**1144-Secret Agent X-9**, 1936, Whit, 432p, Charles Flanders-a
|       | 9.00  | 27.00 | 54.00  |

**1472-Secret Agent X-9 and the Mad Assassin**, 1938, Whit, 432p,
Charles Flanders-a
|       | 9.00  | 27.00 | 54.00  |

**1161-Sequoia**, 1935, Whit, 160p, photo-c, movie scenes
|       | 7.00  | 21.00 | 42.00  |

**1430-Shadow and the Living Death, The**, 1940, Whit, 432p, Erwin
Hess-a
|       | 23.00 | 70.00 | 140.00 |

**1443-Shadow and the Master of Evil, The**, 1941, Whit, 432p, flip pictures, Hess-a
|       | 23.00 | 70.00 | 140.00 |

**1495-Shadow and the Ghost Makers, The**, 1942, Whit, 432p, John
Coleman Burroughs-c
|       | 23.00 | 70.00 | 140.00 |

**2024-Shazzan, The Glass Princess**, 1968, Whit
|       | 2.00  | 6.00  | 12.00  |

    **Shirley Temple** (See My Life and Times & Story of . . .)

|  | Good | Fine | N-Mint |
|---|---|---|---|

**1095-Shirley Temple and Lionel Barrymore Starring in "The Little Colonel,"** 1935, Sal, photo-c, movie scenes

|  | 8.50 | 25.00 | 50.00 |
|---|---|---|---|

**1115-Shirley Temple in the Littlest Rebel**, 1935, Sal, photo-c, movie scenes, hard-c

|  | 8.50 | 25.00 | 50.00 |
|---|---|---|---|

**1595-Shirley Temple in the Littlest Rebel**, 1935, Sal, photo-c, movie scenes, soft-c

|  | 8.50 | 25.00 | 50.00 |
|---|---|---|---|

**1195-Shooting Sheriffs of the Wild West**, 1936, Whit, 432p

|  | 5.50 | 16.50 | 33.00 |
|---|---|---|---|

**1169-Silly Symphony Featuring Donald Duck** (Disney), 1937, Whit, 432p, Taliaferro-a

|  | 14.00 | 42.00 | 84.00 |
|---|---|---|---|

**1441-Silly Symphony Featuring Donald Duck and His (Mis) Adventures** (Disney), 1937, Whit, 432p, Taliaferro-a

|  | 14.00 | 42.00 | 84.00 |
|---|---|---|---|

**1155-Silver Streak, The**, 1935, Whit, 160p, photo-c, movie scenes (RKO Radio Pict.)

|  | 7.00 | 21.00 | 42.00 |
|---|---|---|---|

**Simple Simon** (See Wee Little Books)

**1649-Sir Lancelot** (TV Series), 1958, Whit, 280p

|  | 3.00 | 9.00 | 18.00 |
|---|---|---|---|
|  | 7.50 | 22.50 | 45.00 |

**1112-Skeezix in Africa**, 1934, Whit, 300p, Frank King-a

**1408-Skeezix at the Military Academy**, 1938, Whit, 432p, Frank King-a

|  | 6.00 | 18.00 | 36.00 |
|---|---|---|---|

**1414-Skeezix Goes to War**, 1944, Whit, 352p, Frank King-a

|  | 6.00 | 18.00 | 36.00 |
|---|---|---|---|

**1419-Skeezix on His Own in the Big City**, 1941, Whit, All Pictures Comics, flip pictures, Frank King-a

|  | 7.00 | 21.00 | 42.00 |
|---|---|---|---|

**761-Skippy**, 1934, Whit., 320p, by Percy Crosby

|  | 10.00 | 30.00 | 60.00 |
|---|---|---|---|

**4056-Skippy, The Story of**, 1934, Whit, 320p, 7" × 9½", Big Big Book, Percy Crosby-a

|  | 33.00 | 100.00 | 200.00 |
|---|---|---|---|

**nn-Skippy, The Story of**, 1934, Whit, Phillips Dental Magnesia premium, soft-c, by Percy Crosby

|  | 8.50 | 25.00 | 50.00 |
|---|---|---|---|

**1439-Skyroads with Clipper Williams of the Flying Legion**, 1938, Whit, 432p, by Lt. Dick Calkins, Russell Keaton-a

|  | 6.00 | 18.00 | 36.00 |
|---|---|---|---|

**1127-Skyroads with Hurricane Hawk**, 1936, Whit, 432p, by Lt. Dick Calkins, Russell Keaton-a

|  | 6.00 | 18.00 | 36.00 |
|---|---|---|---|

**Smilin' Jack and His Flivver Plane** (See Top-Line Comics)

| | Good | Fine | N-Mint |
|---|---|---|---|

**1152-Smilin' Jack and the Stratosphere Ascent**, 1937, Whit, 432p,
    Zack Mosley-a             10.00      30.00      60.00

**1412-Smilin' Jack Flying High with "Downwind,"** 1942, Whit, 432p,
    Zack Mosley-a             9.00      27.00      54.00

**1416-Smilin' Jack in Wings over the Pacific**, 1939, Whit, 432p, Zack
    Mosley-a             9.00      27.00      54.00

**1419-Smilin' Jack and the Jungle Pipe Line**, 1947, Whit, 352p, Zack
    Mosley-a             8.00      24.00      48.00

**1445-Smilin' Jack and the Escape from Death Rock**, 1943, Whit,
    352p, Mosley-a             8.00      24.00      48.00

**1464-Smilin' Jack and the Coral Princess**, 1945, Whit, 352p, Zack
    Mosley-a             8.00      24.00      48.00

**1473-Smilin' Jack Speed Pilot**, 1941, Whit, 432p, Zack Mosley-a
                       9.00      27.00      54.00

**2-Smilin' Jack and His Stratosphere Plane**, 1938, Whit, 132p,
    Buddy Book, soft-c, Zack Mosley-a
                       15.00      45.00      90.00

**nn-Smilin' Jack Grounded on a Tropical Shore**, 1938, Whit, 36p,
    2½″ × 3½″, Penny Book      4.50      14.00      28.00

**11-Smilin' Jack and the Border Bandits**, 1941, Dell, 196p, Fast-
    Action Story, soft-c, Zack Mosley-a
                       17.00      50.00      100.00

**745-Smitty Golden Gloves Tournament**, 1934, Whit, 320p, Walter
    Berndt-a             9.00      27.00      54.00

**nn-Smitty Golden Gloves Tournament**, 1934, Whit, 204p,
    Cocomalt premium, soft-c, Walter Berndt-a
                       9.00      27.00      54.00

**1404-Smitty and Herbie Lost Among the Indians**, 1941, Whit, All Pic-
    tures Comics             6.00      18.00      36.00

**1477-Smitty in Going Native**, 1938, Whit, 300p, Walter Berndt-a
                       6.00      18.00      36.00

**2-Smitty and Herby**, 1936, Whit, 132p, 3½″ × 3½″, soft-c, Tarzan
    Ice Cream cup lid premium    15.00      45.00      90.00

**9-Smitty's Brother Herby and the Police Horse**, 1938, Whit,
    132p, 3¾″ × 3½″, Buddy Book ice cream premium, by Walter
    Berndt             15.00      45.00      90.00

**1010-Smokey Stover Firefighter of Foo**, 1937, Whit, 7¼″ × 5½″, 64p,
    Nickle Book, Bill Holman-a    7.00      21.00      42.00

**1413-Smokey Stover**, 1942, Whit, All Pictures Comics, flip pictures,
    Bill Holman-a             7.00      21.00      42.00

*Smokey Stover the Foo Fighter #1421,*
*© Whitman Publishing Co., 1938*

|  | Good | Fine | N-Mint |
|---|---|---|---|
| **1421-Smokey Stover the Foo Fighter**, 1938, Whit, 432p, Bill Holman-a | | | |
|  | 7.00 | 21.00 | 42.00 |
| **1481-Smokey Stover the Foolish Foo Fighter**, 1942, Whit, All Pictures | | | |
| Comics | 7.00 | 21.00 | 42.00 |
| **1-Smokey Stover the Fireman of Foo**, 1938, Whit, 3¾″ × 3½″, | | | |
| 132p, Buddy Book ice cream premium, by Bill Holman | | | |
|  | 15.00 | 45.00 | 90.00 |
| **1100A-Smokey Stover**, 1938, Whit, 36p, 2½″ × 3½″, Penny Book | | | |
|  | 4.50 | 14.00 | 28.00 |
| **nn-Smokey Stover and the Fire Chief of Foo**, 1938, Whit, 36p, | | | |
| 2½″ × 3½″, Penny Book, yellow shirt on-c | | | |
|  | 4.50 | 14.00 | 28.00 |
| **nn-Smokey Stover and the Fire Chief of Foo**, 1938, Whit, 36p, | | | |
| Penny Book, Green shirt on-c | 5.50 | 16.00 | 32.00 |
| **1460-Snow White and the Seven Dwarfs** (The Story of Walt Dis- | | | |
| ney's . . . ), 1938, Whit, 288p | 13.00 | 40.00 | 80.00 |
| **1136-Sombrero Pete**, 1936, Whit, 432p | 5.50 | 16.50 | 33.00 |
| **1152-Son of Mystery**, 1939, Sal, 400p | 5.00 | 15.00 | 30.00 |

|  | Good | Fine | N-Mint |
|---|---|---|---|
| **1191-SOS Coast Guard**, 1936, Whit, 432p, Henry E. Vallely-a | | | |
| | 5.00 | 15.00 | 30.00 |
| **2016-(#16)-Space Ghost-The Sorceress of Cyba-3** (TV Cartoon), 1968, Whit, 260p, 39 cents, hard-c, color illos | | | |
| | 4.50 | 14.00 | 28.00 |
| **1455-Speed Douglas and the Mole Gang-The Great Sabotage Plot**, 1941, Whit, 432p, flip pictures | | | |
| | 5.00 | 15.00 | 30.00 |
| **5779-2-Spider-Man Zaps Mr. Zodiac**, 1976 (1980), 260p, 79 cents, soft-c, B&W | | | |
| | .50 | 1.50 | 3.00 |
| **1467-Spike Kelly of the Commandos**, 1943, Whit, 352p | | | |
| | 5.00 | 15.00 | 30.00 |
| **1144-Spook Riders on the Overland**, 1938, Sal, 400p | | | |
| | 5.00 | 15.00 | 30.00 |
| **768-Spy, The**, 1936, Whit, 300p | 7.00 | 21.00 | 42.00 |
| **nn-Spy Smasher and the Red Death**, 1941, Faw, 4″ × 5½″, Dime Action Book | 21.50 | 65.00 | 130.00 |
| **1120-Stan Kent Freshman Fullback**, 1936, Sal, 148p, hard-c | | | |
| | 4.50 | 13.50 | 27.00 |
| **1132-Stan Kent, Captain**, 1937, Sal | 4.50 | 13.50 | 27.00 |
| **1600-Stan Kent Freshman Fullback**, 1936, Sal, 148p, soft-c | | | |
| | 4.50 | 13.50 | 27.00 |
| **1123-Stan Kent Varsity Man**, 1936, Sal, 160p, hard-c | | | |
| | 4.50 | 13.50 | 27.00 |
| **1603-Stan Kent Varsity Man**, 1936, Sal, 160p, soft-c | | | |
| | 4.50 | 13.50 | 27.00 |
| **1104-Steel Arena, The** (With Clyde Beatty), 1936, Sal, hard-c, movie scenes adapted from *The Lost Jungle* | | | |
| | 8.00 | 24.00 | 48.00 |
| **1584-Steel Arena, The** (With Clyde Beatty), 1936, Sal, soft-c, movie scenes | | | |
| | 8.00 | 24.00 | 48.00 |
| **1426-Steve Hunter of the U.S. Coast Guard under Secret Orders**, 1942, Whit, 432p | | | |
| | 5.00 | 15.00 | 30.00 |
| **1456-Story of Charlie McCarthy and Edgar Bergen, The**, 1938, Whit, 288p | 7.00 | 21.00 | 42.00 |
| **Story of Daniel, The** (See Wee Little Books) | | | |
| **Story of David, The** (See Wee Little Books) | | | |
| **1110-Story of Freddie Bartholomew, The**, 1935, Sal, 4½″ × 5¼″, hard-c, movie scenes (MGM) | 7.00 | 21.00 | 42.00 |
| **1590-Story of Freddie Bartholomew, The**, 1935, Sal, 4½″ × 5¼″, soft-c, movie scenes (MGM) | 7.00 | 21.00 | 42.00 |

|  | Good | Fine | N-Mint |
|---|---|---|---|
| **Story of Gideon, The** (See Wee Little Books) | | | |
| W714-**Story of Jackie Cooper, The**, 1933, Whit, 240p, photo-c, movie scenes, "Skippy" & "Sooky" movie | 9.00 | 27.00 | 54.00 |
| **Story of Joseph, The** (See Wee Little Books) | | | |
| **Story of Moses, The** (See Wee Little Books) | | | |
| **Story of Ruth and Naomi** (See Wee Little Books) | | | |
| 1089-**Story of Shirley Temple, The**, 1934, Sal, 160p, hard photo-c, movie scenes | 8.50 | 25.00 | 50.00 |
| 1319-**Story of Shirley Temple, The**, 1934, Sal, 160p, soft photo-c, movie scenes | 8.50 | 25.00 | 50.00 |
| 1090-**Strawberry-Roan**, 1934, Sal, 160p, hard-c, Ken Maynard photo-c, movie scenes | 10.00 | 30.00 | 60.00 |
| 1320-**Strawberry-Roan**, 1934, Sal, 160p, soft-c, Ken Maynard photo-c, movie scenes | 10.00 | 30.00 | 60.00 |
| **Streaky and the Football Signals** (See Top-Line Comics) | | | |
| 5780-2-**Superman in the Phantom Zone Connection**, 1980, 260p, 79 cents, soft-c, B&W | .50 | 1.50 | 3.00 |
| 747-**Tailspin Tommy in the Famous Pay-Roll Mystery**, 1933, Whit, 320p, Hal Forrest-a (#1) | 10.00 | 30.00 | 60.00 |

*Tailspin Tommy the Pay-Roll Mystery, nn,*
© *Stephen Slesinger, 1934*

**nn-Tailspin Tommy the Pay-Roll Mystery**, 1934, Whit, 52p, 3½″ × 5¼″, premium-no ads, soft-c; another version with Perkins ad, Hal Forrest-a          12.00          35.00          70.00

|  | Good | Fine | N-Mint |
|---|---|---|---|
| **1110-Tailspin Tommy and the Island in the Sky**, 1936, Whit, 432p, Hal Forrest-a | 8.00 | 24.00 | 48.00 |
| **1124-Tailspin Tommy the Dirigible Flight to the North Pole**, 1934, Whit, 432p, H. Forrest-a | 9.00 | 27.00 | 54.00 |
| **nn-Tailspin Tommy the Dirigible Flight to the North Pole**, 1934, Whit, 436p, 3-color, soft-c, premium-no ads, Hal Forrest-a | 15.00 | 45.00 | 90.00 |
| **1172-Tailspin Tommy Hunting for Pirate Gold**, 1935, Whit, 432p, Hal Forrest-a | 8.00 | 24.00 | 48.00 |
| **1183-Tailspin Tommy Air Racer**, 1940, Sal, 400p, hard-c | 8.00 | 24.00 | 48.00 |
| **1184-Tailspin Tommy in the Great Air Mystery**, 1936, Whit, 240p, photo-c, movie scenes | 9.00 | 27.00 | 54.00 |
| **1410-Tailspin Tommy the Weasel and His "Skywaymen,"** 1941, Whit, All Pictures Comics, flip pictures | 7.00 | 21.00 | 42.00 |
| **1413-Tailspin Tommy and the Lost Transport**, 1940, Whit, 432p, Hal Forrest-a | 7.00 | 21.00 | 42.00 |
| **1423-Tailspin Tommy and the Hooded Flyer**, 1937, Whit, 432p, Hal Forrest-a | 8.00 | 24.00 | 48.00 |
| **1494-Tailspin Tommy and the Sky Bandits**, 1938, Whit, 432p, Hal Forrest-a | 8.00 | 24.00 | 48.00 |
| **nn-Tailspin Tommy and the Airliner Mystery**, 1938, Whit, 196p, Fast-Action Story, soft-c, Hal Forrest-a | 18.00 | 55.00 | 110.00 |
| **nn-Tailspin Tommy in Flying Aces**, 1938, Dell, 196p, Fast-Action Story, soft-c, Hal Forrest-a | 18.00 | 55.00 | 110.00 |
| **nn-Tailspin Tommy in Wings over the Arctic**, 1934, Whit, Cocomalt premium, Forrest-a | 10.00 | 30.00 | 60.00 |
| **3-Tailspin Tommy on the Mountain of Human Sacrifice**, 1938, Whit, soft-c, Buddy Book | 12.50 | 37.50 | 75.00 |
| **7-Tailspin Tommy's Perilous Adventure**, 1934, Whit, 132p, 3½" × 3½", soft-c, Tarzan Ice Cream cup premium | 15.00 | 45.00 | 90.00 |
| **L16-Tale of Two Cities, A**, 1935, Lynn, movie scenes | 10.00 | 30.00 | 60.00 |
| **744-Tarzan of the Apes**, 1933, Whit, 320p, by Edgar Rice Burroughs (1st) | 18.00 | 55.00 | 110.00 |

|  | Good | Fine | N-Mint |
|---|---|---|---|
| **nn-Tarzan of the Apes**, 1935, Whit, 52p, 3½″ × 5¾″, soft-c, stapled, premium, no ad; another version with a Perkins ad | | | |
|  | 25.00 | 75.00 | 150.00 |
| **769-Tarzan the Fearless**, 1934, Whit, 240p, Buster Crabbe photo-c, movie scenes, ERB | 15.00 | 45.00 | 90.00 |
| **770-Tarzan Twins, The**, 1934, Whit, 432p, ERB | | | |
|  | 42.00 | 125.00 | 250.00 |
| **770-Tarzan Twins, The**, 1935, Whit, 432p, ERB | | | |
|  | 27.00 | 80.00 | 160.00 |
| **nn-Tarzan Twins, The**, 1935, Whit, 52p, 3½″ × 5¾″, premium-no ads, soft-c, ERB | 27.00 | 80.00 | 160.00 |
| **nn-Tarzan Twins, The**, 1935, Whit, 436p, 3-color, soft-c, premium-no ads, ERB | 28.00 | 85.00 | 170.00 |
| **778-Tarzan of the Screen** (The Story of Johnny Weissmuller), 1934, Whit, 240p, photo-c, movie scenes, ERB | 15.00 | 45.00 | 90.00 |
| **1102-Tarzan, The Return of**, 1936, Whit, 432p, Edgar Rice Burroughs | 12.50 | 37.50 | 75.00 |
| **1180-Tarzan, The New Adventures of**, 1935, Whit, 160p, Herman Brix photo-c, movie scenes, ERB | 12.50 | 37.50 | 75.00 |

*Tarzan Escapes #1182,*
*© Edgar Rice Burroughs, 1936*

|  | Good | Fine | N-Mint |
|---|---|---|---|
| **1182-Tarzan Escapes**, 1936, Whit, 240p, Johnny Weissmuller photo-c, movie scenes, ERB | 15.00 | 45.00 | 90.00 |
| **1407-Tarzan Lord of the Jungle**, 1946, Whit, 352p, ERB | 10.00 | 30.00 | 60.00 |
| **1410-Tarzan, The Beasts of**, 1937, Whit, 432p, Edgar Rice Burroughs | 12.00 | 35.00 | 70.00 |
| **1442-Tarzan and the Lost Empire**, 1948, Whit, 288p, ERB | 11.00 | 32.50 | 65.00 |
| **1444-Tarzan and the Ant Men**, 1945, Whit, 352p, ERB | 11.00 | 32.50 | 65.00 |
| **1448-Tarzan and the Golden Lion**, 1943, Whit, 432p, ERB | 12.00 | 35.00 | 70.00 |
| **1452-Tarzan the Untamed**, 1941, Whit, 432p, flip pictures, ERB | 12.00 | 35.00 | 70.00 |
| **1453-Tarzan the Terrible**, 1942, Whit, 432p, flip pictures, ERB | 12.00 | 35.00 | 70.00 |
| **1467-Tarzan in the Land of the Giant Apes**, 1949, Whit, ERB | 11.00 | 32.50 | 65.00 |
| **1477-Tarzan, The Son of**, 1939, Whit, 432p, ERB | 12.50 | 37.50 | 75.00 |
| **1488-Tarzan's Revenge**, 1938, Whit, 432p, ERB | 12.50 | 37.50 | 75.00 |
| **1495-Tarzan and the Jewels of Opar**, 1940, Whit, 432p | 12.50 | 37.50 | 75.00 |
| **4056-Tarzan and the Tarzan Twins with Jad-Bal-Ja the Golden Lion**, 1936, Whit, 7″ × 9½″, 320p, Big Big Book | 70.00 | 200.00 | 400.00 |
| **709-10-Tarzan and the Journey of Terror**, 1950, Whit, 2½″ × 5″, ERB, Marsh-a | 6.00 | 18.00 | 36.00 |
| **2005-(#5)-Tarzan: The Mark of the Red Hyena**, 1967, Whit, 260p, 39 cents, hard-c, color illos | 2.50 | 7.50 | 15.00 |
| **nn-Tarzan**, 1935, Whit, 148p, soft-c, 3½″ × 4″, Tarzan Ice Cream cup premium, ERB (Scarce) | 48.00 | 145.00 | 290.00 |
| **nn-Tarzan and His Jungle Friends**, 1936, Whit, 132p, soft-c, 3½″ × 3½″, Tarzan Ice Cream cup premium, ERB (Scarce) | 44.00 | 140.00 | 280.00 |
| **nn-Tarzan in the Golden City**, 1938, Whit, 68p, Pan-Am premium, soft-c, ERB | 12.00 | 35.00 | 70.00 |
| **nn-Tarzan the Avenger**, 1939, Dell, 194p, Fast-Action Story, ERB, soft-c | 23.00 | 70.00 | 140.00 |

|  | Good | Fine | N-Mint |
|---|---|---|---|

**nn-Tarzan with the Tarzan Twins in the Jungle**, 1938, Dell, 194p,
Fast-Action Story, ERB          23.00          70.00          140.00

**1100B-Tell Your Fortune**, 1938, Whit, 36p, 2½″ × 3½″, Penny Book
                                                 2.30          7.00          14.00

**1156-Terry and the Pirates**, 1935, Whit, 432p, Milton Caniff-a (#1)
                                                 12.00          35.00          70.00

**nn-Terry and the Pirates**, 1935, Whit, 52p, 3½″ × 5¾″, soft-c, premium, Milton Caniff-a; 3 versions: No ad, Sears ad & Perkins ad
                                                 13.00          40.00          80.00

**1412-Terry and the Pirates Shipwrecked on a Desert Island**, 1938,
Whit, 432p, Milton Caniff-a          9.00          27.00          54.00

**1420-Terry and War in the Jungle**, 1946, Whit, 352p, Milton Caniff-a
                                                 8.00          24.00          48.00

**1436-Terry and the Pirates the Plantation Mystery**, 1942, Whit,
432p, flip pictures, Milton Caniff-a          9.00          27.00          54.00

*Terry and the Pirates and the Giant's Vengeance #1446,*
*© Whitman Publishing Co., 1939*

**1446-Terry and the Pirates and the Giant's Vengeance**, 1939, Whit,
432p, Caniff-a          9.00          27.00          54.00

|  | Good | Fine | N-Mint |
|---|---|---|---|

**1499-Terry and the Pirates in the Mountain Stronghold**, 1941, Whit, 432p, Caniff-a — 9.00 — 27.00 — 54.00

**4073-Terry and the Pirates, The Adventures of**, 1938, Whit, 7″ × 9½″, 320p, Big Big Book, Milton Caniff-a — 53.00 — 160.00 — 320.00

**10-Terry and the Pirates Meet Again**, 1936, Whit, 132p, 3½″ × 3½″, soft-c, Tarzan Ice Cream cup lid premium — 19.00 — 57.50 — 115.00

**nn-Terry and the Pirates, Adventures of**, 1938, 36p, 2½″ × 3½″, Penny Book, Caniff-a — 5.00 — 15.00 — 30.00

**nn-Terry and the Pirates and the Island Rescue**, 1938, Whit, 68p, 3¾″ × 3½″, Pan-Am premium — 10.00 — 30.00 — 60.00

**nn-Terry and the Pirates on Their Travels**, 1938, 36p, 2½″ × 3½″, Penny Book, Caniff-a — 5.00 — 15.00 — 30.00

**nn-Terry and the Pirates and the Mystery Ship**, 1938, Dell, 194p, Fast-Action Story, soft-c — 19.00 — 57.50 — 115.00

**1492-Terry Lee Flight Officer U.S.A.**, 1944, Whit, 352p, Milton Caniff-a — 8.00 — 24.00 — 48.00

**7-Texas Bad Man, The** (Tom Mix), 1934, EVW, 160p (Five Star Library), movie scenes — 14.00 — 42.00 — 84.00

**1429-Texas Kid, The**, 1937, Whit, 432p — 5.50 — 16.50 — 33.00

**1135-Texas Ranger, The**, 1936, Whit, 432p, Hal Arbo-a — 5.50 — 16.50 — 33.00

**nn-Texas Ranger, The**, 1935, Whit, 260p, Cocomalt premium, soft-c, Hal Arbo-a — 7.00 — 20.00 — 40.00

**nn-Texas Ranger in the West, The**, 1938, Whit, 36p, 2½″ × 3½″, Penny Book — 4.00 — 12.00 — 24.00

**nn-Texas Ranger to the Rescue, The**, 1938, Whit, 36p, 2½″ × 3½″, Penny Book — 4.00 — 12.00 — 24.00

**12-Texas Rangers in Rustler Strategy, The**, 1936, Whit, 132p, 3½″ × 3½″, soft-c, Tarzan Ice Cream cup lid premium — 14.00 — 42.00 — 84.00

**Tex Thorne** (See Zane Grey)

**Thimble Theatre** (See Popeye)

**L26-13 Hours By Air**, 1936, Lynn, 128p, 5″ × 7½″, photo-c, movie scenes (Paramount Pictures) — 10.00 — 30.00 — 60.00

**nn-Three Bears, The**, nd (1930s), np (Whit), 36p, 3″ × 2½″, Penny Book — 1.50 — 4.50 — 9.00

**1129-Three Finger Joe** (Baseball), 1937, Sal, Robert A. Graef-a — 5.00 — 15.00 — 30.00

|  | Good | Fine | N-Mint |
|---|---|---|---|
| **nn-Three Little Pigs, The**, nd (1930s), np (Whit), 36p, 3″ × 2½″, Penny Book | 1.50 | 4.50 | 9.00 |
| **1131-Three Musketeers**, 1935, Whit, 182p, 5¼″ × 6¼″, photo-c, movie scenes | 8.50 | 25.00 | 50.00 |
| **1409-Thumper and the Seven Dwarfs** (Disney), 1944, Whit, All Pictures Comics | 11.00 | 32.50 | 65.00 |
| **1108-Tiger Lady, The** (The life of Mabel Stark, animal trainer), 1935, Sal, photo-c, movie scenes, hard-c | 7.00 | 21.00 | 42.00 |
| **1588-Tiger Lady, The** , 1935, Sal, photo-c, movie scenes, soft-c | 7.00 | 21.00 | 42.00 |
| **1442-Tillie the Toiler and the Wild Man of Desert Island**, 1941, Whit, 432p, Russ Westover-a | 8.00 | 24.00 | 48.00 |
| **1058-Timid Elmer** (Disney), 1939, Whit, 5″ × 5½″, 68p, hard-c | 7.00 | 21.00 | 42.00 |
| **1152-Tim McCoy in the Prescott Kid**, 1935, Whit, 160p, hard photo-c, movie scenes | 13.00 | 40.00 | 80.00 |
| **1193-Tim McCoy in the Westerner**, 1936, Whit, 240p, photo-c, movie scenes | 12.50 | 37.50 | 75.00 |
| **1436-Tim McCoy on the Tomahawk Trail**, 1937, Whit, 432p, Robert Weisman-a | 7.00 | 21.00 | 42.00 |
| **1490-Tim McCoy and the Sandy Gulch Stampede**, 1939, Whit, 424p | 7.00 | 21.00 | 42.00 |
| **2-Tim McCoy in Beyond the Law**, 1934, EVW, Five Star Library, photo-c, movie scenes (Columbia Pictures) | 14.00 | 42.00 | 84.00 |
| **10-Tim McCoy in Fighting the Redskins**, 1938, Whit, 130p, Buddy Book, soft-c | 15.00 | 45.00 | 90.00 |
| **14-Tim McCoy in Speedwings**, 1935, EVW, Five Star Library, 160p, photo-c, movie scenes (Columbia Pictures) | 14.00 | 42.00 | 84.00 |
| **nn-Tim the Builder**, nd (1930s), np (Whit), 36p, 3″ × 2½″, Penny Book | 1.50 | 4.50 | 9.00 |
| **Tim Tyler** (See Adventures of . . . ) | | | |
| **1140-Tim Tyler's Luck Adventures in the Ivory Patrol**, 1937, Whit, 432p, by Lyman Young | 7.00 | 21.00 | 42.00 |
| **1479-Tim Tyler's Luck and the Plot of the Exiled King**, 1939, Whit, 432p, by Lyman Young | 6.00 | 18.00 | 36.00 |
| **767-Tiny Tim, The Adventures of**, 1935, Whit, 384p, by Stanley Link | 9.00 | 27.00 | 54.00 |

*Tiny Tim and the Mechanical Men #1172,*
*© Stanley Link, 1937*

|  | Good | Fine | N-Mint |
|---|---|---|---|
| **1172-Tiny Tim and the Mechanical Men**, 1937, Whit, 432p, by | | | |
| Stanley Link | 8.00 | 24.00 | 48.00 |
| **1472-Tiny Tim in the Big, Big World**, 1945, Whit, 352p, by Stanley | | | |
| Link | 7.00 | 21.00 | 42.00 |
| **2006-(#6)-Tom and Jerry Meet Mr. Fingers**, 1967, Whit, 39 cents, | | | |
| 260p, hard-c, color illos | 2.00 | 6.00 | 12.00 |
| **5787-2-Tom and Jerry under the Big Top**, 1980, Whit, 79 cents, 260p, | | | |
| soft-c, B&W | .50 | 1.50 | 3.00 |
| **723-Tom Beatty Ace of the Service**, 1934, Whit, 256p, George | | | |
| Taylor-a | 8.00 | 24.00 | 48.00 |
| **nn-Tom Beatty Ace of the Service**, 1934, Whit, 260p, soft-c | | | |
| | 8.00 | 24.00 | 48.00 |
| **1165-Tom Beatty Ace of the Service Scores Again**, 1937, Whit, 432p, | | | |
| Weisman-a | 7.00 | 21.00 | 42.00 |
| **1420-Tom Beatty Ace of the Service and the Big Brain Gang**, 1939, | | | |
| Whit, 432p | 7.00 | 21.00 | 42.00 |
| **nn-Tom Beatty Ace Detective and the Gorgon Gang**, 1938?, Whit, | | | |
| 36p, 2½″ × 3½″, Penny Book | 4.00 | 12.00 | 24.00 |
| **nn-Tom Beatty Ace of the Service and the Kidnapers**, 1938?, Whit, | | | |
| 36p, 2½″ × 3½″, Penny Book | 4.00 | 12.00 | 24.00 |

|  | Good | Fine | N-Mint |
|---|---|---|---|
| **1102-Tom Mason on Top**, 1935, Sal, 160p, Tom Mix photo-c, movie scenes, hard-c | 12.00 | 35.00 | 70.00 |
| **1582-Tom Mason on Top**, 1935, Sal, 160p, Tom Mix photo-c, movie scenes, soft-c | 12.00 | 35.00 | 70.00 |
| **Tom Mix** (See Chief of the Rangers, Flaming Guns & Texas Bad Man) | | | |
| **762-Tom Mix and Tony Jr. in "Terror Trail," 1934, Whit, 160p, movie scenes** | 12.00 | 35.00 | 70.00 |
| **1144-Tom Mix in the Fighting Cowboy**, 1935, Whit, 432p, Hal Arbo-a | 8.50 | 25.00 | 50.00 |
| **nn-Tom Mix in the Fighting Cowboy**, 1935, Whit, 436p, premium-no ads, 3 color, soft-c, Hal Arbo-a | 13.00 | 40.00 | 80.00 |
| **1166-Tom Mix in the Range War**, 1937, Whit, 432p, Hal Arbo-a | 8.00 | 24.00 | 48.00 |
| **1173-Tom Mix Plays a Lone Hand**, 1935, Whit, 288p, hard-c, Hal Arbo-a | 8.00 | 24.00 | 48.00 |
| **1183-Tom Mix and the Stranger from the South**, 1936, Whit, 432p | 8.00 | 24.00 | 48.00 |
| **1462-Tom Mix and the Hoard of Montezuma**, 1937, Whit, 432p, H. E. Vallely-a | 8.00 | 24.00 | 48.00 |
| **1482-Tom Mix and His Circus on the Barbary Coast**, 1940, Whit, 432p, James Gary-a | 8.00 | 24.00 | 48.00 |
| **4068-Tom Mix and the Scourge of Paradise Valley**, 1937, Whit, 7″ × 9½″, 320p, Big Big Book, Vallely-a | 32.00 | 95.00 | 190.00 |
| **nn-Tom Mix Riders to the Rescue**, 1939, 36p, 2½″ × 3½″, Penny Book | 4.50 | 14.00 | 28.00 |
| **6833-Tom Mix in the Riding Avenger**, 1936, Dell, 244p, Cartoon Story Book, hard-c | 14.00 | 42.00 | 84.00 |
| **nn-Tom Mix Avenges the Dry Gulched Range King**, 1939, Dell, 196p, Fast-Action Story, soft-c | 16.00 | 47.50 | 95.00 |
| **nn-Tom Mix in the Riding Avenger**, 1936, Dell, 244p, Fast-Action Story | 16.00 | 47.50 | 95.00 |
| **4-Tom Mix and Tony in the Rider of Death Valley**, 1934, EVW, Five Star Library, 160p, movie scenes (Universal Pictures), hard-c | 14.00 | 42.00 | 84.00 |
| **7-Tom Mix in the Texas Bad Man**, 1934, EVW, Five Star Library, 160p, movie scenes | 14.00 | 42.00 | 84.00 |

|  | **Good** | **Fine** | **N-Mint** |
|---|---|---|---|
| **10-Tom Mix in the Tepee Ranch Mystery**, 1938, Whit, 132p, Buddy Book, soft-c | 15.00 | 45.00 | 90.00 |
| **nn-Tom Mix the Trail of the Terrible 6**, 1935, Ralston Purina Co., 84p, 3″ × 3½″, premium | 10.00 | 30.00 | 60.00 |
| **1126-Tommy of Troop Six** (Scout Book), 1937, Sal, hard-c | 4.50 | 13.50 | 27.00 |
| **1606-Tommy of Troop Six** (Scout Book), 1937, Sal, soft-c | 4.50 | 13.50 | 27.00 |
| **Tom Sawyer** (See Adventures of . . . ) | | | |
| **1437-Tom Swift and His Magnetic Silencer**, 1941, Whit, 432p, flip pictures | 10.00 | 30.00 | 60.00 |

*Tom Swift and His Giant Telescope #1485,*
*© Whitman Publishing Co., 1939*

|  | **Good** | **Fine** | **N-Mint** |
|---|---|---|---|
| **1485-Tom Swift and His Giant Telescope**, 1939, Whit, 432p, James Gary-a | 10.00 | 30.00 | 60.00 |
| **540-Top-Line Comics** (In Open Box), 1935, Whit, 164p, 3½″ × 3½″, 3 books in set, all soft-c: | | | |
| Bobby Thatcher and the Samarang Emerald | 12.00 | 35.00 | 70.00 |
| Broncho Bill in Suicide Canyon | 12.00 | 35.00 | 70.00 |

|  | Good | Fine | N-Mint |
|---|---|---|---|
| Freckles and His Friends in the North Woods | | | |
| | 12.00 | 35.00 | 70.00 |
| Complete set with box | 44.00 | 132.50 | 265.00 |

**541-Top-Line Comics** (In Open Box), 1935, Whit, 164p, 3½″ × 3½″, 3 books in set; all soft-c:

| Little Joe and the City Gangsters | 12.00 | 35.00 | 70.00 |
|---|---|---|---|
| Smilin' Jack and His Flivver Plane | 12.00 | 35.00 | 70.00 |
| Streaky and the Football Signals | 12.00 | 35.00 | 70.00 |
| Complete set with box | 44.00 | 132.50 | 265.00 |

**542-Top-Line Comics** (In Open Box), 1935, Whit, 164p, 3½″ × 3½″, 3 books in set; all soft-c:

| Dinglehoofer und His Dog Adolph by Knerr | | | |
|---|---|---|---|
| | 12.00 | 35.00 | 70.00 |
| Jungle Jim by Alex Raymond | 17.00 | 50.00 | 100.00 |
| Sappo by Segar | 17.00 | 50.00 | 100.00 |
| Complete set with box | 53.00 | 160.00 | 320.00 |

**543-Top-Line Comics** (In Open Box), 1935, Whit, 164p, 3½″ × 3½″, 3 books in set; all soft-c:

| Alexander Smart, ESQ by Winner | 12.00 | 35.00 | 70.00 |
|---|---|---|---|
| Bunky by Billy de Beck | 12.00 | 35.00 | 70.00 |
| Nicodemus O'Malley by Carter | 12.00 | 35.00 | 70.00 |
| Complete set with box | 44.00 | 132.50 | 265.00 |

**1158-Tracked by a G-Man**, 1939, Sal, 400p

| | 5.00 | 15.00 | 30.00 |
|---|---|---|---|

**L25-Trail of the Lonesome Pine, The**, 1936, Lynn, movie scenes

| | 10.00 | 30.00 | 60.00 |
|---|---|---|---|

**nn-Trail of the Terrible 6** (See Tom Mix . . . )

**1185-Trail to Squaw Gulch, The**, 1940, Sal, 400p

| | 5.00 | 15.00 | 30.00 |
|---|---|---|---|

**720-Treasure Island**, 1933, Whit., 362p

| | 10.00 | 30.00 | 60.00 |
|---|---|---|---|

**1141-Treasure Island**, 1934, Whit, 160p, 4¾″ × 5¼″, Jackie Cooper photo-c, movie scenes

| | 8.00 | 24.00 | 48.00 |
|---|---|---|---|

**1100B-Tricks Easy to Do** (Slight of hand & magic), 1938, Whit, 36p, 2½″ × 3½″, Penny Book

| | 2.00 | 6.00 | 12.00 |
|---|---|---|---|

**1100B-Tricks You Can Do**, 1938, Whit, 36p, 2½″ × 3½″, Penny Book

| | 2.00 | 6.00 | 12.00 |
|---|---|---|---|

**1104-Two-Gun Montana**, 1936, Whit, 432p, Henry E. Vallely-a

| | 5.50 | 16.50 | 33.00 |
|---|---|---|---|

**nn-Two-Gun Montana Shoots It Out**, 1939, Whit, 36p, 2½″ × 3½″, Penny Book

| | 4.00 | 12.00 | 24.00 |
|---|---|---|---|

| | Good | Fine | N-Mint |
|---|---|---|---|
| **1058-Ugly Duckling, The** (Disney), 1939, Whit, 68p, 5" × 5½", hard-c | | | |
| | 7.00 | 21.00 | 42.00 |
| **nn-Ugly Duckling, The**, nd (1930s), np (Whit), 36p, 3" × 2½", Penny Book | 1.50 | 4.50 | 9.00 |
| **Unc' Billy Gets Even** (See Wee Little Books) | | | |
| **1114-Uncle Don's Strange Adventures**, 1935, Whit, 300p, radio star-Uncle Don Carney | 6.00 | 18.00 | 36.00 |
| **722-Uncle Ray's Story of the United States**, 1934, Whit, 300p | | | |
| | 7.00 | 21.00 | 42.00 |
| **1461-Uncle Sam's Sky Defenders**, 1941, Whit, 432p, flip pictures | | | |
| | 5.50 | 16.50 | 33.00 |
| **1405-Uncle Wiggily's Adventures**, 1946, Whit, All Pictures Comics | | | |
| | 8.00 | 24.00 | 48.00 |
| **1411-Union Pacific**, 1939, Whit, 240p, photo-c, movie scenes | | | |
| | 8.00 | 24.00 | 48.00 |
| **1189-Up Dead Horse Canyon**, 1940, Sal, 400p | | | |
| | 5.00 | 15.00 | 30.00 |
| **1455-Vic Sands of the U.S. Flying Fortress Bomber Squadron**, 1944, Whit, 352p | 5.00 | 15.00 | 30.00 |
| **1645-Walt Disney's Andy Burnett on the Trail** (TV Series), 1958, Whit, 280p | 3.00 | 9.00 | 18.00 |
| **711-10-Walt Disney's Cinderella and the Magic Wand**, 1950, Whit, 2½" × 5", based on Disney movie | 6.00 | 18.00 | 36.00 |
| **845-Walt Disney's Donald Duck and His Cat Troubles** (Disney), 1948, Whit, 100p, 5" × 5½", hard-c | 7.00 | 21.00 | 42.00 |
| **845-Walt Disney's Donald Duck and the Boys**, 1948, Whit, 100p, 5" × 5½", hard-c, Barks-a | 20.00 | 60.00 | 120.00 |
| **2952-Walt Disney's Donald Duck in the Great Kite Maker**, 1949, Whit, 24p, 3¼" × 4", Tiny Tales, full color (5 cents) | | | |
| | 4.50 | 14.00 | 28.00 |
| **804-Walt Disney's Mickey and the Beanstalk**, 1948, Whit, hard-c | | | |
| | 7.00 | 21.00 | 42.00 |
| **2952-Walt Disney's Mickey Mouse and the Night Prowlers**, Whit, 1949, 24p, 3¼" × 4", Tiny Tales, full color (5 cents) | | | |
| | 4.50 | 14.00 | 28.00 |
| **845-Walt Disney's Mickey Mouse and the Boy Thursday**, 1948, Whit, 5" × 5½", 100p | 7.00 | 21.00 | 42.00 |
| **845-Walt Disney's Mickey Mouse the Miracle Maker**, 1948, Whit, 5" × 5½", 100p | 7.00 | 21.00 | 42.00 |
| **845-Walt Disney's Minnie Mouse and the Antique Chair**, 1948, Whit, 5" × 5½", 100p | 7.00 | 21.00 | 42.00 |

|  | Good | Fine | N-Mint |
|---|---|---|---|

**1435-Walt Disney's Pinocchio and Jiminy Cricket**, 1940, Whit, 432p

|  | 11.50 | 35.00 | 70.00 |
|---|---|---|---|

**845-Walt Disney's Poor Pluto**, 1948, Whit, 5″ × 5½″, 100p, hard-c

|  | 7.00 | 21.00 | 42.00 |
|---|---|---|---|

*Walt Disney's Pluto the Pup #1467,*
*© The Disney Company, 1938*

**1467-Walt Disney's Pluto the Pup** (Disney), 1938, Whit, 432p,
Gottfredson-a        12.50      37.50      75.00
**1066-Walt Disney's Story of Clarabelle Cow** (Disney), 1938, Whit,
100p        7.00      21.00      42.00
**1066-Walt Disney's Story of Dippy the Goof** (Disney), 1938, Whit,
100p        7.00      21.00      42.00
**1066-Walt Disney's Story of Donald Duck** (Disney), 1938, Whit, 100p,
hard-c, Taliaferro-a        7.00      21.00      42.00
**1066-Walt Disney's Story of Mickey Mouse** (Disney), 1938, Whit,
100p, hard-c, Gottfredson-a, Donald Duck app.
        7.00      21.00      42.00
**1066-Walt Disney's Story of Minnie Mouse** (Disney), 1938, Whit,
100p, hard-c        7.00      21.00      42.00
**1066-Walt Disney's Story of Pluto the Pup** (Disney), 1938, Whit,
100p, hard-c        7.00      21.00      42.00

|  | Good | Fine | N-Mint |
|---|---|---|---|
| **2952-Walter Lantz Presents Andy Panda's Rescue**, 1949, Whit, Tiny | | | |
| Tales, full color (5 cents) | 4.50 | 14.00 | 28.00 |
| **751-Wash Tubbs in Pandemonia**, 1934, Whit, 320p, Roy Crane-a | | | |
|  | 8.00 | 24.00 | 48.00 |
| **1455-Wash Tubbs and Captain Easy Hunting for Whales**, 1938, Whit, | | | |
| 432p, Roy Crane-a | 7.00 | 21.00 | 42.00 |
| **6-Wash Tubbs in Foreign Travel**, 1934, Whit, soft-c, 3½″ × 3½″, | | | |
| Tarzan Ice Cream cup premium | 15.00 | 45.00 | 90.00 |
| **nn-Wash Tubbs**, 1934, Whit, 52p, 4″ × 5½″, premium-no ads, soft-c, | | | |
| Roy Crane-a | 11.00 | 32.50 | 65.00 |
| **513-Wee Little Books** (In Open Box), 1934, Whit, 44p, small size, | | | |
| 6 books in set | | | |
| Child's Garden of Verses | 2.00 | 6.00 | 12.00 |
| The Happy Prince (The Story of) | 2.00 | 6.00 | 12.00 |
| Joan of Arc (The Story of) | 2.00 | 6.00 | 12.00 |
| Peter Pan (The Story of) | 2.50 | 7.50 | 15.00 |
| Pied Piper of Hamlin | 2.00 | 6.00 | 12.00 |
| Robin Hood (A Story of . . . ) | 2.00 | 6.00 | 12.00 |
| Complete set with box | 17.00 | 50.00 | 100.00 |
| **514-Wee Little Books** (In Open Box), 1934, Whit, 44p, small size, | | | |
| 6 books in set | | | |
| Jack and Jill | 2.00 | 6.00 | 12.00 |
| Little Bo-Peep | 2.00 | 6.00 | 12.00 |
| Little Tommy Tucker | 2.00 | 6.00 | 12.00 |
| Mother Goose | 2.00 | 6.00 | 12.00 |
| Simple Simon | 2.00 | 6.00 | 12.00 |
| Complete set with box | 17.00 | 50.00 | 100.00 |
| **518-Wee Little Books** (In Open Box), 1933, Whit, 44p, small size, | | | |
| 6 books in set, written by Thornton Burgess | | | |
| Betty Bear's Lesson-1930 | 3.00 | 9.00 | 18.00 |
| Jimmy Skunk's Justice-1933 | 3.00 | 9.00 | 18.00 |
| Little Joe Otter's Slide-1929 | 3.00 | 9.00 | 18.00 |
| Peter Rabbit's Carrots-1933 | 3.50 | 10.00 | 20.00 |
| Unc' Billy Gets Even-1930 | 3.00 | 9.00 | 18.00 |
| Whitefoot's Secret-1933 | 3.00 | 9.00 | 18.00 |
| Complete set with box | 23.00 | 70.00 | 140.00 |
| **519-Wee Little Books** (In Open Box) (Bible Stories), 1934, Whit, 44p, | | | |
| small size, 6 books in set, Helen Janes-a | | | |
| The Story of David | 1.35 | 5.00 | 10.00 |
| The Story of Gideon | 1.35 | 5.00 | 10.00 |

|  | Good | Fine | N-Mint |
|---|---|---|---|
| The Story of Daniel | 1.35 | 5.00 | 10.00 |
| The Story of Joseph | 1.35 | 5.00 | 10.00 |
| The Story of Ruth and Naomi | 1.35 | 5.00 | 10.00 |
| The Story of Moses | 1.35 | 5.00 | 10.00 |
| Complete set with box | 13.00 | 40.00 | 80.00 |

**1471-Wells Fargo**, 1938, Whit, 240p, photo-c, movie scenes

                                       7.00      21.00      42.00

**L18-Western Frontier**, 1935, Lynn, 192p, starring Ken Maynard, movie scenes      14.00      42.00      84.00

**1121-West Pointers on the Gridiron**, 1936, Sal, 148p, hard-c, sports book      4.50      13.50      27.00

**1601-West Pointers on the Gridiron**, 1936, Sal, 148p, soft-c, sports book      4.50      13.50      27.00

**1124-West Point Five, The**, 1937, Sal, 4¾″ × 5¼″, sports book, hard-c

                                         4.50      13.50      27.00

**1604-West Point Five, The**, 1937, Sal, 4¾″ × 5¼″, sports book, soft-c

                                         4.50      13.50      27.00

**1164-West Point of the Air**, 1935, Whit, 160p, photo-c, movie scenes

                                         7.00      21.00      42.00

**18-Westward Ho!**, 1935, EVW, 160p, movie scenes, starring John Wayne      27.00      80.00      160.00

**1109-We Three**, 1935, Sal, 160p, photo-c, movie scenes, by John Barrymore, hard-c      6.00      18.00      36.00

**1589-We Three**, 1935, Sal, 160p, photo-c, movie scenes, by John Barrymore, soft-c      6.00      18.00      36.00

**5-Wheels of Destiny**, 1934, EVW, 160p, movie scenes, starring Ken Maynard      14.00      42.00      84.00

**Whitefoot's Secret** (See Wee Little Books)

**nn-Who's Afraid of the Big Bad Wolf, "Three Little Pigs"** (Disney), 1933, McKay, 36p, 6″ × 8½″, stiff-c, Disney studio-a

                                    22.00      65.00      130.00

**nn-Wild West Adventures of Buffalo Bill**, 1935, Whit. 260p, Cocomalt premium, soft-c, Hal Arbo-a

                                      8.50      25.00      50.00

**1096-Will Rogers, The Story of**, 1935, Sal, photo-hard-c

                                       7.00      21.00      42.00

**1576-Will Rogers, The Story of**, 1935, Sal, photo-soft-c

                                       7.00      21.00      42.00

**1458-Wimpy the Hamburger Eater**, 1938, Whit, 432p, E. C. Segar-a

                                      12.00      35.00      70.00

|  | Good | Fine | N-Mint |
|---|---|---|---|

**1433-Windy Wayne and His Flying Wing**, 1942, Whit, 432p, flip pictures
5.00    15.00    30.00

**1131-Winged Four, The**, 1937, Sal, sports book, hard-c
5.00    15.00    30.00

**1407-Wings of the U.S.A.**, 1940, Whit, 432p, Thomas Hickey-a
5.00    15.00    30.00

**nn-Winning of the Old Northwest, The**, 1934, World, High Lights of History Series
5.50    16.50    33.00

**1122-Winning Point, The**, 1936, Sal, (Football), hard-c
4.50    13.50    27.00

**1602-Winning Point, The**, 1936, Sal, soft-c
4.50    13.50    27.00

**710-10-Woody Woodpecker Big Game Hunter**, 1950, Whit, by Walter Lantz
4.50    13.50    27.00

**2010-(#10)-Woody Woodpecker-The Meteor Menace**, 1967, Whit, 260p, 39 cents, hard-c, color illos    2.00    6.00    12.00

**2028-Woody Woodpecker-The Sinister Signal**, 1969, Whit
2.00    6.00    12.00

**23-World of Monsters, The**, 1935, EVW, Five Star Library, movie scenes
10.00    30.00    60.00

**779-World War in Photographs, The**, 1934, photo-c, photo illus.
5.50    16.50    33.00

**Wyatt Earp** (See Hugh O'Brian . . . )

**nn-Zane Grey's Cowboys of the West**, 1935, Whit, 148p, 3¾″ × 4″, Tarzan Ice Cream cup premium, soft-c, Arbo-a
15.00    45.00    90.00

**Zane Grey's King of the Royal Mounted** (See Men of the Mounted)

**1103-Zane Grey's King of the Royal Mounted**, 1936, Whit, 432p
9.00    27.00    54.00

**nn-Zane Grey's King of the Royal Mounted**, 1935, Whit, 260p, Cocomalt premium, soft-c    10.00    30.00    60.00

**1179-Zane Grey's King of the Royal Mounted and the Northern Treasure**, 1937, Whit, 432p    8.50    25.00    50.00

**1405-Zane Grey's King of the Royal Mounted, the Long Arm of the Law**, 1942, Whit, All Pictures Comics
8.50    25.00    50.00

**1452-Zane Grey's King of the Royal Mounted Gets His Man**, 1938, Whit, 432p    8.50    25.00    50.00

|  | Good | Fine | N-Mint |
|---|---|---|---|
| **1486-Zane Grey's King of the Royal Mounted and the Great Jewel Mystery**, 1939, Whit, 432p | 8.50 | 25.00 | 50.00 |
| **5-Zane Grey's King of the Royal Mounted in the Far North**, 1938, Whit, 132p, Buddy Book, soft-c | 15.00 | 45.00 | 90.00 |
| **nn-Zane Grey's King of the Royal Mounted in Law of the North**, 1939, Whit, 36p, 2½″ × 3½″, Penny Book | .50 | 14.00 | 28.00 |
| **nn-Zane Grey's King of the Royal Mounted Policing the Frozen North**, 1938, Dell, 196p, Fast-Action Story, soft-c | 14.00 | 42.00 | 84.00 |
| **1440-Zane Grey's Tex Thorne Comes Out of the West**, 1937, Whit, 432p | 5.00 | 15.00 | 30.00 |

*Zip Saunders King of the Speedway #1465,*
*© Whitman Publishing Co., 1939*

| **1465-Zip Saunders King of the Speedway**, 1939, 432p, Weisman-a | | | |
|---|---|---|---|
|  | 5.00 | 15.00 | 30.00 |

# ABOUT THE COVER ARTIST

## *Kevin Maguire*

Kevin Maguire started his career by entering the Marvel art internship for new artists, called Romita's Raiders, under art director John Romita. Very soon thereafter, he became the regular artist on *Justice League International*. After a successful stint on that title, he did posters and other projects. He will be the artist on the new Marvel mini-series *The Adventures of Captain America*, due out in 1991. He currently resides in Florida.

**Cover characters:** Captain America, the patriotic super-hero, along with the Red Skull, his arch enemy, were created by Joe Simon and Jack Kirby in 1940 and were very popular during World War II. Captain America has survived five decades and is celebrating his 50th anniversary with a special movie release in 1991.